Beating the Odds

❑

BEATING THE ODDS

The Untold Story Behind the Rise of ABC: The Stars, Struggles, and Egos That Transformed Network Television By the Man Who Made It Happen

Leonard H. Goldenson

with Marvin J. Wolf

Charles Scribner's Sons *New York*

Collier Macmillan Canada *Toronto*

Maxwell Macmillan International
New York Oxford Singapore Sydney

Charles Scribner's Sons
Macmillan Publishing Company
866 Third Avenue, New York, New York 10022

Collier Macmillan Canada, Inc.
1200 Eglinton Avenue East
Suite 200
Don Mills, Ontario M3C 3N1

Library of Congress Cataloging-in-Publication Data
Goldenson, Leonard H.
Beating the odds : the untold story behind the rise of ABC : the stars, struggles, and egos that transformed network television by the man who made it happen / Leonard H. Goldenson; with Marvin J. Wolf.
p. cm.
Includes index.
ISBN 0-684-19055-9
1. American Broadcasting Company. 2. Television broadcasting—United States. 3. Goldenson, Leonard H. I. Wolf, Marvin J. II. Title.
HE8700.8.G63 1991 90-8700
384.55'06'573—dc20 CIP

Macmillan books are available at special discounts for bulk purchases for sales promotions, premiums, fund-raising, or educational use. For details, contact:

Special Sales Director
Macmillan Publishing Company
866 Third Avenue
New York, New York 10022

10 9 8 7 6 5 4 3 2 1
Printed in the United States of America

Table of Contents

Foreword ix

Preface and Acknowledgments xi

1. Father Time 1
2. Scottdale 6
3. Harvard 15
4. Paramount 22
5. Hollywood 53
6. Divestment 69
7. Cookie 75
8. Merger 95
9. Shotgun Marriage 116
10. Treyz 138
11. Sports 181
12. ABC International 214
13. Moore 235
14. Sharks 251
15. Network News 272
16. Radio 298

Contents

17. **Rule** 314

18. **Number One** 341

19. **Stations** 375

20. **Team Arledge** 392

21. **Media Empire** 420

22. **End Game** 441

Afterword 468
Index 471

FOR ISABELLE,
who has always been there for me.

Foreword

by Warren Buffett

I look at Leonard Goldenson and marvel. At age eighty-four he is fit, keen-minded, and charged with energy. It almost seems unfair. Having accomplished all that he has, this man should appear at least a shade tired. The explanation may be that he is having so much fun; I've never seen Leonard other than upbeat.

He was to need this attitude when he took over ABC thirty-seven years ago. An analyst assessing the business at the time would have had to conclude that, at best, fun would be the only reward arising from the undertaking. ABC was fourth out of four in an industry that looked as if it would support two. And there was no doubt who those two would be.

CBS and NBC were laden with program talent, affiliates, and financial strength. ABC had Leonard and little else. Leonard's assets in turn were vision and energy, nice to have but scarcely slingshot power in this David-and-Goliath replay. Furthermore, though the David-Goliath saga has inspired many would-be Davids over the years, few have met success. (As Leonard, an early movie exhibitor, might say, the original version had "legs" but the sequels haven't worked.)

Undismayed, Leonard rolled up his sleeves. He patched together a few affiliate stations and, in programming, substituted creativity for cash. Often crucial deals with program sources were made more in response to Leonard's personal qualities than by the logic of committing to ABC. Like the general of an undermanned army, he had to outmaneuver the opposition rather than outgun it. You're going to enjoy reading how he pulled it off.

It's fitting that Walt Disney and Leonard were good friends and that the prosperity of the two companies was often linked. Both Disney and Goldenson entered their industries from positions so weak as to be presumed fatal: In the movie business, the major studios had strong distribution and exhibition systems that were thought to doom the "independent."

In network distribution, CBS and NBC had locked up the strongest affiliates. Both Disney and Goldenson were underfinanced as well: Midway though vital projects they often needed to scurry to the banks. Finally, Disney and Goldenson both lacked a stable of stars such as those under contract to their major competitors. These two men had to create their marquees from scratch.

But both Disney and Goldenson had a rare edge: They could see a little further into the future than the next fellow. They also possessed a business savvy that enabled them to keep meeting payrolls while nursing their visions toward reality. Over time, these personal assets overcame all the initial handicaps under which they labored. Today the market value of Disney is far greater than that of any movie company, and the profits of Capital Cities/ABC exceed those of any other broadcaster.

My years of association with Leonard have been few. But they have told me volumes about him, starting as they did with the Capital Cities/ABC negotiations. At such a moment, men reveal much about themselves. Some negotiate for the shareholders, and some negotiate for themselves. That second approach to negotiation—what will be the titles, the consulting contracts, the future use of company facilities, etc.—is not as uncommon as one might wish. Lawyers have their own term for the drill: resolving the "social issues." Frequently the CEO will have some third party raise these issues discreetly. If the wrong answers float back, the deal doesn't progress.

Not a hint of a "social" issue surfaced in the ABC sale. Leonard had two concerns: the welfare of ABC shareholders and finding the best home for a very special enterprise, one that had an impact on society far beyond that of the ordinary business. He sought a buyer worthy of taking over a public trust, and he found what he was searching for in Capital Cities and its managers, Tom Murphy and Dan Burke. In effect, Leonard displayed the same combination of vision and commercial savvy in transferring the company that he had displayed in building it.

Business management can be viewed as a three-act play—the dream, the execution, and the passing of the baton. Leonard Goldenson will be remembered as a master of all.

Preface and Acknowledgments

❑

What follows is both the story of my life, and the story of my life's work. The latter includes the building of American Broadcasting Companies from its modest origins into the nation's most successful broadcasting entity, and cofounding one of the country's most essential charitable organizations, United Cerebral Palsy.

I could not possibly have accomplished my life's work without the assistance and support of a great many other people. Accordingly, I sought to include and acknowledge their individual and collective contributions by presenting their recollections and insights along with my own.

I concluded this formidable task would best be carried out by a skilled interviewer and journalist. I chose Marvin Wolf, who also helped organize and present my own thoughts, to conduct interviews and distill their product into the recollections presented in the following pages. He interviewed more than a hundred of my friends, colleagues, and business and professional associates. Without exception they were candid and cooperative. I am extremely grateful for their contributions, which have enriched this work immeasurably.

This work would never have come into being without the kindness and help of a great number of people.

My daughter, Loreen Arbus, provided the essential impetus to launch the project. Her insights, suggestions, and comments during preparation of the manuscript were most helpful.

Roann Rubin provided extraordinarily thorough research, fact checking, and proofreading. The manuscript reflects her attention to subtle detail and her well-founded criticisms. Any errors or omissions, however, are my responsibility. Of equal importance, Roann's tact and sensitivity were instrumental in helping to arrange dozens of interviews with some of the most influential and important people in broadcasting.

Patricia J. Matson, VP, Corporate Communications for Capital Cities/ABC, was unstinting in her support and assistance, and provided unhindered access to historical records and to biographical material. Her enthusiasm for this book vastly simplified the research and facilitated the interviews, which supplemented and enhanced my own recollections of events long past.

Joan Polhamus, my administrative assistant at Capital Cities/ABC, went far beyond the call of duty in coordinating movement of mountains of documents and manuscript material between my home in Florida, my office in New York, a writer in California and a researcher in New Jersey.

Mike Hamilburg, my literary agent, became one of the earliest supporters in this project. His enthusiasm and insights were instrumental in arranging a most fruitful marriage between author and publisher.

Catherine Bostron provided helpful legal insights and displayed infinite patience in negotiating an equitable contract.

Lys Chuck of Mead Data Central was of great assistance in providing training and techniques to get the most from Nexis, the extraordinarily useful electronic data base her company maintains. I am also grateful to Jane Maxwell of ABC News, who made possible the special arrangement with Mead Data Central.

Julie Hoover, Catherine Foti, Kimberly Robinson, and the entire staff of Capital Cities/ABC Corporate Communications department, provided a myriad of small kindnesses and courtesies.

Cheryl Carelock in the Capital Cities/ABC Legal Department caused the contents of an entire New Jersey warehouse to be moved to recover important historical files.

Cindy Lewis and Ursula Gibson did yeoman service transcribing dozens of recorded interviews, and Julie Wheelock provided much editorial assistance. Dot Hendler provided several small but important administrative services.

Alex Cantor, executive director of the American Society of Authors and Journalists, provided many courtesies.

Joseph B. Treaster and Barbara Dill, Sol and Janice Hopkins Tanne, Jack and Carol Gelber, and Joseph and Theresa Galloway were most generous with hospitality to Marvin Wolf.

In addition to those people whose recollections appear in the text, I also wish to acknowledge information and insight provided by Graham

Allison, former dean of the John F. Kennedy School of Government at Harvard; Dana Atchley, retired president of Microwave Associates Inc.; Jim Aubrey, former president of the CBS Television Network; Seth Baker, former president of ABC Publishing; Norman Brokaw, head of the William Morris Agency; Bob Burton, president of ABC Publishing; Sid Cassyd; my cousin, Julius Collins; Martin Davis, CEO of Paramount; Barbara Greene, associate executive director of United Cerebral Palsy Associations; Jerry Golden, retired ABC corporate secretary; Clare Heider of WLS-TV; Dennis James; Marvin Josephson, head of International Creative Management; James McKenna, former counsel to ABC; Ellis Moore, former head of ABC Public Relations; Al Schneider, head of Standards and Practices for Capital Cities/ABC; Morris Schrier, retired general counsel of MCA; Dr. Leon Sternfeld, medical director of United Cerebral Palsy Research and Educational Foundation; Donn Tatum, a director of the Walt Disney Company; Bill Warren, retired president of KOMO-TV; Lew Wasserman, chairman of MCA; Sonny Werblin, retired head of MCA's New York division; and Tom Werner, former ABC Entertainment executive and partner in Carsey-Werner.

Special thanks to Ned Chase of Charles Scribner's Sons, my editor, for his support, enthusiasm, and insights.

L.G.

Beating the Odds

❑

1

Father Time

❑

There's much to be learned by reading newspapers. Browsing *The Wall Street Journal* on a crisp, autumn New York morning in 1984, I learned that the company I'd run for thirty-one years was in great danger. The Bass brothers, four young tycoons out of Fort Worth, suddenly had acquired enough of ABC's common stock to mount a takeover attempt, were they so inclined.

I've fought off a few raiders in my time, including the mysterious and eccentric Howard Hughes, and Norton Simon, collector of art and companies, in his day one of the country's most fearsome corporate raiders.

But this move from the Bass brothers was a stab in the back. I wasn't so much worried as I was burned up. Several of Wall Street's deeper pockets were interested in taking control of ABC, but I thought the Basses were out of line.

The Basses' billions controlled the Walt Disney corporation, a company that had profited greatly from its thirty-year relationship with ABC. Just a few months earlier, at my instigation, ABC had made a deal with Michael Eisner, Disney's chairman and CEO, to broadcast "The Disney Sunday Movie."

This was more than just an entertainment package. At the top of each program, before the movie, Eisner spent a few moments telling the audience about new developments in Disney's empire of theme parks and motion pictures. It was a reprise of a technique originally applied by Walt Disney himself on the ABC Network in the 1950s.

Eisner's low-key remarks were the Disney company's postcard to America, their way of staying in touch with the millions of people the then-troubled company needed to buy tickets to its movies and amusement parks.

Eisner was an old friend. He became Disney's CEO when the Magic Kingdom was a debt-ridden giant, drifting aimlessly as it slowly sank. As he manned the pumps and fixed the rudder, the Sunday night program was Disney's most important show, its anchor to windward in heavy seas.

I put down my newspaper and called Eisner in California. Obviously surprised to learn the Basses were moving in on ABC, he said, "This is wrong."

Michael called Sidney Bass, eldest of the brothers, to say their move was not in keeping with the friendly relations between ABC and Disney, and that he wanted no part of a hostile takeover of a company that had treated him so well.

Upset and embarrassed, Sidney said he didn't know what Michael was talking about. He quickly discovered that brother Robert, acting on his own, was behind the move on our stock.

A few days later Robert Bass came to see me. I didn't feel it necessary to remind him that in 1954, I had been Walt Disney's last chance to build Disneyland. The banks and the other networks had dismissed his dream as a crackpot notion, but I'd had my company put up collateral to guarantee the huge loans he needed. Nor did I feel it necessary to recall that, as a condition of our guaranty, I insisted that the reluctant Disney become the first Hollywood studio to create a program series for network television.

I merely told Robert Bass I felt it was unfair for them to meddle with ABC when we were trying to help Disney return to profitability. Robert, very conciliatory, said he didn't want to undermine the warm relationship between Disney and ABC. I got the impression brother Sidney had spoken to him. Robert agreed to sell off their ABC stock and leave us alone.

ABC, the company I had built—with the help of a great many talented and dedicated people—from the brink of bankruptcy to the largest advertising medium in the world, was safe. For the moment.

I had served as ABC's chief executive officer since 1953, when it was a collection of stumbling radio and television properties and an anemic network feeding a pitifully small group of affiliated stations. In 1953, ABC was a basket case, dead last among the four networks, and fading.

We built a young, vigorous, and creative team, and in the 1950s, 1960s, and 1970s we challenged the broadcasting Establishment, changing or ignoring many of their most cherished assumptions. Our success totally reshaped the industry.

We arranged a marriage between broadcasting and the movie industry, and gave birth to new entertainment concepts. We wrested program and schedule control from the hands of advertisers. We made sports viewing a national pastime. We brought news of the world and the nation into America's living rooms in boldly innovative ways.

By 1984 ABC's empire included the world's most profitable group of network-owned television stations. Our TV network provided programming to 212 affiliated stations, reaching more than 99 percent of American households. We owned twelve very profitable radio stations, and our seven radio networks provided programming to more than 1,800 affiliates. ABC's cable networks were viewed in tens of millions of homes. Our movie division produced Oscar-winning theatrical films. And ABC Publishing produced more than 100 magazines and book titles a year, while selling more advertising pages than virtually any other American publisher.

ABC enjoyed its most profitable year ever in 1984. Ironically, the same period marked the three networks' first decline in viewership, as the public responded to a panoply of competing program sources. With VCRs commonplace, video rental stores were springing up everywhere. Cable networks were available to nearly all the nation's most demographically desirable households, and many cable networks were producing their own programs or showing top-quality movies. Independent producers created scores of good programs for national syndication.

In the early 1980s broadcasting lost its most potent defense against hostile takeovers. Under the Reagan Administration, the Federal Communications Commission (FCC) had radically changed its role. Led by doctrinaire deregulators, the FCC dropped some restrictions on station licenses, creating, in effect, an open market for broadcasting properties. For the first time it was possible to buy a station with the sole intention of reselling it as quickly as possible.

Then the FCC raised the limits on the number of stations any corporation could own. About the same time, Reagan appointees in the Justice Department's Antitrust Division signaled their intention to allow virtually any merger.

Now, it seemed, almost anyone with money could own a station—or a network. Traditional considerations—moral fitness, conflict of interest, and the potential for anticompetitive effects—became far less important.

Wall Street reacted quickly to the new climate in Washington. Junk bonds—high-risk, high-interest corporate IOUs—became widely acceptable to investors. It was easier than ever for corporate raiders to take over even the largest companies without risking a cent of their own money.

But a network is a powerful medium of communication, and so infinitely attractive to all sorts of demagogues. A network is also a public trust. I could not allow our company to fall into the wrong hands.

Broadcast properties had long been attractive investments, but ABC was peculiarly vulnerable to takeover. We had more cash than long-term debt. Furthermore, 1984 was a record year for our company. At $3.7 billion, our revenues were 26 percent greater than 1983, and after-tax earnings had risen 22 percent to $195 million. Yet our stock was selling for only about nine times earnings, considerably less than most broadcasting companies. ABC's stock was widely held—but management, including myself, owned less than 2 percent of it.

Our major assets included stations owned for decades and carried on our books at far less than their real value. For example, just *one* of our TV stations, KABC in Los Angeles, was probably worth $1 billion on the open market, while ABC's *total* book value was only about $2.3 billion. So a raider could buy ABC with borrowed money, then quickly sell off its assets to reap an enormous profit.

ABC was ready to deal with changing technologies and audience demographics. I was not so certain we could deal with Wall Street's newest breed of corporate raiders.

When I turned back Robert Bass's attempt to gain control of ABC, it was only one of several takeover bids. A few years earlier, Larry Tisch, head of Loews, acquired an uncomfortably large amount of our stock. I relied upon our many years of close friendship to persuade him to sell it.

Investor Saul Steinberg, also a friend, made a run at the company. I asked him to back off, and he did.

I turned aside my good friend Lew Wasserman's repeated overtures to merge ABC with his company, MCA, which owns Universal Pictures.

Martin Davis, head of Gulf + Western, who in a few years would make a play for Time Inc., proposed a friendly merger. I had similar offers from Gannett, Coca-Cola, which then owned Columbia Pictures, and Pepsico.

I told them all, "No thanks." And they left ABC alone.

Then, late in 1984, I was shocked to discover one of my most trusted executives secretly discussing a leveraged buyout with a group of investors. Concerned about the possibility of more takeover attempts, I consulted some of Wall Street's most influential figures. Their consensus was that none of the executives available to succeed me as CEO had sufficient stature to fend off a serious takeover attempt, but the company probably was safe while I remained in charge.

It was cold comfort. Were I even ten years younger, my course would have been clear: I would fight any raider with all my resources. But although I remained enthusiastic about ABC's future, as December 7, 1984, my seventy-ninth birthday, drew near, I became painfully aware that I could not fight Father Time forever.

If I was to keep ABC intact, my only alternative was to make the most of the inevitable. But finding the right merger partner would not be easy.

As the year ended, my top executives became increasingly distracted by the unfolding possibility of a hostile takeover. Uncertainty about their own futures interfered with the day-to-day operation of a large and complex business. This made us even more vulnerable. I knew then that if I was to save ABC from takeover and dismemberment, I had to make a move. And it had to be soon.

2

Scottdale

❑

Coke ovens littered the countryside, hundreds of them, giant beehives with tall chimneys belching woolly columns of dark smoke over the rolling farmland as they turned soft coal into coke. On still days the pall sometimes obscured the sun. When there was too much wind, housewives scrambled to take the wash in before it was blackened by soot. Yet I don't recall that anybody ever complained. Busy smokestacks, in the early decades of this century, were a sign of prosperity to Scottdale's 6,000-some residents.

Scottdale, Pennsylvania, was a prosperous little town of well-kept brick and wood houses and shops. The streets were paved, and nearly everyone had electric lights. A rail depot and electric trolley service linked the community with adjacent towns. It was a place where farmers, steel-mill and coke-oven workers, and coal miners came to shop, bank, worship, or take in a movie.

Those hardworking, grimy men were the reason my father, Lee Goldenson, moved to Scottdale in 1896, when he was nineteen, to open a store with Isadore Marks. Marks & Goldenson sold men's clothing, shoes for the whole family, and a few other items.

My grandfather, Levi Goldenson, was born in Russia. He came to Pittsburgh as a little boy. Before my father was born, in Pittsburgh, Grandpa Goldenson opened a general store in suburban Greensburg.

My father, a humble, easygoing man, spent most of his time at work. Mr. Marks was his partner for about fifty years, but in all that time there was never even a scrap of paper for a partnership agreement. It was all done on a handshake.

My mother, Esther Broude Goldenson, was born in Russia in 1887. She came to Pittsburgh as a small child. Her father had a picture-frame business;

before her marriage, Mother was his bookkeeper. I never learned how my parents met, but they married on June 14, 1904, and honeymooned in Atlantic City.

I was born in Scottdale on December 7, 1905. My sister Sylvia came along five years later, and then in 1915, Madeline. As big brother, I was expected to help with their homework, especially arithmetic, and to look after them. Like many big brothers, I was idolized by my sisters. This was not so unpleasant, as I recall.

We lived in a spacious, two-story house of wood and brick at 613 Chestnut Street. Across the street was the home of the president of H. C. Frick Coal & Coke. Next door lived Charles Loucks, head of the First National Bank of Scottdale, a descendant of eighteenth-century pioneer settlers.

Mother, thoughtful and kind, was the driving force in our family. Dad frequently sought her advice on business matters. She was very ambitious, especially for her children, and continually looked for ways to motivate us.

An astonishingly worldly and cultured woman for such a small town, she was very full of life. She must have read virtually every book in the Scottdale Library. When new volumes came, the librarian telephoned. Mother would immediately walk over to bring them home.

Mother was very open about everything. When the time came, she sat down with each of my sisters and explained the facts of life. She told them that, when she married, at age seventeen, she had no idea what to expect on her wedding night. She wouldn't let that happen to Madeline and Sylvia. So she explained, in the most matter-of-fact manner, the mechanics of menstruation and the vocabulary and syntax of sex as it would be explored after marriage. Remember, she lived in a small town, half a century before sex education classes were first taught in big-city high schools. Mother's sophistication left quite an impression on Madeline.

OTHER RECOLLECTIONS:
Madeline Goldenson Seder

I came home from high school one day and Mother said, "Sit down, I want to talk to you. I just finished reading *The Well of Loneliness*, and I want to explain it to you. I'm sure you'll want to know what it's all about."

Mother mentioned two women that everyone in town knew well. One was Miss Dick, my English teacher; the other, Miss Lowe, worked at a bank. They both dressed rather mannishly, were rarely seen around town except together, and they displayed what seemed to most an exceptional degree of affection toward each other.

"Miss Dick and Miss Lowe are lesbians," she explained. Until I read the book, which described and discussed the realities of lesbian life, I had no idea what she was talking about. But then I understood. This was Mother at her best, a very progressive lady in a small, conservative town, a woman who never left anything important unsaid if she thought it was something we kids needed to learn.

❑ ❑ ❑

Mother involved herself with all sorts of community and charitable organizations, including Amaranth, a women's auxiliary of the Eastern Star Masons. She taught all her children the value of community service, and at a very young age it was plain that helping the less fortunate was an obligation to be taken most seriously.

By way of example, when her sister Lily died of cancer, leaving three small children, Mother just took over. On every Jewish holiday, every Thanksgiving, every special day, we either went to visit our cousins, or they came to see us. Mother remembered all their birthdays, saw to their Bar Mitzvahs, and made sure those kids missed nothing their own mother would have provided.

Until I was well into my teens there were only four Jewish families in Scottdale. So when I was twelve, I began going to Pittsburgh—forty miles by train—for religious education. My father's distant cousin, the illustrious Dr. Samuel Goldenson, became the rabbi at Rodef Shalom Congregation just before my Bar Mitzvah in 1918. He was probably the first rabbi in the world to appear on radio, broadcasting a weekly message on KDKA, Pittsburgh's pioneer station. In his later years, Dr. Goldenson was chief rabbi at Temple Emanu-El in New York City, and emerged as a leading voice of American Reform Judaism.

As a few more Jewish families arrived, my mother became sort of the Perle Mesta of Scottdale. Dinner at our house was almost obligatory for every new Jewish bride or family. By the time I was in college and Scottdale boasted nine Jewish families, Mother led fund-raising activities—bake and rummage sales, newspaper drives, card parties—so the congregation could buy a small building that became our synagogue.

I was never a particularly observant Jew, perhaps because I was exposed to a wide variety of other religions as a boy. One of my father's closest friends was the Roman Catholic priest, Father Jobilski. Often Dad would stop at the rectory after work to deliver a few items the priest had ordered from our store. When Dad came home, Mother would know where he'd been. His cheeks were flushed from the schnapps they drank, and his pockets full of the Havana cigars that Jobilski always pressed on him.

The years of my childhood coincided with a period of national bigotry that has left emotional scars on many of my generation. My sister Sylvia has an especially vivid memory of those times.

OTHER RECOLLECTIONS:
Sylvia Goldenson Weill

When I was six or seven, our father came home from the store one night and said to Mother, "The Ku Klux Klan is starting here." I didn't know what that meant. Later Dad said, "These Ku Kluxers, they're getting so bold that they're marching without their hoods."

Then they began burning big crosses on the hillside behind our house on Saturday nights. Saturday was payday at the mills and mines, and so Dad's busiest day. He always worked very late. When the Klan lit their flaming crosses, Mother would turn out all the lights and take us kids into a small sitting room next to the parlor. We'd all huddle together in the dark, speaking in whispers, until Dad got home.

❑ ❑ ❑

Most of the kids in town were Protestants of one kind or another, and it was from them that I first heard the ethnic slurs reserved for Jews. When I went to the first grade, a couple of kids called me "sheeny." I didn't quite know what they were talking about. I went home and asked my mother about it. She said, "They're obviously talking about you being of the Jewish faith. You have no reason to be anything but proud of your faith, just as they, whether they're Catholic or Protestant, may have reason to be proud of theirs. They're ignorant people if they're trying to make fun of you by calling you 'sheeny.' "

The next time some boys called me sheeny, I started a fistfight. I went after them hammer and tongs. I came home a little bloody, but after that I never heard that word again in school. Those kids became my friends. When I was nine or ten and they were going to Sunday school, I asked my parents if I could go along. They agreed, and I began attending, on an occasional basis, both Baptist and Presbyterian Sunday schools. I even went to a Presbyterian summer camp for three years. I was the only Jewish boy there, but I never felt out of place. In that way, at a very early age, I developed an appreciation for people with different religious beliefs.

My father learned the retail business working in his own father's store, and he had adjusted his business outlook to the realities of small-town life. Many years after I had grown up and left Scottdale, Dad had a heart attack. While he was convalescing, I went over his business books and accounts and was astonished to learn that he'd been carrying several farmers on credit for upward of five or six years. They owed him thousands of dollars.

I asked Dad how he could run a business that way. He said that in a small town like Scottdale, it was the only way. Over the years some of these farmers went through tough times, but he knew each one of them quite well and was sure they'd eventually pay him back.

"In the long run it's worked out all right," he said. "I don't have to be rough and tough, I can see them through." That was his approach to life.

But I remembered the hard times he endured during the Depression, when cash-poor farmers bartered bushels of apples, strawberries, huckleberries, sweet corn, jugs of fresh milk, and eggs in exchange for clothing from his store. They'd leave them on the back porch with a little note. Mother toiled late into the night, canning fruit and vegetables before they spoiled. Much of this she gave away to relatives or to the needy—there was too much for the family to eat. But Dad had to dip into his savings for cash to pay for his goods, or the wholesalers would soon have cut him off.

Even before I was old enough to look over the counter, Dad insisted I work in his store. I worked Saturdays, the Christmas season, during inventories or sales—any time he needed extra help. When they were old enough, my sisters joined me. I found the work tedious. To put it plainly, I hated it. I didn't see any point in it. It wasn't stimulating. I served my time only because I felt a family obligation.

Dad also owned a one-seventh interest in both Scottdale movie theaters, the Strand and the Arcade. They were fairly small, fewer than 400 seats each. It was unusual for that era, but neither theater had a piano or organ. It was all pantomime, with subtitles. Today, few people would bother going. But movies were still new then, and there was an alluring novelty about them that often packed the house.

The Strand showed feature films; the Arcade, open only on Saturday, offered serials. A typical episode ended with the hero or a girl hanging over a cliff by the fingernails, or lashed to railroad tracks with a train bearing down, that sort of thing. The idea was to get people to come back next week and find out if the hero escapes certain death. In that sense they were like today's television soap operas, which use different situations to create cliffhangers.

I found the theater business fascinating. I pestered Mr. Buttermore, the manager, with all kinds of questions. It must have seemed strange, but I often talked to people as they came out of the show, wanting to know what they liked or disliked about the picture.

Although we all worked very hard, life in Scottdale had a leisurely quality to it that now seems to have vanished. After supper I would often go for a long walk with my father. We kept a fine old apple tree in our backyard, and every evening, returning from my walk, I'd pick an apple. Just before bedtime, I ate it. Thus I formed a habit which continues to this day. Wherever I am in the world, if I can find an apple, I eat it just before retiring.

When still in elementary school, I built a crystal radio receiver and tuned in KDKA. In those years, before there were stations all around the dial, and before every home was full of electric appliances, that signal often reached much of the continent. Sitting in my own home while listening to live performances and hearing the news of the world, I was filled with a wonder that has never quite left me.

When I entered high school, I decided to go out for football. Although I would also play high school basketball and baseball, it somehow became extremely important to me to make the football team. But I weighed only 135 pounds and stood about 5 feet 7 inches. To better compete with the brawny sons of miners and steelworkers, I decided to become as strong as I possibly could.

With the goal of getting into great physical shape, I went to our neighbor, the president of H. C. Frick Coal & Coke, and persuaded him to give me a summer job. A new telegraph line was coming to Scottdale, and he put me to work digging post holes for it. Every morning I drove my father's Buick about twenty-five miles into the countryside. I was fourteen, and my three colleagues were college men. Manhandling post-hole diggers, we all worked up a good sweat every day, five days a week.

Through working Saturdays at my father's store, I knew practically everybody in Scottdale. So the next summer, when I was fifteen, I convinced the head of the U. S. Steel mill in Scottdale to give me a job.

What a way to make a living! My task was to stand at the end of a block-long line, where white-hot steel plates emerged from massive rollers in stacks of glowing sheets about 1/16 inch thick. With a long, pointed tool grasped between heavy leather gloves, I turned up the corners of each sheet to separate the stack. I had to move quickly because there was always another stack coming down the line, and I had to take the plates apart before they cooled and fused together.

It was hot, dangerous work, the hardest physical effort I've ever experienced. I was glad that I was just going to be there for the summer, toughening up for football. The men who worked with me were not so fortunate. This was how they earned their living, six days a week, for years on end.

All that sweat produced the desired result. I made the football team, and played quarterback for all four years of high school. My mother and sisters often came to home games, but I don't think they ever really understood the sport. In those days Scottdale High didn't even have bleachers around the field, and spectators just stood around on the sidelines. If I was tackled while carrying the ball, my mother would sometimes cry out, "Those boys are killing my son!" But she never asked me to quit.

Sam Bulick coached both basketball and football. A clean-cut man, very religious, he always insisted we play fairly. He often told me, "You're light, you're small, you have to work harder." Later, when I went off to college, he said, "You'll want to go out for football and basketball, but based on your size you're not going to be able to make the team. You'd better adjust your thinking. But that doesn't mean you shouldn't try."

When I was very young, I read about a Princeton coach who said, "A team that *won't* be beat *can't* be beat." This became my doctrine, and still is.

We were a small school in a small town, so it surprises me now to recall playing against towns like Connellsville, 18,000 people, Greensburg, about 40,000, and Uniontown, population 35,000, and winning football games more often than not.

In basketball we were even better. In those days, boys of all sizes played the game; it was a sport of speed, not height. Only centers were especially tall. I played guard.

Once we were to play in West Newton, about ten or twelve miles away, at 8 P.M. We had only six or seven players and the coach, so after supper we all crammed into one car and set out into a howling blizzard. Somewhere along the way our car broke down. We trudged through the storm for a long time, until we came to a general store.

Inside a group of men huddled around a wood-burning stove. Two were playing checkers, using some kind of lozenge or candy, one pink and the other white, in place of the usual wooden pieces. When one would jump the other's piece, he'd take it off the board and pop it into his mouth.

Eventually, one of the men around the stove offered to try to fix the car, and we all walked back through the wind and snow. We stood around shivering until finally the engine came roaring back to life.

When we got to the gym, it was past midnight—but the West Newton team was still there. The bleachers were still packed. We played the game, and when it was over, somewhere past two in the morning, we ran off the court victorious.

That was the year our team made it to the last game of the Pennsylvania State Tournament. We defeated teams from much larger towns and cities to take the Western Section title. The last game, for the state high school championship and lifetime bragging rights, was against Braddock. They played rings around us. I had to guard a fellow so fast he always had me gunned. They killed us. I'm still not sure how we got by all those other teams to get into that final game.

As I entered my last year of high school, for the first time I began to think about what might come next. My mother held strong opinions. She felt stifled by living in such a small town, and yearned for the sort of business, cultural, and educational opportunities available in a large city. But my father's roots were firmly embedded in the fabric of rural Western Pennsylvania. She felt it was too late for her. But for me, she said, everything was yet possible. She advised me never to settle in a small town, to finish my education, and then go to a large city.

My father's friends included a congressman, who offered me an appointment to West Point. I was also accepted at the Wharton School, in Philadelphia. But my mother's sister lived in Boston, and I had several cousins who had gone to Harvard. The notion of somehow remaining close to kinfolk while away from home and the idea of attending the best university in the country fused into a powerful urge to attend Harvard.

It was unexpectedly easy. Scottdale High School had a rule that I still don't understand. If a student was getting certain grades in daily classes, he was not required to take exams. So even though I hadn't taken an exam since I was twelve years old, I was graduated at the top of my high school class. I never did figure out how they could award grades without some kind of test, but that's the way it was.

About the same time, Harvard adopted a new admissions policy for students in rural schools. Those who finished in the top tenth of their graduating classes could be admitted without taking the usual tough and competitive entrance exam.

In the autumn of 1923 I became a Harvard freshman. I looked forward to floating through four years of fun and football. Instead, I came close to ruining my life.

3

Harvard

❑

Entering Harvard was like plunging into a swift, cold river on the hottest day. After the initial shock came a chilling period of adjustment until my senses refocused, and I learned to enjoy the exertion required to stay above water. As I became comfortable, I swam confidently with the current. I left the river refreshed and enlightened.

But oh, that initial shock.

Competing with the children of mill workers, farmers, and factory hands, I had excelled. But the curriculum in our tiny country high school was geared to the limited horizons set by rural community life. Now I found myself among the top graduates of New England's toniest prep schools—Exeter, Andover, St. Mark's, Choate, and Groton, to name a few—whose standards reflected the greatly expanded expectations of the scions of America's corporate captains and kings.

They wore the most fashionable Brooks Brothers suits, double-breasted creations with wide lapels, cut from the finest English wool.

I was a hayseed, *sui generis,* sporting a Norfolk jacket, belted at the back, with box pleats front and rear, and oversize pockets at the side.

Prep-school graduates arrived on campus with many of their former classmates, and attached themselves to even larger networks of older prep-school grads. These closed cliques rarely mixed with outsiders, even in sports.

Aside from my cousin, Julius Collins, a senior, I knew almost no one at Harvard. But having grown up in a town full of hyphenated Americans —Scotch, Irish, and Polish—I had learned to get along with all sorts of people. In time, I made friends.

One of them was the brilliant, diminutive fellow in the apartment next door to mine at Drayton Hall. Though only a year behind me, he was three years younger. Johnny Green, a protégé of George Gershwin, played his piano long into the night, composing, practicing, and enjoying his art. He went on to write such songs as "Body and Soul" and "I Cover the Waterfront," and to win five Academy Awards for movie scores.

I went out for football. As Coach Bulick had predicted, I didn't make the varsity. I sat on the bench for four years. During practice sessions, I quarterbacked the scrub team.

In preparation for crucial games, the head coach turned me into his scout. On Saturdays, while the varsity teams played, I often drove over to our Ivy League competitors at Yale, Dartmouth, or Holy Cross to observe their action. I took copious notes on how their plays were designed and how they unfolded. I returned to Harvard to outline my observations to the scrub coach, and during the week before each big game, we would run those plays in practice scrimmages, the scrubs against the varsity.

High school courses had been a breeze, but I was neither challenged nor stimulated until I got to Harvard. Now I was actually forced to start thinking. Like Oxford and Cambridge in England, Harvard used a tutorial system to supplement and enhance classroom work. Each dormitory was assigned a tutor, usually an assistant professor or a lecturer. Several evenings each week, our tutor would call us together for an informal discussion. These sessions enriched my life as much as anything else I was to experience at Harvard.

As the tutorials went on, my mental universe expanded astronomically. I started thinking about events that were happening elsewhere, problems involving the whole country or the entire world, matters beyond those linked to the routines and rhythms of life in Scottdale.

My fellow students were from all parts of the country, and the range of their backgrounds and the opinions they each expressed were fascinating. Our tutor followed what was important in the news of the week, but he also went into the arts, into science, into history. For example, we talked about the realpolitik of the League of Nations. We discussed the problems of the Weimar Republic. We explored stories from the newspapers, not necessarily those on the front pages but also briefer accounts that appeared on the back pages, and those in magazines.

We were all encouraged to voice our opinions, and we spoke up as we wished. He never called on anyone, so we were free to listen or participate. At first I didn't speak up at all. I felt less than ignorant. The other students, having come out of prep schools, were well grounded in many of the issues we explored. I wasn't. I felt awkward, even a little delinquent. I began to feel deficient in so many ways. I thought I had wasted a lot of my life up to then, because I had concentrated on sports.

It was a very hard time for me, but eventually I got hold of myself and became very interested in most of the topics that we discussed. Gradually, my sense of self changed. My competitive spirit reemerged. I became more confident.

During that first autumn I played football, made some new friends, and in general enjoyed myself. I attended all my classes and often took notes at lectures, but when the opportunity to have a good time arose, I took it.

Then came November, and our first examinations.

The typical Harvard freshman had survived competitive culling for four years at prep school. Long, hard study, punctuated by frequent examinations, had prepared him for Harvard's rigorous academic standards.

I had no idea what a Harvard exam would be like. As I had in high school, I attended classes and took notes, but I did almost nothing else to prepare for the examinations. I supposed that they would be easy.

I flunked every single exam. The dean put me on probation for the rest of the academic year.

It was the first time I'd ever failed at anything important. I was embarrassed and more than a little angry at myself. In my darkest moments, I contemplated returning in disgrace to face my parents, a frightening prospect.

There was no way I would let that happen without a struggle. I canceled plans to go home for Thanksgiving and Christmas, and began to study virtually around the clock. I made myself more familiar with the innards of Harvard's magnificent library. I hired a tutor to help me unravel the mysteries of test taking, because I had come to realize by then how little I knew about preparing for examinations and how critically important they were.

These sacrifices and efforts paid off. When February came around, I got solid Bs on all my midterms.

The effect of my early failure has never left me. I decided then that I would never allow myself to be humiliated for lack of effort.

In high school, my favorite subjects had been math and history, and so in my first year at Harvard, I decided that my major would be in economics.

This dovetailed nicely with a summer job I had in Pittsburgh. My father had gone to high school in Greensburg with Charles McKenna Lynch, a retired naval officer and a partner in Moore, Leonard and Lynch, Pittsburgh's largest stock brokerage firm. They handled the Mellon family's accounts. When Dad began dabbling in stocks and bonds, he traded through Lynch. In time, Lynch offered me a summer job in his firm.

The summer following my graduation from high school I began working in the Moore, Leonard and Lynch statistical department, analyzing companies' performances. The second year I went to the bond department. My third summer took me to the unlisted department, which handled companies too new or too small to trade on stock exchanges. (Today they are called "over the counter" stocks.) In my fourth year, I became a roving substitute "customer's man," filling in for a succession of salesmen as they took their annual vacations.

Sometime during that third summer, Mr. Lynch called me in to his office and offered me a job with the firm after my graduation from Harvard.

I was reluctant to accept any job at that point, because I hadn't really settled on what I wanted to do with my life. So, being very diplomatic, I told Charles McKenna Lynch that I was seriously considering graduate school. While I would like to continue working at the brokerage, I couldn't make any career commitments just yet.

When he pressed me, I agreed that I would take extra courses during my last year at Harvard, graduate in February, 1927, and work for him until the autumn. Then I would either resume my studies or come into the firm full-time.

So in February, my Bachelor of Science degree in hand, I returned to Pittsburgh and again worked as a substitute customer's man. After five or six months I came to the conclusion that I could never feel comfortable about pursuing a career in the securities business.

The reason was very simple: Having learned how to analyze a company's investment potential, I was surprised and then disillusioned when I saw some of the companies that the salesmen I substituted for had recommended to their customers. Far too often they sold stock in companies that had little chance of growth, less chance of reasonable dividends from earnings, and a very good likelihood that the investors would lose some or all of their investment. These investors, in general, were unsophisticated working people who relied on their salesmen for advice. It seemed that often the salesmen's selections were solely predicated upon the size of the commission they could earn from a particular issue.

This made me feel very uncomfortable. Unless I was free to tell people what I thought were good stocks, apart from what I made on the sale, I wasn't interested. Unfortunately, that did not look like the way to succeed in that business. Instead, as brokerage firms came out with new issues, some of which were plainly quite risky, every salesman in the house was expected to push them. It often appeared that the poorer the stock's prospects, the greater the commission offered to sell it.

I wasn't prepared to sell anything I didn't believe in. That meant that I wasn't going to become a stockbroker. The experience, however, left me with a healthy skepticism about the character of those who choose Wall Street as their path to riches.

I discussed my educational options at great length with my parents. My desire was to get into business, so I considered pursuing either an MBA or a law degree. Once again my mother gave me the benefit of her wisdom. She said, "You can go to law school and still get into business. And as long as you have a law degree, you never can lose it. It's something to fall back on." That settled it. I went to law school.

When I told Mr. Lynch I had decided to go to Harvard Law, but that I could continue to work summers while I was in law school, he graciously offered to help get me into the law firm representing his brokerage, after I graduated.

Working summers at Moore, Leonard and Lynch gave me an opportunity to dabble in the stock market. Having been through the statistical, bond, and unlisted departments, analysis became second nature. I found I could anticipate trends. I can't claim any special talent, because I believe almost anyone can get a revealing picture from the bits and pieces that can be culled from newspapers like *The Wall Street Journal* and from other sources like news magazines.

Buying on margin—only 10 percent, in that era—I invested most of my salary in stocks, and by carefully analyzing each stock and following it very closely on an almost daily basis, I made some money. By the start of my second year of law school I had accumulated between $15,000 and $20,000. To get an idea of what that would buy today, consider that working men in that era earned somewhere between $10 and $25 a week.

The transition to Harvard Law was not as difficult as the trial I had undergone when I first came from Scottdale. Nevertheless, it was hard work. Professor Williston, who taught contract law to first-year students, startled the class on our first day by announcing, "Look to your left. Now look to your right. Next year one of those you see on either side of you won't be back. One third of you won't make it."

He was right, but I made a pact with myself: I would not be among the missing. I had learned how to study, how to write exams, and how to pace myself.

So although I did work pretty hard, it still left me time to enjoy what became a lifelong hobby: high stakes gambling. We played poker, red dog, and bridge. We even played craps. I have to admit there were more than a few weekends when I stayed up nearly all night. I discovered that you can learn a lot about someone when you sit across the table from him with big money about to change hands.

In October 1929, on what has come to be known as Black Tuesday, the speculative bubble that had driven Wall Street for nearly a decade finally burst. Stock prices, which in many cases far exceeded the underlying value of the issuing company's assets, plummeted.

A few weeks earlier I had liquidated my entire portfolio. I claim no particular prescience. Anybody who'd been in the market for a few years might have known that sooner or later reason would apply itself, and there would be a downward correction in prices. But *I* got out because I couldn't spare the time, on a daily basis, to follow the market and still do justice to my study of law. So I cashed in my chips.

That provident act may have been the difference between my finishing law school and having to leave because of a lack of funds. Most of my father's operating capital was in the First National Bank of Scottdale, headed by our friend, Charles Loucks. Like many in our town, Dad thought *that* bank was as safe as a government bond. But the First National went under in the panic that followed the Crash. Federal deposit insurance did not yet exist. Dad, who had lost virtually everything he'd had in the stock market, then lost nearly all his cash. He didn't have enough left even to pay his business insurance.

To keep the family business afloat, I lent most of my nest egg to Dad. When his business came back, I was repaid.

Upon graduation from law school, I returned to Pennsylvania. On the way, I stopped off in New York City. My interest in the movies had grown stronger since the days I hung out at Scottdale's theaters, and I thought a job with one of the giant motion picture companies headquartered in New York would be wonderfully interesting. I visited the offices of Fox, Metro, Paramount, and Universal to apply. But these were uncertain times, the base of the Great Depression, and the major theatrical enterprises were retrenching. There were no jobs for cub lawyers.

So I went to Pittsburgh and took the bar exam. While I was waiting for the results, I sat down with Charles McKenna Lynch, whose brokerage retained two law firms. He felt I would be more comfortable in the smaller.

I accepted a job in this firm. But soon after starting I learned that they had also just hired two other young men, each the son of a sitting federal judge. I don't mind competition—I thrive on it—but it occurred to me that I might be starting behind the eight ball.

I shared my concerns with my parents. As always, they were supportive. Mother agreed with my assessment of limited prospects. After some discussion, she told me, "Why don't you go to New York? It's the largest city in the country, and there are surely more opportunities there than in Pittsburgh." And my parents, despite their reduced circumstances, agreed to back me financially for a year.

I quit and moved to New York. I took up residence, with three Harvard classmates who were also looking for jobs, at the Hotel Chalfonte, on 70th Street near Broadway. As a citizen of Pennsylvania, however, I had to reside in New York for six months before I could take the bar exams. In the interim I set out to find a place as a law clerk.

Though I was still imbued with the rural values that would guide me for a lifetime, I was no longer a hayseed. Having survived the trials of Harvard and Harvard Law, I joined a fraternity of Harvard men that would provide me with friendships, business contacts, and entree into polite society as long as I lived.

With regard to finding employment, however, it made little difference where I had gone to school. The national and world economies plunged into the Great Depression. Breadlines were forming in the big cities as the government struggled to cope with an unprecedented crisis. Millions were unemployed, and there seemed to be no jobs at all.

4

Paramount

❑

As 1931 came and went, America sank inexorably deeper into Depression. Banks closed, factories and mills shut down, stores emptied, and workers were laid off. The mighty engines of commerce slowed to an idle. With less demand for the services of lawyers to help lubricate these engines, even the wealthiest law firms began laying off staff.

I had arrived in New York with letters of introduction from Charles McKenna Lynch to several senior partners in the city's leading law firms. Each of them took time out from busy schedules to see me. They shared their personal and professional philosophies, offering insights into New York's business and legal hierarchies. After expressing regret that they had no position available to offer me, each sent me on to a friend or colleague in another leading firm. Eventually I met virtually the entire elite of New York City's legal Establishment.

In this unexpected way, pounding the New York City pavements provided me with a unique education. I gained a wide circle of personal contacts and an insider's perspective of the legal profession. I never stopped looking for a job, but after a time I began to perceive that whatever my future held, I probably would not find the practice of law very interesting. It seemed a boring, often pointless business, long on details and short on excitement and drama.

However, the kindness that I was shown during this period led me to take on an obligation, in the form of a personal vow. I resolved that if I ever became the head of a company, or achieved some special status, I would always make the time to meet with young people just starting out, and help them get established. I have kept this vow for nearly sixty years, and will continue to do so.

After nine months of fruitless interviews had exhausted the list of New

York City's big-league law firms, I started on the lesser-knowns. One day I walked into a tiny office at 165 Broadway and floated out as Charles Franklin's new (and only) law clerk.

Franklin was the retired general counsel of the Southern Pacific Railroad. His practice was essentially a business of bringing claims against various railroads. These were typically matters of $5,000 to $20,000, suits to settle disputes arising from carloads of spoiled soybeans, bushels of rotted romaine, or crates of damaged damascene. I came to appreciate that most of these cases amounted to chicken feed. In fact, some of the claims were literally over sacks of corn. Franklin handled all the courtroom work, depending on me to organize the detail needed to prepare his cases. I found this about as stimulating as working in my father's store. The job paid around $50 a week; glad as I was to be working at last, I quickly became bored.

So I was delighted to be suddenly handed an opportunity to participate in a Broadway production.

Some years earlier my father had put up the money for Burk Simon, his cousin, to attend the Baker Dramatic Workshop at Harvard. (George Pierce Baker later moved his school to Yale, where it lives on as the Yale School of Drama.) Burk earned a reputation as a successful director while working under David Belasco, undoubtedly the most flamboyant theatrical impresario of his era. When Belasco died, in May 1931, Burk went out on his own. One Sunday in 1932 Burk called to say he had a play he wanted to read me, and asked me to come over.

He lived three blocks away, at the Hotel des Artistes, right across from what was then an equestrian stable on West 67th Street, just off Central Park. About twenty years later I would have cause to remember those stables.

The play he read was about a hillbilly family. As he recited the script by Jack Kirkland, Burk delivered a pretty fair rendition of what I imagined Georgia Crackers sounded like. I thought the play was terrific. Burk said, "You know, we could produce it for five thousand dollars."

He wanted me to put up the money, or at least some of it. I had the funds, and I was inclined to invest them, but I told Burk that, although I personally liked the material, I wasn't qualified to decide whether it would be successful, whether it would attract an audience.

But my roommate, Stan Joseloff, worked for Shubert, the Broadway impresario, and I valued his opinions. I telephoned to ask him over, and Burk obligingly read the play aloud for a second time. I liked it even more. Joseloff differed.

"I don't think it has a chance," he said. His reasoning was founded in dialogue and characterizations that were, for that era, very strong and sometimes shocking material.

Unwilling to back my untried instincts against Joseloff's experience, I passed up this opportunity to invest in *Tobacco Road*, based on Erskine Caldwell's novel.

When that play opened at the Masque Theatre on Broadway in December 1933, *New York Times* critic Brooks Atkinson called it "one of the grossest episodes ever put on the stage." But he also said, "It has spasmodic moments of merciless power where truth is flung into your face with all the slime that truth contains." He added that the male lead, Henry Hull, gave the performance of his career. *Tobacco Road* was a Pulitzer Prize finalist in 1933, and returned to Broadway more than a dozen times after its initial run.

Show business is always a gamble. You never know when to fold your cards or raise the ante. You can spend a lot of money and effort on research, but no one can ever tell for sure what the public will pay to see on any given day. You have to make that decision in your gut. That's the fun of the business, the excitement.

In passing up *Tobacco Road*, I learned to respect my own instincts and to back them instead of depending on others. That is a principle I've followed ever since, whether selecting shows for TV, motion picture theaters, or the stage. It cost me the chance to make a lot of money when I let that play go, but with almost sixty years of hindsight, it seems to have been a very good bargain.

After a dull and dogged year or so with Franklin, I got a call from Sam Rudner, whom I knew from Harvard, where he'd been on the *Law Review*. Sam told me Root, Clark, Buckner, and Ballantine was hiring lawyers on behalf of its client, the trustees of Paramount Pictures, which was in reorganization under the bankruptcy code. These lawyers were needed to help the trustees straighten things out. Sam suggested I contact Leo Gottlieb or Henry Friendly at Root Clark.

I jumped at the opportunity.

I sat down with Gottlieb and Friendly, whom I also knew from Harvard, though they had been some years ahead of me. These were brilliant fellows. Both had made the *Law Review*, and Friendly, who would go on to a long and distinguished career as a U.S. Court of Appeals judge, had set Harvard academic standards eclipsed only by the great legal scholar and Supreme Court justice Louis Brandeis.

Paramount

In July 1933, I joined Paramount. It was soon decided that I would go to Boston to help reorganize the Paramount theaters and circuits in New England.

Initially I met with Stephen A. Lynch, a former pro baseball player. Everyone called him "S.A." He had built up a huge circuit of theaters in the Carolinas, Georgia, Texas, Virginia, and Alabama, then sold them to Paramount for cash and stock. As was the case with many circuits Paramount bought in the 1920s, the deal included a guaranty that if Paramount's stock wasn't trading at $85 a share within a given number of years, Paramount would buy it back at that price.

After the Crash of 1929, Paramount's stock, which had sold as high as about $70 a share, took a dive. By the early 1930s it was selling for under $9. One after another, the former circuit owners demanded that Paramount repurchase their stock for $85 a share. It was like a run on a bank. There just wasn't enough cash. The company went into bankruptcy court, and a judge appointed trustees. They brought in S. A. Lynch to run and reorganize Paramount's theaters.

My interview with Lynch was very brief. A financial wizard, he was a little Napoleon with a blunt, no-nonsense manner. He drilled me with a glance and said, "Young man, I've checked your record. You're very bright, and you're going to go far with Paramount. I have four simple rules, and I expect you to follow them.

"First, I want you to report to me once every week and tell me just what you're doing.

"Next, don't ever fool around with the talent. Stay away from those movie stars. In other words, don't crap on your own threshold." (This is the language he used!)

"Third, I won't pay more than fifteen percent of the gross for theater rentals. If you can do it under that, fine." That is, 15 percent of box-office receipts was the most I could pay for theater rent.

"And last, let me tell you a story. When I sold my circuit to Paramount, half was in stock and half cash. I put all the cash into Coca-Cola. I was probably the second largest stockholder to Robert Woodruff, who controlled the company. I thought therefore I should be on Coca-Cola's board of directors. I came in and made a presentation; I was getting along just fine, except one man kept needling me and asking questions. I could feel he was against my coming on the board. Finally I blew up, picked up my papers, walked out, and slammed the door behind me. And immediately I sold all my stock, every share.

"That cost me millions and millions of dollars, because that's what my stock would be worth today. The lesson I learned, young man, was that you *never* slam the door. In other words, in trading out a deal, *keep that door open*."

That was probably the most important principle anyone in business could ever know. I profited greatly by applying it.

As for Lynch's second rule, I made it a strict practice never to discuss deals with talent. Only with their agents. Before I married, however, much temptation was put into my path by agents who offered me dates with their clients. They were very lovely young ladies. A few went on to fame and fortune, but there's no reason to damage any reputations by naming them. In any case, I can never be sure whether the agent spoke on his own, trying to get his actress or model a break, or if the lady would even have agreed, had I been willing.

I was young. I was single. I admit to being tempted. I always said no. In short order the word got around Hollywood, and the offers stopped. What a relief!

If ever I had cause to doubt the wisdom of S. A. Lynch's dictum, I merely recalled the story of John Otterson, head of Electrical Research Projects, Inc. (ERPI), a division of Western Electric, which became part of AT&T. ERPI developed the sound system that Paramount used when talkies came along. When Paramount went into reorganization, ERPI was one of the biggest creditors, and Otterson came in as president of Paramount Pictures. In Hollywood, he became infatuated with Marlene Dietrich, then under contract to Sam Goldwyn, and made overtures about bringing her over to Paramount.

When Goldwyn learned Otterson was trying to interfere with one of his actresses, for revenge he stole Paramount's biggest star, Gary Cooper, and put him under contract. That was the end of Otterson. The Paramount board voted him out.

Dave Wallerstein, who became a close friend, joined Balaban & Katz Theatres (B&K), Paramount's Chicago-based subsidiary, when I was still at Harvard. He went on to head B&K, and later joined Paramount Theatres' board of directors.

Dave witnessed at first hand the early growth of the motion picture business. He worked for Barney Balaban, my mentor and friend, the man who gave me my big chance. And he rubbed elbows with Adolph Zukor, to me the most important figure in the creation of the American movie industry.

OTHER RECOLLECTIONS:
David Wallerstein

I started with Balaban & Katz November 1, 1926, just before talkies came along. This was a time when people didn't yet live in suburbs. Radio was just coming along. There was no television. People amused themselves by going to movies. They didn't travel. Theaters were where ordinary people experienced grandeur: magnificent buildings with plush ladies' rooms, ushers in fancy uniforms. Lots of atmosphere.

There were seven Balaban brothers. Barney, the oldest, was the most successful. He was a bookkeeper with Central Cold Storage in Chicago. A.J. was the creative one. When nickelodeons came along, A.J. got a job in one playing the piano.

When their mother, who had a little grocery store, saw that a theater was a place where people paid in cash—and paid *before* they saw the show—she said, "That's a great business." In 1908, Barney put up some money, and they opened a nickelodeon.

Sam Katz, who also owned a nickelodeon, married Ida, the only Balaban girl. Katz was an aggressive guy, full of energy, very dynamic, a real promoter. The Balabans and Katz combined their interests. Katz was the showman, A.J. was the artistic force. Max was the film guy. David, Harry, and Elmer also worked in the theaters. John was the operator. Barney kept his bookkeeping job until they had two theaters, then became the manager, the money guy.

Katz went to the Coast on his honeymoon in 1917 and saw Grauman's Chinese Theatre. He said, "That's what we need in Chicago." He went to Julius Rosenwald, the father of Sears. A philanthropist. In Chicago in those days, Rosenwald was the god, the money provider. He sent Katz to his brother, Morris, and then they had backing.

They wanted to start fresh, so they got an architect who'd never built a theater and put up the Central Park Theatre on Chicago's West Side. It combined the best of the new ideas Katz brought from New York and Hollywood—a grand, showy presentation of movies, stage shows, and a symphony. When it opened in 1918, it was an instant success.

After that, the guy building the Riviera Theatre defaulted on his construction loan. B&K took it and embellished it like the Central Park. It, too, was successful. With big syndicators like Hertz,

Parmalee, and Wrigley as backers, B&K sent architects to Europe to copy details from famous cathedrals and castles, then built the Tivoli, on the South Side.

In the meantime United Artists put up the Rivoli, and Warners built the Strand in New York, and the idea of having what were called stage presentations—as opposed to vaudeville-type shows with a master of ceremonies—spread across the country.

The big guys making movies in those days were Sam Goldwyn, Sid Lasky, Adolph Zukor, Marcus Loew, Carl Laemmle, and William Fox. They began battling to control distribution and exhibition, which meant controlling theaters. Goldwyn and Loew combined, Loew in the theaters and Goldwyn making pictures. When Loew got control of MGM—by this time Goldwyn had been forced out and had started his own company—they became one of the big circuits. Bought up theaters all over the country. B&K grew out of the nickelodeon stage just at the time when these big circuits were forming.

Before World War I, in most parts of the country vaudeville and movie theaters closed in the summer. But Barney worked in a cold storage plant where every summer they made a hole in the wall between the storage area and the office, put in a fan, and blew in cold air.

Barney had the idea to do that in theaters, probably the biggest contribution he made to American life, because after theaters got air conditioning, it was used in all kinds of public buildings. B&K's Central Park Theatre was the first—he built an ice-making plant next door and blew cold air through ducts into the theater.

Almost immediately the business changed. With year-round audiences, the studios could make more on a picture, so they made more of them. As they got more theaters, they needed more product, so the studios turned into factories, turning out films as fast as possible. Paramount was making fifty pictures a year by the end of the thirties.

The big movie producers, who now had their own theater chains, kept a stranglehold on pictures. They wanted to eliminate independents like B&K. The producers demanded outrageous rental fees, and to get even one movie you had to take all their pictures in *all* your theaters. Their idea was to lock up the product so you had to sell them your theaters or go broke.

When B&K had trouble getting the right kind of movies for its theaters, they got together with other independent circuits and formed First National Company to make their own.

Adolph Zukor's Paramount became the biggest movie company in the world. Zukor controlled 2,000 theaters, including 350 in Canada. Loews is out buying theaters, Fox is out buying theaters. Everybody is building big palaces in major cities.

By 1926 Zukor needed somebody to run all these theaters. In order to get Sam Katz, whom they considered the best thing going and because he was giving them such a hard time in Chicago, Paramount bought control of B&K. Katz is sent to New York to form Paramount Publix Corporation and operate all Paramount theaters. He proceeds to centralize operations, dictating ticket prices, usher uniforms, salaries, everything.

Paramount was buying circuits that were suing them on antitrust grounds, and settling by buying them out. As we acquired circuits, the guys who put them together were buying up individual theaters and building new ones. In the smaller towns, B&K would buy property, or maybe just an option, and put up a sign, "Watch for the new air-conditioned Paramount Theatre."

It would be the middle of August. They'd put the sign across the street from the other theater. So then they'd go over and see the owner. "We really don't want to build another theater in this town, we'd rather buy yours," they'd say. "But it's up to you. If you don't sell to us, we'll build across the street. We've got the money, we've got banking power." Paramount was a money machine. And they'd say, "Take your time, think about it. We'll be back in fifteen minutes for your decision."

In the larger towns, between Paramount Pictures and First National Pictures, B&K could get plenty of movies. But an independent, maybe a guy has a lovely theater in this town, maybe two—he can't get good pictures. That's how they got Abe Blank, in Des Moines. They said, "Look, Mr. Blank, we'll start building theaters in your towns. Sell to us or else."

In addition to all that, this was the roaring twenties, and along comes Al Capone. The Mob took over the projectionists' union, they tried to take over Hollywood.

Now out of nowhere comes Warner Bros. with talking pictures. One day Barney Balaban, president of B&K, calls me in and says, "We've got contracts for these goddam short subjects but people don't want talking pictures; they like orchestras and an organ. Mr.

Zukor doesn't believe in it. Get rid of these goddam things." So I did, and I got a raise because I got more for them than we paid.

Six months later talking pictures arrived, *Lights of New York* and *The Jazz Singer*. And I have to go and buy the contracts back. Then we had to borrow a lot of money to put sound in all our theaters.

This was the Golden Age. In the big cities, downtown theaters had elaborate stage shows—Bob Hope, Jack Benny, the Marx brothers—all the top acts. We had Fred Waring and the Pennsylvanians, the Ritz brothers, dancing girls, ballets. Money was flowing in. Katz is still building palaces like he didn't care what they cost.

The big studios—Loews, Warners, Fox, and Paramount—divided the country. We bought movies from each other but wouldn't sell to independents. There was a "gentleman's agreement." Those chickens all came back home to roost, but that's later.

Then the Crash comes, and we still do business but then comes 1930 and 1931. Then Katz is after Zukor. The next thing you know, Zukor is out as president, and Katz is in, because he thinks he can run the studio. He puts his own man in the studio. That doesn't work. Finally he brings in John Hertz, who started Hertz Drive Yourself and sold it to General Motors. He wants to save the company by cutting expense accounts and waste. But there are these fantastic rents they've accumulated and very high interest rates on borrowed money.

At B&K we tried to survive by cutting salaries and then by going without salaries and everything else. We thought the 1933 [Chicago] World's Fair would bring it back. It didn't help. There wasn't any money. The empire that Zukor built fell apart. The people who Paramount owed all this money to came in. When Paramount went into reorganization, Blank, Karl Hoblitzelle, E. V. Richards, and other former owners of some of the circuits Paramount had acquired, took back 50 percent interests in their old circuits, and operated them. Everything was decentralized again.

❑ ❑ ❑

My own apprenticeship in the business of theatrical exhibition began in Boston, where my first tasks were to learn what we owned, what we leased, what our partners had, and what the problems were. Then I had to learn the theater business.

One of the bankruptcy trustees was Harry LeBaron Sampson, a partner in Hutchins and Wheeler, the second oldest law firm in the country, which also represented the Cabots and the Lowells. Although he was a model of rectitude—and a very wealthy man—Sampson also set a standard for what New Englanders call "thrift." His offices were Spartan, with bare walls and wood floors that cried out for carpeting. At our first meeting I asked to go through the files to see what the theater grosses were, what they were losing or making, and so forth. That first day I worked straight through until Sampson came in and said, "It's almost midnight. You've worked long enough for the first day. Let's go home."

I had a room at the Copley Plaza. He lived in Cambridge. It was so late I had decided to take a cab, so I offered to share it and drop him off on the way. "Oh no," he said. "I'll take the subway." And in the years that followed, though we often worked even later, he always insisted on taking the subway. He was a rich man but he was "old money" and wouldn't dream of spending a few dollars for a cab.

Many of our theater buildings were leased, so early on I traveled throughout New England to visit every landlord. I needed to negotiate adjustments to our leases, because by then, three years into the Depression, our business was down to almost nothing. I have to give due credit to those Yankees for having greater faith in their properties than we did. They all said, "The theater business is going to come back. You come talk to us again if it's not doing well at the end of a year." Thus I got relief virtually everywhere, but only for a year. I gained the greatest respect for those Yankees. They were tough, but they were good people and fair-minded.

Because of the way Paramount had acquired individual theaters and circuits, we owned some outright but had only a 50 percent interest in others. For example we were fifty-fifty partners with Joseph P. Kennedy, father of the future President, in a circuit of mostly small-town theaters in Maine and New Hampshire, and fifty-fifty with Publix Netoco Theatres, a circuit in greater Boston controlled by Sam Pinanski and his family. In addition, we had many different partners in individual theaters.

There were almost 300 Paramount theaters in New England, and while Sampson as trustee was responsible for reorganization, he turned operations over to Pinanski and his partner Martin Mullen. I had to recommend which theaters to drop, which to keep. I didn't have control. I had to consult with Sampson, I worked closely with Pinanski and Mullen, and I was in constant touch with Lynch in New York.

Until I went to Boston for Paramount, I had never had reason to appreciate all the things that went into making a theater profitable. After going through the financial records of hundreds of theaters, however, I began to detect patterns of success and failure. When I went into the field to look at the actual theaters, I saw them in an entirely new light.

For example, I started looking closely at concession stands. To my surprise, among dozens of items, I didn't recognize the name of one national brand.

I bought several packages, and saw that some had only a few pieces of candy but should have had a dozen. In other cases the candy bars were of decidedly inferior quality. It was clear our concessionaires were ripping us off. And our patrons. I said to myself, "We may have a captive audience, but the public is not going to buy this crap." You can't sell anything that's not quality, no matter what it is.

So I told the circuit managers, "This is ridiculous." We threw out all our concessionaires and handled the candy ourselves. We gave the public their money's worth, and of course they bought more. Almost overnight, our concession sales nearly quadrupled. S. A. Lynch ordered all Paramount's American theaters to get rid of their outside concessionaires.

Concessions are important profit centers for theater owners. Improving our sales helped pump money into the company at a time when it was desperately needed. Nowadays, when theaters must pay huge percentages of box office receipts for exhibition rights to movies, concession sales provide most or all of their profit margins.

To learn the theater business, I sat down with bookers, buyers, theater managers, and advertising people. These were men of great experience, individuals who had developed their instincts in the rough and tumble of vaudeville, nickelodeons, silent features, and the early talkies. Through decades of competition, they had learned what an audience would watch. My years reorganizing the New England theaters helped lay the best foundation I ever could have had for a career in the picture business and later in television.

One of the first pictures I discussed with them was a film about the life of the poet Robert Browning. I thought it was just great. But the bookers and buyers said, "No, that's a class picture, it won't go well."

It went into the New York City Music Hall, and was a modest success, but everywhere else people stayed away in droves. The bookers told me, "You can't judge a picture from the standpoint of your own personal interests. That's not the way to look at a picture. You must ask yourself, 'Does it have mass appeal?' "

From that day on, when considering both movies and television programming, I have tried to set aside my personal tastes to look at each show's potential for mass appeal.

From the start of my time in Boston, I returned to New York almost every weekend. There I would consult with Lynch and Y. Frank Freeman, the Georgia Tech–trained engineer who had helped Lynch build theater circuits while serving as his second-in-command. After a time Lynch had me reporting weekly by telephone to Freeman, and I went to New York less frequently.

On one of those trips I made the acquaintance of Si Siegel, a young Paramount accountant. We would become very close in the decades ahead. Years later, after I had moved into television, he would become my right hand on financial matters, one of the principal architects of the survival, growth, and success of American Broadcasting Companies. Looking back, I can't imagine how ABC could have overcome all the obstacles in its path without Si Siegel as my alter ego.

Si rose from very humble origins. Born in Denver, he came to New York as a small boy. When he was eleven, his father died, leaving his penniless mother to raise six children. Determined that her four girls would never have to suffer welfare's indignities, she resolved that they would become self-sufficient through education. Si left school at age sixteen to help pay for his sisters' schooling. For years he toiled by day and took night classes to complete his own education.

OTHER RECOLLECTIONS:
Si Siegel

By my early twenties, I had finished a two-year accounting course. I got excellent marks, and I really knew accounting. Everybody else in the class was preparing for the CPA exam, but I needed practical experience. I got a job at $15 a week, and I took the Civil Service Exam.

Later an employment agency sent me to Famous Players, which became Paramount after I was hired on June 6, 1929. A few months later I was notified that I passed Civil Service and could get a job with a salary a few dollars a week more than Paramount paid. I told Fred Mohrhardt, the assistant comptroller, that although I liked the company, I'd been offered more money and intended to leave. He said, "We'll match it." So I stayed.

I remember very well the first time I met Leonard. I was in Auditing. The comptroller called me in and said there was a wire from Boston, where Goldenson was reorganizing the New England theaters. "I can't make head or tail out of what he did. So many debentures, so much stock, and I just don't understand it, I don't know what it comes to. Go sit down with the guy and make some sense out of what he's saying."

I took Leonard to a vacant office and said, "Let's start at the beginning, what you're settling each claim for." I used an eleven-column sheet and listed all the items. When we finished talking about each claim, I added it all up. It came to exactly the amount Leonard had said we had to pay out, so much in preferred stock, so much in debentures, and so on. I took it to Mohrhardt.

He said, "That's the way it should be. Now I understand."

Leonard said, "I guess you're more surprised than I am." He was quite young but very sure of himself. He thought he was good—he *knew* he was good—he was very cocky.

I saw very little of him for the next three or four years. He went back to Boston, and then he returned to New York. When he became head of theaters, he asked for me. As I understand the story, and I'm making myself a great guy, Mohrhardt told Leonard, "I'll give you any two men you want, but you can't have Si." Leonard told Mohrhardt, then treasurer, that if he couldn't have *me*, he couldn't run the department.

Leonard didn't tell me what I was to do, just that I was to work for him. So I just made myself useful. In all the years that followed, no matter what title I had, my duties were always the same.

Leonard always knew what he wanted, where he was going. He went out and did it.

❑ ❑ ❑

In 1937, Paramount, still the biggest motion picture company in the world, emerged from reorganization. I'm proud to say I had a small part in the result: In New England, every creditor was paid 100 cents on the dollar. Those Yankees were right. The business did come back.

Adolph Zukor, who had built a single theater on 14th Street in New York into a tremendous empire, and who once owned a large block of stock, ended up with almost nothing. I attribute this to the failings of

Paramount's treasurer, Ralph Kohn. Kohn came up with the scheme whereby Paramount helped finance its expansion by, in effect, betting on the continuing rise in the price of its stock. Had Zukor had a good financial mind running his fiscal affairs, the company would likely have stayed in Zukor's hands.

In that case, of course, I might well have ended up with a dull career in railroad law. I'll never know.

Among Zukor's holdings had been a 50 percent interest in a small but growing radio network called CBS. The trustees, anxious to raise cash, sold it to William S. Paley for $6 million, a ridiculous, fire-sale price even then.

Reorganizing Paramount was a coast-to-coast struggle. When it became clear that Sam Katz didn't have all the answers, the trustees hired financier (and small-time theater owner) Joseph P. Kennedy as a consultant. According to my old friend John Hertz, Kennedy said the first thing to do was fire Paramount's largely Jewish board of directors. Hertz said Kennedy didn't much care for Jews. The trustees thanked Kennedy, paid him, and in 1936 brought in Barney Balaban, an orthodox Jew, as president. He got things moving, partly by selling, merging, or liquidating some 100 companies Paramount owned or controlled.

By the autumn of 1937 Lynch had accomplished most of what he had set out to do and things were starting to roll. He moved on to manage his extensive real estate interests, and Frank Freeman took charge of all Paramount theaters. Mullen and Pinanski wanted to keep me in Boston as general manager of Paramount Theatres. Thinking this would limit my options, I declined.

Then Frank Freeman asked me to come to New York as his assistant. That was the job I wanted, because from New York I could involve myself with theaters all over the world.

When Barney came in to head Paramount, the studio production chief was Buddy De Sylva, an industry legend who started as a songwriter for Al Jolson. Later, De Sylva wrote film scores, then turned to producing—including five Shirley Temple films—and near the end of his life became chairman of Capitol Records. In 1938, when De Sylva became quite ill, Barney sent Frank Freeman out to help him run the studio.

Frank had a wonderful personality. There was a warmth about him. A good-hearted fellow who often joked around in a pleasant way, he enjoyed a wide reputation as a most honorable man. Much revered by Paramount's theater partners, he was an ideal person to head up the studio. The talent liked and respected him. He had terrific good sense about public relations.

These personal qualities propelled him forward to become one of Hollywood's most outstanding leaders, and a highly respected industry spokesman.

With Freeman in Hollywood, Barney Balaban said, "I expect you to supervise all the theaters." In effect, I had the job on probation.

Post-reorganization Paramount was decentralized; circuit partners ran semiautonomous operations. These were all men who had survived the chaotic beginnings of the movie industry by being stronger and more ruthless, and exercising greater cunning than their competition. In a sense they were all buccaneers. They had built these businesses up from nothing. They were rough and tough, hard-headed men who didn't want any interference. They wanted to run their businesses. I could understand this. If a young punk like myself, twenty-five or thirty years their junior, were to try to tell them how to run their business, they would have told me to get lost.

Instead I set out to establish that I wanted to help them. I pointed out events and circumstances in the industry and things happening in our other circuits which they might use to their advantage, so they could hardly object.

For example, we got daily reports by telegraph from certain key theaters all over the United States, consolidated them into a single report, and telegraphed summaries to all our circuits. I was on the phone almost daily to ask how a new picture was doing. If it was earning well in certain markets and not in others, I'd try to find the reason and let everyone know.

If I saw that a circuit had overpaid on one picture, compared to another, I got in touch to let them know. These kinds of things made their jobs easier, just as it improved Paramount's overall profitability.

That's how I got their respect. After a while, as I was right more often than not, they began to appreciate what I was saying. It got easier.

Hardly before my new seat was warm, however, I became aware of several circuits that still had major problems. The most urgent of these was United Detroit Theatres. Our twenty-five-odd theaters there were losing huge sums every week.

Our man in Detroit was George W. Trendle, who also owned, with partner John King (né Kunsky), the Kunsky–Trendle Radio Network and radio station WXYZ.

Trendle was supposed to operate our Detroit theaters. In actuality he was ignoring them to concentrate on radio. I looked at the prices he was paying per film and the overhead of his union employees. Nobody could make money the way he had run things. I said, "George, you've got to make up your mind. Either run our theaters or run your radio business. If you don't want to give up radio, you're going to have to give up the theaters." Since Trendle had a financial interest in the station and network, he elected to stay with radio.

Trendle went on to earn a place in show business history by creating "The Lone Ranger," "The Green Hornet," "Ned Jordan, Federal Ace," "Challenge of the Yukon," and several other radio serials. Those shows, recorded on disks and mailed around the country for broadcast on dozens of local stations, became the basis for the Mutual Radio Network.

I put Earl Hudson, who'd been Trendle's theater publicity and advertising man, in as general manager. I told him I would run the circuit until we reorganized, and when I was satisfied with things I'd turn it over to him.

The key to putting Detroit back in the black was the Madison Theatre, downtown. Trendle had been negotiating for the lease renewal, but was so distracted by his other interests that he let it get away. Just before I arrived, a group of about 120 independents, the Co-Op Theatres, took over the lease.

Paramount owned all but one of the other downtown theaters: the Michigan, United Artists, and State. The other belonged to Harry and Elmer Balaban, who used different suppliers and wouldn't bother us. But if the Co-Op controlled the Madison, it could compete with us downtown for first-run product. That would allow the distributors to play us off against each other and keep rentals high. I needed the Madison in our hands so I could try to correct the film deals Trendle had made. He was paying up to 70, 80, 90 percent of the gross. We couldn't possibly make a profit.

It was time to play hardball. I went to the Co-Op people and said, "Gentlemen, you've had a field day here for a long time with Trendle. Now you've taken the Madison Theatre away. I'm telling you that unless you return that to us, I will break the prices in this town down to twenty-five cents. And I'll do it tomorrow." I would have done it, too. I had no choice.

First-run tickets then were about $1.25; if I had dropped my prices, their business would have gone to pot, because they would have had to match us. As a collection of small independents, they couldn't get by very long on 25 cents. We were a big, rich company that could have sustained losses indefinitely. In any case, we would lose a lot more if they continued to hold the Madison.

Then and there they knew I wasn't fooling. Almost immediately they returned the Madison. Later, I would come to know these people very well, and we became good friends.

Since I wasn't going to continue paying highwayman rates while I negotiated to get film rentals down, I would be unable to get first-run films for the Madison until the situation was corrected. I put in a policy of "proven pictures"—old pictures from every company. Naturally these didn't attract the large audiences the theater needed to make a profit, and each week we went $500 to $750 into the red at the Madison. I didn't care.

With the Madison back in hand, I stopped paying film rentals. No matter what the contract said, they were so far from reality that we couldn't possibly make any money. I got wires and phone calls from all the distributors and producers. Threats, lawsuits—the usual. But I told them, "We're not going to run your films unless we can at least break even."

Meanwhile, I also had to fight the unions. They had four stage hands in each theater, and there was absolutely nothing for them to do except collect their paychecks. All they did was play gin rummy backstage. All day. Every day. That's why they needed four, I guess. I told the union that was three stage hands too many, that I wouldn't allow it. They threw up picket lines and went on strike. We just ran the theaters without them. We really didn't need anybody back there. Eventually they came to understand that one paycheck is better than no paychecks, and we settled the strike on my terms.

I went to New York every Saturday and had lunch with Barney Balaban. After a while he started to needle me about the losses at the Madison. "We can't keep on losing $750 a week on a theater. What kind of a deal did you make?" he asked.

I knew that Paul Raibourn was behind this. An engineer and statistician, a bright man, he had Barney's ear. Barney watched every penny. Even when he ran the whole company, he personally went over executive expense accounts and studio invoices, looking to save $10 here or $200 there. Raibourn went to Barney every time he saw a red figure. Naturally he showed him the Madison Theatre's numbers; every week for three or four weeks Barney asked me about it.

Finally I blew my top. "Barney, you gave me the job of correcting the theaters in Detroit. I'm going to do it. But I won't be needled every week on the Madison. That one theater doesn't concern me. My interest is the overall profit that we can return from all of Detroit, without considering individual theaters. You give me a year, and if within the year this isn't working, get yourself a new man."

Barney backed off and gave me rope enough to hang myself.

At the start we were losing $7,000 a week in Detroit. By the end of a year, the film distributors had caved in on their percentages. We negotiated a much more equitable arrangement. Thus we made a profit of $7,000 a week, or $350,000 a year, on those same theaters. The next year we made almost $1.5 million. From that time on, Barney never bothered me.

After I'd won his respect, Barney began grooming me to succeed him as chief executive of Paramount. He became my mentor, my strongest advocate, and my friend.

Barney Balaban was a vigorous, barrel-chested man of average height who was very health-conscious. He took daily steam baths, was faithful to an exercise regimen, and drank alcohol quite sparingly. When I knew him, he was bald.

Though Barney had a wide reputation as a tightwad—and he worked very hard to maintain it—he could also be generous. I can't think of a single charitable cause he ever turned down, and they usually didn't have to ask. He was a staunch supporter of Zionist causes; during and before Israel's War of Independence, Barney dug deep into his pocket—and stuck his neck way out—to help get weapons to the Haganah.

Barney was also a patriot who felt a strong obligation to his country. On his own initiative, he located the private collector who owned the original manuscript of the Bill of Rights. Barney bought it in 1943—with his own money—and immediately donated it to the Library of Congress for every American to enjoy. He also paid for 250,000 replicas to be printed and distributed to schools to help sell war bonds.

In 1946 he arranged for the original Bill of Rights to be exhibited in towns and cities all over the country on what came to be called the Freedom Train. The exhibition, conceived by Barney, was initially funded with $35,000 out of his pocket and Paramount's corporate coffers.

One of my earliest friendships at Paramount was with a brilliant showman, Bob Weitman. A Cornell graduate, he recruited a squad of young men when he went into the Brooklyn Paramount to straighten things out. When he later took charge of the New York City Paramount, he brought them along.

One of them was a Fordham law student named Irving Kaufman, who eventually quit Paramount to finish law school. Not so many years later Judge Kaufman presided over the espionage trial of Julius and Ethel Rosenberg. Another of Bob's team was Gene Pleshette, whose wife unexpectedly went into labor and delivered a baby girl in the Brooklyn Paramount Theatre. Weitman, the manager, hailed a cab and rushed mother and infant to a hospital. The baby, Suzanne, grew up to become a well-regarded actress.

In 1937, during the darkest days of the Depression, the New York

Paramount Theatre was a sea of red ink. Bob was sent in to rescue it. I helped him whenever I could.

OTHER RECOLLECTIONS:
Bob Weitman

The Paramount Theatre was in the Paramount Building, 1501 Broadway. And that theater was then grossing, with first-run pictures, $7,600 a week, which was nothing. Almost depressing. It was left to me to figure a way out of this. I told Frank Freeman we would put in a new band for the run of each show, two weeks, three weeks, whatever. And I described all this to him. He says, "None of these dancing girls where you'll need all those stage hands." He knew everything.

I said, "Oh, no. We're going to make new deals."

The long and the short of it, I called Dick Walsh, the president of International Federation of Stage Hands and Operators. He was the guy that took on the gangsters, Bioff and Browne. He says, "Hello, kiddy, aren't you the kid that was out at the Brooklyn Paramount?"

I said, "Yes. I'd like to see you. Can you come down tonight at midnight?" He came down, and all we've got is a work light and emptiness. I said, "Push that button." He pushes the button and the curtains close. I said, "Push the other button." He pushes that button and the pit comes up. I said, "You see that bank of lights in front of the balcony? That's the lighting and the projection room."

He says, "I know what you're going to ask: how come six stagehands?" That's how I got rid of the extra stagehands. And we became fast friends.

Then I went with Lenny Goldenson to meet with Mr. James Caesar Petrillo. Little Caesar, the guy who ran the American Federation of Musicians. He was an old pal of Barney Balaban, they grew up together in Chicago. Petrillo's kid died of peritonitis, and nobody ever explained this to him correctly, and from then on he was so afraid of germs he wouldn't shake hands.

When we came in to his office, he opens a desk drawer and takes out a pistol. Six shooter of some kind. Just lays it out on the desk, and we go on about our business like it never happened.

So I tell him, we're going to have a new band policy, play all the bands, and if it hits, he'll be a tremendous man in the country because musicians will be working.

He said, "You listen to me, college boy. If you have Local 802 musicians in the band, you've got no problem. If you have a band with fifteen fellows that are 802, one or two are not but they're traveling, you've got to pay standbys, for a total of the number in the band."

So I said to him, rather irately, "You're crazy. You're in America, you know."

He turns to some guy, I don't know him from third base, and says, "How do you like this kid?"

I said, "I don't care if you like me."

He said, "I'll tell Barney, and then he'll call, and you're out of a job."

I said, "That's up to you. But I'll tell you something. I'm not going to pay that standby. That's featherbedding." I didn't know what the hell featherbedding was, but I'd read about it. "I'm not going to pay for nothing. You give me musicians, and I'll pay them, but let them stand on the grand stairway and play as people walk into the theater."

He said, "I never heard of that before."

I said, "Well, I just heard of it myself. I'm not going to pay and not get musicians. You do anything you like, but if this thing hits, your music guys are going to have a lot of work."

He says, "Let's have a drink. This is show business, you know."

We sat in the bar at the Longchamps. He had beer, we had an iced drink, and we went on. The first band that we booked was Casa Loma, Glen Grey, and we charged 25 cents until 1:00 P.M. My objective was to create a want and a panic, make people think they get in for nothing. The theory behind it, if they're buying these stinking pictures, $7,600 per week, and you give them that plus a popular band for a quarter until 1:00—at any rate, we took in $56,000 the first week.

We had an accordionist who would play in the lobby. We put musicians on the sidewalk. The entertainment started the moment they put their two bits on the window sill. Afternoon prices were higher, evenings still higher. This thing started to mushroom incredibly. We had a huge sign in the lobby, "Vote for your favorite bands." This thing became a big smash.

❑ ❑ ❑

Weitman's new policy was tremendously successful. He booked such bands as Glenn Miller, Tommy Dorsey, Eddy Duchin, Woody Herman, Charlie Spivak, and Stan Kenton. At the time, few of these dance bands or their leaders were well known. But playing the Paramount Theatre put them before the New York press, helped them to get bookings on network radio shows, and thus exposed them to a wide audience. It put them on the map. They became the biggest bands in America and the world.

The Paramount's Depression-era talent budgets didn't allow for many big stars. So Weitman booked unknowns and built them into stars. One of his biggest successes was a skinny New Jersey kid with a big voice named Frank Sinatra.

Bob was a master showman, who knew how to promote a personality. He set out to make Sinatra an instant success by recruiting a few dozen teenaged girls to sit in the front rows for each performance. In exchange for free admission and choice seats, they were expected to shriek and make a big fuss when Sinatra appeared on stage and began to sing.

Before each performance, Weitman took two or three of these girls aside, handed each a dollar bill—a healthy sum for a Depression teenager—and told them that when Sinatra crooned, they were to swoon. After a few well-publicized front-row faints, newspaper reports of Sinatra's mesmerizing voice and its effect on adolescent girls soon propelled him to stardom.

Using other kinds of promotion, Weitman did the same for such unknowns as Danny Kaye, the Andrews Sisters, Tony Martin, Perry Como, Nat King Cole, Frankie Laine, Billy Eckstine, Tony Martin, and Betty Hutton. They all got their start at the Paramount.

OTHER RECOLLECTIONS:
Bob Weitman

So this policy is going like gangbusters. We're booking Martin and Lewis, you name them. It was extraordinary. Warners' Strand, after two years, put in the band policy. The Roxy—owned by Fox—after a couple of years, them too.

So it achieved its purpose, but now everybody was doing it.

So I got hold of Ed Sullivan, and we booked him into the New York Paramount, and we booked Walter Winchell into the Brooklyn Paramount with Ben Birney, they were good friends.

Winchell introduced the acts. We used his column, because if Winchell was on the stage, you never knew who the hell was going to be in the audience. The stars would come, and we'd put a spotlight on the audience and introduce them all.

We did the same with Sullivan; he was writing a column then for the *Daily News*.

Sullivan said, "What'll I do?"

I said, "You'll point and you'll say, 'And now we introduce so and so.' " So Ed did nothing, but like some guy said, I don't remember who, he did it the best in the business. Later on I told him, "Why don't you get into television?"

❑ ❑ ❑

Thus did Bob Weitman create another legend. I came to enjoy Ed Sullivan's friendship and admired his unfailing showmanship. But in the 1950s and 1960s, after we went into television—Weitman headed up ABC's talent and program department—we spent much time and effort trying to find a program that wouldn't die merely because it ran opposite Sullivan's Sunday night show on CBS.

After Barney put me in charge of the theaters, I was incredibly busy. We had about 1,650 theaters; I had only been to about 400 of them; my plan was to visit each of them as soon as possible.

After finishing up in Detroit, I began visiting the various theater partners. Among the first was E. V. Richards in New Orleans. He had theaters in Mississippi and Louisiana. A big, portly fellow, very congenial, he was known as a stickler for detail.

E. V. wanted to know everything about every facet of the theater business, and he expected his managers to know no less than he did. His pursuit of knowledge knew no limits. Some years after I first got to know him, just after World War II, Paramount started a management training school in the South. E. V., who had built a substantial empire out of nothing but his own energies, enrolled in this school. The other trainees were mostly young men just out of the service, but when everyone put on overalls and climbed onto the roof to practice patching leaks in the tar paper, E. V. went right up there with them. He got good and dirty—and enjoyed every minute of it. He insisted that tests be identified by number, so no one would inflate his scores, and then proceeded to rack up scores that were never equaled.

When I got to New Orleans to see him, E. V. was living in a room above one of his theaters. He had a projectionist's school for his managers, and he made me go through it! I learned to run a projector, to name all of its parts, how to fix a broken machine and mend film. At the end he awarded me a diploma to prove I was a full-fledged projectionist.

From the time I joined Paramount in 1933, work consumed all my days and nights. I loved just about every minute of it, and had little time for anything else. I dated a few women in Boston, but these were very casual arrangements, because I wasn't looking to get involved. I had no time for that. I was too anxious to learn the theater business and get on with my career. But after returning to New York, I began to wonder if there shouldn't be more to my life.

There was. My sister Sylvia and her husband were friendly with a couple named Greenfield. In the middle of 1938 they threw a big party. I was asked to pick up a young woman named Isabelle Weinstein at her home, and take her to the party.

I didn't know Isabelle, but like many people in New York, I'd heard of her father. Max Weinstein was born in Russia. He came to this country, alone, as a boy of ten. He sold candy on the streets of New York to earn money. He subsisted for years by grazing on the sandwiches saloon keepers put out to attract beer drinkers, thus saving money to bring over the rest of his family. He almost went off to the Alaskan Gold Rush, but his father begged him not to go. An entirely self-made man, he got into the ladies' coat business, and by his early twenties he had become one of the largest coat manufacturers in the United States.

His footnote in history is that early in 1917, he hired a Russian immigrant to work in his factory. Almost immediately, this immigrant organized his fellow workers and led them out on strike. Weinstein tried to fire him, but the workers stayed out on strike. Eventually, Weinstein had to close this factory and go out of business. Soon afterward, this fellow returned to Russia, where he joined Lenin as a Bolshevik revolutionary. His name was Leon Trotsky.

Max Weinstein, a very capable man, became a millionaire before he was twenty-eight, and retired when he was thirty-five. Bored, he started a bank in the late 1920s; after the Crash of '29, he merged it with another. About that time he bought a majority interest in Russeks, an upscale New

York ladies' clothing store with branches in Chicago and Philadelphia.

I now know someone was playing Cupid, but as far as I was concerned at the time, my introduction to Isabelle in 1938 was strictly a matter of transportation.

Of course I felt an attraction; she was a very pretty young woman. New York was full of pretty women, but I was drawn to Isabelle's bold curiosity and forthright ways. She was very offbeat, very provocative, a bucking bronco in the sense that she would not accept an answer of yes or no. She really wants to ferret out exactly what you mean by everything that you say. She's not being argumentative; she just wants to learn, and platitudes never satisfy her. She can be supercritical about things, but she's just as often supercomplimentary.

Isabelle was very unusual for a woman of that era, and she is far from common now. I think she's one of a kind. Her father, upon hearing some of the things she had to say, often said, "You should have been a boy, to talk that way." It is precisely that quality, her blithe contempt for boring conversation, that has kept me fascinated for over fifty years.

After our first meeting, however, I didn't call her for quite some time. I was constantly on the road. You can't run a theater circuit from a swivel chair, and we had dozens of big circuits. But eventually I did call her, and we began to date, whenever I was in town.

Isabelle always had it in for Frank Freeman. I had said to him, "I think I ought to think about getting married soon," and he had replied, "No, you're going to be traveling all the time."

When I told this to Isabelle, she said, "If you can't handle marriage and me and your business at the same time, you're having a problem." She was right.

OTHER RECOLLECTIONS:
Isabelle Weinstein Goldenson

The name "Goldenson" attracted me, I must confess, a little bit. Because of Rabbi Goldenson, I knew he had a good family. I wasn't going to date just any Tom, Dick, or Harry.

The morning after our first meeting, my mother said, "Did you have a good time?" Now, my parents never interfered or said anything about who I went out with. I said that I had a very pleasant time. And Mother said, "That was a nice young man. Your father and I liked him very much. There was something about him."

For her it was like saying, "Marry him." I was so stunned I

couldn't answer, but I felt there must be something extraordinary about him, or my mother wouldn't have said anything. She was a very good judge of character.

I thought Leonard was very nice, but I wasn't seriously interested in anybody. I really didn't know who would be equal to all the different things that I had in mind. I was spoiled that way. I went out only with fellows who were wealthy, because I wanted to be sure they weren't after me for any money. Our daughters, Loreen and Maxine, had the same type of concern. I don't think they're quite as bad as I was.

The fact that my parents, especially my father, liked Leonard was really quite unusual, because he had a deep prejudice against people in the movie industry.

Lewis J. Selznick—the father of David—tried to bring my father into the motion picture business as his partner. Father liked new things, and so he was tempted. He knew Selznick from a Sunday afternoon card game they played in. It was a friendly game but they played for very big stakes. My father always lost, but he accepted that he was not a good card player. Selznick always won. Some of the other players got suspicious and decided to examine the cards.

But my father was like Leonard, very trusting and very exacting about honesty and keeping your word and not saying anything you don't intend to do. Well, they found Selznick had marked the cards. From then on my father would have nothing to do with movie people. He was very conscious of reputation. That meant a lot.

Leonard took so long to call me that my sister and brother-in-law wanted to find out why he didn't go after me, hook, line, and sinker. At that time I was considered a very, very attractive catch.

Leonard didn't seem too interested in me. I became curious to find out why I wasn't creating a lot of excitement, why he didn't press for a date or anything like that. He took me for granted and treated me like I was a sister. My family was amazed. What was wrong with him? But he was just very busy and he wasn't interested in tying himself down to anybody. He had one thing in mind, his business, to be successful.

I was curious about him, and I don't give up so easily. So I chased *him*. Then he said he could not get married, but if he married anybody, it would be me! I thought, "That's a little overconfident." I resented that. He wanted me to wait a year while he went to visit hundreds of theaters. He couldn't take a girl from a wealthy background on such trips, he said, because in many places there were no adequate hotels. So I should sit and wait while he traveled all around!

Leonard and I were married October 10, 1939, and went to Asheville, North Carolina, for our wedding trip. Barney Balaban, who forgot to congratulate me in person, telephoned about midnight. That was the first disturbance.

❑ ❑ ❑

When we left for our honeymoon, I made the mistake of leaving the name of our hotel with my office. The fact that I was on my honeymoon didn't seem to make much of an impression on anyone. The next day I got a call from three of our theater partners, who were having trouble with Paramount's distribution division. They were fairly close by, so they hired airplanes and flew to Asheville to see me.

The partners insisted that I argue it out with Paramount, and *now*. They had me on the phone practically the whole time we were in Asheville.

I was getting calls from partners all over the country, all on the same subject. It looked like these would continue until I'd talked to every partner, and every partner knew I was on top of the situation. I decided the only way to get off the phone would be to get out of there at once.

Since I hadn't yet had a chance to visit all the theaters, I decided to go through the Texas theaters with Bob O'Donnell.

O'Donnell was general manager for Karl Hoblitzelle, a showman of the old school who owned half of Interstate Theatres. Hoblitzelle was also chairman of the Republic Bank, a fact that I would come to appreciate greatly many years later. O'Donnell took us in hand, and we set out from Dallas in his car.

OTHER RECOLLECTIONS:
Isabelle Weinstein Goldenson

A New York executive in those days did not put himself out to call on a local theater owner. The motion picture industry was so glamorous that the people seemed untouchable. So when Leonard came out and the owners found they could talk to him, he fit in perfectly. He didn't seem to realize he said things that were too nice or too trusting. But after a while it was contagious.

Yet he was like a big star. They treated him like royalty. Like their "golden son." They just adored him.

He was very fair. He listened to them. And then he'd cut right through some problem, suggest what to do, and do it. They weren't used to such fast action. They'd never met a person who'd been to Harvard and could act like that. I knew I'd married someone who was different from everybody else.

These people were always joking, always kidding. They had a great sense of humor, some of them, like Bob O'Donnell, who could have been a performer. And it seems I took it very well. I answered back, which amazed them, because they thought, Here's a little hothouse flower. That's how they were treating me.

Once, I asked for a Coca-Cola—I was dying of thirst—they said, "Here," and handed me the bottle. I got very insulted. I said, "Well, where's the glass? Or a straw?" They said, "Glass?" Leonard led them off to one side, and they were hysterical. So I learned to drink out of a bottle.

Wherever we went they were always entertaining me. I had a luncheon arranged with all the society ladies of Beaumont, Texas. These women sat around the table comparing guns!

I thought they were kidding, trying to show how wild Texas was. But they proved to me they never traveled without a gun in their car. It was very hard for me to understand at first, but they were sincere. They had to protect themselves.

They were pretty aggressive, these Texans. In some of the B theaters, the audience would shoot into the screen. I thought Leonard was kidding when he told me about that. Then I started looking, and there were bullet holes in screens in a lot of theaters. They didn't advertise these things. But I saw this. They would just pull their guns out and shoot if they didn't like what was happening, or they'd get so wrapped up, they thought the story was happening to them.

❑ ❑ ❑

It was hot as hell going from San Antonio to and through the Rio Grande Valley, rattling over washbasin roads in a closed car. Almost every place we went, the district manager and his wife came out to meet us. Often they got in and rode along to the next district.

On the way from San Antonio to Harlingen, we went through a tiny little town. In it was a big, beautiful theater—brand new—and Isabelle asked Bob O'Donnell how such a small place could support a grand theater like that.

"You know, Isabelle, there isn't a jury in Texas that would convict a fellow who catches his wife in bed with another man and shoots her," said O'Donnell.

"That's very interesting," said Isabelle, "but what I asked you about was that theater—"

"Well, I was getting around to that. Seems that the fellow I'm speaking of, name of Ben Something, put up that theater. Named it after his wife."

"But why such a big theater in such a small town? That's what I want to know," said Isabelle. "How could anyone afford it?"

"Well, Ben's wife had quite a lot of insurance, and he collected on it after she died—which is what happened after he came home one afternoon and caught her in bed with the RKO motion picture salesman. And like I said, there's no jury in Texas wouldn't find that justifiable homicide. So that's how he got the money to build that theater."

In Harlingen we had three theaters, one strictly for last runs. When we got there, O'Donnell told us another story. At that time there was a movie called *Scarface*, about Al Capone, and it did so well in some parts of the country that we kept bringing it back. One day, after this particular theater had shown it for the umpteenth time, an old man, a regular patron, came out of the theater, shook the manager's hand, and said, "Boss, you know these *Scarface* pictures are getting to be so they all look alike."

Bob O'Donnell was a very compassionate man. He was a close friend of Johnny Harris, one of the original movers and shakers of the Variety Clubs. For years O'Donnell served as National Chief Barker, the organization's president.

Variety Clubs began after a desperate mother, facing starvation and poverty and frantic for a way to save her infant daughter, left the tyke in the foyer of a Pittsburgh theater with a prayer that "show people" would care for her. They did more. They founded a national organization to care for underprivileged children, and to provide rehabilitation and aid for anyone who needed it. Today Variety Clubs in every major American city continue the good works Johnny Harris helped start.

O'Donnell was also quite a character. He was drawn to beautiful women, and they to him, and he married three or four that I can recall. But his lasting claim to fame is what he did for a young and struggling vaudeville comic in 1928.

OTHER RECOLLECTIONS:
Bob Hope

I got going in 1928 in Chicago. I was doing a pretty brash act. I opened down in Fort Worth, Texas. And I walked out on the stage, did the same act real fast, and they weren't laughing. So I just kept working faster. I came offstage and I was wearing a brown derby in those days and I threw it down and I said, "Get me back to my country," which was also a brilliant thing to say. And then I had to go out and emcee the WLS Showboat—that's actually why they had hired me, for a radio program out of Chicago.

I finished that, went in the dressing room and slammed the door, and all of a sudden there was a knock on the door. I said, "Come in," and a guy said, "Where are you going, Fancy Pants? What's your hurry?"

He called me Fancy Pants, because I was wearing a dark coat and a white pair of pants. By the way, we did a picture by that name, years later, Lucy and I, and that's how we came by the title.

"What are you talking about?" I said.

"What are you working so fast for?"

"Who *are* you?"

"I run this circuit. My name is Bob O'Donnell, and I enjoyed a lot of things you did out there, but this is Texas"—this is 1928 now—"and these people are out in the sun all day working. They want to come in and sit down a while. They want to enjoy you, but you're rushing and doing your act so fast nobody can understand you."

So I thought that over, and I started to slow down, and the first thing you know, I started to get the pace of this whole thing. I went to Dallas the next week and started to score pretty good and went to Houston, then San Antonio. And Bob called me on the phone and said, "How're you doing, Fancy Pants?"

"Just fine."

He said, "You're doing better than that, you're doing great."

What O'Donnell did for me, I almost cried. Because here was a guy, for no reason, telling me this. God, it helped me a hell of a lot. When I got into New York, I found out that he had told the New York chief's office, "Take a good look at this guy right away, because he's valuable."

He helped me again because I got my pick of the theaters. I had been in New York with my partner in 1925–26, so I knew where the nice audiences were. Then this agent called me, Lee Stuart. He said, "The chief's office wants to see your act."

I said, "Why?"

"Well, Bob O'Donnell told him," and he told me the story.

And so I got the chance to pick Proctor's 86th Street. It was bigger than the others—3,000 seats in a beautiful theater and in a residential neighborhood. I did one show there, and I got a three-year contract from Keith (which became Radio Keith Orpheum, RKO) out of it.

Years later, in the 1960s, the Motion Picture Pioneers of America honored him at the Waldorf in New York, and they invited me and Ginger Rogers to emcee. I was in London doing *Roberta*, and I flew back just for this one night.

And by then Bob [O'Donnell] was getting on in years, and he went to the cocktail party, and by the time he got to the dinner, he put his head on his table and slept. And I talked about him as he was sleeping, right next to me. And people cheered, because they loved him so much.

The next day he called me up and said, "Will you come up and do that act for me?"

And so Ginger Rogers and I went up to his suite in the Waldorf and did the same act for him that we had done on the dais. I had to tell all the jokes again.

Bob O'Donnell was a sensational guy, just a marvelous man, and everybody loved him. You couldn't help it. He had that kind of personality. And he changed my life.

❑ ❑ ❑

After my honeymoon trip with Isabelle, I continued to visit all the Paramount theaters. By the time the war came along, I had seen every single one. Thus I came to learn much more than managers' names. I knew what each building was like, what each town held, the nature of the competition—if there was any—how each of our theaters was managed, and so forth. I judged the individual abilities of the managers by what I saw and heard, and I made suggestions accordingly.

I never made notes. I found them unnecessary, and even fifteen years ago I could have recited quite a lot—virtually everything I ever knew—about almost any theater I'd ever visited. But Father Time has a way of collecting his debts, and I'm afraid I no longer remember many details.

I got news of the Pearl Harbor attack while celebrating my thirty-sixth birthday on Barney Balaban's boat. A few months later I reported for a preinduction physical, where it was discovered that a painful operation was required to repair damage to the aft end of my digestive tract. I was therefore exempted from military service. Isabelle was very relieved, but then *I* was the one who had trouble sitting down.

In June 1942, at our annual meeting in Hot Springs, Virginia, Barney Balaban announced that I was now a vice president of Paramount Pictures and a member of the board of directors.

With the war on and travel restricted to essential business, people stayed close to home. Movie theaters were the chief diversions of a mobilized nation, and even with many of the industry's top performers and directors in uniform, business had never been better. I looked forward to a long and uninterrupted career in the motion picture business.

5

Hollywood

❑

After I became head of Paramount's theaters, it occurred to me that the relationship between Paramount's studio and the men who ran the theater circuits needed to evolve. When Paramount owned these circuits, the operators were our employees. After reorganization, they were partners and associates. Our studio's output provided more than 20 percent of what played in our theaters, and the success of these exhibitors directly influenced the whole company's earnings. I felt it would be better if we all worked more closely together.

Accordingly, in the early 1940s I began to bring our circuit partners out to Hollywood to meet with production people and see the films the studio would release in the months ahead. It was also an opportunity for these exhibitors, as canny a group of showmen as the world has ever seen, to offer their insights to producers and studio executives. This had never been done before. The studio was free to ignore exhibitors' ideas, but my impression was that from then on Paramount's product reflected, in part, our partners' suggestions.

One good idea from an exhibitor came late in the 1930s: One of our partners observed that songs from movie sound tracks could become popular through the sale of records. I took that to the studio, and from then on, every new Paramount film had a distinctive theme song. Publicity efforts expanded to promote this music, which also served to promote the picture. Today, the whole industry does this.

When Barney Balaban put Frank Freeman in to head the studio, Henry Ginsberg came in to handle production. Ginsberg, while very astute in business matters, was a remote and distant figure, and cold as they come. But this is a people business. Dealing with talent—and I include not only actors and actresses, but also directors, producers, writers, set designers, cinematographers, the host of people whose creative collaboration is required in filmmaking—requires more than mere tact and diplomacy. Inspiring artists to rise to their highest standards means evoking their desire to please, which requires a high degree of personal warmth.

Ginsberg, with no feelings for talent, succeeded only in alienating them. After three or four years, some of the most creative left, and most of the others were just going through the motions. Studio output slowed to a trickle. Quality declined. Our theater partners began to feel desperate.

When I brought this to Barney's attention, he asked me to go to Hollywood and spend time with Frank Freeman. I urged Frank to find somebody else to head up production, and he asked me to scout around. In time I found Sol Siegel, head of production at Republic Pictures. Republic was never a major studio, but it did make the immensely popular John Wayne Westerns and such. I felt Siegel would be better than Ginsberg, and Frank brought him in. Siegel oversaw production of a classic series of musicals starring Bob Hope, Bing Crosby, and Dorothy Lamour—the *Road* pictures. Working with Freeman and Siegel, I got to know all these performers, along with Betty Hutton and many other stars of that era.

I also became acquainted with Paramount's leading producer-director, Cecil B. DeMille. He was one of the most meticulous men I've ever known. He would make detailed drawings of each scene in advance, and pin them up all over the studio. This practice, refined somewhat, is called storyboarding. Today it is common, but DeMille was one of the first to use it.

After the war, the motion picture business went into a little slump. Some of the best young talent had been in uniform, devoting their energies to the war effort. When they left the service, some went out on their own. Others took some time off. The quality of our product dropped off. Although wartime audiences would watch almost anything, the postwar theatergoer was more discriminating. Box office receipts fell. Movies played to smaller audiences; typical first-runs shortened from over a month to only one or two weeks.

What we needed was more product. In 1946, I went to England and met with J. Arthur Rank. A most religious man, he had made his fortune in the flour business. After the war, he went into film production and made very high-class movies. I persuaded him to come to America, where I set up meetings with distributors.

Rank's movies helped Paramount's theaters, but not much. English pictures of that era tended to present understated emotions, dramas of the interior, conflicts of the soul. Americans crave action. Rank films didn't do very well here.

So I went to Italy, where I met Carlo Ponti and Dino de Laurentiis, then partners in a Rome studio, and persuaded them to start making movies for American screens. Ponti wasn't yet married to Sophia Loren—though he was indeed married—and he seemed to have a girl-of-the-week policy.

Out of this expedition, in time, came the "spaghetti Westerns" that helped Italy's postwar film industry recover. De Laurentiis eventually moved to Hollywood, where he produced several blockbuster hits. He made—then lost—a fortune.

To keep things moving at Paramount, I suggested to Barney that we acquire a little production company called Liberty Pictures. Its principal assets were the three greatest directors of that era: Frank Capra—the genius who put Columbia on the map—William Wyler, and George Stevens. Sam Briskin, the best studio manager of that time, was executive VP. This quartet had spent the war years in uniform, making Army films. Capra was responsible for a magnificent series, *Why We Fight*, which did much to boost our fighting men's morale. The scripts were written by a so-far-unsuccessful novelist, a youngster named Irving Wallace. After the war, these four filmmakers got together and started Liberty.

A problem with many of the best directors is that they would prefer to live in a world all to themselves. They want acclaim from their peers—but the sort of pictures that win Oscars are not always appreciated by mass audiences. Freed of the restraints of the big studios where they had honed their craft, and hungry for prestige, Liberty's directors began making pictures they hoped would win Academy Awards.

Capra, at first, was stymied. He made *It's a Wonderful Life* with Jimmy Stewart. In recent years this film has earned recognition as a classic and, along with *It Happened One Night*, is among his best-known pictures. But at first it did poorly at the box office, and for a time, Capra lost his way. He couldn't think of what to do next. Liberty's first few pictures all flopped. They were deep in red ink.

After Paramount acquired Liberty, at my suggestion we also bought Leo McCarey's Rainbow Films. McCarey, a fine director, had made *Going My Way* with Bing Crosby. This gave Paramount a hot team whose first films included Capra's *Broadway Bill* and Wyler's *Friendly Persuasion* and *Roman Holiday*.

Around this time I got to know John Wayne. He had been under contract to Republic for several years when Warners approached him. Instead of matching the high salary Wayne was getting from Republic, they offered Wayne a smaller guaranty plus a good share in the profits on his films.

John Wayne was a lovely man, but at the time he was a babe in the woods when it came to money. He went to Bob O'Donnell, whom he knew, to ask for advice. Should he take the Warners offer, or stay with Republic? O'Donnell sent him to me.

Paramount's theaters had played virtually all his pictures. They always did extremely well, so I had some idea what kind of gross revenues could be expected. After looking over his Warners offer, I said, "John, if I were shooting craps, I'd say this was the safest bet I could make. I'd go with Warners." So he did, and made much more than he'd ever earned on salary. We became lifelong friends. Not incidentally, after that, until he started his own company, Batjac, Wayne stuck to percentage deals, and became quite wealthy.

Another friendship rooted in that period was with a young man who worked as a Paramount office boy.

OTHER RECOLLECTIONS:
Art Buchwald

In 1940, when I was fifteen years old and living in Queens, I got a job at Paramount. I was in high school, but I lied and said I was in college. I was on duty in the mail room from 4:00 to 8:00. I got Leonard his sandwiches from Lindy's, picked up his wife's dresses at the dry cleaner, those kinds of important things.

About a quarter of eight I took the last mail to the post office. Then I'd buy myself a potato pancake for dinner and go home on the subway. But the fact that I could tell everybody I worked for Paramount Pictures made me an important guy. I made $8 a week, and I got two free tickets to the Paramount Theatre. Sinatra and everybody of importance played there, so I was a big man in Queens.

I saw Leonard almost every day, but it was only "Good evening" and "How are you?" For a top executive he was a very gentle man. We never did any mergers together.

When the war came, I joined the Marines. When it was over, I went back to Paramount, still wearing my uniform. Walking down the hall, Barney Balaban recognized me and said, "How are you?"

"I'm fine."

"What are you doing now?"

"I'm in the Marine Corps, in the air wing."

"Oh, are you? Come in my office."

I was sure he was going to make me a vice-president. I came in, he told me to sit down, looked over at me and said, "I'm thinking of buying a private airplane. What would you recommend?"

I said, "I don't think I'm qualified to recommend an airplane." And he never said a word about the vice president's job.

I have a feeling, if the war hadn't come, I might have stayed at Paramount and eventually become a famous executive. I kind of liked the movie business, and I was a smart kid. But the down side is I might not have gone to college. Which is what I did after the war, for three years on the G.I. Bill. Then I went to Paris and stayed almost forever.

About 1950, when I was a newspaperman, Leonard came to Paris, and I went to see him. I said, "Mr. Goldenson, do you know me?"

He said, "Yeah—did you ever interview me or something?" And I said, "No, I was an office boy at Paramount when you were in the executive suite." And we became sort of pals after that. When he came to Europe, we'd go to dinner, we'd talk. I was always fascinated with him and his business, but we never got down to the nitty gritty or anything. Today I think of Leonard as a man in search of a tennis game. He loved to play. But he told me a story which I tell everywhere now.

He said his wife, Isabelle, read every *New York Times* from start to finish. She wouldn't throw it away until she had finished it. Once, when she was about ten months behind, she was reading in bed and suddenly turned to Leonard, very upset, and said, "My god, Lumumba has been killed."

❑ ❑ ❑

My arena was exhibition, and my base was New York. But I went to Hollywood often and made it my business to get to know the top people in all the studios, among them the near-mythical moguls of Hollywood's Golden Era. Many became good friends.

They were all individualists. They weren't educated people—none were college graduates or were trained in the arts. What they had in common was a sense of what people wanted to see and the ability to put this in films. They brought their visions to mass audiences, people like themselves of humble origins. That was their gift and what made them successful.

Louis B. Mayer, God bless him, never heard of S. A. Lynch's dictum about not fooling around with the talent. Mayer fooled around with more talent, I guess, than anybody else in Hollywood, although Darryl Zanuck may have given him a run for his money. Both of them had that casting couch going all the time. Yet both were great showmen.

I spent a lot of time with Mayer. Every time I went to California we had breakfast together, either at his home or at MGM. The studio had many young stars under contract: Judy Garland, Mickey Rooney, Ava Gardner, and others. They were just kids, but he had trained them at MGM's talent school. Mayer would parade them in front of me as he tried to sell me on pictures they would be appearing in. He was a terrific salesman, and these were little command performances.

He did the same thing *to* his talent. If an actor balked at appearing in some picture, if an actress wouldn't do what he wanted her to do, he'd stage his own command performance. Mayer would get down on his knees. He'd shed real tears, he'd do anything and everything he could think of to convince them. He'd sob, "You're destroying me. If you don't do this, I'll be penniless." I told myself, here was a man in charge of a studio who was actually an actor.

Mayer was supposedly kept under control by Nick Schenck, the head of Loews, but Nick never really had a handle on him. As time went on, Mayer spent more and more on his pictures. Some lost money. Schenck began to ride him. They became pretty tough on each other. Eventually, their relationship folded.

Schenck, looking for a way to force Mayer out, brought in Dore Schary. Dore had developed under Selznick as a writer and producer, and became head of RKO's production. He was very articulate, but he had one glaring weakness: Every film had to have a "message," which sometimes meant sacrificing entertainment values so the message would emerge clearly.

The Cohn brothers, Jack and Harry, owned Columbia. Jack, pleasant and easygoing, stayed in New York, while Harry ran the studio in Hollywood. I knew both very well.

Harry was a hard man. But smart. He always showed good judgment in his choice of talent and stories. He discovered Rita Hayworth, and made her into a superstar before the term was coined. His business manager, Sam Briskin, as savvy an operator as ever came to Hollywood, helped Harry hold on to the studio's top talent. But Cohn, tough and rude, was widely feared and disliked. Before the war, Cohn had Frank Capra under contract. He kept him in line for years by playing on his insecurities. He denigrated his talents, often calling him "dago" to his face, even in public.

Harry was a tough trader, but because I was his customer, I never had a problem with him. I was never the object of his abusive temper.

I also became good friends with Jack Warner. His genius was in cutting a film. I'd sit with him after dinner, and he would have a rough cut of a picture brought in. He had nothing to do with production and probably never read the script, but looking at the screen he instinctively knew where to cut, how to pace, and then how to present and promote a film. He was a brilliant editor, maybe the best of his era.

Warner, known as "J.L." to his chief underlings, had a few unbreakable rules about what could be in his films. One was about yawns: He believed a yawn on the screen, even for comic effect, always brought yawns from an audience. So every time he saw a yawn it was left on the cutting room floor.

Jack was not an educated man; curt and opinionated, he made great use of the four letter words. We had lunch in Warners' executive dining room many times, and though he had top people working for him, when he made a statement, nobody ever spoke up to question it. Like most of the other moguls, in time he became obsessed with power and as a consequence became dictatorial in his approach to people under him. He told the same jokes over and over, but everyone laughed, even though they'd heard the story fifteen times.

Jack and I often played tennis, usually doubles. He had his own court and always kept a pro on hand to play on his side. If Jack didn't feel like exerting himself, he'd let the pro do most of the chasing. Nevertheless, it was fun.

Isabelle and I spent many summer vacations at Cap d'Antibe. We played tennis nearly every day and in the evening visited the casinos. I never gambled in Europe, but I liked to watch while Jack played chemin de fer. One night he broke the bank in Monte Carlo.

One thing always puzzled me. He threw a lot of dinner parties over there, and his guests included a bunch of phony counts and countesses, royal pretenders, and so forth. One day I asked, "Jack, here you are the head of a motion picture company, and your product must appeal to the masses. How can you surround yourself with a bunch of phonies like this, people who have no concept of what ordinary people think or want or desire? It makes no sense to me, knowing that you have a feel for the masses and they for you."

He said, "Oh, it doesn't disturb me. I just have them around for color."

I kept telling him, "Jack, these people can color your judgment." And then I realized that maybe he kept those phonies around because he didn't have many other friends.

For the opening of Disneyland, in 1955, I brought my company directors and their wives out to California, along with Harry Hagerty, vice chairman of Metropolitan Life and one of our company's biggest financial backers. I wanted to show my directors the life-style enjoyed by some of the California producers. Jack graciously invited all these people to dinner at his home.

Jack's wife, Ann Alvarado, a talented decorator, filled their home with period furniture from France. The doors, for example, had once belonged to Louis XIV's opulent Versailles palace. It was a magnificent setting for a dinner party.

Jack's other guests that evening included Marilyn Monroe and other top stars. Before we sat down to eat, I took him aside and said, "Jack, I'm going to thank you for your hospitality, but I don't want you to make a speech. I'll just say, 'Thank you very much,' and you'll say, 'I appreciate it.' "

I thanked him, and he got up, started talking, and nothing could stop him. Four letter words by the dozen. He thought he was talking to his buddies, telling those same jokes for the *sixteenth* time. John Coleman, one of our directors, and Harry Hagerty, staunch Catholic churchmen who went to Mass every day, were stunned. I could see the color draining from their faces. I was ready to crawl under the table, but he went on and on and on. It's just another example of the inconsistency of man. Here was a great film editor who didn't know when to stop himself, and who allowed no one to edit him.

After Barney Balaban replaced Sam Katz as head of Paramount, he brought Adolph Zukor back as chairman emeritus. Zukor had built Paramount from a single theater on New York's 14th Street to the biggest company in the industry by daring to be different. Under him, Paramount had been the first to induce stars from the legitimate theater to make movies, first to make movies in Hollywood, first to produce feature-length films, first to distribute and exhibit color movies, first to import foreign talent for American movies, and first to introduce American films abroad.

Zukor had a lot of courage. Even after he was wiped out, the old man never lost his bearings. Until he was ninety-seven, he went into the studio every day for a few hours. He had an almost innate sense of what people wanted to watch.

Once, Isabelle and I went out to Hollywood with Zukor to attend a charitable affair. We took the 20th Century Limited, then considered the epitome of luxury and style in transcontinental travel. It kept a strict schedule, and like all trains, at times the cars shook and swayed a little. As dinner time approached, however, Zukor called the conductor, and they slowed the train until he finished eating.

Returning from California with Zukor on another occasion, it happened that Mary Pickford was also aboard. Zukor had discovered her, along with Douglas Fairbanks, Sr. She became his first star, "America's Sweetheart," and the talent foundation upon which the early Paramount studio was built. Pickford, Zukor, Isabelle, and myself sat together for much of the trip, and I noticed that Pickford downed glass after glass of tomato juice. I was still an innocent. I whispered to Zukor, "Gee, she drinks so much tomato juice." He said, "Tomato juice? That's vodka. Bloody Mary."

To me, Adolph Zukor was the greatest showman of his generation. His appreciations of programming, promotion, and advertising remained unfailing almost up to his death. I went to see him every time I went to Hollywood. Before he tired in early afternoon, his mind remained crystal clear. He wanted to know everything about each picture. Not only Paramount's films but those of the other studios as well. He made the most astute observations as to why a picture didn't do well. His counsel benefited the company almost to the day he died, at age 103, in 1976.

In the mid 1940s I tried to buy the RKO theaters from Howard Hughes. He was somewhere on the Coast, but nobody could find him. I finally got word to him that I wanted to negotiate. Weeks later word came back that he would talk to me. I was to go to the Irving Trust in Manhattan, contact a certain vice president, and he would give me instructions.

He told me to come to the bank on a particular date and at a certain time. When I arrived, the banker took me up to a conference room, and said, "I'd like you to sit here." I sat. Shortly a phone call came in from Howard Hughes. First he confirmed that I was sitting in this exact room in this exact seat. It was very strange, almost eerie. I said I was, and he said, "I understand you want to buy my theaters."

"Yes. Do you have a price in mind?

"What do you think they're worth?"

"Around twelve or thirteen million."

"No, I won't sell them."

He hung up without another word, and I never had any further conversations with him. Many years later, however, I would lock horns with his emissaries.

* * *

Walt Disney loved *young* children—I don't think he loved teenagers quite so much. His entertainment philosophy was wonderful. Once he told me a story to illustrate it: When he was a small tot, his stomach was upset. His mother needed to give him castor oil. He couldn't stand the taste, so she gave it to him with orange juice. He said, "Basically what I do in films is educate children. The orange juice is the entertainment. The castor oil is the educational portion."

Walt was sometimes like an overgrown kid. He had a miniature railroad running all around his estate. He'd sit on top of a little engine about three feet high, and ride it all through the grounds. He got a big kick out of this.

But he was smart as a whip. Walt ran the showman's side of the studio, but he was business-wise. It never paid to underestimate Walt. He had his brother Roy run the business, and he may have used Roy to do all the hammering, but Walt knew everything that was going on every minute of the day.

Up until the 1970s Disney made few theatrical pictures, but those he did make went very well. He put a lot of money into *Snow White*, and didn't see a profit on the first run, but Disney brings it back every seven years, and it has done extremely well for them. That's true of many Disney pictures, but then Walt always had a very long view.

Joe Schenck, Nick's older brother, cofounded Twentieth Century-Fox with Darryl Zanuck. He was one of the most powerful men in the film industry, well-connected with local, state, and national politicians. He was also immensely wealthy and capable of great ruthlessness. Until 1942, when he was convicted of tax evasion and perjury—in connection with an extortion scam by Willie Bioff, a Capone mobster—Schenck ran Twentieth Century-Fox. After serving a few months in prison, he was paroled. Then he became very active in raising money for the March of Dimes and other charities. A few days after World War II ended, President Truman granted Joe a pardon.

Schenck was a proud man, but never flamboyant, a very quiet type. His life-style was typically Hollywood. I often dined at his home, but there were always other people around, usually movie stars. Whenever he dined out, he always had a beautiful woman on his arm, usually an actress. For a time, long before she became a star, Marilyn Monroe lived in a guest cottage on Joe's estate. By then he was well over seventy, but when he felt up to it, Joe sent his butler to fetch her to his chambers.

Joe had a penchant for very long walks. He also liked to learn foreign languages. Once, late in his life, he invited a young Fox producer, Pete Levathes, to his Palm Springs house. Pete was fluent in Spanish. Before sunrise one morning, Joe asked Pete to go for a walk so they could practice Spanish. Joe didn't turn around until after they'd passed a sign that said, "Palm Springs, 18 miles." Levathes was exhausted, but Joe never slowed down.

Joe must have been a showman, but I could never figure him out. I never dealt directly with him, but he was part of the Hollywood Establishment, a power behind the scenes.

Darryl Zanuck, who founded Twentieth Century with Schenck, was a brilliant writer—he started as a Warners scriptwriter—and very capable. He was always very businesslike. No fooling around, except with women, but that seemed to be the leading indoor sport out there.

I found Zanuck egotistical and opinionated, always boring in with questions about the types of pictures I thought would do well or wouldn't. Every time I went to see him, he'd put me through an inquisition. He was all business.

He made a picture called *Wilson*, about the president. It died at the box office. He should have known that political figures are usually deadly to audiences. Obviously he thought he was going to do something exceptional. But although he made some mistakes, Zanuck had a pretty good sense of showmanship.

Few would suppose that a man like Sam Goldwyn, with only a few years of schooling and a career that began as a wholesale glove salesman, would have great taste. But he never made a picture in bad taste.

Goldwyn was instinctively meticulous about selecting the right director, the right talent, the writers, and stuck very close to his budget. He couldn't have been more thorough.

He made only two or three pictures a year. He finished each one and then came to New York and sat down with the magazine and newspaper people—this was long before television—and he did a super job of selling the film.

Soon after becoming head of Paramount's theaters, I had dinner with Goldwyn. He said, "I'd like to have you come with me. Run production. I'll give you part of my business."

I said, "Sam, you're a very stubborn man, and I am too. I want to be friends with you for a long time to come, but I'm afraid our friendship wouldn't last very long if we were in the same company and you were the boss and I wasn't."

We maintained our friendship until his death. Whenever I went to Hollywood, we'd have dinner and then he'd either show a picture or we'd have a poker game. At that time I was a little guy just coming up, and this was pretty heady stuff.

The games were great. I played against David O. Selznick, Darryl Zanuck, Jack Warner, and Nate Blumberg of Universal. At times there were a few others. Table stakes, and I had to play very close to the belly. But sitting there I got very interesting insights into the character of those people.

Usually when it got to be midnight, if Goldwyn was winning, he'd stop the game. But if he was behind, he'd insist we stay at the table, sometimes until very late, or until he broke even. Jack Warner could be unpredictable; every once in a while he'd go off the beam. Zanuck and Blumberg were pretty steady players. Dave Selznick was extremely wild. If we played stud poker, and he had only a deuce or three in the hole, he'd try to bluff everyone out with nothing to support it. Unlike his father, he always lost.

When it came to getting a beautiful picture on the screen, Selznick was Goldwyn's equal. On the other hand, while Selznick was meticulous about the people he selected, he'd pay anything to get them into a picture. He was wild in the handling of his money and wild in the way he approached things. Just the way he played poker. He went way over budget and had to sell off part of *Gone With the Wind* to Jock Whitney. Then he had to sell half to Mayer, his father-in-law, to finance its finishing.

Whenever he promoted a picture, Selznick sent me a wire which went into the smallest details, everything about it. He could have told me all I needed in ten words—but to Selznick, a picture was worth several thousand words.

Luck enters into many things in life. I've been very lucky at being in the right place at the right time. When you sit down at the poker table, there's an element of luck, but it's mainly skill. You have to know the odds of drawing what you need to win, and you must learn to judge the cards others may have in the hole by the way they play.

There are parallels in the entertainment business. When you select a script for a multimillion-dollar movie, or a pilot as the basis for buying a season's series of television programs, you're shooting craps. It helps to know the odds.

The game is trying to be ahead of everybody else on trends in public taste. It's true in television and in the movie business. Sometimes you're wrong. If a run of bad luck goes on too long, you're history. The only people who stick around are those whose guts are right more often than not. I always found that to be the excitement of show business. It has kept me enthralled all these years. I love it.

Ned Depinet, the head of RKO, became a very good friend of mine. He came up through sales. One day he invited me over to see a new picture. It was awful, and before long I was saying to myself, "My God, what a turkey!" Ned had his salespeople there, and after the lights came back on, he stood up and started to sell that movie. He told them what a great picture it was and why, picking up on various elements he thought were terrific. When the salesmen left, I said, "Ned, how do you have the nerve to get up and sell this thing?"

Depinet started thumping on the table. "Leonard, there's never been a bad picture made," he cried. And *he* believed it. No matter how bad a picture was, he would sell it. That's a lesson everybody in the picture business should learn.

In the end, if a movie really *is* a turkey, it will die quickly, no matter what is done. But that doesn't excuse a person from trying to sell any picture. Movies cater to different people under different conditions. If you can sell the right angle, you can meet those conditions.

I have seen movies come in without being properly promoted and die, even though they're good pictures. And I've seen mediocre films come in with fantastic promotion, and do reasonably well. In the last analysis, word-of-mouth is the greatest advertising. But if you don't get the opening, if you don't get those first audiences in, you're doomed. So I've always said that motion pictures and television are a hokum business—but with a tremendous amount of enthusiasm.

When I was in the movie business, it was a jungle. Tooth and claw. Everybody was out to get everybody else. Yet, if Warners had somebody under contract and Paramount wanted to put him or her in a picture, the studios might make a deal. These could be very lucrative. Talent was under long-term contracts at fixed salaries, and the moguls often demanded stiff prices for a loan-out, which made them a terrific profit. They also traded in screen plays or rights to books. So even though on a day-to-day basis they tried to cut each other's throats, they still had to deal with each other.

As head of Paramount's theater organization, I was able to start keeping the personal pledge I'd made upon coming to New York in 1932. I made my office available to any young person who had the initiative and fortitude to seek me out.

As often happens, my private predilections coincided with company goals. With the war over, I began looking around for young people to help build the company's future. I didn't care if they had experience elsewhere. I wanted bright, inquiring minds that could learn the business and generate the good ideas that progress demands.

Not everyone I hired this way was guaranteed to succeed, but I made it my business to keep an eye on those in whom I saw special potential. I kept in touch by stopping by or phoning to say hello and discuss how they were getting along on the job. I regularly inquired of their bosses and others in a position to know how they were progressing.

Right after the war we hired eight or ten such young men. All had served in uniform, rising in the ranks from private to officer. Henry Plitt was clearly the most outstanding.

Plitt finished law school at age twenty and enlisted in the Army before Pearl Harbor. He put his career aside because he, personally, could not rest until Hitler was stopped. He became one of the first American paratroopers. On D-Day, 1944, when 175,000 Allied troops waded, glided, or parachuted into Fortress Europe, the very first among them was Henry Plitt. He led the 101st Airborne's Pathfinders, the elite troops who jumped behind German lines to secure drop zones for the rest of the division. Later he was the first Allied soldier to jump into Belgium.

Plitt, a major at age twenty-three, was wounded five times. The Army brought him back for a thirty-day "hero's tour," a series of war-bond rallies. Most who went on this tour took advantage of their special status and wangled reassignment to the Pentagon or a base near home. Plitt could hardly wait to get back to the fighting. Before shipping out, however, he had a routine physical exam. A dentist observed that after months of combat, his teeth were so bad they needed at least two weeks of treatment. Rather than chance missing his ship, Plitt had every one of his teeth pulled. A few months later, just after Germany surrendered, he single-handedly captured war criminal Julius Streicher, publisher of *Der Stürmer*, Nazi Germany's virulently anti-Semitic newspaper.

OTHER RECOLLECTIONS:
Henry Plitt

When I sold war bonds on the Paramount Theatre circuit, I met Barney Balaban, Bob O'Brien, Bob Weitman, and Leonard Goldenson. They told me, if I came back in a workable piece, to give them a call. But as I said when I told the dentist to pull my teeth, our missions were pretty rough, and I'd been wounded so often by then that I didn't think I would live out the war. So I listened to Barney, but I went on my merry way.

After the war I became an executive trainee in Paramount's theater division. I went first to the Brooklyn Paramount, where I was everything from the outside doorman to an usher and a janitor. Everything you can think of.

Then they sent me off to New Orleans to E. V. Richards, who probably had more to do with shaping my life even than Leonard. E. V. adopted me. He was known as the Big Bad Wolf of the exhibition industry, the model for the central character in *The Huckster* with Clark Gable—the guy who took his straw hat off, opened the window, and threw it out. It was his way of making a point.

E. V. was a big man. Very, very stout. He would walk into a theater lobby and if the manager had an 8 × 10 production still down low, beneath a 30 × 40 poster, he'd get down on his belly to look at the still. He wouldn't say anything—but this would indicate, "You stupid son of a bitch, why are you putting a picture down there where no one can see it?" This was his way.

One day New York decided they were going to put cash registers at the candy counters. Richards came to New York, went to the Paramount Theatre, bought a couple of candies, and gave the girl a $20 bill. She turned around to go to the cash register, and E. V. swept all the items off the top of the counter into his hat. He went upstairs to Leonard's office on the twelfth floor, walked in, and said, "Say, Lenny, you having a sale downstairs?"

Leonard said, "What are you talking about?"

E. V. said, "Look what I bought for twenty cents." He threw the whole hat full of stuff on Leonard's desk. We never had cash registers in the South. E. V. wouldn't put them in. He thought it was silly. We used a cigar box, just as we had always done.

❑ ❑ ❑

Henry Plitt did very well as a management trainee, and rose rapidly through the ranks. In the late 1940s and early 1950s, as television stations went on the air all over the country, movie box office receipts went into decline. Henry acquired a reputation as an outstanding manager. When he ran Paramount Gulf Theatres, headquartered in New Orleans, his circuit seemed almost immune from the effects of television.

In wasn't until many years later, after our company had gone into television, that I learned the special telephone cables then required to send programs over a television network didn't extend below Memphis until late in the 1950s. So Henry didn't have to compete with network programming, which was far better than what the local stations could produce. He was much too smart to mention this at the time.

Not long after I became head of theaters, the U.S. Department of Justice filed suit against Paramount, Loews, Columbia, Fox, RKO, United Artists, and Universal. The government argued that the broad basis of the way we conducted our business violated the Sherman Antitrust Act. The practices that had led to the rise and immense success of the entire motion picture industry were challenged. These charges had been raised many times before, over the years, and each time the industry had dealt with them. Nobody at Paramount, and least of all me, was seriously worried about the suit.

But had we listened carefully, we might have heard the sound of chickens returning to their roost. Before the decade was out, the eggs they laid would hatch into changelings which would devour the most cherished assumptions of the American film industry.

6

Divestment

❑

Paramount had become the largest movie company in the world by merging with or buying theater circuits across the country. Most of this occurred between 1912 and 1929, using business tactics that most people today, including me, would find abhorrent. But those were different times.

One of Paramount's important partners was Abe Blank, who operated theaters in the Midwest. Abe was profoundly hard of hearing—a handicap he often turned to advantage when there was something he didn't want to hear. Widely respected for his business acumen, he had far-ranging acquaintances with key producers and exhibitors.

Abe got into the picture business in 1908 with a store-front nickelodeon on the Des Moines city square. Like many small cities of that era, all the trolley lines met at the courthouse square, and riders transferred from one to another. Usually there was ten or fifteen minutes between cars.

Nickelodeon shows then ran around ten minutes. Customers came in to sit down, watched the film, then went out the back door to catch their trolley home.

Blank was a pretty good politician with a very sweet way about him. He gained the confidence of backers to build new theaters, paid off his debts quickly, then borrowed more to keep growing. He built or bought more than 100 theaters before Zukor bought his company in 1927.

His son Myron, who is my age, grew up in the business, and is now president of Central States Theatres in Des Moines.

OTHER RECOLLECTIONS:
Myron Blank

Until 1950 we bought pictures for one to three years at a time from MGM, Universal, Warners, Paramount, or the other majors.

We bought each studio's entire yearly output, with the right to cancel maybe three or four pictures a year. We didn't know what the hell they were going to make. We wouldn't know which pictures we'd bought until they arrived. All we knew was the stars a studio had under contract and that they would release thirty-five to sixty pictures a year. This was called block booking.

Because of these booking practices, in 1940 the government brought antitrust suits against the studios. They went after Paramount first. Then the war began, and everything went on the shelf. When it was over, in 1945, they resumed the case.

❑ ❑ ❑

The exhibition business in that era was quite different from today. First-run theaters were in downtown areas. The second run, in suburbs, would not start until at least thirty days after the first run ended, what we called a thirty-day clearance. These theaters usually took a thirty-day clearance over the third run in the smaller cities and towns. This was all done by agreement between the various exhibitors and with the producers and distributors. As Myron Blank and David Wallerstein have explained, the studios sold their product through block booking, pooling agreements, and master agreements.

All of these served to assure the studios that they could sell virtually every picture they made, on very favorable terms. It also meant that in many communities, moviegoers had little choice about which theaters to attend, because the newest movies were only available at theaters associated with one of the major studios.

These were the standard industry practices. I never knew of any understanding between the various major companies, but since the major studios all followed an almost identical pattern, independent theaters rarely got first-run pictures.

A group of independents, the Allied Group of Theatres, brought suit against Interstate Theatres, a partnership between Paramount and Karl Hoblitzelle. Allied won, and got the Justice Department to join in prosecuting the entire industry.

President Truman's Attorney General, Tom Clark, brought suit against Paramount, Fox, Loews, RKO, Columbia, United Artists, Universal—all the major companies. The government argued that under the Sherman Act, the way exhibition and production of motion pictures were combined constituted a monopoly to fix admission prices and exclude competitors. And prosecutors argued that although there was no tangible proof of an agreement among the majors—and I never knew of any such agreement—the practices amounted to a conspiracy in restraint of trade.

In 1947, the case was heard in the Southern District of New York, in Manhattan. The government won.

Paramount and the other majors appealed, and the appellate court reversed most of this decision. The Justice Department countered with an appeal to the Supreme Court.

The movie industry's arguments, reduced to essentials, were that the government had no proof of any conspiracy, and that the Justice Department was applying the wrong laws and the wrong precedents to support its contention that industry practices violated antitrust laws.

On May 3, 1948, the Supreme Court ruled that the studios could no longer own theaters, and every picture had to be put up for bid individually. Every theater owner had to have the opportunity to bid on every picture. The practice of block booking was banned. Henceforth, a circuit with five theaters—or one—could compete for first-run product on an equal basis with giant circuits with hundreds of theaters.

This landmark decision became required reading in every law school in the land, and still is. More important, it ended an era. The giant studios were stunned. At one stroke the system that had served Hollywood since the 1920s was finished.

In a very few years the nature of the production business changed dramatically. The big studios had functioned like assembly-line factories, turning out A pictures in eight weeks and B's in six. They had enormous overhead, much of it in salaries for technicians, writers, producers, and directors. Without theaters of their own, however, studios could no longer be sure of selling any particular film. With every picture put out to bid, producers had no guaranteed minimum prices from exhibitors. The greater risk meant fewer films. The burden was now on the studios to make each production more competitive. Fewer films meant that much studio overhead could no longer be justified. Thousands of salaried employees were laid off. About the same time, the courts overturned another long-standing industry practice, the long-term personal service contract, which bound talent to studios at small salaries long after they had become major stars.

By the 1960s, most talent was hired by the project, so small studios and independent producers were free to bid for the services of the best directors, writers and stars. In the long run the new system was better for producers and distributors. The fees they charged exhibitors soon went to 90 percent over "house nut"—the expense of renting and operating the theaters. Often exhibitors were obliged to make minimum payment guarantees of 60 or even 70 percent of the first week's gross box-office receipts.

For the first few years, with exhibitors paying fantastically larger sums, theaters became less profitable. Today, however, admission fees are six or seven times what they were, and even after discounting the effects of inflation, theater grosses are now quite big. With the evolution of multiple-screen theaters, exhibitors are still doing well.

The decree also ended the system of theater clearances. Today nearly all films are shown on a first-run basis. Except for a handful of "art" films, mostly foreign-made, and a dwindling number of theaters that play classics, there's no such thing as second run. After the first-run, almost everything now goes to videocassette, pay cable, or cable television.

But when the Supreme Court decision came down in 1948, all that was many years in the future. I didn't know what was going to happen, and I was quite angry about the way the government had thrown a wrench into the movie business.

The Supreme Court left the details of divestment to be set by the lower court that had originally ruled. In practice, this meant things were to be worked out, studio by studio, with lawyers in the Justice Department's Antitrust Division. The task of negotiating this consent decree for Paramount fell to the only theater man on Paramount's board—me.

I went to Washington with Bob O'Brien, a former Securities and Exchange (SEC) commissioner and the theater division's chief financial officer, and Walter Gross, our general counsel. I made arrangements to see Attorney General Clark, whom I knew through my friendship with a young Texas congressman named Lyndon Johnson. Clark turned us over to the Antitrust Division, and eventually we met the man who would do the actual negotiation, Bob Wright.

I told these trustbusters it was terrible to break up a company, to make the theaters and production separate. I said the court had done a great disservice to the public.

They said, "We'll tell you one story. American Tobacco was broken into five separate companies by an antitrust decree, years ago. Each of those companies today is bigger than the original American Tobacco." (This was in 1948; today they are even bigger than that.)

At the time, I replied that maybe they were right, but I didn't agree. But now, all these years later, I see they *were* right. The motion picture companies that were broken up are stronger than ever. I love a monopoly—if it's *my* monopoly—but the truth is, competition always stimulates people to do a better job.

Bob Wright, son of architect Frank Lloyd Wright, was one tough cookie, a very difficult fellow. He insisted that since the Supreme Court decision indicated competition was to be established, we were not merely required to divorce exhibition from production. After forming a separate theater company, we were obliged to create competition in every community where we'd had a monopoly. And, by Wright's fiat, we could no longer own a part interest in any theater.

Together we went through our holdings, town by town. We then had whole or partial interests in 1,475 theaters in forty states, including 1,024 partly owned and 451 wholly owned. We were allowed to keep 651 wholly owned and a small handful of jointly owned. It was up to us to decide which to sell and which to keep. Where we had partial ownership, we had to choose whether to sell our interest, buy out our partners, or split the assets with them.

Under the decree, Paramount would be split into a "theater company" and a "picture company." I was the only member of Paramount's board who went to the theater company. The theater company's new board voted to make me president.

Just before the split became official, Barney took all the cash out of the theater company and put it in the picture company. He then put up the theater company's assets for collateral to borrow $30 million from Manufacturer's Trust. Barney's picture company took $18 million of this loan. Our theater company got to keep $12 million—but *we* had to pay back the whole $30 million. Barney justified this by saying that he needed the cash to continue film production, and the theater company could count on a steady cash flow. I didn't like it, but until we separated, it was Barney's candy store, not mine.

All of this left us in something of a bind. In order to meet the Justice Department's mandate of no more than 651 theaters, I had to go around to all our partners and work out deals. I found myself going head-to-head with the old buccaneers, men like Karl Hoblitzelle, Bob Wilby, H. F. Kincey, Abe Blank, and E. V. Richards. These were men I liked and admired, but also tough traders who had clawed their way up in the theater business over the bodies of their competitors, so to speak.

They knew the circuits they wanted to keep and the ones they wanted to unload—but often both parties were more disposed to sell than buy, or vice versa. It was something like a grand game of table-stakes poker, but we were all wagering the future of our companies.

But when you play table stakes—if you play to win—you need money in front of you to call a hand. So I had to sell off as many theaters as I could, as fast as possible, to raise the cash it took to trade out fair deals on the rest.

I spent a lot of time on the road, haggling and bartering, all the while trying to keep daily operations running smoothly. It was a tough time for me.

It was about to get even tougher. For several months Isabelle and I had become increasingly anxious about our baby daughter, Genise. Something was seriously wrong with her, but nobody could tell us just what.

7

Cookie

❑

Genise, the first of our three daughters, entered our lives on October 16, 1943. Early on, she acquired a family nickname. We called her Cookie. She was a beautiful baby, and like any new parents, we were bursting with pride. Cookie seemed slow to walk and talk, but almost until her second birthday, I was telling my parents she was perfectly normal.

Long before that, however, Isabelle's mother had begun to sense that she was not developing properly. When Cookie was a little over a year old, Isabelle said, "Something is wrong." She spoke to our pediatrician, who assured her nothing was wrong. Nor did I take her very seriously. Perhaps I just didn't want to believe it. I replied that since this was our first child, and we had little experience with infants, maybe she expected too much.

As more time passed and Cookie had yet to walk or talk, Isabelle became convinced that something *was* very seriously wrong. For a time, I shrugged it off. I just refused to consider any possibility that our child was anything but normal.

Not long after that, I read something in *Time* magazine about an epidemic of rubella—German measles—in the South Pacific. Hundreds of American G.I.'s wives were infected. A surprising number of those who came down with it in the early months of pregnancy bore children with cerebral palsy (CP).

I suddenly recalled that Isabelle, too, had had rubella early in her pregnancy. I made the logical assumption, and we started to investigate. But we found very few doctors who knew anything at all about Cookie's condition. Most doctors of that era, even pediatricians, had little or no experience or training with CP.

Eventually, at Johns Hopkins in Baltimore, we located one of the handful of physicians who knew something about CP. He confirmed that Cookie had CP, explaining that her lack of motor skill development—the ability to control certain muscles—resulted from brain damage. Rubella was the cause.

Cookie's intelligence was normal. Her inability to control the muscles required for speech and walking, however, meant she would have a very difficult time learning these fundamental skills, if ever she could. Naturally we wanted to do everything we could to enhance her life. Without holding out much hope, the doctor referred us to specialized therapists.

An atmosphere of ignorance about cerebral palsy then pervaded both the medical community and the public. Few people outside the most remote corners of the medical establishment then even knew the condition as "cerebral palsy." Instead it was called "palsy." Sufferers were often called "spastics," a term derived from the jerky, spasmodic way that many moved their limbs.

A whole body of folklore had grown up about "spastics." It was whispered that the condition resulted from venereal disease, or that CP children were the product of "bad blood." None of this was true. Some people even believed that CP children were possessed by evil spirits, or that they were divine punishment for some ancestor's sin.

Few parents spoke about a child with cerebral palsy, or invited inquiries. Many—perhaps most—of these children were institutionalized, as much to keep them out of sight, where they couldn't embarrass their families, as to provide proper care. Isabelle visited many institutions. She found that most were in mental hospitals where conditions often seemed like scenes from Dante's *Inferno*. Cerebral palsy children shared wards with the feeble-minded, with catatonics, and with the violent or dangerously deranged. Public institutions were often little more than malodorous human warehouses, filled with inmates neglected beyond basic food, clothing, and shelter.

Things were worse still in small towns and rural communities. There it was not uncommon to find CP children literally locked away in a closet or basement of the family home. Kept in darkness, often deprived of even the most elementary human kindness, they existed as little more than animals. God alone knows what thoughts might have coursed through their minds. Though more than 77 percent of all CP children are of normal intelligence, the absence of parental nurturing in early years could hardly help to develop their potential.

Isabelle understood the simple truth of Cookie's affliction, but she also knew how most people regarded it. As the nature of Cookie's condition became clear, Isabelle became very defensive about it. For a long time she refused to discuss Cookie, even with her family. It seems strange now, in light of what we learned about CP.

We were very fortunate in one respect, however. When Cookie was less than one year of age, we hired Miss Karen Hansen as her nurse. A native of Denmark, she had lost her own baby in childbirth. Not too long afterward her husband, a doctor, had died as well.

Miss Hansen came to us when she was about forty years old. She was a warm, loving person, and completely devoted to Cookie. In time, Miss Hansen, as she preferred to be called, became virtually a member of our family. For the rest of her life she was a second mother to Cookie and to our other daughters, Loreen and Maxine. To Isabelle and me, Karen Hansen was the most selfless and wonderful person in the world.

Once we knew that Cookie had CP, we tried to find ways to help her learn to talk and walk. We sent her with Miss Hansen on frequent—sometimes daily—visits to therapists in New York and in Philadelphia.

Although we could well afford this care, it was very expensive. After Cookie had undergone several months of therapy—with little to show for it—Isabelle said to me, "What about the poor people? If their children have CP, how can they afford to take care of them?"

I had no immediate solutions, but I knew how Isabelle loved a challenge, and that gave me the beginnings of an idea. When Franklin Roosevelt was President, I had gone to the White House with several other theater industry leaders. The President spoke at length about polio.

Most people today don't remember—or they were born too late—but until development of the Salk vaccine, in the 1950s, polio was like some Old Testament plague. People, especially those with children, feared it the way we now dread AIDS. Summer after summer, great epidemics washed over all the big cities. Health officials, panicked by public outcry, often closed schools and public swimming pools.

Franklin Roosevelt told us of the need for polio research, and asked the theater people to help fund it. Out of these discussions came the March of Dimes. Theaters all over the country showed a little trailer, before the feature film, about polio and the need for more medical research. Ushers went up and down the aisles asking people to put their nickels and dimes in March of Dimes cans. Paramount, the largest theater organization in the country, raised the most money.

In 1948 there were about 75,000 new polio cases every year. The total number of CP cases was estimated at over 500,000. I thought if we could raise money to fight polio, we should be able to do the same for CP.

So I said to Isabelle, "I'll tell you what. If you want to do something about this, why don't you go out and raise some seed money. If you can do that, I'll try to establish a national organization to help CP children and their families. And we'll get research started into the causes." Isabelle agreed that she would at least try.

Since I didn't want to have to invent the wheel, I went in search of information. I visited the Mellon Institute and the Rockefeller Foundation, and then I made an appointment to see Albert and Mary Lasker.

Albert was on the board of directors with me at Paramount Pictures. He was the father of modern advertising, and had owned Lord, Thomas, and Logan Advertising. In exchange for creating campaigns for some of his clients, he'd taken a piece of their companies instead of a fee. Lasker became very wealthy. When he retired, he turned his agency over to his employees. He just walked away and wouldn't take a dime from them.

Mary Lasker, at this writing still alive though ailing, is one of the most remarkable women of all time. Many New Yorkers know her name because she was responsible for getting trees and flowers planted along Park Avenue and many other city streets. That was the least of her accomplishments.

Mary earned a fine reputation and a lot of money designing women's fashions. After she divorced her first husband, she started a New York art gallery. She met Albert, a widower, and after they married, she told him, "I wasn't trained to be a housewife. I want to do something constructive. I could work on medical research."

He said, "Well, I could let you have five million or so, but that's chicken feed. What you've got to do is get the government involved. They spend two hundred million dollars a year on hoof-and-mouth-disease research —but not a dime on human diseases.

"I think if you went to Congress, and to the President, and got them to establish a place for research on human diseases, you could make a real contribution."

Mary got some of her friends involved, and they worked the Washington front. In 1944 she came up with a radical notion: Scientists as well as ordinary citizens should testify before Congress to educate the lawmakers. Today this is routine, but it took Mary Lasker to think of it and make it happen.

By World War II, Mary was the unofficial spokeswoman for those who urged both government and the private sector to expand the horizons of publicly funded medical research. Her legacy can be understood by noting that in 1989 the federal government appropriated some $7 billion for medical research on human diseases. Before the Laskers got involved, the government spent virtually nothing at all.

Mary got my theater people involved, too. In the forty states where we operated, our partners, associates, and theater managers contacted congressmen and senators to push for establishment of the National Institutes of Health. Eventually, legislation created specialized centers for studying diseases of the cardiac, respiratory, and neurological systems, cancer, arthritis, and other serious conditions. Isabelle and I were pleased to serve on their advisory council for several years.

Long before personal computers, Mary was a walking data base. She carried a notebook a foot thick everywhere she went. In it were the names, addresses, phone numbers, and fields of specialization of virtually every American doctor working in research. People all around the country called or wrote her for referrals.

Mary was also one of the earliest and most avid supporters of planned parenthood, a term coined by Albert.

Albert and Mary created the Lasker Foundation, initially funded out of their own pockets. Among many other things, since 1946 the foundation has given annual prizes for medical research. Such is their prestige that they have become known as the American Nobel Prizes.

I had lunch with the Laskers in their wonderful Beekman Place town house overlooking the East River. I explained that we were thinking of setting up a national organization for CP. Since they had been active in starting the American Heart Association and the American Cancer Society, I wanted suggestions about ways to go about it.

Albert tried to discourage me. He said the hesitating style in which these children spoke, their trembling hands, inability to walk, and tendency toward uncontrolled drooling and facial grimaces—their general unattractiveness—would put people off. "I don't think you can sell it to the public," he said. And he made some strong arguments about how many other obstacles we would have to overcome.

The more he tried to discourage me, the more I kept pressing. There had to be a way. I could no longer stand around and do nothing. Every time I saw Cookie, it was a reminder that upward of half a million American children, to say nothing of their families, were suffering far more than my family had. We got the best medical treatment that money could buy, I said, and yet there was little hope for our child. Something had to be done, I said. Albert repeated his opinion: CP would be a very difficult sell.

We argued in this manner for hours. Finally, Mary, God bless her, opened her mouth. She said, "You're not going to convince Leonard. Why don't you tell him how you think he might start, even if you don't think he can succeed."

Albert thought for a few minutes. Then he said, "If I were you, I'd try to organize in New York, Chicago, and Los Angeles the first year. Use that as a base, because most of your publicity and promotion emanates from those cities. We did that for heart disease and for cancer." And he went into some further details about how we might get the right people to serve as national officers.

I went home and told Isabelle, "I have a perspective now on what has to be done to start, so you ought to go ahead and try to raise seed money."

"How much will we need?" she asked.

I really had no idea. Actually, the initial amount wasn't important. What was important then was to begin. So I said $100,000, a figure that seemed achievable.

Around this time we received a letter from someone named Jack Hausman, of M. Hausman & Son, a textile manufacturer. He and his wife, Ethel, had a CP boy. The letter asked for a contribution to a local organization they had started in New York City. Isabelle invited Ethel to join some of her own friends at a luncheon.

OTHER RECOLLECTIONS:
Isabelle Goldenson

I gathered about twelve friends at the Harvard Club and tried to explain what CP was about.

But I had to do something to attract more people, so I borrowed one of the Annenbergs, Evelyn. There were seven girls and one boy, Walter. I was friendly with them from when I was a teenager, and we all lived in the same apartment building.

Evelyn's husband, Bill Jaffe, was a great art collector. He bought very expensive paintings. Of course the Annenbergs had loads of money, and they just bought everything. I told Evelyn, "Nobody's going to come to a meeting in John Smith's home. You're very exciting. Could I have my meeting there? They'll look at your paintings, and then I'll talk to them about CP."

Evelyn would have done anything for me, so she said, "Yes, of course."

When these friends came over, I explained about CP. I had to define the terminology.

I brought in anybody I thought could do something. If one wanted to see another's house, or wanted to say she knew so-and-so—I could tell the social climbers from those who were aggressive. I thought, "If one comes and does nothing, but attracts another who does something, it's worthwhile." I concentrated on that until I had about forty women.

Minnie Mohrhardt, the wife of Leonard's associate, Fred, came across with the Larchmont Shore Club. They gave us everything without charge, including food, which was remarkable.

We had an auction there in the spring of 1949. My friend, a very funny girl named Virginia Graham—her last name was Guttenberg then—was auctioneer. Leonard brought many of his friends, including Barney Balaban, Spyros Skouras, head of Fox, Ed Weisl of Simpson, Thacher and Bartlett, and Danny Arnstein, who owned the Terminal Cab Company in New York. All four donated cars. We auctioned them off, along with fur coats and all sorts of other donated merchandise.

That first affair at Larchmont Shore Club was very successful. About 400 people came. We raised almost $65,000.

❑ ❑ ❑

When Isabelle said they were planning an affair at the Larchmont Shore Club, I immediately thought of Bob Weitman. During the war, he had been the dominant behind-the-scenes figure in staging giant benefit shows at Madison Square Garden for Army and Navy Relief, and the famous Night of the Stars for United Jewish Appeal.

So I asked Bob to get Ed Sullivan as emcee. Sullivan brought several stars, including Dennis James, then very popular on the DuMont TV Network.

Isabelle had to get up and speak before all these people. She had never done anything like it before. After she got over her stage fright, she was terrific. It was a liberating experience, the best thing that ever could have happened to her. Afterward, for the first time since Cookie's diagnosis, she could again be herself. She no longer felt any hesitancy about discussing cerebral palsy or Cookie.

At the Larchmont affair I met Jack and Ethel Hausman for the first time. We became very close friends, and remain so.

By making contact with the Hausmans, I discovered that we were not the only ones concerned about CP. Small groups of concerned parents had banded together in many communities. By 1946 there were enough local groups to support a statewide association in New York.

These community groups primarily concerned themselves with easing the crushing financial burdens on families with CP children. They provided rudimentary group therapy, day care, and to a very limited extent, vocational training. They were unable to address, however, the problem of educating the public about the true nature of CP. Nor had they been able to stimulate much interest in medical research.

Cerebral palsy has been with us from the dawn of time. It was not until 1861, however, that an English orthopedist, Dr. William Little, first described the condition in clinical terms. In 1916, during the worst polio epidemic in American history, authorities urged parents to take all children crippled by paralysis to their doctors. Some of them had CP.

Independent of each other, Dr. Bronson Crothers of Harvard and his former student, Dr. Winthrop Phelps of Johns Hopkins, realized that CP's origins were quite different from those of polio. They began the first medical research into CP's causes.

The Hausmans had founded a support organization in Manhattan. Like virtually all local CP organizations, run by parents with little or no fund-raising experience, they struggled to raise even $50,000 a year. It wasn't enough to get off the ground, even for this one center.

We got in touch with several other concerned people. One was Marie Killea, who had a CP child. Marie was very active in her local Catholic church diocese's efforts to help educate people about CP. She later wrote a book about her daughter, *Karen*. Marie suggested I speak at a meeting of the New York State Association for Cerebral Palsy.

The meeting, in August 1948, at the New York Statler Hotel, drew representatives of community CP groups from throughout the state. I got up and spoke about the necessity of creating a unified national organization. I asked the people present if they thought there was a need for such an organization. They responded almost unanimously and enthusiastically that there was.

One of the first things I did afterward was call Walter Winchell, whom I knew quite well, Drew Pearson, and several other syndicated writers and radio broadcasters. I said, "The public just doesn't know anything about CP. Many cases are never diagnosed, so we don't know the exact number of people affected, but it's more than five hundred thousand children and adults. Many have withdrawn from society. Their families believe CP is something to be ashamed of. We've got to bring them back into America's life stream." They ballyhooed that all over the country. It was a start.

To raise the balance of our initial goal of $100,000, I called all the top theater executives. I didn't have to beg anybody. They dug into their pockets to come up with $35,000, enough to hire Pat Rooney as the first executive director of United Cerebral Palsy (UCP).

Next, we needed an office. So Ethel Hausman, full of charm, waltzed into the Savoy Plaza. She literally went in and said, "This office is empty, and we'd like to have it. Please give it to us." And they did, rent-free.

The Hausmans turned into sensational fund-raisers after Bob Weitman, who knew everybody, began to introduce them to New York's show business elite, including Jinx Falkenberg, Tex McCrary, Arlene Francis, and Sloan Simpson O'Dwyer, wife of the former mayor.

Jack and Ethel are quite a team. First, Ethel charms them, then Jack goes in and closes the deal. The Hausmans deserve a lot of credit for what they've brought to UCP, and they're still at it. Jack Hausman became the most outstanding charity fund-raiser I've ever met. It's been a real pleasure working with him, not only in United Cerebral Palsy, but in later years when he was one of ABC's outside directors.

Now that we had an organization, I set up a meeting with the head advertising people from the major movie companies. I told them about establishing UCP. Then I asked them to tell me how to make it happen. They reached a quick consensus: To get the message across, we had to glamorize cerebral palsy. If we could get movie stars involved, the public would pay attention to our message and respond with support.

OTHER RECOLLECTIONS:
Bob Weitman

I get a call from Lenny one day and he says, "Hey, macher, have you got a minute? Come on in." And he's as white as a sheet. He says, "We've got a problem."

I says, "Is it company or personal?"

He says, "I think we have a cerebral palsy child."

I said, "What is that, Lenny?"

So he explains, and then he says, "What do the poor people do, Bob?"

Now we're becoming philosophical. I said, "What have they always done? They acquire a taste for suffering. What are you going to do?"

He says, "What can we do?"

I say, "Len, let me think about it." I'm talking to a guy who has a broken heart.

Next day I was having a meeting with Bob Hope. Bob and I were very close friends. This was in Springfield, Massachusetts; we took him up there to break in a show. We come back to New York, and it's snowing. We check into the Waldorf. The next day he has to open at the Paramount.

I'm sitting on a wicker basket in the bathroom, and he's shaving. He says, "Hey, how do you think we're going to do tomorrow with the snow?"

I said, "They'll come with sleds, with rickshaws. If they don't, then you ain't what you're supposed to be."

He says, "What's on your mind? You look a little pensive."

I said, "I'm going to ask you something, and the answer has to be 'yes,' because I'm involved emotionally with this guy. Cerebral palsy."

And he says, "What's that?"

I said, "Lenny Goldenson, you're going to meet him tomorrow in between shows. He'll explain it to you."

We get like an hour and a half sleep. We go to the theater, there's a big mob, he's happy.

I call Len and I say, "Len, be free, I want you to meet Bob Hope. It's going to be all right."

❑ ❑ ❑

When Hope came to see me, he said, "Leonard, I know you want me to head up a charity, but I'm handling so many now, I just can't do it."

"Bob," I replied, "all I'm asking is that you sit down and hear me out. If, after ten minutes, you decide you just can't handle this, there will be no hard feelings."

I told him that every year more than 10,000 children were born with CP. And that older people, and those susceptible to strokes, as well as victims of accidents involving head injuries, also become CP victims. I explained why many people felt having CP was shameful, and what the real causes were.

"We've got to free these people from their guilty feelings," I said. "Get them out into their communities. To overcome all the superstition and prejudice, we've got to glamorize it. And you, Bob Hope, in my opinion, can do more by heading up this campaign than anybody else in America.

"If you agree to take it, I'll get Bing Crosby, Jack Benny, and Kate Smith to be cochairmen with you," I added. Now, I hadn't talked to those people, but I was sure that if I could tell them Bob Hope was on board, I could talk them into helping us out. I did. It was easy.

I give Bob Hope all the credit in the world. He didn't merely take on an honorary chairmanship, as most stars would have. He put his heart into it. In those years Bob traveled all over the country, performing in theaters, and everywhere he went, he had us set up meetings with local business people. He'd have lunch, tell a few gags, and then talk about CP. He's been the honorary chairman of United Cerebral Palsy every year since and helped raise many millions of dollars. And, as I had hoped, he helped to bring in the most glamorous names in American show business.

At that time, our company, United Paramount Theatres, owned one television station, WBKB, in Chicago. I called John Balaban, who was on our board and also head of B&K theaters, our subsidiary. Like his brother Barney, John was a very charitable man. I asked him to broadcast an eighteen-hour telethon for UCP, and he agreed. Later we got New York's NBC station to put on a three-hour program, emceed by Milton Berle. It was also aired on several other stations around the country.

A year or two before, Berle had put on a national telethon to raise money for cancer research. The tally board, which showed the total of pledges, went to $16 million. When I checked with Berle, however, he said they actually collected only between $3 and $4 million. That is, many people had called in pledges and then later reneged.

I thought that was outrageous. We had to do better. We had to be credible. I asked Price Waterhouse, then Paramount Theatres' accountants, to make an analysis and recommendations. I wanted a way we could ensure we got all or most of the pledged money. They agreed to work *pro bono publico*, and came up with a system which included a confirming call, with provision for mail and telephone follow-up, when necessary. So successful was this system, which nets more than 95 percent of all telephone pledges, that it's still in use by UCP.

For the first New York CP telethon, Danny Arnstein, owner of the Terminal Cab Company, got volunteer cab drivers to pick up any donation over $25 that very night.

In the same manner that we had raised money for the March of Dimes, we showed a CP educational trailer in 10,000 theaters, then passed baskets through the audience.

That first year UCP raised $1,050,000, about $50,000 more than the first year of the March of Dimes, backed by Roosevelt. Three fourths of that went to help set up local affiliates. Today there are 275 UCP clinics throughout the country, and UCP is among the five largest national charities.

OTHER RECOLLECTIONS:
Jerry Ball
UCP Telethon Executive

In the 1950s we had a staff here of about thirty-five. We were called telethon fund-raisers. We went into communities, worked with local people and with television stations. We set up the whole thing, raised the money, and then left.

When I first started, nobody ever heard of cerebral palsy. They certainly couldn't spell it. We went around the country to develop affiliates. We first sought out parents of CP children to form a nucleus. Then these parents would get business friends and associates to form a little group. They would get together and say, "Okay, now we're ready to render services, but how are we going to raise the money to pay for them?"

We said, "We'll tell you. We have a TV station in this town. We'll have a telethon to raise money. We'll bring celebrities into your town."

At that time there were many closet cases. People had a disabled child with CP and didn't know what was wrong. They kept the child secluded, and the community never saw them. I'd see this a lot, wherever I went in the country.

We did a telethon in Rome, Georgia. Back thirty-five years ago, that was really in the Deep South. No sidewalks. There was a television station, believe it or not, in a Quonset hut. We got CP parents to bring their children, show what cerebral palsy is.

Then we would get sometimes dozens of calls: "My child looks like the child on television."

These things used to tear me up. I remember an incident during a telethon. A woman came to the stage carrying an infant dressed in baby clothes. She talked about her child. She said that the tiny bundle in her arms was actually twenty-six years old.

When she finished and turned to leave, a baby shoe fell on the floor. I went over to pick it up and give it to her. As she walked up the aisle, and for several minutes afterward, there was nothing but dead silence in the auditorium. I was in tears and had to leave the stage.

I don't think her child had CP. It was probably some other kind of affliction. But our telethon had made it possible for this poor woman to overcome her misplaced shame, to again lift up her head, and to have hope.

We coined the term "coming out of the closet" for parents with children who appeared on our cerebral palsy telethon. These people came forth with their disabled children and for the first time were not ashamed of them. They realized they could get some help.

I credit our public education via television for bringing that all to light. We had a very strong, very dramatic impact. Through television we were able to tell this story. Nobody else did. And what we did in those days could be a book unto itself—the dozens of very well known performers, out of the goodness of their hearts, went into these tiny communities to help raise money.

We became a window to the world.

❑ ❑ ❑

In 1953 I attended a Variety Club affair in New York. We honored the brilliant Dr. Sidney Farber of Harvard Medical School for his work with Rh factor blue babies. His pioneer experiments with massive blood transfusions led to a procedure that saved thousands of infants.

Afterward, Isabelle suggested that we ask him to head UCP's research council. So I made an appointment for her, and she and Miss Hansen went to Boston to see him.

OTHER RECOLLECTIONS:
Isabelle Weinstein Goldenson

I went to visit Dr. Farber, ostensibly to see the blood bank that the Variety Clubs had donated. I didn't know what I was going to do. I never knew. I just said whatever came into my head. I had nothing to be afraid of. I never worked. I couldn't get discharged. I knew my husband would feed me and take care of me, and if I'd come back a broken spirit, he wouldn't do anything to destroy me further. So I always took a chance if I thought I could do some good.

When I told Dr. Farber my UCP story, he told his secretary, "Don't disturb me unless it's an emergency. I'm going to spend the rest of the day with Mrs. Goldenson and show her what we're doing here."

That's how he started. He was doing what he thought was helping cerebral palsy, but it was rehabilitation therapy for polio victims and wounded soldiers. He had them climbing in and out of a bus. He put them in swimming pools to learn how to walk again. Things like that.

I thought, Absolutely nothing to do with CP. This is for the armed services, not for CP.

My reaction didn't satisfy him. He said, "Let me call Miss Trainer, one of the greatest therapists who ever lived. She will explain it to you."

She started to tell me a few things, and I said, "Well, it's very wonderful that you do this, but it's not good for CP. It doesn't mean anything to my subject. I would never have my daughter go here and get such treatment. From my own experiences, I know more about this than you."

I was nervous. I felt terrible. I heard myself say, "You're not doing anything for CP. It's ridiculous. You think you're doing it, but you're not." The poor man turned pale.

But I wanted him to do something for CP. Nobody was doing anything. Nobody knew anything. No doctor wanted to see CP children, or they dismissed them right away, because they didn't know what to do. They didn't want to look foolish. The biggest baby specialist, Dr. Leopold, told me, "Well, this child won't be walking. You'll be happy if she's able to hold on and be sort of dragged on her feet."

What good does that do?

Dr. Farber said, "I will get in touch with you. I will call you."

And I thought to myself, He's getting rid of me now, throwing me out. I've been thrown out of places before. I felt sorry for my husband, hearing about how I was thrown out of Boston Children's Hospital, where the Variety Clubs gave this wonderful blood bank. I thought, This is terrible. This man will never look at me again.

He called me at home a few days later. He said, "I now know as much as anybody does about CP." We discussed how to pronounce it. We used to call it cer-*ee*-bral and he said, "The correct pronunciation is *cer*-e-bral."

I said, "That's easier to say."

Then he said, "I have now spoken to everyone on the staff at Harvard Medical School who is working in an appropriate specialty. Come up and meet with them."

"I can't do anything like that. I don't know the first thing about medicine. I can't speak to doctors."

"All you have to do is tell them what you told me. You don't have to say anything else, just speak to them the way you spoke to me. Don't be the least bit afraid. They'll be very polite and nobody will bother you.

"There's only one doctor who might cause a little trouble, Dr. Bronson Crothers, of Boston Children's Hospital. He's very sarcastic, and he may say something you won't like."

When I came to his office, all these Harvard Medical School doctors were sitting around. They tried to make me feel at home. I said they were doing nothing for CP, while they had a misconception that they were. Then the door opened.

Dr. Crothers stood in the doorway and pointed his finger at me and said, "Young lady, you don't know anything." Just like that, in front of all these doctors. That was the best thing that could have happened to me. I became furious.

I said, "Well, if you know so much, why can't you show me what you're doing? You're not doing anything. Just show me what you're doing here to help CP." I don't know what got into me.

So he said, "Come with me," and he walked me around the hospital. He showed me all the worst cases. "What do you do with this one? What do you do with that one? You just tell me what you do," he said. And he showed me movies—he was the first one to take motion pictures of the cases.

Soon I realized he was really trying to help.

As I was walking through the hospital, I noticed a little plaque on the wall near the elevator. It said, "Donated by Julius Rosenwald." I had a thing about Rosenwald because my father admired him so. They met when Father was very young, and Rosenwald taught him all about charity. He was among the most philanthropic people who ever lived, and he practically adopted my father.

It turned out Rosenwald gave the first sum of money for research into CP, as he did for so many other things. His granddaughter had CP, a relatively mild case, and Crothers found it was different from other neurological disorders. So Rosenwald gave $25,000 or $30,000 a year for him to learn what made this particular disorder different from other neurological disorders.

We were so impressed that, through UCP, we gave Dr. Crothers $50,000 to write the first book on CP for the medical profession.

There was nothing else. Up to that time, medical students received an average of only thirty minutes instruction on CP. Dr. Crothers later trained the nation's first specialists in CP.

❑ ❑ ❑

After Isabelle's visit to Boston, Dr. Farber agreed to head UCP's new research council, and brought in a great number of doctors from outstanding medical schools. Dr. Crothers also joined, as did Dr. Houston Merritt, head of neurology at Columbia Presbyterian and dean of the Columbia Medical School. In all, twenty of the finest physicians in the world were on this council.

In 1967, Isabelle and I attended a dinner party in New York. Seated next to Isabelle was Dr. Lee Arnold, chairman of the Department of Aeronautics and Astronautics of the Guggenheim School at New York University. He was one of five advisers to NASA director Jim Webb. At the time, NASA's big mission was to send a man to the moon. Dr. Arnold's role was to find ways to spin off technology from this program into other fields.

Isabelle seized this opportunity to tell him, "You know, it's amazing. You talk about sending men to the moon, but I've seen these poor women carting fifty-pound wheelchairs, trying to put their children in a car. There's got to be an easier way—a lighter metal they could use."

Dr. Arnold replied, "You know, since we aren't sure whether man can walk on the lunar surface, we developed a special vehicle. It moves on lightweight metal legs linked to a small computer. Controlled by a joystick, this thing can go over boulders, through mud, up stairs, almost anywhere."

So Isabelle and I went out to the Aerojet lab in Downey, California, to see it demonstrated. A twelve-year-old boy drove it around, and as Dr. Arnold said, it could go anywhere. We thought that it might be adaptable for handicapped use. It could be a way to get shut-ins out of their homes by allowing them to use stairs.

That has yet to happen. However, modified versions of the moonwalker's joystick controller today allow thousands of handicapped, formerly housebound, to operate a van or car with the use of only one finger.

Also, prodded by Isabelle, NASA-developed technology contributed to the development of a twenty-five-pound wheelchair, using new titanium alloys. This may be NASA's single most important contribution to improving the quality of life for the handicapped.

Moreover, once physicians and prosthesis designers became aware of this alloy, they began to use it in other ways. In 1989, when Isabelle required surgery to replace an arthritic knee joint, the device was made from this very material.

Dr. Arnold arranged for us to visit the Jet Propulsion Lab, where we saw the way they used computers to enhance television images. Isabelle, only interested in what could help the handicapped, was not impressed. But in a very few years this very technology was being used to enhance X-ray pictures of soft tissues. It also became the basis for MRI—magnetic resonance imaging—a noninvasive diagnostic tool very useful for brain scans.

In 1971, Isabelle suggested that UCP sponsor a conference at NASA's Ames Research Center, bringing together physicians and scientists from NIH, the Veterans Administration, and the leading medical schools. Dr. Arnold arranged a meeting with Jim Webb, head of NASA. After hearing her out, Webb agreed to sponsor the meeting jointly with UCP. After she left, Webb told Dr. Arnold, "Give this lady anything she wants."

About eighty leading scientists and physicians came to Ames. Dr. Arnold and Dr. Bill Berenberg, who succeeded Dr. Farber as head of UCP's research council, chaired the conference. NASA demonstrated several useful innovations. Among them was a device to stimulate the human bladder with an electrode implanted near the kidneys. By pressing a button, an individual can void his or her bladder. When the physicians saw that, they stood up and cheered. It has since proved useful to many neurologically handicapped people.

What amazed Isabelle, however, was that this device, developed in a government lab with government funds, was previously unknown to officials of other government agencies, among them the National Institutes of Health.

Isabelle suggested to Dr. Farber that a further synergy of science and medicine might occur if Harvard and the Massachusetts Institute of Technology got together. MIT students should be encouraged to take certain courses at Harvard Medical School, and vice versa, she said.

Farber agreed, and with the head of MIT established cross-disciplinary programs. This marvelous idea has since spread to institutions around the country.

In 1973, Dr. Berenberg and I brought several noted researchers to testify before the House Appropriations Committee, chaired by Indiana's John Brademas. In response, Brademas pushed legislation to provide $30 million to do research on orthopedic equipment.

Subsequently, on a visit to Secretary of Transportation John Volpe, who served in the Nixon Administration, Isabelle eloquently described how wheelchair-bound citizens were denied access to public transportation and buildings. In response, new laws were passed. These led to development of "kneeling" buses, which allow wheelchair access, and to ramps at crosswalks and in public buildings. Today, every time I see a blue "handicapped only" parking sign, I think of Isabelle, because she was the one who pushed Secretary Volpe to lobby for laws requiring them.

UCP-supported research has helped medical science make enormous strides in virology, neurology, orthopedics, and related specialties.

One of the breakthroughs was isolating the rubella virus. Drs. Weller, Ender, and Robbins, partly funded by a UCP grant, did this at Harvard Medical School in the early 1960s. The first effective vaccine was field-tested between 1965 and 1969. UCP and other public interest groups successfully lobbied the government to begin nationwide vaccinations for children under twelve. This greatly reduced the recurrence of rubella epidemics, and thus the number of children born with cerebral palsy. From 2,000 or more annually, brain-damaged births once associated with rubella have dwindled to a few dozen.

In the early 1950s, Dr. Edward Hon, supported by a UCP grant, developed the first fetal heart monitor. Today most obstetricians routinely use this device—in far more sophisticated form—to aid in the prevention of infant brain damage during difficult or protracted births.

Athetoid CP—a form of the condition characterized by constant movement of the extremities—used to claim one child in every 3,000 births. UCP-sponsored research led to effective control of surplus bile pigment, found in Rh-negative blood, in expectant mothers. Now this type of CP is very rare.

Another breakthrough came after researchers, partly funded by UCP, discovered how to treat neonatal jaundice. The condition, common in premature births, often leads to brain damage. Premature babies are now routinely placed under broad spectrum light, which eliminates most of the blood toxins that stunt brain development.

Ruptured blood vessels in premature infants' brains used to cripple thousands. Now researchers at Washington University Medical School in St. Louis, funded by UCP grants, have developed techniques to prevent these ruptures until the child outgrows the condition.

Other UCP projects have included funding vocational centers to give young adults with CP marketable skills. Today there are hundreds of computer programmers who learned their skills at New York City's UCP center.

Others have found work in electronics assembly. Dozens are attorneys or engineers.

Federal and state legislation pushed by UCP, in cooperation with other handicapped organizations, have resulted in "mainstreaming" school programs. Today, most CP children attend neighborhood schools, many sharing classrooms with unimpaired children. Thanks to forty years of UCP public education, CP's awful stigma is little more than a memory.

Much remains to be done. There are still about 9,000 new cases of CP annually; 750,000 Americans of all ages are afflicted. Science does not yet fathom all CP causes. There is no way yet, for example, to treat prenatal brain damage after it has occurred.

Finally, a residue of prejudice against all handicapped still exists. Some restaurants and other businesses systematically discriminate against people in wheelchairs, people who move or speak awkwardly, people who are different. This must be changed through public education.

All of this progress has been immensely satisfying. Yet it did little to diminish the tragedy of Cookie's condition. I still weep to think of her innocence and her helplessness.

When Cookie was growing up, little was known about cerebral palsy. For about ten years Miss Hansen regularly took her to therapists in Philadelphia and New York, searching for ways she could learn to speak. Nothing helped.

Dr. Martin Palmer of the Logopedics Institute in Wichita, Kansas, was developing new techniques that we hoped might help Cookie speak. Having exhausted every other possibility, Cookie, accompanied by Miss Hansen, went to Wichita.

They stayed for five years. Isabelle and our other two daughters made frequent visits, and I usually stopped off to see Cookie on my way to or from the West Coast. In the end, however, it accomplished very little of what we hoped for. Cookie never spoke an intelligible word. Nevertheless, she communicated her feelings in a multitude of nonverbal ways.

Eventually Miss Hansen, great lady and devoted surrogate mother that she was, concluded there was nothing further to be done. She returned to New York to ask if we would allow Cookie to live with her in her own apartment. Miss Hansen felt they would both prefer that to living in Mamaroneck, about an hour by train from New York City, because therapy was more readily available in New York. After some anguished family discussions, we went along with her request.

Late in 1972, while Isabelle and I were on the West Coast, an epidemic of pneumonia swept the East Coast. Cookie caught a bad cold, then developed pneumonia. Miss Hansen, suffering from the same condition, became too ill to attend Cookie.

Miss Hansen was a real Trojan, very strong in her ways. She'd always handled whatever came up. This time she decided to bring in another nurse to care for both of them. She never bothered to tell us until later. Unfortunately, Cookie's lung capacity, stunted by a lifetime without benefit of aerobic exercise, was unequal to the strain. Our daughter died on January 4, 1973.

Soon after Cookie's passing, Miss Hansen was stricken with an inoperable brain tumor. The nation's leading specialists examined her and concluded nothing could be done.

Our friend, Dr. Houston Merritt, indicated Miss Hansen's condition would worsen. She might linger for months or years. He was of the firm opinion that we would not be able to care for her, and suggested the best nursing home in New York.

There she spent her last days. Before Miss Hansen died, she said, "I know I had to come here, but please believe me, don't ever allow yourself to get into a place like this." Losing her was like losing a sister.

Honoring her last wishes, Miss Hansen is buried next to Cookie in our family plot.

As much as we grieve Cookie's loss, Isabelle and I take great comfort from her brief life. She inspired creation of a movement that mobilized armies of volunteers and legions of scientists to improve almost a million lives. For decades UCP has helped ease the burden of all handicapped Americans and of their families, and has helped to change public attitudes toward the handicapped. Cookie's legacy to humanity, rich in compassionate achievement, will serve many generations to come.

8

Merger

❑

The separation of Paramount Pictures and United Paramount Theatres became official January 1, 1950. By that time it was plain to me that television would become the leading entertainment medium of the future. The signs were everywhere. Americans had already spent more than $1 billion on TV sets. Forests of TV antennae sprouted from rooftops coast to coast.

The small screen's popularity made a big dent in movie box offices. Receipts plunged. Hundreds of theaters closed. The big movie studios, reeling under the double whammy of television and forced divestment of theaters, pulled out all the promotional stops. Movies were ballyhooed as never before. Theaters staged "bank nights"—cash drawings—and elaborate merchandise giveaways to lure audiences. It seemed to make little difference at the box office.

Anyone could see that things would get worse before they got better, but the movie moguls just dug in their heels. Television became the enemy. Jack Warner put out the word: No Warners film scene would include a TV receiver, no Warners script would use the dreaded "T" word, and no Warners executive would have a TV set in his office.

I thought television was here to stay. Why not go *with* this irresistible tide? So, almost from the moment we worked out the separation from Paramount Pictures, I was hell-bent to get our company into television.

Television had fascinated me since 1939, when I attended the World's Fair in Flushing Meadow, New York. As I stared at the grainy image of Franklin Roosevelt, conveyed by special telephone lines from the White House to appear on a tiny, flickering tube on Long Island, it occurred to me that here was a way to bring entertainment into virtually every American home. It also seemed like a terrific way of attracting audiences to see new movies.

Even before that, however, when television was still only a laboratory toy, I had been curious about it. In 1937, B&K was offered an experimental television broadcasting license in Chicago. John Balaban, head of B&K, asked me what I thought. I saw it as a great opportunity. "Jump on it," I said. Barney Balaban agreed, and we established a station in Chicago. It went on the air in 1939, as W9XBK, the third American television station. In 1943 the call letters changed to WBKB, Channel 4. Soon after the war, Paramount Pictures started KTLA, Channel 11, in Los Angeles. To mark the event, lightning flashes were added to Paramount's famous mountain peak logo.

World War II interrupted television's development. WBKB's manager, Bill Eddy, became a commander in the naval reserve, and the facility became a Navy school for radar operators and technicians. By war's end, more than 86,000 sailors graduated from WBKB, the electronic eyes of the greatest fleet the world has ever seen.

After divestment, our theater company kept WBKB, which was part of B&K. Barney kept KTLA as part of the picture company.

In 1948 the Federal Communications Commission (FCC) froze applications for new station licenses until it could reorganize its channel allocation system. For the moment, the only way to get into television was to buy an existing station.

So I started looking around. I approached Dorothy Schiff, owner of the *New York Post*, about buying her station in Los Angeles. I spoke with Jack Flynn, who ran the New York *Daily News*, which owned Channel 11 in New York. Neither was anxious to sell to us or anyone else, but they each agreed to talk. In the midst of these discussions, I got a call from Earl McClintock.

Earl, an old friend, was on the board of Sterling Drug and close to Ed Noble. He said that Noble was anxious to make a deal to sell the American Broadcasting Company.

American Broadcasting was created in 1927 by RCA as the NBC Blue Radio Network. Gen. David Sarnoff, head of RCA, used the Blue Network to try out new programs and to serve some of the smaller markets. NBC also had a Red Network, which included more powerful stations in the larger cities. The best programming went to the Red Network.

In 1941, the FCC ruled that no single entity could simultaneously broadcast on more than one network. RCA could operate either the Red or the Blue, but not both. The Blue Network went on the market.

Ed Noble, head of a candy conglomerate, saw the Blue Network as an extension of his other businesses. He approached General Sarnoff and offered to buy it.

Some forty-two other parties, including Paramount Pictures, the Mellon family, Marshall Field, Dillon, Read & Co. and American Type Founders, had bid on the Blue. Sarnoff might have sold to any of them, but he fixed the price at $8 million and refused to accept a dime less. All forty-two eventually withdrew their bids.

Like the other bidders, Noble felt that $8 million was far too much. Sarnoff, replied, in effect, "Take it or leave it, the price is the same." Noble played a waiting game, expecting Sarnoff, after finding no other takers, would lower his price. Months went by before Noble realized he was wrong. Sarnoff, who didn't want to sell at all, was in no hurry to satisfy the FCC's fiat. Noble finally gave in and met Sarnoff's price. The deal was closed in 1943.

Noble renamed his acquisition American Broadcasting Company. It included a radio network of 116 affiliates and stations WJZ New York, KGO San Francisco, and WENR Chicago, a night station that shared a frequency WLS used by day.

(In 1944, WENR gave a young announcer named Paul Harvey his first job in radio. Today, Harvey, who mixes news and conservative political commentary in his ABC Radio network broadcasts, is heard coast-to-coast. He is America's most listened-to radio personality.)

Ed Noble was already something of a legend in the business world. A salesman of subway and transit car advertising space, he and a partner bought a tiny, failing candy company for $1,900 in 1913 and turned its sole product into a world-famous trademark: Life Savers. After solving a perplexing packaging problem, Noble turned his attention to sales. With no money to pay salesmen's salaries, he devised an ingenious plan. He recruited thousands of youngsters all over the country to sell candy on commission. This proved to be a master stroke. Life Savers became a household name. Noble's notion has been successfully copied by dozens of companies.

During the First World War there was a sugar shortage. To get more product out of less material, Noble enlarged the center hole. Now the lozenge had a larger surface area. It tasted sweeter—and dissolved faster. Noble upped the price, and became known on Madison Avenue as the man who made a fortune out of selling "the hole in the donut."

In 1928, Noble sold Life Savers to Drug, Inc., a holding company, for $22 million. He stayed on to run it.

People today think of the Crash as a time when great fortunes were lost. This is true, but a few canny investors also *made* great fortunes out of the chaos that overtook Wall Street. Noble was one of them. In the aftermath of the 1929 Crash, Drug, Inc., dissolved. Noble came in to help pick up the pieces. The result was a new company, Life Savers Corporation. Later he acquired control of Beech-Nut.

(Noble, chairman of Life Savers, groomed a protégé, Justin Dart. Dart nurtured visions of becoming a political kingmaker. Thirty years later he was at the nucleus of a small group of businessmen that persuaded a washed-up actor to run for governor of California. He won. After two terms, Dart's "kitchen cabinet" persuaded the same actor, Ronald Reagan, to run for President of the United States.)

Unlike today, the Depression Era was a time when government attracted the best and the brightest. In 1938, Noble, one of a handful of men in the world who could fly an autogyro, became the first chairman of the Civil Aeronautics Authority. He was later appointed undersecretary of commerce, but resigned in 1940 to campaign for Wendell Willkie.

Frank Marx, a broadcasting pioneer, was head of ABC engineering, and helped get the company into television.

OTHER RECOLLECTIONS:
Frank Marx

I was chief engineer with WMCA when Ed Noble bought the Blue Network. About the time TV was starting, I came to ABC. Applications were open for anybody, so I filed for five TV station licenses. Filing cost nothing, so I didn't ask permission. When Noble found out, he said I would be having him go broke. He fired me. In a day or so one of his associates convinced him to bring me back.

When the first license hearing convened, we were in competition against Howard Hughes in Los Angeles. I had to go on the stand and testify against him. Then Hughes got up there and testified against us. I think that must have been about the last time he ever did testify in public.

Hughes wanted a Los Angeles television station. His studio was out there. He had a lot of money, and he said he could put programs on all day. But we won the hearing. They gave us the license.

There were many hearings at that time on what frequencies would be allocated. The FCC took Channel 1 away, reserved it for mobile broadcasts, and added Channel 13.

I wanted the ABC stations in all five cities on the same frequency. I thought it would be a good thing for people traveling around the country. They could always tune in the same channel. The only channel available in all five ABC markets was Channel 7, so I grabbed it.

Our first TV antenna went on top of the Hotel Pierre. We wanted to put it on the Empire State Building, where the signal would reach much further. The top floor was leased to RCA Labs, and they said no. There were seven stations in New York then, and we all wanted the same thing, so I found out when RCA's lease expired and told the building manager he should charge RCA seven times the rent, unless they allowed us all up there. Then RCA gave in and let us all put up antennas.

At first we didn't have network video transmission capabilities, so we used air freight to ship programs. After AT&T put in video cables, we could transmit live from New York. But because of the time difference on the West Coast, we had to find a way to delay network transmissions.

So I helped develop Kinescope. We were among the first to build a facility in Chicago to make Kinescope recordings of programs before retransmitting them to the West Coast two hours later. That was one of Kinescope's first uses.

❑ ❑ ❑

By 1951, Noble was almost desperate to sell ABC. After buying another radio station, WXYZ Detroit, and building five television stations, the company was losing money. After the banks refused to extend more credit, Noble lent ABC $5 million out of his own pocket to keep them going. Soon they'd eaten that up. Noble didn't want to advance any more money.

So when McClintock said, "He's ready to make a deal," it was because otherwise ABC might have gone into bankruptcy.

I took Bob O'Brien along to see Noble. After some small talk, Noble said he wanted $25 million for the company.

ABC's book value was perhaps $10 million. Certainly, even being generous, it was not worth more than $15 million. And of course, they were losing money.

So I told Noble $25 million was too much. We argued the point back and forth, but he wouldn't budge. Finally, I said I'd like to think about it. I thought I'd let the deal cool. Given time, I felt, Noble would come down off $25 million, and we could really talk turkey.

It was exactly what Noble had thought eight years earlier when he tried to wait out Sarnoff.

Bob O'Brien was as anxious to make a deal as I was. He kept hearing rumors about different people talking to Noble. One day he came into my office and said, "CBS is in the process of making a deal with Noble to take over ABC."

I said, "That's crazy. CBS can't own two networks and the FCC won't approve collapsing one. And even if they did, CBS would have to sell ABC's New York and Los Angeles stations."

Then I saw what Bill Paley might be up to. CBS had been very slow in acquiring television stations. They had dozens of affiliates, but owned stations only in New York and Los Angeles. If they bought ABC, they'd get stations in Chicago, San Francisco, and Detroit. But for the life of me, I couldn't believe the FCC would allow CBS to shut down a network, even one as small as ABC. But maybe Paley knew something I didn't. Or maybe, he thought he did.

I called Noble and told him, "I understand you're flirting around with CBS. Well, you don't have a chance in the world of getting a thing like that through the FCC. They'll never allow it."

He said, "You handle your own business, and I'll handle mine." And he sort of kissed me off. But a few days later he called to say he'd thought about what I said.

"Maybe you're right," he said. "Let's sit down again."

We met again and talked out a deal. He was still as firm on $25 million as Sarnoff had been on $8 million. I knew it was too much, but I was also pretty sure there wouldn't be another television network coming on the market any time soon.

Eventually I gave in. We shook hands on $25 million, half in UPT preferred stock, and half in UPT common stock. And then I found out how tight Ed Noble really was. Ev Erlick, who would eventually become ABC's general counsel and executive VP, had dealt with Noble long before I met him.

OTHER RECOLLECTIONS:
Ev Erlick

Before I came to ABC, and way before its merger with Paramount Theatres, I was in the program department at Young & Rubicam (Y&R). Beech-Nut Foods, owned by Noble, was one of my accounts.

I liked Ed Noble. He was brilliant. Very subtle. A very farsighted man. He knew exactly what he was doing at all times. He could be Machiavellian. Few people, if anybody at all, could read his intentions unless he wanted them to.

But he was such a cheap S.O.B. that he wouldn't buy programs for Beech-Nut anywhere but ABC.

Every buy was agony. Negotiations were always a circus. I would get beat up by Noble because he was never satisfied with a deal until he pushed ABC flat against the wall. He'd say, "Go back and get this, get this, get that."

But as ABC's biggest stockholder, Noble wasn't about to buy at NBC or CBS. He didn't want to see his money going across the street.

Noble had a way of trying to get more, even after a deal was set. For example, Y&R printed his stationery at their cost, but after they delivered it, he would renegotiate the price. So he'd get it below Y&R's cost.

❑ ❑ ❑

In his later years, Noble gave generously to a number of worthy causes through a foundation he established. But when I knew him, he was a world-class tightwad. Frank Marx was also among those who saw his parsimony up close and personally.

OTHER RECOLLECTIONS:
Frank Marx

Ed Noble was mighty tight with a dollar. He fired his purchasing agent because the man got some new envelopes that had a little aroma to them, a little perfume. He called him in and said, "Anybody who'd spend my money like that, I don't want him." He got rid of him, just like that.

Noble never carried any money. When he went out with associates, he never covered the check. Same thing with taxis. He never paid.

He lived in the Waldorf Astoria Towers, and he was always polite: "Frank, I'm sorry, I haven't got enough money." "Frank, I'm sorry, get me a cigarette," and so forth. We went over to the Waldorf for lunch one day, and he says, "My God, Frank, I'm sorry. I've got only a hundred-dollar bill here, and they can't change that. Do you have change?"

So I reached into my pocket and changed it for him. He damn near died. It wasn't my $100, by the way. I borrowed it from the company treasurer, because when Noble invited you to lunch, he always did that number with the $100 bill.

He was forever sending stuff to Georgia. He owned a huge estate on St. Catherines Island. He thought sending things by mail was too expensive. He'd tell me to take care of it. I'd get it bundled up and take it to Penn Central, and give some guy $5 from petty cash to drop it off down in Georgia when the train went through. Noble never knew that. But every damn package he sent down there cost him five bucks, when it could have cost 50 cents.

❑ ❑ ❑

After I had agreed to Noble's price, I said, "Ed, since Paramount Theatres owns WBKB, after the merger we're going to have to sell ABC's station in Chicago."

That's when I learned he'd made a deal with Frank Stanton and Bill Paley at CBS. If UPT and ABC merged, he'd sell CBS *our* station, WBKB (Channel 4) for $6 million!

I said, "Ed, I'm not going to sell Channel 4. We're making money, and your station is losing money. If CBS wants to buy a station, let's sell them ABC's Channel 7, WENR-TV."

Noble insisted we had to give CBS Channel 4. "This is crazy," I said. "Why should we sell WBKB?"

He said, "I've made a commitment; I've got to do it."

Just then I worried most about the deal falling apart. Maybe Noble counted on that. Or maybe he was just stubborn.

So I said, "Okay, Ed, we'll sell them WBKB, but you're going to have to make an adjustment in the price." We finally agreed he'd take $500,000 less in preferred stock.

But CBS got a bargain. WBKB was easily worth twice what they paid —it earned about $1.5 million in 1951. It took us many years to get Channel 7 up to that. In the 1970s, Channel 7 Chicago became the number 1 station—and still is. But even today it makes me angry to think about that deal. The nerve of Ed Noble—selling off a station he didn't own!

Although I had met Noble's price, and although I reluctantly went along with the sale of WBKB, Noble had one more joker in his deck. He kept coming back to the point that this was to be a merger, not an acquisition.

To seal the deal, he extracted a promise that I would leave ABC's management intact for three years. UPT and ABC would merge assets, but ABC would operate autonomously.

I was comfortable with this kind of arrangement from my years of dealing with theater circuits, so I went along.

Thus Noble's man, Bob Kintner, a former partner of columnist Joseph Alsop, remained in charge of ABC. In exchange for this concession, I proposed that three UPT executives go in under Kintner. Bob O'Brien, a brilliant administrator and financial man, would become ABC's executive VP. Bob Weitman would take charge of talent and programming. And Earl Hudson, who had ably served us since the Detroit Theatres affair, would be in charge of West Coast administration and operations, though he would not be involved with programming.

Noble said he'd have to check with Kintner before agreeing. Kintner told him, "I don't need them, but if they are part of the deal, I'll take them."

In hindsight that was a clear signal of the antagonism Kintner felt toward UPT. It's really unfortunate, because he was in many ways a brilliant man. Had he welcomed his new associates, had he opened his mind to their advice, things might have gone better for everyone. But that was all in the future. At the time, I was confident that O'Brien, Weitman, and Hudson would make important contributions to ABC.

So, finally, the negotiations were over. We agreed that the resulting company would be called American Broadcasting–Paramount Theatres (AB-PT). The deal, of course, was subject to approval by both boards of directors. Noble was the majority stockholder in ABC; his board was no more than a rubber stamp. My board, however, was another story entirely.

On June 6, 1951, I took our agreement to the UPT board of directors.

The board members sat around a long, polished table as I got up to make the most important sales pitch of my career. As I began to speak, I saw the faces around the table change, and realized the majority of them opposed the merger.

I recalled my childhood coach's dictum: "A team that *won't* be beat *can't* be beat." I never stopped talking. Afternoon gave way to evening as I laid out my rationale for the merger, and answered questions. The frowns around the table deepened. The queries got tougher and more pointed.

My board included Bob O'Brien, UPT secretary-treasurer, Walter Gross, UPT VP and general counsel, and four outside directors. This arrangement had been forced on us by the terms of our consent decree with the Justice Department. We could have no directors with previous connection to Paramount Pictures, and the majority of directors had to be outsiders.

Nevertheless, this was as astute and able a group of businessmen as ever sat around a board table. John Coleman, a partner in the brokerage firm of Adler Coleman, was also chairman of the board of governors of the New York Stock Exchange. Walter Marshall headed Western Union. Chester Gersten was president of Public National Bank. And William Kilborn was president of Flannery Manufacturing, a Pittsburgh auto and train parts manufacturer.

What had this flint-eyed bunch exercised went far beyond the issue of whether $25 million was too much to pay for ABC. They worried most of all that ABC would never be able to compete with NBC, CBS, and DuMont.

Virtually all network television was live in 1951. The biggest shows were those boasting headliners like Ed Sullivan, Edgar Bergen, Jack Benny, Bing Crosby, Arthur Godfrey, Groucho Marx, Burns and Allen, Kate Smith, Bob Hope, Amos and Andy—the glittering panoply of stars that had built huge audiences on network radio before coming over to television.

And except for Ozzie and Harriet Nelson, virtually all these big stars were on CBS and NBC.

So how, asked my directors, did I expect ABC's lackluster lineup to compete with the networks of the stars?

I said I intended to get our programs from the entertainment capital of the world. From Hollywood. We would get stories from the world's finest screenwriters. On-camera talent would come from Hollywood's legions of aspiring stars. We would put programs on film, and show them on the network the same way we showed feature films in theaters.

To me, then and now, a TV station is much like a theater. And a good story is a good story. The size of the screen people watch really doesn't make that much difference. So if Hollywood could produce entertainment for theaters, they could do the same for millions of people watching at home.

I knew there would be some resistance to this, but I was well acquainted with the heads of all the major studios. I was sure I could convince them that television was not their enemy, that it was inevitable that broadcasting and film production should get married.

The board heard me out. Then they raised the subject of relative audience size.

ABC, with five stations and nine primary affiliates, reached only about 35 percent of American television homes. NBC and CBS, with upward of sixty primary affiliates each, were already in virtually all American television homes. DuMont, the third network, had slightly more coverage than ABC.

My hopes for ABC hinged on the fact that the industry was young and growing. In time there would be enough advertising to support three networks. The trouble was, to most of my board, it was more likely this would be DuMont.

Allen B. DuMont was a protégé of Dr. Lee DeForest, after Thomas Edison the most important American inventor of electronics. Dr. DuMont invented the first practical cathode-ray tube, basis of all television. He also developed the first TV cameras capable of capturing motion picture images, and pioneered many other important television technologies. DuMont Labs manufactured America's first TV sets. They established TV stations in New York, Pittsburgh, and Washington.

DuMont started a television network in 1946. As the earliest network, it claimed an impressive number of innovations. Jackie Gleason made his television debut on DuMont's "Cavalcade of Stars." Mike Wallace's first network news job was on DuMont. DuMont ran the first network soap opera, "Faraway Hill." TV's first science fiction serial, "Captain Video," was a DuMont production.

In sports, too, DuMont was first. In 1951 they aired NFL football from coast to coast. They also introduced America to network baseball, basketball, and wrestling.

With affiliates, DuMont and ABC had roughly the same amount of coverage. DuMont, however, programmed their network over thirty-two hours a week while ABC had only twenty-four hours.

And Paramount Pictures owned a substantial interest in DuMont.

Thanks in part to the cash Barney had scooped out of the theater division's till just before we parted companies, Paramount had plenty of money to pump into DuMont. They had legions of writers, producers, actors, directors, and other talent under contract, enough to create the kinds of shows any mass audience would find appealing.

But Paramount had one more thing, and that was *my* ace in the hole.

Paul Raibourn was Paramount Pictures' vice president for budget planning and television. He was Paramount's liaison with DuMont. This was the same fellow who had whispered in Barney Balaban's ear about the Madison's losses while I was working to turn the Detroit Theatres around in 1937.

Before UPT was separated from Paramount Pictures, I attended many meetings where Raibourn told Barney how he could save a few hundred dollars here and there at DuMont. Usually, the money came out of program budgets. Barney almost always went along. His supreme skill was cutting budgets.

Now, old Dr. DuMont was a nice gentleman. Technologically speaking, he was twenty years ahead of his time. But when he sold part of his company to Paramount Pictures, he lost control of his pocketbook. Backed by Barney, Raibourn constantly nitpicked and needled him over the smallest expenditures. DuMont came to the point where, psychologically, he thought he couldn't do *anything* without Raibourn's approval.

But the name of the television game is programs. If you won't put money into programs, you can't succeed. I was convinced that Paramount would never get anywhere with the DuMont network because Barney depended on Raibourn to run it, and Raibourn's primary interest was saving money.

So on that day in June 1951, I told my board we had nothing to fear from DuMont. Their hole card was Raibourn, but in this game he was a joker. DuMont might try to bluff us out, but if we raised the stakes with better programming at higher costs, they'd fold their cards and walk away.

I'd started my presentation at 4:00 in the afternoon. Now it was about 9:30, everyone was tired and testy, and I had yet to convince a majority. But I'd told Noble I would have my board's approval by the next morning, or the deal was off.

Then John Coleman, God bless him, said, "Maybe I can get hold of Harry Hagerty. I'd like to hear what he has to say about this before I make any decision."

As vice chairman of Metropolitan Life Insurance Company, Hagerty was responsible for all their loans and investments. He was probably the biggest lender in the country. His son later married Coleman's daughter. The two families were close.

Hagerty had lent money to CBS. He was also on RCA's board, a close adviser to General Sarnoff. We all agreed he would have a good feel for this deal.

Hagerty had already gone to bed, but he agreed to meet us at Coleman's Park Avenue apartment, right across the street from his own.

It was raining hard, and we had a tough time finding enough cabs, but by 10:30 we were sitting in Coleman's living room. His family had left for their summer home, and all the furniture was covered with bed sheets.

Coleman laid out the proposed deal, explaining to Hagerty why he felt a merger might break UPT. ABC had so little coverage. It was losing money. It would take years to become truly competitive with CBS and NBC. There was still the question of DuMont. And, he said, while UPT had about $40 million in cash, the network could eat that up very quickly.

Hagerty turned to me and said, "What's your position?"

After outlining the facts I'd presented to the board earlier, I pointed out that television was in its infancy. There were still tens of millions of homes without sets, but that would change. People would buy sets, and then they'd demand more programs to watch. That meant more advertising, and in time the present networks wouldn't be able to handle it.

Someone said, "What do you mean, they won't be able to handle it?"

"There are only twenty-four hours in a day," I said. "No one can make more. The *Saturday Evening Post, Life* or *The New York Times* can add pages to accommodate increased advertising sales. They never have to turn anyone away because they don't have room. But there's a finite amount of broadcast time. There are only so many commercials NBC and CBS can fit in.

"So, as demand grows they'll raise rates, but eventually they won't be able to handle the demand." So, I said, there will be room for a third network. It's going to happen.

"We'll lose money for five, maybe six years. But this is the chance of a lifetime. We should take it," I said.

Then I explained my feelings about DuMont's prospects, and my plan to get programming from Hollywood.

I said I was convinced we could get the programming needed to be competitive. Moreover, I believed the motion picture industry's survival ultimately depended on marriage with television. The studio moguls would resist, but it would happen sooner or later. UPT, with hundreds of theaters, still wielded some muscle in the movie business. I said I believed we could nudge the studios to the altar, so to speak, and hold the shotgun while the moguls mumbled their vows.

After some discussion, Hagerty turned to the board and said, "I agree with Leonard. In our lifetime, I believe there will only be three television networks. I think you should make the deal, and if you need it, I'd be willing to lend you some money."

There was one more issue. Some of the board were concerned that Noble, who after the merger would have almost 9 percent of the stock, would get control.

Hagerty dismissed this with a wave of his hand. "If you gentlemen don't know how to control the situation, then you don't deserve to be in business," he said. In other words, he was telling us, "Just run the business and ignore him."

That's exactly what we did.

The merger, which was conditional on FCC approval, was headline news around the country. I was widely quoted as saying I would be looking to Hollywood to provide programs.

In the first days after the announcement, I took several phone calls from leading figures in the movie and broadcasting industry. Three of them stick in my mind.

Nick Schenck, CEO of Loews, which owned MGM, asked me over for lunch. No sooner had we sat down when he said, "Leonard, you're a traitor to the motion picture business."

I was a little shocked. I asked Nick what he meant.

"Obviously, you're going to go after writers, producers, and directors that make motion pictures and try to get them into television. It's going to increase our costs. And you'll be competing with movie theaters for the audience's time. Leonard, you'll drive us out of business."

"Nick, if I were to tell you today that I could get a trailer for MGM's next Clark Gable picture, or your next Greta Garbo picture, into virtually every home in this country, what would you give?"

"I'd give a fortune."

"Nick, I rest my case."

He recognized what I was saying, but disagreed. It took a long time to get MGM into television, and so they never did as well in the medium as other studios. But today every studio *depends* on television to sell their films. I wonder what Nick might have said if I could have told him that, in 1989, ABC would be advertising network programs in movie theaters!

Another call was from David Sarnoff. We knew each other from the theater business. He asked me to come over for lunch.

"Leonard, what are you going to do for programming on the ABC network?" he asked.

"General, you don't give us much choice. You and CBS have tied up all the top talent which came out of radio. All we have is 'Ozzie and Harriet.' So I'm going to try to bring Hollywood into the picture."

Sarnoff was incredulous. "Hollywood? This is a medium of spontaneity. Who's going to watch film? Audiences want to watch things live."

"General, the public doesn't care whether it's on film or it's live, as long as it's entertaining."

He argued with me for a time. Finally he said, "I've been thinking about your problem. I'd like to suggest that you take the best programs off CBS and NBC, after we play them, and show them on ABC."

"General, I appreciate your thinking of us, but I'm not interested in having a second-run network. I want to be competitive with both NBC and CBS."

The third call was from Adolph Zukor.

"It's true," he said, "that I was one of the pioneers in the picture business. But you now have a great opportunity to reach many more people than we could ever reach with motion pictures. I want to tell you how much I admire what you're doing in trying to establish a viable third network."

Zukor's blessing banished all the doubts I'd harbored since I first went after ABC.

After our board approved the merger, I set out to visit the five ABC TV stations. I hadn't done this earlier out of fear that if word got around I was looking at their properties, somebody else might beat me to a deal with Noble.

Chicago didn't concern me. WBKB was in the State and Lake Building, and the facilities were first rate. Even though we sold Channel 4 to CBS, we were really selling the license. After the sale we planned to move Channel 7's operations into our facilities.

But looking at the rest of what we'd bought was shocking. In Detroit, all the equipment was sitting around some hallway they'd leased. The San Francisco property had been an Elk's Club. There was still sawdust on the floor. I went to Los Angeles to look over what had originally been the Vitagraph Studio, where Warner Bros. had made such silent epics as *The Phantom of the Opera* and the first talkie, *The Jazz Singer*. Vacant for years before ABC moved in, it was falling apart. Rats scampered across the rafters, and piles of droppings were everywhere. I felt sick to my stomach.

Back in New York, I told my board we had a major problem. We would need to spend a lot on facilities. "But if we're going to build ABC into a truly competitive network," I said, "we really have no choice but to spend it, over a period of time."

The board went along with me. These directors, and the ones that followed them through the years, were sensational. I believe they developed great trust in my judgment. Thank God for that, because I regularly asked them to approve enormous programming budgets without knowing what the shows were going to be, and they almost always did.

That didn't mean, however, that they lay down before everything I proposed. To the contrary, they always raised arguments when they had reason to question something.

ABC's strength has always been that we had far more outside directors than management directors. The latter always want to run the company for themselves instead of the stockholders. That's the worst mistake you can make in business.

After our boards approved the merger, there were two more obstacles. The first was approval by stockholders of the two companies. Noble, with

58 percent of ABC, could have held his stockholders meeting in a telephone booth. We had ours in a hotel on July 27, 1951, and although some serious questions were raised, the merger was overwhelmingly approved.

That left only the FCC. We submitted our paperwork to the Commission in July. Leo Resnick was appointed hearing examiner in late August. Although up to that time this was the largest issue ever to come before the FCC, we expected the proceedings would take no more than a few months.

But the hearings turned into a marathon, a nightmare, prolonged torture. Instead of merely satisfying itself that a merger between UPT and ABC would be in the public interest, convenience, and necessity, the FCC set off on an expedition into terra incognita.

Resnick elected to package DuMont's pending application for the purchase of stations in Cleveland and Cincinnati with our merger, and to tie both to an investigation into Paramount Pictures' past. Paramount had applied for renewal of KTLA's license and for a new television license in San Francisco.

This all-star package generated tremendous media attention. An unlikely assortment of interests, ranging from disaffected inventors of television hardware to independent theater owners to the American Civil Liberties Union rushed forward to put their comments before the FCC.

The ACLU initially said they questioned the whole idea of a marriage between the movie industry and broadcasting. It would put too much power over public opinion into too few hands, they said. If UPT were to own a network, the ACLU thought MGM, Fox, and the other major studios might want to buy CBS and NBC. The result, they said, would be a near monopoly with little competition. Commissioner Frieda Hennock adopted this line of reasoning for her own, and throughout the proceedings kept bringing it up.

Looking back, the ACLU sounds silly. UPT no longer had anything to do with movie production. But silly or not, we had to take such challenges seriously. We argued that ABC, revitalized by UPT's capital, would in time become competitive with CBS and NBC. Echoing arguments that the Justice Department had made to us four years earlier, we said a strong, competitive ABC would stimulate CBS and NBC to do better. By the end of the hearings the ACLU had swung completely around and backed our merger as in the public interest. Hennock, however, had no such change of heart.

The first witnesses to testify were from Paramount Pictures. The FCC contended Paramount Pictures controlled DuMont. If they did, the FCC reasoned, then Paramount's KTLA, plus the San Francisco license they sought, combined with DuMont's three stations and the two DuMont wanted to buy, far exceeded the five UHF stations that any single entity could own.

Witnesses from both DuMont and Paramount Pictures testified that while Paramount might be able to veto certain DuMont transactions—anything requiring a large expenditure—they never had a majority of the board of directors.

DuMont opposed our merger, trying to depict a combined UPT-ABC as a giant that would dominate the industry. We fervently wished this were so, but even after merging we would remain a minnow to the whales called CBS and RCA.

Encouraged by massive media attention, the Commission began to sift through all the dirt that had been excavated during the landmark antitrust case against Paramount Pictures.

Barney Balaban was grilled for four days. One of the first things he was asked was to characterize the relationship between UPT and Paramount Pictures.

Barney testified that for the last six months no Paramount Pictures films had played at the New York Paramount Theatre. It was true. Our two companies couldn't agree on terms. Moreover, he said, he and I were "as far apart as the poles."

That was the truth. Neither of us was glad about it.

When we first opened negotiations for ABC, we knew we were in for heavy expenses in the months and years ahead. It was going to take a lot of money to put ABC in the black.

At this time theater earnings were declining. That was because on the one hand we were selling off theaters to comply with the Justice decree to create competition, and on the other the whole country was in an economic slump that hurt the theater business a little more than other industries.

So I felt very strongly that we should conserve our cash. We were going to need it. We discussed this at a board meeting, and decided to reduce our 1952 dividend from $2.00 to $1.00. Competing theater companies, as it happened, followed suit.

Barney held 80,000 shares of UPT stock. We had several thousand stockholders and a little over 3.25 million shares, but because of his unique status as the head of Paramount Pictures, he was the only one allowed to own both Paramount Pictures and UPT stock. It was held in trust. Under the terms of the consent agreement, he had a few years to dispose of it.

After we voted to reduce the dividend, I called Barney to tell him. He became very angry.

"You should have told me this before the meeting, so I could have given you advice about it," he said.

"Barney, we're two separate companies now," I replied. "I can't possibly consult with you before our board meets. If I were to discuss such things with you, and you were to influence our board, they might as well get rid of me. I'd no longer be responsible as head of the company."

Barney said that lowering our dividend would cause the value of his stock to drop. This indeed happened after the dividend announcement. But I could hardly have given Barney advance notice of our intentions and not given them to everyone else who owned UPT stock. Even then there were laws against insider trading.

I told Barney that his brother John, a member of our board, had voted for the dividend reduction. Barney stubbornly insisted that I should have consulted him first.

I think that in Barney's head I had once been his man and was always going to be his man. He may have felt that even after the Justice Department forced us into separate companies, I should continue to do whatever *he* felt was best.

Now, I regarded Barney as a second father. He'd given me my big opportunity. I felt a great obligation to him personally. Yet I knew I was right in what I'd done. I'm sure he must have felt he was equally right, and I couldn't dissuade him. I felt terrible about our breach. It troubled me no end. In fact, all these years later, I'm still upset about it.

A mutual friend, Ed Weisl, Paramount Pictures' outside counsel, spoke to Barney. He told Barney he was wrong, suggesting he just forget about it.

But Barney remained stubbornly determined neither to forgive nor to forget. For over sixteen years he refused to speak to me.

Not until the twilight of his life did we patch things up. Barney lived near me in Mamaroneck, and in the late 1960s, when he became quite ill, I went with Spyros Skouras to call on him. After that, until his death in 1971, we had some friendly discussions. Even then, however, our relationship was never as close as it had been before 1952.

On the stand Barney was questioned about agreements he'd made in the 1920s, when B&K was first acquiring theaters and working out exhibition contracts. Trying to prove that Paramount was a habitual antitrust violator, and hence unfit to own TV stations, FCC counsel James Juntilla dug up old documents originally subpoenaed for the antitrust case. And he put my friend David Wallerstein on the stand to testify.

OTHER RECOLLECTIONS:
David Wallerstein

The government's big question was whether we could be trusted. They were afraid we might corner the market on film, or use our theater power, even though we had restrictions and had to sell many theaters.

My virtue was that I was responsible for operating B&K under John Balaban, the president, but I was not part of the old regime that did all of these horrible, horrible things.

I was the younger generation. I wasn't tainted by the monopoly practices, by dividing up the country, by putting up signs, "We're going to build unless you sell," or dealing with the hoodlums, or the union corruption. I was not part of that conspiracy. I was clean. I was a kid at the time all that happened. Now I was running the theaters. I was responsible for B&K's good record.

❑ ❑ ❑

Wallerstein's testimony helped to convince the FCC that UPT indeed was no longer connected to Paramount Pictures. But Paramount was also accused of influencing DuMont, which distributed films to independent TV stations, to force customers to buy packages of several films just to get one. The film booking practices Paramount used before the consent decree were rehashed. It was ugly stuff.

Abe Blank was called to the stand to justify his business practices thirty years earlier. Disgruntled widows and sons of small-town theater owners who had been driven out of business by Paramount's subsidiaries in the 1920s came forward to complain about the pioneers' buccaneering tactics.

I had been a schoolboy while Paramount was built and had not joined the company until after the era of the buccaneers, but I was not immune from attack. When my turn to testify came, George W. Latimer, a man I'd outbid on a 1941 theater lease deal in Salt Lake City, testified against me. He was now a Court of Military Appeals judge, and he had some pretty stiff things to say about the way Paramount looked after its interests in those years.

(Latimer was to get another moment on the national stage in 1970, when he defended Lt. William L. Calley, accused of mass murder at My Lai, South Vietnam. Latimer said Calley was "a fine boy." A court-martial found him guilty.)

The FCC's counsel absurdly suggested that UPT wanted to buy ABC so we could help strangle the infant television industry in its cradle. Our proposed merger, they suggested, was a sinister plot to help the movie industry and the theater business!

During the dog days of the summer of 1952, our attorneys slaved over petitions to the FCC, trying to get the commissioners to sever our merger from the rest of this long-running soap opera. Meanwhile Barney's lawyers were trying to get the FCC to stick to the issues. Paramount Pictures wanted the antitrust angle dropped, on the ground that it had nothing to do with the present situation. DuMont, of course, argued that it had everything to do with Paramount Pictures and UPT's fitness to hold broadcast licenses.

There was a background issue, not much discussed, but important. Some of the FCC commissioners' noses were out of joint. When Justice forced the breakup of Paramount, and I worked out a consent agreement with Bob Wright, no one consulted them about transferring the license for WBKB to UPT and KTLA to Paramount Pictures. It was a technical error, of course, but some of the commissioners were going to get their pound of flesh. Barney's and mine.

By late August 1952, a compromise on the antitrust issues was reached. The FCC would forget about any alleged antitrust abuses that occurred more than three years prior to August 7, 1951, the day we filed our original petition for merger.

Unfortunately, out of 531 antitrust cases filed against Paramount Pictures since 1920, 234 were filed after August 1948. In addition, the FCC wanted to discuss a handful of other lawsuits Paramount was defending.

U.S. Attorney General James McGranery, corresponding with FCC Chairman Paul Walker, tried to pressure the FCC into widening the antitrust probe. But bureaucrats fight ferociously for their own turf. Walker told McGranery to keep his nose out of the matter.

The hearing examiner, Leo Resnick, abruptly halted the hearings August 20, 1952. After more than 3.5 million words of testimony, Resnick gave all parties thirty days to submit proposed findings.

Trade newspapers optimistically predicted a decision by October 1952. We fervently hoped this was so, because things at ABC had gone from bad to terrible. Advertisers, unwilling to make commitments amid all the uncertainty, were backing off in droves. By one estimate ABC had lost over

$20 million in business. Running short of cash, Noble took draconian measures. He froze hiring and pared the payroll. Many of ABC's best qualified executives and technicians began looking for new jobs. Some went to the other networks.

Every day that passed saw ABC sinking deeper and deeper into debt. To keep the company out of bankruptcy, Noble had to guarantee major creditors that he'd personally make good on ABC's mounting debts if the merger failed.

The FCC did not rule in October. The seven commissioners were unable to agree unanimously. Editorials in *Business Week, The Wall Street Journal*, and *The New York Times* focused the attention of the national business community on the delay. Not until February 1953, eighteen months after our boards had given approval, did the FCC render its decision. We could merge, said five commissioners. Frieda Hennock and Eugene Merrill penned dissenting opinions.

CBS and NBC had used this time well. The license freeze had ended in July 1952, and virtually all the dozens of new stations around the country had affiliated with one or the other. Advertisers flocked in, eager to get their commercial messages before these burgeoning audiences.

On February 9, 1953, we entered the business of network broadcasting. Our network headquarters and studios were housed in what had once been a riding stable on 66th Street. The scent of equine manure still permeated the establishment. That scent was all too plain to Wall Street and to Madison Avenue, where we were regarded as a lost cause. We had no hit shows, no stars, and nothing in prospect but struggle.

9

Shotgun Marriage

❑

ABC had been in limbo for twenty months, unable to plan or go forward with the sort of growth that CBS and NBC had accomplished. We owed money all over the place, short-term debts that we settled within the first few weeks. We also repaid the millions owed to Noble personally. Suddenly our $40 million war chest didn't look so big. And this was just the beginning.

Including our five owned and operated (O&O) television stations, ABC's network had only fourteen primary affiliates. By then CBS had seventy-four, NBC seventy-one. Since the number of viewers exposed per message determines the price of advertising, this meant one hour of CBS programming brought in about five times as much as an hour on ABC. But the cost to create that programming was about the same for all networks.

Our first priority was programming. Weekdays, ABC had almost nothing on until 6 P.M., when we presented John Daly with fifteen minutes of news. Until network programming resumed at 7:30, individual affiliates aired programs of their own. Some nights ABC programmed until 11. On others we finished at 9 or 9:30.

Weekends were only a little better. Sunday afternoon we aired a few shows and stayed on through 11:00 P.M.

So Bob Weitman's first task was to start filling those hours with programs. I helped him every way I knew. So did Bob O'Brien, ABC's new executive VP.

O'Brien's chief assistant was Jason ("Jay") Rabinovitz. A Harvard Business School graduate, he drafted quarterly and annual report statements, and helped O'Brien answer stockholder correspondence. Before the merger Jay was UPT's resident television expert, which meant that he knew a little about the business. The rest of us knew almost nothing.

A couple of years before the merger, the NCAA had declared a moratorium on network-televised football games. Jay knew O'Brien had played college and semipro football and was well connected with college sports figures. Jay suggested that O'Brien try to get Big Ten games into those of our theaters equipped with projection TV. O'Brien met with Tug Wilson, Big Ten athletic director, and made a deal.

We did all right with it in a few big Midwestern cities, but after one season the NCAA went back to the networks.

Now *we* had a network, so O'Brien went to the NCAA and got them to let ABC televise several important games in 1954.

OTHER RECOLLECTIONS:
Jay Rabinovitz

I came over to ABC in 1954 to help set up a budgeting system—cost control. I was hatchet man. People assumed that I was there to spy for Leonard. It became a very difficult situation.

At the time we used to say that Kintner was very bright but a lousy administrator. Not very good at running a company.

But in retrospect he was probably as good an executive as I've known. He understood the importance of communications in a company. Leonard might kill me for saying so, but of all the places I've been, Kintner had the best internal communications.

O'Brien's vision of television was contrary to Kintner's. They locked horns very early on.

O'Brien thought sports would play a very important role in television. Kintner didn't see that at all. It may well be he didn't think it was important because it wasn't his own idea. Or because O'Brien was much more conversant with sports.

Kintner emphasized news very heavily. O'Brien also believed in news, but he thought there was room for feature motion pictures in television. That was anathema to Kintner and to many top broadcasting executives.

O'Brien and I drafted a statement submitted to the FCC, our view of television's future. We said it should be like a good magazine. We saw television as going into movies, sports, and features, but the kinds of features you used to get in *Life* magazine. Actuality, not fiction. We didn't see the dramatic series as being so rooted in American culture as it has turned out to be.

So when O'Brien made a deal with the NCAA, there were great

differences between him and Kintner. When it came time to go out and sell the program to advertisers, Kintner took off for Europe on vacation. On his orders, the network sales force sat on its hands. He'd told them NCAA football program sales would not earn them bonuses.

When O'Brien realized what was happening, he put together a special sales force to go out and sell it. They were able to sell only half the program. ABC took a big belt. O'Brien went back to the parent company in disgrace, a failure, and Kintner was left triumphant to rule over ABC.

❑ ❑ ❑

We lost our shirt on NCAA football, but, even worse, the whole matter caused Bob O'Brien to think I no longer had confidence in him. This was not true.

I could not allow him to continue in a situation where he and Kintner were at odds, and I'd promised Noble I'd leave Kintner alone for three years. So I brought O'Brien back to UPT, where there was much for him to do, and took no action against Kintner. O'Brien, dear friend and faithful executive, felt I should have done more to back him. He left ABC about a year later to become financial vice president under Joe Vogel, president of Loews. When Joe died, a few years later, O'Brien became president of Loews.

Within weeks of the merger, I went out to Hollywood and made the rounds of the major studios. I was trying to sell television as an opportunity to rejuvenate the movie business. Nobody was buying. Television was the enemy. I came back to New York empty-handed.

Back in New York, I called Abe Lastfogel, head of William Morris, the largest and most successful theatrical agency in the world. Abe and I had enjoyed a fine relationship for years. Paramount Theatres booked William Morris acts in New York, Detroit, Chicago, Dallas, Houston, Atlanta, and Miami—wherever we had stage shows in addition to movies.

I said, "Abe, I need help. All ABC has is 'Ozzie and Harriet.' Everything else is advertiser controlled, and we've got to build up some assets of our own in programming."

Abe came up with Ray Bolger, Sammy Davis, Jr., Joel Grey, George Jessel, and a fellow out of Detroit who had done well in nightclubs. We created variety shows for Bolger and Jessel, which debuted in the fall of 1953. They died in the ratings. Joel Grey, a big name on Broadway, did nothing for viewers on the small screen.

Sammy Davis, Jr., was another story. Probably the most gifted performer of his era, he could sing, dance, play instruments, do standup comedy—everything. And he was eager to go into television. We built a pilot around Sammy's family, all entertainers. But no advertiser dared to back a "colored" star at that time. We couldn't sell it, so "The Sammy Davis, Jr., Show" never went on the air.

That left the nightclub performer.

He lives today in a wonderful Beverly Hills mansion overlooking Hollywood. His living room is almost the size of Madison Square Garden. Almost. Enormous murals of the Lebanese countryside cover the walls. It's very appropriate. After all, Danny Thomas's mother was a cousin of Kahlil Gibran, mystical author of *The Prophet*.

Danny has come a long way from Detroit. There, in the 1930s, as Jacob Amos, he went into show business doing an act in beer gardens. In those days his ambition was to become a character actor on radio. He signed with WXYZ, but the only thing they'd let him do was help the sound man. They gave him a pair of coconut shells, and Danny became the horse's hoofs on "The Lone Ranger."

OTHER RECOLLECTIONS:
Danny Thomas

I was working the Copacabana in New York, staying in the Fourteen Hotel, next door on 61st. That was my dressing room. You came down in the elevator and wound up in the kitchen of the Copa. Uncle Abe Lastfogel came to me and said, "Sign this."

"Sign what?"

"This contract with ABC. They want Bolger, but if they want him, they have to take you, too. You're an entry, one and one-A, like in the races."

Well, they wanted Ray Bolger and wanted him badly. It was the day of the White Protestant American United States, and a guy like me wasn't exactly family fare. I believed it, too, until we made the pilot of "Make Room for Daddy."

I created that, accidentally, myself.

I was talking to Lou Edelman. He'd produced a couple of movies I was in at Warners, *I'll See You in My Dreams*, the life story of the songwriter Gus Kahn, and *The Jazz Singer*, Jolson's life.

Uncle Abe had asked Edelman to see me. We talked about a

series for ABC, a fledgling network which had no station lineup at the time. We were talking about a concept. With us was Mel Shavelson, who wrote, with Jack Rose, *I'll See You in My Dreams*.

We kicked around a theatrical boarding house, a street corner fruit stand—someplace you could meet other people. An Allen's Alley type of thing.

Mel said he had no time to write a pilot. Then I made an impassioned plea. Whatever we came up with, I said, I'd spent so much time on the road, doing clubs, that now I wanted to stay home.

I used to play those clubs a lot. I was gone twelve weeks at a time—no weekend dates in those days. I played the Chez Paree for seventeen weeks. I played the Martinique, my first time in New York in 1943, from Labor Day to New Year's Eve.

From my musings and recollections evolved the private life of a man who had no private life—a nightclub entertainer who was always on the road. His children outgrew him, and his dog attacked him when he came home. His kids called him Uncle Daddy.

He wasn't really a schlemiel so much as he wanted to be a hero to his kids. And that was me, in our old house on Elm in Beverly Hills. When I came home the kids would come flocking, "Daddy, Daddy, Mommy did this." Mommy was the disciplinarian, and Daddy came home with presents. Mr. Hero.

Mel said, "Hell, I could write that overnight," and he did.

Nobody knew much about television then. We invented it as we went along. Sheldon Leonard, my partner, and Mel and I would stay up until 2:30 A.M., tearing up pages. Scripts aren't written, they're rewritten. Some weeks someone would say, "My God, we're not doing *Gone With the Wind* here." I'd say, "Yes, we are." We did marvelous shows.

"Make Room for Daddy" opened on ABC in the fall of 1953. Jean Hagen played the wife, Rusty Hamer the son, and Sherry Jackson played the daughter.

We hit very quickly with whatever audience we had. We were on only twelve weeks the first year and won an Emmy. We certainly hit with the industry, the press, and the producers.

I mean this show put me in such a spot that everybody thought I was a genius. Uncle Abe Lastfogel used to bring everybody to me. From "Make Room for Daddy" came the "Andy Griffith Show," the "Dick Van Dyke Show," "Real McCoys," and "Mod Squad."

My partner, Sheldon, gave Bill Cosby a start in "I Spy." When "The Cosby Show" went on, I told Bill, "It's like old times. You're doing 'Make Room for Daddy.' " He said, "What's the matter with that? You went eleven years. I ain't going to go no eleven years."

"Make Room for Daddy" built St. Jude's Children's Research Hospital. How could I have managed to get people interested in what I wanted to do if I didn't have access to the national public?

In our fourth year of "Make Room for Daddy" wherever I went, I autographed everything. I went to towns I'd never seen before. On my way to do a St. Jude's benefit in Orlando, I went into a restaurant with my wife, and I was swamped. And this was the year we were in 107th place in the ratings! That's why I never believed in the rating system. I didn't believe it when we were on the bottom, and when I got to the top, I didn't believe it either. Mr. Nielsen must have been very upset with me.

That was our last year on ABC. We were on forty-one stations live and forty-four delayed. The delays went on at 2:30 Sunday afternoon, and the live went up against Bob Hope every fourth week, and Burns and Allen every other week. No way we could get ratings. The numbers just weren't there. So we were canceled.

My partner and I owned two thirds of the show. ABC owned the rest. But Leonard Goldenson is not the kind of man to say, "Well, whatever we can make as one-third owners of this show, let's keep it." That wasn't his thinking. He gave us back ABC's share of the profits. Amazing is the word.

❑ ❑ ❑

Late in 1953 I got a call from Walt and Roy Disney. They wanted to come see me. I already knew why. Dave Wallerstein at B&K had told me.

OTHER RECOLLECTIONS:
David Wallerstein

Walt Disney used to say I was a good showman. That's the best reference I could get. And I have done a few showmanlike things in my life. I helped get Ronald Reagan into the Knute Rockne picture by persuading Warner Bros. to produce it.

I knew Disney because I played his pictures.

I started Disney world premieres at the B&K theaters. We

premiered *Fantasia, Cinderella*, and *Mary Poppins*. He was very happy with our promotion, the ads. We got to be very close friends.

Walt was always hard up for money, so I used to advance film rental to him. Understand, that wasn't so kosher. We were supposed to be out of production. But I'd still advance Walt maybe $300,000 against film rentals.

Leonard always used to say, "You're such good pals with Disney, let's see if you can't get us his stuff for television."

One day I said, "Walt, you know we have ABC now."

He said, "Look, I've done a special for NBC, and I had some talks with CBS. I've got to show you something. Come with me."

He takes me to the back lot in Burbank and shows me a pony. "What does this have to do with it?"

He said, "That's a five-eighths scale horse."

Then he shows me some sketches. He takes me across the street, there's about four acres. He says, "This is going to be Disneyland. I've always felt these amusement parks for kids were no good. I'm going to build something five-eighths scale and I'm going to originate my television shows from Disneyland."

He says, "I'll need financing. So that'll be one of the conditions when I sell any of my stuff."

"Well, what'll I do now?" I said.

"Just rely on me. I'll call you."

❑ ❑ ❑

The Disneys said they wanted to build an amusement park in a dusty little California town called Anaheim. Walt had always had something like this in mind. After he brought in Stanford Research, however, he'd decided not to put it next to his studio in Burbank.

ABC was really Disney's last hope. He'd gone to the banks, and when he tried to explain what he wanted to build, they just couldn't grasp the concept. They kept thinking of a place like Coney Island. Very risky. They turned him down.

Walt and his wife, Lily, borrowed against their life insurance to pay for a scale model. They'd gone to see Sarnoff at NBC, offering to give him access to the Disney film library if he'd finance the park. "Cartoon films? Television will never be a medium of entertainment," said Sarnoff, showing them the door.

Then they'd gone to see Paley at CBS. For months he kept them on a string, refusing to say yes or no, but extracting Disney's promise that he wouldn't talk to anyone else about it until CBS decided. Finally, Paley said, "No."

I asked Walt how much they thought it would cost to build Disneyland. He said, "About four million dollars, maybe five million at the most."

That wasn't going to be nearly enough, I said. Probably it would take more like $10 million or $15 million. After construction they would have to staff it, train people, and operate at a loss for some time. (As it turned out, it cost $17 million, the first year alone.)

I offered to take the Disneys in to see our board. But as a condition, I said, "I want a one-hour program, every week." And of course I wanted access to their 600 animated-feature film library. In exchange I offered one minute each week, free, to promote Disney's latest film. With hundreds of UPT theaters to show these movies, that wasn't a bad deal for us.

At first my board opposed the deal. After all, they said, CBS had turned Disney down. NBC had turned him down. And the banks had said no. More to the point, where were *we* going to get financing?

I talked to some of the New York banks. They were reluctant to lend us $10 or $15 million for Disneyland. Then Sid Markley, my Harvard Law roommate, who was in charge of UPT's southern theaters, suggested we talk to Karl Hoblitzelle.

Karl was Bob O'Donnell's boss, owner of Interstate Theatres. He'd started his career as a booker for Keith-Orpheum, and wound up with several theater circuits, a fortune in oil—and chairmanship of the Republic Bank in Dallas.

I got to know Karl very well when I was in charge of Paramount's theaters. He was a very big man in Texas, widely known for unstinting philanthropy, and active, behind the scenes, in state politics.

In 1946 Karl had called me from Dallas and said, "Leonard, there's a young fellow, schoolteacher, running for Congress in the Johnson City area. I'd like Paramount Theatres to support him with $10,000 for his campaign."

I said, "Karl, you're running things down there. You know the situation. If you think it's right, we'll support him."

This young fellow, Lyndon Johnson, won his seat by a handful of votes. Not long afterward he came up to New York, and I met with him. I brought Ed Weisl along, and they became quite close. Ed became his counselor, in a sense.

Dave Wallerstein also knew Karl pretty well. Dave had a German cook at his Chicago home, and whenever Karl came up, he dined at Dave's. Sid and Dave went down to see Karl.

Karl agreed to have Republic put up $5 million. After that, other banks got in line to lend us the rest.

Then I hammered out a deal with the Disneys. We would put in $500,000 and guarantee the loans. In exchange we took 35 percent of Disneyland, and all profits from the food concessions for ten years. I knew that could be a gold mine.

And of course there was programming. That's what I really wanted from them. We agreed to a seven-year deal, with an option for an eighth, at $5 million a year. At $40 million, it was then the biggest programming package in history.

"Disneyland" went on the air in 1954. Hour-long dramatic segments tied in to Disneyland theme areas such as Frontier Land, Tomorrow Land, and Adventure Land.

The following year Disney gave us "The Mickey Mouse Club." This was followed, in the fall of 1957, by "Zorro."

At the end of the seventh year, Walt and Roy came to me and said they'd had an offer from NBC—really from RCA—to go into color with "Walt Disney's Wonderful World of Color." RCA was willing to pay a phenomenal sum. For RCA it was a way to sell color television sets. They owned all the patents and got a royalty on every color set sold in the world. The Disneys offered us the opportunity to match RCA's deal.

I said that we couldn't afford to do that. We just didn't have the kind of money that would allow us to bid against RCA. Furthermore, I thought it was time we reevaluated our whole relationship with Disney. The only reason we'd taken a position in Disneyland was to get them into television, but the Disneys had turned out to be terrible business partners. Disneyland had become enormously successful, but Disney kept plowing his profits back into park expansion. I feared that it would be a very long time before we started seeing any return on our original $500,000 investment.

Since ABC needed cash to finance its own growth, we made a $17 million deal to sell back our share of Disneyland, and we parted company. We took $7.5 million in cash and Disneyland's concession profits for five more years. I felt they would bring in about $2.5 million a year, and I wasn't far wrong.

After I had made the deal with Disney in 1954, I called Jack Warner again. We had dinner at the LaRue Restaurant on the Sunset Strip. We ate and talked and talked. I was trying to persuade him to go into television.

Jack said, "Leonard, I made those quickies thirty years ago, and I'm not going to make 'em again."

I said, "I don't want you to do that either. This is different. I want to use your library. I want you to put young management in charge of this. And I want to give you one minute a week in every program to promote your motion pictures."

After four and a half hours he finally agreed. Jack put his son-in-law, Bill Orr, in charge of television, reporting to Ben Kalmenson, executive VP and general sales manager. Kalmenson and I sat down and went through their entire library, looking for films upon which we could base an hour-long series. We selected *Cheyenne, Kings Row*, and *Casablanca*.

OTHER RECOLLECTIONS:
Bill Orr

I don't think Jack Warner had ever seen a television show. He'd come home, and if his wife was watching a show he'd say, "What do you want to look at that for? Go into the theater and see it on a big screen, now pictures are getting bigger."

None of us knew much about television. There was very little talk about it except, "Those dirty dogs, they're taking away our box office."

Finally, Jack had a conversation with Leonard. I was outside the loop, as they say today. Benny Kalmenson came to the studio, and we had a big meeting. Benny said, "We have to get into television." Mort Blumenstock, in charge of advertising and publicity, said that Gary Stevens, in our PR department, had worked in television.

It turned out that his connection to television was as a PR man bringing people to breakfast at Sardi's and things of that kind. But he spoke fluently about ideas we didn't understand. "Cross-commercialization" and "logo," and other terms that none of us were even aware of.

So Gary was put in charge of television. I was to be liaison with the television division.

I was to find out what their needs were and hire for them. I would suggest somebody and set up interviews, and usually they hired whomever I sent, because Gary didn't know any of the local talent.

And I was to keep track of them and see they did things the Warners way, and didn't spend too much money. Help them find writers to do scripts.

One day I'm in Steve Trilling's office. We'd just got a squawk phone, a speaker phone, first time we ever had that. Jack is in the south of France and every few days he called in, and Steve reported what was going on. I would throw in whatever Steve hadn't said.

Every week he was away, Jack got a packet from the publicity department. Things that might interest him from *Variety* and the local papers.

Jack said, "Did you read the thing in the *Times*?" Gary Stevens gave an interview to a columnist, saying, "Now that Warner Bros. had gone into television, their expertise should lead to the finest television ever made."

But at the end the columnist said, "I like Gary's enthusiasm and desire. However, television isn't all that easy, and I would hate to see Jack Warner running around in a white zip-up suit taking parking tickets."

In other words, if we failed, as was likely, we'd have to turn this place into a parking lot.

Jack said, "Fire that dumb S.O.B. Get him out of there right away. Now, who's going to take his place?"

Steve says, "I don't know anything about television. We'll have to try to find somebody."

Jack says, "What about you, Bill? Do you know anybody?"

I said, "No, I don't."

Steve said, "Bill's the only one who knows anything about television."

So Jack says, "Fine, put him in charge."

So in twenty minutes I'm over in the television division looking around to see what they were doing.

Jim Aubrey was in charge of ABC programming. He sent Bob Lewine out, and he explained the mechanics of a television show. A teaser up front, a cliffhanger for the end of an act, things of that kind, the fundamentals of television.

He was very helpful. He said our scripts weren't very good. We agreed. We were working on it.

There'd been no supervision, so they were running off in all directions. That first year I spent all day at the studio and three quarters of the night at my house with writers and producers, going over the stuff we had and what were we going to do next.

Then we got into casting. The network wanted us to take George Montgomery, who had been my neighbor and friend since before the war.

I didn't want to use somebody who had already established himself. He'd got this far in pictures, and I felt that if we put him in "Cheyenne," it would hurt him. At that time going into television was like, "You couldn't get a job in the picture business, so you were in television."

So I looked around for someone new. An agent brought Norman Walker in to see me. I wanted to test him. He'd done nothing except carry a spear at Paramount. He'd been under contract to De Mille for twenty minutes; they were perfectly willing to let us pick him up. I saw the test and said, "Wait a minute. You sluffed this guy off."

Dick Bare, in charge of testing, said, "Well, the producer said to just do it and get rid of him."

I said, "Test him again, and test him right." We did another scene, with Walker and a guy named Lee Marvin, the first time I'd seen him.

We screened Norman's second test, and Jack liked him. The producer said, "Impossible. We can't have this rank amateur. I'll eat every foot of film that this guy makes after the pilot."

But Jack had the final say. Then we sat in the projection room talking about how Norman was no name for a Western star. Arty Silver, who made all the promotional trailers, said, "Remember *Saratoga Trunk*, with Gary Cooper? He was Clint Maroon. Why don't we call him Clint Walker?"

❑ ❑ ❑

Originally we called the program "Warner Bros. Presents" and rotated each series in turn through the same time period, starting in the fall of 1955. No one had ever done this kind of programming before. Almost everything then was live. We were breaking a lot of new ground, so of course we were making a lot of mistakes as we went along.

Kings Row and *Casablanca,* though very successful feature films, were doomed to fail as television series. Working on "Cheyenne," however, was a brilliant young writer-turned-producer, Roy Huggins.

OTHER RECOLLECTIONS:
Roy Huggins

After the war, I had written three or four novels. One of these was *77 Sunset Strip,* which was really a collection of novellas.

My books were serialized in the *Saturday Evening Post*. I had also written screenplays, and directed one called *Hangman's Knot* which is still shown in retrospectives.

In the early days television was really like radio. Programming was done live in New York, just like radio. Everything was in half-hour units, just like radio. TV was run by the same people who had run radio for twenty-five years, advertisers.

But TV is a film medium. A storytelling medium. It shouldn't be in half-hour chunks and shouldn't be run by advertising agencies.

The man responsible for modern TV is Leonard Goldenson. No one had ever thought of doing it any other way until Leonard came around and said, "Hey, this is crazy, they are doing radio with pictures, and that is not what TV is."

So we started making one-hour shows that told stories very similar to the way we do in movies.

I wanted to do "Cheyenne," but they had somebody else on it. It had not gone on the air yet, but a few shows were finished. Then the sponsor, Monsanto Chemical, sent Warners a telegram like a phone book—it was that long—criticizing "Cheyenne."

The gist of this telegram was they wouldn't pay for the show and were going to sue Warner Bros. for practicing television without a license. The telegram was so beautifully written that I wanted to hire the guy who wrote it.

Monsanto demanded total changes, so Bill Orr asked me to look at the shows. They were awful. They were aimed at children. A mistake. If you're doing a 7:30 show for children, give them something they'll like, but tell stories *parents* will like. Children don't object to good stories if there are ingredients like horses and guns and action.

I looked at these and said, "Jesus, you're telling stories for children, you are not even telling B movies, you are telling *C* movies. And you have this silly sidekick, L.Q. Jones."

They said, "He's gotta have a sidekick because he's got to have someone to talk to."

But that was what was wrong with it. They don't have sidekicks in A movies because the people who make A movies know the hero doesn't need somebody to talk to. And that the scenes where he's talking to his sidekick are the boring, deadly scenes that tell you this is a B movie.

Next, Cheyenne was a map maker. I said, "Get rid of his occupation. What kind of stories are going to come out of a man who makes maps?"

The man has to be a Western hero. Did the Western hero have an occupation? Hell no, unless he was a sheriff or cowboy. Mostly he just drifted.

So I said, "If you let me make all of these changes, get rid of the sidekick, and get rid of these stories—these shows must never get on the air—and do adult stories, I will do 'Cheyenne.' " Which was what I had really wanted from the start.

So they gave me "Cheyenne." The only thing I kept was Clint Walker, who had been a rent-a-cop in Las Vegas, a security guard. He was a nice man. A natural-born actor. He grew up on Western movies, and he knew how those heroes acted and what they did.

"Cheyenne" was a big hit. It ran seven years, because it had Clint, it was a Western, and it came on at 7:30. It was the first hour-long Western.

❑ ❑ ❑

"Cheyenne," the first Western series made for TV, was a watershed. It started the Western trend. CBS and NBC countered with their own shows, most notably "Gunsmoke" in the fall of 1955. By 1959 there were twenty-eight prime-time Westerns on the three networks.

Walt Disney instantly grasped the power of television promotion for his theatrical features, and he used his weekly free minute very effectively.

Jack Warner went on *once* to promote his pictures, and after that he said, "Aw, who wants to bother." It cost him millions of dollars. But Warners was soon providing us eight hours of weekly programming—40 percent of our prime-time schedule—a highly profitable arrangement for them.

Early in 1954, when we were still acutely desperate for programming, we grabbed anything we could put on. We got the "Voice of Firestone," a half-hour concert series, and aired it Monday nights. The sponsor was Firestone Rubber. The show's opening and closing theme was a lovely piece of music written by Harvey Firestone's mother.

It was a very highbrow show and very well done. For three or four years we loved it. But as we came along with newer programs, we had to pay more attention to ratings and to audience flow. "Firestone" went on at 8:30, but had such a low rating that almost nobody was watching ABC after 9:00.

So I had to call Harvey Firestone, chairman of Firestone Rubber. I said,

"Harvey, your show is wonderful. But it doesn't have the proper flow for us. I'd like to suggest that we move it to Sunday afternoon."

"Sunday afternoon?" he said. "Impossible! Everybody's playing polo on Sunday afternoon."

We had to cancel the show.

Lawrence Welk, another of our early shows, was phenomenally successful in a way that has never been duplicated. He and his band established themselves performing live at the LaMonica Ball Room in Santa Monica. Our Los Angeles station, KABC-TV, put him on the air locally at 9:00 Saturday night. In the summer of 1955, we picked this up for the network.

The Dodge people saw this show, fell in love with it, and asked to sponsor it as "Lawrence Welk's Dodge Dancing Party." So we created a *second* network program, starting in the fall of 1956. "Lawrence Welk's Top Tunes and New Talent," aired at 9:30 Monday night. That show ran through the fall of 1957.

I don't believe there's ever been another individual with musical variety shows on a network two nights a week.

It couldn't go on forever, of course. In the middle of 1960 Dodge suddenly decided they wanted a change. The program had outlived Dodge's interests in it. Welk was very upset. He had been with them so long that he felt like they'd taken away his life.

Then I got a call from Matty Rosenhaus of J. B. Williams Company, the makers of Geritol. He said he'd asked Welk if Geritol could sponsor his show, and Welk turned him down. Welk said he didn't know the product, and he wasn't going to allow himself to promote anything he didn't have confidence in. I haven't heard that kind of television talk in a long time.

I called Welk. I said, "I want to come out and see you. Matty Rosenhaus is a very upright man. I've known him for years, and I think you should consider accepting his product."

Matty flew out from New York, and the three of us spent several hours together. Matty brought some samples and showed him that Geritol was mostly vitamins, including iron. The very worst thing you could say about it was that it was like chicken soup—it couldn't hurt you. But more important, Welk had a chance to see Matty wasn't a phony.

In the end Welk said he was assured Matty was of good character and that Geritol was perfectly proper. We shook hands on a deal.

From the time J. B. Williams began sponsoring part of "The Lawrence Welk Show," Geritol became a household word. When we changed our network strategy to go after younger audiences, we took Welk off the air, in 1971, even though he had sixteen years of solid ratings. Welk went into syndication for another dozen years. Geritol sponsored him till the end.

I was a good friend of Billy Rose, one of Broadway's most colorful figures. In 1944 Billy bought the old Ziegfeld Theatre. Dorothy Hammerstein, Oscar's wife, completely redecorated it. Billy put in an office that was really an apartment. He took me through the whole place. I had to go up in the booth while he showed me how the lighting worked.

I got to know Billy better after he started coming by to see me about television programs. He had had a show on ABC in the fall of 1950, "Billy Rose's Playbill," an anthology drama series, but it ran only one season. He never did come up with anything we could use, but he was an interesting fellow, and we enjoyed each other's company.

Billy was a completely self-made man. At age sixteen he was probably the fastest shorthand stenographer in the world. He could write with both hands simultaneously.

Billy had a lot of moxie. He got himself introduced to Bernard Baruch, the kindly wizard of Wall Street who advised every president from Wilson to Johnson. Baruch was so taken with Billy that he hired him to be his personal secretary.

When Billy went into show business, he quickly became Mr. Broadway. He was a newspaper columnist for the New York *Mirror*, and a songwriter, and he ran nightclubs. He eventually became a producer and impresario in the mode of Florenz Ziegfeld. He married and divorced five times. His first wife was the incomparable "Funny Girl," Fanny Brice, his childhood friend.

In the early 1950s, General Sarnoff gave Billy $100,000 to write a "crystal ball" report on television's future. He spent weeks watching everything on the screen. Then he wrote that TV, then 90 percent live and 10 percent filmed programs, would eventually be 10 percent live and 90 percent filmed. And he said that the biggest shows on the small screen would be old Hollywood movies. Sarnoff was aghast. The Rose Report was quietly locked away in some basement vault.

Billy remained friendly with Baruch for the rest of his life. Baruch constantly advised him on investments. One day Billy told me Baruch had decided to invest heavily in AT&T. He said everyone took AT&T for granted, but it was undervalued. And so Billy, too, became a big AT&T stockholder. He was worth over $30 million when he died.

Through my friendship with Billy, I was invited to some of Baruch's cocktail parties. Baruch and I ran into each other once or twice in the 1940s, sailing to or from Europe on the *Queen Elizabeth*. We spent a fair amount of time circling the deck, talking. He pressed me on my views of different people and about the motion picture industry.

One thing about Baruch—he wouldn't surround himself with older folks. It wasn't in his nature. His philosophy was to think young by being with young people. Now I'm far older than Baruch was when we knew each other, and I feel the same way. I prefer to associate with younger people.

So desperate for programs were we that even by 1955 we had practically nothing on before the evening newscast. "The Mickey Mouse Club" signed on at 5 P.M. in the fall of 1955, and was successful, but it was hardly enough.

We wanted to put feature films on during the day, but the major studios stubbornly refused to release even the oldest features in their libraries to network television. The few movies we could get were either old or all too forgettable.

One day in 1955 I went to visit my dentist, Arthur Epstein. He's eighty-seven now and still my dentist. His office has been in the Paramount Building since 1934. Nobody has been there longer.

When my mouth was full of all sorts of dental gadgets, he said, "The movies on your network are awful! Why don't you do something about that?"

But let him tell it.

OTHER RECOLLECTIONS:
Dr. Arthur Epstein, D.D.S.

Leonard had a show on every Sunday night, "The Sunday Night Movie." He had an appointment on Monday morning, and when he came in I said, "Leonard, how come you have such bad pictures?"

"We can't get any good pictures."

"I can get some good movies."

"Where can you get them?"

"I can get you some of the Rank movies."

"You could do that? How?"

"A friend of mine is the attorney for Rank here in this country."

"Who's that?"

"Bob Benjamin."

"Well, try. How much do you think it would cost?"

"Nobody knows any prices. There's never been any sales. The field is free."

"I suggest one-and-a-half million dollars."

Well, that sounded like a lot of money to me. Especially when you don't have it. But Leonard said, "Go ahead and try."

I called up my friend Bob Benjamin. "Bobby, I have a patient here who would like to use some of Rank's pictures on television. Three, four, five years, whatever you can swing."

"Well, who is it?"

"I can't say. He asked me not to tell."

"Well, how much is he willing to pay?"

"I think a million bucks." A nice round figure.

"Let me call up Rank and find out," he says.

Now, I know he's not going to call Rank. It's too new. At that time, nobody knows prices. An hour later he calls me back. "They want two million."

"I don't think he'll pay that, but let me go back and ask."

I wait a half hour, and I call him back. "Bobby, I just spoke to them, and I think I can get them. You asked two million, they offered one million. Why don't you compromise and make it a million and a half?"

"I'll have to call Rank again. I'll call you back."

An hour later he calls me. "Okay, you talked me into it. Rank says he'll take a million, five. By the way, who is the buyer?"

"Leonard Goldenson."

"You son of a bitch, I could have gotten three million out of that guy!"

"Come on, don't be greedy. You didn't even know if a million was too much."

"Okay," says Benjamin, "have him come up and sign the papers."

I call Leonard and I say, "It's a deal. Send over somebody with authority, he'll tell him what to do." So he sends over Sid Markley, who's also a patient of mine. He comes over and says, "So what do you want out of this deal?"

"Well, ten percent?"

"You've got it."

Then I had another idea. I owned a theater. So I asked Sid if

I could play the movies in my theater as well, and he said there would be no problem.

❑ ❑ ❑

Thus was born the ABC "Afternoon Film Festival." It included several Alec Guinness comedies, some of David Lean's earliest dramas, including *Great Expectations*, Carol Reed's *Odd Man Out* and *Fallen Idol*, Laurence Olivier in *Henry V*, and, of course, *The Red Shoes*.

These films were far better than any American movies that the studios would allow to be shown on a network. They were modestly successful on ABC, though there's no relationship between the English spoken in Britain and that in the American interior. Over the years that has changed some, but it's still true that most Americans can't relate to the English dialect. I mentioned this to Winston Churchill once. He told me, "It's not an English dialect, it's an American dialect."

One more thing. In 1955 ABC was so starved for cash that we made our executives travel coach. We cut staff to the bone. We sliced nickels and dimes out of budgets. We did anything we could to save a few dollars. I'd always believed Bob Benjamin, who represented United Artists, paid Epstein's commission. But in 1988, when I started researching this book, I learned that ABC paid him the $150,000. Oh, my.

In our early desperation for programming we tried all sorts of things.

Bob Weitman's wife, Sylvia, was very religious. She insisted he spend Friday nights in temple or at home. But Bob was very open-minded about other creeds, and he knew a spellbinding showman when he saw one.

OTHER RECOLLECTIONS:
Bob Weitman

One day I say to Lenny, "I've got an idea. I want to go after Bishop Fulton Sheen."

Sheen had done radio and was on television periodically, on DuMont.

Lenny says, "Go."

I tell O'Brien, and point to Kintner's office. O'Brien says, "Well, it's a question, who'll convert who?"

O'Brien was a Knight of Malta, a big Catholic. Kintner was Episcopalian.

So I pick the phone up and called the bishop at the Propagation of the Faith office on Fifth Avenue.

I go over, and sitting there is a man with a fedora pulled over one eye and a very beautiful lady. And the bishop is playing a piano.

I said to myself, "Well, when you're a priest, this is it."

I said to the bishop, "How would you like to be on television?"

He said, "You're going to have trouble for me and trouble for yourself."

We became very fast friends, and he said yes, he'd go on ABC.

I said, "It's none of my business, Bishop, but who is that gentleman sitting out there with the fedora, and who is the beautiful lady with him?"

He said, "That's Clare Luce." The man in the fedora was Fritz Kreisler, one of the greatest violinists in the world. Kreisler and the bishop were buddies. Clare Luce was there because he was going to convert her or something.

I had an Irish-Catholic secretary who was with me for many years. The next day I say to her, "I expect a gentleman here tomorrow." I don't tell her who. When she ushers him in, she falls to her knees and kisses the bishop's ring.

I said, "Julia, how long have you been working for me? You never kissed me." Naughty. But I knew the bishop had an extraordinary sense of humor.

He said that whatever we paid him, that went to the Church. Propagation of the Faith. Heathen, take a quarter. So we decide he'll be on a Sunday night at 8. But we'll film it first, then decide if he's on the network.

For the opening, we gave tickets away. It's raining outside. The theater is jam-packed, teeming. I thought this guy must have something.

He meets my wife, Sylvia, backstage. She says, "Bob, he's beautiful."

He introduces me to a black cardinal, Oxford-educated, and he says, "Do you mind if at the end of the show, I bring him out for a bow?"

I said, "Whatever. You don't have to tell me your subject matter. It could be baseball, whatever you want, but these are the nays: no pitch for the Propagation of the Faith. No talk about money."

With that the stagehand comes in and says, "Bishop, you have a shine on your nose."

He says, "You mean sheen."

He had Fritz Kreisler write his entrance music, which we recorded. A simple stage, nothing churchy, nothing bizarre, nothing cathedral, just a black curtain. He got dressed in his garb. You say sometimes the suit makes the man, but he had it all.

Music swells up, he walks out, and there is insanity in the theater. All sects, all religions, whatever. And he talks. Thirty minutes. No breaks, no commercials. No teleprompter, nothing but a little bit of a watch that he put on so he could see the time. He gets all through, and he says, "I'd like you to meet His Eminence, Cardinal Whatever."

Comes Monday, Tuesday, we get bags and bags of mail with checks, cash. All made out to "Sheen, Propagation of the Faith." And look at the names: Jews, Protestants.

I shlep this over, and Lenny comes in and says, "What is this?"

"It's the bishop. We've got to put this guy on."

He says, "You're right." We put him on.

❑ ❑ ❑

In that same era we had another religious show, a mixture of anti-communist politics and fundamentalist Christianity. The star was Dr. Billy Graham. He had a half-hour show, "Hour of Decision," from 1951 to 1954. Eventually, however, I came to believe a network isn't a proper place for regularly scheduled religion. I could see that we could still allow it occasionally, however.

I went to see Billy Graham at the St. Moritz Hotel. I'd asked him to go on when we desperately needed programming. Now I had to go back to him and say, "Billy, I put you on television. But the ratings for your program are poor. We need better audience flow for our entertainment shows.

"I think you could be on from time to time with your crusades and get a very good audience, but we can't continue on a regular basis. We must discontinue your show," I said.

Billy was a real gentleman about it. He's remained a very good friend.

Toward the end of 1956, ABC's chances for success were enhanced when DuMont, after years of red ink, folded its network. The stations continued to operate, but in a few years they were sold off to raise cash for DuMont's faltering manufacturing division. DuMont should have sold the factories and kept the stations. Today, after changing hands a number of times, those stations are immensely valuable. DuMont Labs, still losing money, eventually sold its manufacturing interests to Emerson and just faded away.

Those first three years, Kintner's years, I pretty much stayed out of his way. I went after Hollywood's programs and talent, but I left the rest of it to Kintner. Not until 1955 did I even establish an office at ABC's 66th Street studios. But as the "hands off" period I'd promised Noble came to an end, I became painfully aware of how much we needed a change.

Kintner, a very tough guy, was nobody's fool, and he knew Madison Avenue, or as Bob Weitman used to call it, the Gaza Strip. He knew the network business, but he had no vision.

He also had a disconcerting way of dressing down his subordinates in front of their peers. I dropped over, once, unannounced, around six in the evening, and found him sitting around with his department heads. A bottle of whisky went around the room as Kintner described each of their shortcomings, often in four-letter words. He was a little tipsy.

Now, it's one thing to tell your people what they've done badly, but embarrassing someone publicly is not the way to keep good people. It's not a way to nurture and develop executives who are willing to risk making mistakes. This is a business where, if you don't risk, you don't win.

For example, in 1955, Ben Kalmenson at Warner Bros. wanted to sell us Warners' whole film library, everything up to 1950, for $15 million. And after we got our money back, ABC would split profits fifty-fifty with Warners.

We could have made that deal. I wanted to go ahead with it. But Kintner was against it, and I feared he would have handled Warners' films the same way he handled O'Brien's NCAA football games.

That library would have been worth a fortune to ABC. But I worried then that Kintner might take the matter to the board or to Noble, claiming I was trying to second-guess him. During that early period, I felt I was in no position to force the issue. I've kicked myself many times since. I should have overridden Kintner and dealt with the consequences.

But that's hindsight. What I knew by 1956 was that ABC was still struggling mightily. And every time I proposed a solution to some problem, there were twenty ABC executives coming up with 120 reasons why it wouldn't work.

What I needed at ABC was *one* executive who could find reasons why things *would* work, even if he had to invent them himself.

I found such a man. His name was Ollie Treyz.

10

Treyz

❑

In all of broadcasting's long and colorful history, there has never been a character to match Ollie Treyz. He was brilliant. *Is* brilliant. Charismatic, ebullient, a born salesman, Ollie, when I knew him, worked twice as hard as anyone else and would never take no for an answer.

Never did one man rise so far and so fast in broadcasting. And never did one man fall so low, or so quickly.

Ollie had wonderful programming instincts, which he credits to a brief association with Alexander Woollcott. Woollcott, the celebrated *New York Times* drama and book critic, author, and frequent contributor to *The New Yorker*, employed Ollie one summer while he was a graduate student at Columbia.

Woollcott's criticism often contained such zingers as, "*Number 7* opened last night at the Times Square Theatre. It was misnamed by five." Immensely influential, Woollcott was the inspiration for *The Man Who Came to Dinner* and for the literary critic in *All About Eve*. His literary praise was infrequent but assured the success of formerly obscure books by such formerly obscure writers as James Hilton and Thornton Wilder.

One day Ollie, then twenty, asked Woollcott, "How do you judge a book or a drama? What are your criteria?"

He replied, "On the basis of how it delivers suspense, empathy, or conflict."

That was as insightful and succinct a summary of guidelines as I can imagine, and Ollie successfully applied it to sports events, news stories, television programs, and movies.

In 1939 Ollie joined one of Madison Avenue's premier agencies, BBD&O, to work in radio research. There he became acquainted with

Sarnoff and Paley, and with top management at Mutual, Westinghouse, and everywhere else.

As a twenty-one-year-old, Ollie devised the basis of broadcasting's advertising charge system, the cost-per-thousand listeners or viewers. He admits to borrowing the concept from magazines, which had long billed at cost per page or line for each thousand circulation.

Ollie came to ABC in 1948, during Kintner's tenure, to write sales presentations for the radio network. He did a little work for television as well, but this new medium was still a curiosity, a mere sideline to radio.

Soon Ollie wangled the manager's chair in Research and Sales Development. This was a high-visibility post, where his talents were quickly apparent to management.

In the early days of television, advertisers bought entire programs—thirty or sixty minutes. Sometimes they bought only half of an hour-long show or half of a half-hour. But ABC didn't have enough network affiliates to provide the national coverage that advertisers find desirable. Some of our shows couldn't get into communities with only one or two channels, and if our programs did get in on a delayed basis, the stations usually broadcast them at the least desirable times.

But advertisers who sponsored a one-hour show that didn't get enough coverage became dissatisfied. Often we'd lose their business. So it was difficult for ABC to sell full or half sponsorship of many shows.

When Ollie was in Sales, he devised the idea of scatter buys. Instead of buying a one-hour show, which then included six minutes of commercials, sponsors could scatter their six minutes over two, three, or four nights a week. By eliminating the risk of sponsoring any specific program, Ollie changed broadcasting's entire selling strategy to the sale of generic commercial time.

Another of Ollie's fundamental, strategic contributions to ABC came in 1954, just before he left the company for a couple of years. He devised the concept of bridging—starting network programming at 7:30. NBC and CBS had shows on then like the "Camel Newsreel," "Perry Como," and "Leave It to the Girls." CBS ran the highly rated "Arthur Godfrey Show" at 8. Ollie said, "Let's open our store with 'Disneyland' at 7:30."

Similarly, he suggested we start "Cheyenne" at 7:30 to bridge NBC's "Milton Berle," which went on at 8.

It was simple and obvious, but Kintner resisted it. In radio, hour shows always started on the hour. I supported Ollie's position, and as it turned out, he was right.

OTHER RECOLLECTIONS:
Ollie Treyz

The Blue Network was NBC's experimental network, a dumping ground for programs the Red wouldn't take or was ashamed to air, like Walter Winchell. And for cultural things. Most of the radio affiliates were smaller cities, low-power stations. I think Sarnoff sold it to Noble because he felt he could never be an effective competitor. He never dreamed Noble would sell it to someone as aggressive and resourceful as Leonard.

To compete we took whatever we could get. Instead of soap operas, we ran "My True Story" and "Modern Romances," which were regarded as shlock.

To get a modicum of income and to show a modest profit, ABC took a relaxed view of standards established by NBC and CBS. We took spots for deodorants and laxatives, which the other guys wouldn't take. We called ourselves the Blue Network, but the other guys called us the Brown Network, because we took laxatives.

I worked for Bob Kintner, and he was a brilliant guy. He was great in news. He held nobody in awe, because he'd met all the great figures of his time. He was a good administrator but had no feel for programs or promotion. He started drinking and became irascible. Angry. He was under tremendous pressure, and you can't be under pressure and drink vodka from a water glass at your desk. But he thought he was fooling people.

He often called me to his office to listen on an earpiece to his conversations with agency heads or television buyers. Never had to swap memos. Didn't have to tell each other what was said—he'd pick up nuances that I wouldn't, and vice versa. In my role as head of Research and Sales Development, I was, as much as anybody, his strategist. I made a lot of sales myself. And I became very close to Bob.

One day Kintner called me in while he was on the phone with Jimmy Neal, of Dancer Fitzgerald & Sample, which had the General Mills account.

Then I had to go to the john. It was down the hall, but I had diarrhea, and I didn't think I could make it. So I walked into Bob's private john. I didn't ask permission. Maybe it wasn't polite, but I wasn't about to soil my trousers.

When I came out, Bob was off the phone, glaring at me. Livid. He lectured me about politeness and about consideration and courtesy and invasion of privacy. He cut me six ways from Sunday.

I was shocked, because I thought he sensed what I had seen. He was very shrewd. And in the john I'd seen a glass, identical to the one on his desk.

I probably shouldn't have done it, but I picked up the glass and smelled it. Vodka. And it wasn't even diluted. No ice, nothing.

After that I was not invited to meetings and was cut off from all memos. I was "promoted" and got a raise. He sent out a lavish memo and made me director of the Radio Network, but took me away from the seat of power. I didn't like it. Otherwise, I would have stayed there forever, because I was never the kind of guy to go out and hunt for a job.

Being cut off that way hurt me. When I heard the Television Bureau of Advertising (TVB) was hiring, I applied for a job and became its first president.

In the early days a lot of people thought television wasn't for real, that it would go away. Leonard himself used to say, "Some of my friends think it's like selling land underwater."

The intangible value of television wasn't readily accepted. It was still new and unproven. You had to sell the medium. You had to transfer advertisers from print. You had to create television budgets. Only top management could okay television appropriations. That's why, in those days, you had to go to Henry Kaiser or George Romney or to the executive VP of General Motors.

Over time, some of the more sophisticated advertisers, like Procter & Gamble, accepted TV. The Television Bureau of Advertising, a nonprofit business association to develop television appropriations, raised over a million dollars in dues. They hired me as president because I wanted to work on the guys who were *not* yet in television.

I went to the owner of Clorox in San Francisco. I actually located the homes using liquid bleach and automatic washing machines and so forth. Through Nielsen, I showed him how they viewed television, how many hours a day they watched, what they watched and when, and correlated that with his market. Except for liquor companies, Clorox became television's biggest advertiser in 1954. They spent $3.5 million, all on spot buys, not networks.

❑ ❑ ❑

In 1954, Bob Weitman accepted an offer from Frank Stanton at CBS. Bob couldn't get along with Kintner, and his health was suffering. The CBS offer was much too good to turn down, and we both knew it. Weitman and I parted friends. After some years at CBS, he went out to Hollywood. Over the next few decades he ran production for MGM. Later he was an independent producer for Columbia. He died in 1988, just six days after sharing his recollections for this book.

Kintner replaced Weitman with Bob Lewine, who was very effective in getting the most out of Disney and Warners. But after three years under Kintner's stewardship, ABC was still floundering. The Disney and Warners programs were doing very well, but weren't nearly enough to fill prime time, let alone the rest of the schedule. Overall we remained a distant third in ratings. But everyone from Kintner on down, saddled by negative attitudes and preconceptions arising out of long careers in radio, kept insisting nothing could be done.

I was worried to distraction. For months I had sleepless nights of tossing and turning, racking my mind for answers.

In October of 1956 I told several individual board members the time had come to change ABC's management. Most agreed with little persuasion. I carried this message to Noble. He continued to back Kintner and the inner circle of executives retained after the merger. Noble threatened a proxy fight.

I said, "That's your prerogative. But my neck is out, and I'm going to have to correct this situation." Noble took his views to those board members he thought would back him, but these were not enough. When he saw he would lose if the issue ever came to a vote, he backed off.

I asked for Kintner's resignation, and he left to join NBC to take charge of conversion to color broadcasting. In a few months he moved up to become NBC's network president. He did very well for several years.

I brought Ollie Treyz back to ABC in 1956 as network president. I gave him his head. Only thirty-eight, he was full of ideas and strategies, brash but enthusiastic, exciting and often unpredictable. Ollie became ABC's driving force, supplying the lively leadership so long lacking. We were soon on the move.

When Kintner left, he took Lewine with him, so after Ollie became president, I called Earl Hudson on the West Coast and asked him to scout around for programming talent. He recommended Jim Aubrey, manager of KNXT-TV, the CBS station in Los Angeles. I interviewed Jim and hired him as head of programming. He recruited a young friend, a CBS film salesman named Tom Moore, who came in to head our sales department.

We were still desperate for programming and experimenting with all sorts of strange ideas. We were trying to come up with something totally different. One of our worst ideas was giving Orson Welles $200,000 to do a pilot. Abe Lastfogel brought him to see me, and after some discussion I agreed that Welles would have full artistic control of a show called *Orson Welles at Large*. We found a sponsor more than eager to back Welles. Welles was vague about what he planned to do. But he was *the* Orson Welles, and nobody pressed him too hard.

I should have known better.

Welles went off to Europe, and we heard nothing for several months. Finally I sent Jim Aubrey over to find him and report on when we might expect our pilot show.

Aubrey caught up with him at the Grand Hotel in Rome. From early in the morning until late evening, Welles was busy making a movie. He was writer, producer, director, and star. The only time he could see Aubrey was late at night.

Aubrey sat around with him in the hotel lobby until the wee hours of the morning. Welles, who weighed well over 300 pounds, put away several steaks, drank vast quantities of Napoleon cognac, and smoked huge cigars, all the while loftily expounding his vision of television programming. All, of course, in the broadest generalities.

After several days Aubrey realized he was getting nowhere and returned to New York. We kissed off the $200,000.

About a year later Welles turned up with a single reel of 16 mm film. His grand idea, as it turned out, was a sort of precursor to "Lifestyles of the Rich and Famous." Except that it was very poorly done. In fact, it was little more than a home movie of splendid homes and ostentatious yachts belonging to obscure European royalty. In plain language, Orson Welles conned us out of $200,000.

We had better luck with Hollywood. After seeing *Ma and Pa Kettle at Home*, a Universal theatrical film about hillbillies, I thought it had potential for television. Aubrey and Universal developed it as "The Real McCoys." It debuted in October 1957 and became such a hit that five years later, at CBS, Aubrey copied the concept three different times, with "Beverly Hillbillies," "Green Acres" and "Petticoat Junction."

Aubrey had good instincts, but he had been trained at CBS, and in his heart he always thought their ways were best. It's hard to fault him, since CBS had at the time been the leading network for years. Jim always had a yen to go back to CBS, and after about a year with us he did just that. He quickly rose in their organization, and ran their TV network for several years with much more than competence. Tom Moore took his place as head of ABC's programming.

Before leaving ABC, Bob Weitman went with me to see Frank Sinatra, then appearing at the Riviera Club across the Hudson River in New Jersey. Weitman had made Sinatra a star in the 1930s, but when we went to see him, Frank's career was in the doldrums. He'd just finished working on *From Here to Eternity*, but it was months away from release. Nobody yet knew it was going to be the smash hit that would restore Sinatra to superstardom.

Sinatra was married to Ava Gardner. They'd been living in Spain, taking it easy. He'd become her stooge over there, lying around all day, partying at night, and not working. He finally came back to America to film *From Here to Eternity*.

During that period Ava didn't call or write him, and there were all sorts of rumors about her running around with various men. There may have been nothing to the gossip, but Sinatra couldn't handle it. He was still very much in love with her, and the day I dropped in to see him, he was in tears.

I said, "Frank, do you have any money?"

He said no. I said I wanted him on ABC. Perhaps we could work out a deal where, instead of a straight salary, he could make a capital gain. (Income tax upper brackets were then about 70 percent, capital gains only 25 percent.)

Sinatra told me to talk to Abe Lastfogel. Eventually we agreed to form a production company together. ABC put up $3 million in cash. Sinatra put up his profit-sharing interest in certain movies he'd already made or had contracted to do.

Now, everyone in the picture business knows that accounting practices being what they were—and are—it's rare that talent ever sees much in the way of profits, even with blockbuster hits. So Sinatra made $3 million when he had nothing in the bank. This was not from the kindness of my heart. It was business. I thought a musical variety show hosted by Sinatra held great promise.

We put the show together as a thirty-minute program for 9 o' clock Friday nights.

After we made the deal with Sinatra, *From Here to Eternity* was released. It was a big hit. Sinatra won an Oscar. He got all kinds of offers. And he kissed off the television show. He paid it scant attention, devoting hardly any time to rehearsals. Even when he showed up, the day before broadcast, he just went through the motions. He spent most of his time kibitzing back stage with his Rat Pack retinue.

With Sinatra doing nothing to make it work, the show flopped. It was poor television, and people wouldn't watch.

The situation was not hopeless however. I felt we might work out something in place of a weekly show. Perhaps, I thought, a series of specials. Or something else that would allow ABC to get some return on a $3 million investment.

So I called Abe Lastfogel and made an appointment to sit down with Sinatra at The Sands in Las Vegas. Tom Moore, then in charge of programming, came along with me.

OTHER RECOLLECTIONS:
Tom Moore

Leonard and I get on an airplane and go out to Las Vegas. We're supposed to have a meeting on Sunday night. Sammy Cahn, Sinatra's songwriter, came down and said, "Frank won't be here tonight, but he'll catch up with you in the morning."

The next day Leonard and I called his room, but there was no response.

We cooled our heels. Everybody knew what was happening except us. Sammy would come down and say, "He'll be down soon, in a couple of hours."

Juliet Prowse was there. We talked to her. He was shacked up with her—but how much shacking up can you do?

Sinatra left us sitting three days. Finally I said, "Leonard, we won't see this son of a gun. He has stood us up." We walked up to the front desk, and Leonard borrowed a piece of hotel stationery.

❑ ❑ ❑

I wrote Sinatra a letter in longhand. "Never in my life have I experienced such treatment," I said. "I have no respect for anyone who lacks the character to appear for an appointment. When you were down on your luck and had no money, we went out of our way to make a capital gain for you.

Because the program has not succeeded, I wanted to try to develop some alternatives. You did not show. I've never heard of anybody less considerate of my feelings than you. I want nothing further to do with you."

The desk clerk put the letter in his room box.

For twenty-five years I swore I'd never talk to Sinatra. Then a few years ago he appeared on a UCP telethon. He'd contributed $10,000 or so, and he said, "I want to be sure that Leonard Goldenson knows I made this contribution."

Of course, by then $10,000 was pocket change to Sinatra.

After that, Sinatra made some other overtures through mutual friends. There's always a dinner hosted by the Hausmans, Isabelle, and myself on the night of UCP's annual telethon. A few years ago, Jack Hausman invited Sinatra and his wife, Barbara. That evening, during the meal, I said, "Let's bury the hatchet." We shook hands on it. I haven't heard from him since. I still can't say I'm very fond of him.

With "Cheyenne" and "Disneyland" doing extremely well in early evening, we still needed something capable of competing after 9, when CBS and NBC continued to dominate the ratings. We turned to Columbia's Screen Gems for "Naked City," a 10 P.M. show that won critical acclaim and helped launch the careers of Dustin Hoffman, Robert Redford, Jon Voight, and several other stars. We put it on in the fall of 1958. "Naked City" was one of television's first dramatic crime series.

For the same season Warners gave us "77 Sunset Strip," which we aired 9:30 Friday nights. This series launched the "caper" trend—such shows as "Bourbon Street Beat," "Adventures in Paradise," "Hawaiian Eye," and others. This type of show, still popular today, became for a few years as ubiquitous as Westerns had been earlier.

OTHER RECOLLECTIONS
Roy Huggins

> After a year on "Cheyenne," I didn't want to do it anymore. We had another show on ABC, "Conflict," which was, like "Cheyenne," the first of its kind. It was an anthology, what amounted to a series of one-hour movies connected by a theme—conflict.
>
> I told Bill Orr we ought to do a private-eye episode, à la Raymond Chandler. We called it "77 Sunset Strip." I had met Efrem Zimbalist, Jr. He was so terribly Eastern. Elegant, classy, the an-

tithesis of a private eye. And I thought, what a great idea to cast this guy against the image of the hard-boiled private eye.

I wrote the story that became the basis of the pilot. In it was a standard heavy, a miserable son of a bitch who killed people for money. I brought in Marion Hargrove (author of *See Here, Private Hargrove*) as a writer, and I told him the story.

He came back and said, "Roy, you know something is going wrong with the postwar generation. They are monsters. These kids are scary."

He wanted to make a nineteen-year-old boy the heavy. I said, "Marvelous—let's make him a sociopath." So he became a cold-blooded killer. When the story was over, that kid was going to the gas chamber—he was irredeemable, unconscionable, amoral. Charles Manson with a comb.

So Marion wrote the script—and this kid was wonderful. Since the success of "77 Sunset Strip," four or five people have taken credit for his combing his hair. But in Marion's original script, while waiting to kill people, he habitually ran a comb through his hair. That little affectation became a part of our culture for a few years.

In the original script we'd called the Edd Byrnes character something, but we didn't dignify him with a real name. As I sat and edited the picture, I referred to him as "when the 'kook' comes in." I kept on calling him "the kook," and that became "when 'kookie' does that, da da da."

Hugh Benson, Bill Orr's assistant, sometimes sat in the back of the room watching this, and he got the idea that the character's name was Kookie. So that's what we used in the series.

At that time producers got royalties on any first-run show that made a profit. But Jack Warner had told Bill Orr, my pal, "Don't ever get into a situation where you have to pay a royalty."

So Bill calls me up and very sweetly says—and I love Bill—"Roy, let's do this as a movie." Suddenly we were doing a movie called *77 Sunset Strip*.

We previewed in Huntington Park, near East Los Angeles, with Efrem, Edd Byrnes, and the other guys sitting in the back rows.

When the show was over, the teenagers in the audience took one look at Edd and went wild. They recognized one of their own. A guy who kills parents and combs his hair before doing it.

These were the kids who made *Rebel Without a Cause*—parents were the heavies—such a hit. They surrounded Edd, screaming. He was their hero. I never had a hand in the writing of a more monstrous heavy in my life, but they loved him. In their hearts they wanted to be just like Kookie.

After the preview, we showed it to ABC. They bought it as a series, but insisted it had to have Edd in it. This is a wonderful example of an audience dictating to moviemakers.

Warners had this movie shown in some little town in the West Indies. It ran a week and was sold to ABC as the pilot that opened the series. Since they could now claim the series was based on a theatrical film, I was not eligible for any royalties.

When the first series episode after the pilot came on, Kookie was a parking-lot attendant. Efrem came on first and said, "We previewed this show, and because Edd Byrnes was such a hit we decided that Kookie and his comb had to be in our series. So this week we'll just forget that in the pilot he went off to prison to be executed."

❑ ❑ ❑

Ollie Treyz had a great regard for research. One of the first and most important things he did was commission Dr. Paul Lazarsfeld, a Columbia University professor, to create an analysis of television audiences.

Our objective was to learn how we could beat CBS and NBC. Lazarsfeld, one of the world's outstanding researchers, came back with what was then a startling insight: The top programs at CBS and NBC, built around stars that came out of radio, appealed mostly to older audiences.

But this was not the audience most sought by advertisers, said Lazarsfeld. Older persons are more set in their ways, and less likely, for example, to switch brands of toothpaste or laundry detergent. They are also less likely to change their television viewing habits. They tend to watch what they've become accustomed to watching.

Younger audiences, those between eighteen and forty-nine years old, are more open to change. They are more willing to turn the dial looking for something new and different. And they are more open to experimenting with new types of products and new brands of familiar products.

Even better, suggested Lazarsfeld, younger audiences spend more money per capita than older ones. These are the people with growing families, those who buy most of the household products which are the staples of mass-market advertising.

Up to that time TV had not used demographic profiles. Lazarsfeld's research helped us establish techniques to create such profiles, and we sold the concept to advertisers. Today this profile is an important, industrywide practice.

Lazarsfeld recommended we go after the young audiences. We should build programs around casts of young, virile people, he said. Beautiful women and handsome men. And create programs with stories that younger people could identify with.

This was a lightning bolt to us. We began programming for the young families of America, and in so doing revolutionized television. With this strategy we transcended the medium's traditional limitations to come up with new program concepts.

But for our new programs to succeed, they had to be more than different. They had to be significantly *better* than anything on CBS or NBC, so they could be easily promoted. Without sufficient primary affiliates to show our programs, in one- and two-station markets we had to depend on stations affiliated with other networks to run our shows. But unless our programs were far better than those of CBS and NBC, we couldn't expect to get them on in competitive time slots. Furthermore, without our own stations in these markets, we had to use other media to ballyhoo our programs. Nobody had ever done this before, so it was risky. But we simply had no other choice.

The success of this strategy was slow in coming and did not become apparent to the ossified bureaucracies at CBS and NBC for several years. Not until a new generation of executives took control at the other networks did our competitors see how effective this strategy was. Then Bob Wood at CBS canceled such shows as "Petticoat Junction" and "Beverly Hillbillies." Even though their ratings were respectable, they were not attracting the younger audiences that advertisers found most desirable.

But that was years in the future. In the 1950s we were still struggling to make progress against what seemed insurmountable odds.

Creating new programs for young audiences required a special breed of executive. I wanted youngsters with plenty of wrinkles in their bellies —up-and-comers who hadn't become satisfied with success and who were willing to experiment and take risks. People out to make names for themselves.

Dan Melnick was one of these bright youngsters. Before he was drafted, he'd worked briefly at CBS. In 1956, on the eve of his discharge, he met Bob Kintner at a party. It wasn't love at first sight.

OTHER RECOLLECTIONS:
Dan Melnick

Kintner was an aggressive, bullying man, but interesting. I thought he was some sort of journalist. I was a wiseass, arrogant kid. He was an overbearing, feisty veteran of the political wars. We took each other on. We argued about politics.

As he was leaving, he said a gruff good night and asked, "What are you going to do when you get out?"

I said, "I think I can go back to CBS."

"Well, if you've got time and you're interested, give me a call and we'll talk about it."

When he left, I asked my mother-in-law, "What does Mr. Kintner do?"

"He's the president of ABC."

I went to see him. He gave me five minutes and sent me to Bob Lewine, head of programming.

As I sat down in Lewine's office, the intercom buzzed. Someone said, "The mouse got killed in Philly."

And I thought, It's another world. What does that mean? Later I found out "The Mickey Mouse Club," a new show, got bad initial ratings in Philadelphia.

Bob hired me as manager of program development. I wasn't quite sure what that meant, but the process intrigued and fascinated me.

When I showed up for my first day of work, Kintner had just left to go to NBC. Two days later Lewine joined him.

I wandered around. There was only one other fellow there to talk to, a lovely man named Ted Fedder. We tried to sort out what had to be done and stumble our way through it. I knew someone would replace Lewine. Since new bosses want new teams, I figured the first thing he'd do was get rid of me.

After six weeks of speculation about who and what, I wanted to get on with my life. So I summoned up all my courage and asked for an appointment with Leonard Goldenson.

I walked into his office and said, "How do you do, Mr. Goldenson?"

He looked at me very, very seriously and said, "Let's get something straight."

I thought, My God, he's not even going to give me a chance to quit, he's going to fire me first!

I said, "What is that, sir?"

"Mr. Goldenson was my father. I'm Leonard."

At that point I became the man's servant for life. I kind of phumphered through my prepared comments about leaving.

He said, "Look, I've examined your background very carefully. I've spoken to a number of people. I would like to believe that if I had been in Bob Lewine and Bob Kintner's place, I would have been smart enough to hire you. Please stay."

I stayed. It was a very exciting time. The atmosphere was very much like that of a bunch of students putting out a college newspaper.

We were competing under such difficult circumstances. ABC was a relatively new company competing with the two giants, CBS and NBC, but it didn't have the stations. It was as if *Newsweek* competed with *Time* but couldn't be on the stands in Miami, Boston, Phoenix, and half the other cities.

I decided the only way to make my mark was to do shows completely unlike those on other networks. It wasn't really counterprogramming, putting a drama against a comedy or musical variety against a quiz show. Instead, our entire fare had a different, younger look. We did shows which, in retrospect, seem like the Establishment. But in those days shows like "The Fugitive," "Ben Casey," "Maverick," and "77 Sunset Strip" were very innovative, totally different from what was available on other networks.

To get Bing Crosby Productions to let Bing do specials for us, I had to agree to do some pilots with them. It was a throw-in, a sweetener.

I wanted to explore the possibilities of a medical show that looked unlike all the soft, traditional programs that had been tried over the years. I wanted to do the equivalent of *Naked City* built around a medical environment.

A former literary agent and story editor, Meta Rosenberg, and a very talented writer, Jim Mosher, came up with the notion of "Ben Casey."

We commissioned a script. It was a very tough, reality-based series with what became the first of the medical antiheroes. Everything was set to make the pilot, except we couldn't find a Ben Casey.

I told my wife I was stymied. I had a terrific script but couldn't find a leading man. She said, "Remember that picture we saw five or six weeks ago—we all were very impressed by the guy who played the killer?"

I tracked it down, a B movie starring Vince Edwards. I ran it again thinking she was totally off-track. Edwards was too much of a killer type.

But I showed it to Meta and Jim, and they wanted Vince right away.

It took a long time to get sponsorship, because "Ben Casey" was so realistic that people didn't want to put their products on it.

One evening when it was getting very close to going on the air and we were only half-sponsored, Ollie called and said, "Stick around. I'm running the pilot of 'Ben Casey' for a possible sponsor. I'm going to want you to come up and talk about series direction and all the creative stuff."

They're screening upstairs, and I'm in my office waiting to be called when the door bangs open and Ollie comes running in.

"Get a doctor, quick," he says.

I said, "What's the matter?"

"I think the sponsor's son had a heart attack."

So we called an ambulance. By the time it arrived, this strapping, 6-foot-3-inch college football player had recovered. He had merely fainted watching Ben Casey put a needle into a patient's heart.

A little later Ollie, back upstairs with the sponsor, called to ask if I thought he should finish screening the pilot.

I said, "It would be in good taste not to."

That was a glorious time to be in television. When we discussed types of programming or a specific program, Leonard always drew on his incredible memory. He could recall every picture of that type ever made, and what their grosses were, as an indicator of public tastes.

I always suspected that, depending on how committed I seemed to a particular subject, program, or pilot, he would select a piece of data to support my point of view. But he could as easily have found three to indicate it was a bad idea.

And I was always aware that he enjoyed my youth, my energy—and probably my arrogance. I think he related some of this to himself when he was my age.

When I told Leonard I was going to leave ABC, I was very concerned about hurting his feelings. A part of me felt I was letting him down.

He was very gracious and recounted all the things I had accomplished while I was there. He said, "If you're willing to stay, you'll end up being president of this network. But my personal advice to you as your friend is to get out now. You have a wonderful, exciting life ahead of you."

❑ ❑ ❑

Dan's contribution to ABC programming was enormous, and though I hated to see him go, I could well understand why. He had probably the most demanding position in the industry. He spent nearly all his time at it—weekends, late evenings, birthdays, anniversaries, and all the little moments people want to treasure with their families. Dan spent most of his life watching the other networks, reading scripts, viewing pilots, and always having to make tough decisions. It's a young man's job. After four or five years, even the best—and Dan was one of them—must move on.

Dan went on to a marvelous career in film. He produced *That's Entertainment, Straw Dogs*, and *All That Jazz*, among many others. As president of Columbia Pictures, he was involved with such blockbusters as *The China Syndrome, Midnight Express*, and *Kramer vs. Kramer*. Still quite active, he's one of Hollywood's more important independent producers.

Shortly after "Ben Casey" debuted in the fall of 1961, NBC came out with "Dr. Kildare." This was the beginning of a three-network "medical trend." Some of the most exciting shows of the 1980s, like "St. Elsewhere" and "China Beach," can trace their roots to the gritty realism of "Ben Casey."

Early in 1960, we stole a march on CBS and NBC when we outbid them for a Screen Gems sitcom pilot. This was a kind of "Cosby" precursor, the show that virtually defined the genre. It was about a widower raising his children alone. The star was Fred MacMurray, and "My Three Sons" became a big hit. It ran on ABC through the summer of 1965. Then the sponsor, General Motors, switched it to CBS, which had far greater distribution.

In 1957 Isabelle and I went down to Greenbriar, West Virginia, for a meeting. We arrived on a Saturday morning. As we were unpacking in our hotel room, the phone rang.

"This is Henry Kaiser," said a voice. "I want to see you."

"Well, Mr. Kaiser, I'd be glad to see you. I'll be back in my office on Monday morning," I said.

"I want to see you this afternoon."

"Well, you can't. The only way you can get to this place is by train, and the next one in or out is tomorrow."

"I've checked, and they have an airport there. I can get my own plane in there, and it'll be there in two and a half hours. I'll have a car meet you at La Guardia. I'd like to see you at the Waldorf Towers this afternoon."

I had never met Henry Kaiser, but I certainly knew who he was. Well over six feet tall and 300 pounds, with a bald, bulletlike dome, he was one of America's true pioneers. Henry Kaiser made his fortune paving highways in Cuba in the 1920s. He built Bonneville Dam, Hoover Dam, Grand Coulee Dam. He built the Liberty ships in World War II, a monumental feat. An undersecretary of the Navy once told me that we couldn't have beaten Hitler without Henry Kaiser. Without Kaiser's revolutionary methods of turning out hundreds of ships, England would have been starved into submission long before we could have launched the Normandy invasion.

Now Kaiser owned the third-largest aluminum company in the world and half the hotels on Waikiki Beach.

I told Isabelle to stop unpacking.

When I got to the Waldorf, I met with Kaiser and Pete Levathes of Y&R, which represented his firm. "Kaiser is well known only on the West Coast," he said. "Mr. Kaiser believes if his company were to become known nationally, the price of his stock would be much nearer its real value. He'd like to sponsor a feature picture from 8 to 10 on Sunday nights. Because of your theaters, you're the biggest buyer of motion pictures in the United States," he added. "If anyone can buy good movies to put on television, it should be you."

I said, "Up to now the motion picture industry hasn't been willing to do anything like that. But I'll try."

I called all the major companies, and every one turned me down. I went back to Kaiser and told him that the only movies available were quite old and unsuitable. So we started looking for something else to interest Kaiser in.

A couple of months later Ollie and I looked at a series pilot. It was the most unusual Western we'd ever seen.

OTHER RECOLLECTIONS:
Roy Huggins

After doing "Cheyenne," I hated the format of the traditional Western.

I was on "Conflict," and one show involved a no-good con man with an ironic attitude toward himself and life. He was the brother of the heroine—not very important in the story. He was called "The Man from 1999." In those days that was science fiction.

Bill Orr asked me to use Jim Garner. I had already used him in a bit part in "Cheyenne." I thought he was terrible. Awful. Bill said, "Come on, we like him, he's a good-looking guy. He'll come around." I gave him the part of the brother.

I had written some funny lines for this character—subtle, cynical, antiheroish lines. Watching Jim Garner read these lines in the dailies, I realized they were much funnier than they should ever have been.

His understanding of that character and his delivery were absolute perfection. Lines I thought would never come off on film were funny as hell, because Jim understood that character perfectly.

I left the screening room saying, "I've found something!" It's the greatest feeling in the world, knowing you've just discovered Cary Grant or someone like that. I immediately started thinking about doing a Western with that kind of character.

And about that time Bob Lewine from ABC asked for a meeting at Warners. He said, "We want more product. Have you got any more ideas?"

I said I wanted to do a Western about a gentle grifter—to use a title from O. Henry—the absolute antithesis of the Western hero.

Lewine said, "Well, how do you mean?"

I said, in a traditional Western, if a girl runs up to this guy and says, "I need help," he would take her side and say, "How can I help you?"

My character would say, "You need help? You see that building right over there? That's the sheriff's office. Go over there and tell *him* you need help."

Or he's in a saloon and someone comes in and says, "Hey, Jack Slade is out on the street"—the heavies were always named Slade—"looking for you."

Our hero says, "He is? Where is he?"

"He's over on the east side."

"Thank you," he says, and goes out a rear window, gets on his horse, and rides west out of town.

That is what I want to do, I said.

Silence. Bob Lewine looks at me and says, "That isn't a bad idea, let's try that."

So I wrote a script, and by this time I was calling him "Maverick." It's what he was.

❑ ❑ ❑

When we saw the pilot, I said to Ollie, "This is Henry Kaiser. He is a maverick, just like James Garner." I called Kaiser in Hawaii, and we went out to see him there. We showed him the pilot, and sure enough he threw out his chest. He could really see himself as James Garner.

I left Ollie in Hawaii and returned to New York. Over the next several days we stayed in almost constant touch. In those days there were only a few telephone circuits between the islands and the mainland. Calls were placed through operators, and often it was hours before a line was available. One day, faced with the very complex job of putting together a package to present to Mr. Kaiser and needing to speak to several top ABC executives, Ollie decided to keep the line from his hotel room open to ABC's switchboard all day.

After several hours, the phone charge had reached astronomical proportions. The hotel manager presented himself at the door to Ollie's suite and demanded that he settle the bill immediately.

"Doesn't Mr. Kaiser own this hotel?" asked Ollie.

"Yes, he does," said the manager.

"Well, I'm doing business on his behalf, and I need to keep this line open. We'll settle up when we check out."

"I don't care about that. I've got to have some cash right now, or I'll have the operator break the connection."

So Ollie gave him all the money he had, a few hundred dollars, and sent one of his assistants out to cash a check.

OTHER RECOLLECTIONS:
Ollie Treyz

Selling Henry Kaiser on ABC was the proudest moment of my life. He was a monumental figure, one of the really great men of his time. I became an admirer of this unbelievable, fantastic, eighty-year-old man. The mere fact that he was even interested in buying a program on ABC made me feel proud.

I courted him for three weeks, hanging out with him in Hawaii, listening to his stories, soaking up information. We offered him a third ownership in *Maverick*. Warners had a third and ABC a third.

Kaiser wasn't sure what he was going to do. Y&R had a different proposal for Kaiser. Sig Larman, Y&R's president, was coming out to make the pitch. We went back to Oakland for a final showdown.

I told Kaiser, "I'd love to sit in that meeting when they're recommending against ABC. And I'd like to know what it is they're recommending."

Kaiser says, "You're invited."

So I think I have an order. I knew Kaiser wanted "Maverick" because I said, "I think we gotta change that title, Mr. Maverick. I mean, Mr. Kaiser."

"What do you mean, change the title?"

"Oh, it's not a good title, it's a working title."

He said, "Wait a minute, *I'm* a maverick."

When he said that, I knew he was hooked.

"If you buy, Mr. Kaiser, you can have the title."

Now he's coming around very slowly. But Edgar, his son, president of the aluminum company, is resisting it.

These Y&R guys came out with an army of people. I am sitting in the meeting, and Larman suggests that since I'm an outsider, I should be excused.

Mr. Kaiser says, "No, I invited him."

Larman says, "I'm sorry, Mr. Kaiser, but it's our policy not to have networks at our meetings."

Kaiser says, "This is not *your* meeting, Mr. Larman, this is *my* meeting. Mr. Treyz will stay."

So I sit there, and Larman gets up with a fantastic offer, something that nobody else has—half of the "Ed Sullivan Show."

Lincoln Mercury's going to give up half the show. But I knew they had given up half a long time before to several cosponsors —and they'd all canceled. It was a premium-price show. But it was a sure bet. It had a record, no risk, nothing bad.

And they have an option. They got CBS to withhold this valuable property for the exclusive benefit of Kaiser, but he must act by noon tomorrow or lose it.

They get up there with their charts, and not only show "Sullivan's" in the top ten, the third- or fourth-ranking show, but it's got a rating of 35. In "Maverick's" proposed time period, ABC has a rating of 2 for "Omnibus" and "Meet the Press."

And Larman keeps saying what a gamble ABC is, that throughout its history has never had more than a 2 or 3 rating, it's not a habit, it's overlooked. And he kept saying third network, third network, third network.

I was getting mad sitting there. Really mad. I can see my weeks of work going down the drain. I'm being pushed back to my 2-foot line.

Kaiser says, "Ollie, anything you want to say?"

Everybody looked at me kind of sympathetically. I'd just been wiped out by these masterful guys.

I figured I had nothing to lose, so I allowed myself to lose my temper. I stood up and said, "Everything that Mr. Larman has said is true. The only thing is, he's omitted a few things.

"I acknowledge that we're a young network. Goldenson's only taken over three or four years, and it's true we are still the third network.

"We're not as good maybe as Young and Rubicam, they're the second advertising agency. But I'll tell you, Mr. Kaiser, we have something in common: You're the third aluminum company."

I said, "Mr. Kaiser, I'd like to ask you a few questions. Sullivan has a thirty-five rating, it sounds very tempting. It's had various cosponsors." I named them—Lorillard and the others.

"Why did they cancel?"

I knew why, but I said, "I don't know why, ask Lorillard Tobacco, why did they cancel. It'd be interesting to ask them."

Kaiser said, "Maybe we should ask them."

I said, "There's another question I would like to ask. Why does this agency suggest that you cosponsor with Lincoln Mercury when one of Kaiser's leading products is going to be the Jeep?"

He had just bought Willys, which made Jeeps.

"They have a ninety-five percent sponsor identification. Are you going to spend money for Jeep to sell Lincolns and Mercurys? Is that good business? They've had this thing for years. They will laugh at you. You'll be selling *their* cars, not *your* cars."

That got to him. He was coming around. I said, "What does it take to buy 'Ed Sullivan'? You know, all it takes is money, and God knows, you've got plenty. But what did you do when you built Grand Coulee Dam? Give somebody a few hundred million dollars and say, 'Build it'? The hell you did. You were out there with the steam shovels, testing the currents, wading in the muck with the engineers.

"You've got enough money, Mr. Kaiser. But to build something and own it takes the kind of a man who built Bonneville Dam. That built the Hoover Dam. It takes a man who could build a bridge across the Columbia River when all the best engineers said it couldn't be done. The kind of man who hired a fool kid just out of Stanford—a kid by the name of Edgar Kaiser—and he built the damned bridge because nobody told *him* it was impossible."

I hadn't been around this guy for three weeks for nothing.

After I pause, Kaiser says, "Mr. Larman, will you comment about what Ollie just said?"

"I don't have any comments, except he's wrong."

"Well, why is he wrong?"

"He's wrong, that's all. His facts are wrong."

"Well, what facts are wrong? The fact that I built Hoover Dam, is that wrong? The fact that I'm to have a one-third interest, is that wrong?"

I interrupted. "Mr. Kaiser, I'm not through yet."

Larman didn't know I had arranged for Leonard to call Jack Warner and have him available for a conference call. And I had my assistant get on the line in another room and tell Leonard what had just happened. I wanted him to get Jack to accept the challenge of beating "Ed Sullivan."

Leonard gets him really steamed up. Jack didn't like what he heard. It was a carom shot. Leonard made a sale, then Jack Warner made the sale.

I said, "We have Mr. Jack Warner on the phone."

We put him on one of those loudspeakers. "Jack?"

"Yeah, yeah."

"Got Mr. Kaiser here, Dusty Rhodes, Mr. Kaiser—Edgar and Henry Junior—Mr. Larman, Pete Levathes." God, there must have been twenty people.

And I say, "Y and R claims, Jack, that you can't put out a show that can beat 'Ed Sullivan.' "

"They do, eh?"

Now his ego is involved. Oh, Jesus Christ.

Warner said, "My show isn't out yet. You give me the stage, and I'll be the fucking winner."

Kaiser thinks this is great. He loves it. He was always for the underdog. So he says, "Well, do I still have a third?"

Jack says, "Far as I'm concerned, you've got a third."

And Leonard, who has been quiet on the line up to now, says, "Yes, you have a third."

I closed with Churchillian blood-sweat-toil-and-tears. "Mr. Kaiser, with all due deference to the number-two advertising agency, we two number-threes will join forces. Together we'll ascend the mountain top, and both of us will become number one."

So we made the deal. And it wasn't just "Maverick," it was Sunday night, a strategic position at 7:30. We bridged, as we had with "Disneyland" and "Cheyenne." "Maverick" knocked "Ed Sullivan" and "Steve Allen" out of the box by starting a half-hour earlier.

❑ ❑ ❑

Producing each episode of "Maverick" took seven calendar days, but Warners couldn't afford to pay the overtime required for weekend work. So, even if nothing went wrong, every episode produced cost them two days out of the following week. But this was the infancy of series television, and in many ways Warners was inventing it as they went along. Mistakes were inevitable. Soon they were lagging far behind schedule.

Roy Huggins finally concluded that to complete the twenty-six episodes ABC had purchased, he had to have two episode productions going simultaneously. Since we couldn't expect Garner to work in both, he needed another Maverick.

Thus he created the character of Bart Maverick, the equally roguish brother of Bret, Garner's character. Jack Kelly, whom Huggins knew from "Kings Row," was cast as Bart.

This change was cleared with Y&R, but not until the sixth episode did Kelly make an appearance on the show.

The morning following Kelly's first appearance, I got a call from Henry Kaiser.

"Leonard, I want to see you."

I said, "Sure, what about?

"I want to see you in Oakland, tomorrow."

Before I got on a plane, I checked with my people and then I checked with Y&R. Nobody knew what the problem was.

I took Ollie along; we met with Henry and his son Edgar.

Kaiser started in, "Leonard, I bought from you a bushel of red apples," he said. "I like red apples. But after I got through the top layer of red apples, I found nothing but green apples. I don't like green apples."

"Mr. Kaiser, if you're referring to the fact that we have Jack Kelly along with Garner, this was cleared with your advertising agency."

"Leonard, I made that deal with *you*. Not with my agency. I expected you to contact me if you're going to make any change involving Garner."

I replied that I'd assumed Y&R would clear all that through him. I had no contact with the agency. Warner Bros. and our sales department worked with them.

Eventually ABC had to pay Kaiser $600,000 to keep him happy. But it was worth it. "Maverick" became the foundation of our growing success on Sunday nights. And it launched not only Jim Garner, but also helped Roy Huggins, who brought many fine programs to ABC over the years following.

In 1957 we were making progress, but we were not yet truly a full-service network. We had nothing on in the daytime to speak of. That was a problem, because it was very difficult to attract new affiliates without being able to offer them a full schedule. We had our hands full developing prime time, so I asked Ollie to see if we could pick up something from our affiliates, a local show that could go on the network.

OTHER RECOLLECTIONS:
Ollie Treyz

Being an old researcher, statistically oriented, I used to read ratings books. I'd take them home and study them. And just scanning, I noticed in the Philadelphia book a show called "American Bandstand," with a 15 or 16 rating.

It's a local show. And it's on non-network time, in the afternoon. And we had just dropped "Mickey Mouse," which we would bring back later at 5:30, although I didn't know it then.

I thought to myself, What in hell is this? I never heard of this. It's not in any other market.

So I called Roger Clipp, a good friend, the guy who hired me to come to ABC in 1948. He ran Channel 6, Philadelphia, for Walter Annenberg.

I said, "Roger, let me see 'American Bandstand.' "

"Oh," he says, "I put the show on the air, and the host got drunk on the air. I had this young kid come in and replace him. He's doing fine. His name is Dick Clark. His father runs a radio station."

I said I don't know the kid. Dick was then twenty-five, twenty-six. And I said, Well, tell me about the show.

"Oh, the girls come and dance in the studio. He's got all these kinds of new dances. He gets singers to come down and lip-sync their records. I don't think it's for the network."

"Well, Jesus, it's got a fifteen or sixteen rating."

What intrigued me about it was that Dick Clark was unknown in Philadelphia. If he'd been an established personality and had a successful show, that's something else. And the show had been on the air only a few weeks before he took over. Had he been a radio announcer or something—but all of a sudden, he looms as a tremendous area personality.

Now, you can't tell me that something that works that fast in Philadelphia is not transferable to the rest of the country. Human nature is human nature. I don't believe in regionalism to that extent. It got a 15 or 16 rating in Philadelphia consistently. That has my full attention.

Roger says, "I'll send you a Kine."

I saw the Kine, and I thought, I can see why. I had a 16 mm Kine projector at home, so I showed it to my kids, and they liked it. I told them, Bring in all your school friends, the girls, get them to come over. I was interested in the girls' reaction, because I saw girls dancing with girls.

And they loved it. They asked to see it again. They loved that kind of music and the dancing, the Twist and all that.

"Would you come home and watch that right after school?"

Oh, yes, they would.

I didn't want to act anxious. I called Roger and played dumb. I acted like, "I guess you're right, it's probably not for network. But we need something. Maybe we ought to experiment with it. It might help you out."

We made a deal for $1,500 a *week*, plus Dick got a certain

number of spots for himself. But we sold the national spots for $1,500 a *minute*.

I made a deal with him on the phone. Leonard put me up to this. Dick was selling scrapbooks for $2 apiece. Thousands of girls wrote in for these Dick Clark scrapbooks. We sold them all over the country. Dick kept a dollar and sent a dollar to us.

❑ ❑ ❑

"American Bandstand" was an extraordinary part of ABC's history. It became an anchor for the whole daytime lineup. It got huge ratings, whipping all competition. It drew people to the network who weren't there before. It became ABC's longest running show—the longest running show on *any* network—thirty years on ABC.

Dick Clark became a national institution. When ABC celebrated its 25th anniversary, Dick produced the show for us.

There was a time, however, when it looked like Dick and "Bandstand" might go down the drain. It had nothing to do with his talent or his ratings. It had to do with a sordid chapter in broadcasting history called "payola," and the outsized egos of some of Capitol Hill's most powerful figures.

Dick Clark held an interest in companies that produced records at the same time he was doing "American Bandstand."

There was therefore the possibility that he could have used his show to promote his own records, though he never did so. But having the potential was inconsistent with ABC's conflict-of-interest policy.

What brought this to my attention was the November 1959 Congressional investigation into payola, which was the use of cash and other inducements to get disc jockeys to play certain records. A special subcommittee of the Committee on Interstate and Foreign Commerce began holding hearings. It turned into a three-ring circus. The committee began to concern itself with all sorts of claims about evil influences from rock music on teenagers' behavior.

As chief executive of a company that owned radio stations and a TV network that carried "American Bandstand," I was subpoenaed to testify. Before going down to Washington, I wanted to be very clear about Clark's role.

I'd never met Dick before, so I invited him up to my house with his lawyer, Marv Josephson. They came in at nine o'clock on a Saturday morning. For greater privacy, we used the projection room of my home theater.

My daughter Loreen was a teenager then and a big fan of Dick Clark.

She kept trying to find ways to come in and watch. Somehow she got an idea of what we were doing, and became very worried that some harm might come to Dick.

Si Siegel and Ev Erlick, our general counsel, and I went at it all day long and well into the evening. We grilled Dick in great depth, went over everything related to his record business and his ABC show. I most wanted to know if he had ever promoted his own records on "Bandstand."

When the day was over, I satisfied myself that Dick was clean. And he agreed that he would divest himself of his music holdings. So I went down to Congress to testify on his behalf. I said he shouldn't be blackballed from television. And the committee went along with my recommendations.

OTHER RECOLLECTIONS:
Dick Clark

I worked for ABC before it was ABC-Paramount. The first job I ever had was at an ABC radio affiliate, in 1947. I used to tell a joke—years ago, before they became number one—that I had been with ABC through "thin and thin."

The payola investigation was a witch-hunt. Congressmen were anxious for publicity after the quiz-show scandals. It was also a reaction to the tremendous popularity of rock music with young people.

Rock was unpopular with older people. They began saying it was a bad influence on children, that it contributed to delinquent behavior. The Old Guard felt it was losing control. So they put huge pressures on the Congress to investigate why young people listened to this kind of music.

Most of the investigation went to local radio disc jockeys. They took money for playing records. I was heavily involved in the music business. Writing, publishing, artist management. Horizontally, vertically, sideways, crossways. Because of "Bandstand's" success, I was the guy in the spotlight.

The record companies I had an interest in *paid* payola. It was legal. Nothing wrong with it. Had been done since the dawn of time.

But nobody ever paid *me* to play records. I was doing very well. It wasn't necessary. My income was substantial. I was a giver, never a receiver.

As the chairman of the Congressional committee said, I was an entrepreneur, and there wasn't anything wrong with that. But perhaps there was a conflict of interest. Maybe I should choose one or the other—television or music. There wasn't any choice for me. I wanted to be in television.

The hearings were some kind of a shuck. After I testified, Robert Lishman, chief counsel of the subcommittee, who for days had grilled me on the witness stand, stopped me in a corridor and asked me to give an autograph to his teenaged son!

I gave Mr. Goldenson my word, "As long as I do the 'Bandstand' on your network, I will not go into the music business." There's no way to project this, but the music publishing companies I had to sell would have been worth many millions of dollars today, if I had invested the same kind of energy I did in television.

But I don't have any misgivings. From the time I was thirteen, all I ever wanted to do was to be involved in broadcasting. Music was a sideline, another way to make money until I made it in television. It's a crime, when you look back at it, that I couldn't have done both. At one time I was invited to run ABC's record company. But then someone, maybe Ev Erlick, said "Let's not get near that one again."

It would have been very easy to say, "Let's get rid of this Clark guy, and we'll clear the slate and move on." But after that meeting at Mr. Goldenson's house, they decided to back me, which was pretty daring. Leonard Goldenson is one of my idols. He stood by me. He had to be a brave man to do that.

❑ ❑ ❑

During the Treyz era I was down in Washington at the FCC practically every week, trying to get more "drop-ins."

A drop-in was a way to get ABC programs into markets where there were only one or two stations. By FCC order, those stations, affiliated with the other networks, could be forced to clear some of our programming during prime time. The problem was that without a shove from the FCC, these stations either wouldn't clear our programs at all, or would run them in time slots like midnight or Sunday morning at 6.

At this time there was a controversy about UHF stations. VHF channels were quite limited. The FCC allowed only twelve VHF channels and required 125 miles of physical separation between transmitters on the same channel.

More channels were available on UHF, a less desirable band of frequencies with limited range. But very few television sets in that era were equipped with the tuner for receiving UHF signals.

Manufacturers were reluctant to build sets with UHF tuners because the biggest television markets had only VHF stations. Adding a tuner would make the sets more expensive and so less attractive to buyers who didn't need UHF.

I went to various congressmen and senators, those on committees dealing with the FCC, about drop-ins. I met often with Newton Minow, chairman of the FCC, on the subject.

When the UHF issue began heating up, Minow asked me for help. We made a deal. I would get ABC's affiliates to ask their congressmen to push for a law requiring all new TV sets to have both kinds of tuners. In return, ABC would get drop-ins in the fourteen largest two-station markets.

I carried out my end of the bargain. Phone calls and letters lobbied congressmen. The other two networks, with plenty of stations, were pretty much indifferent to the UHF bill. They sat on the sidelines. I don't know what effect our lobbying had, but we pushed hard for it, and the law passed.

But when I went back to Minow and asked for the drop-ins, he told me it was impossible. There was too much pressure from television-set manufacturers, he said. They wanted new UHF stations to come into these markets, which would help sell their new sets. Putting ABC's drop-ins on VHF stations would discourage new UHF stations from starting up there.

I was flabbergasted. I said, "Newt, how in the hell can you make a commitment to me and then back away from it? I never heard of a government official lying like that." I really let him have it, and he walked away.

Now, Minow was the fellow who said, in 1961, "Television is a vast wasteland." That will be his footnote in history. I thought he was wrong when he said it, and I think he'd be wrong if he said it now. There are an enormous number of series programs on television. You have to look at them in perspective. If you're feeding three networks so many hours a day, 365 days a year, there are bound to be some bad shows.

ABC funds twenty-five or more pilots a year. We usually select five or six to air, and if only one is a hit, we're in pretty good shape. If it's two out of five, my God, we're in clover!

Of course there are lousy programs—perhaps 40 percent of what's on the schedule at any given time is junk. But that leaves 60 percent that isn't. Moreover, no one claims that more than 60 percent of all the books published in America are wonderful, enlightening, inspiring works of art. Many, including many best-sellers, are worse trash than anything on television. Yet that's what people want to read, so publishers give it to them. Television is no better and no worse than book publishing.

Minow is part of an articulate, educated minority that can afford and appreciate highbrow cultural entertainment. He can attend operas or ballets, go to university lectures, or see Broadway-style theatrical productions.

Most Americans can't. They can't afford the ticket prices, and they haven't the educational background to appreciate the fare. For the majority of Americans, broadcast television is their chief entertainment.

So this isn't a Tiffany business. It's Woolworth and K-Mart.

There's a place for the articulate minority—on public broadcasting (which I have long supported). Every once in a while the networks can also afford to present shows that appeal to Minow's school of watchers. But we'd go broke if we tried to appeal to the articulate minority all the time. The proof of this is that public broadcasting is perpetually in the red.

One dire consequence of our lack of affiliates and inability to get drop-ins was the tendency of sponsors to move their shows to other networks after we had invested great sums of money and much energy developing them.

As an example, in 1953 Kintner got U.S. Steel to sponsor "The U.S. Steel Hour," a dramatic anthology series. Where ABC competed, the show did very well. But where we had to rely on secondary affiliates, it ran in poor time slots. In the fall of 1955 the sponsor moved the show to CBS, which could offer much greater distribution and consequently good ratings.

I went to my board and said, "We've got to know that those programs are licensed to us and can't be taken away. We've got to control audience flow. We can't allow advertisers to yank programs around to suit themselves. We must be able to schedule as we wish, so nobody can force us to move a show into another time slot against our best interests."

But this is exactly what advertisers did on all three networks. As a condition of coming to ABC, for example, sponsors often insisted on a particular time slot. It was routine, a legacy of network radio.

You can't run a business that way. I told the board, "We've got to commit to a fixed time slot for every program we air. If we can't sell it, then God bless us, we're in trouble—but I think we can sell it. But we can't compete the way things are now." The board backed me.

We told our advertisers: Take it or leave it. They screamed bloody murder. Of course, we didn't have many advertisers then. But as I saw it, we had no choice, and so we gave them none. This decision changed the whole scheme of our business. In a few years, ad agencies lost their grip on scheduling. For the first time networks could shape their own futures with programming decisions unhindered by advertisers.

(Oddly enough, now that agencies have become enormous conglomerates, they're trying to get back into programming. In 1988 Saatchi & Saatchi announced a plan to develop its own programs and place them on European networks.)

In 1958 our daytime programming was limited to "Mickey Mouse Club," "Do You Trust Your Wife?" (formerly "Who Do You Trust?"), and "American Bandstand." We had nothing before 3 P.M. AT&T, however, required us to lease cable time in eight-hour blocks, so we were paying for many hours of unused time.

We had trouble finding both daytime programs and sponsors. ABC was considered a very risky buy. Then a very bright fellow, Pete Levathes, thought of a way to get ABC into daytime with a bang. We called it Operation Daybreak.

OTHER RECOLLECTIONS:
Peter Levathes

> I was director of media and television at Y&R. We bought newspapers, magazines, radio, television. We had many clients, but the daytime situation was very tight. Only CBS and NBC had daytime network programming, and their rates were increasing. It was a seller's market. There was just no place to go. We were getting desperate to find other places to put our clients.
>
> ABC was just starting as a network. It was hard to go to General Foods or Procter & Gamble and say, "Let's buy some shows for you on ABC."
>
> They'd say, "They're not even in business."
>
> I went to Leonard and Ollie and asked if they'd open up network daytime if we could put a package together. They said, "Sure."
>
> The fatality rate in daytime is very high. In those days if you went to a client and said, "I want to buy a show for you that starts at eleven and goes until eleven-thirty" no matter what the show he'd say, "How will it do?"
>
> When I went to see General Foods' advertising manager, he said, "Tell me about the shows."

"Are you so smart that if I told you the shows, you would know if they were good or bad?"

"God, no, we make mistakes all the time picking shows."

So I suggested that he buy, say, ten spots. The first spot would be at 10:05. The next at 10:30. Then 11. So if they rotated from 11 to 5, in the course of a month, his spots would appear everywhere on the schedule. That was the clincher. Instead of gambling on a particular program, we could sell them the *average* audience for the entire schedule. It was a new concept.

I'd gone to the head of Y&R, Sig Larman, and told him what I was doing. Later I went back and said, "We've got it together."

"Well, Peter, I don't know," he said. "Some of the senior executives have come to me and said that this is so big it might be in restraint of trade. That Y&R is making such a big purchase we will have an undue influence on the medium."

I guess the lawyers had gone to him. When we bought, the word got around.

Larman was of Swedish extraction. I said, "Well, Sig, if this is too much for the Swedes to handle, we won't do it."

He smiled. "It's not too much for the Swedes. Go ahead."

We assembled almost $18 million worth of orders from seven clients. In 1958, that was a lot of money. I took it to Lenny and put it on his desk. We had General Foods and Procter & Gamble, some of the top advertisers. He was completely awed.

The fact that Y&R was buying showed that it was acceptable. Once the word got around, the other agencies jumped in. By the time we went on the air, I'm sure ABC had sold almost $50 million in spots.

Lenny, a very thoughtful man, did a very sweet thing. The day after I delivered the orders, he called my wife. He didn't know her. *I* hadn't told her anything about this deal. Lenny told her about it and how happy he was with everything. My wife will never forget what Lenny did. He made me a hero in her eyes. She was very touched.

❑ ❑ ❑

Pete Levathes helped save ABC by putting us into daytime with shows like "Liberace," "Day in Court," and "Beat the Clock." He left Y&R in 1959 to run Fox's studio production.

One of ABC's brightest young men in the Treyz years was Julie Barnathan. Trained in mathematics, a brilliant statistician who did a Brooklyn College term paper on the odds in crapshooting, Julie hides a Phi Beta Kappa mind behind a rough-and-tumble exterior. Ollie hired him shortly after the merger with UPT, at the precise time when, at my request, Si Siegel, trying to staunch the red ink, was going through ABC's payroll with a very large ax, laying off dead wood.

Julie had Ollie's old job in Research. Ollie saw his potential and found a way to hide him. He kept him off the payroll for two months, paying him with expense advances until he was safe from further cuts.

The business that Operation Daybreak brought in was predicated on a discounted daytime rate that Ollie and Julie dreamed up. Sitting around Haley's, a bar near ABC's studio, they decided that if we could offer a lower rate, that would bring in new advertisers who couldn't afford the rates CBS and NBC were getting. But the only way we could live with this lower rate was to get our affiliates to accept less station compensation.

OTHER RECOLLECTIONS:
Ollie Treyz

The order from Y&R provided for a new Class D rate, which was one third of the prime-time rate.

This was because in daytime, the Homes Using Television (HUT) level is only a third of prime time. So at night, if the HUT was 75, then during the day it would be 25.

But in radio, advertising rates for daytime were *half* of nighttime, reflecting what the industry agreed was the approximate ratio of listenership between night and day. When television came along, everyone applied the radio rate structure, which was all they had.

But it didn't make sense anymore. Our research indicated that daytime television audiences were only a third of prime time. I had to get our affiliates to attune themselves to the realities of modern television. So I called a meeting of our affiliates' advisory committee. I thought I could handle this, so Leonard didn't come.

I ran into a buzz saw.

Roger Clipp, the guy who gave us Dick Clark, was a little sore at me because he'd realized we got the show for almost nothing, and it's making us a lot of money. He said we had a contract going back to 1926, the first days of the Blue Radio Network, which called for 50 percent station compensation.

I argued that that was radio, and we were now in television, and I showed him the figures to prove that the ratio of day to night was 1:3 in TV, not 1:2. Radio's ways did not apply to television.

But Roger is all worked up. He says that with a one-third rate he'll be getting $9.50 for a one-minute spot, and he's selling his own, locally, for $25 to $30. He says I'm cheapening the medium, I'm bastardizing the business. I'm moving backward.

And soon they were all ready to hang me. They were getting so hot I had to adjourn the meeting. I said, "I'll think about this, you think about it, maybe we can find a way to work it out. Because it's very important that the network gets into programming daytime. And the economics of this deal is that we cannot afford to pay you 50 percent."

And they indicated that they'd rather forget about network daytime until the advertisers became realistic. They said they'd be goddamned if they were going to sell their spots for that kind of network compensation.

Now I'm really frustrated. I can't see any way out of this. And I'm getting angrier and angrier because they just don't see it, and if they don't, then daytime goes down the drain.

An old friend saved me. Saved ABC, really. I called up Ed Kovac, who was the retired executive VP of NBC, and was on the board of Gillette. He was a dear friend, almost a father to me.

I said, "Ed, you once told me that when you worked for McGraw-Hill in 1926, and when old man McGraw went to see Dick Ellsworth, president of NBC, you went along with him. And you wrote the first rate card for NBC."

He said, "Yes, that's right."

Before that, Kovac had written rate cards for the *Saturday Evening Post, Collier's*, and the leading newspapers. But NBC didn't become a network until 1926, so this was the first network rate card.

"Let me ask you something. When you wrote that card, did you have nighttime to daytime, two to one?"

"Absolutely."

"Are you sure?"

"Absolutely sure."

"Wait a minute. You didn't have any ratings in those days."

"That's right. No ratings. Hadn't come along yet."

"If you had no ratings, how did you know it was two to one?"

"Oh, that was simple. I told them that in the daytime, the wife is home and the man is working. At night, the man and his wife are both home. So that's why I made it two to one."

I almost fell out of my chair laughing.

Now, every one on our affiliates advisory committee knew Ed Kovac. Some of them had worked for him at NBC. They revered him, respected him. But I was younger than all those guys, and they figured I must be dangerous, a wild-eyed liberal.

I said, "Ed, would you mind telling that story to a group of ABC's affiliates?" And I told him about the trouble I was in.

He agreed to come to our meeting, and they were very surprised to see him. "I've come to protect Ollie," he said. And with a fine sense of whimsy and his natural, folksy humor, he told the story.

And all their hostility turned into laughter when Ed Kovac had finished. Roger Clipp said, "Oh, hell, let's let Ollie have his folly. Why don't we let him do it. He'll learn better."

Before anybody could argue, I put it to a vote, and they went along with the one-third rate.

❑ ❑ ❑

Even with reduced compensation to stations, however, we were going to lose money on our D rate because a minute cost only $2,500. Thank God for a flint-eyed auditor named Mike Boland, who recommended we add a "networking charge" of $500 to integrate the commercials with the programs.

Another good thing that came out of Operation Daybreak was that I had an opportunity to meet Ev Erlick, one of Y&R's young attorneys. Several months later, when we needed a general counsel, I thought of Erlick and persuaded him to come aboard. He stayed with us until he retired in 1985. Ev's contributions to the rise of ABC were enormous.

In 1959 Dan Melnick and Tom Moore saw "The Untouchables," a segment in a Westinghouse anthology series. Federal agents against the Chicago Mafia, set in the 1920s. I saw it, too. We all agreed that it would make a terrific series. Quinn Martin did it for us. Very quickly, it became one of our biggest hits.

The show went like gangbusters for three years. Then I got a call from John Pastore, the Rhode Island senator in charge of communications under

Senator Warren Magnusson. He said he'd like to bring some people in to talk to me.

OTHER RECOLLECTIONS:
Ollie Treyz

I got word from Marion Ayer, Leonard's secretary, to see Leonard immediately. When I heard the word *immediately*, I knew it was very serious. Leonard was not one to cry wolf.

I walk into his office. There were about thirty guys there, all leading Italian-Americans—judges, lawyers, businessmen, manufacturers, doctors, even the publisher Generoso Pope—father of the man who would a few years later turn the *National Enquirer* into something quite unlike any other newspaper.

All well-dressed. Not yelling, not screaming. Cultured men who came quietly with soft voices to express their deep concern and displeasure at what they regarded as a growing anti-Italian sentiment generated by "The Untouchables." This, they said, was unfair to the Italian-American community.

These men said we were doing a disservice to Italian-Americans that reflected not only on them but their children. They felt we ought to consider this problem and take action.

Leonard was shocked. I was too. We hadn't even thought about this when we put the show on. It grew awfully fast, and I think it got away from us. We should have been more sensitive.

They could see we felt bad. Leonard had great empathy for their point of view. Leonard says, "Let us look into it." He didn't commit to anything.

Before we could change all these names, make some of the bad guys Anglo-Saxons and some of the G-men Italians, I got a wire from Terry Klein at McCann-Erickson: "Cancel 'The Untouchables' immediately, do not run the commercials tonight."

They had two minutes. They had a right to tell us not to run the commercials, but they had to pay. It was too late to sell the time to somebody else.

When I got this wire, I couldn't believe it. I thought it was a ruse. So I called Terry Klein. He wouldn't take my call. I ran over there, but he wouldn't see me. I was told later that he went downstairs and hid from me.

Leonard had some good analysis and good advice what to do. We take out all the Italians and make them Greeks. Then the Greeks get mad, so we change the Greeks into Anglo-Saxons, and all the bad guys were named Smith. And the show died. Everyone knows very well that Al Capone was Italian. So we take the show off the air.

❑ ❑ ❑

Not all of the Italian-American protest about "The Untouchables" was as genteel as an office full of distinguished businessmen saying, "Wait a minute." The same sort of Italian-Americans that Elliot Ness battled conveyed threats of violence against me and my family. I'd planned a family vacation to Italy, and when we were told it would be "unhealthy" to visit Sicily, I thought it wiser to reroute to Corfu.

A few years ago Hollywood released a feature film version of *The Untouchables*, starring Kevin Costner and Sean Connery. Connery won an Oscar for best supporting actor. But what interested me most about the movie was a little disclaimer that ran before the titles. It said that not all gangsters are Italians, and not all Italians are members of the Mafia. Looking back, I wish we'd thought of doing something of that nature with the television series *before* my office was three deep in distinguished Italian-Americans.

For all the years I knew Ollie, he worked long, long hours. We often traveled together, sharing hotel suites. I came to regard him almost as a son or younger brother. When I brought him in as network president, he was the right man at the right time. Without Ollie, ABC might very well have failed to achieve parity with the other networks. At the very least it would have taken many years longer.

Ollie was a unique character, who often seemed larger than life to those around him. Practically everyone who worked at ABC in those days had a favorite Ollie story.

Tom Moore worked closely with him for several years, and recalls many of Ollie's escapades.

OTHER RECOLLECTIONS:
Tom Moore

Ollie was the kind of guy who was always running a tremendous head of steam. Time was nothing, and he was always late, always running out, grabbing a cab, always, "Do it this way, do it that way."

Once we went to Chicago to see Phil Wrigley, the chewing-gum king. By the time we checked into a hotel, we were already late for our appointment.

Running through the lobby to get a cab, I reminded Ollie that Leonard had suggested that he get a haircut. In fact, his hair was very long.

Ollie ran back to the hotel barber shop. "How fast can I get a haircut?" he said.

"I can have you out of here in ten minutes," said the barber.

"I don't have ten minutes. Put some extra guys on the job, I'll pay whatever it takes."

Ollie sat down and one barber worked on one side of his head while another cut the other side. He was out of there with a flattop in three minutes.

Once we were all out at Swift, in Chicago, trying to sell Peter Pan Peanut Butter on renewing "Disneyland." The meeting was running late. We had to be back in New York that night, but all our luggage was at the hotel, and we didn't want to miss the plane. Ollie called one of the guys with us, Don Coyle, and told him, "Go in our rooms and get our clothes, pack them and meet us at the airport."

Don threw everything into our suitcases, hailed a cab, charged out of the hotel, and met us at the airport. We barely made it.

We got off the plane in New York and a guy comes on the loudspeaker and says, "Will Oliver Treyz please see the agent." He said, "Mr. Treyz, you have to get your luggage and separate out what isn't yours, because there's a man back at a hotel in Chicago who doesn't have a damned stitch of clothes." They had rented the room again after we left, and this guy was in the bathroom when Coyle came in and packed everything up.

Another time Ollie and I were negotiating a deal with the agency that had Alka-Seltzer. As we got to the fine points of the contract, right at the most crucial point, Ollie had to use the toilet.

The bathroom was between Si Siegel's office and Ollie's. A door on each side. Locking one side automatically locked the other. When Ollie tried to get out, the solenoid jammed. He was locked in.

While we wait for a maintenance crew to fix the lock, Ollie continues negotiations by screaming through the door. The Alka-

Seltzer guy is screaming back, "No, I can't live with that, word it this way." Then they slid the contract back and forth under the door and screamed some more. We closed a $2 million deal with Ollie locked in the john.

❑ ❑ ❑

Not everyone thought Ollie was a genius. He was headstrong, and many thought he had become increasingly arrogant. One man who never got along with him was Si Siegel. By the early 1960s, the company had become far more than a network and a collection of movie theaters. I depended on Si to run the day-to-day affairs of the corporation.

OTHER RECOLLECTIONS:
Si Siegel

Treyz was his own worst enemy. He was a good salesman, but he didn't know when to stop selling. Once I got into a discussion with an ad agency executive, and we were comparing ABC to the other two networks.

He said, "If I bought a show from ABC and asked Treyz for the merchandising rights and the billboard rights, Treyz would say, 'You've got them.'

"If I went to NBC and said the same thing, they'd say, 'Wait a minute.' They'd call a lawyer in and say, 'Look this up and see what we can give them.'

"If I went to CBS they wouldn't have to call a lawyer in, they'd say right off, 'You can't have them, we don't have them to give you. The producer of the show has kept them for himself."

So Treyz would say, "You've got them," but two months later you'd be fighting with him, "But Ollie, you said . . ." And Ollie would say he couldn't have said it.

That was Ollie. He would sell things he didn't have, and reinvent history to justify his actions.

I went in and talked to Leonard about it. I said, "If we're going to be a mature company, we've got to have mature people. Not a bunch of wild guys promising anything to anybody."

At that time I was financial vice president. I was doing what I thought I had to do, and Leonard always backed me.

Ollie tried to go around me. To him, I was "the bookkeeper."

He said, "I don't report to a bookkeeper." That's what he called me to the bulk of the people who worked for him.

We had a fight while Leonard was in Europe. Ollie ordered me to do something. I said, "Go to hell."

When Leonard returned, Ollie went in and complained. So we had a meeting in Leonard's office, and Leonard said to Ollie, "Si is my alter ego. When I'm not here, he's in charge."

Ollie said, "You can't put him in charge. I can't be reporting to a bookkeeper, a financial man."

Leonard said, "We'll make him executive VP of the corporation."

So in a way he did me some good. But the title didn't mean anything. My duties the day after I became executive VP were no different from the day before. I was still running the inside. I was still the guy who said yes or no.

In 1961 we aired "Bus Stop," based on a successful Broadway play and a movie that starred Marilyn Monroe. Early in its first season, I had another call from Senator Pastore. This time he was objecting to what he called the show's emphasis on violence and sex. In particular he objected to one episode, which starred Fabian, the teenaged singing idol.

That episode is quite tame by today's standards. But in 1961, some public figures perceived television as growing too powerful. They made all sorts of assertions. Some said young people's behavior was negatively affected by what they saw on the tube. Any show that featured alcoholism, hinted at sexual deviation, or implied violence was an easy target for those charged with "protecting" Americans from television's "evil influences."

Senator Pastore's committee chose to make an example of the Fabian episode on "Bus Stop." There were hearings, and Ollie testified that, with hindsight, maybe we should have toned the show down a bit. We canceled it at season's end.

Not long after that, for reasons explained below, I had to fire Ollie. In his mind there was a strong link between the FCC's "Bus Stop" hearings and his sudden departure from ABC. Ollie persuaded himself that he was a human sacrifice, that I got rid of him to appease the Congress and the FCC.

But that is only in Ollie's mind. There was no connection between the two events. No connection whatever.

OTHER RECOLLECTIONS:
Dan Melnick

For a long period there was enormous upset within the whole industry. The perception was that Ollie interpreted the truth very loosely.

Ollie once asked me to come to a meeting at an ad agency. We were in the agency's boardroom, Ollie and I on one side of the table. Facing us were seven account executives and the head of the agency, who began by rattling off an "Ollie, You Said" litany.

"On the fourteenth of the month you said . . . and this is what happened. On the twenty-third of the next month you said this, and this is what happened." Incredible. Like the "Catalogue Aria" from *Don Giovanni*. They went through a whole indictment ending up with, "And you *said* this, and you *did* that."

Without missing a beat Ollie says, "Well, yeah. Now Dan wants to talk about the new programs."

At one point there was a full-page ad in weekly *Variety*, or maybe *The New York Times*, a big banner across the top, "But Ollie, You Said . . ."

It listed the names of a half dozen different ad agencies. They all got together to do it.

It became an intolerable situation. Our credibility was becoming suspect. I would make representations to the talent—producers, writers, and production companies I dealt with—and Ollie would ignore them. There were just countless things. Everybody was embarrassed. And it got to the point where the network was chaotic.

I got a call from Tom Moore, who said, "Some of us are getting together to have a discussion about what to do at the network." It was clear what he was talking about.

The heads of all key departments met. We agreed we couldn't stay unless there was a change. It wasn't that Ollie had to be fired, but there had to be somebody between him and the rest of the world.

One of us told Leonard what we had agreed.

Ollie was coming back from some place and the car that met him, instead of taking him home, brought a note that said please come to the office, there's a meeting going on and we want you to be there.

When he arrived, Leonard had a private conversation with him and told him that this wasn't going to work anymore.

Ollie came into the conference room afterward, wished everybody well, said a few gracious words, and left. Leonard announced that Tom would be filling his responsibilities.

It must have looked like a palace coup. I think we all felt, no matter the justification, that we were just a little bit dirty.

❑ ❑ ❑

I had heard murmurs about Ollie for some time before Dan Seymour of J. Walter Thompson, one of the biggest agencies, told me that they couldn't do any further business with ABC.

"Ollie is just not telling us the truth. We can't rely on him. He makes one statement and then does something else. We just have to back away."

I had Ev Erlick make an analysis of all the top agencies, and I found this to be true. The agencies were very skeptical of him. They thought he was brilliant but couldn't trust him.

After the department heads had met—they told me afterward—I called another meeting at my house in Mamaroneck on a Sunday morning. I invited Si Siegel, Tom Moore, Julie Barnathan, and Ev Erlick.

The consensus was that Ollie had to go.

I dislike firing people at any time, and in those days I usually had Si do this for me. But Ollie was very special. When he flamed out, it was a tremendous disappointment. I felt terrible about it, but I saw no other course of action.

I got Ollie a job with Warners at a comparable salary, but he held that for only a few months.

The bottom fell out of Ollie's life after that. He had a ruinous bout with alcoholism. His wife suffered a long, agonizing death from cancer. Ollie was left to pay a fortune in medical bills. He lost all his ABC stock and his options, when, in the aftermath of a failed takeover bid, our stock plunged, and Ollie couldn't meet a margin call.

He lost his home. For an extended period he depended on the kindness of friends. He has many, and they, like me, choose to remember his many fine qualities and forgive his unlimited capacity for self-delusion.

Ollie slept on a lot of living room sofas, a few nights at a time. He survived countless crises by begging "loans" from practically everyone he knew.

And then, a few years ago, he rallied. He landed a job with an advertising publication, which helped get him back on his feet. Now in his early seventies, his mind is still sharp. He can still sell ice to Eskimos. His fabulous ability to "read the tea leaves," to spot trends and opportunities in voluminous ratings reports, is undiminished.

Ollie spends his days as a consultant to such media giants as Fox, Westinghouse, Taft, Storer, and Mutual. Too often, however, he spends his nights recalling the six glorious years when he was president of the ABC Television Network.

11

Sports

❑

ABC's long, often agonizing growth into a competitive third network got a mighty boost from sports. In the process, we reinvented, redefined, and reengineered sports broadcasting to bring an entirely new dimension to television. This new programming soon attracted huge audiences, including many who had previously paid little attention to sports.

The NCAA football fiasco did nothing to discourage me from seeking ways to get sporting events on ABC. We needed programming of all sorts. I was very sure that if Kintner hadn't played power politics by trying to embarrass Bob O'Brien, we would have done quite well with the package. Nevertheless, this episode revealed how ill-equipped we were to deal with sports. We had no executive expertise, few sports-oriented sales people, and little production capability.

The man who changed all that, who put us on the road to world leadership in television sports, was an intense, well-spoken former advertising executive named Edgar Scherick.

OTHER RECOLLECTIONS:
Edgar Scherick

In late 1950 I came to New York looking for a job. I knew no one at the networks and had no experience in broadcasting. I saw a newspaper ad for a job at Dancer, Fitzgerald & Sample. "Wanted: Time-buyer. $60 dollars a week, must know Nielsen." I had a vague idea of what a time-buyer was. I knew how much $60 a week was. But I didn't know where I had to go to meet this guy Nielsen. I got the job anyway.

My boss was Jimmy Neale, a broadcasting pioneer who had been among NBC's first thirty employees. He was in charge of broadcast media buying.

One of our accounts was Falstaff Beer, an up-and-coming regional brewery. I'd always been interested in sports, and so it occurred to both Jimmy and me that baseball and football games would be natural vehicles for Falstaff. We acquired the rights and took the shows to the networks for distribution.

In the early 1950s, television was just exploring sports. Only NBC, whose sports director was a legendary character named Tom Gallery, had a stable presence in sports broadcasting.

After becoming very involved with Falstaff and sports, I left the agency to spend a few months at CBS as their sports specialist. Then I went into business for myself as Sports Programs, Inc.

❑ ❑ ❑

Scherick's company produced such programs as football pregame shows for Wheaties. These featured the Wheaties spokesman, Olympics pole-vault champion (1952, 1956) Reverend Bob Richards. Armand Grant, who worked for Jim Aubrey when Jim was head of programming, brought Scherick in to talk about producing some events for ABC. Scherick produced a few football games as special network events.

When Aubrey left, Tom Moore, who had been head of sales, took over programming under Ollie Treyz. Unlike Aubrey, both were very anxious to get ABC into sports, as was I. Since ABC still had no sports department, Moore began to rely on Scherick for more and more production. In effect, Sports Programs, Inc., functioned as our sports department.

In 1960, NBC canceled Gillette's "Friday Night Fights." Gillette felt the regular exposure of a weekly show was very important to its goals. Gillette secretly approached Scherick to see if he could get ABC to carry the fights.

ABC wanted to get NCAA football back from NBC. But because of what had happened the last time, we weren't about to bid on the rights without knowing we had a sponsor.

So Scherick made a deal on our behalf. In return for bringing "Friday Night Fights" to ABC, Gillette agreed to sponsor NCAA football—if we could somehow acquire the rights.

OTHER RECOLLECTIONS:
Edgar Scherick

Tom Gallery of NBC had produced NCAA football for a long time and was very buddy-buddy with all the NCAA people, especially the football committee, headed by Asa Bushnell, commissioner of the Eastern Area, a very important man. It was more or less assumed that he would retain the rights for NBC. The only competition they saw was CBS.

To have any realistic prospects for success in the bidding, we had to make NBC think it was unopposed. Otherwise it could easily outbid us. So I told Moore, "Let's mentally go through the whole company and come up with the most innocuous fellow we can find, someone who could melt into the wallpaper."

We chose Stanton Frankle from the controller's office. I toyed with the notion of sending him to the bid meeting in a tuxedo so he might be mistaken for one of the waiters who served coffee. I discarded that because it was *too* deceitful.

Moore and I put together what we hoped was a reasonable bid. ABC's board approved it. Since our only chance was to surprise NBC, we didn't want any leaks. When we typed up the bid letter, we left the amount blank until the last minute, when we wrote it in longhand.

I told Frankle, "A limousine will be waiting for you in front of the ABC building. At one o'clock, go to the Manhattan Hotel on Eighth Avenue. Go upstairs and join the meeting. Keep your bid envelopes in an inside pocket. Linger in the background. Don't volunteer any information. If anybody asks who you are, tell the truth—but don't volunteer anything else.

"You will see a bald man who weighs about two hundred and twenty pounds, a very garrulous and outgoing fellow, whom everyone will know. That is Tom Gallery. When Asa Bushnell calls for the bid, you remain in the background. Do nothing.

"What will probably happen is that Gallery will look around to see if CBS is there. If they are not, he will bid his low envelope. Don't move until you see him put it on the table in front of the committee.

"The moment that envelope hits that table, you are to rise from wherever you have been making yourself obscure. You are to say, 'My name is Stanton Frankle; I represent the American Broadcasting Company, and here is our bid.' "

As Frankle tells it, when bids were asked for, Gallery looked around the room. CBS was not bidding. He selected an envelope from his pocket and laid it on the table.

Frankle, carrying two bids, came forward and laid the smaller of them on the table. The committee went a little berserk. They retired to a back room for about an hour. When they came out, someone announced that ABC had won.

❑ ❑ ❑

Around the time we acquired NCAA football, Ed saw a Kinescope pilot for a sports magazine show, "For Men Only." Ed decided the show wasn't right for ABC, but he liked the way it was put together. He asked to meet the producer, a young man who had produced shows for DuMont and NBC stations.

Ed liked him immediately and offered him a job. The fellow's name was Roone Arledge.

OTHER RECOLLECTIONS:
Roone Arledge

For several reasons I was determined to leave NBC, and coincidentally, in the space of a week I had five job offers. One was to go to Sports Programs, Inc., a rinky-dinky company with about six people. It operated out of a place on 42nd Street, which looked like a bookie joint.

In the spring of 1960, I took that job. Then the company became part of ABC. To show how far behind we were, ABC had obtained rights to several major sports events but later reneged on the deals. One was the Squaw Valley Winter Olympics in 1960. After ABC decided it couldn't sell the Games, Walter Cronkite and Walt Disney persuaded CBS to do it. Another deal ABC reneged on was the Sugar Bowl, which it had bought rights to for $5,000.

I came from NBC's local station in New York. I produced their most important program, but if I saw the station's general manager once a month, that was a lot. I had met General Sarnoff, but that was because my wife worked for him. Otherwise I never saw any of the top NBC people.

When I had been at ABC about a week, I had lunch with

Leonard. Right after that I went to a reception at a sales guy's apartment. Leonard showed up in blue jeans and a sweater. I thought to myself, This is a totally different place.

I had heard, "Don't ever go to ABC. You walk on eggs all the time. You don't know who your boss is. They're cutthroats, pirates. NBC is stable and safe."

At ABC there was a sense of adventure but also a sense of family. You didn't have to go through channels. There weren't all these elaborate offices. Leonard's office, and those of Ollie and Si, were tiny. The conference room was their lunch room, there was no executive dining room. I still had the sense from NBC of awe, so I didn't go wandering into Leonard's office. But it was not unusual to go to meetings there, or in Tom Moore's office. I can't imagine that happening at NBC or CBS in those days and at that level. It was part of what allowed us to cut through bureaucracy and get decisions made quickly.

After I accepted Ed's offer, I went to say good-bye to Bud Rukeyser at NBC, who now works for Grant Tinker. We had been in the Army together. Bud asked me what I was going to do over there.

Because there was somebody sitting in his office, I told Bud I really didn't know. Bud said, "It's fine, he's not going to say anything."

So I said ABC just got the NCAA football package, and I'd be producing it. The guy sitting there said, "What are you doing now?"

I said I produced and directed a local program with Shari Lewis and her puppets.

A few days later a trade publication called *Anny* ran a story that Roone Arledge was leaving NBC to produce and direct NCAA football.

That created an insurrection over at Gillette, because I had never done a sports program. Moore had to go up to Boston to see Gillette and personally disown me. He had to say I would have nothing to do with NCAA football.

So for about half of that summer I hired producers and directors for various sports packages that ABC had suddenly acquired. We were juggling the AFL, the NCAA, a bowling show, and boxing.

In midsummer it occurred to the people at ABC that they really had to do something different. People were raising questions about what they were going to do with the package. Tom was putting pressure on Ed Scherick.

I had shared many of my ideas about NCAA football with Ed. He came to the conclusion that I should become involved.

But ABC was very skittish about trying to get me onto the NCAA package. They'd told Gillette I was going to have nothing to do with it. It's not like I was a big star in this business. I came from a local station and was only twenty-nine years old.

Jack Lubell, a veteran of CBS, was scheduled to produce NCAA football. He refused to work with me. He said I knew nothing about remotes. The only one I had ever done was lighting the Christmas tree at Rockefeller Center.

So there was a shakeup. ABC decided I would produce NCAA football. To explain to a reluctant Gillette how we were going to do it, Ed asked me to write a memo on all I had planned.

I wrote out a concept. Essentially I said television had succeeded in bringing the game to the fan—but now we would bring the fan to the game.

Instead of just focusing on the action, we'll give viewers all the experiences they'd have if they were at the game. We would use all the technology we could find to show them what it's like to be there. We will show closeups. We'll show people in the stands. We'll humanize the participants. We'll use sideline cameras and hand-held cameras. And we will use sound in new ways, such as shotgun mikes to let the audience hear the actual sound of a football being kicked.

I said, in short, that we will add show business to sports. We will add elements of news coverage and entertainment to what had been the traditional coverage of sports. We will also add journalism. No one had ever done that. They were all afraid to.

Hand-held cameras were developed for political conventions. We began using them for sports. We developed slow motion, instant replays, color slow motion, freeze frames, superimpositions, blimp shots, and underwater shots. We were the first to put cameras in race cars and first to miniaturize cameras for ski jumpers' and skydivers' helmets.

All these innovations grew out of this desire to get people inside the game. To do things that before were only done in magazines and books by still photographers, or in motion pictures with carefully contrived practice sessions.

It all seems so basic today—but in 1960 this was brand new. Out of that memo came all the things that we later did on "Wide World of Sports" as well as "Monday Night Football."

Writing the memo took me about two hours. The ideas had been incubating in my head for years.

I first became fascinated with television's possibilities with sports around the time when the Giants lost the 1958 championship to the Colts—the NFL's first overtime championship game. Television was becoming important to sports because of the NFL, but particularly in New York where, for a time, being a Giants fan was almost a religion.

Around the same time, in 1954, Bob Reger and others started doing very insightful and visual things in *Sports Illustrated*. I liked that.

The NFL was very fortunate the team that people all fell in love with was in New York, which has all the big advertising agencies and television networks. This quickly led to astronomical fees for rights. Advertisers paid incredible sums. It might have happened someplace else, but it wouldn't have had the same impact as in New York.

About a year before that, I went to the Army–Notre Dame football game in Philadelphia with my first wife, who didn't care much about football. It was a very close game. In the last thirty seconds one team was lining up for a game-winning field goal. Then my wife borrowed my binoculars.

I thought, This is great, she's really into the game. I asked what she was looking at, and she said, "The Notre Dame band has gold tassels!"

She didn't give a damn about who won the football game. But she still loved the experience of being there. I realized there must be many people who don't care that much about sports. But if sports is to have the impact that it should have, it can't appeal only to hard-core fans who will watch anything.

When I first mentioned I was going to be in sports, everybody said, "You'll hate it. There's nothing creative you could possibly do. You just open up three cameras and cover a baseball game."

I said, "It's not really true." There are so many different aspects to sports. There is the physical beauty. That is true of the popular sports, but equally true of hundreds of lesser-known sports we ultimately brought to television.

Then there is the degree of excellence required in any confined arena. This is an artificial situation, specifically created to force greatness out of people. There is nothing divinely inspired about 100 yards of chalk stripes, or an eighth-mile cinder track, or the specific dimensions of a baseball diamond.

But once you put people in there with a clock that runs out or nine innings of play, it forces almost superhuman efforts. It creates conditions like war, but it is not war.

I also loved the historical sense and the romance of places I had never been. Ann Arbor, Michigan, or Palo Alto, California—magical places I'd heard about on radio. I thought this could be translated into a television experience.

Ultimately "Monday Night Football" was where we put this concept to the test. With NCAA football we had to involve other people—Gillette and the NCAA—and, of course, our concept was not something that sports purists automatically loved. Nor did our critics at the other two networks.

When I started producing the games, some called up the NCAA every other day to say, "This guy is going to destroy everything for everybody. He is shooting cheerleaders, ushers tearing tickets in half, people selling hot dogs, babies in strollers—and all this before the game starts."

And I was, because if you walk into Madison Square Garden for a basketball game, you don't focus your eyes on the court and ignore everything else. You watch the court when there is action, then you look around. You have a total sensory experience. What I did was attempt to capture what it was like to be there in person.

Watching a game in the rain is totally different from sitting there on a beautiful day. If it's raining, we want to see raindrops rolling down people's faces. Now the person at home can see what it is like to sit in the stands.

If you carry that a little further to the contest itself, television must personalize the players, so viewers know who they want to root for—or against.

Then we have to show how difficult it is to achieve whatever the athlete is trying to do. And how, in the athlete's own world, this is so important.

For a time, ABC broadcast the annual World Barrel Jumping Championships at Lake Placid, a little novelty on "Wide World of Sports."

Trying to break the seventeen-barrel barrier is as big an event in a barrel jumper's life as Hank Aaron breaking Babe Ruth's home-run record or Roger Bannister cracking the four-minute mile.

If you can get that across to people, make it possible for them to recognize how difficult it is, give them a sense of where it is happening, and a reason to want the person to succeed—or fail—then the viewer can become involved.

That is the hallmark of what we have done over the years at ABC Sports.

❑ ❑ ❑

One of the stations carrying our NCAA football was in Austin, Texas. The owners were Lyndon and Lady Bird Johnson. I knew them pretty well, going back to when Paramount Theatres had supported Lyndon in his first congressional election.

Long before Paramount was broken apart, we owned radio stations in New Orleans and in Alabama. After his election to the Senate, Lyndon Johnson bought a radio station in Austin. It was losing money when the Johnsons went in. There came a time when they asked me to help them turn it around.

I looked over their programming and found it basically sound. So I got in touch with J. Walter Thompson and a few other New York agencies and asked them to throw some advertising their way. Most did, and the station prospered. In time the Johnsons acquired a television station license.

When Johnson became President after Kennedy's assassination, our friendship continued. I had lunch with Lyndon at the White House from time to time. Once, arriving a few minutes early, he said, "Let's have a swim before lunch."

I said I liked to swim, but hadn't brought a bathing suit.

"Bathing suit? Who needs one?" said the President of the United States. We went skinnydipping in the White House pool.

Afterward we went up to his bedroom to talk privately. Johnson suffered from constipation, and complained about it endlessly. He went into the bathroom to sit on the toilet. I sat on a bedroom chair, and he sat on the can, and we carried on a face-to-face discussion through the open bathroom door.

He said, "You know, Leonard, I don't understand. They're always after me in the press about the fact I control that television station in Austin. You know, and I know, that it's in a blind trust, so I really don't have any control over it.

"But the Kennedys had a blind trust, and I know that Jack Kennedy and Bob Kennedy were very active in everything in it. They knew exactly what was going on. So I think the press has been very unfair to me on that."

Only one end of him was constipated, so he went on in that vein for quite a long time. Not knowing what to say, I just listened.

A few months later ABC's station relations people recommended we switch NCAA football away from Lyndon's station to a competitor which had been clearing several of our other programs.

Since the Johnsons' station carried very few ABC programs, if any, I approved the change. Almost as soon as Johnson's station manager got the word, Lyndon called me. "Leonard, you and I have been good friends for years," he said. "You can't do this to me. If you put that football on little UHF stations which don't broadcast very far, the public won't be able to see the games."

I said, "Mr. President, I appreciate what you're saying. But my understanding is that your station's not carrying any of our programs, or none to speak of. We should support any station, even a UHF, which carries our programs."

"Oh, I'm sure that we're doing better than what you say."

"Why don't you check into it, Mr. President?"

A few hours later he called back. "Well, Leonard, maybe it wasn't as good as I thought it was. But I've talked to my people, and we'll do some rethinking. We'll be clearing a lot of your programs. But I've got to have those football games."

In a few days he sent Clark Clifford, very soon to become Secretary of Defense but then just one of Lyndon's lawyers, to meet with our affiliate relations and network program people. Clifford went over the ratings books and said that the Johnsons would start taking more of our shows.

So we let him keep NCAA football, and, true to his word, Lyndon's station began clearing more of our programs.

I thought about reminding him how critical he'd been of the way the Kennedys ran their blind trust. Here he was, involving himself in the day-to-day management of a station that was supposedly in his own blind trust. But I didn't.

Soon after Roone Arledge came to ABC, he started pushing Frank Marx in Engineering to develop the hardware that would revolutionize television sports.

OTHER RECOLLECTIONS:
Roone Arledge

In the first year of NCAA football, we played videotape highlights of the first half at halftime. That was new. Later we began playing little highlight segments right after a particularly outstanding play. This would become known as "instant replay."

Around the same time, I was over in Japan and watched something in slow motion on film, nothing to do with sports at all. It occurred to me that if we could ever do that on tape, we could show if somebody stepped out of bounds, if someone was safe or out at a base. Or on a great run we could show who missed the tackle and who didn't.

Not long afterward I produced a boxing match in Los Angeles and met with Bob Trachinger, our West Coast engineer. I told him about my notion of somehow using slow motion to look at things again to see if something actually happened instead of having to wait for film to be processed.

He thought if we photographed a videcon (television) tube with another TV camera and then slowed that to half speed, we'd see a lot of things. We tried it, but it flickered too much.

We stole some money from various budgets, and Bob worked on solving that problem. He kept making it a little better, and I looked at it from time to time. We used it for the first time on Thanksgiving Day 1961, for a Texas vs. Texas A & M game.

It was a very dull game, 3 to 0 at halftime. Just to show we could do it, we ran the only score, a field goal, in slow motion. It flickered, but it was slow motion.

The following weekend we had Syracuse *v.* Boston College. I produced, Bill Bennington directed, and Curt Gowdy and Paul Christman announced.

Boston's quarterback, Jack Concannon, later played for the Chicago Bears. The most exciting play of the game was when he faded back to pass and couldn't find anyone open. He made a great run, about eighty yards, for a touchdown. We ran it back in slow motion at halftime. Watching this in the booth I saw the future open up.

If you watch a football game today, they all look pretty much alike. But in those days we were the only ones doing any of that.

NBC and CBS derided it. They had all the big events. They had a bureaucracy who had never thought in those terms. They said we were kids playing, that what we did detracted from the enjoyment of the game. It was sour grapes, but it was also mind-set.

❑ ❑ ❑

In 1959 Harry Wismer owned the New York Titans, an American Football League team. He had a severe drinking problem, and he said and did things no man in the public eye—and especially no one connected with professional sports—could expect the press to ignore. And so they really gave him the business. For a time he was one of the least popular men in New York, and that didn't help his football team one bit.

The AFL wanted to cash in on the growing popularity of televised football because they desperately needed to find more revenue—their teams played to half-empty stands. The league had approached NBC and CBS, but since they carried the NFL, they didn't want any trouble, so they said no.

Then Harry Hagerty at Metropolitan Life called to ask me to come over and talk about the AFL. Harry said, "The AFL will fold unless they can get on television, and the other networks won't touch them. What can you do about it?"

"I'm not sure it's readily salable, commercially," I replied. "But I would be willing to make a sliding scale deal, where a percentage of our sales go to the AFL. That way we're sharing the risk proportionally. If we sell 100 percent, I'm sure we'll both be happy. If we sell less, at least ABC won't have to bear big losses."

Hagerty agreed, and we worked out a deal for five years, with the right of first refusal thereafter. It took some time to build an audience, but Roone's innovations succeeded in attracting many new viewers. The league eventually prospered, attracting better players and coaches.

After a few years, Joe Foss, the AFL commissioner, called to say Wismer was selling out and the Titan franchise was available. "Since you really saved this league, we want to offer you the first opportunity to buy the team," he said.

"What kind of price are you talking about?"

"One million dollars."

"I'd like to think about it, Joe."

My feeling was I wanted to be free to bid on NFL games. I didn't want to limit ABC to having a secondary league—this was, of course, a few years before the leagues merged. I told my directors, "I still hope to get the NFL on ABC. I want to go first class in everything. If we owned an AFL franchise, that opportunity might not be available, because we might have a conflict of interest." They agreed.

A few days later Sonny Werblin called. Sonny, a top talent agent and head of MCA's New York office, was an old friend and we did a lot of business. Sonny represented Ed Sullivan, among many other show business greats.

Sonny said he was part of a small group, which included Leon Hess, an oilman and a member of ABC's board, which was buying the Titans. And he offered ABC the opportunity to join this group. I said we'd already been offered the whole team and had decided to pass.

OTHER RECOLLECTIONS:
Sonny Werblin

The Titans were not a very successful team, and so it was not a strong franchise. I was able to get into this personally only because the package wasn't worth very much. But New York is the biggest market in any sport, and with television I thought they had a chance.

I didn't much like the name "Titans," so I engaged the J. Walter Thompson advertising agency to find a better one. They held a contest, which produced a list of eighty-seven suggested names. Scanning this, it occurred to me that our stadium was between La Guardia and Kennedy. The jet plane was just coming into vogue then, and I could see no better name than the Jets.

I was born on St. Patrick's Day, and green is my favorite color, so we changed the team colors to green and white.

❑ ❑ ❑

Sonny changed more than the team's name and colors. He recruited Broadway Joe Namath from Alabama, a marvelous athlete and one of the most colorful men who ever put on a uniform. Joe personified the Jets, and all New York fell in love with the team.

ABC kept the AFL alive and prospering through five seasons. We had the right of first refusal to renew in 1965. When I learned that NBC had offered $35 million, several times what we had paid, I decided that for this kind of money we could go first class and acquire NFL rights. My board saw things the same way, and we said good-bye to the AFL.

In 1970 the AFL and NFL merged. In hindsight, we might have done well keeping the AFL. But at the time, with far fewer affiliates than either CBS and NBC, we couldn't afford to bid for rights to a league we had helped make competitive with the NFL. In a sense we were the victims of our own success.

With NCAA football, "Friday Night Fights," a weekly baseball game, and the American Football League, ABC needed its own sports department. We created it with a stroke of the pen by buying Ed Scherick's company. Ed and all his people became part of ABC, with Ed coming in as network VP for Sales.

In early 1961 Tom Moore and Ed Scherick came to see me to propose a one-hour show for Saturday afternoons which would present different sporting events from all over the world. They talked about soccer matches from England, alpine skiing from Switzerland, bicycle races from Italy, Formula One races from France, golf from Scotland, and so forth. Video tape was still in its infancy, and there were as yet no commercial communications satellites. Everything would have to be filmed, then airfreighted to New York for editing.

I thought it was the screwiest idea I'd ever heard. Why, I asked, would people want to watch a race or a football game that was a week old, or more, and the results long known?

Ed was very persuasive. His idea was to show sports that few Americans followed regularly—events whose outcome might well be unknown in this country to all but a few diehard fans. It would be a way of introducing sports enthusiasts to things they'd otherwise never get a chance to see.

I still thought they were crazy. But I've never considered myself infallible, and both Ed and Tom were very excited about this. I said I'd be willing to give them a chance. We'd put on "ABC's Wide World of Sports" for six months, as a trial.

As the six-month trial period drew to a close, we still had few advertisers for "Wide World," but Ed was convinced the show had great potential. He and Tom Moore asked for another thirty days. I gave them the additional month.

When Ollie left and Tom Moore became head of the network, Ed Scherick, who had moved over to sales, asked to take over programming. I thought this was a little strange, since he had come into ABC to work in sports. But I gave him the opportunity to prove himself, and he was much more than competent.

Ed recommended we put Roone Arledge in to head sports. That was one of the best things that ever happened to ABC.

OTHER RECOLLECTIONS:
Roone Arledge

We had a great deal of trouble trying to get "Wide World of Sports" on the air in the first place. Everybody thought it was a semicrazy idea.

I went to see Scherick in sales and told him that we were in great trouble. I feared we would lose this program. We had thirty-day options on event rights; if we postponed the show, CBS, which had been nosing around, might come in and get them away from us. Then we would never get it on the air.

It was a month before our scheduled debut. Ollie Treyz finally said that if, by the close of business Friday afternoon, it wasn't half-sold, that was the end of the program.

NCAA football had become a very hot package and had four advertisers. One was L & M cigarettes. Then they changed ad agencies. Like all new agencies, they wanted to show they were different. So they canceled their quarter of NCAA football. Everybody immediately wanted it.

A quarter of "Wide World of Sports" was already sold to Gillette. Two tobacco companies wanted that last quarter of NCAA football. Ed told them that whoever bought a quarter of "Wide World of Sports" could have the football.

I was in Ed's office on the final Friday afternoon when he took a call from Brown & Williamson Tobacco. They said they didn't want "Wide World of Sports" at all, but would take an eighth of it if they could get the quarter of NCAA.

Ed talked to Ollie. Ollie wanted to take it because he had been through all this stuff of losing advertisers, and he didn't care that much about our program anyway.

I said, "We can't do that."

And to Ed's everlasting credit, he said, "I know. We are not going to take it. Let's wait and see if anyone else calls."

A few minutes before 5, R. J. Reynolds called and said, "We don't want it, but dammit, we'll take a quarter of your sports show if it's the only way to get NCAA football." That's how close we came to never getting it on the air.

All of a sudden we had one month to get it ready. We had no announcer. We had only options on events, no deals consummated.

We hadn't done any surveys. We had to get directors and producers. In the middle of all that I wrote the show's opening, "Spanning the globe . . ." and "The thrill of victory, and the agony of defeat . . ."

We went through the summer, then off in the fall for football. At first we were mildly received. That changed when we went to Russia. No one had ever done that in sports.

There was a big element of adventure in going to Russia. We played up being behind the Iron Curtain. And we presented what then was a classic confrontation: the U.S.–Soviet track meet. These competitions were like Dodger–Giant baseball games—a special electricity always in the air.

Ampex had just developed video tape recorders and didn't like us taking the equipment into the Soviet Union. They worried about the Soviets stealing the technology. So every night we locked the tape heads in a vault at the U.S. embassy.

Our last event that summer was an AFL practice game where we put microphones on quarterbacks. We positioned cameras to look into the huddle. You could see the huddle, the quarterback talking, and the players talking about the play. We used radio mikes, and they got jarred pretty badly when the quarterback hit the turf.

We had to be very careful then about language. So we did everything on a few seconds delay. As the team walked up to the line of scrimmage you could still hear them in the huddle, talking about what they were going to do.

But it was interesting enough that Red Smith wrote an article about it. People started to notice different things. When we came back on the air in the winter of 1961, "Wide World of Sports" became a hit immediately. Football season was over, and there weren't all the sports that are on now. It was clear then that this was a program that would last.

❑ ❑ ❑

After a few years of "Wide World of Sports," practical video recording devices became widely available. Commercial communications satellites came along a few years later and allowed quick transmission of pictures and sound. Programs were broadcast live or taped, edited, and shown within days.

And this began to attract interest overseas. Once, while visiting England, I was summoned to Windsor Castle to see the Queen, who wanted to talk about how the American public would perceive Prince Charles's investiture as Prince of Wales. Then Prince Philip, an avid horseman, asked me why "Wide World of Sports" didn't carry more polo. He thought Americans would be very interested in the sport. I had to explain that Americans, except for Harvey Firestone and his friends, just don't follow polo.

"Wide World of Sports" is still on the air. In recent years NBC and CBS put on similar shows, so the genre is much more competitive. And the prices we pay for rights to once-obscure sports events are far higher.

"Wide World of Sports" was tremendously important to ABC because, until it succeeded, our sports image was one-dimensional: football. There were still many who recalled our fiascos with Squaw Valley and the Sugar Bowl.

Even more important to ABC's future, "Wide World of Sports" became a training ground for our future success in covering the Olympics. This is where our technicians developed the hardware and techniques they would later use to show worldwide audiences the beauty and challenge of Olympic sports.

CBS turned down the 1964 Olympics in Innsbruck, Austria, because they didn't think they could find enough advertising support. The Olympics Committee came to us. Initially, we passed—it seemed like too much money—but when no one else was ready to step in, we reconsidered. We paid $650,000 for rights, which did not include European distribution.

Since ABC had reneged on Squaw Valley, and since we were still a question mark to the financial community, we had to put front money into what amounted to an escrow account. They just didn't trust us.

Our broadcast of the 1964 Winter Olympics became the foundation of our network's hard-earned identity with sports. ABC Sports transformed the Olympic Games from events of mild interest outside the locale where they were staged to colorful, major-league spectacles enjoyed by hundreds of millions of people around the world.

It would be impossible to overstate the contribution made to sports telecasting by Julie Barnathan, who in the mid 1960s became head of Broadcast Operations & Engineering. Julie is the sort of fellow who always thinks months and years ahead of everyone else. When he started looking at the problems we might encounter trying to televise sports action on snow-covered mountains or mile-long golf courses, he'd bring them to our attention. Invariably we'd turn around and ask him to provide solutions. He always came through.

OTHER RECOLLECTIONS:
Julius Barnathan

The impetus for many of our developments was "Wide World of Sports." When we went to Grenoble and I saw what we had to do in alpine events, it was a nightmare. Terrible. Nobody could appreciate how difficult that was.

Our old camera cables were almost 3 inches thick and held eighty-two different wires. They could not withstand extremes of temperature, and they were unreliable. The cables came in sections 200 feet long. We couldn't go longer because they were so heavy a man couldn't carry more than that. The farthest you could go was 2,000 feet.

No matter what kind of sleeve we put on to protect junctions, water would get in and short-circuit. So you had to go up the mountain to replace equipment, and you needed people who knew how to ski, you needed a rack truck, Sno-Cats.

We developed a multiplexing system, and sent all those signals down a single cable less than half an inch thick. This extended the distance we could cable up to 15,000 feet. That allowed us to do golf matches, and to go to the tops of mountains for downhill skiing, bobsled, toboggan, all that.

Then we convinced Ampex to build us the first color slow-motion device. We put up some of the development money, and Max Berry went out to the Coast and worked with them. Then we got them to build a hand-held model. Then, in 1967, wireless microphones and wireless cameras.

We had hand-held color cameras and slow motion for the 1968 Olympics. Viewers just went crazy because nobody had seen anything like that.

❑ ❑ ❑

One of the unsung heroes of ABC Sports is a congenial man named Marvin Bader. After joining WBKB, Chicago, as a camera operator in 1951, he became the logistical genius who planned and supervised the enormous support system underpinning ABC's coverage of the Games. Through more than two decades and ten Olympics, Bader worked full-time to bring the drama, suspense, and spectacle of the Games into living rooms around the world. A tough and often thankless job, he did it very well.

OTHER RECOLLECTIONS:
Marvin Bader

ABC was a mom-and-pop company. We took a lot of needling from other guys in the industry. They joked about us, "Put the Vietnam War on ABC, in thirteen weeks it'll get canceled."

Leonard and Si Siegel built this company. In the early days our accounting department couldn't buy a calculator unless Si approved it, personally. And we couldn't hire anybody unless it went through Si. But it didn't bother anybody. We were lean but not mean. Everyone knew everyone else in this company.

I was the only one who did Olympics year to year. The others went back to doing football and baseball or whatever else we did. Thank God for Leonard and his pocketbook. He was the one who took the chances on buying the Olympic Games. Leonard gave me my career for twenty-five years.

If ABC Sports was an army, I'd be the quartermaster. In the army, riflemen get all the medals, the credit, the glory. You never saw John Wayne play a motorpool sergeant or a company clerk. He never played a quartermaster. He carried a rifle. He was the hero. George Patton ran out of gas at the Rhine, and had to stop until his quartermaster gave him some more. But you never hear about quartermasters.

That's what we do. We're the guys behind the scenes. I break a job down into manageable pieces, get the best people I can to manage the pieces, and watch what they are doing. Logistics is just planning. It's not brain surgery—if you are organized.

The biggest Olympics we ever did was Los Angeles. We brought 5,000 people. We had 2,360 hotel rooms in twenty-eight hotels. There were almost 2,900 people at the venues. Not counting motorcycles, mobile units, and tractor-trailers, it took 1,016 vehicles ranging from compact cars to trucks to move these 5,000 around every day over 4,500 square miles. I lost a lot of sleep over that.

But I had great people. Everybody working for me was terrific—or they didn't stay. But they did it. They were the best.

Every game I did was terrific in one way or another. Leonard and the powers-that-be allowed me to do my job. Nobody messed with me, or questioned my budgets or the monies I spent. I was allowed to do what needed to be done. I don't think there is another company in the world that would have let me do some of the things I was allowed to do.

❑ ❑ ❑

In 1972, ABC Sports went to Munich to cover what became the most horrifying chapter in Olympics history. Palestinian terrorists invaded the Olympic Village and took the Israeli team hostage. ABC Sports suddenly became a news organization. Everyone rose to the occasion magnificently.

OTHER RECOLLECTIONS:
Marvin Bader

At 7 A.M. I was in a barber chair getting my hair shampooed at the Munich Sheraton. One of our engineers, Jacques Lesgards, called me. He said, "You better get out here. Something is going on. I hear shots."

So I wipe off my head and grab my jacket and bag. The barber thought I was wacko. I speed to the broadcast center, and bit by bit, we find out what is happening.

I knew that if something really big was going down, the authorities would close the village. So I started handing out walkie-talkies and getting people into the village. Anybody I could grab.

I called John Wilcox, the guy who produced "Up Close and Personal," and his production manager, Tony Brown. I said, "Find your crews and get them over here."

I called New York and told somebody in News to order up a satellite channel.

I called Roone's hotel room. His daughter answered and said I better not wake him. I said, "I think you'd better." I gave him what I knew.

He said, "Find Cosell, find Peter Jennings and Jim McKay." We got Peter into the village.

When we found Jim McKay, he was taking a swim in the pool with his wife. This was an off-day for him, because there was no track and field.

He came in wearing a wet bathing suit under his clothes and stayed on the air for fourteen hours, straight through without a break.

From our broadcast center we could see the balcony where

one of the terrorists, in a white hat, talked to the German authorities. Throughout the day I sat next to McKay, coordinating logistics.

We went from "Wide World of Sports" to "Mission Impossible." There was an ice-cream truck sitting next to our broadcast center. Jacques bought their signs and put them on our electronic newsgathering unit—a minivan that carries cameras. The signs were paper, and he just pasted them on our truck. Jacques found a back entrance and took the truck into the village. We knew damned well if it said ABC or television they wouldn't let us in. But they let an ice-cream truck in. Go figure that one.

One of my people, a young woman, bought a uniform from a hostess and went in with tape stock, film, food and soft drinks.

Another guy, red hair and freckles, a face like the map of Ireland, conned a Pakistani athlete out of his uniform. The Germans took one look and said, "Wait a minute." He got arrested three times. He'd get thrown out of the village and go back again.

Nobody could have done what McKay did that day. At the very end, exhausted, almost in tears, McKay said, "They're all dead." He was incredible, mind-boggling, touching. When I look at the tapes, it still shakes me up.

❑ ❑ ❑

Even by 1972 there were few communications satellites. ABC had booked some time on one, and as the hostage story unfolded, we sent pictures and sound back to our network. We had an exclusive, but of course CBS and NBC kept asking for access to our feed. They were dealing with one of ABC's midmanagement types in New York, and this fellow let his loyalty to ABC get in front of his broadcaster's obligation to the public interest. He refused to share with CBS and NBC.

But as the day wore on, CBS's turn on the satellite was coming up. They offered to relinquish it to us, if we'd share our feed. Our man in New York again said no, and we lost the satellite to CBS. In place of the breaking news story in Munich, they televised an English soccer match. I suppose they were trying to make a point, because I doubt if anyone in America watched that soccer.

While all this was going on, Isabelle, uncharacteristically quiet as a church mouse, sat in the broadcast center control room and watched. I was supine in my hotel room with a high fever when somebody knocked on the door and asked me what to do about sharing with the other networks.

I said I thought it was wrong to keep it exclusive to ABC. It was imperative that we get the continuing story through to the American public, and the best way to do that would be to share our feed with the other networks. I let Roone handle the arrangements, and drifted back into a feverish slumber.

OTHER RECOLLECTIONS:
Roone Arledge

When you televise in Europe, you never get enough sleep because you're always covering live events and airing complete broadcasts five or six hours later. I had two of my children with me and was trying to spend time with them in the mornings. But I didn't get to bed till 4:30 or 5 every morning.

Three days in a row I was awakened by the telephone. Somebody in Arkansas complained that their local station was not carrying the Olympics one day because they had an Arkansas Travelers' baseball game. I'd like to know how they found me.

Then Bing Crosby called. "Hello, Roone, boo, boo, be doo." I thought somebody was putting me on. I was in no mood for it. But it really was Bing. He wanted tickets to Mark Spitz's seventh gold medal race that night. I told my daughters that except for emergencies, I was not available until 9, when we had breakfast.

Every night after we went off the air, we had a production meeting about our plans for the next day. The night before the terrorists struck, we got off the air at 4 A.M. The meeting went till about 4:30, everybody left, and I was alone in the broadcast center. A German driver was waiting for me outside. I went back to my office for some mail that had come in from the States and to get some things ready for the next day. So I stayed for another ten or fifteen minutes and then went outside.

I was in a little parking area just outside the broadcast center. There was a gorgeous moon, and the lights were on in the stadium. The Olympic Village was just next door, and I told the driver that it was such a lovely sight, we ought to stand here and enjoy this for a moment.

We got in the car, and as we turned around, the headlights swept across a grassy area in front of the fence around the Olympic village. Between the car and the fence, the ground sloped off into a little ravine and then rose again.

I later learned this was the exact spot where the terrorists climbed over the fence. This occurred within five or ten minutes of the time I had finally left the broadcast center.

So the terrorists must have been down there in that ravine, less than fifty yards away, while we were standing there looking at the moon.

These were guys wearing hoods, carrying automatic weapons, and getting ready to go over a fence and kidnap the Israeli athletes. I've often thought that if, for some reason, we had wandered over there, we would have been killed.

❑ ❑ ❑

ABC Sports was associated with all but four Olympics after 1964. We passed on the 1972 Winter Games in Sapporo, Japan, and Summer Olympics in Tokyo (1964), the Soviet Union (1980), and Seoul (1988).

ABC's last Olympic participation was the 1988 Calgary Games, for which we paid a record $309 million. Long before we arrived in Calgary, however, it was apparent that many in the international Olympic community had allowed greed to overpower common sense. They were killing the goose that lays the very golden eggs that have sustained them for decades.

We decided against bidding for the 1988 Summer Games. The political situation in Korea was too unstable to risk the huge sums the Koreans demanded. NBC met their price, and lost a bundle on the package, despite respectable ratings.

Before "Wide World of Sports" and ABC's presentations of the Olympic Games, few Americans were more than slightly acquainted with the bulk of Olympic sports. For example, educating viewers to the nuances and subtleties of gymnastics did more for this sport than anything previously attempted. There's little question that our coverage of gymnastics on "Wide World" and of Olga Korbut in the 1972 and Nadia Comaneci in the 1976 Olympics encouraged an entire generation of young American women to take up gymnastics.

I would also wager that exposing mass audiences to this and other sports—especially women's sports—helped raise public consciousness about physical fitness in general. It cannot be an accident that our "Wide World of Sports" coverage of track events and our Olympic decathlon and marathon racing broadcasts coincided with the running boom in this country.

And I believe ABC Sports played a major role in getting American women more involved in sports and fitness. Until we televised the U.S.–Soviet track meet in 1961, no one paid much attention to women's track and field events. Aside from those involved in figure skating, golf, tennis, and, to a small degree, swimming, only a handful of American women pursued sports. Women were never seen sweating. They rarely demonstrated muscular dexterity in public. It was considered unfeminine. All that changed in the 1960s and 1970s. American women began looking at their bodies in entirely new ways. They began to admire athletic skill and fitness. I believe ABC Sports led the way.

The same sort of thinking that made "Wide World of Sports" and the quadrennial presentations of the Olympics went into the creation of "Monday Night Football." Many people, including some at ABC, believed there was little chance a football game in prime time could succeed, especially on a Monday night.

The original idea came from Pete Rozelle, commissioner of the NFL. For years he'd tried to get networks to carry games in prime time. Few people will recall this, but NBC did telecast a few NFL exhibition games in prime time, during the 1960s. From the standpoint of ratings, they were a disaster.

Some sages said wives would never allow their husbands to watch yet another game on a Monday night after they had spent all of Saturday and Sunday watching college and NFL football.

Others maintained that we couldn't depend on finding a game every week that pitted teams of championship quality against each other, or that was important to league standings.

The fact was that even with a great matchup of traditional rivals, or a game to decide division leadership, we still couldn't guarantee the game wouldn't be a one-sided rout.

Moreover—and this is the most important reason the other networks refused to consider putting football on during prime time—*any* program in the 9:00 slot would be competing with some of the strongest programs either network could present.

When "Monday Night Football" kicked off in the fall of 1970, it was up against Bob Hope or "Movie of the Week" on NBC and a lineup of CBS's successful comedies: Andy Griffith and Don Knotts (on "Mayberry R.F.D."), Doris Day, and Carol Burnett.

Roone's challenge was to find a way to keep people involved in the game no matter what. And the way he went about this was to add one more ingredient to a mix that had already begun to revolutionize sports.

That ingredient was a loquacious, opinionated, often argumentative man with an encyclopedic memory and virtually total recall.

Howard Cosell came to ABC shortly after the merger. He has a brilliant mind and graduated from law school while still in his teens. A sports buff, he was the lawyer who handled all the details for the original incorporation of Little League Baseball. And he can talk about anything.

OTHER RECOLLECTIONS:
Howard Cosell

While I'm proud of my achievements, my role in the company's development, I've always regarded Leonard and Si Siegel as virtual fathers. I wouldn't be anything without them. They took to me, believed in me, felt I was very bright.

I was the attorney for Little League. I got a call one day in 1953 from an executive at ABC Radio asking if I would do a Little League Saturday morning show with a panel of Little Leaguers. As a hobby. No pay.

I brought in the greatest stars of the sports firmament. The Little Leaguers questioned them. Their answers were often written up in the newspapers. We stayed on the air for six years.

My first director on that Little League show was a big gambler, always borrowing money from people all over the country—which finally got him fired. Then I got him a job as a janitor in a Stamford, Connecticut, theater. That led him into becoming an actor. He did very well in the profession. His name is Telly Savalas.

After a time, ABC offered me a whole series of radio shows. I discussed it with my wife and decided to leave the law profession. I loved broadcasting, loved the immediacy of it. I agreed to do the shows and finally get paid.

In 1956 John Charles Daly was head of ABC News. He put me on television, the first national television nightly sports show and the only one in the history of this country. I went back-to-back with John, fifteen minutes of news and fifteen of me.

In 1969 I was having lunch in a restaurant, Jimmy Weston's, when I was paged. It was Roone. He wanted to talk about "Monday Night Football," which we had just signed. Rozelle has always contended it was he who recommended me to Roone. I think Roone had made up his mind about me long before that. He had started using me on "Wide World of Sports" and on boxing. Roone Arledge is a brilliant man. A goddam genius if you want to know the truth. Were there major personal differences between us through the years? Of course. But I never discounted him. I didn't agree with many of his judgments, which was my right, and I told him how I felt. He had the option of firing me at any time. But he never did. He was too smart for that.

He knew the dimension I could bring to a telecast because of my mentality. And he knew it would be a different and enduring dimension.

Then in 1972 at Munich. I'll never forget Roone saying to me, "Do you want to go in the studio?" I said, "No, I'm emotionally undone." I could see this happening. I had grave misgivings about even coming to this country. "No, I don't want to go on. This is a place to use McKay."

I am Jewish, brought up in Brooklyn, through the Depression. The age of Hitler. I have all the Jewish insecurities normally attached to such a person. Unquestionably a better spot for McKay than for Cosell. And McKay proved to be exactly right. He gave the finest performance I've ever seen.

❑ ❑ ❑

When we got "Monday Night Football," Roone elected to put Howard, Keith Jackson, and Don Meredith on as a team. It seemed a very odd mix, but Roone knew exactly what he was doing.

OTHER RECOLLECTIONS:
Roone Arledge

Our affiliates opposed "Monday Night Football" from the beginning. They thought we would be giving up the NCAA in all the markets away from the major cities. So it was clear we were going to have to find a way to make this different.

Also, we were the first and for a long time the only people who would not allow organizers to tell us who the announcers should be. The classic example is when the Masters Golf people made CBS fire Jack Whitaker because he called the crowd there a mob. CBS had to go along because the Masters had announcer approval in their contract.

When I first met Howard Cosell, I was surprised that all the top athletes seemed to know him. He seemed to have great credibility with them, which came from his own persona. So he would always get the best guests on his program and always get the right interview, the main story.

He worked for a poor stepsister of a network, which did not have much clout, and for Howard to get these people on the air with such regularity was extraordinary. I finally put him on a baseball show, and he was very, very good.

I got him to do some boxing. At first everybody screamed and yelled and said he didn't know anything about boxing—just like they later would scream he didn't know anything about football.

The 1968 Olympics, in Mexico City, is where he first became controversial. Tommy Smith and John Carlos gave Black Power salutes when they were awarded their medals. Howard covered all that. He interviewed them. Many people didn't think we should have them on the air. We put them on anyway. Then came the Ali years when he was so close to Ali. Many thought Ali was a traitor and draft dodger, not to mention a Black Muslim, and Howard was in the middle of all that.

For "Monday Night Football" I wanted another ingredient. The things Howard could do would add a touch of journalism, controversy, excitement, and interest. He was the first person I hired, but he was neither a play-by-play announcer nor an expert commentator in the sense of being a former athlete or coach. So, to accommodate him, I had three announcers instead of two. Nobody had ever done that.

I wanted to change the role of the play-by-play man. Make him less important. Instead of having a golden-throated, play-by-play man, with a color man who came in every now and then, the real act would be Howard and X. The play-by-play man would be like a stadium announcer and give the downs, how much time to go, substitutions, injuries, and the score.

I had made a run at Curt Gowdy and Vin Scully, but Curt couldn't get out of his contract, and Vin didn't want to travel. We couldn't use Chris Schenkel because he was doing college football, and I had promised the NCAA I wouldn't steal from their package. They were furious at us for doing "Monday Night Football" games anyway.

I had been trying to get Frank Gifford away from CBS for quite a while, but he had a year to go on his contract. He's a close friend of Pete Rozelle, and so he knew all about our plans. When we flew down to Augusta for the Masters—Frank was going to do the opening—he told me he would rather be on this package than anything he could think of.

I told Frank I wanted somebody who would be irreverent, a counter to Howard, someone just recently out of football, but particularly somebody with humor. I was tired of hearing the NFL treated like it took place in a cathedral. It's a football game. I wanted people to have fun.

Frank said, "The guy you ought to get, a man who really needs a job, is Don Meredith."

Don had recently retired from pro football, had been unable to find the right job in broadcasting, and was unhappily pursuing a career in insurance.

Frank arranged a lunch for the three of us and then left early. Don and I sat and talked. He was funny and irreverent, and I came to the conclusion right off that he was the guy. I hired him right then and paid him more than I had intended. I said, "You just had a ten-thousand-dollar lunch."

Don said, "It's the best money you'll ever spend." It was.

With Don and Howard aboard, I now wanted an announcer who would fit in in a different way. Keith Jackson was very good, but had been doing primarily regional NCAA games. I hired him with the idea that he would change style, become short-spoken and succinct. He would give information and the other two would entertain and inform.

The first few games were only a little rough. The third game of the season was St. Louis at Dallas. They were very strong rivals. I told Don Meredith that I wanted him to get much more anecdotal. I said, "You played with the Cowboys a year ago, so you know all these players. I want to hear stories. I want it amusing, and I want you to be a country boy who does what you do."

We were up against a good movie and a Johnny Carson special on NBC, plus the usual heavy stuff on CBS. Our game ended up 33 to 0, St. Louis. With everything going wrong for the home team, the Dallas crowd was sullen. Altogether it was the worst possible conditions you can imagine. Instead of merely telling anecdotes, as the game wore on Howard and Keith taunted Don. The longer things went badly for the Cowboys, the funnier Don became. He was moaning and groaning. For the first time he was just being himself. Everything jelled, and the show became a hit, with a 38 share of audience.

I've always believed that when you have a great game—the score is close, the outcome is important and meaningful, and great athletes are performing incredible feats—you can bring somebody in off the street, and they could announce it. But you really need talent in the booth when the situation is like it was in Dallas.

That game demonstrated to all the cynics that we could hold an audience with a lemon of a football game. It came from the chemistry between Howard and Don, and to a lesser extent Keith.

The next year I finally got Frank and brought him in to replace Keith. One reason for the change was that by this time it became apparent that Howard was going to deal with controversy, personalities, and journalism, while Don was going to be Don. That meant he was up-to-date some weeks and some weeks he wasn't. Half the time he didn't know who the players were, but he still was interesting and informative. I envisioned Frank as being a combination play-by-play and expert. I still wanted Howard and Don to be the act that they had become, but I thought adding Frank to it brought another dimension. Frank was the embodiment of class, and he was a bridge to the old NFL.

In addition to being very good and doing all that I asked of him, Frank is one of the few people in the world with an ego that could handle everything that went on in the booth. By the time he came aboard, the package had begun to attract huge crowds, and with them came the pressures from all our promotional hoopla.

Howard and Don both had the luxury of not saying anything if they didn't want to. Howard would get annoyed every now and then, and you wouldn't hear from him for a whole quarter. Or Don would be on the phone or something. Frank had to keep his sanity in the middle of all this, call the game, carry the telecast, lead to the commercials, get the promos in, be sure that the score and all the basic stuff got out to viewers, and at the same time contribute humor every once in a while. He had to be the catalyst to get these guys going, and sometimes he had to be the referee and step in when things had gone too far.

Frank's first ABC football game was the Hall of Fame game in Canton, Ohio. I picked it because it's low profile, a Saturday afternoon in August when people are not paying that much attention.

But suddenly the NFL decided to get Richard Nixon to dedicate the Hall of Fame. He came on a Friday night before the game, and we had to interview him, and the guy to do it was Frank.

So the very first thing he did for ABC, amidst these flashing lights and all the excitement attending the event, was interview the President of the United States. It was an augury of what was to come, the kinds of things which characterized our Monday nights. They became happenings, where the unexpected was typical.

There was an intensity to it. A large part of that was Howard and the chemistry among the three announcers. The novelty of nighttime. The way stadium lights reflect as halos from helmets. It was crowds that were proud to be on Monday night. It was players who were aware that everybody in the league was watching. It was astonishing what an institution "Monday Night Football" became.

❑ ❑ ❑

The first "Monday Night Football" telecast was September 21, 1970, from Cleveland. At the top of the show, Howard introduced Don. Roone had put together a "low-lights" film clip, a compendium of Don's worst moments as a Dallas Cowboys quarterback. As Howard sang Don's praises as an athlete, the audience watched him fumble hand-offs, throw interceptions, and slam into the turf under beefy linemen. Don, who wasn't told in advance, took it with his characteristic good humor. By the way, the Browns beat the Jets, 31–21.

The next morning I got a call from a sponsor, Henry Ford II, head of Ford Motors. "Take that guy Cosell off," he said. "He's hogging all the time. He and Don Meredith talk so much I can't enjoy the football game." I agreed to look into it.

I called Elton Rule, who had succeeded Tom Moore as head of the network in 1968, and Roone, and told them about Ford's call about Cosell.

Roone said, "Give me four or five weeks, I'll monitor it pretty closely. If Howard is hogging the mike, I'll cut him off. But I think we ought to give this a fair trial."

I agreed. I called Ford back, and told him, "We're going to give him a few weeks, and if at the end of that time, it's not working out, I'll get back to you." I made no promises.

Three weeks later Ford called me back. He said, "Leonard, I apologize, I really enjoy the patter that's going on between these two guys. I withdraw my objection."

Howard is very opinionated. Half the audience likes him; the other half hates him. But they all talk about him. I don't know how "Monday Night Football" would have succeeded without him.

Nor can I imagine the show without Frank Gifford, who, since he joined the program, has never missed a game. Together with Don Meredith, they made Monday nights magic.

OTHER RECOLLECTIONS:
Frank Gifford

When I came over from CBS, I immediately noticed how much more alive ABC was. It was on the move. We were doing things that no one else thought could be done. It wasn't always great, but we were able to roll the dice. Roone pretty much got carte blanche from Leonard.

We made sports entertaining. We created a special kind of postcard, and sent it back from wherever we were. That's the edge Roone has always had. He's brilliant at presenting something to an audience.

"Monday Night Football" changed American popular culture. It got so some restaurants started closing on Monday nights during football season. PTA meetings would be rescheduled because everybody was staying home to watch us.

That became part of our mystique. We'd go into a city, and it became a big celebration. In 1988, after Indianapolis got the Colts, we went in to do their first Monday night broadcast. They had a luncheon for us, and they gave us Indy 500 helmets. They passed out 60,000 Frank Gifford face masks. It was crazy, like going back to the early 1970s, when a whole culture developed around us.

What it did for ABC was allow us to concentrate on six nights of prime-time programming. For twenty years we've almost been able to forget about Monday night during the football season. And it's still one of the top-rated shows each week, still going strong.

Even when we get beat, we still hang in there with a 15, 16, 17 rating and dilute a very expensive piece of programming on the other networks. They know that even if they beat "Monday Night Football," they're going to get hurt. It's very expensive for them to do it. When we get a good billboard or the Bears playing the Giants or something like that, it kills whatever they've got.

Not only do we pick up many other kinds of viewers besides football fans, but the rest of the league, all the players, are watching.

The coaches watch. They use it as a way to scout, because they're coaching on Sunday and can't watch any of the other telecasts.

And the sportswriters who usually cover the Sunday games watch "Monday Night Football."

About 25 percent of our audience is women, which is remarkable. Many are wives. They're happy to have their husbands home with the kids watching it.

One of our continuing trademarks is that at the beginning of each game we create a storyline—conflict, suspense. "This team must do that, this team must do this." This is required because the audience includes people who don't follow it week to week except on Monday nights.

Not all of our Monday night games were memorable football. In fact, most of them weren't. But you only need a few, and every once in a while it would be like lightning in a bottle.

The best of all was in November 1978, in the Astrodome. The Oilers and Dolphins. Miami's great quarterback Bob Griese threw three touchdown passes. Every time Miami scored, Houston battled back, driving the length of the field, giving the ball to a rookie named Earl Campbell again and again. He ran for three touchdowns, but when it came down to the last few seconds, the Oilers were down 30 to 28 on their own 19-yard line.

They ran a sweep, and Campbell went eighty-one yards for a touchdown to win it. I don't even remember calling the game. We became part of it. It was great theater. You only have to see one of those to endure many more that aren't too good.

"Monday Night Football" is different now. Everything is different sociologically, too. We went on the air right at a time when this country was being torn apart. Cosell would make bizarre statements about bizarre things, or bizarre statements about real things and just drive people up the walls. Whether he was right or wrong, it was the way he did it, a pronouncement from on high. Sometimes Meredith would chop him right off at the crotch with "Come on, Howard, don't do that to me."

Throughout the 1970s and even today to a lesser degree, if you went to work and didn't talk about what happened on Monday night, you just weren't with it. I'd be walking down the street and people would ask me, "Was Don really pissed off at Howard?"

I'd say, "I don't think so." We never were.

All our problems came later when Don had left and come back and Howard wanted to leave. It's the biggest fishbowl in television. You get whacked whether you do it right or wrong, so you have to be fairly solid with yourself. Howard decided to leave because he was exhausted. He had to keep defending himself. People were always taking shots at him—in many cases wrongfully so.

We traveled so long and so hard. The repetition of doing it over and over is a grind. Don got to the point where he couldn't even go to the airport. For Don and Howard it became more show business than football. I think they both felt like, "What the hell am I going to do for my act next week?"

❑ ❑ ❑

"Monday Night Football" was very successful. It continued to grow until, in four or five years, NBC and CBS essentially stopped trying to compete and wrote off their Monday nights, filling them with the sort of movies and shows for which they entertained limited expectations.

The tremendous success of ABC Sports underpinned and supported the rest of the company for many years. People tuned to ABC for football games and "Wide World of Sports" and the Olympics, and they stayed to watch our other programs.

But times change. I may be all wet on this, but I believe the day is not far off when football, baseball, and other top sports, and perhaps even feature pictures, will be on a pay-per-view basis. This is because as costs continue to escalate, the three networks will no longer be able to retrieve that money through advertising alone. That may be ten or fifteen years down the line, and I may not be around to see it, but I think it has to happen. It's all but inevitable.

12

ABC International

❑

When I first went into television, my frame of reference was that of a theatrical exhibitor, and my model was Paramount, a company with extensive interests abroad. Paramount owned, usually with partners, theaters in Europe and Canada. It licensed technology to foreign exhibitors, and it sold picture distribution rights around the world.

So I felt that television, like motion pictures, would become a worldwide medium. Hence I set out to acquire partnerships in foreign television stations and to make foreign licensing agreements for our programming. My planning began before the development of satellites, so I envisioned several international networks, linked by cable.

I made no secret of these plans, and as usually happens, the word got round quickly. It happened that a young Australian, scion of a distinguished publishing family, came to hear of them. Not long after this young man graduated from Oxford, his father, Sir Keith Murdoch, head of the Melbourne *Herald*, died. Quite suddenly this man, still in his twenties, inherited a large share of News Limited, an Adelaide newspaper company that also owned a radio station. On his own, he picked up a few other newspapers. Then he wanted to get into television.

The young man's name was Rupert Murdoch, and in 1956 he came to New York for one day only, hoping to meet with people at all three networks. His first stop was ABC, where he called on our syndication department. The man in charge brought him over to see me.

Rupert was full of energy and bursting with ideas. I liked him immediately. After we chatted, I said I wanted to buy a piece of his company. He said, "Foreigners can only have fifteen percent. Perhaps I could let you have six percent."

"Whatever it is, I'll buy it." And I did.

OTHER RECOLLECTIONS:
Rupert Murdoch

We had just won the franchise for a TV station in Adelaide, the fourth-biggest city in Australia. Television was very new to Australia. NBC and British companies—suppliers—were after me. All wanted a piece of the television company. Leonard, too, was trying to get into worldwide television. He took me to lunch at Sardi's, he and I and Si Siegel.

It was a pleasant lunch. They said, "How about a share holding?" in what was then News Limited. This was our holding company, of which my family owned 45 percent. In a sense, it was a small, family company. My father had run a much bigger company, but this was his personal investment.

I was very attracted by their offer. Leonard later introduced me to one of his directors, John Coleman. He seemed to be a very nice fellow, too. So they bought some shares.

Some years later ABC were having struggling days, and they saw an opportunity for a good profit in selling their share back to us. Even so we've always remained very good friends.

After we first met, Leonard and Isabelle came out to see me, along with Don Coyle, a friend of mine who was at ABC, and his wife. They spent a couple of weeks with us in Australia. I took them around Sidney and Melbourne and to our little, tiny station in Adelaide. Then I took them to Alice Springs in the center of Australia, to Ayers Rock, and to Darwin. Then we went to Arnhem Land, up in Crocodile Dundee country. Leonard wouldn't shoot, but Isabelle shot a [water] buffalo. Wounded it, and our guide had to track it down and finish it off. We had a great time together those two weeks.

❑ ❑ ❑

More by accident than by design, ABC backed into international broadcasting just a few months after the merger with UPT. The biggest scheduled news event of the year was Queen Elizabeth's coronation on June 3, 1953. CBS and NBC had made costly arrangements. NBC even leased a special plane from the Venezuelan air force. They planned to rush film of the coronation by motorcycle to the London airport and develop it over the Atlantic. The plane would land at Boston, and their network would broadcast from Logan Airport. All that would cost over $1 million.

We were so desperately poor then that sending an international telegram required Si Siegel's permission. For $10,000, however, we arranged a special trunk line from Ottawa to Buffalo, New York. The Canadian Broadcasting Corporation agreed to provide us with a Kinescope broadcast of the BBC film. We would feed the network from our Buffalo affiliate.

NBC's plane was delayed by weather. Less than half an hour before broadcast time, NBC called Bob Lewine in our programming department and begged to copy our feed from Ottawa. Lewine said, "Sure, pay us $10,000 and it's all yours."

We went on the air at 4:14 P.M. with the first international television broadcast in history. NBC somehow missed the feed cue, and so began their network transmission several minutes later. CBS, which spent close to $1 million on their own arrangements, did not broadcast the coronation until later that day.

I was surprised to learn that neither CBS nor NBC had tried to establish a presence in Latin America, though they successfully sold programming around the world. I began to visit the capital cities of each Central American country, speaking to broadcasters and generally testing the water. We wanted minority positions in stations. Eventually we bought interests in four or five.

As our foreign interests grew, we set up a separate division to handle things. Si suggested Don Coyle to run it. A bright, extremely personable young Canadian, he began in Research, and later became VP and general manager of Sales. In 1959, he became the first president of ABC International.

OTHER RECOLLECTIONS:
Don Coyle

Leonard's thinking was based on the fact that the Owned and Operated (O&O) stations of all three U.S. networks were profitable. Actually, for years ABC's O&O's made more money than our network lost. So he thought there was a parallel. If we owned interests in stations abroad and could help make them profitable, we could expect part of the profits.

There were several things going against us. CBS was the number-1 network, and they were so strong that in dealing with any producer, they invariably got foreign rights for their shows. Their foreign syndication became a very important factor in dealing with stations abroad. This led them into deals where they acquired part ownership in certain stations.

NBC, as part of RCA, had a different point of view. RCA was in the equipment sales business. They were prepared to sit down with anyone anywhere and build a complete station. That led them to financing and in some cases to equity positions in foreign TV companies.

ABC had neither of these possibilities. So we approached it from the notion of building an international network. We hoped to convince people that their strength would be the strength of the network.

The prototype was Central America. A Costa Rican group—an engineer, a radio station owner, and the operator of a department store—had spoken to ABC's engineering department about helping to build a station in San José.

We put some money in and helped with technical advice and training. They spread the word to other Central American stations. Soon they were all asking to meet with us.

Each Central American country had at least one station. They were unable to get good product and didn't know how to sell, so all operated at a loss. They asked us to work with each of them. We responded with a proposal to form a network of Central American stations. They could program as a group and sell circulation larger than in any one country. In 1960 this became Cadena Centroamericana.

There were stations in Guatemala, Honduras, El Salvador, Nicaragua, and eventually in Panama and Costa Rica. When we put the Costa Rican station on the air, it joined the network. We financed the network and then traded off bits and pieces to each of the stations in exchange for part ownership. We ended up with 51 percent of the network and a piece of each station, except Nicaragua. We made no investment there because we were very concerned about the country's stability.

This worked so well that we developed a concept called Worldvision and applied it to stations all over the world.

We programmed Cadena's stations partly by buying programs for them as a group. This gave us far more buying power than any station going individually to CBS or NBC or a production company. We became their buying agent for programs not produced in their country.

We attempted to sell their air time to international advertisers as a group. In this way advertisers like Exxon or General Motors could get access to different parts of the world.

The TV network in Venezuela had gone bankrupt, and the workers took over the operation. At that time there was quite a strong Communist element in Venezuelan labor unions. The group running the station became very militant. After about five months the government decided that, to satisfy creditors, the network should be auctioned to the most competent and highest bidder.

I formed a group with some ad agency people to make a bid. We stipulated that if we could not take possession of the facility for any reason—because of labor unrest for example—our proposal would be void.

Our bid was highest, but because of the stipulation, a judge awarded the station to the second bidder, a partnership of Diego Cisneros and Goar Mestre.

Cisneros was the Pepsi-Cola king of Caracas, probably their biggest bottler. Mestre, a self-exiled Cuban married to an Argentine, was one of Latin American TV's major moguls.

A month or so later I had a call from our lawyer, Loraga. Would I talk to Cisneros about the facility, if he were to come to New York?

Diego came and said he just couldn't do business with Mestre. "He wants this, he wants that, he wants everything," he said. Mestre owned the top station in Buenos Aires. For political reasons, Argentina banned networks, so his channel was the country's leading station.

Mestre had his own ideas, among them how great it would be if Venezuela and Argentina joined in a network. But the Caracas facility had to be a Venezuelan operation. Diego asked ABC to go into a deal with him, because he had to get out of his arrangement with Mestre.

Cisneros was almost comical looking, very dark, with wispy hair. Short and squat, with a pot belly. Around Caracas it was whispered he was a *mestizo*. It might have been true.

But he was very astute and an interesting negotiator. When we sat down to work a deal out in New York, his suit jacket came off. Soon he took his cuff links off and rolled up his sleeves. He loved cigars, and asked if I minded if he smoked. When I didn't object, he lit up, filling the room with blue smoke. The longer we talked the more he undressed. His collar opened up and his tie came off. It was like a strip tease, almost, but not done as a distraction. He would hammer away at points he wanted to make, emphasizing each with the physical act of removing his clothing.

Diego got out of his deal with Mestre, and we formed a partnership. We got 35 percent, and put up the necessary money. It was a good arrangement.

We had to screen every employee. Some were very pro-Communist, and we had to try to keep them out. We let many people go. The National Guard established itself as facility security behind a Cyclone fence. They mounted machine guns on the roof.

Cisneros brought in some very astute people, as did we. I went down for a month or so, helping to train them, and we got off to a very good start.

Because of his clout with Pepsi-Cola, Diego arranged to have Joan Crawford, then married to Pepsi's president and herself vice president of public relations, attend the station's grand reopening. She conducted herself beautifully and made quite an impression.

Cisneros was a fine businessman. He got good people, we gave them know-how, and that really bucked up the facility. Before long, we were outrating the government station.

❑ ❑ ❑

In Argentina we had to deal with the Jesuits, which was fascinating but troublesome. A Jesuit, Father Grandinetti, had got the last license for Buenos Aires. He believed his station should be supported by as broad as possible a cross section of Argentine society. So he passed the plate, so to speak, seeking investments from everyone, a few pesos here and a few there. He really had no idea what it would cost to mount this project and then support it.

There was a terrible problem in doing business in Argentina then, and I don't suppose it's too different today. Few, if any, advertisers settled their accounts in less than nine months. So besides the investment required to build a facility, one had to have resources to operate that long before any cash flowed in.

Don met with Father Grandinetti to talk about our investing in his station. Don soon realized Grandinetti would be terribly difficult to deal with because he had no appreciation of television's commercial aspects. The station license was in the name of the church, but Grandinetti ran it as though it was his own. Finally we got his superior, Father Sojo—a far more business-minded person—involved. Sojo sat on Grandinetti, and we started to get a few major investors together. ABC wound up with around 25 percent of the package.

A semiretired gent from our Chicago station, Matt Veracker, looked after our Argentine interests. Every so often the Argentine military would revolt, and take over all the broadcasting stations. Don recalls talking to Veracker on the telephone and hearing strange sounds in the background.

"Matt, what's that noise?" asked Don.

"The tanks are rolling down the streets, and we're being invaded again."

It happened so often it became sort of a joke. Whenever the tanks rolled, the Air Force temporarily took over the station. The same group of airmen, whom the station came to know very well, always came in. Mostly they just sat around with their guns and did nothing for a few weeks. Sometimes the leader of the latest coup would make a speech, which everyone televised. There was much posturing, commercial activity fell off a bit, and then things went back to normal.

Eventually, the generals took over for good, and at that time they invited us to leave Argentina.

To a Norteamericano like myself, used to doing business with buttoned-down Madison Avenue M.B.A.'s, the tempo of Latin American business was often frustrating. Schedules were interpreted quite loosely. Deadlines were never final. But sometimes it was amusing, too.

For example, our Costa Rican partners didn't have enough money to build a new studio, so we got a warehouse beside a railroad track in San José. There was a train every afternoon, and as it chugged into town past the station, the engineer blew the whistle. That blast was heard for sixty miles on our broadcast. You could almost set your watch by it. So Coyle's people called the station "Tele Tica," since *tica* is local slang for a small locomotive. They used Tele Tica cartoons to promote the station. It worked very well for them.

In Guayaquil, the Ecuadorean seaport that ships most of the country's bananas, I visited a very unusual television station. The owner, a German Jewish refugee named Rosenberg, built it with his own hands, with a little help from his wife and kids. It was a fantastic, ramshackle building through which strolled all manner of livestock—chickens, goats, and pigs—clucking, bleating, and snorting. Recalling my horror upon first inspecting ABC's stations in 1951, I had to smile.

It was impossible to believe, but the equipment inside was first rate. The man had built it all himself, using a mail-order book as a guide. After surviving the Holocaust, he'd started in Ecuador by selling all sorts of goods in the street. Eventually he opened a store, and the profits went to building his dream television station.

We made most of our investments in Latin America, where commercial television was allowed to develop in much the same way as in North America. And, since their time zones were close to our own, if we ever got around to providing an international feed, that could become very important. And unlike Europe or Asia, the entire continent used only two languages, which simplified dubbing.

We became involved in every South American country except two. Paraguay was a dictatorship, virtually a police state, where all the media were under government control. Bolivia allowed free enterprise, but the country was so poor there was little hope of getting advertisers.

ABC was the only foreign company to make investments in Japan. After meeting with top management at the Asahi Shimbun and the Mainichi Press, each of whom were just starting in television, we made an agreement in principle to invest in NET, a Tokyo station, and MBS in Osaka. I sent Si Siegel and Don Coyle over to work out the details. They were very difficult and tedious negotiations that went on for weeks, though we took only 5 percent of each station.

Both stations were in the same network. It was the youngest and most aggressive, so in that regard these stations shared a common outlook with ABC. Part of the deal was an agreement to bring a few people over here and train them.

OTHER RECOLLECTIONS:
Don Coyle

When Kennedy was shot in Dallas, Jiro Maeda, a young man from Mainichi Television, came to my office to express his condolences. As we talked, I was struck by how affected he was. We all were, but it seemed strange to see this Japanese gentleman feeling so bad. He said, "Is there anything you can do to bring this event to Japan?"

At this point there were a few *non*synchronous satellites operating on an experimental basis only. I knew there was an opening on the satellite that would give us twelve minutes during which we could transmit to Japan.

We were still getting pictures out of Dallas from our affiliate, WFAA, and we had used several announcers to narrate these images over our network. But for Japan, I decided, we should do something different.

Jim Hagerty was then in charge of ABC public relations. When he was Eisenhower's press secretary, the President had sent him to Japan to determine if he should accept the Japanese government's offer of a state visit. Hagerty's car was stoned by an airport mob. He told Eisenhower the time was not right to go there.

Knowing this, and that the Japanese had lost a great deal of face when Eisenhower decided not to go to Japan, I called Jim and asked if he would be available to narrate over a few minutes of pictures about what was going on in Dallas.

Hagerty agreed, and AT&T let us use the satellite during a pass over the Pacific. There was, however, no audio capability, so I arranged to get telephone lines to Japan. I had Jiro Maeda watch a monitor as Hagerty spoke. We interspersed a head shot of Hagerty with footage out of Dallas. Maeda, on a telephone, translated Hagerty's comments. I had another line to Japan through which I could hear the narration coming through in Japanese.

This patchwork arrangement was the world's first satellite telecast. Because of this and because of the nature of the news, in twelve minutes Jiro Maeda became a national hero in Japan. They made him a vice president at MBS.

❑ ❑ ❑

On my way to China in 1972, I stopped in Hong Kong and met with Sir Run Run Shaw, the biggest filmmaker in the Far East. I've known him since my years at Paramount Pictures. When Run Run's son wanted to go to Harvard, we helped to get him in.

Paramount had a studio in Hong Kong before the war. Run Run was eight or ten years old and spoke no English when he began working there as a messenger. His boss would hand him some papers—a script or some invoices, whatever—and say, "Run, Run!" and he'd deliver it. So he became known as Run Run. As he became older, he went along to better things.

One day, his little brother, a few years younger, came along and asked for a job. He had no more English than Run Run. He said, "Run me, Run me." He got the job running errands, and became known as Run Me Shaw.

Run Me is now based in Singapore. Between them, the brothers control most of the motion picture production in the Far East. Run Run also dabbles in coproduction. One such film was *Blade Runner*, which did quite well in the United States.

We tried to make a deal with Run Run and Run Me, but they had no interest in television in those days.

Then we tried to get Channel 7 for a station in Hong Kong. We were dealing with the Postmaster General, and for a time it looked very promising. And then out of the blue, Ollie Treyz, who was working on this for me, learned there was no chance for us on Channel 7. The American Navy had objected, because they used that frequency for guided missiles. We then talked about a UHF station, but that is mountainous terrain, and the signal doesn't do very well there.

Equally important, the government required majority ownership by British subjects, and we would have had to put up a lot of money for a very small percentage.

There were two stations then, one owned by the British government, and the other by George Ho. He was half black, half Chinese, and reputedly the basis for Ian Fleming's villain in the James Bond book, *Dr. No*. Ho had interests in a cable system and a radio station. We talked to him, but it was a very difficult market. It was also so far away we would have to be on our toes always to ensure our partners didn't cook the books. So nothing came of it.

In the early 1960s we acquired a half interest in a group in Beirut that wanted to start a TV station. This was a very peaceful time, when Lebanon was a relaxed and lovely country. Don Coyle almost bought some land there because it was so delightful. There was then only one television station in all Lebanon. It was owned by the French government, and many of its programs were broadcast in French. So we thought that an Arabic-language station had possibilities.

We didn't anticipate that we were going to get rich on this station, however. The French channel operated with a considerable government subsidy, so we couldn't charge advertisers full market rates. But we thought there were still possibilities if we kept our investment around $700,000.

Unfortunately, our partners, a consortium of Greeks living in Lebanon, insisted on going first cabin. They put in red marble floors in the foyer and all kinds of things we didn't need. Our share of this palace came to $1.5 million.

The best-known Lebanese in the world then was undoubtedly Danny Thomas, because of "Make Room for Daddy." Just before the facility was ready, Don Coyle suggested that I ask Danny to come over and open it for us. He was happy to oblige.

Don went to General Foods, American sponsor of Danny's show, and got them to sponsor the program for broadcast in Beirut. Opening day was a mob scene. It looked like half of Lebanon turned out to welcome their prince, Danny Thomas.

Then we aired the first episode of "Make Room for Daddy." It was a disaster. The distributor, Screen Gems, was selling product to the other station and mistakenly assumed this program should be dubbed in French. But to Lebanese who came to see Danny Thomas, watching him on the screen speaking French was the worst blow possible. They were offended. We eventually got shows dubbed into Arabic, but by then, out of pride I suppose, hardly anyone would watch. After twenty-six weeks General Foods dropped their sponsorship. That really set us back.

We didn't have that many local sponsors, but oddly enough, a few were Israeli companies, including a gasoline retailer. Israel had no television at all then, yet there were about 10,000 Israelis in the northern part of the country who could receive television broadcasts from Beirut. So we sold time through ABC International in New York. It was all handled by telephone, and the Israelis paid their bills.

We eventually sold our Lebanese interests—at a nice profit—to Roy Lord Thompson, the Scottish media baron. He once said, "TV is merely a machine to make money." He didn't make any in Lebanon after he bought our half of the station.

What I really wanted to do in the Middle East was to set up a network spanning all the Arabic-speaking countries. Because the countries were fairly close together, two or three well-sited and very powerful transmitters could cover most of the region. Perhaps I was a little naive, but in the late 1950s I thought regional peace was a very real possibility. I thought that television could be an agent for peace, a way to open windows between these neighboring countries. I even thought that one day Israel might be part of this network, because there are many Arabic-speaking Israelis.

So I planned a trip to Beirut, and asked Don Coyle to arrange for representatives of various Middle Eastern countries to come there to meet me.

One of the people I sat down with in Beirut was the Emir al Sabah of Kuwait. We said we wanted to talk about establishing a television station in his country, as part of our network. He said, "I want to talk to you about a television set. I want to buy a solid gold television set."

We kept saying, "Well, we're not in the manufacturing business; we're only broadcasters." He wouldn't believe it. We never got anywhere. We never got to the question of a network. All he wanted was a solid gold TV set. And that's the way it ended. It's thirty-odd years later, and I still find the whole thing unbelievable.

From Beirut, Isabelle and I went to Jerusalem, by way of Cyprus, to see David Ben-Gurion, prime minister of Israel. We made an appointment, and after some pleasantries I said, "I've been to England to see Sir Isaac Wolfson and the Rothschilds. They're willing to finance the building of a television station in Israel."

Ben-Gurion said, "Television? I won't allow my people to watch television. They've got to work!"

"Well, Mr. Prime Minister, you have 10,000 sets in northern Israel right now, and they're watching Lebanese stations. In the Negev they watch Egyptian programs. Why wouldn't you have your own station?"

"Oh, no, I'm not going to let my people spend their time that way."

"I think you're kidding yourself," I replied.

I never got anywhere with him.

Israel had to wait many years before they put up their first TV station.

When Golda Meir became prime minister, we became friends. She used to come to New York two or three times a year, and on those occasions she was in the habit of visiting with Punch Sulzberger and his people at *The New York Times*, or Kay Graham and her people at *The Washington Post.*

I asked myself, "Why shouldn't she sit down with the broadcasting people as well?"

And so I arranged to see her in Israel. She came in a few minutes late, explaining she had been working all night to convince Moshe Dayan not to bolt the party. She finally convinced him.

I told her, "When you come to New York, why don't you speak to all the top media people? You may speak to the leading newspapers, but broadcasting reaches far more of the population. And magazines are important, too. I can arrange for all of them to come to lunch. You can tell your story and let us ask questions."

She agreed to think about it. Six weeks later she called from Israel and said, "I'll take you up on your offer."

From that time on, every time she came to New York, we arranged a luncheon in our fortieth-floor executive dining room, and invited the top people from the New York media to attend.

At one of those luncheons, shortly after OPEC had begun raising the price of oil and boycotting sales to the United States for its support of Israel, the head of Exxon got up and asked Golda a question. He said, "Mrs. Prime Minister, regarding this oil boycott, what would you do?"

She said, "I'm only the head of a very small country. But if I was the leader of the United States, I wouldn't let *any* country knock me around."

She said she'd take a very strong position with them and wouldn't let them dictate terms.

I got to know her fairly well. As a person, she was really very homey. I think she would have preferred to be with her grandchildren than be Prime Minister, but she felt an obligation to serve her country. She was in there fighting all the time.

Later on, after the Camp David Accords, Isabelle and I spent some time with Pope John Paul II. Our news department had covered his first visit to Poland after he became Pope, and I brought him a videotape. On it were a great number of his old friends, people whom he knew in Poland from his youth.

When I presented it to him, he said, "Ordinarily, I'd let this thing go into the Vatican files, but because it has all these Polish faces I miss so much, I will keep it in my own room so I can look it from time to time."

We talked about a variety of things, nothing very important. Just before we finished I said, "We're going from here to see Sadat and then Begin, in that order. Is there any message you would like us to deliver to either or both of them?"

"Yes," he said. "I wish you'd convey this message: I hope they can work out the problems between them in peace."

When we got to Egypt, Sadat was at the summer palace. We drove up and spent about two and a half hours with him. Before I even met him, I was impressed with his statesmanship, the way he had handled himself by going to Israel.

I had driven up one side of Egypt and back the other, and it was all desert. And I had been to Israel several times and saw how they converted their desert to green fields. When I mentioned this, Sadat spoke about how he wanted to work together with Israel to restore life to the soil of Egypt.

When I went to see Begin, I told him he was being too rough and tough in approaching Israel's problems. I said, "Far be it from me to tell you how to handle yourself, but I only know one way to tell you what I think. People in the United States are very pro-Sadat, because of the way he's handling himself, and they're very anti-Begin because of the way you're handling yourself. They see only your stubbornness, that you're not willing to listen.

"Mr. Prime Minister, as far as the United States is concerned, I think it behooves you to take stock of your public relations approach. Israel has had fantastic support and properly so, but if public opinion in our country turns against you—the Congress may not go against public opinion."

I think it went in one ear and out the other. He is a very stubborn man. I told him what Sadat had said, and in reply he went into a long story about his life in Poland, the Holocaust, and the suffering of Jews.

We were with him well over an hour, and when we left his office, his aides came out with us. Outside they said, "We know you're right, but we can't seem to convince him. We don't know whether you've accomplished anything here or not."

In time we developed a program-buying arrangement for overseas. Our program people invited program managers from abroad to come to Los Angeles while our domestic operation was screening product for the coming season. This became valuable, because these foreign stations got quite a jump on their competitors. They could sign up for the best shows before they were broadcast in the United States.

The sales end wasn't as successful. We thought that American advertisers, who had grown up with television, would see the value of applying what they learned in the States to foreign markets. We could supply them with programming, and we thought they would support it.

Perhaps we were a bit ahead of the times, because we encountered animosity from the foreign affiliates of American ad agencies. For example, while Y&R is an international agency with affiliates or subsidiaries around the world, those people did not want New York to dictate what they should be buying. And their clients, who might also buy time in the United States, didn't want to be told what to buy. A Swiss agency might say, "We know our market best, so we will recommend to Nestlé what programs we think they should buy." The sales end of our international operation never did as well as we hoped.

Prior to 1970 it was legal for a network to syndicate its own programs. We could also share ownership in programs with producers. In 1958 I moved Henry Plitt over from UPT, where he had done an admirable job running theater circuits, and put him in charge of ABC Films. This was ABC's syndication and production arm. It operated worldwide.

OTHER RECOLLECTIONS:
Henry Plitt

I made a hell of a deal with ABC. My salary was minimal, but I got a percentage of profits. My comptroller, who (in 1989) had been with me over thirty years, laughed at me. He said, "This is real smart. You get a minimal salary, but you get ten percent of the profits. This company has never had a profit, and not only that, its losses are tremendous." I'm his boss and he's telling me how stupid I am.

When I've been on the job six or seven months, Leonard says, "Henry, we're going to have to close the company. I made a pledge to the board that if the losses at ABC Films ever reach a million dollars, we close it down. Don't worry, you'll have a job for the rest of your contract or longer."

I said, "This is because we're going to lose in excess of one million dollars by the end of the year?"

"Yes."

"If I bring that down, what happens?"

"Oh, then we'll just keep right on going."

So he agreed to let us go on to the end of the year. Now, this million-dollar loss was the result of my agreeing to thirty-nine episodes of "Congressional Investigators," a series produced by Dave Wolper, Sandy Howard, and Harvey Bernhard. These are three names to conjure with in this business today. In that day, when a half hour was running $25–30,000, we produced it for $10,000. But the thing was a total, absolute disaster. We couldn't sell it.

We're still in business, and doing some dubbing into French for a show we had, and the guy who does this for us comes in. Up to now he wanted our business. Now, suddenly, he's very arrogant.

I said, "What's the matter with you?"

"I've got a deal to dub one hundred and thirty pictures."

In other words, "I don't need you any more." I said, "Oh, one hundred and thirty pictures is a big deal any year."

He said the Bon Ami Corporation—cleansers, detergents—bought 130 pictures and were going to distribute them worldwide.

I wondered why the hell they would go into this, so I got the Bon Ami guy on the phone, and said, "I understand you have one hundred and thirty pictures. What are you going to do with them?"

"We're going to distribute them worldwide."

"Do you have a distributor?"

"No. We've gotten calls from a few people."

"Has anybody offered you any money?"

"No."

"I'm going to make you a large offer."

So we met. I offered him $570,000—$500,000 of it was represented by a show which up to that time had never been seen anywhere, it was brand spanking new, "Congressional Investigators." The $70,000 was in cash. They took the deal.

Now our books pick up the distribution value of 130 features and drop the $500,000, as it belongs to Bon Ami as a guarantee against distribution.

So the company stayed in business.

As the years went by, I was earning more money than Leonard Goldenson, Ollie Treyz, Si Siegel. More than anybody at ABC. All because I had a percentage deal. When we got to a million dollars, I had $100,000 over and above my salary. It got well over $100,000. It became an embarrassment to them, because here's Leonard getting $72,000 a year and Si getting $56,000. Fortunately I wasn't on the board so they didn't have to publish my salary.

When Rupert Murdoch came to New York, I would drive him up to Leonard's home for screenings on Saturday nights. Rupert bought some of our shows for his operations in Australia.

Then Murdoch reneged on a deal. I wanted to sue him. Leonard said, "You can't sue him. We're partners, forget it."

So I forgot it.

About three years later, we had some top-rated shows like "Combat," "Ben Casey," and "The Fugitive," We were really riding high. Then Rupert asked to get together.

In Australia then, the TV operators had made a gentleman's agreement. A half hour was $3,000, an hour was $6,000. Nobody would pay more than that for anything. First you had to sell the show, but once you sold them, that was the price.

Now this little boys' club apparently was going to break up. It was going to become a competitive business. Rupert comes to New York and tells me he wants to buy the shows we're presently running on another Australian network.

I said, "If I do that, I'll never be able to sell a show in Australia again."

He said, "I wouldn't worry about that. I'll take all your shows."

"Well, that's fine for one year, but what about next year and the year after that?"

"Let's fix a time now."

"Five years."

"You've got it."

"For five years *everything* I produce or distribute will be bought by you?"

"Correct."

For this he was getting "Combat," "Ben Casey," and "The Fugitive." And everything else. Those three were a piece of cake, but I had *dreck* like "26 Men" and "Expedition" and all kinds of crap that I couldn't sell to anybody else. He had to take it all. That was the deal.

We shook hands. He was about to leave the office. I said, "There's one little problem."

"What's that?"

I said, "You could renege on this deal. I had a problem with you a couple years ago. Leonard interceded and wouldn't let me sue. What I want now is to get in a position where I never have to sue you."

"How do you propose to do that?"

"I want you to deliver five million dollars."

This was 1962. People are buying things for billions now. But then $5 million was money.

"You deliver five million to us now. You will work against that for the next five years. So, then, under no circumstances will I have to worry about you defaulting, because I've got your money."

He was pissed, and he's Rupert Murdoch and I know what his credit is. I said, "I know everything you're telling me. But if we're going to make this deal, I want five million."

Murdoch sent us $5 million.

He delivered it to ABC Films, and we put it in the bank and drew interest on it.

In 1963, it came time to get my ass out of New York. I think they were embarrassed by my salary. Si said, "We want you to go to Chicago and take over the Northern Theatre Division."

I didn't want to go. I loved New York. I had a beautiful penthouse on 72nd Street, my eighty-year-old mother lived nearby, and my daughter was at the University of Bridgeport, forty-five minutes away.

So if I had to go, I wanted them to make it worth my while. I prepared a list of things I wanted. A new Cadillac every year, a new office, all sorts of crazy things that would make them say, "Forget it."

Si gave me everything I wanted, until we got to salary. I wanted $150,000 a year. Now remember, even Leonard isn't earning that.

He said, "We can't do that."

"Why not? I'm on a contract. It's $40,000 a year plus 10 percent of the profits."

"Yeah, but how do you know what the profits are going to be?"

"I not only know, I've got the money here."

He said, "Tell me."

So I told him about Rupert Murdoch and our deal. I went to Chicago with $150,000 a year.

❑ ❑ ❑

In 1970 the FCC put restrictions on network ownership of programming and on domestic syndication. ABC Films activities were limited to overseas sales. Several years later, this activity was merged into our Video Enterprises division.

By the mid 1970s we decided to get out of the theater business. Over the years, virtually all theater earnings went to subsidize television losses. We deferred all but the most essential theater maintenance and cut costs wherever we could.

All the while the business was changing. People were moving to the suburbs. Downtown theaters became opulent dinosaurs. Exhibitors put in multiple screens in new, down-sized suburban movie houses. Rather than invest in these when we needed our money for television, we sold off our Northern Theatre group to Henry Plitt in 1974. In 1978, with partner Thomas Klutznick, a Chicago land developer, he bought the Southern group. ABC was finally out of the theater business.

The Plitt Theatres did very well. In 1987 Henry sold them to Cineplex Odeon, and turned to producing motion pictures.

Meanwhile ABC International continued to bring American programs to worldwide audiences. We pioneered the use of satellites to distribute both programs and world events to every corner of the globe.

Without question, ABC's most important international transmission was the first moon walk, in 1969, sent to at least sixteen countries by satellite. We could only send video, so we opened phone lines to each country for the audio. It sounds a little clumsy, but the result was spectacular.

Afterward, our station manager in Santo Domingo called to say a woman viewer had begged him to tell us what a wonderful thing it was to see men on the moon. She was crying. The drama of watching those men take the first steps on the moon, and the suspense of wondering if they'd return safely, had greatly affected her. We got hundreds of letters from people around the world complimenting us on this achievement.

Neither CBS nor NBC transmitted this event internationally. When Americans walked on the moon, hundreds of millions of people around the globe watched ABC's telecast of this monumental event.

In the late 1950s, John Bassett, a Toronto newspaper publisher, came to see me. He had started a TV station, his technical end was in good shape, but he was losing his shirt in programming. He asked me to make a fifty-fifty deal. I said I didn't want more than 25 percent, but we agreed to train his people. Several worked at WXYZ-TV, Detroit, under the tutelage of Jimmy Riddell, a master of the broadcasting game, and we also sent some of our people to work with Bassett in Toronto in sales and programming. In a year we put him well in the black.

Then the board of governors, Canada's equivalent of our FCC, decided foreign interests shouldn't be involved in Canadian broadcasting. In the early 1960s they invited us out.

This is essentially what happened throughout Central and South America in the early 1970s. A rising tide of nationalism focused on foreign investors. In broadcasting we were more visible than most. Even though we had only minority positions, we felt they'd eventually want us to get out. The Japanese didn't want us to leave, but our 5 percent holdings there meant very little.

In the mid 1970s we sold off all our international interests. In general we made money on our investments. In hindsight, however, running international networks would have been more viable than station ownership.

In the early 1970s Robert Maxwell, one of Britain's more aggressive publishers, called me. I didn't know him. He said he wanted to buy our stock in News Limited (Murdoch's original Adelaide company).

"Why do you want it?" I asked.

"I want to buy the London *Sun*. Murdoch is also trying to buy it," said Maxwell. "If I can get enough stock to control his company, I can call him off."

"You have no chance of that. Rupert is our partner. If he wants our News Limited stock, he can have it. Otherwise we wouldn't sell."

I called Rupert in London, told him about the call from Maxwell, and offered the stock at whatever it was going for that day on the London Exchange. He was glad to take it.

Robert Maxwell failed to get either the *Sun* or control of News Limited. However, he now owns the company that published the book you are reading.

Rupert's acquisition of the *Sun* brought him to international attention. He later picked up *The Times*, bought a large number of American publishing properties, then acquired Twentieth Century Fox. After becoming an American citizen, he bought television stations. In 1988 he launched a fourth network, Fox Broadcasting. There's a good chance it might one day be competitive with CBS, NBC, and ABC.

When we went international, Europe was not open to private investment in broadcasting. So we joined with a group of bankers and built production companies in several countries. The idea was to produce programming there for sale to the government systems. We produced an hour and sold it to, say, the German Number 2 network. These were mostly one-time shows because Europeans didn't then appreciate series the way we did here. So we never made any real money.

All that is changing now. Most of Europe is opening to cable systems, which are, in the main, privately owned. European audiences have developed a craving for American programming, and many of our top series get terrific ratings in England, Germany, and Italy. The development of satellite networks has opened the way to provide truly international programming to any home with cable. Rupert Murdoch has jumped on this and has very ambitious plans to bring American programs to European viewers. The only obstacle to his success is the resolution of international political issues.

In the final analysis, however, what counts most is what's on the screen. If Rupert can bring the right programs to his audiences, he will finally create what ABC set out to do thirty years ago: the first truly viable international network.

OTHER RECOLLECTIONS:
Rupert Murdoch

Leonard was about twenty years ahead of his time. He had the right idea; it just took longer to happen. I think Leonard will be remembered as a pioneer who was the first to bring and maintain real competition in television. A man with imagination and the guts to do things differently.

He was in many ways a role model, though we came from very different backgrounds: he through entertainment and business, and I from journalism, publishing, and general media inclusive of broadcasting. Leonard's success was always an inspiration and encouragement.

He proved you *can* buck the odds.

❑ ❑ ❑

13

Moore

❑

When Ollie Treyz left, our head of programming, Tom Moore, became president of the network. A tall, heavyset fellow with a courtly demeanor, he spoke in a rich Southern accent that instantly proclaimed his Mississippi roots.

I had high hopes for Tom. While he wasn't a visionary in Ollie's mold, he was a solid manager with a good sense of showmanship and excellent contacts in Hollywood and on Madison Avenue.

I wasn't sure that Tom would be a strong enough leader, however, so I put Julie Barnathan in as executive VP of the network. That didn't work out, however. Tom and Julie disagreed about almost everything, and soon they were squabbling in public.

Accordingly, I moved Julie over to head our O&O division, which supervised our five television stations. After a few years, Si Siegel suggested that Julie's raw energy and restless imagination would best serve ABC as head of Broadcast Operations and Engineering. By 1965, when Frank Marx retired and Julie took over the department, this department had grown from half a dozen people to hundreds.

Ed Scherick took over programming from Dan Melnick. He filled his department with highly talented people, among them Douglas Cramer, Harv Bennett, Paul Picard, and Leonard Goldberg. Later, all of them would become very well known.

Before he came to ABC in 1957, Tom sold filmed programs to independent stations for CBS. Working out of Hollywood, he got to know the Disney organization. In 1953 he wrote a long memo to Bill Paley, suggesting CBS should bankroll Disneyland. But Tom was a voice in the wilderness, and Paley paid him little attention.

Early in 1963, Tom made a deal with Jerry Lewis to do a two-hour variety show for Saturday nights. Lewis was very full of himself, and he wouldn't tell us what the show's format was. He kept giving us double-talk and double-talk and double-talk, insisting it would take the country by storm. I had some misgivings about this, but Jerry Lewis was one of the premier comedy talents of the era, so I let him have his way.

OTHER RECOLLECTIONS:
Tom Moore

Saturday night was date night, when many young people go out to dinner or take in a movie. We couldn't get many advertisers. So we decided to try a two-hour Johnny Carson–style show with Jerry Lewis. To convince Lewis to do it, we had to buy the old Capital Theatre near Sunset and Vine, in Hollywood.

Lewis also insisted on full control of his program. He refused scriptwriters and tried to wing it, but he doesn't have that kind of talent. It was amateur city. The worst program you ever saw. The ratings and reviews were awful.

Lewis kept repeating, "What a brave crowd this ABC is, my friend Leonard Goldenson let me have these two hours," and so on. He would say, "Lenny, are you listening?" He must have used Leonard's name ten or twelve times, which rankled Leonard terribly. He told Jewish jokes, but they were in terrible taste. I'm not a Jew, but I took exception to those.

I went to see him and said, "You've got to script this show. No ethnic jokes, none of that. And quit referring to Leonard's lineage."

Lewis regarded me as a go-fer. He would call Leonard and repeat everything I had said.

After three weeks I had the horror of flying out with Ed Scherick, head of programming, and telling Lewis we were pulling him off the air. We let him do only two more shows.

So, after having bought a theater to put this guy in, now we've canceled the show. I had to go back and face the board and Si Siegel.

I've always felt that if you've got a lemon, make lemonade. I told Ed, "Let's be aggressive." On the flight back to New York, Ed had an idea: Stay on the air in the same time slot, keep the theater, but change the name from the Jerry Lewis Theatre and make it the Hollywood Palace. We would have variety, with rotating emcees, and it would be like *Ed Sullivan*.

I said, "This rotating emcee is the problem, that's where the hitch is."

Ed called Leonard and told him what we wanted to do. Ed said he wouldn't have done that in a million years, but we had to get moving because we had a show to do in three weeks. Leonard said, "Let's go."

I told Ed if we could set a precedent with a good emcee and a good opening show, it might get off the ground. So I called Bing Crosby at his ranch in Nevada and asked him to do the first one.

Bing said, "God, I never fancied myself as an emcee. Why don't you get Pat Buttrum?"

"Bing, you don't know everything." And I explained the situation.

Bing said, "I'll do it if you really want me to, but I think it's dumb."

"Bing, we're really in trouble, we've got problems, you can help us."

He never asked what it paid. He never asked a thing. That son of a gun came to town, and worked his ass off. It worked out great. He got on the phone himself and got Peggy Lee, and we never looked back. We got George Burns, we had the best series of emcees you could ever imagine. Soon we could get anybody. It became the "in" thing. And suddenly we were getting ratings. We salvaged a disaster, paid the theater off, and later sold it and made a profit.

Years later, my son, Tom, got a job writing for Johnny Carson. One night Jerry Lewis comes in as the guest host. In a session with the writers, he did a parody act of my firing him. He did it like a red-neck Southern sheriff, "Ya'll got to stop tellin' those Jewish jokes, boy, he, he, he." And of course by then he's done this routine at least a million times.

He didn't know it was my son, and Tom said nothing. Two weeks later Lewis came into Tom's office, shut the door, and said, "I just found out I was hurting you, and I'm sorry." That's more than I thought he would ever do.

❑ ❑ ❑

"Hollywood Palace" ran through the fall of 1969 and, considering its hasty origins, did rather well. Tom Moore's son has gone on to a marvelous career in television, writing and producing such ABC shows as "Hooperman" and "Doogie Howser, M.D."

Ever since my days as head of Paramount's theaters, I had regularly visited the West Coast, calling on all the major studios and most of the better independents once or twice a year. It was my way of maintaining personal relationships with Hollywood's movers and shakers.

When I got into television, I continued this practice. I hoped to get an early look at whatever shows were in the works. I might have left this to ABC's programming people, but as the network with the smallest potential audience, I felt we had to give program producers some reason to offer us their best shows before CBS and NBC took them.

Early in 1963 I planned yet another trip. On my list of must-sees was the producer of "Cheyenne" and "Maverick," the brilliant Roy Huggins.

OTHER RECOLLECTIONS:
Roy Huggins

When I left Warners, I didn't want to do any more Westerns. I was tired of them and didn't think they would last much longer. I was wrong by only about fifteen years.

To a writer, the appealing thing about Western heroes is they never have a job. So they are never compelled to stay in one place. That allows a writer to use all kinds of locations and to introduce characters at will.

But while I was tired of the whole Western thing, I asked myself, "How do I get a hero character, with all the freedom they have in a Western, into a contemporary environment?"

In a contemporary setting, a man without a job is a drifter or a bum, and can't be a hero. But I wanted to do a show around a guy who could move from place to place. The answer was, he must move around because he's been falsely accused of a capital offense. If it was some lesser crime, the audience would say, "Hey stupid, fight it. Take your chances." So this must be a man who has already been found guilty and has escaped. He's got nothing to fight; he's going to go to the gas chamber. That man can behave like a Western hero.

But he couldn't be a private eye. So I wrote a three-page treatment of a story built around an innocent fugitive from justice.

Then I got a call from Ollie Treyz.

"Roy, how would you like to run television at either Metro or Fox? Or you can set up your own company, and we'll support you," he said.

"I'd be very bad casting as head of a company. I'm a writer, not a businessman," I said.

"You'll be hearing from both Metro and Fox."

I signed with Fox. Pete Levathes had just become head of the studio. We flew out to California sitting side by side, and I told him my idea for this show. It was the first time I'd ever told it. Pete just looked at me, but I felt as though I could read his mind. He seemed to be saying, "What have I got myself into here? Who have I hired to run television, when he comes up with an idea as repulsive as that?"

He said, "We'll talk about that later," and didn't speak to me for the rest of the trip. When we got to Fox, he put me in a tiny office on the third floor of a separate building. Very soon he fired me. Soon after that he was fired.

I had been telling my story to close friends, people I could trust. Everyone reacted the same way. Usually, they were embarrassed for me. My agent hated it. Every time I mentioned it, he changed the subject. One of my closest friends said, "Roy, you have a really big reputation in television. Don't tell that idea to anybody, or you will lose that reputation."

Everyone thought it was in grotesque bad taste. A man had been found guilty of killing his wife, and he escapes. Finally, I thought I had been mistaken, and I gave up on it.

My brother was a professor of literature, a very happy man. I also intended to teach. I graduated from UCLA, Phi Beta Kappa, and did two years toward a Ph.D. in political theory. Then the war came. Since I was myopic, I was 4F and didn't go into uniform. Instead, I was given a government job. With too much free time, I started writing novels. Then I went into movies and was seduced by the money. I didn't think I was very good, but soon I had such a great reputation I couldn't quit.

But for years I'd said, "This will be my last year." I wanted to finish graduate school.

When I was fired by Levathes, I thought, Here's my great opportunity. Fox owes me a year's salary. I will go back to school.

Then I get a call from Dan Melnick at ABC. "Leonard Goldenson is coming out to talk about our programming and wants to meet with you."

I said, "Dan, I'm in graduate school at UCLA. I've been out of television for a year. There's no reason for Leonard to meet with me."

Melnick sounded desperate. "Roy, you're not telling me that you won't meet with Leonard?"

"Wait a minute. I love Leonard. He's a nice guy, he's bright, but I'm not in television."

"I can't tell Leonard you won't meet with him."

I liked Dan. He had been very nice to me. And he hinted that I owed him something.

"Okay, Dan, I'll tell you what I'll do. I have a series idea that I love. Everybody else hates it with a passion. But I will meet with Leonard and tell him this idea. But I warn you, you'll be in deeper shit with Leonard for bringing me in to tell this story than by saying 'Roy Huggins doesn't want to meet with you.' "

"What's your idea about?"

"It's about a guy who has been tried and convicted of killing his wife, and he's running around the country with a cop chasing him."

"Yeah, ah ha. So you'll meet with Leonard?"

We met at the Beverly Hills Hotel. I'm in a bungalow with Melnick, Julius Barnathan, Ev Erlick, Burt Nodella, Leonard—and Tom Moore.

I tell them my concept, beginning with how and why I arrived at it. I explained the hero was found guilty of killing his wife. He claimed he saw a one-armed man leaving the death scene, but they could never find this man. On the way to prison for execution, there is a train wreck, and he escapes. And the story is what happens to the hero as he moves from place to place, one step ahead of the cop who has sworn to bring him in to be executed.

As I tell my story, everyone in the room looks very skeptical. When I get to where the hero escapes and is on his own, Tom Moore gets up and walks out. That jars me a little. But I didn't care, because when this was over, if a miracle occurred and they said, "We want it," I intended to say, "You can have it. Find yourself a producer." So his walking out didn't bother me one bit. I'm telling the story better than I ever did, and getting the usual result.

Then Moore walks back through the room carrying a suitcase. He says, "I've got a plane to catch," and leaves. Everyone clearly understands he wouldn't buy this show if I paid him.

I finish by saying the hero is pursued from week to week, always hoping that someday he'll find the one-armed man. But the story is really about this good man, a doctor, and his wanderings. I wanted to call the show "The Fugitive."

There is silence until Barnathan stands up and says, "I think this is the most un-American idea I've ever heard in my life."

I said, "Un-American?"

"Yes, it's a slap in the face of American justice every week." He was furious.

I said, "That is why we have appeals courts and supreme courts in every state and another Supreme Court in Washington. Because sometimes courts make mistakes. That's America."

"But how do we know he's innocent?"

"There is going to be a narrator, as I told you, an omniscient voice who knows everything. The audience knows his wife was killed, because the narrator tells them. And the narrator says he's innocent. A signature, a little recurring piece, will precede and follow each episode."

That had never been done before. I invented it for "The Fugitive" when I wrote the treatment. Now it is very widely used.

Barnathan said, "Well, I don't like it. I think it is un-American," and he sat down.

There is another silence, and then the gentleman sitting across the room, a man for whom I had tremendous respect, says, "Roy, I think it's the best television concept I have ever heard in my life."

I said, "Do you really mean that?

Leonard Goldenson said, "Absolutely. We'll buy it."

"I am so glad to find someone at last that likes this idea. But I can't do it. I am in the graduate school of government at UCLA, and it is difficult to get in. When they accepted me, they rejected someone else equally qualified. So as much as I'd love to be free to do this show, I won't be able to do it."

❑ ❑ ❑

I was very surprised that Roy wouldn't agree to produce even the pilot. After some discussion, we agreed that Roy would approach Quinn Martin, who had done "The Untouchables" for us, and get him to produce "The

Fugitive." Roy made a deal where he acted as creative consultant. Roy was instrumental in casting his poker pal, David Janssen, in the title role, and it was a marvelous choice.

"The Fugitive" aired in the fall of 1963, at 10 P.M. on Tuesday nights. It did well from the start, and each season the ratings improved. In the final episode, Janssen's character finally finds the one-armed man and establishes his own innocence. By then it was 1967, and viewers nationwide were on the edge of their chairs. This episode was for many years the most watched television show in history.

At my home in Mamaroneck I had a small theater, about thirty seats, and I screened several movies a week, the latest from Hollywood, and usually well in advance of their general release. On weekends I'd screen several films, to which I invited neighbors, friends, business associates, and many of the top people from ABC. I'd done this for many years, going back to my Paramount theater days.

One night I saw *Imitation of Life* with Lana Turner. It was nothing more than a deluxe soap opera. At the time, the other two networks had several soap operas, mostly shows which had come over from radio. But they had them on in the daytime. I said to myself, "My God, if we could put a deluxe soap opera on television, it would go great in *prime* time."

So I called in Scherick and Tom Moore to look at the picture. I asked them to dig up a property at one of the studios. And they tried for several months, but they couldn't come up with anything suitable.

Spyros Skouras, the head of Fox, lived nearby. Two or three times a week we'd drive in to New York together. Sometimes I'd drive him, and sometimes he'd drive me. One Monday morning he picked me up, and I said, "Spyros, I'm looking for a deluxe soap opera to make into a prime-time series. Do you have anything in your library that possibly could serve that purpose?"

He said he thought so. It was called *Peyton Place*, based on a sensational novel. I said, "That's it! I'll send Moore and Scherick over today, and see if we can't tie up a deal."

OTHER RECOLLECTIONS:
Edgar Scherick

We had a marvelous cast, including Mia Farrow and Ryan O'Neal. But everyone was very nervous because the title suggested sex. They were scared to death. Somebody suggested changing the name of the program before it went on. I said, "Change the name and we've got nothing. The only thing going for us now is the title."

Finally someone at *The New York Times* wrote a very perceptive article about the way "Peyton Place" reflected our society and mores. That took the curse off it. Bristol Meyers bought part of it. Then Leonard Lavin, who ran Alberto Culver, saw the pilot and also came in.

❑ ❑ ❑

"Peyton Place" premiered as a half-hour show, Tuesday and Thursday evenings at 9:30 on September 15, 1964. In the summer of 1965 we added a third episode on Fridays. The show was a major development in television, forerunner to such long-running programs as "Dallas" and "Dynasty."

In launching "Peyton Place," we tried something unusual in scheduling. Instead of waiting for the end of September to put on our new fall lineup, we had a "sneak preview" week, starting September 14. For the next three weeks, for the first time, ABC led both CBS and NBC in ratings. When the others came out with their own fall schedules, of course, we went back to our usual ranking.

Preceding "Peyton Place," and helping feed it a happy audience, was a Screen Gems show that we had to outbid the other networks to get. "Bewitched," starring Elizabeth Montgomery, was the adventures of an ordinary man and his benevolent witch of a wife. The show got huge ratings and stayed on the network through the summer of 1973.

If Failure is an orphan, Success has many fathers. Years after "Peyton Place" had left its mark on television, Bobby Lehman, head of the investment banking firm of Lehman Brothers and a very close friend, called to say he'd had a long conversation with Darryl Zanuck. "Incidentally," said Bobby, "Zanuck claimed credit for developing 'Peyton Place.' "

I said, "Bobby, he's out of his mind. Spyros Skouras is responsible for that. I'm going to send you a letter, with a copy to Darryl." And I did. In it I said that I knew of my own knowledge that Skouras was responsible for "Peyton Place," and no one else. I said that while it was one thing to go around announcing one's own triumphs—and Zanuck had quite a few—claiming somebody else's achievements was beneath him. The next time I met Darryl, however, we were still as good friends as ever.

By 1965 ABC's headquarters at 7 West 66th Street was jammed to the rafters. With more growth in sight, we had been looking for another piece of property on which to build a new corporate headquarters. I gave this task to Si Siegel.

Si learned of a forty-story apartment building, still under construction, at 1330 Avenue of the Americas, at the corner of 54th Street. While the building wasn't exactly what we had in mind, the location offered a wonderful opportunity. It was a block north of CBS's headquarters and three from Radio City, NBC's corporate eyrie.

It occurred to me that establishing a visible presence for ABC in the heart of the broadcasting district would announce to the broadcasting and advertising industries that ABC was finally on an equal footing with the other networks. In many ways, of course, we were not yet fully competitive, but this is an image business. Si negotiated a lease with an option to buy the property, and late in 1965 we moved in. The old facilities on West 66th were turned over to News, Sports, and Broadcast Operations & Engineering.

Ted Shaker, who left CBS to become head of our owned and operated television stations in the 1960s, recalls the impact our new building had at CBS.

OTHER RECOLLECTIONS:
Ted Shaker

People at CBS didn't like us moving into their neighborhood, and they didn't care much for our building's looks. A joke made the rounds at Black Rock: We had taken the packing crate that the CBS building came in and put it across the street to be the ABC building.

The CBS sports department was right across from Roone Arledge's office. One winter afternoon it was dark, and the CBS sports executives could see into Roone's office. A guy from the PGA was talking to Roone. This guy was supposed to be at CBS for a 4:30 meeting.

The PGA guy called CBS Sports and said, "Sorry, I can't be over there. I've been held up in a meeting. I'm calling from a pay phone."

The CBS Sports guy, Bill McPhail, said, "We can see the pay phone you're calling from."

Roone got some blinds for his office shortly after that.

❑ ❑ ❑

Our new building was a small triumph. As a morale booster to those who had worked so long with so little recognition, I had large ABC logos affixed atop the building, including one on the south side, where CBS executives couldn't miss it whenever they looked out the window. It was our way of saying, "Watch us, because we're coming after you." I'm told that sign was particularly irritating to Chairman Bill Paley.

Probably the most oddball success story in ABC programming history was a show based on a comic book character. I give Ed Scherick credit for having the panache to see the potential, then argue the idea past all the roadblocks that sprang up when he announced he wanted to do Batman —not as a cartoon, but as a series.

OTHER RECOLLECTIONS:
Edgar Scherick

Yale Yudoss, now a highly successful Hollywood screen writer but then a very junior fellow in the program department, came into my office and said, "Let's do 'Batman.' "

I threw him out, of course.

But Yale came back. We got involved in a discussion, and finally we decided, "What the hell." At that time we had a departmental credo. When we put a project into development, we always asked ourselves the question, "To the best of our ability in television, is this project touched with singularity?"

"Batman" certainly answered that criterion.

So on our next trip to the coast, we went to Fox, where we had a lot of development and production. Bill Self was head of Fox television; David Gerber worked under him. We told David we wanted to develop "Batman." He said, "You're out of your mind."

"Batman," the comic book, had been around for a long time. It wasn't beginning from scratch. This was a piece of the American culture. But to my knowledge, nothing like it had ever been done before in television. It was a chance to do something wildly singular.

Eventually Fox decided to go along, and we suggested Bill Dozier, one of their staff producers, take charge. When told what we wanted, he said, "You're crazy." But he came around.

After everybody thought about it for a while, they suggested Lorenzo Semple to write it. We brought him back to a New York meeting, which included Leonard and the network management. Semple described the approach we all had agreed upon. He spoke around the stub of a burned-out cigarette clenched between his teeth and found his own presentation so amusing that he kept interrupting himself with a high-pitched "tee-hee" giggle. He explained we would play it tongue-in-cheek, and camp was our watchword.

I was on the stage at Fox while we were shooting it and got a great charge out of the whole thing. Frank Gorshin, an impressionist who was billed as "the man of a thousand faces," was in the first episode as a character called The Riddler.

Before adding "Batman" to the schedule, we decided to test it for audience acceptance. A California research organization, ASI, maintained a special screening room. Members of the audience sat in chairs with dials on the armrests. Watching a big screen, they responded to the program by rotating the dial. Composite responses were recorded electronically in the control booth and correlated second by second with the program.

The test was a disaster—the lowest score on record at ASI. If the audience could have taken the dials and forced them below zero, they would have done so. They hated the show.

I said, "Look, there's something wrong. The audience is in one universe, and our show is in another. We've got to promote this show so when the audience comes to it on the air, they won't be jarred out of their conventional expectations, as they were in this test."

Then I wrote an internal memo that included a slogan, simply: " 'Batman' is coming. So is Robin." I said, "If we promote this show correctly we could open with a 40 share. So I want to see 'Batman is coming. So is Robin.' everywhere. I want it so people can't turn around without seeing or hearing it. When Leonard Goldenson goes to his private john, I want there to be a strip across the toilet seat that says, 'Batman is coming. So is Robin.' "

In that era, most program promotion was done on the network itself. But "Batman" was so different it lent itself to unique promotional techniques. We bought ads in newspapers, we put up posters. We tried to exploit every medium possible.

❑ ❑ ❑

Until 1966, all networks usually stuck with fall schedules no matter what. There was little jockeying and tinkering with time slots, and there was little, if any, thought to canceling programs halfway through the season.

Parts of our 1965 fall lineup hadn't worked. In fact, it was a disaster. In desperation, we decided that "Batman" would debut as the first network midseason replacement series.

We had retained Grey Advertising to handle our promotion. We explained that we were going to try something new, that we would be introducing programs in the middle of the season, and needed a way to promote the idea. A copywriter, Irwin Fredman, coined the expression "The Second Season."

"Batman" debuted as a thirty-minute show on Wednesday and Thursday at 7:30 P.M. on January 12, 1966. As Scherick had predicted, by that time audiences had an idea of what to expect. And, as Scherick had promised, we opened with a 40 share. It was a huge hit.

Ed recruited a young fellow named Len Goldberg from BBD&O, where he was liaison between the agency's program and media departments. Len had worked briefly at ABC as a research department clerk in the late 1950s.

After rejoining ABC, Goldberg became Doug Cramer's assistant. Doug, a meticulously organized individual, would go on to become one of Hollywood's leading program suppliers. Doug trained Len Goldberg in ABC's ways. After a few years, Goldberg became very important to us. Scherick made him head of daytime programming.

OTHER RECOLLECTIONS:
Len Goldberg

ABC was about to leave the daytime business. It was doing so poorly, it was hard to get the affiliates to carry programs. We weren't making any money. They wanted to make one more try at it, and they offered me the job of VP in charge of daytime programming. I understood it would probably be a one-year job because, if we didn't substantially improve, the department was out of business. Much to everyone's amazement, I took it.

In the summer of 1965 we started with "Where the Action Is," a half hour of rock 'n' roll with Dick Clark, at 2 P.M. It didn't make the long run, but it gave us a quick little burst.

Chuck Barris had been head of ABC's West Coast daytime programming before I arrived. Chuck, a very bright guy, was doing a lousy job. I said, "Why are you doing this?"

He said, "I really don't want to be an executive. I want to be a producer."

Because I didn't think it through, I said, "Okay, you've got to leave." We might have done the shows he eventually created right in-house.

So he left and came back with a couple of ideas. We went forward with one: "The Dating Game." This became our first success.

About the same time I saw a run-through of a game show, which was terrible. I told our guys to buy the rights to it, because there was one element in it I thought was terrific. One couple on the show was newlywed, and I found the byplay between them fascinating. I wanted just that element in the show. I called Chuck and said, "What can you do with the fun and uncomfortableness of newlyweds?" He came back with "The Newlywed Game."

We tried other shows. I decided a teenage serial would be a great idea. I went to our Hollywood studio and said, "We're going to do a boardwalk show, like the bikini movies, on the beach." So we tore up the parking lot and filled it with sand and built a boardwalk. They thought I was nuts. Thirteen weeks later, when "Never Too Young" didn't work, I came back and said, "Okay, you can fill it back up again."

"General Hospital" had been a very big hit, and then it died down. We resuscitated it with new characters and better scripts.

From my BBD&O days I knew Dan Curtis, then a golf producer. He called me one morning and said, "I have to see you. I dreamed a serial."

He came in and told me the story. I said, "Dan, you dreamed *Jane Eyre*."

He said, "Well, is it on the air?"

"No."

"Well, let's do it." So we did the first Gothic serial. But after it went on the air, it didn't do too well.

Dan said, "Look, if we continue doing it this way, you'll have to cancel the show. So let me pull out all the stops and go all the way."

I said, "Okay, we've got nothing to lose."

So he made it really Gothic, and the ratings started to climb. "Dark Shadows" became a cult hit, and then a big audience hit—a smash.

We were in California for a big affiliate meeting, and we were sitting around the Bel Air Hotel—Tom Moore, Leonard, and myself—and we were early. Leonard said, "I'd like to see some of our daytime shows."

I knew he hadn't seen "Dark Shadows" yet, so I said, "Well, we really should be getting along because of traffic."

He said, "No, no, we have plenty of time."

Tom said, "Come on, turn on the show."

I said, "Well, I'm not sure what time it's on here."

But as it happened "Dark Shadows" was just starting. We watched for a few minutes, Tom and Leonard open-mouthed, and Leonard said, "Why is that fellow looking at that girl like that?"

I said, "Well, he's imagining what it would feel like to sink his teeth into her neck."

"Why would he want to do that?"

"Because he's a vampire."

"Is he a regular on the show?"

"His name is Barnabas. He's the star."

Tom said, "It's getting late. We'd better go."

For years afterward Leonard teased me about that show. Whenever a programming meeting ran late, Leonard always said, "It's getting dark. Shouldn't you go home now? You know you're not allowed out after the sun goes down."

Those four shows were the basis of ABC's daytime turnaround. Daytime became very successful and very profitable.

Leonard was always very enthusiastic. Once, when I was a little discouraged after some of our new pilots hadn't gone well with management, he said, "We're not in the business of building a bridge from one point to another, where you know you've done well if the bridge reaches between the points and doesn't collapse when cars run over it.

"We deal with flickering images on a screen, and who knows if they're good or bad? That's why you have to be very enthusiastic. What you convey to us and in turn to the audience is somehow understood and picked up."

After Edgar and Doug Cramer left, Tom made me head of programming. I was only twenty-eight. Leonard took me into his office and told me something I'll never forget.

He said, "You know, this can be a very complex business. Lots of meetings. Lots of business. There's the affiliates, there's Washington, there's sales, there's engineering."

Then he pointed to his television set and said, "Remember only one thing. All the audience sees is what comes over that tube. All they know about us is what they see on the screen from their local station. That's how they will judge us. And that's all that matters. Keep your eye on the screen. Don't ever be diverted from what's on that screen."

It's stood me well through all my years.

❑ ❑ ❑

Ed Scherick was head of programming for just over three years, and though I'd had a few misgivings when he came over from Sales, he performed outstandingly well.

Aside from having a demanding basic job, however, the head of network programming has to have his hands in so many pies simultaneously that it's difficult to concentrate on any one program. So it's hard to leave a personal mark on any show in particular. This became a source of frustration to Ed. Soon after "Batman" debuted, he resigned to start his own company. Doug Cramer left two days later.

Today Ed is one of Hollywood's most successful independent producers, with a long string of miniseries and motion pictures to his credit.

Doug Cramer, on his own and in association with Aaron Spelling, became one of television's most important programming suppliers.

Tom Moore put Len Goldberg in as head of programming. While Len continued to do a terrific job, his new position brought him into almost daily contact with Moore. For some reason, relations between these two key managers quickly deteriorated. Before long, they were openly quarreling.

Unfortunately, I learned, this was not an isolated case. I gradually became aware that Moore's leadership abilities were questioned by several of ABC's key executives. By 1966 he had headed the network for almost four years, but I had begun to suspect he was not the right man for that job. Tom continued to make rosy forecasts, but we didn't seem to be making progress on many of our most serious problems.

Mentally, I began casting about for a replacement. Before I got very far along in my thinking, however, I was forced to concentrate on more urgent matters. Quite suddenly, it seemed, ABC was at war. The field of battle was Wall Street.

14

Sharks

❑

Once television grew out of its infancy, networks and stations became highly attractive investments. Since there were never more than a few networks, corporate raiders found them irresistible. In the 1960s, an era of turbulent social change, these sharks came after ABC. Our troubles arose, in part, out of our need to compete with color programming.

Large numbers of color sets did not appear in American homes until the early 1960s. Just as RCA had pioneered radio networks in the 1920s as an inducement to buy radio receivers, they now began creating reasons for consumers to buy color TV sets. NBC, as part of RCA, began to schedule color programming.

In 1961, when our contract with Disney ended, Sarnoff offered the studio a huge sum to come over to NBC as "Walt Disney's Wonderful World of Color." Walt gave me the opportunity to match NBC's offer, but we had no color broadcasting equipment, and in any case it was just too much money for us.

CBS, which had suffered huge losses from its brief fling in manufacturing, also began installing color transmitters and adding color programs to its schedule.

Soon both networks were giving preference to producers of color programming. Advertisers, bowled over by how much better their products looked, began favoring color shows.

The motion picture industry had always withheld its best movies from network television. But the studios had gone through a decade of financial reverses, and now they saw an opportunity to recoup some of their losses by selling color films at greatly increased rates. NBC and CBS, anxious to fill their schedules with color, were asked to pay as much as four times the previous license fees for movies.

NBC and CBS responded by doubling their movie schedules. In 1961, NBC debuted "Saturday Night at the Movies." In 1963 they added a second night of movies. In 1965, "The CBS Thursday Night Movies" began. CBS supplemented this with film specials on other nights throughout their schedule.

I took no pleasure recalling that in 1953, when I was the new kid on the block and regarded as somehow tarnished by my association with Hollywood, Sarnoff had insisted on telling me that "television is a medium of spontaneity" and audiences would "never" watch filmed programs.

In 1962, we began a year of Sunday night movies. In black and white. Despite the impressive improvements in ABC's programming wrought during the Treyz years, we were still the third network. While ratings proved we captured 33 percent of the available audience—compared to just 15 percent in 1953—our advertising went for $10,000 a minute while CBS got $25,000 and NBC $22,000. So our $15.5 million annual profit was only a third of what CBS netted.

Soon we would have to face the music. Either we added color or we died. The cost of converting all our equipment was a mind-boggling $50 million.

Once we had color, of course, we would have to add a second night of movies. The Hollywood studios, who among themselves controlled virtually the entire supply, wanted $50 million for a three-year deal. And they wanted it in advance.

Before I could address these problems, however, I had to deal with a force more immediately threatening. His name was Norton Simon. He was known, then, as a collector of art and companies.

Simon used Hunt Foods & Industries, which included companies for grocery products, packaging and containers, and building products, as a base to build a powerful and diverse empire. This included McCall Publishing, which had *McCall's, Redbook*, and *Saturday Review* magazines, and a printing business that produced books and advertising brochures. Simon also had interests in meat packing and soft drinks.

By 1964 Simon had emerged as a formidable figure. *The Wall Street Journal* began to refer to him as an "industrialist," a "financier," and "a rugged corporate proxy in-fighter." I saw him as a troublemaker, a pain in the nether regions.

Simon's activities followed the classic pattern of raiders. Often using third parties to disguise his intentions, he acquired a strong minority interest in the shares of a publicly traded company. Once his activities were discernible, he maneuvered himself or a surrogate onto the board of directors. From there he was in a position to carry on a campaign of intimidation, agitation, and harassment.

Thus he would sow dissension and attempt to rally enough support from other board members to gain control of the board and hence the company. If this failed, he would make a tender offer to buy outstanding shares of the company. Inevitably this led to a proxy fight. These measures did not come cheap, but most of the expenses were borne by the stockholders.

Simon was somewhat successful at this sort of thing. But once in control of a new company, he often displayed a remarkable lack of aptitude for managing his prize. He had left more than one successful company floundering in his wake as he moved on to seek his next challenge.

George Jenkins, then chairman of the finance committee at Metropolitan Life and also a member of ABC's board, had had previous dealings with Norton Simon.

OTHER RECOLLECTIONS:
George Jenkins

Simon was trying to be a busybody, trying to make himself out as a major investor. I suppose in today's parlance you might call him a raider, although in those days maybe you would have called him a semiraider.

Metropolitan Life had a loan to the Wheeling Pittsburgh Steel Company. Simon decided that the business wasn't being run properly, so he bought a big block of stock. He got on the board and put forward all his good ideas on how to run a steel company, which were zero.

Soon Wheeling Pittsburgh was ready to go down the drain. We maneuvered to get Simon to sell his stock. We knew he wanted to get out, because he didn't know anything about the steel business and was in over his head, but he wanted to save face. We gave him a way to withdraw, and the company revived.

❑ ❑ ❑

I got word of Simon's interest in ABC in February 1964, when Gus Levy, senior partner at Goldman Sachs and a good friend, came to see me. Gus said Simon, through his companies Hunt and McCall, had been buying ABC stock for months. He was now among our biggest stockholders and wanted a seat on our board.

I said, "Gus, I have no objection to *you* going on our board, but I don't want Norton Simon on it."

"Do you mind meeting with him?"

"No."

With John Coleman, one of my directors, I went over to Simon's Fifth Avenue apartment, where he and several of his top associates awaited us.

One of Simon's surrogates was Herbert Mayes, president of McCall Corporation. Mayes started the meeting by telling Coleman, then considered New York's outstanding Catholic lay leader, how smart Catholics were to support Jewish charities.

"You contribute ten dollars to a Jewish charity and get back a hundred dollars from the Jews," he said.

Coleman, normally the most mild of men, almost had a fit. I had to restrain him from going after Mayes.

The meeting went downhill from there.

Simon asserted he could make a real contribution to ABC. He had purchased our stock, he said, because it was undervalued and had great upside potential. By changing certain accounting methods, he said, we could increase our apparent earnings and increase the value of our stock.

But more important, he said, an interest in ABC could help promote Hunt Foods. His competitors were giants, Del Monte and Heinz, and Hunt could not truly compete in their arena. But control of ABC, he said, could offset his size disadvantage by using broadcasting's power to persuade.

This was either very fuzzy thinking or double-talk. ABC didn't own the airwaves. We were licensed to operate on them in the public interest, convenience, and necessity. We couldn't turn the network into Simon's private advertising arm without putting our licenses in jeopardy, and I had no intention of letting ABC become anyone's tool.

I said I agreed our stock was undervalued, but we would never permit such an abuse of public trust as he suggested.

Simon replied, "You fellows have cumulative voting. I now have enough stock to entitle me to one seat on your board."

Cumulative voting was a little-used provision of a corporate charter based on one we inherited from Paramount Pictures. Under cumulative voting, each shareholder has one vote per share for each seat on the board of directors. He could vote all of them for any one board seat.

Simon said he wanted Herbert Mayes to have a seat on our board. I said I didn't believe the present members of the board would ever allow it. But, I added, we would be glad to accept Gus Levy if he could assure us that he would be representing all our stockholders and not just one interest.

To his everlasting credit, Gus said that under the circumstances he would have to represent the Simon interests. But, he added, his greatest desire was *not* to serve on our board in any capacity whatsoever.

When John Coleman and I left Simon's apartment, we decided that we must somehow get rid of cumulative voting.

OTHER RECOLLECTIONS:
Si Siegel

Leonard, John Coleman, and I met to discuss how to get rid of cumulative voting. The big problem was getting the financial houses to go along. They hate to give up any of their rights.

One of my jobs through the years was stockholder relations, even though somebody else was officially in charge of that. I spent a lot of time with our biggest stockholders. There were never unhappy surprises for them. If things were bad, they knew it well in advance.

I told them what the future held and how long something was going to hurt us. I predicted our earnings, and when we came out with these earnings, they developed a lot of faith in me.

So I had a lot of friends in the financial houses. I went around the country to see them. Mutual funds in Denver and Chicago, Fidelity Trust in Boston, all of them. They went along with us on cumulative voting. They believed me when I said it was best for the company.

❑ ❑ ❑

Simon made his move late in our fiscal year. By the time we could get ourselves together, our annual meeting was almost upon us. There was a real question whether we could get our ducks lined up in time.

It was a different world in those days. There were far fewer important stockholders to deal with than today. We knew many, and could call and talk to them.

So we got on the phones, Si and John and myself. We said, "We have enough real problems without having to deal with Norton Simon and his agenda. Simon is disruptive. He's out to tear this company apart. We won't be able to do the things we need to do. We are really getting our act together now. Go with us on this. You'll be better off in the long run. You'll make more money." And most of them supported us.

Simon continued to woo us. He invited me to a meeting at his Hotel Pierre suite on May 17, 1964. I brought Si. Simon brought Mrs. Stella Russell, a McCall Corporation director.

When it suited him, Simon could turn on the charm. This sly rascal began by trying to make us feel sorry for him! He'd been trying to acquire Canada Dry, he said, and had far more of their stock than he had yet bought of ours. But Canada Dry's directors had refused even to meet with him or to give him any information at all about their company.

We had been more forthcoming, he said. He was glad to be doing business with such helpful people. But since we had rejected his bid for a board seat, his lack of success with Canada Dry might cause him embarrassment. He wanted our help in cooking up a plan to save his face on Wall Street.

The fellow had a lot of nerve, I'll give him that.

Next, Simon apologized for Mayes's remark to John Coleman. The meeting had gotten off to a bad start, he said, and he wanted a chance to start over.

Then he began questioning Si about our accounting methods. He asked to send someone over to take a look at our books.

Si wore his poker face and said only that he'd be glad to answer specific questions, but he wasn't going to have outsiders poking around in our books.

My own inclination was to run, not walk, out of that hotel room. But I remembered the story S.A. Lynch told me when I first joined Paramount in 1933, about the way he'd lost millions by walking out of a Coca-Cola board meeting and slamming the door behind him.

I left, but I didn't slam any doors.

After talking it over with Si Siegel, however, I decided we didn't want to dicker with Simon over anything.

We pulled out all the stops to get rid of cumulative voting. This required a special meeting immediately before our annual meeting. By law, we had to give a certain amount of notice, but we didn't want to tip our hand early. We waited until the last possible minute to mail notices.

At the special meeting, several people, perhaps seeing a chance for a short-term gain if Simon went on to make a tender offer, backed Simon's bid for a board seat. When the motion was made to eliminate cumulative voting, there were shouts of "Unfair! Unfair!" from the floor. When we put it to a vote, however, we won by over 6 to 1.

Cumulative voting was gone, but Simon was still a threat. He went on buying stock.

In October 1965, Simon made yet another pass. He replaced Herb Mayes, president of McCall, with Arthur Murphy. Raymond Rich, McCall's chairman, asked to have lunch with me. I invited him to our executive dining room.

Murphy and Rich oozed cordiality as they recounted McCall's successes. Rich mentioned that Murphy had experience in television. When he was at Time-Life, Murphy had something to do with the *March of Time* newsreels.

As lunch was served, Rich brought up the subject of Curtis Publishing, a rival to McCall. Curtis had about $50 million in tax losses that they'd carried forward from previous years. Rich suggested that since there didn't seem to be much chance of them making enough profit in publishing to offset that, they should go buy a few television stations. These would be good investments even if they had to pay more than market value, he said, because with the tax loss factor, the government, in effect, would be helping to pay for them.

I knew that Rich hadn't asked to meet with us so we could discuss a company that neither of us had an interest in. He was trying to open up the subject of buying ABC.

So I told him that under a proposed new FCC rule, if another company acquired ABC, there was no guaranty the FCC would transfer all our station licenses. In fact, I said, it was likely that they wouldn't. That would mean that as many as three of our stations, all in the top fifty markets, would be up for bid to anyone else who could qualify for the license.

Ray Rich should never play poker, because his face gives him away. He was very surprised.

I thought this was a good time to mention that I was aware that he'd met with Alger Chapman, one of our directors, earlier in the week. "All the members of my board are quite loyal to management, and they make it a point to apprise me of this sort of thing," I said. "And so I also know that you've been trying to meet with John Coleman, but he's not interested in such a meeting."

Rich turned red and mumbled something about having a very pleasant meeting with Chapman.

Come to think of it, I would have loved to see Rich across the green felt. I might have made quite a killing.

Then Rich said McCall owned the rights to many stories, published in one or another of their magazines, which could be made into good television programs.

"That was tried by *Reader's Digest* and *Saturday Evening Post*, and they were not successful," I said. "That doesn't mean the idea has no merit. If you can come up with a format, our network program people would be glad to discuss it."

Murphy said he'd send us a proposal within a month. We never heard from him again. But Simon kept buying stock.

There were others interested in acquiring ABC. I got a call from someone at General Electric, who said they were exploring the possibility of a merger. I suggested there might be antitrust problems, and they should look into this. I never heard from them again.

The first overture from ITT came by way of Fidelity Fund, when Gerry Tsai came over to chat about a possible merger in late 1964. ITT wasn't offering very much money, and I wasn't much interested in a merger, so nothing came of it.

Meanwhile, our lack of color broadcasting had begun to erode our competitiveness. We still needed to buy movies. We had little prospect of borrowing the kind of money we needed from banks. And then I heard from Harold Geneen, head of ITT.

I was playing tennis with my good friend Larry Tisch, head of Loews, when he told me that Geneen, whom he knew very well, had put out some feelers about a merger.

Geneen had been trying to buy a network for some time. He met with Frank Stanton twice. Stanton, CBS president, was mildly interested. Bill Paley, their board chairman, was not.

ITT had started in Cuba in 1920. By 1925 it was a holding company for telephone and telegraph operations there and in Puerto Rico. Then it bought Western Electric's international manufacturing division. By World War II it was a big company. It lost some of its overseas holdings during the war, and took big losses in a couple of consumer-product ventures, and by 1959 it was on the ropes.

Geneen, who was everything Norton Simon aspired to be, was executive VP of Raytheon. ITT hired him as president, and he turned the company around. He started buying companies and building them up. Eventually he would acquire more than 350 corporations and turn ITT into a very profitable company.

I met with Geneen and found him very interesting. He'd commissioned Roth, Gerard & Company to do an analysis of ABC, and they were very high on our potential. They concluded that, with enough working capital and some time, the network could become very profitable. My feelings exactly.

At first I wasn't much interested in a merger. I didn't want to work for somebody else. Equally important, I was concerned about the potential for abuse of broadcasting's power.

ITT was about 6 percent foreign-owned and had extensive holdings around the world. Would its management allow the network's news division, for example, to report unflattering truths about countries where ITT's investment could be affected by that country's government? Would ABC executives, knowing their promotions and perquisites were at the mercy of those concerned with ITT's bottom line, be willing to broadcast programs that might cut the parent company's profit?

I raised these issues with Geneen. He assured me that ABC would have "complete autonomy."

Geneen indicated that he wanted ABC for several reasons. We were the smallest company in a young and growing industry, so we were a good investment. But there was an even more important reason. Geneen believed that ITT's stock was not selling for anywhere near its true value because the company was perceived as a foreign corporation. It was not well known to small investors. But if ABC became part of ITT, the parent company's name would be in America's living rooms every day.

During our discussion Geneen sweetened the pot. His first offer was about $70 a share, which was above the current market price. When I didn't immediately accept, he raised it to $80. I thought he would go higher. Each time I refused to make a deal—but left the door open—he kept going up. Finally, at $85.50, he indicated there would be no higher offer. I was inclined to believe him.

I was ABC's chief executive, but I didn't control the company. I thought that at some point ABC's board of directors would be vulnerable to legal sanction if we didn't consider a price that was far above what our stock was selling for. We couldn't simply reject an offer that benefited stockholders.

All the while, Norton Simon continued to accumulate our stock. I sent Si Siegel over to negotiate with Geneen.

OTHER RECOLLECTIONS:
Si Siegel

Geneen was a helluva bright guy. I thought we had a good chance with him, but I worried about who he would send to ABC to represent ITT if a merger went through. Who would be his Bob O'Brien? Who would be his Si Siegel?

Geneen had a very fine financial man, Hart Perry. We worked out the deal. Perry was very bright and very realistic, so I said I wanted him named as part of the deal.

Geneen refused. That always worried me. That was a clue as to how much he would take over.

When we signed the deal and the board approved it, it was a very sad day. I saw it as the beginning of the end of what we had built.

❑ ❑ ❑

On December 7, 1965—my sixtieth birthday—I presented the deal to the board. I said that we'd also had an offer from Litton Industries. It was somewhat less than ITT's. I reminded everyone that Norton Simon was still in the picture. Then Si got up and spoke about the business aspects.

As a subsidiary, ITT's automated accounting department would be available to us and would save us millions because we wouldn't have to build our own. He talked about ITT's expertise in telecommunications engineering, which would be invaluable to us in many areas, not least in converting to color. Si also discussed how ITT, as an international company, could assist the growth of ABC International. Finally, he pointed out that affiliating with a larger company would enhance our image in the advertising community. We could expect to attract more affluent sponsors, which would increase our earnings.

Part of the deal was that Si and I would join the ITT board, and ITT would put two people on ABC's. Si and I were to be guaranteed long-term employment. If for any reason Geneen wanted us out, it would cost him a great deal of money in the form of cash settlements to us.

From a business perspective it made perfect sense. Personally, however, I did not relish the idea of reporting to anyone, even Harold Geneen. Nevertheless, with a heavy heart I recommended we take ITT's deal. The board voted to accept.

Our stockholders met on April 27, 1966. Norton Simon's minions made a last-gasp attempt to derail the merger, but they were voted down. The merger was approved.

ITT's stockholders met the same day to consider the merger. Geneen made a curious comment at this meeting. He said the subject of autonomy for ABC had been "overemphasized" and the FCC had indicated that ITT must be "responsible" for ABC. I wasn't worried, however. I had demanded and got a contract from Geneen guaranteeing ABC total management autonomy unless there was "material deterioration" in our company's affairs. It was the first and only time Geneen gave such a guarantee. The merger was approved by ITT's shareholders.

There was much curiosity about us at ITT and vice versa. So executives from the two companies began meeting. The idea was to give everyone a chance to get used to each other's corporate culture.

OTHER RECOLLECTIONS:
Edgar Scherick

We met all the ITT executives, among them a couple of guys who later went to jail in the bribery scandal. We invited them to a cocktail party at our offices.

Geneen had a reputation of being very tough. Our controller, Mike Boland, was a tough little Irishman. I was standing with Leonard and Geneen, so I called him over and said, "Harold, I'd like you to meet our controller, one of the sweetest, most decent, lovely men in the whole world."

All the blood drained from Boland's face, because "sweet and decent" are the last things any controller wants to be known as.

❑ ❑ ❑

The only hurdle to our merger was the FCC. The hearings were scheduled for September 1966. We expected little opposition. In a departure from routine, the commission had announced that the merger would be considered for approval in *one* day of oral hearings.

I testified for almost four hours. Many of the questions were points I had raised to Geneen concerning ABC's autonomy and our ability to report international news without bias. As many had predicted, the proceedings ran over the allotted time and were continued for a second day. When the hearings were recessed, FCC Chairman Rosel Hyde indicated that a decision would be announced in a few days.

It was not. There was concern in the Senate and in the Justice Department that the ITT merger was not in the public interest and that it might be anticompetitive.

Senator Gaylord Nelson wrote to the FCC, asking Hyde to look further into ITT's possible influence on ABC's news reporting. He said the very fact of their assurances to the contrary confirmed that they did have such power.

Senator Wayne Morse also wrote to the FCC. He said that he'd seen evidence that ITT officials disguised campaign contributions to Lyndon Johnson in 1960 by funneling them through reimbursable executive expense accounts.

On December 20, 1966, Donald Turner, chief of the Justice Department's antitrust section, sent a very peculiar letter to Chairman Hyde. He raised ITT's entry into cable broadcasting as a possible conflict of interest. He also asserted that ITT would be able to use unsold network advertising time to gain unfair advantage over its competitors.

Couched in elliptical terms, Turner seemed to be saying that, while he doubted Justice could win a court case to stop the merger, he hoped Hyde would nevertheless do the right thing and either disapprove it or convene further hearings.

Bureaucrats are by nature territorial animals. Hyde was no exception. The very next day the FCC approved the merger. The three Democratic commissioners, however, voted against it.

It was like 1951 all over again. Two days before the decision was to take effect, Justice put aside their white gloves and issued a stiffly formal petition to the FCC, urging reconsideration and calling for further hearings.

Faced with the prospects of a court case where Justice would argue the FCC hadn't been thorough, Hyde reluctantly scheduled new hearings for April—seven months after the original hearings, which had been expected to last only a single day.

This time the proceedings lasted two weeks. All the old issues were raised in more detail. The most important matter, of course, was whether ITT could be trusted to own a network. A lot of dirt was dredged up about ITT's past dealings.

The Justice Department got the hearing administrator to rule that all witnesses were to be sequestered in a nearby room until they had testified. Years later, I learned an ITT executive had hidden a tape recorder in her oversized handbag. After secretly recording the proceedings, she passed the tapes along to ITT's outside counsel to give to Geneen.

These attorneys were smart enough to destroy the tapes immediately. Geneen didn't know about them until the executive who made the recordings, Dita Beard, asked if he'd enjoyed listening to them. Beard became notorious in the 1970s when her secret memos revealed that ITT had at least attempted to bribe Nixon Administration officials to settle an antitrust case in ITT's favor.

The hearings were very heavy-handed, but when the votes were counted, the merger was again approved. The same three commissioners voted against it.

In July 1967, Justice filed suit in the Court of Appeals to stop the merger.

The trial opened on October 17, 1967. By that time Geneen and I were both nervous as well. Our arrangement had included an escape clause. If FCC approval was not forthcoming by January 1, 1968, either one of us could pull out.

ABC had the most to lose if the merger was called off. Since the merger agreement prohibited us from borrowing long-term capital from the banks, we were still stymied on color conversion. ITT had become our bankers, and we were into them for $25 million. Worse, since we were still a black-and-white network competing with two nearly all-color networks, our income was down and our earnings declining.

Meanwhile ITT, with far greater resources, had continued to expand. Propelled into the public eye by the storm surrounding the proposed merger, their stock had risen from around $70/share when the merger was announced to nearly $110/share. With good income from operations and with two new domestic mergers in the works, their price-to-earnings ratio had risen threefold. Geneen had accomplished one of his goals without even consummating the merger.

The courtroom portion of the Justice suit was over quickly. Very little new information was argued by either side. The judges retired to deliberate, indicating a verdict might come in December. Nobody doubted that whatever the ruling, either side might appeal, causing further delay.

December came and went without a decision.

Over the holidays, Isabelle and I took a little vacation. We went to Nassau, where my friend Larry Tisch had just opened Paradise Island, a resort hotel. On New Year's Day, I was on the tennis court, playing a game with Larry.

I heard my name over the public address loudspeakers. An overseas phone call was waiting for me in the lobby.

It was Si Siegel in New York. He'd heard a radio bulletin. Geneen had called together his directors that morning, and they had voted to back out of the merger.

I didn't know whether to laugh or cry. As I walked back to the tennis courts, I passed Gerry Tsai, the fellow who had first suggested the merger with ITT. I gave the news to Larry Tisch, who had set up my first meeting with Geneen.

Much later in the day, Geneen telephoned to make it official. He gave no reason for backing out. I could think of nothing to say except, "Good luck."

But we didn't part enemies. We get along well even today. Several years after the merger was called off, I went to a Banker's Trust advisory board meeting. He's on that board. We had dinner, and he said, "What happened at ABC? You fellows have been going ahead by leaps and bounds, daytime, nighttime. . . ."

"It's very simple. You didn't give us any choice. After you called it off, we rolled up our sleeves and went to work."

At the time, however, it was an unpleasant shock. Nor was I pleased to learn that Norton Simon, who had practically driven us into ITT's arms, dumped his ABC shares when the deal was called off but still made $10 million.

ABC was in a lot of trouble, no doubt about it. It was going to get worse before it got better. Our stock, which had soared to $80 a share in December, fell to $45 by March.

Still hoping to merge ourselves out of harm's way, we talked to a few other corporate suitors. One was Monogram Industries, a rapidly expanding California conglomerate. But when we learned that the company had built its expansion on the manufacture of aircraft toilets, we lost interest. It was a good company, but we were in show business. Toilets of any kind presented exactly the wrong image.

Feature film prices had continued to rise, and locking up the inventory we needed would now cost $125 million. We worked out a deal with Manufacturer's Trust to factor the sale. They paid the studios and held film rights as security. We paid them for each film as we aired it.

But we still needed at least $50 million to convert to color transmission. The banks were not about to lend it. After some discussion, we decided to issue debentures—in effect, corporate IOU's—to raise this money.

The very day we registered our intention to sell these debentures with the Securities and Exchange Commission (SEC), an order was issued from a Las Vegas hotel penthouse. On July 1, 1968, Howard Hughes, the most mysterious figure in America, tendered a $150 million offer to buy control of ABC.

I hadn't spoken to Howard Hughes since the 1940s, when I tried to buy RKO's theaters from him. But several times in the preceding year I had been contacted by various emissaries, each time a different person.

The previous October, after the Court of Appeals heard the ITT merger case, Gregson Bautzer, an attorney for Hughes Tool Company, had called to suggest that if the ITT merger failed, Hughes would like to step in and take their place. I told him we weren't interested.

Just after ITT withdrew, another Hughes lawyer called. He asked me to go to Las Vegas. Howard Hughes wanted to meet me.

I might have hopped on a plane and satisfied my personal curiosity about this enigmatic character. After all, he reputedly saw no one outside a tiny circle of top aides. I resisted the temptation. I had better things to do.

I wondered, then and now, what Hughes wanted with ABC. Perhaps he was seeking a forum for his political views.

When he was younger, Hughes had a good feeling for the entertainment industry. He liked the glamour, and he certainly knew how to promote a movie. Look what he did with *The Outlaw*, a very poor film from beginning to end. He saved it by spreading the idea that he'd used his engineering background to develop a special brassiere for Jane Russell. That made it controversial. People came flocking in to see her cleavage.

After Hughes's first approach, Max Rabb, later United States ambassador to Italy, John Loeb of Loeb Rhodes, and several other attorneys approached me on Hughes's behalf. They said he wanted to buy our television stations.

I told them all, "That's crazy, why would we want to sell our stations?"

Loeb came to see me on Friday, June 28, and again said Hughes wanted our stations. Still not interested, I said. Three days later, on Monday morning, Hughes made his tender offer. Loeb hadn't said a word about it on Friday. This still bothers me.

We had to deal with the tender at once. Worried, I called in John Coleman, Si, and Ev Erlick, ABC's general counsel.

OTHER RECOLLECTIONS:
Ev Erlick

The Hughes tender offer was to become effective on the same day that ABC went into registration on a new debt issue. But when you're in a registration period and securities are offered for sale, by law no officer of a public company may make any statement beyond that in the registration statement.

Hughes's people thought that since we were in registration, we could make no response to their tender. Whether it was good, bad, or indifferent, whether the values were there or not. Theoretically, we were barred from saying anything. That turned out to be a boomerang.

As soon as it happened, we realized we had a helluva problem. Leonard asked for an appointment with SEC Chairman Manny Cohen. We went to him very early in the morning.

We said, "Look, we know you're a fair man, we know you want to see equity done. You're not going to decide on the spot, but please hear our position."

"What do you have on your mind?" he said.

We said that we were constrained from speaking out, but we needed to make a public statement.

Cohen said, "What do you want to say?"

I just happened to have an ad in my pocket. He read it and said, "I'm chairman of this commission. I don't approve ads. Go see so-and-so." And he said, "What else are you going to do?"

"More things along these lines."

"Well, I don't approve ads, but you go see so-and-so, and tell him what your problem is, and maybe we can work something out."

While we were on the way down, obviously, Cohen picks up the phone and calls this guy, and says, "Look, these guys have a point, and they're really in a tight squeeze. It's wrong that they shouldn't be able to state their point of view."

We got in, and this guy adds a couple of chicken scratches to our ad. He said, "I'm not going to clear it. I'm not going to tell you it's okay, but I'm not going to do anything about it."

So we cleared the SEC that way.

The FCC is in charge of transfer of licenses, but Hughes didn't go to the FCC to make an application for transfer simultaneous with his tender.

Leonard and our Washington attorney, Jim McKenna, went to see FCC chairman Rosel Hyde. Leonard said, "We're going to fight this. We're not asking you to do anything, right now. Just understand our position. We're going to lay it out on the table for you.

"We think it's wrong that some guy in a green eye shade sitting out in Las Vegas should control one of the three great communications mediums in this country. We'll fight, hard as we can, everywhere we can. FCC, court, in the press, on the beaches, on the hills, we shall never surrender."

He nodded and listened and said he understood our position. Then he told his general counsel, Henry Geller, to follow this very closely.

❑ ❑ ❑

On the morning of July 3, Hughes's attorney, Greg Bautzer, showed up at my office. Bautzer said he couldn't understand why we were so upset. Hughes just wanted to help us. We needed money to buy color equipment and movies, and he could provide it. He said that Hughes wasn't out to get rid of ABC's management, and that he really wasn't interested in profits. He just wanted to help out.

I don't believe in Santa Claus, the Tooth Fairy, or the Easter Bunny. I saw no reason to believe in Howard Hughes.

"That kind of help we do not need," I replied.

When Bautzer left, I renewed some discussions I'd had earlier in the year with CIT Financial Corporation. If we did not stop Hughes in court, our sole remaining option was to find a white knight, a merger partner who would prevent us from being swallowed by Hughes. CIT had offered to make a tender offer of its own for our shares, but if there were to be a merger, I wanted ABC to be the surviving corporation.

So I made a counter offer. I proposed that ABC issue $1.2 billion in convertible bonds in exchange for all CIT's stock, then worth about $800 million. If shareholders later chose to convert their bonds to stock, CIT's shareholders would wind up with about 75 percent of the merged corporation.

CIT's board agreed to consider my offer. After a day-long meeting, however, they turned it down. They believed the activities of Howard Hughes made the situation far too complicated and risky. He had huge resources, and there was some chance he could have swallowed us both.

It looked like our last chance to stop Hughes was in court. We beefed up our legal team with several outside firms and presented our case to Judge Dudley Bonsal in federal court. We argued that Hughes should have gone to the FCC first, since the issue was within their jurisdiction. And we said his hands were dirty because he came in at midnight the day we went into registration. We said the court shouldn't permit this sort of underhanded tactic.

Our struggle against Hughes was one of the toughest times of my life. I was very worried about what would happen to ABC if he took us over. The possibilities were so catastrophic that I just couldn't leave the matter at the office.

OTHER RECOLLECTIONS:
Isabelle Goldenson

It was a terrible thing. I was so afraid. It was like fighting a tidal wave. I've never understood how Leonard could hold up under that. He was terrific. He had so much to take care of, and this did not allow him to attend to his business, except with great strain. I was really worried about his health.

He got very attractive offers for his company from big financial companies—you'd be amazed. Nobody knew about them. They called him at home and wanted to meet at hotel suites so nobody would know.

These people wouldn't show their faces, because if this ever got out they would be in terribly ill repute. It was disgraceful, to make an offer behind the back of their company. They hinted that he could make millions, himself. This was like a bribe.

And Leonard wasn't the least bit interested. He just kept repeating, "If you want to meet me, everybody is welcome in my office. I'll be happy to discuss it there." Of course they wouldn't come to the office.

These people are all very greedy. You don't find Leonard trying to gain control of any company that's helpless. It demonstrates a lack of character. He's always told our girls that character is just as important as brains and work. You have to have character or you cannot succeed.

❑ ❑ ❑

During the court proceedings a newspaper reporter noticed a tall, gaunt, somewhat disheveled man sitting on a back bench. He bore an extraordinary resemblance to what few photos were available of Howard Hughes. The reporter, sensing a scoop, went to speak to him. Without replying, the man hurried out of the room. Soon he was pursued by a pack of reporters and photographers. Cornered at last, he turned out to be an insurance salesman named Bill Donovan.

This incident helped to crystallize our thinking about a strategy to defeat Hughes. He was a recluse who hadn't been seen in public for many years. If Judge Bonsal would stop Hughes from making a tender offer until he was approved for broadcast license transfer by the FCC, we might persuade the FCC to insist Hughes personally appear for questioning before the commission. We were betting he'd never show his face.

On July 10, Judge Bonsal ruled. Our request for a temporary injunction was denied. We immediately filed a request for a *permanent* injunction. Bonsal denied it as well. Now our only hope was an appeal—and that could take weeks or months. Hughes would use that time to buy up our stock.

ABC filed a writ with the U.S. Court of Appeals. By great good fortune, the presiding justice was Henry Friendly, the same fellow who was instrumental in getting me hired by Paramount in 1933. We asked the court to conduct an immediate full hearing on the merits of our case.

OTHER RECOLLECTIONS:
Ev Erlick

A couple of Hughes's attorneys went to see the administrative judge of the Court of Appeals. They started to argue the case! They told him, "Let the market work its will. You shouldn't interfere with a tender offer." So while apparently talking procedure, Hughes's lawyers were actually arguing substance.

But this judge was not about to rule on the merits of the case. He was administrative. His job was to decide whether an appeal should be heard now, next week, or next year. (Of course, if you let the thing go and have an appeal next month, and in the meantime don't enjoin it, the company's gone.)

So Hughes's people made a big mistake. It was poor form, and it went down very hard. Our guys just said, "This is a vital question to this company, its stockholders, and its 7,000 employees. We urge you to hear this as soon as possible." That's all it's proper to say on a procedural presentation.

A day later I get a call from our outside counsel: "They've set this thing down for a full hearing on the merits on Monday." This was Friday. Such speed was unheard of, if not unprecedented. Certainly very, very unusual.

This was a three-judge court, Judge Friendly presiding. He was a marvelous, articulate, corporate lawyer who should have been on the Supreme Court. After a full hearing on all the issues, he looked at his cohorts and said, "Let's go into the back room." And he told everyone in the courtroom, "Stay here for a few minutes. Don't go anywhere."

In about half an hour they came back. Judge Friendly says, "We're going to render a decision from the bench. We'll write it up formally in due course, but in the meantime, this is it:

"Number one, the FCC should have full jurisdiction over this proceeding. One cannot transfer licenses in this fashion. A full application should be made for transfer—if that's Hughes's intent. The FCC should move immediately to have full hearings to determine the fitness and character of the licensee, his financial capabilities—everything it usually does to determine qualifications.

"Second, ABC can say whatever it wants.

"Third, nothing is going to happen in the meantime, and this court will retain jurisdiction of the proceeding. If the FCC does not act, *we* will act. And we grant your request for a stay."

That weekend wires went out from the FCC to Hughes and to his principal associates, including Bautzer.

They said, "Show up for a full hearing on Monday morning at 10. Be prepared to testify openly and publicly, to everything involved in your tender. We're going to treat this as an application for license transfer."

Well, Mr. Hughes didn't care for public testimony. Never did. And by the time this happened, the scale had tipped. People then realized there was no way the FCC would approve handing over the ABC network and those stations to a guy pulling the strings from behind closed doors. No way.

Hughes wouldn't have got one vote. How do I know? I know.

When Hughes got the telegram, "Testify publicly on Monday," he knew the war was over.

❑ ❑ ❑

Within hours Hughes's outside counsel called our outside counsel, asking for a meeting. They said, "Howard Hughes wants to withdraw his tender offer. If he does, will you agree not to sue him for damages and costs?"

We had a quick meeting and agreed that if he withdrew unconditionally and without qualification, we would just drop the matter. Hughes agreed, and that ended his threat.

(Many years later, as this book went to press, I learned that Bautzer had convinced Howard Hughes to go after ABC by telling him that his close friend, Jim Aubrey, would be the perfect man to run ABC. This happened just after Aubrey had been fired from his job as head of the CBS Network.)

Dealing with Norton Simon, Howard Hughes, and Harold Geneen was both expensive and distracting: It set us back, no question about it. But I thank my lucky stars ITT pulled out.

In the early 1970s it was discovered that ITT helped foment a coup in Chile, and there followed a host of shocking revelations about ITT's involvement in corporate bribery. Had we been part of that company, our credibility would have been zero. In the early 1980s ITT faltered. It lost momentum just at the brink of a new era in communications technology.

Despite what happened in the aftermath, not merging with ITT was one of the best things that ever happened to ABC. And I learned how to swim with sharks.

15

Network News

❑

Senator Joseph McCarthy of Wisconsin brought his anticommunist witch hunt to a climax in 1954, with thirty-six days of hearings into "Red influence" in the Army.

ABC aired all 187 hours of hearings, live, from the moment McCarthy gaveled the room to order to the minute he ended the Fort Monmouth, New Jersey, proceedings. Lawyers, politicians, and witnesses—the cast of McCarthy's scripted but unrehearsed melodrama—became as familiar to viewers as movie stars.

This exercise in public service cost us upward of $600,000, which we could ill-afford then. But I felt very strongly—as I feel right now—that McCarthy was no good.

I watched most of the hearings, often cringing as McCarthy and his cohorts browbeat witnesses, pontificated absurd assertions to the cameras, and made innocent people seem like traitors.

McCarthy's conduct was so outrageous that to this day I carry images of the hearings in the back of my mind as a reminder of what can happen, even in this country, if a demagogue gets control of the mass media.

For years McCarthy had abused his office to advance his own political career, in the process stifling much dissent. He succeeded for a time in intimidating and frightening America's creative community. Many lives and careers were ruined.

Eventually, backed by Stanton and Paley at CBS, Edward R. Murrow courageously attacked McCarthy's demagoguery. But during the Army hearings, since both CBS and NBC had extensive daytime schedules and ABC had little or nothing on the air, NBC and CBS presented only highlights of the proceedings on their respective evening news programs.

I felt that if the public could see just how McCarthy operated, they would understand just how ridiculous a figure he really was. That was the greatest contribution we could have made at that time. I also saw this as an opportunity for us to establish the presence of ABC News.

In truth, there was very little presence to establish. Under Kintner, ABC News was primarily the creature of John Charles Daly.

OTHER RECOLLECTIONS:
Julius Barnathan

> Kintner hired John Daly, who will always be known as the voice of Pearl Harbor. He was on CBS, on Sunday morning, the first voice everybody heard: "We interrupt this program. . . ." At ABC he was God. He was VP of News, he was executive producer, he was the on-air talent. How could you say anything about what he did? You couldn't. He had a quick temper and a contract such that, if Kintner ever criticized, he hung up on him.

❑ ❑ ❑

We had no film crews overseas. Instead we relied on Fox Movietone or Hearst Telenews. When we could get a reporter to the scene, the correspondent narrated over the pictures. But we could afford few foreign correspondents. Often our news came from wire-service reports that Daly read into a studio camera.

CBS and NBC dominated broadcast news. In the 1930s and 1940s, when network radio came of age, those networks practically invented news broadcasting.

Unlike entertainment viewing, news viewing is a habit, and the older the audience, the stronger its loyalty to a particular newscast. When I came to ABC, most news viewers watched the other networks. They soon became glued to Cronkite or Huntley–Brinkley, and would be for years. There was little we could do about it. I knew it would take us a long time to build an audience for ABC News, because we would have to start with the younger people, who are more likely to switch channels, and get them in the habit of watching us.

In local news, ABC stations didn't fare much better. We slowly acquired new affiliates, but most were the newest or least competitive in their respective markets. Often the stations were UHF channels, with weak signals and limited audiences. They couldn't afford to spend as much on news as their competitors, the more strongly entrenched stations.

We had so much to do to make ABC a competitive third network—

and such limited resources—that I decided to concentrate our funds and talent on building entertainment programming. That was, I felt, the surest way to attract bigger audiences and better affiliates. We put development of our news department on the back burner for a time.

But that didn't mean we ignored news. I'd inherited a weekend news commentary program featuring Drew Pearson, the Washington newspaper columnist. He presented a very distinguished appearance, and he was a gifted speaker. But he had a right-wing, conspiratorial viewpoint. Some of the things he said on the air were of dubious authenticity. I have little doubt *he* believed everything he said, but after a few years his credibility had so diminished that I had to take him off.

Starting in 1957, Mike Wallace—whose style, in those early years, was sometimes akin to that of Geraldo Rivera in the 1980s—had a thirty-minute interview show on Saturday nights. Mike's guests once included an avowed Mafioso, shown in silhouette to protect his identity, who revealed how the Mob did business in New York, Chicago, and Las Vegas.

In 1958, one of Wallace's guests was Drew Pearson. Pearson dropped a bombshell: He said Senator John F. Kennedy had *not* written his Pulitzer Prize–winning book, *Profiles in Courage*. He said Theodore Sorensen actually wrote the book, and allowed Kennedy to claim authorship.

Immediately after that broadcast, John Coleman got a call from Joseph P. Kennedy, Senator Kennedy's father. Joe Kennedy, a former ambassador to Great Britain, was a multimillionaire shipbuilder and financier, an extraordinarily influential Catholic layman who knew Coleman quite well.

Kennedy said that his son and Clark Clifford, their attorney, wanted to meet me in my office at 9 Monday morning.

I had done a little business with Joe Kennedy back in the 1930s, when I helped reorganize Paramount's New England theaters. And I'd met his son John a few times in Washington. The moment I heard Joe Kennedy had called, I realized he must already have decided that John would run for President. They weren't taking any chances with his reputation.

I agreed to see them. In the meantime I had our news department checking Drew Pearson's statement. Our Washington bureau found that Pearson had overheard part of a Sorensen conversation at a cocktail party. I asked to have Sorensen come to New York as soon as possible and arranged for our outside counsel to interview him. I wanted to know if he'd actually made that statement, and if so, why.

John Kennedy and Clark Clifford appeared promptly at 9 Monday. I told them, "It will take about three hours for us to complete our investigation. Do you want to come back?"

"Oh, no," said Kennedy. "We're going to sit here until you give us an answer." And they camped in my office.

Sorensen told our attorneys that Kennedy, bedridden in Georgia while being treated for a chronic back injury, sent him requests for certain books and papers from the Library of Congress. Sorensen found the material and sent it to Kennedy. As Kennedy wrote drafts of each chapter, he sent them back to Sorensen for editing. Sorensen's principal contribution was improving Kennedy's punctuation and spelling. He had nothing to do with the creative side of the book.

In similar circumstances, networks had made air time available to various individuals so they might tell their side of the story. But in this case, the error was ours, not Kennedy's. I felt it was our responsibility to set the record straight. The next Saturday night Ollie Treyz, then head of the network, appeared at the top of Wallace's show to apologize and to say we had been mistaken.

Not long afterward, Wallace quit and went to CBS. Upon learning this, I called to ask why. He said, "John Daly's in charge of news. If a plum assignment comes along, he takes it himself. Nobody has a chance. The man running the news shouldn't be on the air." He was absolutely right. At that moment, however, my priorities had to be elsewhere.

The Presidential election of 1960 was the first to use television in a significant way. The candidates, Nixon and Kennedy, agreed to a series of four televised debates. The three networks drew lots, and CBS won the right to broadcast the first, in Chicago. NBC had the second, in Washington, and ABC got the last two in New York. I attended all four.

In advance of the New York broadcasts, I sent word to each candidate that we would make our facilities available for three hours before each debate. Their respective adversary would not be present, and each would have free rein to look at anything in the studio and to do whatever he wished.

Kennedy came with his brother, Robert, and with their own producer and director. They used virtually all three hours, carefully checking each rostrum and the lighting. Robert got up in the control booth and directed Jack, suggesting gestures, body language, and small movements around the rostrum.

Nixon showed up twenty minutes before the debate. I said to myself then, "Here's a man trying for the most important office in the world, and he's giving it short shrift."

* * *

Just after Kennedy was elected President, in November 1960, I had a call from Senator John Pastore. He chaired the Senate Communications Subcommittee, which had oversight of the broadcasting industry.

Pastore asked me down to Washington. "I know you're making some progress, and I know you've been losing money, but I think you've got to start addressing yourself to the news problem," he said. "If you're ever going to build ABC in the eyes of the Senate and the House—in Washington, generally—you're going to have to build your news operation."

I agreed. We had deferred action until we could afford it, but I could now see we had do something.

I went to see President Eisenhower, whose term expired in a few months. I said I wanted to offer Jim Hagerty, his press secretary, a job as head of ABC News after the President left office. The possibility of coloring Hagerty's judgments in dealing with ABC's correspondents couldn't be ignored, so I didn't want to make an offer while Hagerty was still press secretary unless Eisenhower approved.

Eisenhower said, "Go right ahead." I contacted Hagerty, and we made a deal to bring him to ABC.

Shortly after Lyndon Johnson became President, Hagerty and I visited Eisenhower in Washington. Johnson invited us all over to lunch. Johnson asked Eisenhower what he thought about the Vietnam situation. Eisenhower said, "Mr. President, my advice is to stay out of it. Maybe you could send a few advisers, but don't get us into it."

Sadly, this advice was too late, and Johnson chose to ignore it. I thought Johnson was terribly misguided. I'll never know for sure, but I think he believed winning in Vietnam was going to be his crowning glory, his big chance to make a mark in history. He thought Vietnam would be his Alamo.

Johnson telephoned often, on a variety of subjects. He was very thin-skinned, and sometimes he objected to the way he was treated in the news. I don't mean to single him out on this. While I never heard from Eisenhower or Jerry Ford in this regard, every other President since 1960 has felt, at one time or another, that ABC's reporting hadn't quite measured up to his own view of events. I got calls, from time to time, from each of them.

Usually when a President called, I'd say, "I'm sure our people are trying to be objective and fair, but I'll check it, and if they're not, I will certainly bring it to their attention very forcefully."

And, on occasion, I did speak to the head of news or his deputy. But I always said, "You're running the news department, and if you feel you've been objective, I'm satisfied." And that was it. I never reported back to the White House. We never bowed down to any President.

But when it came to calling me, Johnson was in a class by himself. It was just his nature. He was thinking of Lyndon Johnson first, last, and always.

After hiring Hagerty to head ABC News, I asked John Daly to resign. Jim brought in several top people, including Howard K. Smith, a Rhodes scholar who had been with CBS. Smith became our evening news anchor.

Two years after Nixon lost to Kennedy, he ran for governor of California and lost again. He called a news conference and told the reporters, "You won't have Nixon to kick around any more," because, he said, he was through with politics.

Howard K. Smith came up with a documentary, "The Political Obituary of Richard M. Nixon." Nixon, who had risen to national prominence while in the Congress, became famous for his attempts to root out communists in government. One of the people he went after was Alger Hiss, who was prosecuted for perjury as a result of Nixon's investigation.

Howard K. Smith offered Nixon an opportunity to come on the program, but he refused. Alger Hiss, and several others invited to appear, accepted.

Even before the program aired, I received calls from leading right-wing Republicans. Many advertisers called also. All protested our intention to put Hiss on television. They said it was a disservice to Nixon, an outstanding citizen, while legitimatizing Hiss, a traitor to his country.

I asked Hagerty, who knew Nixon very well from their years in Eisenhower's White House, if he was absolutely sure our program was fair and objective. He assured me it was.

When the program aired, I got dozens of calls. Many, many people called me at home that evening to tell me, in the strongest terms, that we should not have allowed a convicted perjurer like Hiss to appear on the program. Kemper Insurance, a sponsor of our evening news, canceled all its ads. We lost several million dollars in advertising.

Despite the political obituary show, Nixon couldn't have been more friendly when he became President. He called quite often, and I still hear from him from time to time.

There's no question Nixon had the best grasp of foreign affairs of any President since World War II. He understands the issues very well and knows what to do about them. Years after he was out of office, when he had begun to reemerge as a public figure, I saw him speak for at least ninety minutes, including a question-and-answer session, without once consulting his notes. He was always right on the mark.

Nixon was also the most professional politician of all Presidents since

Roosevelt. I'll never understand how he could have allowed Watergate to happen. What were his people trying to accomplish? He had the election locked up. The polls were overwhelmingly in his favor. It was the stupidest thing a man could have permitted.

In 1961, I agreed to see a young documentary filmmaker who wanted to show me a film he'd made. By the time he came to see me, David Wolper's project had been rejected by all three network news departments, including ours.

OTHER RECOLLECTIONS:
David Wolper

I went to ABC with "The Race for Space" in 1959, but I couldn't get it on the network. None of the networks would show independently produced documentaries about contemporary events.

I was stunned when "Race for Space," which included exclusive footage of the Soviet space program, was turned down by all three networks. I thought I'd lost all my money.

But I had been in the television business then for ten years and knew the owners of every television station in America. I got them on the phone and had them clear an hour of time in the same week in every single television market. It was cleared in 120 markets, often preempting major network shows. It was the first time anything like this had ever happened.

Jack Gould, the *New York Times* television critic, called for an interview. He said it would be in the paper the next day, so I went out and got one, turned to the television section, and it wasn't there. I became very depressed.

I thought, That son of a bitch! I drove all the way up to his house in Connecticut for the interview. I turned to the front page, and it said, "Fourth Network Formed by Documentary Film Maker." Big story.

Then I bought the rights to Theodore H. White's Pulitzer Prize–winning book, *The Making of the President, 1960*. It came out of my pocket. I believed very strongly that it couldn't miss. It was a great election and a prize-winning book.

The film was terrific. I sold it to a sponsor, Xerox, and went to CBS. White was their political consultant. They said, "We don't play films of that nature unless we do them ourselves."

I went to NBC. They said the same thing.

The head of ABC's news department said, "Absolutely not."

I knew somebody who knew Leonard, and he set up an appointment for me. I said, "You have to see this film. It's written by Theodore H. White. You'd hire him for your news department, if you could, to write a documentary, wouldn't you? You couldn't make this film better than I made it, because nobody could report it better than White."

Leonard saw the picture and overruled the news department. "Making of the President, 1960" went on the air in 1962. At that time the industry had a "Super Emmy." My film won that. It was *the* number 1 program of the year. It was ABC's first Program of the Year Emmy. And it won three other Emmys, for best documentary, for best musical score (by Elmer Bernstein), and for best editing.

❑ ❑ ❑

I thought Wolper's film was great. I went to our news department and said, "The news departments of the three networks don't have a monopoly on brains." If a documentary is as good as Wolper's "Making of the President," we ought to put it on the air, as long as we could review it for editorial control. I insisted we show it, and that ended the network policy of excluding outsiders from making documentaries.

David Wolper went on to do many, many more documentaries for us. In the next two seasons alone, we bought twelve of his shows. The other networks had turned them all down.

OTHER RECOLLECTIONS:
David Wolper

I told Leonard that because of ABC's support of "Making of the President" and those twelve documentaries in the second and third years of my career, for the next two years they would get first crack at everything I did. I held to that for twenty years. And so they got "Roots," "The Thorn Birds," the 1984 Olympics, Liberty Weekend. I felt an obligation.

One day I was looking at some underwater footage on television, and I said, "A TV screen looks like a fish tank. The fish look like they're alive, swimming around in my tank. It would make a great series, an underwater thing. I'm going to go make a deal with Jacques Cousteau."

I went to see him, and he said, "I can do a fifteen-minute show from my museum."

I said, "No, no. Nothing like that. You're going to go around the world on your boat."

He agreed to outfit the *Calypso* the way I wanted it. It had to be all jazzed up and painted and have closed-circuit television screens and helicopter platforms. It couldn't look like what it was, a dunky old boat.

I went to New York and saw DuPont and Encyclopaedia Britannica. I personally went to the advertising agency and showed the program. The sponsors said they would buy only four shows. But Cousteau couldn't redo his boat and go around the world unless he had the money from twelve.

CBS agreed to buy the four shows I had sold to sponsors, but nothing else. I said, "I can't do it. I have to sell twelve."

I went to ABC, and talked to Tom Moore. He was a member of the Explorers Club of New York. He knew of Cousteau, who had invented the Aqualung.

Moore liked the four shows. A lot. We talked about what was going to be in the others. I think he was going to buy it anyway, but he said, "I'll tell you what. If you can get Cousteau to come to the next meeting of the Explorers Club, you've got the deal."

Cousteau came on the next plane, and ABC bought the show. That was in 1967.

❑ ❑ ❑

ABC's association with Wolper proved rewarding in ways that neither of us could have imagined. At the 1972 Olympics in Munich, for example, ABC Sports needed more camera positions than our hosts, the German Olympic Committee, would give us. Dave, doing a documentary of his own, had more positions than needed. He gave us the extras. If the Germans had known this, they might have taken them for their own use. So for two weeks, many ABC Sports technicians walked around wearing jackets that said "David L. Wolper Productions."

Perhaps the strangest chapter in television news history was written in October 1962, during the darkest hours of the Cuban missile crisis. Four days after President Kennedy stunned the world by revealing that the Soviets had put nuclear-tipped missiles in Cuba, ABC diplomatic correspondent John Scali was summoned to a furtive meeting by one of his sources, a Soviet diplomat.

Over lunch at the Occidental Restaurant, two blocks from the White House, the Russian asked Scali to convey a Soviet offer to top United States officials in hopes of resolving the crisis: If the United States would promise not to invade Cuba, the Soviets would remove their missiles.

The Soviet knew Scali had access to U.S. Secretary of State Dean Rusk. Apparently, he suspected Scali was secretly an American intelligence agent. After some discussion and a veiled threat that, if the United States didn't accept the proposal, the Soviets would join with the Chinese to make further trouble, Scali agreed to pass the proposal along to Rusk.

First, however, he had to resolve an ethical dilemma. Scali was an ABC newsman, not a diplomat or a spy. Becoming a conduit between the Soviet and United States governments required utmost secrecy, which would mean he could not report the scoop he had just been handed.

Scali went to his boss, Jim Hagerty, and explained the situation without revealing the content of the Soviet proposal or the identity of the Soviet diplomat. Hagerty brought Scali to see me.

John told me only what he had told Hagerty. Frankly, I didn't want to know any more than that.

I said that while it looked like he had a helluva story, the world was teetering on the edge of nuclear war. Anything we could do to prevent that war was more important than any story. I told Scali to put aside his newsman's role and do what he could to help resolve the crisis.

Scali carried the Soviet message to Roger Hilsman, director of State Department Intelligence and Research. Hilsman immediately took him to Dean Rusk.

There followed a series of clandestine meetings between Scali and his Soviet contact, and between Scali, Rusk, and President Kennedy. Scali became more than a messenger. At one meeting the Soviet attempted to introduce further conditions into the settlement. The Russians, he said, would allow the United States to confirm through inspections that the missiles were gone—but only if the Soviets could inspect United States bases in Florida to ensure that no preparations were being made for an invasion of Cuba after the missiles were pulled out.

Scali bristled, reminding the Soviet that Russian missiles in Cuba were the real threat to world peace, not the United States countermobilization. The Russian backed down.

Scali reported all this to Rusk, who clapped him on the shoulder and said, "John, you have served your country well. Remember, when you report this, that, eyeball-to-eyeball, they blinked first."

It was not the end of the crisis. Hours after Scali delivered what seemed to be Soviet acquiescence, a message came from Khrushchev: The Cuban missiles would be removed only if the United States pulled its own missiles out of Turkey and Italy.

Scali met again with the Soviet "diplomat." The Russian seemed mystified by Khrushchev's offer. Perhaps, he suggested, it was because of the long delay required for replies to messages sent from the Russian embassy in Washington to the Kremlin. There were hundreds of cables going back and forth over a single circuit.

Returning to the State Department, Scali met with Kennedy. After some discussion, Robert Kennedy, then Attorney General, suggested that the President ignore the Cuba-for-Italy-and-Turkey offer and instead *publicly* acknowledge agreement to the proposal conveyed through Scali. JFK went on the air with this.

After many anxious hours, Khrushchev replied with a broadcast of his own. The Scali offer was genuine. The crisis was resolved. There would be no nuclear war.

Scali's role in the negotiations was a closely guarded secret, known only to Jim Hagerty and myself at ABC and to a handful of people around the President, until 1964, when Hilsman wrote a book revealing Scali's involvement.

Scali then wrote a magazine article describing his participation in greater detail, but omitting the fact that he had consulted Jim Hagerty and me before delivering the message. I believe that small fact has remained a secret until now.

Scali explained that the mysterious Soviet was Alexandr Fomin, officially minister-counselor to the Soviet ambassador. Fomin was actually a deep-cover KGB colonel, director of all Soviet espionage activities in North America.

OTHER RECOLLECTIONS:
John Scali

In April of 1971 Richard Nixon secretly offered me a position as a special Presidential consultant on foreign policy. He said he wanted my assessment of the leadership of the U.S.S.R. and China. He intended to visit these countries.

Hearing Nixon say that he intended to visit the U.S.S.R. and China was like hearing him say he could fly to the moon.

I had always been a newsman, with my nose pressed to the window glass. Now I had a chance to find out what it was like inside.

I went to see Leonard, and while I couldn't tell him about Nixon's travel plans, I asked for a leave of absence.

He said, "John, we'll keep a candle burning in the window for your return. There will always be a place for you here at ABC."

I went to the Soviet Union and then to China as a member of the official delegation.

❑ ❑ ❑

In 1973 President Nixon appointed John Scali as ambassador to the United Nations, succeeding George Bush. After two and a half years, John was offered his choice of several other diplomatic posts. His heart had always remained at ABC, however, and so he asked to come back. We were glad to have him.

In 1989, at the age of seventy-one, Scali signed a new four-year contract with ABC News. He remains the oldest working network television journalist in America.

In the spring of 1963, Jim Hagerty told me, "ABC News is quite an empire. I'm really not trained to run something so big. I'd like to change jobs and concern myself with ABC's corporate public relations."

I didn't disagree. Hagerty, a fine gentleman and a very good newsman, wasn't much of an administrator. Si Siegel and I discussed a replacement. We decided to go after Elmer Lower at NBC News.

OTHER RECOLLECTIONS:
Elmer Lower

When ABC approached me, I was VP and general manager of NBC News. Above me were Bill McAndrew, president of NBC News, and Julian Goodman, executive VP. My big boss was Bob Kintner, a good man to work for. He was an insomniac who came to the office at 6 A.M. His secretary came in at 7. By the time I got in at 9, he'd have a dozen memos on my desk, things he thought we should do. Probably ten of them were worthwhile.

I had a perfectly good job. I had built highly successful election and convention coverage systems for both CBS and NBC. This was capped by the success of Huntley and Brinkley at the 1960 political conventions, when we overtook the great CBS team of Walter Cronkite and Edward R. Murrow.

The initial approach was from Ted Shaker, then in charge of ABC's television stations and spot sales. I'd worked with him at CBS. He asked me to come see Siegel. I said, "I don't want to be seen in your building." I didn't want talk to start. I was happy in my job.

Shaker called again and said, "Would you do me a favor and come over and see my boss?" After the third call I went over and talked to Siegel. I thought then that he was a strange little guy. I have a very high opinion of him today.

Later he called and asked me to meet with him at Goldenson's house on a Saturday afternoon. We had iced tea and cookies on the back porch. I didn't think his house was pretentious enough for a big television mogul.

To keep from wasting his time, I had to find out how serious he was. ABC was just in the process of dropping Telenews and setting up its own camera crews. Had ABC not made that decision, about two weeks before the day we spoke, I would not have been interested. It couldn't attempt to compete without its own crews.

Jack Bush, a close friend, was in charge of ABC's cameramen, sound men, cutters, couriers—everything like that, worldwide. I took Jack to lunch and asked him to level with me and tell me whether these guys were for real. He cited the budget numbers. For 1963, they were impressive figures. Jack was setting up bureaus in London, Paris, Berlin, Moscow, Rome, and Tokyo.

Then I wanted to know what ABC was going to do about an anchor to replace Ron Cochran. Ron was a good friend of mine from CBS, but I didn't think he would ever make the grade competing with Huntley–Brinkley and Cronkite. Jack said ABC was negotiating to get Charlie Collingwood, which impressed me. He didn't say ABC had him, but ABC had offered Charlie $125,000 a year to switch.

The figure impressed me. I happened to know that Huntley and Brinkley were each making $165,000. Considering ABC's reputed financial problems and their weak lineup of affiliates, I thought that was something.

Bush said ABC had got some other people. One was a graphic arts man, still my close friend, Ben Blank. Ben is one of the real creators in television news and to this day runs graphics for ABC Sports and News.

I got the impression that building ABC News was not going to be any piece of cake. But I agreed to come over and try.

My boss at NBC tried to get me to stay. He finally had me talk to Bobby Sarnoff, the head of the company. He really impressed me, but the question was, Did I want to be number 3 man in the number 1 organization, or number 1 in the number 3?

I did a lot of soul searching. I was fifty years old, and I thought I might not get a chance to run things at NBC. My bosses, Julian Goodman and Bill McAndrew, were both younger than me.

As it happened, McAndrew died suddenly, and Goodman got Kintner's job. I would have been president of NBC News. But I never kicked myself.

When I left, Kintner became very upset with me. Word was out that he told Goodman his number 1 task was to make it as hard for ABC as he possibly could.

❑ ❑ ❑

A few months after Lower took charge of ABC News, on November 22, 1963, I was having lunch at the Plaza Hotel. A waiter brought a phone to my table. My secretary said, "President Kennedy has been shot in Dallas." I immediately stood up and excused myself. As I left the dining room, I passed the table where Bob Kintner and Bob Sarnoff were having lunch.

I said, "Have you heard? The President's been shot."

They had not heard the news. They left immediately.

I went to my office and called all my department heads in. I said, "We have no choice now but to take off all our entertainment programs. I also think running commercials would be inappropriate during this time of national mourning." Edgar Scherick was then head of programming.

OTHER RECOLLECTIONS:
Edgar Scherick

We threw out our entire regular schedule. The whole country underwent a metamorphosis, and television, already an integral part of society and culture, changed its face completely. It was television's finest hour.

Between news reports from Dallas and Washington, we did cultural shows. Marian Anderson sang "America the Beautiful." Sidney Blackmere read Lincoln's Second Inaugural Address. Christopher Plummer did the "Goodnight, Sweet Prince" scene from *Hamlet*.

We dug through our files to find a Kinescope of Robert Saudek's "Young Abe Lincoln." I called the important show people in the community to join with me to figure out what else we wanted to do.

Charlton Heston had played many biblical figures. I called and said, "I would like you to fly out here to read Psalms. Work on them, put them into a suitable form." He came.

Other programs were Kinescopes of symphony orchestras performing elegiac pieces.

I was shocked to see that Pete Rozelle didn't cancel the New York Giants football game. It was a disgrace. He is still apologizing for it.

OTHER RECOLLECTIONS:
Dr. Frank Stanton, Retired President, CBS

I was having lunch with the head of our network. When the bulletin came in, I said, "I've got things to do. Get your programming people together and decide what you're going to do. We'll talk in a few minutes."

In the meantime, I put a memo out saying there would be no more commercials. I got a call from Kintner at NBC raising hell with me. He took a contrary view, but said, "Now that you've done that, I have no choice but to go along." He was very bitter about it.

❑ ❑ ❑

Elmer Lower was in the swimming pool of the New York Athletic Club when his secretary located him. Sobbing, she told him that the President had been shot.

OTHER RECOLLECTIONS:
Elmer Lower

I dried off as fast as I could and caught a cab back to the office. I went down to Leonard's office. Si and Tom Moore were there. Howard Smith flew in from somewhere.

I said, "I'm going to run with it." Everybody said, "We'll give you whatever help you need." I'd only been at ABC three months. I barely knew where the water cooler and the men's room were.

Fortunately we had a pretty good affiliate in Dallas, WFAA. That station is next to the Dallas *Morning News*, very close to the Texas School Book Depository, and it was a nonunion station. They handed out 16mm cameras to everybody on their staff who knew how to run one. So we got pretty good coverage.

The minute he learned what happened, our operations guy put a cable through to the AT&T test board in Dallas and then to WFAA. We held the cable, at the fantastic cost of $1.15 per minute per mile, for four days.

We were scrambling to cover the events in Dallas. We were all in a state of shock. People were calling in and volunteering to work. Guys who were off, stringers, part-timers. Anybody would do anything. We paid them eventually, but nobody ever asked to be paid.

There was a comical little Irishman, Mike Boland, who worked under Siegel. After it was all over, Mike came in and talked to my deputy, wringing his hands and saying, "The company is going broke, we've spent all this money, we've canceled all those commercials. That cable to Dallas cost us a fortune," and on and on. My guy took it for about ten minutes. Then he said, "I'll tell you what. The next time they assassinate a President, we'll have 'em do it in Brooklyn."

The networks did a magnificent job. They held the country together immediately after the assassination in a way that the newspapers couldn't. Everybody in the country spent the whole weekend watching television.

❑ ❑ ❑

All America was stunned by Kennedy's tragic death, so I had no corner on grief. The sudden loss of this energetic, witty, warm, courageous man filled me with despair and outrage. The spirited flame of hope Kennedy lighted in our national consciousness was snuffed out. He'd just begun to move forward on so many things. His efforts had not yet begun to show results. Now he would never get a chance to finish. What a terrible, senseless waste.

Devastating as that day was, however, the death of this President and the astonishing, often bizarre events of the days that followed, served to propel ABC News into the modern era of television journalism. George Watson, now chief of the ABC News Washington Bureau, was just starting his career.

OTHER RECOLLECTIONS:
George Watson

Edward P. Morgan was the most prestigious journalist ABC employed, but because this was the paleolithic age of ABC Television, he was heard mostly on radio. I was young and new to broadcasting. I wrote Ed's radio shows.

Morgan was lunching at the Brazilian embassy. When the report came from Dallas that shots had been fired near the motorcade—that was the extent of the first bulletin—I called the embassy.

Ed immediately drove to the White House. Senator Hubert Humphrey was at the lunch as well, and Morgan brought him along. At the White House, McGeorge Bundy, Kennedy's national security adviser, said the President was dead.

Ed thought he had a great scoop, awful news that it was. No competitive journalist, so far as we knew, knew or had reported that Kennedy had been killed. Ed came tearing back to the bureau.

There was a great uproar of engineers trying to figure out how to get ABC Washington into the ABC Television Network. The television and radio studios were not connected, so it was one or the other. We could have got him on radio much faster than on television.

By the time the technical wherewithal to put Ed on the air was established, Kennedy's death had been confirmed from Dallas. So Morgan and ABC News lost the scoop. I think if Ed had had the ability to get on the air from the White House lawn, as we have today, the news that Kennedy was dead would have come first on ABC News.

Then Howard Smith came in from New York. Smith and Morgan are on anybody's short list of first-rate, highly intelligent, enormously literate broadcasters. Together, for the next three days, they performed magnificently.

On the day of the funeral we built a kind of balcony or platform in front of our old bureau, just across from the Mayflower Hotel on Connecticut Avenue. From it Morgan and Smith described the remarkable procession on foot from the White House. De Gaulle, Churchill, Haile Selassie—all the world's presidents and prime ministers—followed Kennedy's casket to Arlington.

That was not only a memorable moment in national history. One could argue that our coverage of the assassination for the first time established ABC News as a competitive force in television.

Ed didn't take to television very well. He was impatient with it. He thought there were too many producers, too many people. He preferred simple, direct, uncluttered radio. So Ed was never as successful in television as Howard. But together on the assassination and subsequently at the 1964 political conventions, they gave ABC a level of intelligent, incisive, often eloquent reporting that concealed some of the shortcomings of a fledgling network that, in staff and resources, was still very much in third place.

❑ ❑ ❑

Even given our increased commitments of funding and manpower, Elmer Lower had a very tough challenge. His first priority was to hire experienced people, and that meant getting them from our competitors. We could never afford enough of the top people, so Elmer also had to find promising newcomers who could be developed, over time, into first raters.

One fellow, who had joined ABC only a few months before Elmer came aboard, was Ted Koppel. At that time he was about twenty-four years old, working on Flair Reports, newsy, radio features for the entertainment department. When Elmer began to pull things together, he asked Si to transfer that whole production unit into his department. That's how Ted got into News, a very lucky break for ABC. Another youngster in the department was Charles Osgood, who unfortunately went over to CBS within a few years.

Elmer also hired a young Canadian journalist. Although he was only twenty-five years old, Elmer immediately saw his enormous potential. His name was Peter Jennings.

OTHER RECOLLECTIONS:
Elmer Lower

Peter first came to my attention through John Scali. In early 1964 Scali went to Toronto with Dean Rusk. When he came back, he said he'd seen two guys on the tube who were quite good, and

I ought to hire both Jennings and Baden Langton. I got a video tape, and I liked what I saw. Eventually we hired both. Langton stayed awhile, then went back to Canada. He ended up playing the bassoon in a symphony orchestra.

Peter joined the staff as a reporter in the fall of 1964. I don't recall ever seeing his résumé, and I learned just a few summers ago that he was a high-school dropout.

He hadn't done much reporting in Canada. He was what they called a "link" man or a "presenter." When Peter came to New York, the assignment desk sent him on stories. He got a big kick out of it.

We lost Charles Collingwood when Paley sweet-talked him into staying at CBS and sent him to London as a kind of super foreign correspondent. They gave him a lot of dough, and he became a boulevardier and was very seldom on the air.

About that time our anchor, Ron Cochran, started developing a tic. I don't think he even knew it. We had nobody in the organization to replace him, so we were looking for somebody. ABC's prime-time lineup played young. One theory was to use a young anchor to capture that audience. If young people were used to tuning in ABC at night, maybe they'd do it for the news, too, if we had a younger person.

I can't say it was my idea, but we had to replace Cochran. Peter Jennings seemed a good gamble.

He didn't particularly want to do it. He enjoyed what he was doing. He was learning how to be a reporter, and he had the makings of a pretty good one. But he agreed to be the anchor, and did it for two and a half years.

If today you were to see the old video tapes, Peter looked so young you'd have to ask how he possibly could have attracted an audience. And wasn't I out of my mind to put him in there? But he didn't do so badly, if you consider we still had only fifteen minutes of news and that the ABC lineup was terribly weak.

❑ ❑ ❑

I suppose many people thought we were crazy to ask a youngster like Peter to go up against Walter Cronkite and Huntley–Brinkley. But Peter, despite his youth, had worked in broadcasting since 1959, when he was eighteen, and had very good camera presence. If he lacked formal education, he made up for it with an inquiring mind and a willingness to attempt almost anything that was asked of him.

These qualities came to Peter from his upbringing. His father, Charles Jennings, was one of Canada's broadcast pioneers, a man of such integrity and talent that he was often compared with Edward R. Murrow.

OTHER RECOLLECTIONS:
Peter Jennings

Leonard cared a lot about young people. He had a very good sense that this was going to be a long haul. One never got the impression, when one was hired here twenty-five years ago, that it was going to be a short-term relationship. ABC were hiring bright young men who would remain with the company for a long time.

When I arrived, Elmer's number 2 was Jesse Zousmer. Among many other things, he had coproduced Ed Murrow's "Person to Person" at CBS.

Zousmer was also enormously caring about young people. He had a very strong sense of what development meant. For example, when Lower made me anchor in 1965, Zousmer believed that I shouldn't do it, a somewhat ambiguous position for a boss to take. He felt I should work as a reporter in the South, I should go to Washington for a year, go overseas for ten years, and then I should come back to Washington. At that point I might be qualified to be an anchor.

Unfortunately, Zousmer was killed in an airplane crash at Narita, Tokyo's old airport, while returning from having visited his ABC correspondents in Vietnam.

I don't pay much attention to that early period of my career, because in retrospect I don't think I learned very much, and I don't think I contributed very much. In looking back, my sense is that ABC was desperately searching for ways to get an edge and to find a sense of itself. In 1965 and 1966 there was an enormous emphasis on youth programming. They thought, probably, "Why not try this guy, he's got his hair and his teeth, and he can string two words together." There were not many people available at ABC at the time.

I think they would have fired me quite shortly, but, in fact, I resigned first. I came back from the Middle East in 1967 and told

Bill Sheehan, who'd replaced Zousmer, "I want a commitment that I get off this thing; if not now, by the end of the year."

I was enormously relieved to get out of there. I felt like a free man within hours. My secretary said, "Go to Tiffany's and buy everybody a small present, then get out of here and go do some honest work." That is exactly what I did. I never believed I'd come back.

I stayed in the United States through the political campaign of 1968. I covered George Wallace and then Gene McCarthy. They called me a national correspondent, but titles have always been a crock at this and every other network. I covered the environment, which I much enjoyed, and then I went overseas, to Rome and then Beirut. I came back to Washington very briefly, and then went to London.

I remember the jokes in those days. We all thought we would be sold to a Chinese laundry. We all knew that we were poor, but it never struck me that way. I, after all, had come from Canada, and one of the reasons I came to ABC was because Canadian broadcasting corporations didn't have the resources to send me around the world.

ABC would put me on an airplane and say, "Go somewhere." I've been all over the world at company expense. We all flew economy, but I thought ABC was rolling in manna.

As a reporter I have never been told that I couldn't do something because there wasn't any money. Mind you, we didn't pay people very much. I was hired at $15,000 a year, less than I made in Toronto. As anchor, I made $39,000.

I don't recall being badly beaten by the enemy on the basis of fewer resources. Sometimes CBS would show up on a story with more camera teams. I don't think it made the reportage necessarily any better.

In those days whenever I came back from the field, Leonard always invited me up to the corporate dining room, where he would sit me down and expect to be briefed about what had gone on in the field. The story behind the headlines.

I remember feeling enormously flattered, as a young person, that the head of the company, even though he was very friendly and warm and supportive of news, would take the time to have me and others up to his dining room. I think he's a complicated man with a multitude of broadcasting business talents, but he always gave us the impression that news was very special to him.

❑ ❑ ❑

ABC went to a half hour of evening news in 1967, almost forty months after CBS and NBC did so and a year before Peter Jennings resigned as anchor. It was yet another reason why getting new or better affiliates was an uphill battle. There was a period of about a year, for example, in the mid-1960s, when our evening news wasn't on a single station in the state of Ohio.

Not long after succeeding Peter as anchor, Bob Young spoke at an affiliates' meeting in California. He made a very bad impression, and Elmer was somewhat embarrassed. Afterward I asked Elmer to come to my hotel room. I asked him if he was happy with Young, and he admitted that he wasn't. "What do you intend to do about it?" I said.

"Look for somebody, I guess."

I said, "How would Frank Reynolds strike you?"

Frank Reynolds had been a local anchor for CBS in Chicago before coming over to WBKB (later called WLS-TV) as anchor. Frank had never done much field work and wanted to go to Washington. Elmer put him on the White House, where he did a fine job. President Johnson liked Frank, and often asked him up to his apartment, where they talked late into the night. Mostly, of course, it was Lyndon lecturing Frank.

So I thought Frank would do a good job as our evening news anchor. Elmer agreed, but he wasn't sure Frank wanted the job. He liked covering the White House very much.

After some discussion we agreed that Elmer and Bill Sheehan would go to Washington and try to induce Reynolds to accept this job. They took him to lunch and told him how much we needed him at the anchor desk. He was reluctant. They offered him more money, but Frank was never the sort who had his agent coming around hustling. It wasn't that important to him. Finally, they appealed to his ego, and he agreed to it.

Frank Reynolds did a very credible job in New York as anchor, at times teamed with Howard K. Smith, until 1970, when he returned to Washington. Then Elmer succeeded in luring Harry Reasoner away from CBS. He was paired with Howard K. Smith, and together they got very respectable ratings. We were still third, but the ratings gap had narrowed to only a few points.

While we grew, our competitors weren't standing still. When we first established a Washington bureau, we maintained only three camera and two sound men. Today each network needs between fifteen and twenty crews available there.

I always thought it was a waste of time, manpower, and money for all three networks to cover certain kinds of events. The public interest could be served equally well by pooling camera coverage of such standard events as Presidential news conferences, conventions, summit meetings, and elections.

This wouldn't, however, relieve any network of the responsibility to control editorial portions of news stories. Content should be handled individually by the respective news organizations.

Toward that end, I asked Lower to look into establishing a pooling arrangement to cover national elections.

Lower had covered elections since his college days, when he reported the 1932 Roosevelt *v.* Hoover contest in Missouri for the United Press. In 1970, he wrote his Columbia University master's thesis on the use of computers to predict presidential election results between 1952 and 1968, a study still cited by those who write about elections.

OTHER RECOLLECTIONS:
Elmer Lower

The wire services had traditionally provided vote counts, but they were so slow—they didn't put much money into it—results might not come in until five the next morning. I had built faster tabulating systems for CBS and NBC. This was important to all broadcasters because we had to report results before most people went to bed.

At ABC, our initial objective was to match the other networks' vote reporting in primaries. We began in New Hampshire the first week in March 1964. Then Illinois, Wisconsin, Washington State, Oregon, and finally California, on June 8.

Some nights we were good, and some nights we weren't so good. Either way it cost ABC a barrel of money. But there were five reporters in every precinct, one each from AP, UP, and the three networks. Leonard kept asking about a pool as a way to save money. I sounded out CBS. It was willing to talk about pooling. NBC was not.

This was mostly because Kintner disliked Goldenson. He was on top of the pile then and was not going to give us any advantage.

Leonard and Frank Stanton sat together at some industry dinner and talked about it. Stanton was sympathetic to the pool idea. Leonard and Frank agreed it was a lot of money and didn't see how counting your own votes gave any advantage. But ABC had never done this before. We had to prove that we could match them before they'd let us in the club.

The wire services, meanwhile, were getting flak from their member papers. In particular, the AP got it from Punch Sulzberger at *The New York Times*. Sulzberger, still a young man feeling his oats, put heat on Wes Gallagher, head of the AP.

I knew Wes very well from World War II. We discussed a pool. UP was interested because it was always running a million dollars a year in the red. Leonard asked me to talk to Fred Friendly, president of CBS News. Fred was interested because Stanton had told him to be interested.

But with all this talking, we weren't getting anywhere. Fred and I even spoke about a two-way pool, but that didn't happen.

The blow came when we all went to California for the Republican primary, Goldwater *v.* Rockefeller in 1964. There are 30,000 precincts in the state. Theoretically, we should have had 30,000 people, one at each precinct.

It's an impossible job. We got the League of Women Voters to help. NBC and CBS sometimes got a church or a junior chamber of commerce, anything that controls lots of bodies. You have to make a contribution. The League asks $2,000 to $10,000, depending on the area it covers.

The election was very close. Goldwater won by an average of two votes per precinct, 60,000 votes among millions cast.

The AP's strength was its stringer organization in Northern California, where Rockefeller was strong. They had few stringers in Orange and San Diego counties, Goldwater country. The New York *World Telegram* ran an AP headline the next morning: "Rockefeller leads Goldwater in California."

We used computer projections and knew Goldwater was going to win, based on our key precincts. But we had so little voting that we didn't call it until later. CBS was faster that night. Leonard got me out of bed in Los Angeles and asked what had gone wrong. He was a little unhappy that our totals weren't as fast as the others. But we just didn't have as many people in the field.

The *World Telegram* was very upset with AP because, while it didn't say Rockefeller was going to win, its vote totals made it look that way. So the newspapers started putting more heat on Wes Gallagher and the AP.

Wes invited five people representing the major news organizations to come to his office to discuss this. We didn't get anywhere. UP was hesitant to commit much money. NBC got flak from some of their affiliates about going into a pool.

We met again in Friendly's office and agreed to start News Election Service.

Having an agreement among five people was getting over a big hump, but the network lawyers were very cautious. Word came that we had to go to the antitrust division of the Department of Justice and get them on board.

The Department of Justice said, "Are you guys sure you aren't doing this just to save money? Convince us that you're doing it because it's a greater public service."

In time, the lawyers persuaded Justice that being able to accurately report the results of national elections almost as soon as the polls closed was a public service.

❑ ❑ ❑

Elmer's planning for the 1968 Presidential election began early in 1966, about the same time ABC planned to merge with ITT. When the deal collapsed on New Year's Day, 1968, I called together ABC's department heads and asked everybody to cut their budgets. I asked Elmer to cut about $15 million.

He was far from unprepared. When things started to go sour with ITT, Elmer had begun planning. He cut back documentaries for 1968 from twelve to eight, but he laid off only thirty people, a minor miracle under the circumstances.

The budget crunch's most visible effect on News was our decision not to cover the political conventions gavel to gavel. Instead we ran the best entertainment programming we had from 7:30 to 9:30, and limited convention coverage to ninety minutes. As it turned out, we got very good ratings for those nights. Not everyone in the country wanted to sit through three and a half hours of speeches and prearranged "spontaneous" demonstrations. We were criticized for cutting back. It was the first time since 1952, when television networks began covering conventions, that a network had less than total coverage. But I thought it was the right thing to do then, and I still believe it was.

Four years later, and every four years since, we reverted to gavel-to-gavel coverage. We needed to establish ABC News as credible and competitive with CBS and NBC, which had full coverage. But I really think that most people don't watch the whole time. After months of media attention focused on primaries, there are few surprises at the conventions.

In my view, by staging these enormous, costly affairs and asking the networks to cover every minute of them, the Republican and Democratic parties operate as if television and radio did not exist. They've stuck with a horse-and-buggy era institution despite modern-day communications that allow the public to see all the boring idle chatter and meaningless, self-serving speeches that almost no one in the convention hall listens to. And the public isn't stupid. They don't want to listen or watch unless there is something of value.

Elmer Lower asked to be relieved of his responsibilities as head of news on Labor Day, 1974. He spent the next three and a half years as VP of corporate affairs, the job Jim Hagerty had left vacant with his retirement.

During his eleven years as president of ABC News, Elmer built an infrastructure of people and organization that even today underpins the news department. In the process, he created an enduring reputation of legitimacy for ABC News. Though we still lagged in the ratings, when Elmer handed his creation over to his successor, Bill Sheehan, it had finally achieved equal status with CBS and NBC.

16

Radio

□

When radio first became popular, during the silent-film era, many theater people thought it would compete for their audiences. It did no such thing; radio and motion pictures flourished side by side.

When talkies came along in the late 1920s, the radio people threw up their hands and said, "This is going to drive us out of business." It didn't. By the 1930s, network radio was big business, and the movie industry was enjoying its Golden Age.

After the war, when television arrived and the movie industry underwent radical changes, many felt that radio was obsolete and doomed gradually to die out. NBC, which pioneered network radio, began selling off radio stations in the 1960s, and even threatened to fold its radio network.

I never believed radio was destined for extinction. I felt very strongly, and still do, that it has an important role in our society, and as broadcasters we ought to foster and develop it. In 1953, soon after the UPT-ABC merger, I addressed a group of broadcasters. I said radio needed to change. While television sets had replaced radios in America's parlors, people now had radios in their kitchens and bedrooms. Almost every car had a radio, and many people took portables to the beach or on picnics.

Since our population was segmented, with different interests and different life-styles, we needed to serve the needs of specialized audiences. I thought radio would prosper if, instead of being a delicatessen, so to speak, offering a little of everything, it became a boutique, with each station purveying programming to a narrowly defined audience. Eventually, this approach emerged as radio's great strength.

At the time of our merger, ABC owned radio stations in New York, Los Angeles, San Francisco, and Detroit, and a "half station" in Chicago where WLS shared a frequency with another station. Our radio network wasn't much. The Blue Network that Ed Noble bought was a poor stepsister to NBC's Red, the dominant network in radio. NBC kept the best stations and sold Noble what it didn't want.

Nevertheless we had some good people at our stations. The best of them was Jimmy Riddell. When he joined WXYZ, Detroit, in 1931, the owners were George Trendle and John King. Trendle was the fellow I'd had to fire in 1937, when I restored Paramount's Detroit Theatres to profitability.

OTHER RECOLLECTIONS:
Jimmy Riddell

I was nineteen years of age, and Detroit was in the depths of despair after the Crash of 1929. There were few jobs. At Christmas time I was working at Hudson's, Detroit's number 1 department store. I heard WXYZ wanted to hire an office boy, so I went to see Barney Kilbride, the Si Siegel of WXYZ—its money and personnel man.

He said, "How much money are you making?"

I said, "I make eighteen dollars a week, plus three or four in commission—so, about twenty-one or twenty-two."

"Well, you won't make that kind of money here."

I didn't know whether he meant I'd make more or less. After a while, he offered me $10 a week. I was still living at home, and money wasn't the all-important thing to me. Radio was a glamorous business, and there was potential, I thought. Of course it was all if/come, as they say.

My father had a cartage company, several small trucks, and he offered me $35 a week to drive. I knew that five years later I'd still be making $35 and still be driving a truck, so I said, "No, I'm going to take this job for $10 a week."

Hal Neal was an announcer at WXYZ. He was on "The Lone Ranger," the voice that said, "A fiery steed with the speed of light, a cloud of dust, and a hearty 'Hi yo, Silver! Away!' " while the sound guys beat gravel pits with rubber plungers.

Another WXYZ announcer was a young fellow with a pock-marked face, name of Mike Wallace. Douglas Edwards was on the staff as well.

Soon I got a raise to $12 a week. Then the bank holiday came. The banks were broke, the cities were broke, everybody was broke. We all took a pay cut. I went back to $10. Instead of cash we were paid in city scrip, but every grocer took it, every candy store, every bar.

In 1944, Trendle and King sold the company to Noble. They made me the manager and then, about 1946, I became president of WXYZ, Inc.

This is bragging time. We had the best station in the entire company. In the early 1950s, when no one else was making money in radio, we were. New York used to call me and say, "Jimmy, can you send us fifty thousand?" They needed it, they were so close to the bone. Finally we worked it out that we just sent them all our money and kept $50,000, which is what we needed for operating.

❑ ❑ ❑

In 1958 Ollie Treyz headed the television network. He was terrific with advertising, scheduling, and programs. Si Siegel knew money management and had an uncanny knack for finding the right people. But I also needed a broadcaster, someone who knew the operating side. I brought Jimmy Riddell to New York as executive VP of AB-PT. I put him on the board of directors.

Jimmy was supposed to run the company, day to day, but it didn't work out that way. In practice, everybody—and especially Ollie—went around him to Si or to me. Jimmy was a team player, and while his feelings were bruised by this sort of treatment, if it meant hurting the company, it wasn't in his nature to assert his perquisites of office.

OTHER RECOLLECTIONS:
Jimmy Riddell

We were trying to get John Daly to say on his newscast, "And now a word from *blank*"—whoever the sponsor was. Daly was resisting. Leonard said, "Jimmy, why don't you see if you can get John to go along with it?" I called him into my office one night, and we had a couple of drinks and talked. We talked for an hour and a half. I kept coming back to it. Finally he said, "Jimmy, I'm not going to do it." And he wouldn't. It was beneath his dignity as a newscaster.

❑ ❑ ❑

For more than a year Jimmy accomplished next to nothing. He just couldn't assert his authority over the pack of powerhouse executives under him. But Jimmy was still valuable to us because the station managers, both radio and television, gave him great respect. He became, in effect, our in-house consultant. I often used him as a sounding board, bouncing ideas at him, especially about station management. So did Si.

In 1959 he said, "Leonard, this isn't working out. I've got to leave New York. My family isn't happy here, and I'm not happy either." The root of the matter, of course, was that he couldn't stand Ollie Treyz. Jimmy was too much of a gentleman to say so, though it was common knowledge that they cordially detested each other.

We decided that he would take over management of our West Coast operations, replacing Earl Hudson, who was well past retirement age. Jimmy ran both radio and television in Los Angeles and San Francisco, and the subsequent success of our stations there reflected his insights and vision.

In 1957 the payola scandal rocked the broadcasting industry. After I had determined the nature of Dick Clark's relationship to the music business and publicly absolved him of wrongdoing, my overriding concern was to ensure that no one at ABC was involved in anything remotely smelling of conflict of interest. This was especially an issue in radio. Many of our stations broadcast popular music of exactly the sort that some record promoters bribed disc jockeys to air.

Beyond payola, however, I became aware there were plenty of other opportunities for broadcasting executives to enrich themselves by taking advantage of their access to the airwaves. As I've said many times, a broadcast license is a public trust. If we allowed anything to compromise the public interest, then we didn't deserve to be broadcasters.

One of ABC's attorneys was Chuck DeBare, in-house counsel for our radio division. I asked him to help draft some very strict conflict-of-interest standards for ABC employees. To my knowledge, no other network, station, or multiple broadcasting entity thought it necessary to go quite as far in this area as we did. But we had far too much at stake to take even the slightest chance of losing our license.

OTHER RECOLLECTIONS:
Chuck DeBare

When the payola scandal broke, Leonard was almost in shock that something like this could happen. After days of hearings in Washington, Leonard set a requirement that we devise a series of rules and guidelines for employees. He said, "I never want to go through an experience like this again." His voice was cracking. He said, "I don't even want the *possibility* of someone thinking there was something wrong."

Our guidelines were the toughest in the industry. Some hindered our ability to operate competitively. When I told him that, he said, "You are better people than they. You operate better. So I'm starting you ten yards behind the starting line."

The first step was to clean up any messes, anything that might have been there at that time. We asked everybody to give us an affidavit that they had no involvement with payola or anything that might have been a conflict of interest.

One of WABC's leading personalities then was Alan Freed, one of the fathers of rock'n'roll radio. He never gave us an affidavit, so we had to let him go. He was a major talent, a great asset to any station, but we didn't want anybody on the air that wouldn't sign an affidavit.

Our stations in San Francisco, KGO-AM and -FM, were big and powerful, but they broke even or made maybe $50,000 or $100,000 a year. And for years, we sold the time from 9 P.M. to midnight to religious organizations. This brought ABC as much as $750,000 a year, and that is what kept KGO in the black.

But, very few people listened to the programs except the members of this evangelical sect, and the broadcaster used the air time for fund-raising.

At WABC, in New York, paid religious programming also brought in a lot of money. "Big Joe's Happiness Exchange" ran from midnight till three or four in the morning. Big Joe, a preacher, bought the time, programmed it, and sold his own products. We had no control over what was going on.

For many years, WABC also sold weekend time to a group of the religiously affiliated blind who used its program to make solicitations. This was its major source of funds.

But in all cases these programs killed our audience flow. We came to the conclusion that the only way to get programming consistency, a format that goes right through the day, was to get rid of paid religion on all our stations.

But religion brought in $1 million a year to the Radio division. ABC needed every bit of it at that time. Leonard never hesitated. He gave us the go-ahead, and we dumped paid religion.

I came into work a few days later to find about thirty blind people with Seeing Eye dogs picketing in front of the building. They were carrying signs protesting us kicking them off radio after twenty years. My heart sank. I thought, My God, I hope Leonard's out of town.

After that, ABC's new radio programmers came through, and our Radio division started to come into its own. We were the first to start paying attention to continuity and programming flow.

Hal Neal took over at WABC, which had been a hodgepodge with no personality, no distinctive shape. He started programming rock 'n' roll around the clock. He hired talent like Dan Ingram, Ron Lundy, and Cousin Brucie Morrow. After a few years it became the most listened-to station in America and very, very profitable.

❑ ❑ ❑

Our radio stations in Los Angeles, KABC, and in San Francisco, KGO, had also suffered from their lack of identifiable format. In 1958, shortly after Jimmy Riddell took charge of our West Coast operations, he set about the long task of turning them around.

His first effort was at KABC in Los Angeles, which was losing money. One reason was the staff. Our announcers included big-salaried radio greats like Jim Ameche and Dennis Crosby—one of Bing's kids—and a full orchestra that rarely played but because of union agreements had to be paid.

Jimmy got rid of the orchestra and brought in Ben Hoberman, who had worked for him in Detroit and in New York, to become general manager of KABC.

Ben had done very well at WABC in New York, and both Jimmy and I expected big things of him in Los Angeles. He surprised me by doing far more than making KABC the leading station in the most competitive radio market in the world. With the help of a few key assistants and some talented announcers, he invented and refined a unique genre of radio programming. Ben became the father of talk radio.

OTHER RECOLLECTIONS:
Ben Hoberman

KABC was trying to find something that would work, struggling to find identity for itself. It had a different musical format every three to six months. Stations were just beginning to start specializing in some kind of demographic format. At that time nobody had ever done exactly what I was considering, though WOR in New York had done monologue programming.

After surveying the Los Angeles market, I knew there was nothing like an all-talk format. It was new and totally off the wall. I thought it would be distinctive and appeal to a small, quality audience, which would give us enough to sell. We could then make some money.

It was a struggle. I made calls with our salesmen, but the agencies weren't too interested in the format. They always asked, "How do you run a radio station without playing any records?"

That was a question we had to continue to answer. It took a few years to catch on. I had total support from New York; management allowed me to make the investment. We continued to grow, and we made money almost every year, but it really started to take off in 1974 when we made a deal to get the L.A. Dodgers. They had been on KFI, which just then was sold to Cox Broadcasting.

We had tried to get the Dodgers for years, but we were a 5,000-watt radio station fighting 50,000-watt, clear-channel KFI. Walter O'Malley, the Dodgers owner, was on the KFI board. I made the deal with O'Malley. There are many stories about his being a tough businessman. But he always made sure the other guy had a chance to make a buck.

When I told Hal Neal, then head of ABC's radio division, about how much I'd given to get the Dodgers—a lot—he thought I was out of my mind. But anybody who has lived in this market knew the value of the L.A. Dodgers. Anybody given the opportunity to move the Dodgers to their station would have made almost any deal. They are that big an attraction. It turned out to be a bonanza for the station and a cash register ever since.

Having the Dodgers gave people a chance to sample our product. People who would never have tuned to talk radio liked the ball games and stayed with us afterward. That broadened our base of appeal. The notion of a small, high-quality audience disappeared; we ended up with a tremendous audience. I was the most surprised of anyone to find it developing that broad an appeal.

In Montreal I found Joe Pyne, first of the shock radio performers. I brought him to Los Angeles. He was startling and quickly created an audience, adding something to talk radio. I soon came to abhor that kind of radio—totally.

Pyne served to bring in an audience that could sample our other talk radio programs. But eventually we had to fire him.

Another big break for us was hiring Michael Jackson [not the singer of the same name]. He'd had an overnight disc jockey show in San Francisco before coming to Los Angeles. He briefly had some kind of talk show on KNX, and then for some reason got fired.

Michael called to asked if he could come see me. He's a little guy and—now—very slender. At that time he probably weighed over 200 pounds. He was trying to make a name as a talk host, and there weren't any talk programs.

I thought Michael would wear very, very well. His English accent was interesting; he had a sense of showmanship and an excellent command of the English language. It was apparent that he was very well-read and seemed to know a great deal about everything. So I signed him up.

Unemployed in a very tight job market, Michael was in no position to bargain. I chose to pay him more than I had to because I felt he was worth it. The money would do something for his morale. I wanted to help build up his ego.

He does his homework. He goes on at 9 A.M., but Michael is in the station by 6 or 6:30. He goes over all the wire copy that came in overnight. He gets East Coast–time interviews out of the way before going on the air. Whatever he does, it is not an act, because you can't act in that format for two, three, four hours a day. What you hear is what you are.

Michael has been with the station for over twenty-two years. He's added something to talk radio that's different from any other performer. It's turned out that most of KABC's performers have been there for well over fifteen years.

❑ ❑ ❑

Under Ben Hoberman and his successor, George Green, KABC became far more than just a radio station. It became a voice of the people of Southern California, a forum for debate on all sorts of critical issues. Never was this more important to the community—and to ABC—than in the late 1970s, when Los Angeles had won the right to host the 1984 Olympics.

OTHER RECOLLECTIONS:
Ben Hoberman

Los Angeles had a plan whereby the city would be financially responsible for the Olympics. This was just a few years after the Montreal debacle, where Montreal lost hundreds of millions of dollars hosting the Games. People there will be paying for them into the twenty-first century. There was no reason why the same thing wouldn't happen in Los Angeles.

KABC was extremely active with editorials and participation by performers and other staff people in various community organizations. We launched an editorial campaign, and used the efforts of our investigative reporter, Hank Konysky, to get the facts out. We succeeded in getting a special initiative on the ballot that prohibited the City of Los Angeles, and hence its tax-paying citizens, from having any financial responsibility for the Games.

Without that initiative, which the voters approved, Peter Ueberroth would still be running Ask Mr. Foster, his travel agency.

The pressure we received during that time was tremendous. I got a call from a very well regarded businessman. He told me if we didn't call off the dogs, he'd cancel his advertising.

I said, "We're presenting all the arguments as fairly as we can, and it has nothing to do with your advertising. If you decide that's what you want to do, there's nothing I can tell you about it." He canceled his advertising.

In New York, Leonard and his top people were getting a lot of pressure from these same people. It was a strange situation. Here's ABC's owned radio station fighting against the City of Los Angeles conducting the Olympics, right after the broadcasting rights to the Games were won by ABC. Leonard asked what we were doing, how we were handling the situation, why we were doing it. It was not a lengthy conversation. The result was that New York said, "As long as you treat everybody fairly, go ahead." That was unusual. The easiest thing would have been for New York to say, "Hey, knock it off."

As a result of the initiative, the city was forced to get somebody to organize a privately financed organization to assume the financial obligations of hosting the Olympics. So, for the first time in the history of the Olympic Games, they were privately financed. And because of that, they were the most successful games ever.

❑ ❑ ❑

In 1979, following the retirement of Hal Neal, we brought Ben back to New York and put him in charge of our radio division. He retired in 1986 and returned to Los Angeles.

In the mid 1950s, radio was in the midst of its post-television identity crisis. One of the first of the new station formats which emerged from this was the Top 40. Todd Storz, an Omaha station manager, built his programming around disc jockeys who played the forty most popular songs.

Radio networks carried a variety of long-form programs, ranging from ABC's "Breakfast Club," a morning variety show hosted by Don McNeill in Chicago, to soaps like "Stella Dallas" and news and public affairs programs, including "Paul Harvey, News and Comment," our most successful radio program ever.

Radio station owners were scrambling for television licenses. They paid little attention to radio and put almost nothing into developing programs. By 1966 our radio stations were marginally profitable. Our network was losing millions.

Some of my managers were suggesting we fold our radio network. I didn't think the FCC would allow it. At that time only radio reached the entire nation. In a national emergency, network radio was the only way to reach into every single community in America. So, although they never came out and said why, the FCC indicated that we had to keep the network to maintain our O&O licenses.

My thinking crystallized when Westinghouse offered us $50 million for our stations. I called in Hal Neal, then in charge of our owned radio stations. I said, "Hal, if Westinghouse thinks they can make money from our stations, then we certainly can do it ourselves. I want you to draw up a five-year plan and a ten-year plan. Within five years I want our stations earning ten million dollars per year. Within ten years, I want to double that."

Hal created those plans, and within three years we had reached the $10 million goal. In the meantime, our radio network was going through momentous changes.

The problem with our network was that we were trying to be all things to all stations. We sold network advertising, so we insisted everything on the network had to be run by our owned stations. That made for very awkward programming. For example, in New York, WABC had a one-hour network news block, 6 P.M. to 7. In effect, this rock 'n' roll station had to tell its mostly teenaged audience, "Go away for one hour and listen to our competition—but don't forget to come back at 7." It was an unreasonable requirement, and our station managers knew it cost their stations ratings.

The man who eventually found a way to put our radio network into the black was Ralph Beaudin. He began his ABC career in 1957 as general manager of KQV, Pittsburgh. He turned that station around by developing a loud, breezy, rock 'n' roll format. For the first time since we'd bought it, KQV made money. Lots of money. Ralph was rewarded by being asked to do the same with WLS, our Chicago station.

Ralph turned WLS on its ear. He switched it to a Top-40 format, and after a few years it was the leading station in its market. In 1966 we brought Ralph to New York and put him in charge of ABC's radio group, which included both our owned stations and our radio network.

OTHER RECOLLECTIONS:
Ralph Beaudin

In 1966 there were many problems in the country. One was racial tension, especially in the major cities. I went to lunch one day with the guy who handled PR for our TV network. He asked me if we could develop another radio network that would be geared toward blacks, to give them a voice and black news. He thought this would make them feel we had balanced newscasts.

I told him that because of the "chain broadcasting rule" I couldn't do it. The FCC had ruled that no radio station could affiliate with a network that operated two or more networks simultaneously. This was the rule that had been used to split up NBC's Red and Blue networks.

I'd been struggling with what to do about our owned stations in the radio network. Radio was becoming very competitive. In some cities there was more than one station using the same format.

Three of our owned stations were Top-40 format—New York, Pittsburgh, and Chicago. Detroit was a middle-of-the-road (MOR) music format. San Francisco and Los Angeles were Talk Radio.

Our network shows included "Breakfast Club" for an hour in the morning, a half hour of news with Paul Harvey at noon, an evening news hour, and short features, including Dennis Day for Archway Cookies and Zsa Zsa Gabor for Maidenform Bra.

Our stations were good and could carry network programming as long as there was no competition in their format. But now our stations were having trouble with ratings as competition came into their markets.

I dug out the chain broadcasting rules. One word caught my eye. "Simultaneously."

I asked myself, "What happens if we do it *sequentially*?" Top-40 stations like newscasts at 55 (minutes after the hour), where we then carried ours. Talk and MOR stations prefer news on the hour. We could do a second newscast for them. Our FM stations, which for a long time had merely simulcast programs from their AM counterparts, were beginning to develop unique formats. We could do a third newscast, at 15, for FM. And, for stations that still had a wide diversity of programs, we could do one at 30.

So we could do four networks. Five, if I could plug one in at 45 for "urban" formats, our code word for stations with largely black audiences.

This was before satellites. We were then spending about $3 million a year on broadcast-quality AT&T lines for our network. We were only actually using the lines a few minutes each hour, but we had to pay for twenty-four hours a day. If we could run four or five networks *sequentially*, it wouldn't cost us any more to get our programming to several stations in the same market.

That would greatly increase our program inventory, and we would have different demographic networks to sell to advertisers. And it would reduce the hours of network programming each station was required to carry, so each could maintain a competitive stance.

❑ ❑ ❑

Ralph took this idea to Si Siegel, prefacing his pitch with a caution and an offer. The caution was that what he had to sell might well strike Si as the craziest idea of all time. The offer was that if Si didn't like it, he'd never bring it up again. Si told him to get on with it.

Standing in the middle of Si's Spartan office, Ralph laid it out. As Si's usual facial expression, stony skepticism, dissolved into comprehension, Si told Ralph to sit down.

One thing Si liked was that Ralph's plan quadrupled networks but added only a few new people. The other thing was that ABC was already losing upward of $2 million a year on its radio network, and Ralph had calculated we wouldn't lose much more than that for the first few years. After that, he said, we might start to make money.

Si brought Ralph into my office so he could again explain the concept. I said, "What the hell, it can't be any worse than what we're doing. And it could help the owned-and-operated stations. I think we ought to pursue it."

The next morning Ev Erlick and Ralph took the shuttle to Washington and met with the FCC. They said, "This is unofficial, but as far as we're concerned, sequential networking is legal. But you must ensure that stations do not tape programming and delay it so it would be on while another station was broadcasting ABC's network programming." Formal approval, of course, would require full FCC hearings. We applied in November 1967; the FCC gave its blessings in December, just days before we were scheduled to start broadcasting.

We decided to start with four networks: the American Information Network for Talk Radio (older audiences); a Contemporary Network for Top-40 stations (the young); the Entertainment Network (MOR stations); and an FM Network (easy-listening stations).

Then came the hard part, selling the idea to stations.

OTHER RECOLLECTIONS:

Si Siegel

We had a meeting with our radio affiliates, about 300 stations, and I told them we planned to form four networks. They were very offended. Many had had exclusive ABC affiliation for years. Now as many as three other stations in their market area would also be ABC affiliates.

So we had to go back to scratch. We canceled all our network advertising and affiliation agreements. Then we formed and acquired new affiliates, not necessarily the same ones as before, but we filled up. And we made money. But oh, was that a crapshoot! The first year, when I saw those losses, no radio business.... I discussed it with Leonard and told him, "Staying with what we've got, we'll just continue to lose. At least this has a chance of making a helluva lot of money."

He said, "If that's the way you feel, go ahead." He was gambling, and so was I. We made more money than I ever believed possible.

❑ ❑ ❑

Almost immediately, the multiple network concept allowed our owned stations to become the highest billing and earning group of radio stations in America.

The advertising community was responsive to the specialized demographics we promised to deliver with four networks. It was a very efficient way to reach specific audiences.

But selling the concept to stations was much more difficult. While we did sign up hundreds of stations, after a few years it became apparent that something was amiss, though we were beginning to make money.

Ed McLaughlin, general manager of our San Francisco station, had adapted Ben Hoberman's Talk Radio concept to his own highly competitive market, turned KGO around, and made a good name for himself. I brought him in to straighten things out with the radio networks.

OTHER RECOLLECTIONS:
Ed McLaughlin

When we first went out to sell this idea, it was seen as good for ABC, but stations didn't just fall over and say, "Oh, wow, we can hardly wait." Building the affiliate base was very difficult, much more so than anyone anticipated.

In many cases we had to take smaller stations, the third or fourth rocker in a town. The more successful stations, and those that already had network affiliation, had no interest whatsoever in our new concept.

We then went to independently owned music stations and said, "We will compensate you to become an affiliate." That got their attention.

But some really only wanted the money. Not the service. They asked, "Can we just run your spots and not run your programming?"

Between 1968 and 1972, ABC built the Contemporary Network. Advertisers reached a youth market they couldn't find through any other medium.

At first there was some misunderstanding—I'm being kind—as to the station's obligation vis-à-vis their network relationship. Many stations said, "Well, if we're not sold out, we'll run your spots. If we are sold out, we won't."

So at some point we realized that maybe the stations weren't delivering what we told advertisers we were offering. We had to explain to advertisers that even stations that didn't carry the newscast could run their commercials.

In 1972 we restructured the division, and I came to New York to be president of ABC Radio Networks. Now, at KGO I ran everything 100 percent clean. At an ABC Owned Station, you must. So I thought everybody did. I was unaware of the marketing problems that had taken place from 1968 to 1972. When I learned we had no systems that would tell us if stations were clearing us, I became nervous. We had no way of proving to advertisers that they had got what we'd sold.

And advertisers were asking hard questions. I learned that sometimes affiliates didn't run our commercials at all. They just took the money.

Frankly, at that point I wasn't sure that multiple networks were a viable concept. If the stations were treating networks in such a fashion, there was just no way I could sell the concept to an advertiser and hold my head up or represent ABC.

I had to tell every station exactly what was expected from each of them. We had to create systems that would confirm what stations reported. Incidentally, many *were* reporting correctly, and we didn't know it. In other cases some honest mistakes were made. Some stations couldn't figure out some of our affidavits. Hell, *I* couldn't figure out some of our affidavits.

So there was a lot of work to be done. I confronted Leonard with the problem. I said, "There are only two things we can do. Either close it, or take the bottom line down considerably."

Leonard didn't kill the messenger. But a lot of people between me and him didn't think my plans were a good idea. I got a lot of heat. But I always thought that the worst thing that could happen to me was to get fired and go back to San Francisco, which is not so bad.

When people criticized or questioned me, I'd say, "Did you bring me back to change things or bring me back to change me? If you brought me here to change things, let me do it. If you brought me here to change me, then send me back to San Francisco."

It didn't take a lot of guts, because I knew the players, and I've always thought I knew what kind of company ABC was.

❑ ❑ ❑

Ed succeeded in cleaning up the mess by getting ABC to lobby the FCC for a rule that said that when a station signed a network affidavit certifying it had broadcast a particular spot, it was certifying this to the advertiser as well. So, falsifying an affidavit to the network could cost them their license. In a remarkably short time, the stations became models of rectitude.

After that we got a chance to show how well the concept worked. The whole radio advertising industry switched around. It was this quiet revolution that brought major national advertisers back into radio. Even so, by having to start all over, we lost $7 million the first year, $5 million the second, and $3 million the third. The fourth year we broke even. Since then we've been making money.

I'd thought the other networks, CBS, NBC, and Mutual, would immediately follow suit. Instead, while CBS and NBC waited to see how things would go for us, Mutual filed a lawsuit. It never came to trial. By the time CBS and NBC could see how things were going, two years had passed, and ABC was the dominant force in network radio.

As satellite technology matured, the cost of distribution came down. In the early 1980s we replaced telephone feeds with a digital satellite network. That allowed us to add networks designed for the new breed of rock stations, for country and western stations, and a "direction" network for longer programs and commentary. In 1990 ABC had seven radio networks serving over 2,200 affiliates among them.

Today, ABC's combination of networks and stations is radio's largest advertising medium.

17

Rule

❑

Defeating Norton Simon and outlasting Harold Geneen diverted my attention for almost two years. Once it was clear we would continue as an independent company, I turned my attention to a critical personnel change.

As president of the television network, Tom Moore had not proved himself a man for all seasons. While knowledgeable and most honorable, Tom no longer seemed to believe ABC could achieve parity, much less leadership. He focused instead on maintaining the status quo, and so became overly cautious.

Negative attitudes at the top inevitably seep downward. Moore had to go. Unlike Ollie Treyz, however, I thought Tom might be of great value to ABC in some other capacity.

I had arrived at this conclusion nearly two years earlier, but when fighting off corporate raiders, a change at the top may be interpreted as weakness. We were vulnerable enough without that kind of a problem, so I waited. When Geneen and ITT backed out, on New Year's Day, 1968, I moved.

The man I wanted to run the network was Elton Rule, general manager of our Los Angeles station, KABC-TV.

Elton, a native Californian, seemed to many an unlikely choice. He had no network experience. He had come up through the sales organization at KABC-TV, and his ABC career had been confined to one station in a single market.

But I thought then, and still do, that the best way to acquire a broad understanding of broadcasting is to work in a station for several years. A network-owned television station, in particular, is in many respects a miniature of the network. They produce programs, including news and sports, buy syndicated shows, sell advertising, and build schedules. Elton had turned KABC-TV into the most successful station in the nation's most competitive television market.

I knew Elton as a charismatic leader who got along well with everyone. That's important in any business, but even more so in broadcasting. He knew how to build a team and keep it moving forward. And he made a fine appearance, always well dressed and immaculately groomed. Although he was only a station manager, Elton *looked* like a network president. This is an image business, and that was important.

OTHER RECOLLECTIONS:
Elton Rule

At KABC, most of our business came from local advertisers. We were very short on national advertisers, so even as general manager, I remained involved in national sales for our station. I spent two weeks of every quarter in New York, and a week between Chicago, Minneapolis, Detroit, and St. Louis. I also made many trips to San Francisco, which then had most of the big West Coast advertising agencies.

Very early on, Leonard suggested that, whenever I was in New York, I stop in and let him know how things were going. I took advantage of that. He was very interested in the progress of the station and listened very carefully to me.

Tennis was a mutual interest. We were both very active. Good gravy, his lob shot was the most destructive thing I've ever encountered. I used to come home with a stiff neck from looking up at his lobs.

His secretary, Marion Ayer, would call me from New York and say, "Mr. Goldenson will be in Los Angeles for meetings later in the week. Are you available to play tennis with him Saturday morning at ten o'clock at the Beverly Hills Hotel?" I always made myself available.

Every year the managers would assemble in Palm Springs, Puerto Rico, or Hawaii—some wonderful place where you could get a little recreation and also do intensive reporting on goals for the next year. Leonard and I always found ourselves together on a tennis court.

I'm sure it helped me. Along with the recognition, our relationship became considerably more personal. He could see how I would react under competitive conditions outside the business. It wasn't intentional, but it helped everything fall into place.

❑ ❑ ❑

I'd been after Elton to come to New York for years, but he always resisted. His roots were in California. His children were still in school, and he had real-estate holdings and other investments that required frequent oversight.

In the early 1960s we offered Elton the number 2 network sales position, with the idea that he would progress from there. He turned it down. Later I asked him to run our flagship television station in New York. He declined. After seeing what he did at KABC-TV, we offered him the presidency of our O&O television stations. Again he said no.

At some point I asked what it would take to bring him to New York. He said, "I'm not at all thrilled about going to New York under any circumstances. But there is one job that would be absolutely intriguing. You wouldn't have to ask me. Just tell me to be there on Monday morning, and I'll come."

"Well, what job is that?"

"President of the television network."

OTHER RECOLLECTIONS:
Elton Rule

I was at KABC-TV for sixteen years. I felt very secure that I might end up being the oldest living station manager in America. When people talked about my career being meteoric, as they did once I got to New York, I'd say, "What about my sixteen years in the trenches?" But pretty nice trenches.

And then came the call from Tom Moore on a Friday morning right after the ITT merger blew up. On my way to work, driving through Griffith Park, my car phone rang.

Tom Moore said, "I'd like to have you come to a meeting in New York tomorrow."

I said, "Tomorrow's Saturday! And why would I come back to talk to you about anything?"

"I want to talk to you about the network."

Well, *all* the talk was about the network. We were at loggerheads with the network a lot of times. We often felt they usurped our autonomy.

Then Moore said, "I'd like to talk to you about *running* the network."

I said, "Jesus! Let's not talk about it on a radiotelephone! Wait till I get to the office. I'll call you back in ten minutes."

I called him, and I said, "What's going to happen to you if I've got the network?"

"Well, I'm going to be promoted. I would be Group Vice President."

I didn't know what he was talking about. But Leonard suggested I come back and talk. It had to be under the utmost secrecy. Nobody could know. Moore had me registered at the Hilton under an alias. A room the size of a shoe box.

They wanted me under wraps completely, so I stayed at the Moores' house Saturday night. And then Tom and I had a meeting on Sunday with Leonard and Si Siegel in Mamaroneck.

And of course, Jack Gould of *The New York Times*, then the dean of entertainment critics, had the whole story in the Sunday evening edition of Monday morning's paper.

I don't know where he got his information, but he was very good friends with Tom Moore.

We talked several hours out at Leonard's. They wanted me to report to Tom. That was the one thing I didn't like. Tom had a hell of a time making up his mind about anything.

I was very aware of where the strength was in the company. It was Leonard and Si. Nobody else. If things were going to get done, that's where the decisions were made. So I felt an extra layer of bureaucracy would make things too cumbersome.

I took Si and Leonard aside, away from Tom, and made an agreement that I would have access to them firsthand. I would keep Tom informed. This was not a subterfuge; it was a question of going where the answers would be forthcoming.

❑ ❑ ❑

There was some grumbling in ABC's upper echelons about Rule coming in to take over the network. It was to be expected. Executives tend to be political animals, and television executives perhaps a little more so than most.

Elton didn't allow this to bother him and quickly established himself as a leader. While taking Tom Moore's counsel on occasion, he mainly sought mine and Si's.

After about six months, Moore decided to move on. He went to California and became a successful independent producer. Among Tom's better-known films is "The Autobiography of Miss Jane Pittman." Today Tom divides his time between the Napa Valley, where he grows fine wine grapes, and Palm Springs. Coincidentally, his Palm Springs home was built by Walt Disney. Tom bought it from Lilli, Walt's widow.

In short order Elton demonstrated a very clear vision of what needed to be done, how to do it, and who should carry out each task. He began by determining who his strongest people were, then put them where they needed to be. He took Fred Pierce out of sales and put him in charge of planning.

Marty Pompadur, a lawyer who had worked in network sales and in business affairs since 1960, had been Moore's assistant. Marty had become so frustrated under Moore that he was on the verge of leaving.

Elton convinced him to stay and made him, in effect, his chief of staff. Marty pulled together the mountain of paperwork generated by the network. And he became Elton's liaison between groups such as the sales and programming departments. These are organizations that by their nature often have opposing views of how to accomplish things. Acting in Elton's name and with his guidance, Marty resolved many differences. He was a facilitator and expeditor.

OTHER RECOLLECTIONS:
Elton Rule

There really hadn't been a plan for the network. It had always been bullshit: "We will overtake CBS this year." Or, "Just wait till next year. We'll end up number one." That's a crock. No way could we overtake CBS in a year.

So, among other things, we developed a plan. We brought in the McKinsey Company, management consultants. We decided our goal was to improve each area by 5 percent per year. That was achievable and recognizable as a real goal. And if we could improve 20 percent in four years—holy Moses, that would really be an accomplishment.

This wasn't just my thinking. I was never a one-man band. My interest was in surrounding myself with the right people, giving them some goals, letting them do the work, and making sure they got the credit for it.

We knew that we had to go after affiliates, but we didn't have anything at that time to entice a station to change over from NBC or CBS to ABC. But we started the process. We planted the seeds. It was like the Chinese water torture. Drip, drip, drip.

❑ ❑ ❑

As Elton's right-hand man, Marty Pompadur played a very important role in formulating ABC's first five-year plan.

OTHER RECOLLECTIONS:
I. Martin Pompadur

We divided the broadcasting day into parts. We're the ones who started that. Our analogy was Time Inc. On the magazine side they had *Time, Fortune, People, Money*, and *Sports Illustrated*. All separate businesses. So why should we treat the network as *one* business? Prime Time is a separate business. News is. Late Night. Sports. Early Morning. Monday through Friday Daytime. Children's.

So we had a portfolio, not a single business. And the business plan we made for each daypart was totally different.

❑ ❑ ❑

In broadcasting, where change is the only constant and where technologies rapidly evolve, it behooves a top officer to be aware always of what *may* happen, and if it does, how to adjust quickly enough to stay ahead of the pack.

So I've always felt that the role of top executives should be to stimulate those around them. They should be provocative. They should seek to be farsighted. They should raise the sort of questions that cause others to think through all conceivable options and explore their likely consequences. It's also an obligation of executives on their way up to stimulate those around them, especially their bosses. The process must go both ways.

With that in mind, the people who have proved most valuable to ABC over the years have been those willing to say they didn't agree with me. When very strong people take that attitude, and when issues are then thrashed out thoroughly, we usually come to the proper conclusion.

I had this sort of interplay with Ollie Treyz, and before he went off the track, it worked wonders at ABC. Over the years, Elton and I developed a similar relationship. Although I alone dealt with the board of directors, in most other things we followed the manner that had evolved between Si Siegel and me. That is, we behaved more like old-fashioned partners than traditional, corporate-style executives.

OTHER RECOLLECTIONS:

I. Martin Pompadur

It was wonderful to watch the give-and-take. Leonard would give Elton a lot of rope. He let him do things that were strange for a CEO or COO to do. But it was Leonard's board, and Elton never tried to woo the directors, as other people had tried.

And it was Leonard's company, and Leonard got the publicity. And Roone Arledge got the publicity. And the talent got the publicity. Elton didn't really get a lot of publicity, and that was not an accident. He wanted it that way. He felt that the stars, if you will, were the Roone Arledges and Fred Silvermans of the world, and the on-camera network talent, and not him. And that played extremely well for the people we had at ABC.

Elton didn't get involved in minutiae and in administrative stuff. He didn't get involved in the financial area. His contribution was holding that place together, and having a relationship with the advertising community and with the affiliates and with the programming community. They were all so comfortable with him. He was an honest guy. He was the right guy. It was Central Casting Time. He was perfect.

Another of Elton's talents was getting these huge egos to work together. It was Central Park Zoo. If you took the ego of a Dick O'Leary running the television stations, and Roone Arledge running sports, and Marty Starger in entertainment, and Jim Duffy in Sales and later the network you'd have to say, "My God, how can all those people work in the same company? And you put them in the same room, and they sit around a conference table? I don't believe it." But Elton got it to work. He's the best people person I've ever seen.

Elton's take on doing things was informational and cooperative. I made it my style as well, and it permeated the company. Also, suddenly the affiliates had somebody in here that had worked at a station and understood the problems they were having. For the first time they were getting information. We had a much closer working relationship with each other, rather than the antagonism that was the norm before Elton.

❑ ❑ ❑

Elton and I became each other's sounding boards. I tend to have a great many ideas. Some are very good, and some are not. Elton became the fellow who said, "Leonard, I think this is a really fine idea, and I think we should forget about that other one." And of course I did the same for Elton.

Which is not to say we didn't make mistakes. Mistakes are part of every business, and especially show business. But I don't waste time feeling sorry. When I fall on my face, I take what lesson there may be from it, and go on to do the next thing.

One of our more notable failures was our decision about a show we had adapted from the BBC program, "Till Death Do Us Part." It was a comedy built around a lower-class Englishman and his long-suffering wife. British viewers found it hilarious. We asked a brilliant young—and then unknown—writer, Norman Lear, to create the pilot for an American version.

We didn't like the pilot, but we felt the project still had potential, so we asked Lear to do another. On the day the program department screened it for me, Elton, Si, and our station relations and sales people, we were in the midst of a strike. There were no union projectionists available, so Len Goldberg scoured the office for anybody who could run a projector. He came up with a young clerk named Michael Eisner.

OTHER RECOLLECTIONS:
Michael Eisner

Elton Rule had just become president, and had agreed to put on a show called "Turn On" in the winter of 1969. "Turn On" was like a stupid version of "Laugh In." Real short clips. It wasn't risqué, just bad. It didn't work.

In those days things would stay on for thirteen or twenty-six weeks before you would ever consider canceling. We canceled "Turn On" the night after it went on. It was the shortest-lived program in the history of network television.

Within six months "All in the Family" came up. The pilot had some very unflattering words about Jews and blacks. Elton got nervous—everybody was still shell-shocked from "Turn On." I think if it hadn't been for that, they would have put the show on. But they chickened out.

I was only a projectionist that day. I did say, "I think you should put 'All in the Family' on the air." Nobody listened. But later, they did listen.

❑ ❑ ❑

Elton and I knew "All in the Family" was funny, but felt it would antagonize certain ethnic groups. We also had serious doubts that advertisers would support the show. Our station relations people expressed strong reservations about getting it cleared by affiliates. It seemed too risky, so we passed.

I give Bob Wood, then president of CBS, full credit. He gambled and picked it up. Instead of antagonizing ethnic groups, they loved it. It was a hit. Thereafter, Lear brought CBS several other ideas, many of which also became hits.

So you can lose. And you can win.

In television, Hollywood's biggest winner is undoubtedly Aaron Spelling. I first met Aaron in 1964, when he was writing and producing for Dick Powell's Four Star Productions.

Aaron was an actor who became a writer and then a producer. Given an original idea, he grasps its central concept at once. His ability to take almost any script and fix it, make it work better, is unexcelled. Often he would put in a full day at the studio, then write a script at home, in bed, working until the wee hours. And it was always terrific.

OTHER RECOLLECTIONS:
Aaron Spelling

At a time when I was barely dealing with ABC's lower echelon, suddenly Leonard asked me to lunch at a Tahitian restaurant. I was absolutely petrified. I asked Dick Powell, "What do I do? What do I say? What did I do wrong?"

At lunch Leonard said, "I've been watching you. I think you're a hell of a writer, and now a producer. I want you to know if you ever leave Four Star, we would be very interested in your continuing to work with us at ABC."

I was then producing a hit for ABC called "Burke's Law." That's why Leonard took an interest in me. He thought it was a fresh idea.

It was the first show that used guest stars as suspects—as "Murder, She Wrote" is doing now, and as we did later in "Love Boat," "Fantasy Island," and "Hotel."

When Dick Powell died, I just couldn't stay at Four Star, so I went with Danny Thomas. My first year, 1968, I did a show called "Mod Squad." In the meantime Leonard was nice enough to call me now and then, and say, "I saw 'Burke's Law' last night, that was fun, it was really nice." Calls like that, you don't expect to get from the head of a network.

I was told that "Mod Squad" would never work. Many people at Paramount, where we were shooting it, said that. Sheldon Leonard, whom I respect very much, said that an audience will never watch a show about kids finking on kids.

I said, "Shelly, you ought to see the show. They don't fink on kids. The 'Mod Squad' is to prevent people from *using* kids."

And here's an action show where none of the kids carried guns. They never killed anybody. They were pacifists from the word go. They were kicked off the police force, suspended, because they picketed the police department against the war. But some people never got that. Too bad.

We made the pilot for 'Mod Squad,' and Leonard called to say how much they enjoyed it.

A little later he invited me to my first affiliates' meeting. I didn't know what the hell that was. I just plopped down at a table somewhere, sitting with strangers. Leonard came by and called me by name. People at the table were impressed. It was my first touch of a four-letter word called FAME.

Leonard played the room like a maestro. He went from table to table. He knew every affiliate's name. If he didn't know somebody, he'd walk over and say, "Hello, I'm Leonard Goldenson," and they'd say "I'm so-and-so, and I'm with so-and-so." Maybe it was a producer, and he'd say, "Oh yes, I like your work." He had seen every pilot, and he knew every show, which amazed me. And if he didn't know someone's work, he wouldn't say anything but "Nice meeting you," and move on. I was very impressed.

About two weeks later, ABC said they wanted to change "Mod Squad" to "The Young Detectives." The person they sent out to tell me ended up being one of my closest friends, Leonard Goldberg.

In those days I was single and didn't have any overhead. I had a dinky little apartment. So I said, "I'm not going to do a show called 'The Young Detectives.' It's going to be 'Mod Squad.' "

For the first time in my life I called Leonard. I said, "They want to change the name, but I don't want to do a show called 'The Young Detectives.' It sounds like 'The Hardy Boys.'

"We're doing a show that has meaning. These kids are social activists. They carry placards, but they don't carry guns. I'm trying to be different."

He said, "Aaron, if you believe so strongly, hold your ground. It'll get up to me."

About two weeks later ABC said, "We agree it should be 'Mod Squad.' "

True to his nature, Leonard never called and asked, "Did you get a call from so-and-so," or "Are you okay now?" None of that. He just didn't take credit. And to this day if you ask him, he'll say, "Oh no, the people who are day-to-day on the firing line, they agreed with you." He would never take credit for it.

We did the show for five years. Nobody ever fired a gun. It's still running on cable.

After three years of "Mod Squad," "The Guns of Will Sonnett," and a few other shows with Danny Thomas, I decided I wanted to form my own company. I wanted creative freedom, and all that.

It was terrifying. Suddenly I have no income. Nothing is guaranteed, yet I have to run an office and pay for telephones. That was not very exciting to me. But my young wife said we should take the shot. So I did.

Then I got a call from Elton Rule, and we met at the Brown Derby. He said, "We would never interfere as long as you were with Danny, because he is an old, close friend of me and Leonard. But since you've started your own company, why don't you become exclusive with us? We will finance you." Music to my ears.

Then he said, "I really want you. But I want you to know it was Leonard who suggested it."

Which knocked me for a loop. I thought, Here's a new man, Elton Rule, coming in and wanting to start something of his own —but Elton is the same kind of man as Leonard, you'll find neither one ever lies about anything. They have the greatest integrity.

I had a stupid, sophomoric question. I said "Gee, I don't know about being exclusive.... Why do you think I should do this?"

He looked me in the eye, as no man ever has, and said, "Trust me." And I trusted him.

We made a deal that day. It was the fastest thing in history. The first year I made three pilots. They bought all three shows.

❑ ❑ ❑

For eighteen years we had an exclusive arrangement with Aaron, a unique and unparalleled situation. Aaron's obligation was to create programs for our consideration, and produce them if we decided to broadcast them. If we didn't want a particular show—and over the years we did turn down several—he couldn't offer them elsewhere. In deciding what to buy, our programming department treated Aaron's projects no differently from others. His pilots were screened in competition with everything else we commissioned, and we chose the shows that best suited our needs.

Aaron became virtually an extension of our programming department. If we made a mistake with a show and it flopped, he could create a replacement and have it ready within five or six weeks. I don't know anyone else who can move that fast and that well. Aaron became our secret weapon when we began to depend on a second season. He was a tower of strength.

I made it a point to get together with Aaron whenever I was in California for a few days. He had his ear to the ground, and by comparing notes I learned a lot about what was going on around Hollywood, including which new writers or producers or talent were hot. Our relationship soon passed beyond business to friendship. Fortunately, our wives became friends as well. We confided in each other.

OTHER RECOLLECTIONS:
Aaron Spelling

Our daughter, Torie, became an actress when she was nine. I was talking to Leonard about something else and he said, "Oh, how's the baby, how's Torie, my actress. . . ."

I said, "I'm really upset, I don't know what to do. She's been offered this great role in a television movie. She is to play a little girl that's been raped.

"I really don't want her to do it. She's playacting, but she gets into her character, and it's all real to her. It could have a very bad effect. Maybe somebody else would think differently, but I don't want my child to go through the rape syndrome, even as an actress.

"Also, it might look like we care only about money to have our daughter take such a role."

He said, "I couldn't agree more. My advice is don't let her play it. I know it is going to break her heart, but don't let her."

So I didn't let her do it.

My son Randy was a preemie. Weighed only two pounds at birth. It was a horrifying time for us because we had to leave him in the hospital. Just consider going to that hospital every day for three months and worrying about him. Frightening as hell.

When Randy was about five days old, I got a call from Leonard. "I'll be in town this week, and I'd like to go see Randy," he said.

I picked Leonard up at the hotel and we went to Cedars–Sinai, then up to the preemie room. We put on caps, gowns, and gloves, because of the danger of infection to the babies.

I said, "You see these lights directly over the baby's crib? The doctor told me the greatest danger to preemies is yellow jaundice. These lights are new, and they prevent jaundice in ninety-eight percent of preemies."

Leonard said, "I know. Through United Cerebral Palsy, I helped raise the money for them to experiment with that light."

He said it with great pride, but it wasn't about the money. It was that it worked. It saved children. I got the cold chills. Here was a man that I dearly loved. And our paths had crossed in so many ways, businesswise, and now he was the man that may have been responsible for saving my baby's life.

That's the closest I've ever felt to Leonard.

❑ ❑ ❑

We kept Aaron very busy for many years. One result is that he is now one of California's richest men. He's entitled. Aaron has produced more film than anybody in the history of motion pictures or television.

And that speaks volumes about his ability to entertain an audience. If so many of his shows hadn't been huge hits, playing to big audiences season after season, no one would have kept asking for more. Bearing in mind the way network audiences have shrunk since the mid-1980s, I doubt anyone will ever come near Aaron's production achievements.

With Elton's accession to the network presidency, our programming department began to evolve. Len Goldberg had moved up from head of daytime to run the programming department after Ed Scherick and Doug

Cramer departed. In line with our strategy of going after young audiences, he hired the brightest young men he could find.

OTHER RECOLLECTIONS:
Len Goldberg

I put together a pretty good staff of killers. I wanted guys around me who were smart and tough.

I was then seeing Marlo Thomas, Danny's daughter. She introduced me to a family friend, Barry Diller. As a kid he had lived down the block from the Thomas home in Beverly Hills, and was close to Marlo's sister, Terry. When I met Barry, he was at William Morris. Just out of the mail room, but not yet an agent.

I met Barry at a party at Marlo's house. We got into a tremendous fight. Not with fists. A verbal battle. I started it purposely. I wanted to provoke him, see what he was really like. I was very impressed with Barry's knowledge—being such a young man—and with his loyalty to William Morris.

I decided I wanted him to come to New York. We had a meeting. I said, "I want you to be my assistant."

Barry said, "And forget being an agent?"

"Nobody wants to be an agent. I mean, if you can't do anything else, you become an agent."

He was very loyal to his company and didn't want to leave, but I finally convinced him to come. After a brief period, Barry became very unhappy with living in New York. He hadn't made many friends yet, and didn't like his job.

He told me, "People say I'm your secretary. They make fun of me."

I said, "Don't worry. In a very short time no one will ever make fun of you again." And I'll tell you, no one makes fun of Barry today.

And then we hired Michael Eisner. I read his résumé. He told me later he had sent out 100 copies, and we were the only ones who had answered. Barry interviewed Mike and sent him to me. I liked him. I said, "Comb your hair, Michael." He was enthusiastic, bright, tough, and didn't know any of the rules. That was great, because he didn't feel bound by them.

❑ ❑ ❑

Len also brought over Marty Starger, who had been his associate at BBD&O, and who would succeed him a few years later as head of programming.

Len recognized that our primary medium to advertise ABC's programs was our own on-air promotion. But as the network with the smallest number of affiliates, our promotion reached far fewer people than CBS or NBC. So he tried to do what he had done in daytime: Come up with radically different types of shows that were promotable in other media.

Aaron Spelling's "Mod Squad" was one of those programs, and it did very well. Len also bought "That Girl," starring one Marlo Thomas. "The Courtship of Eddie's Father" became a successful show. And of course there was "Marcus Welby, M.D."

OTHER RECOLLECTIONS:
Len Goldberg

"Marcus Welby" was developed for another network. They passed on it, and the script was submitted to Barry Diller and Marty Starger by Sid Sheinberg at Universal.

I really liked it and I said, "I know the perfect actor for it. Lee J. Cobb, who did *Twelve Angry Men.*" I thought he'd be perfect for the kind of doctor the script called for. But we couldn't get Lee J. Cobb.

Sid called Barry or Marty and said, "A funny thing happened. Robert Young saw the script, and he wants to do it." Young was a big hit in "Father Knows Best," but had done nothing since.

I said, "That's a terrible idea."

Sid said, "Well, everybody else wants Robert Young, but he won't do anything. Now he wants to come back and play 'Marcus Welby.' "

"He's just wrong. He's good-looking and charming. He's a leading man. This is not written for a leading man."

A week later I get a phone call from Young: "Mr. Goldberg, I understand you don't want me to be in 'Marcus Welby.' "

I was embarrassed. He was a great star. I'd watched him in so many motion pictures, and I loved "Father Knows Best." I said, "You're just too handsome for the part. And you look rich and successful. This guy is struggling."

He said, "I don't think I'm handsome. Maybe I'm charming. But why can't he be successful? Why can't he drive a nice car? There's nothing wrong with that."

"That's just not the character," I said.

"I really wish you'd reconsider."

I said I would. Then I sent word that I still didn't want him. I went to an affiliates convention in Barbados, and Young called me again. "I really want to do this."

"Look, I feel so badly. I mean, you're too good for this part."

"Would you allow me to test?"

"Mr. Young, *you* don't have to test for a television show."

"I want this part, and I'm going to prove to you that I can do it. I'm asking you, would you let me test?"

"Of course."

I saw the test and damned if he wasn't outstanding. He said it had to do with an attitude. Just because we had one thing in mind doesn't mean we couldn't do it another way.

He was absolutely right. I was 100 percent wrong. "Marcus Welby" became one of our biggest hits.

❑ ❑ ❑

When "Marcus Welby, M.D." premiered on Tuesday nights at 10 in the fall of 1969, we were still struggling to get competitive series programming. By then live programming was almost forgotten. Both our network competitors, to say nothing of the motion picture studios, had heartily embraced the idea that programs should come from Hollywood. But as the network ranked third in distribution outlets, any ABC show started with about 30 percent fewer potential viewers.

Since the size of the audience was what kept advertisers happy, any show would have a better chance for a long run on either of the other networks. And shows that played several seasons were far more profitable to their producers than those that went off the air quickly because of startup costs and because of the potential for syndication.

Accordingly, as time went on, we rarely got first look at new ideas from the studios or independents. It was up to us to come up with the new ideas.

Despite a few exceptions like "All in the Family," however, neither of our rival networks was particularly willing to experiment with radical ideas. They didn't need to. They were already winning.

The first movies created expressly for television were the brainchild of Jennings Lang at Universal, in 1962. But ABC just didn't have the money to do two-hour movies. We were still trying to find ways to finance the purchase of rights to theatrical films.

And then we got lucky. On New Year's Day, 1968—ironically, the same day ITT backed out of our merger—Roy Huggins was walking off the effects of his previous evening's celebration on a Malibu beach.

OTHER RECOLLECTIONS:
Roy Huggins

In the old days, many movies ran seventy-five to eighty minutes. I did "Hangman's Knot," which only ran seventy-seven minutes. So why, I asked myself, must we do two-hour movies on TV?

I came up with the idea of doing a show called "Movie of the Week" that would start at 8:30 and run ninety minutes. Without commercials, the film would be about seventy minutes.

I had a contract with Universal, which was run by Lew Wasserman. Under Wasserman was Sid Sheinberg, VP in charge of TV. I presented the idea to Sheinberg. He said, "We don't want anything to do with this, you are on your own."

Under my contract, if they didn't like a series idea, I could sell it anywhere. I went to CBS. We had a meeting that included Fred Silverman and Mike Dann, a great power at CBS and a very opinionated, strong-willed man. Dann said, "Roy, that is the worst idea I've ever heard in my life." He walked out.

Then I took it to NBC. My friend Herb Schlosser was polite but said, "We already have 'World Premiere,'" a two-hour movie series. He just didn't get it. He rejected it.

Then my friend Dave Kaufman called and said, "I heard a rumor you're trying to sell a series called 'Movie of the Week.' What is it about?"

I told him. The next day, March 21, *Variety*'s front page had a story about Huggins's "Movie of the Week." It laid out the whole concept.

I didn't know how important that was. I got a call from Leonard Goldberg. "Roy, I read this thing in *Variety*. Are you interested in presenting it to us?"

I made my presentation at a meeting with Leonard Goldberg and Barry Diller and several others. They asked questions like "What kind of stories would you tell?"

I said, "You must start with hard-hitting melodramas and mysteries until you've got your audience. Then you can branch out and tell character stories or war stories or anything you want. It is an anthology series."

They said, "Okay, Roy, we'll talk to you."

Instead of coming back to me, ABC went to Universal. Management there asked the legal department, "Do we have to do this with Huggins?" The lawyers said, "All we are buying is a concept, which after publication in *Variety* is now in the public domain."

On June 13, *Variety*'s lead story was about ABC doing a ninety-minute "Movie of the Week" show.

I called Leonard Goldberg. He said, "We have decided this is too big for any one person. We are going to do this ourselves."

I said, "How can you do that? I brought you this concept. You and I better get together."

Goldberg said, "We're going to do twenty-six of these, and we think it's too much for any one producer, but we would like you to do a lot of them. How many would you like to do?"

I said, "Twenty-six."

He laughed and said, "The network has to control a show of this importance. How would you like to do eight?"

I should have accepted a guaranty of eight shows a season. Instead, I insisted on doing them all. And I talked about suing them.

A few days later my lawyer called and said, "You can sue them, but you will lose. Since the whole concept was printed in *Variety*, it's now in the public domain. Anybody can use it."

I could have gone back to Goldberg and said, "Okay, you win," and he would have given me eight shows. I would have been in good shape.

I didn't. I had enough to do. There were times when I had three shows on the air and didn't have time to do them all. I really didn't need "Movie of the Week."

❑ ❑ ❑

"Movie of the Week," a seminal notion, became vitally important to ABC, and a number of major careers were launched or accelerated because of it. So one should not be surprised that credit for the idea has been claimed widely. A check of *Daily Variety*, however, confirms Huggins's primacy.

Ideas are important, but in the final analysis it's what you *do* with an idea that counts. Len Goldberg, Marty Starger, and Barry Diller took Huggins's idea and jump-started ABC's television network with their efforts.

For Len Goldberg, "Movie of the Week," with its ninety-minute format, was a godsend.

OTHER RECOLLECTIONS:
Len Goldberg

We made up a presentation—Barry and Marty did most of the work—for the board. We asked for a commitment of $14 million for movies. They said, "Maybe we should try one or two."

I said, "No, it's got to be a series."

There was no pilot, there were no scripts. But Leonard was very enthusiastic. He always liked new ideas. So they committed $14 million just on an idea.

I came out to Hollywood with Barry. We talked to all the studios, but nobody, at first, was interested. Everyone thought it would interfere with their other movies. And the idea seemed strange. The studios wanted orders for twenty-six weeks of a half-hour series. So what was *this* thing? They were very uncomfortable with it.

Except Universal. They had done the "World Premiere" movies for NBC. They saw the potential. We came very close to giving them the entire franchise.

But finally Barry and I decided the only way to get it going was to do it ourselves, since no one else wanted to do it.

A producer, Harold Cohen, came in with an idea about a spy. There was a series of books written, so we agreed to finance him for two back-to-back shows. A way to effect savings.

We got Jimmy Sangster to write them, and we cast Robert Horton, a big star in "Wagon Train," and Sebastian Cabot, star of "Family Affair," and Jill St. John, who gave it a little movie star glamour. So it would sound like we were doing real movies, not just something for television.

In the trades we announced we were going ahead. The phone started ringing. All the guys who'd previously rejected us said, "What do you mean? Where's our order? We want our share. You can't not take Screen Gems . . . you can't leave out Warners."

The first "Movie of the Week" we aired was one by Aaron

Spelling, *Corporal Crocker,* about a guy who came back from the war.

❑ ❑ ❑

Barry Diller had quickly evolved into a tough, capable businessman and a hard-nosed negotiator. His forte was negotiating the purchase of rights to feature pictures from the major companies. Barry made a presentation to the board. While Universal was asking $400,000 per film, Barry said he could produce each "Movie of the Week" for $350,000.

That was a very good price, so we gave him the green light. For a time we thought we would let Universal—a division of MCA—do all the films. But when the deal got up to MCA chairman Lew Wasserman, he insisted on $400,000 each. We turned them down.

OTHER RECOLLECTIONS:
Barry Diller

The wonderful thing about ABC was that it allowed people like Michael Eisner, me—and an endless list of others—to take all the responsibility we wanted. It was never a question of waiting for somebody to *give* us responsibility.

With the responsibility came authority. We could make almost any decision. It allowed me, even at the age of twenty-four, to deal with the heads of all the movie companies. To negotiate directly with titans like Lew Wasserman, Arthur Krim at United Artists, and Charlie Bluhdorn, the industrialist who purchased Paramount.

I was responsible for ABC's movie inventory, buying movies and scheduling them. That's a remarkable load to put on a kid.

When we decided to do movies for television, I thought we should do it ourselves and not turn things over to some movie factory we had no control over.

But the feeling was that we just didn't have any ability to do them ourselves. We got into a negotiation with Universal. Thank God, Universal acted in its normal arrogant manner. Besides asking for more money than we were prepared to pay, they said, "If you do this with us, then evermore, any movies for television you make will have to be made with Universal."

We said, "No, we're not going to do that."

Universal said, "Well, we won't do it."

They didn't mean it, but they said it. So we said, "Okay, we'll take you at your word."

In that little space, I was able, with Leonard Goldenson's help, to push away the people in the company who had wanted this simple, one-stop arrangement with Universal.

Leonard flew to Los Angeles, and we met with each of the companies to encourage them to get into the movie-of-the-week business, this new form. Leonard helped us by godfathering the process, by articulating what we wanted to accomplish with these ninety-minute movies. The next week, in New York, Wasserman became involved, trying to put Universal's deal back together by agreeing to everything we originally asked for and they had said no to.

We said no, and when they came back, we continued to say no. They flew in all their senior people for meetings. We said, "We've decided to go in another direction. If you'd like to participate along with the others, we'll order a few from you."

That's how we built that business. We made arrangements with lots of companies, and we started our own production company. That's how Spelling really began in his independent company. That's how Lee Rich began. The formation of Lorimar resulted from ABC's original seed money for these ninety-minute movies.

❑ ❑ ❑

Lew Wasserman, who rarely indulges in self-criticism, later told me that trying to inflate the price of these ninety-minute films had been a serious mistake for Universal.

By controlling production of the movies ourselves and contracting with several production companies, Barry let competition work in our favor. We stayed within his original $350,000 budget per film. And thereafter, in all the years he worked for ABC, Barry was uniformly successful in meeting fiscal targets. As far as I know, he never went over on any budget.

"Movies of the Week" were programmed strategically at 8:30, bridge programming that maintained audience flow to our few successful episodic series. In 1971 we added a second, ninety-minute film show, "Movie of the Weekend," on Saturday evenings. In 1972, we moved the "weekend" films to Wednesday nights. By 1973 our schedule included three nights of ninety-minute films, including "ABC Suspense Movie" on Saturday evenings.

Until the mid-1970s, theatrical movie nights and made-for-television movies, coupled with Roone Arledge's sports operation, were what kept ABC competitive.

Of equal importance, under ABC's leadership, personified by Barry's supervision, the made-for-television movie became a distinctive genre. Movies exploring current social issues, which would be far too financially risky for big-budget theatrical features, found a place on television. It opened up an entirely new vista for filmmakers. And for audiences.

Out of this genre came such unforgettable classics as *Brian's Song*, the story of Brian Piccolo, whose professional football career was cut short by the cancer that eventually took his life, and his friendship with Gayle Sayers. It was an extraordinary film. It's still aired, from time to time, and draws very large audiences.

Another was *That Certain Summer*, starring Martin Sheen and Hal Holbrook. It was one of the first films dealing with homosexuality to be broadcast in the United States. It won an Emmy for best film of the year in 1971.

Len Goldberg, needing relief from his pressure-cooker job, resigned in May 1969 and went to Screen Gems, a Columbia subsidiary. Marty Starger became head of programming.

By 1970 it was apparent to everyone what kind of a leader Elton Rule was. We still had several serious problems, but ABC was gathering steam. We restructured the company, and Elton became head of a new broadcasting division, which included the television network, our owned stations, and all radio operations. Wally Schwartz, who had been in charge of our radio networks, became head of the TV network.

In 1970 all three television networks were dealt a body blow when the FCC ruled that after January 2, 1971, we could no longer carry advertising for cigarettes. Our general counsel, Ev Erlick, was close to the FCC's decision-making process on this issue.

OTHER RECOLLECTIONS:
Ev Erlick

The problem was that cigarettes began to take a big piece of prime-time television, sponsoring news and anything that would lend respectability. The commercials were often sexual, but not blatantly. The hidden message was, "Smoke, you'll have sex appeal." And, "Smoke, you can be successful." Charming, all these things. They were less obvious in magazine ads. It was part of the mystique. Of the appeal. And they were damn effective commercials, because people were smoking more and more.

The health problem began to surface in the 1960s. The Heart Institute, plus individual researchers and scientists, began to voice concerns.

The networks took the position that if a product is bad for health, then it shouldn't be sold. But as long as it's a legal product, whatever requirements for advertising it are placed on print media, billboards, matchbook covers, skywriting, or whatever, should be the same requirements for broadcasters.

But if it's legal, how the hell can you say networks shouldn't do it? That's blatant discrimination.

To this the FCC replied, in effect, "Screw you." They said that broadcasting is the most effective means of advertising this product.

The government was collecting $4 billion in tax revenue from the tobacco states. And some of that goes back to subsidize the growers.

The networks raised that issue in many, many ways. We said, "Is it logical that you subsidize the growing of the product, but you tell TV networks that we can't advertise it?"

They said, "Maybe not, but you guys are so effective that we think this will have a big impact."

Ultimately the cigarette companies themselves did it in.

Preceding the FCC's outright ban, cigarette commercials were deemed to have violated the Fairness Doctrine. To balance bad things that they implied or said or taught, we had to put on *anti*smoking commercials.

These commercials, created by public interest organizations, were tough, hard-hitting, and ultimately devastating. The networks had to air them without charge, under the Fairness Doctrine. It was like putting a stick of dynamite up the rectum of the tobacco companies. They were really getting gored. They concluded that, if they got off the air, the antismoking commercials would disappear. There would no longer be a necessity to broadcast them.

And they thought they could all save a lot of money. Network time was getting very expensive.

For example, the head of Lorillard Tobacco was then Larry Tisch. He wanted to get out and save a lot of money. But introducing a new product is easy on television. It is not easy when you have to do a whole lot of things that cost a whole lot of money. After the ban, Reynolds and American Tobacco and some of the others started pressing hard on in-store distribution, point-of-sale materials, and newspapers. They started paying off distributors. Lorillard and everyone else had to fall in line, do the same things, to keep their share. All the money they saved on television was spent in other ways, and no one saved any money.

But they didn't know that going in. They thought if they could all withdraw at the same time, there would be no competitive disadvantage. But they could not *conspire* to withdraw from television. That's against the law. But if they were ordered out, then no problem. It's not a conspiracy.

At first, legislation was framed in such a way that it might have run afoul of the antitrust laws. We went to see Senator Phil Hart of Michigan, chairman of the antitrust committee. We said, "You can't do this. Antitrust law is not this flexible." He killed the bill.

But the next week the FCC said, "We'll just rule that you can't advertise a cigarette after January 1, 1971. No law, just a ruling. It'll be very simple: You just can't do it anymore."

Every network, every broadcaster, all the broadcast associations, and some print media spoke out against that ruling because they understood that someday their day might come. People who looked beyond their noses understood that we might be hung separately on this occasion, but there would be a time when we would all go down gurgling.

The ruling was challenged and sustained as being constitutional. I've never fully understood why, nor have a lot of other lawyers.

Pete Rozelle got them to put it over to January 2, so it would keep that NFL season intact.

❑ ❑ ❑

For ABC, the end of cigarette advertising meant an immediate loss of 7 or 8 percent of our prime-time revenues. It was a terrible setback. We were just beginning to get things together in several areas, most notably sports and prime-time programming. Our success was the result of seventeen years of struggle, but our progress was also aided by the growth of the national economy from a two and a half network level to nearly three.

We were not in a position to reach out to the advertising community and demand they increase their budgets to make up for our shortfall. But clearly, we had to do something.

Then, almost miraculously, what the FCC took away with its right hand it gave back with its left—at least for ABC.

For years the FCC had been concerned with the twin questions of network "dominance" and "control of programming."

The game-show scandals of the 1950s had compelled networks to take more control over programming. ABC was not involved in that scandal, but we couldn't avoid responsibility by trying to shift blame on our suppliers. We hold the switch that puts a show on the air; Congress looks to us as a control point. We are licensed. Production companies are not.

By 1970 we were moving toward full control of our program schedule. Advertiser control was fading fast. Then the FCC began active examination of network program "dominance." There was a general perception that network shows were too pervasive. The FCC sought to moderate this by helping independently owned but network-affiliated stations become more autonomous. They assumed that networks could force affiliates to go along with anything we asked.

This was never true, but it was widely believed.

So the FCC discussed various alternatives. Eventually they narrowed the options to two. In the fifty-fifty plan, advertisers would control 50 percent of programming. In the Prime Time Access plan, network-originated programming would be reduced by thirty minutes daily. Prime time would begin at 8 P.M., instead of 7:30, and end at 11. Individual stations would program the additional time to meet local objectives.

OTHER RECOLLECTIONS:
Ev Erlick

This was an era of heavy government regulation toward broadcasting. The Democrats were in control of the agencies and believed regulation was inherently and implicitly good.

We violently opposed the fifty-fifty plan. It was totally unworkable. Network management cannot wait to see what programs advertisers come in with over the course of a summer and then try to have a schedule fixed for sale in the fall. That's sure death.

Publicly, we also opposed reducing network programming time by thirty minutes a day.

But among ourselves, at ABC, we realized there was going to

be a ruling of some sort, and we would all have to live with it. If the ruling mandated a cut in network programming, then all three networks would have to shrink programming inventories.

That would hurt CBS and NBC, but it would help us. After the ban on cigarette ads, ABC couldn't sell all of its available time. But with thirty minutes less each day to sell, advertising time on all three networks would become more precious. We could charge more. And with fewer shows, we would save about 15 percent on program expenses. So ABC would become more competitive, relative to the other networks.

We opposed both plans initially, on the ground that the government shouldn't interfere with a free market. Ultimately ABC's position was understood by a number of people on Capitol Hill and on the FCC staff. We quietly told them—unofficially—that, while we opposed both plans, if there had to be some sort of limitation, we would support a reduction in prime time.

❑ ❑ ❑

As we had hoped, the FCC adopted the Prime Time Access rule. After the loss of cigarette revenue, we came out about even or slightly ahead. And I must give credit to Ev Erlick and our Washington counsel, Jim McKenna, for doing a very effective job in selling this to the FCC. In contrast to the other networks, they worked in a variety of low-key ways that made defeat of the fifty-fifty rule almost inevitable.

While curbing network power, Prime Time Access did little for local stations. Most independents, especially in smaller markets, can't afford to develop and produce prime-time shows. Denied network programs, they turned to other suppliers. American television between 7:30 and 8 P.M. is now filled with reruns of old network sitcoms, syndicated game shows, and tabloidish "reality-based" programs.

All my life I've been blessed with good health. I've never smoked, always watched my diet, and exercised regularly. Since my Harvard undergraduate days, when I learned I was allergic to virtually all forms of alcohol, I've been a teetotaler. For those reasons, and probably because of a fortunate genetic heritage, I've reaped the benefits of being able to put in many, many hours of work each day without undue fatigue. In my sixty-sixth year, however, I learned that my body was not indestructible.

In May of 1971, I went to Denver to attend United Cerebral Palsy's annual meetings. For four days I began each morning with a 7 A.M. working breakfast, then continued steadily throughout the day and on into late evening.

In the mid-1960s, ABC had established a film production division, and at this time several of our projects were being produced overseas. I was scheduled to drop in on them.

On the way, I stopped in New York, where my secretary met me at JFK airport. We spent several hours going over my mail and discussing things that had to be done. After dictating several letters and giving detailed instructions to my secretary, I flew to Stockholm, where the time is six hours later than New York and eight hours later than Denver.

In Sweden, I met with Ingmar Bergman. He was doing a picture with us, *The Touch*, and after he picked me up at the airport, we spent two days in his remote farmstead, where we discussed the picture and our planned promotion for it.

Next I flew to Munich, where we were doing *Cabaret*. For three days I worked late into each night, immersed in details of promotion and scheduling. I gave no thought to rest. I worked as long as necessary, for there was much to do.

Then I flew to London, where we were doing *Straw Dogs* with Dustin Hoffman. Dan Melnick was producing this theatrical film for us, and I spent two or three days with him.

I returned to New York late Friday evening. Because of the differences in time zones, I'd been averaging only two or three hours of sleep a night for about ten days.

I was a little tired. Nevertheless, early Saturday morning I played several sets of tennis. That afternoon several ABC executives came to my home. Our annual stockholders' meeting was scheduled for the following Tuesday, and we spent the afternoon and all the next day discussing questions we anticipated might arise.

I had promised Isabelle that I'd speak to a group of women about cerebral palsy after the ABC meeting. It took a couple of hours. Returning to my office, and later walking back to our New York City apartment, I began feeling pressure on my chest. It was hard to breathe.

The pressure became a steel vise. As it slowly crushed inward, I hailed a taxi. "Columbia Presbyterian Hospital," I gasped. I was having a heart attack.

18

Number One

❑

Once again I was lucky. Very lucky. When I got to Columbia Presbyterian, I asked to see an old friend, Dr. Dana Atchley. By the time he ran some tests, I was feeling much better. The tests seemed to indicate that my heart was quite normal. As a precaution, Dr. Atchley had me admitted to the hospital.

Later that night, when jaws of terrible pain again seized my chest, quickly rendering me unconscious, I was in the best place in the world to have a severe heart attack: a well-equipped cardiac ward. I'm sure that saved my life.

Despite the damage to my heart muscle, my recovery was fairly rapid. I was out of immediate danger in several hours. Within a few days I was out of bed for brief periods. After less than two weeks I returned to Mamaroneck for a brief recuperation.

Given ABC's chronic vulnerability to corporate raiders, Si Siegel, who continued to manage ABC's day-to-day business, decided to clamp a lid on news of my heart attack.

OTHER RECOLLECTIONS:
Si Siegel

We kept it very quiet. Outside of a few people and the board of directors, nobody knew Leonard had a heart attack. John Coleman appointed himself a committee of one to decide who needed to know about Leonard's condition. Until he brought it up, we were not to discuss it. Nobody asked, so there was no discussion.

The only thing in the newspapers was a short item that Leonard wasn't feeling well. We were very lucky and didn't get any calls.

And nobody was panicked. Nobody said, "You better look for a new president."

Whenever decisions had to be made, I made them. And there were no pressing matters, just the things I'd have handled anyway. I talked to John Coleman every single day to let him know what was going on. We issued no reports during the period Leonard was recuperating, but fortunately, none were due. Then Leonard came back, and nobody was the wiser.

❑ ❑ ❑

Surviving a brush with death forced me to think about a successor at ABC.

I knew that Si Siegel would have liked to be president. In many ways, he had earned the job. For many, many years, Si kept us solvent with his shrewd fiscal moves. And Si had raised personnel management almost to an art form. He had an uncanny knack of knowing who would be best to fill key jobs. Often, he knew someone's capabilities and limitations far better than they knew them themselves.

But the years he'd spent immersed in the business side of the corporation, relieving me of that burden, had insulated him from the entertainment side. While I was frequently in Hollywood, maintaining relations with producers and talent, Si was minding the store in New York. He knew little about the programming process or the personalities.

Moreover, Si had always been the one who said no in fiscal affairs, and who said go when someone had to be fired. At heart a sweet and gentle man, and inclined toward shyness, to counter these traits he had created for himself a tough, no-nonsense persona. In consequence all but his closest associates perceived him as cold and distant.

But broadcasting is a people business, and Si, despite his many achievements and important contributions, was not the right man to become president of ABC.

OTHER RECOLLECTIONS:
Si Siegel

Leonard wanted me to become vice chairman of the board. I said, "Forget about it. What kind of management will you have with the chairman of the board an old man, and the vice chairman an old man? Let's put some young men in and get the old men out. I'm ready to go, Leonard."

Leonard was great in his area, and I was great in my area. But when you try to find one guy who is great in *every* area, Elton Rule was the only one we had. But Elton didn't see his future forever with ABC. We had to develop some younger people.

❑ ❑ ❑

Si retired in 1971, though he remained on the board of directors until 1984. He lives now in Westchester County, New York. His son, Bernie, a Yale-trained surgeon, is a best-selling author. Bernie Siegel's *Love, Medicine and Miracles*, and *Peace, Love, and Healing* are very widely admired.

Elton Rule, who had headed the broadcasting division since 1970, became ABC's president and chief operating officer in January 1972. Jim Duffy, who had done a marvelous job as head of sales, became president of the television network.

I became chairman of the board of directors, retaining the title of chief executive officer.

OTHER RECOLLECTIONS:
Elton Rule

After Si left, only three people reported to Leonard: me, his secretary, and our accountant. Everybody else reported to me, and I, in turn, would tell Leonard what was going on.

But anybody in the company who wanted to see Leonard could do so. He would see anybody at all. I made that abundantly clear early on. Leonard always wants to know everything that's going on. It was a hell of a lot easier for someone to tell him than for that someone to tell me and me to tell him.

But I told everyone, "Be damn sure that I know what you've told him. You can tell me after the fact, but don't leave me out there to be sideswiped." I would encourage people to do that. Often I'd say, "We'll go up together, and you tell Leonard." Or, "You go ahead. I know what you're talking about. Go tell Leonard."

Leonard could be a real tough guy if he got his neck bowed. But I haven't seen him angry very often, and our differences were minuscule.

In dealing with situations where someone needed a little motivation, one of Leonard's favorite expressions was, "Let's get out that old pineapple." He meant, "Shove the pineapple where it would do the most good."

For his seventy-fifth birthday, I went down to Hammacher Schlemmer and bought a beautiful bronze pineapple. I gave him this as a talisman.

❑ ❑ ❑

When my mother, then eighty-four years old, learned I had become chairman, she telephoned from California. "Does this mean you're not president anymore?" she asked, almost in tears.

One casualty of my heart attack was tennis. The doctors suggested I take up a less strenuous game, so I turned to golf. With such a late start in this sport, I don't expect to become competitive until early in the twenty-first century, when my age may at last exceed my score.

For years, Isabelle had urged me to take up painting. I constantly rejected the idea. I'd never been able to draw, and couldn't imagine I had any latent talent in that area.

My heart attack changed my attitude. During my convalescence, Isabelle brought me a painting kit. Rather reluctantly, I went to our deck, where I could see a small pool surrounded by bushes and flowers. I tried to paint what I saw, but it was a miserable attempt. I was more convinced than ever that I was no latter-day Picasso, Andrew Wyeth, or even a male Grandma Moses.

But by October, faced with boredom because I was unable to play tennis on weekends, I realized I should be doing something to occupy my mind and my time.

I arranged to take lessons from Alton Tobey, a distinguished artist and gifted teacher. Under his tutelage, I became an ardent amateur painter.

I find it fascinating and exciting. I take pleasure from seeing how colors relate to each other, and what effect the sun has on color. For example, I always thought of tree bark as grayish black, or brown. But looking closely, I now see reds and yellows.

Painting taught me to examine objects in a new way, taking note of proportion and small peculiarities. In other words, I began to open my eyes to things I'd always taken for granted.

Over a few years I moved from pictures of fruit to animals, landscapes, flowers, and then people. In time I stepped away from realism to find an impressionistic style.

Equipped with a new way of seeing, I began to take note of my environment. For a few years I became especially fascinated with New York's seamier side. It was amazing to learn there were some 100,000 prostitutes working the streets. They are found along virtually every avenue. Several of my paintings from the mid-1970s depicted this aspect of the city.

In time, my fascination with painting led me to bring along easel, canvas, and paint box wherever I traveled. Since I've never slept well on airplanes, I now often paint on longer flights. I buy two tourist-class seats, set up my easel, and paint the hours and miles away.

Marty Starger, who became head of programming in 1969, is very talented, and this extends far beyond television. By 1972, when ABC had begun producing live events and theatrical films as well as television programs, it occurred to Marty that since his responsibilities had grown beyond programming the network, we ought to restructure his department. Elton and I agreed. The program department became ABC Entertainment, with Marty as president. To reduce executive travel, we based it in Los Angeles. Within two years, both CBS and NBC copied our idea and created entertainment divisions.

On a trip to London, Marty saw some BBC shows, programs they called miniseries. This was a form then unknown in America. BBC miniseries were adaptations of well-known novels or stage plays, and they ran from one to three nights.

Always on the lookout for something different, Marty saw an opportunity to kill two birds with one stone. Using celebrated works of fiction as source material would allow ABC to present a "quality" image. And in a unique program form, they might attract new viewers through bridging schedules.

Marty outlined his notion, which he called Novels for Television, in a memo to Elton. Elton and I thought it was an excellent idea and gave him the green light. It fell to Barry Diller to bring the concept to fruition.

OTHER RECOLLECTIONS:
Barry Diller

There are wonderful stories in novels. But when you have a really big novel, it's going to take a long form to tell the story. What better place to do that than on television?

The first one we did was *QB VII*, based on Leon Uris's book about a slander trial in England. Anthony Hopkins played the plaintiff. Doug Cramer produced it. A very powerful story, it dealt with the Holocaust—and castration.

That's a very tough subject for television, but I wanted to test this form against something tough, not something easy. We got remarkable results. Then I bought *Rich Man, Poor Man*, the Irwin Shaw novel, simply because I thought it was a good, good read.

❑ ❑ ❑

Starger's plan was to test the limits of the form by starting with a one-night program, then two nights, then three, and so forth. He wanted to see how much an audience would accept before they became bored and tuned out.

In 1976, "Rich Man, Poor Man," produced by Universal, went to six two-hour segments broadcast over a seven-week span. Media critics were generally quite upbeat about the show, but they insisted on calling it a miniseries.

Marty also purchased rights to a number of other novels. Before Marty left ABC in June 1975, he put into development several series projects that would become blockbuster hits.

OTHER RECOLLECTIONS:
Marty Starger

Mike Eisner was head of development at that time. We became very close friends. With our wives, we often spent weekends together in New Hampshire.

Mike would come in with ten ideas, seven of which were absurd. Things like, "Let's turn the building upside down and walk on the ceiling."

I'd say, "Michael, you can't turn the building upside down. What about the furniture?"

But three would be crackling good ideas. He was the ideal development person. You want somebody who's totally free, not someone who edits himself.

Michael and I and our staff had a meeting at my place in Malibu. We were brainstorming, looking for new show ideas. We started with "What kind of an audience?" will we reach.

Someone said, "We all remember our high school days with nostalgia. What if we take a couple in their late twenties and early thirties, our target age, when were they in high school?"

So we came up with a show about high school in the 1950s. If it's well done, people who were in high school will remember those songs and the dress, so why wouldn't they watch?

Garry Marshall had always wanted to do something like this. We called it "Happy Days," a title that was thought out very carefully.

❑ ❑ ❑

If there are truly such beings as geniuses, and I don't know there are any, then Michael Eisner is a genius. He's a wonderful fellow, smart, very creative, and rather offbeat. And he works twice as hard as everyone else, which may be the real definition of genius in show business.

Michael worked in virtually every office on the thirty-seventh floor, the programming department. He was involved in almost everything the department did while he was at ABC. He helped get "Bugs Bunny" away from CBS. It was his idea to create new types of animated programs for children, including "The Jackson Five," "The Osmond Brothers," and "Super Friends." And he was involved with such soaps as "All My Children," "One Life to Live," and "General Hospital," and with television movies and novels.

OTHER RECOLLECTIONS:
Michael Eisner

I was twenty-three when I joined ABC in 1966. The network was not doing well, and we had a lot of turnover, a lot of change. But we were a scrappy group of guys and we truly ran the department. I was only twenty-eight when I autonomously ran daytime and children's programming.

Nobody cared what I did as long as we were successful and responsible, as long as we didn't do junk. If we'd failed, if we had done junk, then we would have been thrown out. No one in any company I've ever associated with ever ran it the way we ran ABC Entertainment.

I could not live that way here at Disney. I had more power at ABC than I was to have at Disney, years later. At Disney, people work for me, but I have to share the running. I wasn't sharing anything at ABC. And before me, to a degree, Barry Diller was running it, and Len Goldberg ran it before him, and Edgar Scherick ran it before him. Every once in a while you'd run into a wall and get thrown out.

We were all in a fish tank, but there was nobody above saying, "This fish, that fish." So the strongest fish dominated, the most creative. I think that's how ABC succeeded. It was unique. We were playing grown-up. And those gentlemen who were allowed to flourish were very good.

There were no long strategy meetings at ABC, endlessly discussing things. Most decisions, as they always are in the entertainment business, were a couple of guys sitting around saying, "Why don't we try this?" and then doing it. That's the way a creative company has to run.

Companies that try to research everything and try to analyze everything and try to anticipate public taste, by some sort of political polling process, fail. We do a lot of research at Disney, but not in the creative areas. And Leonard understood about that.

Leonard always thought of himself as an exhibitor. His style created the environment that allowed our company to be successful.

"Happy Days" was created at Newark Airport, while I was snowbound. I was there with my wife and our three-month-old baby, who is now in college. Tom Miller, Paramount's head of development, was with us, and I said, "We have nothing else to do, why don't we create a show?"

I wrote a five-page paper called "New Family in Town," and later we took it to the people who were doing "Love, American Style."

We did "New Family" as an episode of "Love, American Style," with Ron Howard. It did not get on the air. The research department had reams of paper about why the 1950s wouldn't work.

Then Ron Howard did *American Graffiti*.

We did a pilot, the same characters, but now it was not part of "Love, American Style," it was "Happy Days." Then Garry Marshall produced a second pilot for us, and we put Henry Winkler in that pilot as The Fonz.

We showed it to the affiliates. It was the highest-tested pilot I'd ever been involved with. It went on opposite CBS's "Good Times" on Tuesday night at 8, the beginning of ABC's turnaround, along with "The Six Million Dollar Man," "Charlie's Angels," and "Laverne & Shirley."

❑ ❑ ❑

"Happy Days" premiered as a midseason replacement in the winter of 1974 and did well from the start.

* * *

One of Michael Eisner's most enduring legacies to ABC is in children's programming, an area long neglected by all three networks. Michael, with Brandon Stoddard, opened a programming niche that over the last two decades has quietly but effectively presented some of television's best shows.

The man most responsible for filling and expanding that niche was Squire Rushnell, who had come to ABC via our Chicago station, WLS-TV, in 1969. Squire's background was in talk shows. At WLS he created "Kennedy and Co.," a morning show that was a forerunner to "AM America" and "Good Morning America." Slotted against the "Today Show," "Kennedy" caught and surpassed the NBC program's Chicago ratings in two years.

Soon after Squire came to WLS, national interest began to focus on children's programming. In response, he created a local talk show called "Interesting News for Kids."

WLS's general manager, Dick O'Leary, did so well with WLS that we brought him to New York to head our TV O&O's. O'Leary brought Squire along to run programming for these stations.

Squire inherited from his predecessor a bunch of BBC-produced films and packaged them as "Rainbow Sundae." These were films of American classic stories like *The Deer Slayer*. Squire went on talk shows and made himself available to interviewers, thus generating tremendous publicity for them as children's fare. In 1974 Squire became our VP for children's television, succeeding Brandon Stoddard, who became head of daytime.

OTHER RECOLLECTIONS:
Squire Rushnell

When CBS announced it was taking "Captain Kangaroo" off the air, some parents marched on a CBS affiliate and made enough noise to ingratiate themselves with the Washington power base, then much more liberal and responsive to public opinion. Parents began making an awful lot of noise about children's television, and suddenly the industry was paying attention.

ABC was paying more attention than the other networks. In 1972, when Eisner was head of daytime, he held a workshop on children's television. That brought together teachers, parents, and opinion leaders. The other networks were invited but didn't participate. This was a turning point, the first time a network made a major commitment to children's programming.

The workshop set an agenda for our network and made us visibly committed to better children's television.

One thing that came out of the workshop was the "ABC Afterschool Specials." Stoddard produced about fourteen of them before moving to daytime.

But they were all over the lot. There was a variety show, a documentary, and some were animated. They had no discernible identity. I felt creating that identity needed to come first.

Stoddard had commissioned an "Afterschool Special" drama called "Rookie of the Year," the story of a girl who met with discrimination when she wanted to play Little League baseball. The star was Jodie Foster—her very first film.

That show became a rallying point for legislation permitting girls to join Little League teams in several states.

I told my people if Disney is exemplified by *Escape to Witch Mountain*, then the "ABC Afterschool Specials" will be exemplified by "Rookie of the Year." It became the prototype for all "ABC Afterschool Specials."

I wanted these programs to deal with problems of kids at the junior-high age level. Those children were pretty much ignored by television, but in the eleven-to-fourteen age range they go through the most dramatic periods in their lives. Their pimples are larger, their chests are flatter, their feet are bigger, and every problem is tremendously exaggerated, whether it's the boyfriend who slipped away or the parents who are getting a divorce.

We soon realized we were getting more adult than children viewers. Most of these adults were women. We needed that expanded audience to protect the "Afterschool Specials." Stations would continue clearing them only as long as they provided a positive or at least neutral ratings lead-in to their five o'clock news.

❑ ❑ ❑

Today, 70 percent of "Afterschool Special" audiences are eighteen and over. These programs provide solutions to complicated issues facing young Americans, and are often a basis for family discussions. Sometimes they get terrific ratings. "My Mom Is Having a Baby," which dealt with that age-old child's question, "Where do babies come from?" was the highest-rated daytime special in network history, with a 14.1 rating.

To promote our "Afterschool Specials" Squire arranged for network spots throughout the day. Our spokesperson was Eda LeShan, a noted child psychologist with a bombastic style. She looked viewers in the eye and said, "It's time for parents to take charge. It's time to stop the anarchy in the living room. Television is a shared responsibility between parents and broadcasters."

That slogan became the focus of our promotion and of our program development for children's shows. I believe very strongly that broadcasters have a responsibility to provide safe programming for children. But parents must sometimes turn the television set off and chase their children outside into the sunshine. And they must actively encourage them to read books and magazines.

From the time my own daughters were toddlers until they graduated from high school, Isabelle very carefully controlled access to the television set. Our girls were not allowed to watch just anything they chose, and until their homework was completed, the set stayed off.

Squire Rushnell was also very active in creating animated shows for children, and these became very important to our weekend schedules.

OTHER RECOLLECTIONS:
Squire Rushnell

There is something in animation that kids universally love. Creatively, animation can deliver a better program. Live action usually means limited movement because it's shot in a studio. Inside four walls, talk takes the place of action. Animation is magical. You can do anything, and visual entertainment is much greater than verbal entertainment.

I came to understand that most Saturday morning kid audiences are really no different from adult audiences. Adults tend to watch programs with likable characters we want to come back to week after week, whether it's "L.A. Law" or "Roseanne" or "The Cosby Show" or "The Honeymooners." "Bugs Bunny," "Scooby Doo," "Winnie the Pooh," and "The Smurfs" are all characters that kids like to watch over and over. It isn't so much the stories or even the form of the program, it's the characters. With likable characters, it all comes back to suspense, conflict, and empathy. And kids are more likely to watch things that are humorous.

❑ ❑ ❑

Under Squire's inspired supervision, American kids were introduced to "Richie Rich," a character out of a comic book, and "The Little Rascals" in animation. Working with Disney and Hanna/Barbera, he helped develop or create such television cartoon characters as "Great Grape Ape," "Scooby Doo and Scrappy," "Dynomutt," and "Flintstone Kids."

OTHER RECOLLECTIONS:

Squire Rushnell

An animated canine, "Scooby Doo," was a major hit on Saturday mornings. After a time we needed to freshen it with some newer characters, maybe even a younger one. So I got together with Joe Barbera for a weekend at his house in Palm Springs.

We settled in the pool, two guys paddling around on a couple of inner tubes, trying to come up with a new character. Scooby is a big dog, always voraciously hungry but scared of everything, while the kids he was involved with were always looking for ghosts and mysteries.

We were thinking of a new character, something like Henry the Chicken Hawk in the old Warner Bros. cartoons, a little bird with a strut and a tough-guy attitude who would take on the biggest roosters—and always lose.

So I said, "What if we have a little dog that comes to live with Scooby, and the little dog is tough as nails, a little Jimmy Cagney?"

Joe says, "Yeah, he could be the nephew that comes to live with Scooby, idolizing his uncle, never recognizing that Scooby is frightened of anything."

I said, "Let's call him 'Scrappy Doo.' He's got kind of a little Scooby Doo voice, and he says, 'OK, Uncle Scoob, let's go get 'em.' " Barbera would pick up on that and say something in this little-dog-with-a-big-heart voice.

In Palm Springs, hedgerows often form the boundaries between houses. Floating on my inner tube, I could just picture some little old lady tending her roses on the other side of the hedge, listening to cartoon voices coming through it, wondering what on earth was going on in the pool at Mr. Barbera's house.

❑ ❑ ❑

Squire would present his new characters to our affiliates in a manner worthy of Walt Disney himself. He'd choreograph a stage show, little musical revues, with dancers in the sort of costumes found at Disneyland. And frequently Squire would do several cartoon voices himself. It was all very entertaining, and very, very effective in selling our affiliates on clearing these Saturday morning programs.

Squire's contributions weren't limited to the children's area. As time went on he added late night programming to his responsibilities and became involved with morning shows.

In 1975, we launched "AM America," with which we hoped to challenge NBC's "Today," the unquestioned leader among early morning network shows since its inception in 1952.

"AM America" fell on its face. After nine months we took it off. Our second effort was "Good Morning America."

Bob Shanks, who preceded Squire in the early-morning area, had seen a documentary, "Birth and Babies," produced by and starring David Hartman. Very impressed with Hartman, Shanks hired him to host "Good Morning America," a controversial move at the time because he was known as an actor, and morning show hosts were thought of as news people.

But Hartman soon proved himself. He was a friendly, avuncular presence, a man of obvious intelligence, boundless energy, and a searching curiosity that allowed him to ask the most entertaining and provocative questions of the show's often celebrated guests.

Soon after "Good Morning America" debuted, Bob Shanks left ABC and the legendary Woody Fraser stepped in. Woody, probably the best-known talk show producer in the industry, put the show together as a family concept. He surrounded Hartman with colorful personalities like Erma Bombeck, wacky weatherman John Coleman, chef Julia Child, and other interesting characters. In a sense the show was like a newspaper, in that each character had a distinctive style, and each contributed a segment that was akin to a daily newspaper column.

Woody Fraser's modus operandi is to start things and pass them along to others. When "Good Morning America" was up and running but still uncertain in places, still finding its audience—and still getting beaten very badly by "Today"—Woody moved on. In 1977 Squire Rushnell became executive producer.

In that time slot, "Captain Kangaroo" was getting 2.5 rating points and "Today" was getting 4.5. "Good Morning America" had slowly risen to 2.5 and then stopped.

OTHER RECOLLECTIONS:
Squire Rushnell

I've learned that women between eighteen and thirty-four are the most fickle and curious lot. And after them come women thirty-five to forty-nine. So if you're a young show in search of an audience, this is the place to start. Happily, this is also the audience advertisers most want to reach. If these women have no loyalty to product brands, they also have no firmly entrenched viewing habits. They can be seduced into a new shampoo, a new breakfast serial—or a new show.

So we focused on a thirty-two-year-old working woman, and that's all we thought about. If we were doing an interview with Henry Kissinger or Pete Rose or the Ayatollah's spokesperson, we were always thinking about a thirty-two-year-old working woman and doing the interview with her in mind.

For example, if we had Pete Rose on the show, we knew our audience didn't care much about baseball. So David Hartman would ask something like, "How does your wife feel about you being on the road all the time?" Or, "Is it true that you're taking the grocery money and gambling?"

❑ ❑ ❑

With that kind of a touch, in three years "Good Morning America" went from 2.5 rating points to 6.0, surpassing "Today" and everything else in its time slot.

In 1974, on Elton's recommendation, we again restructured the top part of the company. Fred Pierce became president of ABC Television, with supervision of our owned stations, ABC Entertainment, and the television network.

OTHER RECOLLECTIONS:
Fred Pierce

While the program area officially began reporting to me as head of television, prior to that I had worked parallel to them, offering advice, insights, ideas, suggestions, criticisms. They didn't always act upon my ideas.

I loved being president of television. It was the cat's meow, a lifelong dream come true.

My personal philosophy is that first you compete to be equal. Then you compete to win. Then you compete to be the best. Then you compete and be the best and put something back in.

After establishing believability and a level of performance, by 1975, regardless of the risk, we began breaking new ground, committing big dollars to new projects. Besides changing our whole daytime schedule and adding novels for television—at which ABC had no peer—we wanted to put something back into the medium.

I always had the complete backing and support of both Elton and Leonard in terms of dollars, regardless of the risks and mistakes.

One attempt to bring quality drama back to television was "ABC Theater," which started in 1973 as an occasional series. The first show was Katharine Hepburn's television debut, David Susskind's production of "The Glass Menagerie."

Not only did this series have an aura of quality, as it turned out many of the shows demonstrated good audience appeal: shows like "The Elephant Man"; "Divorce Wars"; "My Body, My Child," about a woman's right to have an abortion; "Women's Room," with Lee Remick; "Shadow Box," directed by Paul Newman; and "Who Will Love My Children," which thrust Ann-Margret into perhaps her first major dramatic role.

❑ ❑ ❑

About the same time Fred Pierce moved up, Barry Diller got an offer from Charlie Bluhdorn. Charlie, an industrialist, had assembled Gulf + Western, an enormous conglomerate which included Paramount Pictures.

Charlie was an intriguing fellow. He was on the heavy side, and wore thick, horn-rimmed glasses. He spoke with a thick Viennese accent, had a pronounced overbite, and was very excitable. When he spoke, saliva sprayed everywhere.

Charlie could multiply astronomical-length sums in his head. He could be, by turns, infuriating, funny, charming, or crazy. He was a devoted family man with a beautiful wife and lovely children. But most of all, Charlie liked to make a deal, and he made quite a lot of them.

He made a small fortune in commodities, and turned it into a big fortune by accumulating companies, among them Gulf + Western, which became an incredibly diverse group of assets. Some wag dubbed the company "Engulf & Devour," which wasn't quite fair but did describe Charlie's activities.

Barry negotiated most of ABC's major movie contracts. He too loved to wheel and deal, and became a very tough trader. Since Charlie lived to negotiate, he wouldn't delegate that to anyone at Paramount. In the process of pounding out dozens of deals, Charlie became very fond of Barry.

Charlie called me in 1974 and asked if I'd let Barry out of his contract. He wanted to make him chairman of Paramount. But before he spoke to Barry, he wanted our approval.

I called Elton in and said, "How do you feel about this?"

He said, "How can you possibly stop a person from accepting that kind of an offer? If you don't permit him to take advantage of this, I'm not sure what his reaction will be, as far as continuing to contribute to ABC. And I think that he can do us a lot of good as head of the studio. It might help us get a preferred position on shows they develop."

I quite agreed with Elton. And I didn't see how we could possibly stand in Barry's way.

OTHER RECOLLECTIONS:
Barry Diller

Becoming chairman of the board of Paramount was a rather large leap of faith for Bluhdorn. When I told Leonard, he didn't even blink. He said, "You have to take this opportunity."

Leonard Goldenson's life began at Paramount Pictures. He understood the company, and he was wonderfully and instantly supportive.

And I really didn't want to go. I think probably the only reason Bluhdorn offered me chairman was because for five or six years before that he had offered me other jobs.

I think he respected me because I was so young but that I wanted to prevail. Winning requires an act of will. There are moments and times when the exercise of my will is strong. And this business is all about will.

❑ ❑ ❑

When Barry left, Michael Eisner was in charge of our West Coast entertainment operation, reporting to Starger in New York. In 1974 Michael hired a young lady who was destined to have a profound effect on television.

OTHER RECOLLECTIONS:
Marcy Carsey

I was thirty, female, and pregnant, and you didn't go to NBC in those days if you were thirty, female, and pregnant. Especially pregnant.

ABC was exactly the place I wanted to be because it had a very scrappy image. They made jokes about ABC. One was, "The reason nobody could find Patty Hearst was that she was on ABC at eight o'clock Friday night." That kind of stuff.

But if you were in the TV production industry at the time, you also knew that ABC was full of wonderful people. It had the smartest and brightest and the best, and it only had to be a matter of time before ABC picked itself up, brushed itself off, and came to the top.

Michael Eisner was the guy I reported to.

I had been recommended for hire by somebody below Michael, and for my final interview I had to pass muster with Michael. I said, "It's nice to meet you, but I'm three months pregnant. I'll have the baby in January. Why don't we talk again in February?"

He said, "Why would we wait until after you have the baby?"

I said I thought people would be more comfortable with me after I had the baby.

He said, "I'm having a baby too. Is this a factor? Why are we talking about this?" It was so refreshing for a guy to take that attitude.

I was hired as a program executive in comedy and assigned three or four on-the-air shows as network liaison.

I told Michael I wanted to be in development, that's why I came, that's what I'm probably going to do best. So he arranged for me to move into development. It was sort of a demotion, but I wanted it.

Michael was the best person I've ever worked for. He taught me what it meant to be a network person. He taught me courage, and I have learned, over the years, that this is the single most important quality you can have as a network executive or as a producer or anything.

With great courage and a sense of humor, Michael would stand up in front of his bosses at the scheduling board and give his rationale for the schedule he was pushing. What shows should be renewed or canceled and where should they go on the schedule?

He made great arguments for it. He said, "Either it's going to work or it isn't. If it doesn't, get some other jerk to do this." You had to be impressed. He always was willing to put his job on the line.

Michael taught me that my job wasn't about making friends and influencing people. It didn't have anything to do with anything except getting a couple of hits a year. Hits that were good and make the network proud and make the audience happy. That was it. He didn't care whether ideas came from the elevator operator or if they came from going to the right parties. It was a fabulous graduate school education in how to be an effective anything.

We ran a casual shop. Instead of using the intercom I'd scream down the hall for somebody. We didn't look great, and we had babies at home so half the time we were covered with throw-up. I often brought my baby to work. We'd take meetings with producers and outside people, and the kid would be in the bassinet in my office. I'd take her to runthroughs in the screening room and nurse her through reruns.

We used to be warned that the guys from New York were coming, Leonard and Elton and those guys. Somebody would slide in and yell, "Leonard and Elton are in town!"

I'd go, "Holy shit! Maybe I better go home and change. And maybe I better not be caught with a mirror and makeup thing in front of me and my hair dripping wet."

But we only did it because we wanted to look spiffy for them. It was okay if they came in, and the baby was crying beside you. The whole office was a little chaotic, but as long as you got your work done, everything was fine.

When I first got there, I was assigned these horrible shows. I said, "Michael, listen. I hate these shows. What happens if they all get canceled, do I get fired?"

He says, "No, by then it will be somebody else's fault."

I said, "I'll trade all the shows you've given me for this pilot on your shelf that you guys never picked up."

I was doing my homework so I'd dusted off all this stuff and looked at what they had passed on. One was a pilot called, at the time, "The Life and Times of Captain Barney Miller."

I said, "Give me that, just put that on the schedule, I just want to work on that."

Michael said, "Oh, I've got to get back into that. That was a good pilot."

I'm sure it was in the back of Michael's mind anyway. I'm sure other people were telling him the same thing. But obviously he liked a person who would say, "These shows you've given me are horrible! How about this one on the shelf that none of you liked." That's probably the reason he hired me. I was a blunt son of a gun. So we picked it up, and I was assigned it.

❑ ❑ ❑

"Barney Miller" debuted as a midseason replacement in the winter of 1975. An immediate hit, it remained on the network for almost eight years.

Marty Starger's contract was scheduled to expire in June 1975. Marty, though quite able, wanted to dabble in every aspect of the entertainment business. He wanted to spread his wings, to produce Broadway plays, make theatrical pictures, *and* be in television. But our business is television. That's what needed Marty's full attention.

By mutual agreement, we decided not to renew Marty's contract. That left us with a major personnel problem. Fred Pierce recommended that we go after Fred Silverman, head of CBS programming. Elton thought it was a good idea, and so did I. Pierce, who knew Silverman slightly, made him an offer.

Silverman was not exactly a stranger to ABC. In 1959, working toward a master's degree at Ohio State, he spent several weeks with Julie Barnathan and Fred Pierce, researching his thesis. His 400-page work, an analysis of ABC programming from 1953 to 1959, concluded with a prediction: "For 1960–61 and the seasons which follow, ABC should provide a balanced schedule ... [and] the most vital image in network television."

In June 1975, Silverman became president of ABC Entertainment.

OTHER RECOLLECTIONS:
Fred Silverman

Everybody was very surprised that I didn't move in here and sweep the place out. But I took a look around and said, "Hey, this is a hell of a good group of people."

Michael Eisner was there. Steve Gentry was head of drama. He had worked for me at CBS in program development. Brandon Tartikoff worked for Michael. Marcy Carsey was head of comedy, and Tom Werner worked for her. Pam Dixon, another person I knew from CBS, was in charge of casting and talent. Squire Rushnell was in charge of the children's area. This was a very good group of people, so I made very few personnel changes. I brought in maybe three people, including Barbara Gallagher, who became my assistant in running special programs.

They just needed a little bit of motivation. They were all doing the wrong things, marching in forty-eight different directions. My job was to motivate these people, get the best out of them.

I worked with Michael Eisner for one week, and I said, "This guy is terrific, the best." I mean, in order for us to move forward, I have to have him here.

❑ ❑ ❑

To meet the demands of developing new shows on the West Coast while working with Fred Pierce on network scheduling on the East Coast, Fred Silverman became bi-coastal. He took a summer house in Trancas, near Malibu, and moved his family out for the summer.

Along with his office, Silverman's Trancas house became the focal point for creative brainstorming within our entertainment division. Often meetings took on the aspects of retreats or workshops, and would run for hours or even days.

Ideas generated from within this group often became shows, which Silverman then farmed out for production.

OTHER RECOLLECTIONS:
Fred Silverman

These meetings were opportunities for the guys three and four layers down to open their mouths and be heard. It was a very open shop. It was very informal.

I saw myself as an orchestra leader or a cheerleader. I made sure everybody was doing the right thing. And after a while you start getting a certain amount of success. The ratings start to come in. And success is like a brushfire. We'd say, "Let's take this successful show and move it over here to another night." Suddenly the fire spreads to another night, and before you know it the whole schedule catches fire. This is exactly what happened.

❑ ❑ ❑

Silverman's prime-time efforts were first felt on the network in mid-season, January 1976. With the end of the football season, "Rich Man, Poor Man" went on at 9 P.M. Monday. "Laverne & Shirley," a "Happy Days" spinoff developed under Eisner, and "Family," an Aaron Spelling show, debuted on Tuesdays. "Bionic Woman" went into the 8 P.M. slot on Wednesdays as a lead-in to two already successful shows, "Baretta," a Roy Huggins offering, and "Starsky and Hutch."

Silverman moved "Welcome Back, Kotter," a hit which had debuted in the fall of 1975 on Tuesday, over to Thursday to lead "Barney Miller," "Streets of San Francisco," and "Harry O," all successful and well-established shows.

Friday evenings began with another new show, "Donny and Marie," followed by our long-running two-hour movie.

Suddenly, from our perennially distant third in the ratings, in the second part of the season ABC began winning the weekly averages as often as CBS.

One of the most important new shows for the fall of 1976 had been in the works for years. "Charlie's Angels" was produced by Aaron Spelling and Leonard Goldberg.

OTHER RECOLLECTIONS:
Aaron Spelling

Goldberg and I believed in it, but at first ABC wasn't excited at all. They said, "Absolutely not, forget it." When Silverman took over he said, "Why don't we try it out?"

We made a pilot, and tested it at ASI. They rated it 57. At that time 75 was considered good, 70 was passing. A 57 was ... foo yuck!

But now ABC saw something in it. They decided to put the pilot on the air in June. Maybe, they thought, if we could get a tuned-in audience, we could bring them back in the fall for the series.

Well, it got a 57 share! They thought that was a mistake, so they ran it again, the same summer, one week before we opened in September with the series, and it got a 46 share.

So you can't go by research, and you can't go by critical acclaim. Read the first reviews of a show called "I Love Lucy" sometime. Lucy told me they were just terrible.

❑ ❑ ❑

Silverman slotted "Charlie's Angels" in on Wednesday nights at 10 to replace "Starsky and Hutch." It had begun to fade the previous season, and he moved it to Saturday evening. "Charlie's Angels" got enormous ratings in the fall of 1976. This was coupled with our established shows and with such other newcomers as "The Captain and Tennille" and "The New Original Wonder Woman," a jiggly vehicle for 1973 Miss U.S.A. Lynda Carter. Suddenly ABC was the prime-time ratings leader. To many in the industry, Fred Silverman looked like a genius.

Just about that time I got yet another call from Charlie Bluhdorn. He wanted Mike Eisner to run Paramount's studio, under Barry Diller. And he was offering him far more in salary and other perks than we could possibly match.

Although Michael had more than two years to go on his contract with ABC, once again, I felt that we could not stand in his way.

OTHER RECOLLECTIONS:
Fred Silverman

> I was very sad when Michael Eisner left. It was never the same. I could never replace him. With him gone, my job was three times as difficult. Three people absorbed his job. We had a head of drama, a head of comedy, and a head of talent, and they all reported directly to me, and that was just hell without Michael.

❑ ❑ ❑

Charlie Bluhdorn died of leukemia in 1983. He was succeeded by Martin Davis, who had his own vision of Gulf + Western's future. Charlie was a dealer; Davis was a builder and operator. He spun off some of the less profitable holdings and brought in strict cost-control measures. In 1984, he offered Diller and Eisner new contracts, with substantially less money than they had been getting. They both resigned.

About that time I heard from a Denver oilman named *Marvin* Davis. He had just acquired control of Fox. He's a strange fellow, and I didn't know him at all until he called me. We are related by marriage; his daughter married one of Isabelle's second cousins.

Marvin wanted to know about Barry Diller, whom he was considering for the chairman's seat at Fox. Of course I told him that he was an outstanding executive in every way, and would be a fine choice to run Fox.

Marvin hired him. He also wanted Eisner to come over and work under Diller, but Mike by that time had decided he needed to be more of his own man. When the Bass brothers, four Fort Worth investors who had inherited a vast fortune built by their father and uncle, took control of the Walt

Disney Company, they hired Michael Eisner to run it. After a few years of struggling, Michael turned that company around and made it far more profitable than Walt was ever able to.

The winter of 1977 was a watershed for ABC. While only a few new series were scheduled to debut—most notably "Eight Is Enough" and "Three's Company"—the most controversial of our novels for television, a property purchased several years earlier, was finally ready to broadcast.

OTHER RECOLLECTIONS:
David Wolper

I had my friends Ossie Davis and Ruby Dee over for dinner at my home. They told me about a book that their friend, Alex Haley, was writing. It was about seven generations of his family, from Africa to today.

I thought that sounded like a terrific idea, and I went after it. But when I called over, I learned the book had been optioned by Columbia.

A few weeks later I walked into a New York restaurant for lunch. I saw a friend sharing a table with a secretary from the William Morris agency and another lady. My friend invited me to join them—and it turned out the other lady was Alex Haley's secretary.

When I mentioned that I had been interested in buying *Roots* for television, Haley's secretary said that Columbia's option had expired.

I got on it right away, and we made a deal.

❑ ❑ ❑

Wolper brought his proposal to Brandon Stoddard, who recommended to Barry Diller that we buy it. Barry took the project to Marty Starger.

OTHER RECOLLECTIONS:
Marty Starger

Buying "Roots" meant spending a big chunk of money. The production costs were high. Every hour was a different era, so there were lots of sets and locations and costumes and talent. It was a big commitment.

I went in to Elton and Leonard and said we were going to do the story of a black slave.

In that day in television, some eyes would glaze over: "Here are those program guys again. This is not what we want to hear."

It was much easier for me to say, "That's interesting," and go see them, than for Elton and Leonard, with all their other problems, to decide if this is the thing we want to do. But they were absolutely supportive. They said, "Do it. Sounds like a good idea."

❑ ❑ ❑

Brandon Stoddard worked closely with David Wolper in developing "Roots." At a lunch with Alex Haley and David Wolper at the Beverly Hills Hotel, he bought a pig in a poke.

OTHER RECOLLECTIONS:
Brandon Stoddard

I had lunch with Alex Haley, Stan Margulies, Lou Rudolph, and David Wolper. Alex never told me the story of "Roots." In fact, "Roots" at that point didn't exist. Alex hadn't yet written page one. Instead, he told me the story of how he came to decide to write it.

I said, "We ought to buy this thing anyway. This is a great American story, an incredible story." I was intrigued with the idea of American slavery from a black's point of view. We'd always seen it from the white's point of view.

So we made a deal with Wolper and Haley. While Alex was writing, our screenwriters, Ernie Kinoy, Bill Blinn, and a bunch of other guys, were writing right behind him.

The only time we got nervous was when our guys would get ahead of Alex. When I got Bill Blinn's first draft of the first three hours, I loved it. You could tell there was something real exciting there.

We got the scripts all ready, and it came to yes-or-no on whether to produce it. I wanted to do it. There weren't a lot of people going "Yay team." There never was on *Roots*. I said, "If you don't want to do it, *you* guys call Alex Haley and tell him. I'm not going to call him." That changed the atmosphere a little bit, because nobody had the guts to do that.

We shot "Roots," and I saw the rough cut. It opened in trees. The sun comes up, and women were washing clothes in an African village.

I said, "Wolper, this African village looks like a part of Disneyland, clean as a whistle. Show me a monkey in a tree. Put a water buffalo in someplace. You've got all your documentaries, you've got all that footage."

So they intercut this stuff, and the first thing you see was the sun coming up. Then you see treetops and a monkey swinging from tree to tree. The camera goes on to the river, and there's a water buffalo. Then a hippopotamus yawns, and now you know you're in Africa.

❑ ❑ ❑

"Roots" was both an opportunity and a risk. As entertainment, the show was compelling. On the other hand, no drama starring blacks had ever succeeded on television. I knew that whether I liked it or not, there were bound to be some people who simply wouldn't watch anything with an almost exclusively black cast. The question was, how many people was that?

But that's the essence of show business. You must take chances. You must have the guts to dare to be different.

OTHER RECOLLECTIONS:
Fred Silverman

I had seen Alex Haley on the Tom Snyder show when I was still at CBS. I would have loved to have bought "Roots," but it was already gone.

Originally, "Roots" was conceived as a five- or six-hour series. Every other week Brandon Stoddard would say, "It is so rich. Can we expand it?" Freddy Pierce and I would say, "All right go ahead, go ahead." We ended up with twelve hours.

Here's twelve hours of a story where the whites are the villains and the blacks are the heroes in a country that is 85 percent white. It doesn't sound like a good idea, at first blush.

But I asked myself, "Why did they buy it in the first place?" That was interesting. They took the risk. They had the feeling that it was a wonderful story that had never been done.

It was nerve-wracking. I didn't know if it would work. I thought I'd look at three or four hours one weekend and three or four the next and finish on a third. I got so caught up in it that I looked at all twelve hours over one weekend. It provided an emotional catharsis.

I still wasn't sure if people would watch it. So we scheduled it for one week, and not a week when sweep ratings were conducted.

My thought was, if people *don't* watch, if it's a disaster, then by doing it in just one week, we protect the rest of the season.

We sliced it up like salami, one-hour episodes and two-hour episodes, starting at either 9 or 10. In that way we didn't preempt the earlier shows, "Happy Days" and "Bionic Woman" and "Welcome Back, Kotter." It was strange scheduling, but it worked like gangbusters.

❑ ❑ ❑

"Roots" aired in January 1977. It got the highest ratings of any miniseries in broadcast history. Even today its final episode still ranks as the third-highest-rated program ever broadcast. In program content and production values, "Roots" became the standard by which all other miniseries are judged.

Even more important, by attracting such a huge audience, "Roots" allowed viewers who normally watched other networks the opportunity to sample the rest of our schedule. Not everyone who watched "Roots" stayed with ABC, but virtually all our prime-time shows reached new levels after "Roots" was over. We were number 1 in prime time.

OTHER RECOLLECTIONS:
Fred Pierce

With "Monday Night Football," "ABC Theatre," our prime-time shows, daytime shows, the mid-1970s was like a rocketship at ABC. The levels of performance in prime time, where almost everything was working, were almost unheard of. The only comparison was back in the early days of CBS. We became the largest advertising medium in the world. Our billings went from $700 million to over $3 billion. The profits went from about $100 million to $400 million.

❑ ❑ ❑

After struggling for more than twenty-four years, we had finally beat CBS and NBC. I was elated. It felt great to know that we had won our gamble against overwhelming odds. ABC, the perennial underdog, the goat of decades of industry jokes, now dominated prime time. We broke out the champagne.

Still, I was well aware of how quickly a network's fortunes can change. So I called in all our top people, and said, "Congratulations. You've done very well, and I'm proud of you. But it puts me in mind of the story about the little boy who sits down to milk a cow. He's doing fine until the milk is up to the top of his bucket. Then he gets up and accidentally kicks over the bucket.

"I think that's applicable to us. We're now number 1, but let's continue to be gracious. Let's continue to think we're not number 1—and let's keep that momentum going."

One of the people who heeded this call was Marcy Carsey.

OTHER RECOLLECTIONS:
Marcy Carsey

When they made me a vice president, the first thing I bought was a show called "Soap."

It was controversial. Billy Crystal played the role of Jodie Dallas, an out-of-the-closet homosexual. He was hilarious, but nobody had ever done gay characters in prime time.

Before ABC scheduled it, we got about 40,000 letters of protest from people who had been urged on by religious leaders. Of course they all wrote before they saw anything. But they wrote anyway telling us not to schedule it.

We also got all sorts of pressure from advertisers and even from some affiliates. They did not want us to put it on.

In the spring of 1977 we screened our pilots for upper management. That's when they decide what to put on in the fall.

When I screened "Soap," I was so nervous I had a tummy ache. It was a landmark show, it broke taboos. And that, by definition, is potentially a hit. So I introduced it by saying something snippy, as usual: "You guys are going to love this or hate it. I don't care how you feel about it. Just put it on the schedule."

There was silence after the pilot. Leonard Goldenson was the first to speak, and he said, "We have to put this one on."

In those scheduling meetings Leonard was a very clear, sane, and smart voice. It was very plain to us that he knew more than anybody else in the room about everything and everybody. There was no way he could, but somehow he did.

For example, when we bought "Taxi," we knew it was a demographically suicidal concept. We bought it because we wanted to make a deal with Jim Brooks and a group that had split off from MTM. We said to Jim and the guys, "A half hour of air time is yours, what do you want to do?" They said, " 'Taxi,' a bunch of guys in a garage."

We said, "Isn't there anything else, any other idea you can get this passionate about?"

"No, there isn't."

"You do understand you're closing out a big percentage of the women and children in the audience?"

"Yeah, but it's what we want to do."

So we said okay. They did it beautifully, and we lobbied heavily to put it on the schedule behind "Three's Company."

For our scheduling meeting I put together a rationale that fooled almost everybody in the room as to why "Taxi" should go behind "Three's Company." I sat down, and Leonard, who happened to be sitting in front of me, turned around and said, "I knew you'd want to put it there. You want to force-feed the audience, don't you?"

I said, "Yeah, I do, goddammit. I'm going to push an audience into that show whether they like it or not. That's okay with me."

I had talked about everything else but that, and nobody in that room but Leonard got it.

❑ ❑ ❑

"Soap," which came on in the fall of 1977, was an enormous hit. Its controversial concept generated so much free publicity that huge audiences tuned in to see what the fuss was all about. Not all of them stayed with the show, but many did, and that helped make Billy Crystal a top star.

On "Taxi," Marcy's argument prevailed, and it debuted behind "Three's

Company" in the fall of 1978. The show won several Emmys and attracted almost a cult following.

One of two areas where ABC remained weak was daytime. To remedy this, Fred Silverman brought Jackie Smith over from CBS in March 1977. They were old friends who had first met at WPIX in New York, where Jackie was in charge of on-air promotion and Fred bought films. When Fred became head of CBS daytime, he brought Jackie in to do children's shows.

OTHER RECOLLECTIONS:
Jackie Smith

"All My Children" had been bought as a half hour. Silverman's first move, in 1977, was expanding "All My Children" to an hour, so that "Ryan's Hope," which had debuted in the summer of 1975, would get sampled.

Next, he expanded "One Life to Live" and "General Hospital" to forty-five minutes from thirty minutes.

Fred was looking at how everything was laid out, and he said, "Now I want 'One Life to Live' and 'General Hospital' to become an hour in January of 1978."

Then he must have looked at the shows and said, "My god, they really are lousy. They're only fifteen shares." They'd just expanded to forty-five minutes, and he was going to expand them to an hour. I think at that moment he must have said, "I've got to bring someone in to get this under control so it's not a disaster."

And that someone was me. I'd been with children and prime-time specials and two-hour movies. But I had two children of my own to care for, and while I took care of my area I wasn't ambitious to learn everything that might be helpful to me. I just didn't have that kind of drive at the time. So I didn't know anything about serials. It was really very brave of him to have brought me in and think that I could have been effective.

❑ ❑ ❑

Silverman's instincts were correct. Although Jackie had always been content to be a very good follower, she soon became a dynamic leader. Jackie inherited Agnes Nixon, the writer who had created "All My Children" and "One Life to Live." She also brought in Gloria Monty, who had become almost an institution in daytime serial programming.

OTHER RECOLLECTIONS:
Jackie Smith

Gloria's career was kind of wandering, and she didn't quite know what to do with her life that was special. She was looking for something to do. Although she had a reputation for being difficult, I liked her a lot.

She took five "General Hospital" shows and five scripts and came in to see me. She said, "I know you have writing problems, so I won't address myself to that. I'll just show you what you could have done with these scripts."

It took her about three hours. She showed me how these scripts could have been redirected. She was brilliant and astonishing. I knew at once we had to bring her in right away.

I was then living in Los Angeles and waiting for my daughter to finish school, so I couldn't get to New York until June—but these shows were going to expand to an hour in January. When I started figuring all this out, I started asking myself what I had got into.

I hadn't seen Fred for months when I finally moved to New York. I walked into his office and he said nothing except "Who are you going to get to produce 'General Hospital'?"

I said, "Gloria Monty." Gloria had worked for Fred as a serial producer at CBS. He had a few comments which I'm not going to repeat. But he let me bring her in.

There were two keys to "General Hospital." One was Gloria Monty. The other was A. J. Russell, a writer from television's Golden Age. I called him in Orleans, Massachusetts, and somehow interested him in the show. He wrote the "bible" for what I call the "New General Hospital" and the Quartermain family. A.J. introduced many of the elements that are still going strong.

❑ ❑ ❑

Producing daytime dramas is like running an enormous factory. Each program requires five shows a week, and the schedule is extremely demanding. Jackie became a catalyst, a sounding board who ensured her shows got good stories and casting. Equally important, she kept peace among the monumental egos that inhabit show business.

Jackie was equally capable at promotion. As ABC began to dominate prime time, she and Fred Silverman used this huge audience to promote our daytime schedule.

OTHER RECOLLECTIONS:
Jackie Smith

I told Fred I didn't want to promote anything until we're very, very good—and when we're good, then we'll promote ourselves.

After our shows improved, I came into his office unannounced. It was full of people—some kind of meeting. He looked up, very irritated, and said, "What's your theme going to be?"

I trilled, "Love in the Afternoon."

He said, "Good."

And that was the way we communicated sometimes to one another. This did not come to me suddenly. I had been working on it. But no one liked it until I *sang* it. "Love in the Afternoon" became enormous. It was everywhere, on T-shirts, bus billboards, and bumper stickers. Macy's had a boutique with a "Love in the Afternoon" sign. It became part of the public consciousness. One day I opened *The New York Times Magazine*, and it had a football picture with the headline, "Violence in the Afternoon." It was a takeoff. They could not have done that if Love in the Afternoon hadn't been so big.

❑ ❑ ❑

Jackie also developed a stable of actors and actresses. From this came such present prime-time stars as Judith Light of "Who's the Boss" (formerly of "One Life to Live") and "MacGyver" star Richard Dean Anderson.

As Jackie blossomed, ABC's serials began to dominate the hugely profitable daytime schedule. By 1979 we were clearly the leader.

Fred Silverman's apparent effect on ABC did not go unnoticed in the industry. But few outside the company properly appreciated his contributions. He was a superb leader, he had wonderful instincts for scheduling and promotion, and proved he could get the most out of what we had. However, much of what appeared to be Silverman's success was derived from the creative team below him, and from management and leadership by Fred Pierce and Elton Rule above him. But by late 1977 Silverman apparently began to believe he could do anything.

NBC, which was having serious problems both with its schedule and in other areas, saw Silverman as a savior. Though he had reassured Fred Pierce on many occasions that he would never accept an offer from another network without allowing us to match it, Silverman began secretly negotiating with NBC. They offered him the sun, the moon, and all the stars, so to speak, if he would become president of NBC.

OTHER RECOLLECTIONS:
Fred Silverman

That period at ABC, and a window of one to two years at CBS, were the most exhilarating points in my life. CBS in 1973 or 1974 was very much like ABC in 1977 or 1978. Two of the most successful prime-time schedules ever.

So I had great confidence. I felt I could walk on water. Kind of a Christ complex. That's one of the reasons I took the NBC job.

That attitude, the confidence, was great at NBC. On the other hand, it was just like going into the Pentagon. ABC was very simple. It was just concentrate on programming. NBC was falling apart at the seams. There weren't good times at NBC like there were at ABC and CBS.

Leaving ABC had nothing to do with money. It had to do with power. And not merely power, it was creating at the number-1 network. And I had lost Eisner. It was wearing me down. I felt like I was repeating myself. I wanted to do some other things. I tälked to Fred Pierce on a couple of occasions about getting into the news area in some way.

❑ ❑ ❑

Silverman's departure was a personal blow to Pierce, who had supported his eccentricities and stroked his ego.

OTHER RECOLLECTIONS:
Fred Pierce

Any man in Silverman's position requires a multiplicity of ideas and approaches. He needs a combination of both business and creative instincts. You must meld good business with good audience appeal, and the cost of those things must stay within a certain range.

But no individual can do that job by himself. When you deal with somebody very creative and who has a very large ego that helps him to keep going, you feed that ego. You give him visibility, you let him take the front position.

Fred Silverman's contract ran though June of 1978. We had been negotiating about his continuing. In conversations before Christmas of 1977, he indicated that we were going to work something out.

It seemed to me, unless I was on another planet, that we were working out a continuation of his contract. We came back from the holidays, and out of left field he says, "I decided to take this job to run NBC."

Obviously, Fred was free to do what he wanted at the end of his contract, but I had gone out of my way to make him comfortable and important at ABC. I gave him all the credit and visibility, almost to a fault. He added insult to injury because, not only was he leaving, he was going to a direct competitor. It left a sour taste in my mouth.

I said, "I feel you've gone back on our conversations. I don't take kindly to that. I am a firm believer in ethics and morality in business deals. So if business is business, we're going to protect our interests. We are not going to let you go over there till the end of your contract." We were playing hardball.

❑ ❑ ❑

After Silverman's departure in early 1978, Pierce put Tony Thomopoulos in as head of ABC Entertainment.

While the unexpired portion of his contract ran out, Silverman took an extended vacation before joining NBC in June 1978. Silverman did not save NBC. He was and is a creative force, but that company needed something more to direct its rejuvenation. In mid-1981 they brought in Grant Tinker, former head of MTM, to run NBC, and let Fred go.

Fred, who still enjoyed a tremendous reputation as a showman, turned to independent production. He had a number of colossal flops. I'm very pleased to say, however, that after drinking from the bitter cup of failure, he learned humility. As this is written, Fred Silverman is one of the world's most successful and sought-after producers of prime-time shows. Even better, Fred Silverman and Fred Pierce renewed their friendship and have begun to collaborate on various projects.

ABC's rise to prime-time dominance was not entirely the result of our success in programming. Without the success of our owned and operated stations, and without acquiring affiliates equal in quality and number to the other networks, we would never have had any chance of equal or greater ratings.

So, while Starger, Silverman, Diller, Eisner, Stoddard, Carsey, Rushnell, Smith, and all the other creative people were working very hard to create and schedule product, another talented team was working hard to develop our stations and to bring in new and better affiliates.

19

Stations

❑

Between 1961 and 1971 the ABC Television Network lost about $120 million. In the beginning, most of that deficit came out of our theater operations. As that part of our business dwindled, the money to continue network operations came from profits earned at the company-owned stations.

At the time of our 1953 merger, those stations—New York, Los Angeles, Chicago, San Francisco, and Detroit—were not doing especially well. It took several years for each to become competitive in its respective market.

The first to start making serious money was WXYZ-TV, Detroit, under Jimmy Riddell. After moving to the West Coast, he played a hand in helping KABC-TV become more competitive.

Elton Rule had a major role in KABC-TV's success. As sales manager and later general manager, he built a terrific team. It's true we got to know each other better by playing tennis, but I kept my eye on Elton because he turned KABC into a money machine. He also developed some very important people.

One of these was a genial, talkative Irishman named Dick O'Leary. Dick grew up in Southern California and in the early 1950s worked in sales at two independent television stations there. Among his colleagues and bosses were some exceptional people, including three future presidents of CBS's television network: Jim Aubrey, John Reynolds, and Bob Wood.

Early in 1954, Dick joined KABC-TV. His boss, Elton Rule, had just become sales manager.

OTHER RECOLLECTIONS:
Dick O'Leary

Just after the merger with United Paramount Theatres, they put in a new general manager, Selig Seligman, who formerly headed a group of Paramount's theaters. He was a Renaissance man, a writer and lawyer and a Juilliard School of Music violinist, altogether an engaging, dynamic, unique fellow. Over the years he conceived and executed shows like "Combat" and "General Hospital," which is still on today.

In the late 1950s Seligman died—he was still in the prime of his life, and it was quite unexpected. Elton became general manager and moved me up to sales manager.

By the early 1960s I had absorbed my job. Things were working to my satisfaction, and I wanted to be a general manager. It didn't appear that Elton was going to go anywhere, so in 1966, when the opportunity arose, I went to WLS-TV, Chicago, as VP and general manager.

Chicago was a four-station market: CBS, NBC, WGN, an independent, and WLS, the fourth station in the market. WLS was a dog. I cannot describe how bad it was. That presented a marvelous opportunity for me. It had nowhere to go but up.

I had learned there is nothing like a customer. Our customer was not the advertising agency that bought the time. Our customer was the viewer—but the Chicago viewer was not being well served.

Up to then WLS had a minimal commitment to news and information programming. We had no ratings, no lead-ins, and no reputation, and going into news and information programming is very expensive. But my thought was that if we could find news talent who could uniquely communicate through the tube, we could start attracting an audience.

Fahey Flynn was one of Chicago's old-time favorites, a beloved figure for years and years, the number 1 newscaster. He was at WBBM, the CBS station.

Flynn's trademark was a bow tie. A new, typically arrogant CBS executive took charge of the station and told Fahey, "Bow ties are old-fashioned. Get a regular tie."

Some enterprising newspaper reporter picked up on it. The paper ran a picture of Fahey before and after. The caption was

"What happened to the bow tie?" Chicago is often wonderfully self-concerned, and so the bow tie became the talk of the town.

I called Fahey at home and said, "Mr. Flynn, it seems to me that you have been treated shabbily."

He said, "Well, CBS has their rights." He was a very nice fellow. But I sensed he was hurt, and hurt can turn to anger, and anger breaks up relationships. So I asked if I could see him at his home in Winnetka, and we took to each other instantly.

I told him what I was trying to do and what our vision was. I said we had an opportunity to do a newscast that would be "people-oriented." And I hired him away from CBS.

Next I got Joel Daly, from NBC's Cleveland affiliate, a Yale man and a remarkable fellow who is now a lawyer, a pilot, a country-and-western singer, and a great writer of commentaries and such.

So now we had an old man and a young man. There was still something missing. We added a cartoonish weatherman, John Coleman, and a young, very virile sports fellow who had done a lot of local radio.

It used to be that TV newscasts inserted commercials in the middle of a segment. For example, the weatherman would say, "That's the weather for today. We'll be right back with tomorrow's forecast after these messages."

I thought it might work better by putting commercials *between* the segments. Then the newspeople could communicate with each other as each took a turn on camera. We also brought in Eyewitness News reporters as part of the team.

For example, there's a train wreck, Flynn gives the main headline, "Ten people killed." Instead of pausing for a commercial before giving details, he takes it to conclusion. Then he says, "Something is wrong here, Joel. There are too many damned train wrecks and equipment failures." And Joel Daly reacts to this. He might follow with a sidebar story but the main thing was reacting, because this is spontaneous, not scripted. It's Flynn daringly set free to say whatever comes to his mind to Joel or to the weatherman, the sports man, or the reporter. By stepping outside the traditional role of reading the news, their personalities came across.

This technique was unique, lively, vital, personal, authentic, compelling. We are not dealing in mere news, we are dealing in information and in people. The viewer dares not miss this.

People watching this say, "That's how I feel, that Flynn is right on," or Joel is this or that or whatever. We tapped into the viewer's need to be talked *with* rather than *at*.

We knew we had it the first night. The next day we hit the streets with full-page advertising: "Will success spoil Fahey Flynn and Joel Daly?" We followed that with our own promos, and we got Chicago's best commercial producer to cast and direct them.

Fifteen minutes led to thirty, and half-hours led to one hour and eventually to three hours. The audience came to us. It just exploded.

It took two years to build, but everything worked. It was magic. We went from dead last to number 1. We got the ratings, and with them came money.

❑ ❑ ❑

Dick built a tremendously effective news operation, and proved that local news could both attract viewers to a station and turn a profit. As word of this spread throughout the industry, other stations picked up on it. Today, around the country, almost without exception, the stations with the strongest news departments lead their individual markets.

In February, 1970, Si called Dick O'Leary, and offered him a new job: head of our owned television stations. As it turned out he was an inspired choice. In the process of building WLS-TV into the hottest station in Chicago, he had created a formula, a programming approach that could be translated to other markets. Dick realized that each station had to build in its own way, with its own people. He couldn't merely copy WLS—but he could use the same principles that worked in Chicago.

He had a formidable task. While we never hesitated to go outside our organization for top people, in general we tried to build ABC by hiring young people and promoting from within. This meant that as O'Leary turned his attentions from one station to the next, he had to work with eager, talented, but often inexperienced station people. It meant traveling a lot, holding many hands, and reserving to his own office many of the key decisions usually delegated to general managers.

Dick was smart enough to know he had no monopoly on ideas. He encouraged people to speak up. In this way he developed a very strong nucleus of station managers at all our O&O's.

One of these bright young men was Dennis Swanson, who joined KABC-TV in Los Angeles in January 1976, as executive producer of our local newscast. He quickly moved up to assistant news director, news director, and then station manager.

OTHER RECOLLECTIONS:
Dennis Swanson

In Southern California, there's no winter, so people are outdoors all year. And there's no mass transportation. In New York or Chicago people buy a newspaper with yesterday's stories and read it on the train on the way home. In Los Angeles people listen to car radios. When they get home, they already know the headlines. We had to give them more than a replay or repetition of radio.

We did a life-style survey in 1977 to learn what kind of information people wanted. We had a promotional campaign: "There's more to life than news, weather, and sports." We had medical information, a law segment, consumer information, style, clothing. And magazine elements, back-of-the-book things like restaurant reviews, travel, and an entertainment segment.

In 1980 we went to a three-hour newscast, then the longest newscast within the owned stations. The longer format allowed KABC greater control of our schedule. We weren't at the mercy of syndicated programming and could better control costs.

We demonstrated that you could put a variety of information segments into a longer form and be successful. Look at newscasts around the country now: It's not unusual to see these kinds of segments. You could say we had some influence.

Southern California is a vast market that includes mountains and valleys. It's very difficult to report news across such a wide area. The population we serve is huge—bigger than many states.

I decided we needed to establish news bureaus. In making a presentation to get the resources, I put up a transparent map overlay of California. If Los Angeles was New York City, then Sacramento would be as far away as Montreal. Those are the kinds of distances we had to overcome in California.

So we had to bring technology in to work for us. We put in a microwave relay system in 1977 and 1978. Then we were ahead of the game. We could deliver live signals from locations our competitors couldn't. In 1980, when torrential rainstorms caused flooding that resulted in hundreds of millions of dollars in damage and sixty fatalities, and when the brush fires came, only KABC could get live signals out of wherever news was occurring. The public recognized that and watched our newscasts.

❑ ❑ ❑

By 1983 KABC-TV was doing exceptionally well. Our Chicago station, WLS-TV, had gone through some management changes, and began to stumble. Dennis was tapped to straighten it out.

OTHER RECOLLECTIONS:
Dennis Swanson

My first week at WLS, Fahey Flynn died. I said to myself, "I didn't read about this in any journalism book." The same week a talent agent called to say, "By the way, your morning show host is leaving."

I looked at the ratings. We were not doing so well, so his leaving didn't break my heart. But I had to find somebody to do that show.

One of our assistant producers was a young lady we had just hired from a Baltimore station, Debby DeMayo. She gave me a tape of the talent on her old station's morning show, which was co-hosted by a man and a young black woman.

I didn't much care about the man, but that young woman was sensational. I brought in all my program people, and they agreed. So I called her.

Oprah Winfrey flew to Chicago on Labor Day weekend, 1983, and we did a mock A.M. show on Saturday afternoon, when hardly anybody was around. Sitting in my office, watching this audition, I said, "Holy smokes. This is something."

I had looked at tapes for years, but never had I seen anything like Oprah. She is a unique personality. So up. So effervescent. So television. So spontaneous and unrehearsed. She was not like anyone else on the tube.

Oprah was exactly what we were looking for. We were up against Phil Donahue, who did his program from Chicago at 9 A.M. and had been beating the brains out of everybody in town. And he's great. We were not going to find another Phil Donahue. Rather than try to out-Donahue Donahue, we had to give the viewer a distinct alternative, and that was Oprah.

I thought, Give her a free-form environment where she can be herself, and she will be the best.

Oprah came to my office. I chased everybody else out. We sat there and looked each other in the eye.

She said, "Dennis, you know I'm black."

I said, "Oprah, it wouldn't make any difference to me if you were green. I think the only problem we're going to have is, can you handle the success?"

"You really think it will go that well?"

"I would bet on it."

Oprah's contract was up at the end of the year. We waited. We put her on on the morning of January 2, 1984. What a sensation that turned out to be! Oprah hit Chicago like a bucket of cold water.

It was amazing. There was no gradual build. We went from last in the time period to number 1 in about four weeks. She just took over the town.

A few weeks later Quincy Jones, the musician, is in town to do something, and he's watching television in his hotel room. He sees Oprah Winfrey and calls the station. He's involved with Spielberg in producing *The Color Purple*. That's how Oprah wound up in the film. That gave her national exposure. It was a great break for her.

❑ ❑ ❑

In 1986 Oprah went into syndication with her show. Debby DeMayo, who had become her producer, stayed with it, and the program has been immensely successful.

Dennis Swanson did more for WLS-TV than discover Oprah Winfrey. Within a few months he had hired news anchor Floyd Kalber for the six o'clock news and put "Wheel of Fortune" on at 6:30. It was like hitting three grand slam home runs, and it helped turn the station around. In recognition of his talents, Dennis became head of our O&O television station division in 1985. Today he is president of ABC Sports.

By the early 1980s each of our TV stations was consistently best in its market. And they all made money. When Dick O'Leary took over the O&Os they were netting about $30 million a year, or just about enough to make up for our network deficits. By 1984 they were earning over $166 million a year, more profit than the CBS- and NBC-owned stations combined.

As early as 1951, when I first sat down with Ed Noble to negotiate the purchase of ABC, I knew that ultimately our success would depend on acquiring enough affiliated stations to allow the network to reach as many television households as CBS and NBC. I also knew it was going to take a long time, because the other networks had a big head start.

When I fired Bob Kintner in 1956, he set out to make things difficult for ABC wherever he could. Kintner was friendly with Otto Brandt, manager of KING-TV, Seattle, the top station there and one of our few competitive affiliates. In October 1958, Kintner got Brandt to persuade KING's owner, an elderly widow, to drop ABC and affiliate with NBC.

KOMO, Seattle, was one of NBC's first radio affiliates, going back to the mid-1920s. When NBC suddenly told KOMO that they were severing their relationship to affiliate with KING, O. D. Fisher, the owner, almost went into shock.

O. D. Fisher was one of America's great pioneer capitalists. After San Francisco was destroyed by earthquake and fire in 1906, O.D., sure the city would be rebuilt and people would need a lot of lumber, went to Washington state and bought logging rights to millions of acres of virgin forest. He built the largest sawmill in the world, and the first to be electrified, at Snoqualmie Falls, in the Cascade Mountains near Seattle. He made an enormous fortune.

By 1956, O.D. owned the Fisher Flour Mills, was Seattle First National Bank's biggest stockholder, owned a big chunk of and was chairman of the board of Weyerhaeuser Lumber, and was principal founder and chairman of General Insurance Company of America (now known as Safeco).

In 1958 O. D. Fisher came to see me in New York. O.D. was absolutely flabbergasted that NBC had dropped him like the proverbial hot potato. He couldn't understand it.

I told him, "We need a station in Seattle, and we have no other choice but to go with you. But if we are going with you, we want you to be the leading station in your area. I want you to do an outstanding promotional job. At the time of the transfer, we'll bring whatever stars or famous people we have to Seattle. I'll come there myself."

We did just that. I brought several Hollywood stars that I knew from my years with Paramount. O. D.'s people did a tremendous job of promoting the changeover. They made it appear that they'd dropped NBC to get this wonderful, new, and growing network called ABC. I addressed a luncheon of about 400 business people in one of Seattle's finest hotels. Everybody in the community knew O.D. Fisher, and I came away with the impression that things would go well for us with KOMO.

KOMO turned out to be one of our best affiliates, consistently number 1 in its market. For almost thirty years KOMO got close to 40 percent of audience share in its market, a record envied by all ABC affiliates. I can't think of any station that did that well for so long. It may have been a shotgun marriage, but it turned into a love match just the same.

Over the years I became very friendly with O.D. and his nephew, Bill Warren, who managed the station. Bill served five terms on our affiliate board of governors, and was its chairman for a time.

In 1962, O.D. heard Isabelle and I were planning a working vacation in Japan. O.D. knew that I customarily throw a cocktail party on these trips, so he asked me to invite his friend, Hidesaburo Shoda, and his wife, Fumiko.

Mr. Shoda had been a moderately successful miller before the war, and his company, Nisshin Flour Milling, had done business with Fisher Flour. The war ruined Nisshin. In 1945, Mr. Shoda was almost destitute. O.D. helped put him back on his feet; by the time we met, Shoda was a billionaire, one of Japan's wealthiest merchants.

In 1959, the Shodas' daughter, Michiko, married Crown Prince Akihito. She was the first commoner to marry a member of the Imperial family, and there was quite a fuss about it.

Fumiko Shoda was quite charming. She said she'd never been to a cocktail party before, since Japanese wives are never invited out with their husbands. They are expected to stay at home with the children.

We asked Mrs. Shoda about her daughter, and her mood changed quite abruptly. She said, "Sometimes I wish she'd died instead of marrying the Crown Prince."

Surprised, we asked her why.

"We are commoners, and so cannot telephone our daughter or visit her palace. Nor can she visit us. The only time we can see her is on certain ceremonial occasions, when we are shown in through a side door. Then, if we are lucky, we can see her at a distance. If we are very lucky, we might be able to make eye contact for a moment. But nothing more. If she was dead, I could at least visit her grave."

Mrs. Shoda died a few years ago. Her daughter, Michiko, became Empress of Japan in 1989.

In the late 1950s, when Ollie Treyz was network president, Julie Barnathan was in charge of station relations. Julie started working on A. J.

Fletcher, who owned the NBC affiliate in Raleigh–Durham, North Carolina. When it looked like he might be willing to switch to ABC, Julie brought me in, and we went down to spend some time with Fletcher.

Fletcher was extremely wealthy, a hell of a nice guy, and he had his fingers into everything in that part of the Carolinas, including a cemetery. The only other television station in the market, a CBS affiliate, was owned by his son.

After a number of meetings, we persuaded him to switch to ABC. We did this by selling him on our potential value and by increasing the rates we paid his station to clear network programs. In short, we bought our way into the market. And he turned out to be an excellent affiliate, one of our best.

Fletcher had very pronounced political views. He was somewhere over on the extreme right. But his station was number 1 in its market, so he was evidently in tune with his viewers. His station manager, a fine broadcaster in his own right, was a young man named Jesse Helms.

Helms shared Fletcher's political leanings, and he wrote and delivered most of the station's editorials. I used to see those editorials from time to time, and so I became very familiar with his views.

I don't subscribe to Helms's vision of America, but apparently many in North Carolina do, because they elected him a U.S. Senator in the 1960s as a Democrat. He's now a Republican, but still in the Senate. A few years ago he formed a committee that attempted to buy CBS, because, he said, he wanted to be Dan Rather's boss. And in recent years Senator Helms has introduced controversial legislation aimed at denying public funds to forms of self-expression he finds offensive.

The Taft family of Ohio has produced several generations of statesmen and politicians, one President, and some notable broadcasters. The current generation is epitomized by Dudley Taft, whose late father owned several radio and television stations. One was WKRC, Cincinnati.

WKRC dropped CBS to affiliate with ABC in 1961. Taft's Birmingham, Alabama, and Lexington, Kentucky, stations also joined our network. With their Columbus, Ohio, station, which had come over a few years earlier, that made four Taft stations in our lineup. Taft Broadcasting became very important to ABC, and I developed a close friendship with Holbert Taft.

Holbert was one of the few multiple-station owners of that era who believed that ABC would become competitive with the more established networks. He worked tirelessly to be part of our success, and his stations were strong competitors in virtually every market he went into. Dudley, Holbert's son, graduated from law school and briefly practiced law in Washington, D.C. Dudley returned to Cincinnati in 1967 and became Taft Broadcasting's corporate counsel.

A month later, Holbert died in a freak accident. He had built a bomb shelter beneath the family home, and somehow natural gas got inside. Holbert went in one afternoon and flipped on the lights. A tiny spark from the switch ignited the gas, and it caused an explosion.

Dudley gradually made his way to the top of Taft Broadcasting. Over the years he became very close to Elton Rule.

OTHER RECOLLECTIONS:
Dudley Taft

Elton certainly did a very good job of pulling it all together. He understood the station business and amongst the affiliates, he was the guy everybody could relate to. Elton started a period of real growth for ABC's network.

There's no substitute for ratings, and after Elton took hold, the network began to arrive. He put deals together with several Hollywood suppliers that stood him in very good stead. The network began to put on competitive programming.

We were very locally oriented operators until the middle 1970s, when Jim Duffy and one or two others came in bitching and screaming at us to carry the network news. So we did, shortly thereafter.

When Elton moved up, I think many people underestimated what he had done for the network. They didn't focus on it. We did. There have been long strings of network presidents—our stations have been affiliated at one time or another with all three networks—but of all those I met over a twenty-year period, Elton was the best-liked. Affiliates wanted to support him. They thought he would succeed.

❑ ❑ ❑

In 1978 CBS aired a very popular show called "WKRP in Cincinnati," which helped make stars of Loni Anderson and Howard Hesseman. One of the show's original producers was John Guntzelman, who, with his brother,

Dan, had worked at Taft's Cincinnati radio station, WKRC. Dudley assures me he had nobody that looked like Loni Anderson at the station. He admits, however, to having more than a few nutty characters around WKRC who might well have inspired the show.

As ABC's programming finally hit its stride in the mid-1970s, Elton put together a very ambitious program. Now that we finally had something concrete to sell—top-rated shows in prime time—we wanted to increase distribution. That meant bringing in new affiliates where we had none, and exchanging our weaker, poorly performing stations for better ones serving the same market. The key to that was the respect that Elton had earned from his years as a station operator.

OTHER RECOLLECTIONS:
Elton Rule

All of a sudden it wasn't "those network guys" they had to deal with at ABC. I had been, man and boy, a station operator, worked in various station sales and management jobs and so forth. And I knew all these guys throughout the country. For years I'd met them at National Association of Broadcasters (NAB) meetings and affiliate meetings. We all exchanged ideas and questions, discussed concerns common to station managers. These were my friends, guys I knew from other parts of the country.

When you boil through everything else, as a station manager, I was interested in the bottom line. You can be the greatest programmer salesperson in the world, but if you don't deliver the owners enough money to keep them in the style to which they are accustomed, it isn't going to work.

To do that, the network has to deliver programming that a station's market has an appetite for, so it can sell local spots adjacent to network programming. The price you can get for those spots is directly related to the size of the audience. It goes back to the ratings.

❑ ❑ ❑

Jim Duffy was Elton's chosen instrument to bring in new and better affiliates. Jim began his career as a public relations writer, switched to radio announcer, then moved up through sales. In 1963, when he was executive VP of our radio network, Tom Moore made him VP of television network sales. This surprised a lot of people, but it was a wonderfully deft choice.

Duffy had won his spurs in an era when the value of radio to advertisers was waning. He knocked on every door and reestablished the value of the medium.

For seven years as head of network television sales, he used the same strategy. To overcome advertiser skepticism about television—and especially about ABC's viability in this young medium—he began calling on the advertisers themselves, and always at the highest level. Recognizing this was going to be a tough nut to crack, Duffy put aside short-term concerns. His approach was to sell the value of ABC as an institution and as an emerging competitive force.

By doing this in a highly systematic way, and by dealing with top people like Lee Iacocca, then president of Ford, and John DeLorean, head of Chevrolet, and spending his time educating these future clients about ABC's potential, he made a very significant impact on sales.

In 1970, Jim became president of the television network, a post he was to hold for an unprecedented fifteen years. In 1976 Elton asked him to boost our distribution as he had boosted sales. Duffy put together a flying squad headed by Dick Beesemyer, our affiliate relations manager, with Bob Fountain as his principal deputy.

OTHER RECOLLECTIONS:
Jim Duffy

We established an office of affiliate acquisitions. We used the same kind of marketing technique as with sales. That is, go to those major markets where we were really weak, or where we didn't have affiliates at all, and meet with owners and general managers of the other networks' stations and let them know what our long-range intentions were.

Beesemyer had contacts all over. Little by little we started to get new stations.

❑ ❑ ❑

All this had to be done quietly. Very quietly. This is the James Bond side of the television business, as Bob Fountain once said. He and Dick

Beesemyer buttonholed station owners at industry gatherings to set up clandestine meetings. They met in hotel rooms, in private planes, around campfires surrounded by thousands of square miles of howling wilderness, at sea on luxury yachts, in tropical resorts—anyplace where the chances of being spotted by someone who knew their identity was minimal.

All this secrecy was necessary, because we didn't want to alarm our existing affiliates, and we didn't want to tip off the other networks. The last thing we wanted was a bidding war with a network on either side and the station in the middle playing "Let's you and him fight" while they jacked up the price to both sides.

It was a long-range program, to be sure, but we began to see results early in 1977. One of the most important stations Duffy brought in was KSTP, Channel 5, Minneapolis. The station was owned by Stanley E. Hubbard, one of the founding fathers of American broadcasting.

Stanley Hubbard went into business at the age of nine, in 1906, fixing doorbells. He carried a business card that identified him as "Stanley Hubbard, Electrical Engineer."

At age fifteen he built Minnesota's first amateur radio transmitter. Still in high school, he became a new car salesman, peddling the now long-vanished Overland for 5 percent commissions to net over $200 a month. At sixteen he learned to fly, and served in World War I as a Signal Corps pilot. After the war he started America's first commercial airline, the Ohio Valley Aero-Transport Company. In 1919, it flew twice daily between Louisville, Kentucky, and Cincinnati, Ohio.

After a barnstorming tour around the South, Hubbard was invited to the White House. Equipped with one Navy biplane, he became the head (and sole pilot) of the Internal Revenue Service's air force, which patrolled the skies looking for bootleggers, drug smugglers, and illegal aliens.

In 1923 Hubbard returned home to Minneapolis and put radio station WAMD on the air, all 50 watts of it. In 1924 he started the first daily news broadcast in the nation. By 1928 he was running 1000 watts, had merged with another station, and was operating as KSTP. He couldn't get wire service reports because the newspaper moguls feared new competition, so in 1928 he organized Radio News Service with bureaus around the country.

Stanley Hubbard was an innovator, a risk taker, a gambler. My kind of guy. He bought the rights to a golf tournament in 1930, long before anybody had thought of doing remote broadcasts, and put a radio transmitter in a baby carriage that was wheeled from hole to hole.

He couldn't get accurate weather reports, so he established his own weather station, which now feeds the government meteorological service. In 1938 he bought a primitive television camera, taught everyone at his radio station how to use it, and set up the world's first commercial closed-circuit transmission to feed scenes from an American Legion parade to seven receivers at the Radisson Hotel.

Hubbard put his television station on the air in 1948 and joined NBC's network, their second affiliate. My first contact with him was in the early 1940s, when Paramount leased him the Minnesota Theater in downtown Minneapolis. I negotiated the lease. We changed the name to Radio City; he moved his offices and radio station into the building. Eventually he asked to buy the property, and we sold it to him.

In 1976, when Duffy and Bob Fountain went to see him, he'd established KSTP-TV in a large structure straddling the line between St. Paul and Minneapolis, and often boasted of traveling between the Twin Cities hundreds of times a day.

OTHER RECOLLECTIONS:
Jim Duffy

We'd got to know Hubbard's son Stan a little in Las Vegas at the NAB convention. We'd sit and talk about where we were going and so forth. But his dad was really running things then.

Stan said, "If you can convince my father, I think we can do some business. I believe ABC is the sign of the future. I like your people. I like Leonard."

Before I went, Fred Silverman had gone to see the old man, but apparently they didn't get along very well. I would soon learn why.

So Bob Fountain and I flew up there. Old Mr. Hubbard sat behind his desk and didn't say anything. He wore a rumpled business suit, not quite seedy. He was no fashion plate. He was a man of himself. Clothes just didn't matter much to him. It was what you were inside that mattered to him.

I said, "Mr. Hubbard, it's nice to see you."

He said, "I'm very disappointed."

I said, "Is that right, sir? What are you disappointed about?"

"I expected an older man."

I was forty-six or forty-seven then, and I was taken aback. I realized he was playing with me. He wanted to rattle me a little. I said, "Well, I'm old in my ways. Believe me, we've been through a lot, but that isn't what we came to talk to you about."

"I'm not especially fond of New York City slickers."

I bit my tongue and said, "Mr. Hubbard, do you know where Moweaqua, Illinois, is?"

He said, "No, I don't."

"It's in the middle of central Illinois, a farm town. That's where I grew up."

"Well, Christ, then, sit down and let's talk." From there, he kind of took over. He was funny. I mean, he was just wonderful.

We went out to eat at their club, and he drove himself. He had a red light that he put on top of his old DeSoto, like a sheriff's light. He's talking the whole time he's driving, and he's all over the road, going in and out of lanes.

He was checking me out, testing me, and I love guys like that.

We went back to KSTP after dinner. He took us into a huge studio where they did live shows and commercials. Hubbard had a new Wurlitzer organ, and he thought it was just wonderful. He sat down and tinkered around with it. He made us sit down and then said, "We just redid this studio, and it's got the best acoustics in America. Watch now."

He went out in the middle of the floor and said, "Can you hear me?"

We'd nod, and he'd back to the edge of the studio. "Can you hear me now?"

He went way down the hall and said, "Can you hear me now?"

Bob and I were sitting there going, "Jesus Christ!" But silently.

We said, "Yeah, this is a beautiful studio."

Back in his office he says, "I'm not sure we want to do business with you."

So we said, "Mr. Hubbard, this has been a delight," and so forth.

Young Stan winked at us as we left, and Stanley said, "We'll call you tomorrow." They called, and they agreed to become an ABC affiliate.

Leonard was very helpful. He talked to the old man on the phone, and to young Stan several times.

But when this was announced, Leonard had Bob and me come up in front of the board of directors. He made the announcement to the board about what a coup this was. That it was kind of the unplugging of the NBC Television Network.

❑ ❑ ❑

When Stanley Hubbard came aboard, it sent shock waves through the industry. Many, many desirable stations approached us. We made deals with WSB, Atlanta, a Cox Broadcasting station, as well as with the Cox station in Charlotte, North Carolina, NBC's oldest affiliate. These were very important additions to our network and a coup for Duffy, Beesemyer, and Fountain. They also brought in KGTV, San Diego, a McGraw-Hill station, the leading broadcasters in California's second-largest city. Then they were on a roll.

If Jim Duffy had done nothing else for ABC—and he did quite a lot—his success in upgrading and expanding our affiliate lineup would have been more than enough to make him one of the company's true heroes. After leaving the network presidency in 1985, Jim became head of ABC Communications, which handles our community service programs. Jim has been a tireless promoter of national and local literacy programs, and travels the country speaking about our industry. He is now a consultant to Capital Cities/ABC on these matters.

Our campaign for improved distribution was an extraordinary success. Between 1974 and the end of 1980 we added or switched some seventy stations, thus bringing almost 2 million new prime-time viewers to our network. With 206 affiliates, for the first time in our history our network had more stations than CBS or NBC.

With our newly powerful distribution pumping out ABC's daytime and prime-time programming to an enormous audience, advertising revenues spurted upward. We made more money than I had ever dreamed possible.

This stream of dollars allowed us, finally, to deal with the one remaining area where ABC had lagged. By the middle 1970s we began looking for ways to make ABC News the world's leading news organization.

20

Team Arledge

❑

In a luncheon speech on the opening day of our 1977 affiliates meeting in Los Angeles, I said that our prime-time schedule was going like a house afire. We were starting to make progress in daytime and in morning; and now, I felt, we could at long last start pumping in the resources to make ABC News competitive with CBS and NBC.

We had put this off for far too long, I admitted. Now we have to score in news. I said, "We will commit whatever resources are required to make ABC News number one."

This process had already begun. Mingling with our affiliates at the 1977 meeting was Barbara Walters, who had joined us in 1976 after many years as the star of NBC's "Today."

Bill Sheehan, who had been Elmer Lower's deputy for several years before succeeding him as head of ABC News in 1974, had helped bring her over.

OTHER RECOLLECTIONS:
Bill Sheehan

We had toyed with the idea of a male/female anchor team before Barbara came into the picture. It was being done on local stations everywhere, but not on any network. Ted Koppel had been anchoring a Saturday night news broadcast; I thought of putting a female anchor with him to test the water. We began looking for someone. We considered Jessica Savitch, Hilary Brown, Pat Harper, and a lot of other women. Then Fred Pierce came in and said he understood Barbara Walters might be available.

❑ ❑ ❑

Pierce's notion that Barbara might be available was the result of a few remarks lobbed into a tennis match that he had with Lou Weiss, a William Morris vice president. Lou mentioned this because of a conversation initiated by my close friend, Jack Hausman, then a member of ABC's board.

OTHER RECOLLECTIONS:
Barbara Walters

Most of the stories that have appeared about why I left NBC and why I came to ABC are all wrong.

I knew Leonard in the same way that I knew Jack Hausman: because of their work in cerebral palsy. I had a sister who died recently. She was retarded, and for a while she went to the cerebral palsy training center on Long Island. Ethel Hausman was very involved with that and helped me. When I needed advice, she was someone I could always turn to. I used to go to UCP events. I didn't know Leonard and Isabelle well, but we shared a very close mutual friend, Lola Finkelstein.

Jack Hausman became more of a personal friend. He had talked to me, superficially, about coming to ABC, but I was never terribly interested. And then, my contract was up at NBC. When Jack again mentioned it, for the first time I was mildly interested. But, at first, he wanted me to come over and appear on ABC's morning program.

I had been working on "Today" for fifteen years, starting each day at 4:00 A.M., and it's tough. You burn out. Diane Sawyer does two years (at CBS) and says, "I want to leave." David Hartman did about eight years (at ABC).

So I would not have left NBC to do another morning program. But then ABC's original offer was followed up in a much more concrete way by Fred Pierce. He said if I was interested in coming, they were very anxious to have me as coanchor of the evening news. I had a young child, and it sounded like the opportunity to have a normal life.

The first time I talked to anyone was in California, when Fred Pierce and Bill Sheehan came out.

❑ ❑ ❑

There were several meetings after the first. At one, Barbara and her agent, Lou Weiss, met with Elton and Fred Pierce in a hotel suite while I remained down the hall in another room. From time to time, one or another would come down and update me on their discussion. Subsequent meetings were at Barbara's apartment or in a hotel suite that ABC maintained at Essex House in New York.

OTHER RECOLLECTIONS:
Bill Sheehan

Fred suggested pairing Barbara with Harry Reasoner, our evening news anchor and ABC's most respected newsman. I said, "That's an entirely new game. In the first place, it would be extremely expensive, because we would be bidding against "Today," and we would have to cover a lot of territory in making Harry happy with the situation."

A period of discussions began. With Harry. With Barbara. With her agent. Then the problem became, "What do we do about Harry?" He was not enthusiastic about the idea, and Barbara would not come unless Harry would welcome her.

We had meetings with Harry and Barbara together, with Harry and Barbara separately, Harry and Barbara with me, Harry and Barbara with her agent. Fred and Elton Rule and I had dinner with Harry. After a few weeks, Harry said he would give it a try. We were convinced that Harry was sincere.

❑ ❑ ❑

Barbara is a very buttoned-up lady. She knew what she wanted and had every one of the things she wanted to discuss on paper. In the end we agreed to pay her $1 million a year, which seemed to make her the highest paid news talent in the world. Actually, half her salary came from the Entertainment division, because Barbara's deal included four one-hour specials in addition to her news anchor duties.

Serendipity attended the announcement that Barbara was television's first million-dollar baby. It was so widely publicized that when she called a statesman on the order of Sadat or Begin, they usually agreed to see her. And she handled herself very well. ABC's million was very well spent.

OTHER RECOLLECTIONS:
Barbara Walters

At that time, ABC was riding high. They were determined to make their news department, which had not been very good at all, into something at least competitive. One of the ways they would do it was to be first to have an hour program; they would start with forty-five minutes and then expand it. There was no question that this would happen. It was a commitment on ABC's part.

I was to coanchor with Harry Reasoner, and the longer format would allow time not only to read the news—which was not my great desire or really what I thought I did best—but also to do a kind of briefing and to do interviews. The sort of things you see on the news now, but for which we were highly criticized when we began to do them.

After I was hired and went to the affiliates meeting, I made a big declarative speech on behalf of the one-hour news. I was practically booed out of there. ABC didn't have the guts to push it through. The commitment evaporated.

❑ ❑ ❑

Pairing Barbara with Harry Reasoner was a bold stroke. Unfortunately, it didn't work. The show never jelled, and viewers tuned out.

OTHER RECOLLECTIONS:
Bill Sheehan

We all have beautiful hindsight in this kind of thing. One person that seemed to have it locked from the beginning was Andy Rooney. I met him at the convention in Kansas City in 1976 and asked how he thought it would turn out. He said, "It's no-win for Harry." That turned out to be true.

If it had been successful, Harry would have got less than his share of the credit. Barbara would have got it all. If it was a failure, then he would go down with the sinking ship. So one of the deals that we had to make with Harry was: If it didn't work, or if he wasn't happy with it, then we would pay off his contract, and he'd be free to leave.

I like Harry, but he didn't pull his weight on this. Barbara did. She worked her butt off.

❑ ❑ ❑

In defense of Harry Reasoner, he was going through some tough times, personally. Moreover, he had been brought over from CBS and "60 Minutes" with the idea that he would be sole anchor. So, as Andy Rooney so perceptively noted, it had all the makings of a situation where Harry couldn't win. But Harry *did* have a choice of which way he would lose.

OTHER RECOLLECTIONS:
Barbara Walters

I don't think it was anything personal. I know that sounds Pollyanna-ish, but Harry came to ABC after being promised he would be the force behind the news, and the only anchor. Shortly after he came, he was teamed with Howard K. Smith. But he didn't want a partner. It didn't work out with Smith, so finally he was able to do it alone.

And, I think, he felt it was a bad news department. He felt it needed new equipment, it needed all kinds of attention. It angered him that ABC spent this money to bring me over, instead of spending it to improve the department.

He also felt I was hired for the wrong reasons. I'm not sure he would have felt the same way if Mike Wallace had come over, although he may have. He was terribly unhappy about it. Unlike others who have had to live with coanchors, it was something he couldn't accept, and it showed on the air.

I'd walk into the studio, and Harry would talk to everybody there except me. He cracked jokes with all the guys about the latest baseball scores—by the way, he was very good with baseball scores—and he would go across the street every day to Des Artistes and spend an hour before the show and an hour after complaining about me. Had I known how violently opposed he was, I wouldn't have come. It was the toughest period of my life.

But I also knew that Harry is not a mean man, not a spiteful man. He was just terribly unhappy. We also know now, as we didn't know then, that he was very unhappily married. Not many years after that he got a divorce. It was a very tough period for him, difficult at home, difficult in the studio. He didn't see any hope for ABC getting better. I was just one more impediment. I suspect he felt almost silly being paired with this woman from the "Today" show. That was a part of an old-boy mind-set that still, to some degree, exists.

❑ ❑ ❑

While pairing Harry and Barbara was Fred Pierce's idea, I must accept responsibility for its failure. I hadn't foreseen what might happen, and when the idea was proposed, I thought it was a good one. But that's the nature of the business. One can't be right every time.

In our failure, however, were the seeds of two triumphs. One was "The Barbara Walters Specials."

OTHER RECOLLECTIONS: *Barbara Walters*

The "Specials," to our amazement, took off. When the ratings came out, I always heard from Leonard the next day. All those years, I would know that if the show did well, I would hear from Leonard. "Congratulations, good for you." It was very sweet and thoughtful. Something he didn't have to do. And nobody else did it. He didn't call when they were bad, but they were very rarely bad.

We started trying to mix celebrities and hard-news interviews. The first was Barbra Streisand with her then-boyfriend, Jon Peters, and President-elect and Mrs. Jimmy Carter. The second had Elizabeth Taylor and her then-husband, Senator John Warner, Barbara Jordan, and the Shah of Iran. As time went on, we found that audiences didn't want the political ones, no matter who we did. We had King Hussein and his wife, Queen Noor. We had Vice President Mondale. That's not what they wanted. They wanted television stars, movie stars.

We were on at 10. Usually there would be a movie opposite us, in which someone would be dying at two minutes of ten. They'd have to switch channels to watch us, so we really had to have the biggest stars possible. That's how it emerged into being all celebrities.

❑ ❑ ❑

Over the years, Barbara has scored many triumphs. She interviewed Fidel Castro, and asked him some very tough questions. Apparently he appreciates this quality, because Castro sent her a copy of the Cuban constitution, with a handwritten note on the bottom attesting to her doggedness.

She's also interviewed some very controversial celebrities for her "Specials" and for "20/20," which she cohosts with Hugh Downs. Probably the most notable was Jane Fonda. In 1988 she succeeded in getting Fonda to discuss her wartime support of North Vietnam for the first time in public.

OTHER RECOLLECTIONS:
Barbara Walters

I had done three interviews with Jane, two for the "Specials," and one for a three-hour *Life* magazine special. We had, from time to time, touched on Vietnam. She never really wanted to talk about it.

My husband, Merv Adelson, had a house in Aspen. Jane and her then-husband, Tom Hayden, went there to ski. Occasionally our husbands skied together. One night we all had dinner together. They invited us over to watch a segment from the miniseries "Amerika," and during the show I said, "If you ever decide to talk about Vietnam, to explore the subject, I hope you'll do it with me."

She said, "If I ever do, I will." A year and a half later she was making a movie, and once again, Jane was criticized for her Vietnam activities. Veterans and others didn't want her to come to Waterbury, Connecticut, where she was scheduled to do some filming.

She called and said, "Look, you said if I ever wanted to talk about it . . . now I would like to."

I said, "We'll have to do it the way *we* want to do it," and she agreed. Probably, the interview would not have happened if negative publicity hadn't been piling up about her movie. I think she felt that sooner or later she was going to have to address it. A prime-time news magazine like "20/20" was as good a place as any.

We never discussed questions in advance, there was no control on her part, no agreement, no attempt. The producer and I both thought it was a tough interview. We showed a lot of old footage of Jane in Vietnam. I mean, you really want to push a pie in her face, to say the least.

I was surprised at the outcry that followed the broadcast. [Veterans' groups, still angry at her Vietnam War position, opposed any publicity for Jane Fonda.] We thought it would be very interesting, but we didn't expect that kind of reaction and all the publicity that we got. We were delighted, of course.

The phones never stopped. And they were picketing us. They called, they wrote letters to Roone Arledge, and I'm sure they wrote letters to Leonard, and they copied us. But I never heard anything from Leonard or Roone about it.

❑ ❑ ❑

The second piece of good luck resulting from the failure of the Reasoner/Walters team was that it forced us to keep looking for bold new ways to make our news competitive. Once again Fred Pierce had an idea. It was one of the best he ever had at ABC, but at first I didn't think so.

OTHER RECOLLECTIONS:
Fred Pierce

There were a lot of eyebrows raised, but I felt there was a natural synergy between sports and news. Roone Arledge had studied journalism at Columbia and was always very interested in that area. He had the utmost good taste and judgment, which he proved at the 1972 Olympics in Munich. For one very long day ABC Sports operated as if it were ABC News, and no one could have done better.

So I went to Leonard and Elton and recommended we put Arledge in as head of News. If we were going to move that area ahead, I wanted a major thrust. There was some initial resistance, but eventually they supported me.

❑ ❑ ❑

Putting Harry and Barbara on as a team was a small gamble. Making Roone president of ABC News was like throwing the deed to the family farm on the casino table. I couldn't be sure we'd win—but if we did, I thought we would win big.

No one was available to replace Roone as head of ABC Sports, so he kept that job as well as his News responsibilities. Roone habitually worked long into the night and was rarely seen early in the day. He had mastered the art of keeping many balls in the air at once, and sometimes made decisions through deliberate inaction. That is, he avoided responding to certain inquiries in the belief that events would sort themselves out satisfactorily without his intervention. With the strange hours he kept, he acquired a reputation as quirky, unconventional, and unreachable.

When ABC announced his appointment as head of News, media kibitzers around the country were quick to say that Fred, Elton, and I had lost our minds. A joke made the rounds: Roone will now have *two* offices where he can't be reached.

OTHER RECOLLECTIONS:
Roone Arledge

When I first got out of college, I wanted to be a writer for *Time* or *Newsweek*. I was interested in politics and world affairs and culture and plays and opera and ballet and symphony orchestras and all sorts of things.

It was also a natural progression. Of all the things I've contributed to sports, among the most difficult, and of which I am most proud, is adding some journalism to sports. That's why I put people like Howard Cosell on the air.

After the 1976 Montreal Olympics were very successful, I was extremely hot. I had five unsolicited offers, any of which would have paid me far more than I could ever make at ABC.

Agents would call me and say, "I will get you this much money from ABC. They'll scream and yell, but they'll have to pay it."

I said, "I can't do that. I have to work with these people afterward."

I believe you have to leave something on the table, although people seem to get away with taking everything and still survive. Working for a company like ABC, the day comes when you have to get programs on the air. You have to have cooperation. You have to get a decent time period, and you must have enthusiasm from people you work with.

In the middle of all that, I was talking to Fred late one night, over coffee, and he asked me if I was interested in running News.

It kind of came and went. We talked about a bunch of things. The next day I called and said, "Were you serious about News last night?"

He said, "Wait a minute, I was just sort of feeling around. News doesn't even report to me."

I said, "That's something I would be very interested in." Meanwhile, everybody was telling me, "You're crazy, go make yourself a fortune."

But ABC News was a great personal challenge. It was a wasted organization. Compared to CBS and NBC, it was like we almost didn't exist in news. It was third because there were only three networks. Otherwise it would have been fifth or tenth.

Leonard was opposed to my becoming head of ABC News. Elton was very worried about it. They all liked me and knew I'd done a good job on sports, but they thought I was kind of erratic and strange and hybrid and charming. Part of the family and all that, but God knows what trouble we're getting into, this guy who puts Howard Cosell on the air.

They had News report to Fred so he would be the one who made the change. That way there was some deniability.

❑ ❑ ❑

Roone's critics were in full cry as he struggled with his new job. Many believed he would turn ABC News into a circus. I know Roone was shocked and disappointed by this. He had won every award one could win in sports broadcasting, and ABC Sports was recognized everywhere as a first-rate, high-class organization. He'd broken through all sorts of barriers and created new forms of television. Despite my misgivings, I was very proud of his achievements.

But I suppose there will always be people who are wary of somebody coming in to head an organization when that individual hasn't worked his way up that particular ladder.

Roone's initial program offerings were far from successful. But he was still learning, and we had to give him a full opportunity to show what he could do.

OTHER RECOLLECTIONS:
Roone Arledge

My top priority was our evening news. Harry Reasoner was not among my fans when I came here. Yet I had the feeling that, if I spent a lot of time around him, I would get to like him very much.

But I didn't want to become his crony, because I knew immediately that he would have to go. Barbara was great at so many things that reading the news opposite a grumpy guy who didn't want her there was not in her best interest.

But there was no way I could take Barbara off that program and keep Harry on it without leaving her tremendously damaged. So poor Harry had to go, even though it would be a major loss, and we didn't have anybody to replace him.

I didn't think the chances of Harry taking a magazine show or something else were good, although in retrospect, maybe if I had spent more time trying to get him to do this, he might have ended up doing "20/20" instead of going back to "60 Minutes" at CBS.

During the few months Barbara and Harry remained on the air, we stopped showing them together. I told the producer that wide two-shots of them trying to "relate" looked silly. So we shot them individually. Barbara would say something, and Harry would say something. We didn't have all this phony "relating."

After looking around to see who I could get, I concluded we would have to proceed with the people we had. It was a major disappointment to many affiliates, to the network, and everybody else who thought I'd steal Walter Cronkite away from CBS. Or pull some other rabbit out of my hat.

Under her contract, Barbara had what amounted to a veto over any coanchor. I wanted to put Barbara in a whole new environment, so I had to come up with something totally different. That's why I began calling people who read the evening news "desks" instead of "anchors."

Barbara was based in New York, but if she wasn't our New York "anchor," we would have none there at all. So I used Frank Reynolds in Washington and Peter Jennings in London. I planned to build Peter into the embodiment of a foreign correspondent. We needed to differentiate ourselves from the other networks, so I came up with a three-desk concept, adding Max Robinson in Chicago. We needed strength in the middle of the country.

❑ ❑ ❑

Roone's three-desk newscast, "World News Tonight," premiered July 10, 1978. It was the first to take advantage of the breathtaking advances in technology that had become available by the 1970s. The three "desks" rotating story presentations were linked by satellites and fed with news tapes from all over the world. It was a new form, and despite all the orthodox criticism this drew, it was apparent even to his detractors that Roone was thinking on a new and broader scale.

As "World News Tonight" evolved, Roone began to look at other shows to increase ABC News visibility on the network.

OTHER RECOLLECTIONS:
Roone Arledge

It was an article of faith that we would have a magazine show. As the date got closer and I didn't have a producer, I hired a guy who'd done only entertainment and talk shows. They were physically isolated from us and had no relationship to the News division at all, and things got away from me.

The producer wanted to do different things, and the program "20/20" was ahead of its time. It also had two offbeat hosts, one of whom was Bob Hughes, art critic of *Time* magazine. He is a hell of a person, but his Australian accent was so thick, you couldn't understand him on television.

The first "20/20," in June 1978, was terrible. I should never have put that first show on the air. There was such chaos in the control room the night of the first broadcast that, while I didn't think it was very good, I couldn't tell. Everybody on the show was ecstatic. They thought it was great.

I told them, "Don't confuse getting it on the air on time with having done something worthwhile."

I couldn't wait to look at a cassette of it, but Fred Pierce was under the gun to get me signed to a new contract. I promised to meet with him at the Dorset Hotel, and that happened to be the day after "20/20" went on the air.

I spent the whole day with Fred in the hotel and went to a benefit party that night. After dinner there was a Neil Simon play, but I sneaked out after dessert, went home, and looked at the cassette. It was even worse than I had imagined.

I thought, We're just not going to do this. We cannot go on the air next week with a program like that. If necessary, I'll just kill it, even though it will be embarrassing. I must find a new host.

I got up the next morning and turned on "Good Morning America." Hugh Downs was substituting for David Hartman. Hugh was somebody we had thought about earlier, but had not picked. I thought, I don't know who I'm going to be able to get in a week that's going to be better than Hugh Downs.

I called him, and we started talking. I came in and fired all the people on the show. By the next week Hugh was the host. He's been there ever since.

❑ ❑ ❑

Harry Reasoner's return to CBS left ABC News with no one of comparable stature to Walter Cronkite at CBS or John Chancellor at NBC. Despite that, we had some good people here. One of Roone's most important contributions—aided, I'm sure he will admit, by some fortunate timing in the occurrence of world events—was to recognize and develop their talents. Such present media superstars as Peter Jennings, Ted Koppel, and Sam Donaldson were playing minor roles at ABC News when Roone became president of the division.

He created a framework in which they could flourish. One element of this framework was built by bringing in top people to design sets and graphics. Another, far more important, was to build strength in our bureaus, and to recruit, train, and lead a team of producers, tape editors, and camera people.

Roone inherited from his predecessors a small group of behind-the-scenes people, mostly producers and directors, who, by surviving all the lean years, had become minor wizards. Toughened by competing with NBC and CBS in their heyday, when ABC was such a poor third, they learned how to do things under the most adverse conditions. They took a perverse pride in battling the competition with only half as many correspondents and camera crews. Roone used this handful of crucible-hardened veterans as a nucleus to build upon.

Once this infrastructure was in place, it became far easier to recruit people of stature and people with promise. And it became possible to develop people like Peter Jennings to their full potential.

After giving up his job as anchor of the ABC network newscast, Peter left New York in 1967 to become a national correspondent. He went to Rome in 1969, and after a few months went to Beirut, where he helped create the first American television bureau in the Arab world. From Beirut, Peter established his credentials as a premier correspondent, scooping the other networks with the first full-length interview of Yasir Arafat broadcast on American television.

Peter was in Beirut for six years. In 1975, after returning from Israel via Cyprus, he and another ABC correspondent, Charles Glass, were jailed by Lebanese authorities.

OTHER RECOLLECTIONS:
Peter Jennings

Journalists based in Lebanon used to go to Israel via Cyprus and to the Occupied Territories, in my case on a regular basis. The Lebanese found out I'd been to Israel because their diplomatic staff in the United States saw my story on a broadcast and reported back to them. The Lebanese were very sensitive about their own permissiveness. Lebanon was getting pounded. They were bombed by the Israelis in the south, and the Palestinians and the Lebanese Army were fighting all the time. They just got fed up, I think, and tried to use me as a test case.

It was a traumatic experience. Charlie and I were marched through the streets in handcuffs. It was awful, but we spent only a couple of days in jail. My wife's uncle was the Lebanese Minister of Defense, which was helpful. That's the way Lebanon worked.

❑ ❑ ❑

Peter left Lebanon shortly after his brush with prison. Charles Glass, a very capable correspondent, also departed. He took a leave of absence in 1987 and returned to Beirut to write a book. Glass was kidnapped by terrorists who subjected him to constant death threats while he lay, blindfolded and in chains, in a Beirut apartment. After sixty-two days, he escaped and made his way to freedom.

Although he was the first and so far only one of dozens of kidnapped Westerners to escape, the Reagan Administration chose to intimate that his escape had somehow been engineered by "quiet, behind-the-scenes diplomacy." I don't believe that, and neither does anyone else who knows Charlie Glass.

In 1973, while based in Lebanon, Peter did a documentary about Anwar Sadat. Up to then Sadat had avoided the press. Peter's one-hour biographical exploration of Sadat's life was America's first glimpse of the man who had emerged from obscurity to replace Nasser as head of Egypt. Broadcast early in 1974, the program won Peter a Peabody Award.

In 1975 Peter came back to Washington to cohost our short-lived "AM America" morning show. He went to our London Bureau in 1976, and the next year, as "World News Tonight" debuted, Roone made Peter, as ABC News chief correspondent, the foreign "desk."

Peter was not rooted in London, merely based there. He traveled the world, reporting international events. In 1978, he was working on a story in South Africa when Roone called.

OTHER RECOLLECTIONS:
Peter Jennings

Because of my documentary, I knew Sadat very well. Bill Seamans, our bureau chief and correspondent in Israel, knew Menachem Begin very well. Roone had talked to several people in Israel, including some members of the Knesset, who said Begin would be willing to talk peace with Sadat if Sadat would come to Israel.

So Arledge, sitting in some Italian restaurant in Manhattan, got a brain wave. He called me in South Africa and said, "You've got to go to Egypt. Charter a plane."

I said, "They won't let you land at the airport if you're coming from South Africa. This is a racist regime. They take that stuff very seriously."

Bill Seamans and I were on the phone all night long. It was one of the most hysterical nights of my life. We finally broke down laughing when we realized that the secret services of both countries were listening to these two correspondents working up enough nerve to call Arledge back and disturb his Italian dinner. But eventually I did. I left on a commercial flight to Geneva. I had a shower there, then got on another plane for Cairo.

I called Sadat from the airport and said, "Can I come and see you, Mr. President?" and he said yes.

When I got there, I said, "Do you want to sit down and make peace on television?"

He said, "Oh, no."

I said, "What about going to Jerusalem? You know, there are all these rumors about Begin wanting to sit down with you and talk peace."

"Go on, go on."

"Under what conditions would you go to Israel?"

"If Begin invites me."

I ran back to the office and telexed Seamans in Tel Aviv, via New York. Those were the days when, if you lived in the Arab world, you referred to Israel as "Dixie" or "New South Wales," because Arab government censors would not allow a message with the word "Israel" to leave the country.

The telex to Seamans said: "Sadat will come when Begin invites him." Seamans ran over to the Knesset with a camera, stuck a microphone under Begin's nose, and said, "Sadat will come if you invite him."

Begin said, "Well, I invite him."

The only trouble was that Arledge had moved my ass around the world like nobody's business and forgot to have a camera crew waiting for me in Cairo. I had no pictures of Sadat saying he would go to Israel if asked. So on the 6 P.M. feed that day, I came on the broadcast from Cairo saying, "Anwar Sadat says he will go to Jerusalem if he's invited, and here's Bill Seamans in Jerusalem."

Bill Seamans introduced his pictures of Begin saying, "Well, I invite him."

The telex began to clatter away with complimentary telegrams, "Congratulations, a great scoop."

❑ ❑ ❑

When I studied philosophy as a boy, I learned the ancient conundrum about a tree falling in the forest. If there is no one in the forest to hear the tree fall, is there a sound? Something like that happened to Peter's scoop.

OTHER RECOLLECTIONS:
Roone Arledge

We actually broke the story, but to this day everybody thinks Walter Cronkite brought about peace between Egypt and Israel. After Peter spoke to Sadat and Seamans spoke to Begin, CBS did separate interviews and put them together electronically. Cronkite talked to one and then the other, although they were all on tape, and he had interviewed them after our people interviewed them.

We were an organization which wasn't used to leading, and so downplayed everything. Peter Jennings, in those days, was not a major player, and nobody had heard of Seamans. Contrast our ratings against those of Walter Cronkite, add the theatricality of the story's presentation, and CBS's broadcast became a landmark in television history. Everybody said, "Cronkite brought about peace in the Middle East." That was totally wrong. It shows how little attention anybody paid to ABC News.

However, in the following weeks, when Sadat went to Israel,

our coverage was so much better than anybody else's that people started recognizing it.

I got Barbara on Sadat's plane from Egypt to Israel. Peter described the landing in Jerusalem, and he was great. Frank Reynolds went to Cairo and described what was going on back there. And Sam Donaldson got another scoop when he grabbed Jimmy Carter coming out of church in Washington.

We were the only network to show the whole event live. We went right from Jimmy Carter talking to pictures of Sadat walking into the Knesset.

Barbara had the first interview with Sadat and Begin together, but our luck was still bad. Barbara had a great interview, and we had no place to put it. It was a Sunday; CBS had "60 Minutes" coming up. Cronkite pleaded for another interview. I really admire Walter for his tenacity in pursuing Begin and Sadat. Finally they agreed to a joint interview with him, mostly because he was Walter Cronkite.

We put on a little of Barbara's interview in the afternoon, just for the record, to be first with it. This was to be Barbara's total scoop and coup.

But when "60 Minutes" producer Don Hewitt saw Cronkite's interview coming in, he put it on to lead the broadcast. We did a longer version of Barbara's interview later that night. But "60 Minutes" was a very popular program, and our broadcast went on the tail end of a movie. It was yet another tree falling in the forest that nobody knew had fallen.

But this proved to everybody here how good they could be. I kept telling them that we will get good, and something will happen, and everybody will turn around and say, "My God, how did they get so good, where did they come from?" This was the first time our people really understood how good they could be if they would just do what we told them to do and went all out after stories. Even though we didn't quite get credit for them.

❑ ❑ ❑

The events that followed the historic meeting between Sadat and Begin, together with the wider audiences our newscasts were reaching in the late 1970s, helped establish Peter Jennings as one of the world's leading journalists.

Another unprecedented event gave Roone the opportunity to expand our daily network news to an hour. It also helped propel talented, versatile—and unheralded—Ted Koppel to stardom.

OTHER RECOLLECTIONS:
Roone Arledge

One of the major combat areas in those days was an hour-long evening newscast. All three network news divisions desperately wanted to go to an hour. Of the three, we were the least able. ABC affiliates, good though they were, had no real network news tradition. It wasn't like you could wave the Holy Grail in front of them, as CBS could, and say, "Let's do this for the general welfare."

We had yet to prove that we could even be competitive with our thirty-minute evening news. The affiliates' argument, which I couldn't disagree with, was, "Go prove you can do a half hour before you talk about an hour." They didn't mean that as an insult. They meant ABC News at dinnertime had never been very successful.

I concluded we were not going to win that fight. Then it dawned on me: Why not do at 11:30 the same thing we do at 6? Why not have local news followed by network news? Everyone was very skeptical.

To prove we could do it I said, "We'll do a whole group of specials. We'll do one every time anything happens of any significance." I had the right to preempt the 11:30 time slot if it was truly important. So if there was a plane crash, a key congressional vote, a visit by a dignitary, whatever it was, we would do a half-hour special. We got to where we were pretty damn good at them.

We continued to do these half-hours. Sporadically, but often. I was trying to demonstrate that we could get an audience, that people would watch a network news program from 11:30 to midnight.

Our anchor for this show was almost always Frank Reynolds in Washington. In November 1979, our people in the American Embassy in Tehran were taken hostage. We did a special: "The Iran Crisis—America Held Hostage."

The hostages weren't released the next day, so we did another special. The next day they were still captive, so we did another one. And another.

After several of these, I began seeing this was a story that people cared about. The United States itself was being held hostage, our embassy and our people. I went up to Lake Placid for a quick press conference in connection with the 1980 Olympics. The press conference started about facilities but turned quickly into questions about the hostages.

I came back that night and asked, "What are we doing tonight for a late night special?"

Somebody said, "We're not doing one."

"Why not?"

"Because the story really hasn't advanced any."

"Look, my elevator man, the taxi driver, the pilot on the plane, the people in Lake Placid who should be talking about the Olympics—all these people care about now are the hostages in Tehran.

"I do not believe that we cannot make an interesting half hour. Don't lose sight of our overall goal, which is to get that time slot. I will make the decision for you. We will do a special every single night until the hostage thing is over."

I called Fred Pierce and told him I wanted to do that, and he said okay. We took a big ad, and we made a pledge that we would continue to report this story every night until our hostages were freed. We all thought it was going to be maybe two weeks.

It went on and on and on. After a while it became obvious it wasn't a daily life-or-death crisis. It was settling in for a long run. We did pieces about the history of Iran, the spread of Islamic fundamentalism, "What's an Ayatollah," and the history of Savak, the Iranian secret police, about the Shah, and everything you can think of.

❑ ❑ ❑

Frank Reynolds, who anchored most of these shows, was dying of lung cancer, though neither Roone, Elton, Fred, nor I knew it. But after months of these specials, it became obvious that he was unable to continue holding down the Washington desk on "World News Tonight" and the nightly specials. Frank kept the nature of his illness a secret, but more and more often he had to call in sick. His replacement was often Ted Koppel, a relatively obscure Washington reporter.

OTHER RECOLLECTIONS:
Roone Arledge

Ted and I had kind of a rocky beginning. When I first started here, he was doing a Saturday news program and was on kind of semileave of absence. His wife was going to law school, and he had agreed to stay home during the week to take care of the children. He was making almost no money at all.

When I became head of News, there was such curiosity about every damn thing we did that I couldn't hold a conversation without it turning up in the newspaper. I needed some place away from the glare of publicity. I needed a show to try out some things. I couldn't do that on the evening news broadcast, and we didn't have a Sunday program.

Nobody paid any attention to Saturdays. I turned the Saturday show into an experimental place where we could see which of the young people were good and which weren't.

That was Ted's show, and I was very heavy-handed and clumsy about it. I should have talked to Ted, but I changed his producer without telling him first. That really annoyed Ted, who looked upon the show as his franchise. He wrote me a letter, resigning.

I just ignored it. Ultimately I had lunch with him, and he told me that he did a lot of other things. I asked him to send me a cassette. He had done things at the conventions, and everything he'd ever done was wonderful. So I started using him on "Good Morning America" to substitute for Steve Bell.

We've been very close friends ever since.

When Frank began to falter from his cancer, I had Ted fill in for him. It became apparent that Ted was a natural. One night we wanted to interview somebody from the Iranian embassy. The guy couldn't leave. He was waiting for something.

He said, "I can't come to the studio, so therefore I can't be on the show."

I told the producer, "Bullshit. We'll go over there and do it." We put a camera over there, and we put him on the screen, and Ted talked to him. That was the genesis of the "Nightline" format.

The other thing that shaped "Nightline" was a program just after Carter's 1979 State of the Union address. Ted moderated it, and we had Harold Brown, then Secretary of Defense, and a guy who was to become President of Iran. We also had Vladimir

Posner—a Soviet news commentator—a senator, and a congressman. They all discussed Carter's speech.

Watching Ted bounce these people off each other and control things, and the manner in which he did it, I said, "You know, that's what this program is going to be." That was the format.

By this time the hostages had been there 230 days. We had been pushing very hard with the affiliates. We wanted a regular program, and we had proved that we could make this program so interesting that people would watch it, even though there was no life-or-death urgency anymore.

The Iran hostage crisis was one of those events that you can't foretell. But when things come along and you're prepared and you seize the opportunity, that's how you make progress. Luck is the residue of design, as Mr. Rickey once said.

❑ ❑ ❑

Roone finally convinced the network and the affiliates, and early in 1980 "Nightline" became a scheduled program four nights a week. In the summer of 1981 it went to five nights and continues to maintain very good ratings.

Among our emerging stars was Sam Donaldson, who as a Capitol Hill correspondent in 1976 had been assigned to cover a Georgia peanut farmer's dark-horse bid to become President of the United States. When Jimmy Carter won, Sam became our White House correspondent. He distinguished himself from his colleagues with an irreverent style and a deft sense of how far he could go in pushing a President or other Administration officials. In an era when government had become suspect, when even ordinary citizens looked upon official proclamations with cynicism, Sam became the voice of the people, daring to ask the questions everybody wanted answered and refusing to accept platitudes in response.

By 1980, ABC News had become clearly competitive with the other networks. Such shows as "20/20" and "Nightline" were drawing respectable ratings, a synergism of good shows exposed over our improved affiliate lineup. And, despite all the naysayers and critics, as Roone's army of newsgatherers, correspondents, producers, tape editors, and camera crews became increasingly competent, the distinctive, three-desk format on "World News Tonight" began to work well.

A great deal of credit for that must go to Peter Jennings. He emerged very clearly as the most effective and knowledgeable foreign correspondent in American broadcasting. Since most world crises occur overseas, as Peter's reputation grew, more and more people tuned to ABC. Audiences began to appreciate how we specialized in world news.

A bloody era of international terrorism dawned in the 1970s and continued into the 1980s. Many of the most dramatic events—airplane hijackings, car bombings, hostage seizures—took place in the Middle East. Peter's wide-ranging contacts and his experience in that region allowed him to play an important role in explaining these events. American audiences came to depend on ABC to report events and explain their background, including the Arab point of view, an element notably absent on other networks.

OTHER RECOLLECTIONS:
Peter Jennings

I did the first interview the Ayatollah Khomeini ever gave to an American network, in France, and when he returned from exile, I flew back to Iran sitting next to him.

I had no inkling of what was to happen, although I'd known the Shah's regime was in trouble since 1969, when I first went there. Anybody who spent time there in those years could see something coming. But not necessarily the Ayatollah.

Khomeini was absolutely lifeless. I sat beside him as we flew across the border into Iranian air space. The camera was rolling, and I stuck the microphone under his nose and asked, "How does it feel?" He just didn't feel anything. It was a stunning revelation. I've never, ever, known a leader to express less. I've never known anyone less communicative in an intimate situation. To a Westerner, at least. But he was an astonishing and inspiring figure to millions of Shiites. I suppose they appreciated his message.

I interviewed him again in Iran, and found it to be the same laborious experience. It was impossible to get a response out of him.

But I must say I've never been one of those journalists who defined what I do by the people I've interviewed. That's never been the way I've approached a story.

In my own approach to understanding places, I've always felt it was more productive to stay at some distance from (a) the palace gates and (b) the American embassy.

I don't seduce very easily, but I want to be at arm's length from predictability and from institutions like the Presidency and the American embassy, which are themselves at arm's length from society.

People sometimes forget that journalists very often have much more access to a society, in real terms, than do diplomats, bankers, or politicians.

A pretty good example of that is when TWA Flight 847 was hijacked in the air en route to Rome and ordered to fly to Beirut. One reason the relatives called people like me all the time is because all they have to do is look at television to realize that ABC's facility on the ground is very often better than that of the embassy. We have more freedom to move around as journalists than the United States government does.

I think anyone who's been in this business as long as I have would agree that, although I make a lot of money, most of us would probably do it for nothing. I'm in it because it's the most opportune profession or craft that I can imagine in which to learn.

The other thing is the wonderful sense of gratification I get from being able to pass what I discover on to others. When someone tells me they have learned something about a place where I've been, or that they came to realize that maybe things were not quite as they had thought before they saw our report, it's very satisfying.

❑ ❑ ❑

As Peter continued to grow in stature, so did Frank Reynolds in Washington. Max Robinson, however, never quite accomplished what we hoped he would.

"World News Tonight," in its three-desk format, improved as it became better defined. In time, Roone and Peter saw it needed a stronger central figure, while remaining faithful to the original concept of shifting between desks. Peter advocated that Frank become that figure, as he was the senior fellow and Washington was much more at the heart of things than London or Chicago. Max had some misgivings about that for a time, but he came to terms with the situation.

Max, a brilliant fellow, was very troubled. He felt pressured by the burden of being America's first black network anchor. When not actually performing as an ABC newsman, he took upon himself the role of spokesman for black causes. This often cast him in an adversarial position to ABC management. These activities further intensified scrutiny of his daily ABC duties by all sorts of outside critics.

And although he was quite good in a studio, Max lacked the particular kind of experience that had prepared Peter and Frank. Max had never done much field reporting, and the three-desk concept was designed to free one of the deskmen, at any given time, to do far more reporting than network anchors normally are able to do.

Moreover, Max did not respond well to the fishbowl environment of a top network news job. This is not always a kind business. Competitors and print critics are far too eager to snipe, and anyone perceived to have a weakness becomes an instant target. Anchors, even when they are called "desks," seem to draw more flak than anyone else in the business.

In the spring of 1980, when "World News Tonight" moved into second place in the ratings for the first time, it marked only the third such shift in modern television history. CBS, long the leader, fell behind NBC's "Huntley-Brinkley Report" in the early 1960s. Walter Cronkite regained leadership for CBS in the early 1970s. When ABC, always dead last, became number 2 for the first time in 1980, it vindicated Fred Pierce's choice of Roone Arledge—but silenced few of Roone's critics.

Besides providing leadership and building the structure which propelled Barbara Walters, Ted Koppel, and Peter Jennings to media superstardom, Roone had a very significant effect on the careers of news people far removed from ABC.

OTHER RECOLLECTIONS:
Roone Arledge

Starting in late 1979, we began trying to recruit someone to challenge Cronkite. All the research and everything else I knew about showed that Dan Rather, on "60 Minutes," was the outstanding young comer. And so I made a major effort to get Rather away from CBS.

I spent much of Christmas Day 1979 rereading Dan's book to see if there was anything I had forgotten about and ought to know. I subsequently met him in hotel rooms, at my apartment, and at several secret rendezvous. God, I can't tell you how many times we met and talked.

I knew CBS would do everything it could to hold Rather. I

thought they would promise that when Walter Cronkite left, Rather would succeed him. I never believed they would go to Walter and ask him to say when he was going to leave, because Walter Cronkite was an icon, a towering, Olympian figure as anchor at "CBS Evening News." He was Mount Everest. There was nobody even close to him.

About February of 1980, Rather finally decided. After a tremendous amount of soul-searching and indecision, and two or three times when he almost said he was coming to ABC, CBS finally asked Walter to name a time when he would leave. They gave Dan the date certain. Even then he was ambivalent, but he agreed to stay at CBS.

I pursued Tom Brokaw, with not quite the same ardor as I had Rather, but very, very hard. After talking to Tom several times, NBC made him the sole anchor. Roger Mudd was shunted off to the side. He didn't stay very long.

❑ ❑ ❑

The departure of Walter Cronkite helped "World News Tonight's" ratings for a brief period, but Dan Rather quickly put CBS back on top. In 1982, "World News Tonight" began to falter. Frank Reynolds's illness was now obvious, but we still didn't know he was suffering from terminal lung cancer. Frank hid his condition from everyone.

For about six months we continued with a format designed for three particular people. As Frank's absences became more frequent, Roone was forced to make do with a variety of substitutes. One was David Brinkley, who had joined us in 1981.

OTHER RECOLLECTIONS:
Fred Pierce

Roone came to me and said he wanted to hire David Brinkley. "He is not happy at NBC. They are treating him like old linen. He's no longer appreciated, he feels he has some good years ahead of him, and I would like to use him in a new format on Sunday mornings."

I went to Elton and Leonard and chatted about it. There were questions about why we didn't get younger people, and wasn't Brinkley over the hill?

I said, "Roone and I think it will pay off. He will give us a classier image."

❑ ❑ ❑

Roone had not only come up with a new format for a Sunday morning show, he had already sold it to our affiliates. Although I was a little reluctant to bring in an elder statesman like Brinkley to join the young team Roone was building, Elton and I decided to back Roone's instincts. If he was to be responsible for making News competitive, we had to support him. And, at worst, a gentleman like David Brinkley could do us no harm.

OTHER RECOLLECTIONS:
Roone Arledge

The show was ready to go, but we were still looking for a host. I wanted George Will, but he didn't want to work Sundays. He felt going to church was more important. He had worked for us, on and off, but he didn't want to work regularly.

I'd heard that David Brinkley was unhappy because Bill Small, head of NBC News, had taken his producer away without asking, then put him on a magazine show that he hated and was not suited for.

Dick Wald, a former president of NBC News who was then working at ABC, knew David. I asked Dick to approach David and find out if he was actually unhappy. He said he was, and David is a very definite kind of person. We offered him the Sunday program, and he leaped at it. It was just what he wanted to do.

When we announced signing him, George Will suddenly had a different perspective. "This Week with David Brinkley" is different from just "a Sunday program." George agreed to be on every week, and we also added Sam Donaldson to the program.

Now it was a thing that people could feel and smell and touch. Sales zoomed up; there was great excitement and interest. When you can put a David Brinkley into a format designed to change the way Sunday programs were regarded, it gives it instant credibility and stature. So we were very fortunate.

During the summer Frank Reynolds was dying, "World News Tonight" languished. Every week the ratings were lower and lower. We sank back to a very distant third place.

There was a short period when David had agreed to fill in for Frank. Then he was scheduled for vacation; he had rented a house in the Bahamas. We were preparing to do extended coverage of some kind of summit in London, so I couldn't bring Peter back. I needed him over there for the story.

I called David on a Friday; I was going to be away the next week, and he was supposed to leave at the end of that week. I called to thank him for everything and to tell him to have a good vacation.

He said, "I'm not going on vacation."

I said, "What do you mean?"

He said, "I signed on to be a team member. You guys are in trouble, and I can see that, and as far as I'm concerned, any time you want me I'm here."

This is a guy who has been one of America's leading television news personalities for decades. Compare his attitude to the egos of some people I could name, who would say, "I'm not going to be on something where the ratings are going down, this isn't my show, I insist on having all my own writers, I will only do this or that."

And David just volunteered. Nobody asked him.

I insisted on paying for the house in the Bahamas he would not get to use, but he would not even let me do that. That's what kind of a gentleman David Brinkley is. And an example like that is contagious, as he full well knew.

❑ ❑ ❑

In 1983 Frank Reynolds lost his long battle with lung cancer. Out of respect for his many contributions to ABC and to the nation, we televised his funeral. Max Robinson, who had been told he was to be seated next to Nancy Reagan during the eulogy, refused to attend the event. He left ABC shortly afterward, and for a time worked at WMAQ, the NBC station in Chicago. In 1985 he was hospitalized for alcoholism and depression. He died in December 1988 from complications arising from AIDS. Max was forty-nine years old, and his untimely death was a loss to broadcasting.

With Frank Reynolds's death and Max Robinson's departure in 1983, Peter Jennings became sole anchor of "World News Tonight." Roone moved the point of origin to New York and brought in a new producer to refocus the program. While superficially resembling a conventional, single-anchor broadcast, "World News Tonight with Peter Jennings" retained its global viewpoint. Peter crisscrossed the world to cover major stories. Wherever he was became the anchor point and focus of the broadcast, an innovation NBC and CBS eventually copied.

By 1984 ABC News became more than competitive; it was well on its way to becoming the world's leading news organization. Before the end of the decade, ABC would emerge as the dominant network in news, and more Americans would get their news from us than from any other medium.

21

Media Empire

❑

Through all the years we battled to build ABC into competitiveness with CBS and NBC, the company slowly but steadily diversified. Not all of our acquisitions proved fruitful, but each was bought with some very clear purpose in mind.

When we acquired ABC, it had four and a half radio stations, the half being WLS, Chicago. A man named Butler owned the other half. That is, his station used the frequency twelve hours a day, while WLS used it the other twelve. Butler also published three of the country's oldest farm magazines, *Wallaces Farmer, Prairie Farmer*, and *Wisconsin Agriculturist*.

When Butler died, his will provided that all these properties would go to his employees, but they couldn't sell them for ten years. After that, if they chose to sell, they had to sell everything together. We were the logical ones to buy, so when the ten years expired, we bought the company for around $4 million. That's how we got into publishing.

I made the deal only because the radio frequency was a clear channel—nothing else on it in the whole country—which reached most of the continental United States. Butler's radio station was unprofitable, but I soon learned the publishing was a cash cow. We got checks in every quarter. I said to myself, "This is a good business. I like this."

Not until the early 1970s, however, when Elton Rule began to work his magic, did we begin to expand our publishing holdings. In 1974 we acquired *Modern Photography* and *High Fidelity*, monthlies that also put out several annual and quarterly special-interest publications such as *Photo Equipment Buying Guide* and *Stereo Quarterly*.

The following year we bought the Wallace-Homestead company, which produced books on antiques and collectibles.

We also acquired Word, Inc., a Texas-based publisher of religious and inspirational books and the country's largest religious music producer. Over the years, Word's author list has included athletes Kyle Rote, Jr., and Roger Staubach, and such national figures as Ruth Carter Stapleton, Eldridge Cleaver, Senator Mark Hatfield, and the Reverend Robert Schuler.

In 1977, Word signed the Reverend Dr. Billy Graham. Despite the fact that I had to cancel his network program in 1954, Billy and I had remained good friends. In 1976, when the National Conference of Christians and Jews saw fit to give me their Humanitarian Award, Billy made the presentation. (Though dying of cancer, another old friend, John Wayne, insisted on coming to the ceremony.)

OTHER RECOLLECTIONS:
Billy Graham

I first met Leonard at Paramount Studios in 1950 when Frank Freeman had a luncheon to interest me in going into motion pictures as an actor. Cecil B. De Mille and his son-in-law, Anthony Quinn, and a number of other interesting people, including Leonard, were at the luncheon.

Shortly after Leonard bought ABC, he asked me to go on television every Sunday night at 8. I did that for two years, either having a little religious skit or interviewing important leaders like senators and congressmen. I believe we were the first religious program on national television. I still have all the old Kinescopes, and they are interesting to watch.

A few years later, Leonard put our Crusades on live television, beginning in New York from Madison Square Garden, Yankee Stadium, and Times Square.

Leonard is one of the great men of American communications in the twentieth century. His years at Paramount, his development of ABC, and the high moral standards of his personal life are deeply appreciated by millions of people. I have the highest admiration for him.

Because of my friendship and loyalty to Leonard, I changed publishers and began to publish my books through ABC Publishing.

❑ ❑ ❑

Dr. Graham's first book for Word was *How to Be Born Again*. Its first printing was 800,000 copies, at that time a record initial press run for a hardcover book. After that he gave us one or two books a year, all extremely successful, with sales generally between 600,000 and 700,000 copies each. In the book business, those are astronomical numbers. Since Word was losing money when we bought it, Billy Graham's books were tremendously helpful in making the company profitable.

Over the last few years, the media have been full of reports of such fallen-angel televangelists as Jim Bakker, Jimmy Swaggart, and Oral Roberts. Dr. Graham, in his personal and professional life, is a shining example of what a televangelist ought to be. He could quite legitimately keep all his book royalties, but despite the huge sums generated by them, he takes only a minimum salary.

I don't know the exact figure, but his personal income is less than he could make teaching college almost anywhere in the country. The rest of his book earnings go to support the cause he serves. Billy Graham could be a very wealthy man, but he's chosen otherwise, and I admire him for it.

In 1976, we bought *Los Angeles* magazine, an upscale city mag that became the model for other such publications around the country. We hired its publisher, Seth Baker, to reorganize our diverse publishing holdings into a single division.

Seth brought coherence and direction to our publishing division, which he continued to expand. In the early 1980s American farmers went through tough times. This was reflected in the sale of advertising at our farm publications, which showed their first losses since ABC owned them. Except for this brief period, publishing earnings continued to grow.

In June 1977 Seth added Hitchcock Publishing, a Wheaton, Illinois, publisher of trade magazines such as *Industrial Fishing* and *Office Products*. In January 1979, we bought the R. L. White Co., a Louisville, Kentucky, organization which provides multiple-listing directories to realtors and publishes *Homes* magazine, with upward of 4.5 million monthly readers. White also provides computer data-base services to the real estate industry.

Our biggest acquisition was Chilton, a Radnor, Pennsylvania, publisher of more than twenty specialty magazines. Chilton is the country's largest publisher of automotive do-it-yourself books. And thanks to Seth's hard bargaining, we bought it for a fraction of its potential value. Chilton has since become one of our most profitable publishing operations.

One of Seth's major contributions was in cost control. He created an extremely strenuous budgeting process, where all previous assumptions were challenged. This is sometimes called "zero-based" budgeting, and it allowed management to scrutinize every cost projection. This only works, however, if the person doing the scrutinizing is both tough and fair. That describes Seth Baker perfectly.

By 1981, Seth found himself thinking more and more about returning to California. He resigned in October, moved to Beverly Hills, and started a chain of unique, upscale weekly newspapers serving the region's toniest communities.

Seth's successor was Bob Burton, who came to ABC in 1980 as VP in charge of the Special Interest Publishing Group.

Over the next few years the division grew at a very good pace, and by 1984 we earned more than $30 million a year in publishing.

This became increasingly important to ABC, because by the early 1980s it was apparent that television would not continue the rate of growth it had over the preceding ten or fifteen years. Publishing was another way of increasing our base, and it has a terrific growth potential.

Just as important, publishing offers a relatively constant cash flow. Unlike broadcasting, revenues don't seesaw from quarter to quarter. Publishing, from an investor's viewpoint, requires very little capital. By 1984, ABC published more than 100 magazine and book titles a month, as well as about twenty-five record titles a year. Our publications, each quite specialized, collectively reached over 20 million readers.

To get Walt Disney into television in 1954, we had taken a 35 percent interest in Disneyland, which we sold back for a handsome profit in 1962. Long before we decided to sell, however, we had begun to add other amusement attractions.

Through Florida State Theatres, our subsidiary, we owned a partial interest in Weeki Wachee Spring, near St. Petersburg, one of the world's unique scenic attractions. There, sixteen feet beneath the surface of a natural canyon filled by 168 million gallons of crystal-clear water, audiences seated in a comfortable auditorium enjoy spectacular underwater ballets. This environment was also ideally suited for production of underwater scenes for motion pictures and television, and these activities also generated some income over the years.

In 1959, we bought out our partners. Weeki Wachee became our wholly owned and operated subsidiary.

In October 1962, we bought the 3,900-acre Silver Springs entertainment park near Ocala, Florida. Until Disney World was constructed in the 1980s, it was the largest scenic attraction on the east coast. The main attraction of Silver Springs is a unique environment where seagoing marine life mix with freshwater species. Visitors can observe this phenomenon through a fleet of glass-bottomed boats.

A third amusement park, ABC Marine World, opened in Redwood City, California, just south of San Francisco, in July 1968. In its million-gallon tank, trained killer whales, sea lions, and dolphins performed for delighted crowds. The sixty-acre park included many other features, designed to both educate and entertain visitors.

One of Marine World's biggest fans was Michael Eisner, who produced an ABC television special celebrating the park's opening. This was Mike's very first production.

Over the long haul, however, these theme parks were never as profitable as we had hoped. By 1984 we had sold them all.

One ill-fated venture, and this must be on my own head, was the ABC Entertainment Center in Los Angeles. In 1968, ABC bought a large property in Century City, a huge complex of office buildings, shops, and hotels developed on what had formerly been Twentieth Century Fox's back lot. Our complex included two movie theaters, office buildings, a retail shopping and restaurant complex, and what would become the Shubert Theatre, a house suitable for Broadway-style plays.

The major flaw was that Century City was isolated from the surrounding communities, and it took many years before the planned office buildings were erected and leased to tenants. In the meantime, few retailers could afford to pay the rents we had to charge. Our theaters played to empty seats. And all the while, of course, we had to make our mortgage payments. When we finally sold our interest in the ABC Entertainment Center in 1984, even the considerable appreciation of the real estate didn't quite make up our losses over the fifteen years we had owned it.

The one silver lining in this storm cloud was that it led ABC into a close and ultimately profitable relationship with the Shubert Organization. The executors of the famed Broadway impresario are Bernie Jacobs and Jerry Schoenfeld. They are partners and friends, so close they're all but joined at the hip, so to speak. They often seem to think and talk alike.

OTHER RECOLLECTIONS:
Bernie Jacobs and Jerry Schoenfeld

JACOBS: When the theater first opened, it was a disaster. We weren't prepared for Los Angeles and Los Angeles wasn't prepared for a full-scale Broadway house. They'd been used to road companies, local productions. The idea of touring productions, New York–style, was something new.

SCHOENFELD: Our association with the lease established a very cordial relationship with Leonard and Elton. One day Bernie gets a phone call. They were taking down the marquee of the Shubert Theater in Los Angeles. *A Chorus Line* was playing, and suddenly here's a crew taking down the marquee. Bernie tried to call Elton.

JACOBS: We knew he was in Puerto Rico because they had meetings there for their affiliates.

SCHOENFELD: The guy Bernie spoke to was Elton's man, and you really couldn't talk to him. He turned us off like that.

JACOBS: He wouldn't tell us where Elton was. "We're doing what we want to do and you can—"

SCHOENFELD: "—drop dead."

JACOBS: It took so much time to find Elton. We had to call every major hotel in San Juan.

SCHOENFELD: We set up an emergency meeting, and the next day we were in Leonard's office. We said, "How can we function in a theater without a marquee? Just because some architect has a concept is no reason to do this. You're taking away the basic identification of the theater. And we rented a theater with a marquee."

Leonard immediately took care of it. Elton didn't, of course, support the removal of the marquee either. It was hardly an act compatible with an interest in theater. But it was one of those corporate decisions that somehow never filtered its way to the top.

When we got involved in production of *Last Licks, Devour the Snow*, and *Zoot Suit*, we invited ABC to invest with us in those plays, and they said yes. The investment was relatively nominal, maybe $75,000 per show between us. To make a long story short, all three shows were failures.

At that point we became interested in coproducing a play called *Children of a Lesser God*. We asked ABC if they wished to get involved. It was playing in California, and we said, "You have a perfect opportunity to see it and make a judgment about going in." After a long time with no response we called a second time. "We're going ahead with the show. Are you going in or are you not going in?" They didn't get back to us. We called a third time. Finally they called to pass.

Of course *Children of a Lesser God* was a major hit, and they would have made up many, many times what they lost on these three earlier shows.

JACOBS: After that they went in with us on a couple of winners.

SCHOENFELD: We took Leonard to the opening of *Ain't Misbehavin'*, and he was delighted. It was a big winner. After that, Bernie and I were asked to come over and meet with Leonard, Elton, Herb Granath, Fred Pierce, and Tony Thomopoulos. They wished to get involved on an ongoing basis.

JACOBS: I said to them, "If you're going to cherry-pick among the projects we offer you, invariably you'll pick the wrong ones, and you'll be unhappy. We believe if you take our package, in the long run, it will turn out positive."

Around this time, 1982, we started negotiating to produce *Cats* and *Dreamgirls. Cats* was such a successful venture, it made over $100 million in the United States, and it's still coming in, so that kind of whetted ABC's appetite for further investments.

We told them they would be the same kind of a partner as we would be, their money would buy the same as our money. In essence, we would ground-floor them and if there was a television aspect to the project later on—

SCHOENFELD:—we'd endeavor to give them first review—

JACOBS:—and we would be a silent partner in the television

SCHOENFELD:—if they wanted us—

JACOBS:—and they would be a silent partner in the theater, recognizing their expertise in television and our expertise in theater.

SCHOENFELD: They were a one-third partner in *Amadeus*. And of course *Amadeus* was a major, major hit and then came *Dreamgirls*, which was a major hit, and *Cats*, which was a bonanza, a once-in-a-lifetime. They have been with us since.

❑ ❑ ❑

Aside from my lifelong, personal interest in the legitimate theater and beyond the investment possibilities, our motivation for joining ABC and the Shubert Organization had a basis in yet another dimension of ABC's long-range strategy. As it turned out, we got a very nice return on our investments, but our interest in Broadway shows was primarily a way to ensure we would have television rights to them.

From a production standpoint, we could not simply film or tape a Broadway performance. Such shows are staged especially for live theaters. We would have to create performances designed for the presence of cameras.

We thought it unlikely that such shows would find the sort of mass audience necessary to support prime-time network broadcasts, although there have been a few. Instead, we supposed that eventually they might be used on cable. When we began doing business with the Shubert Organization, the time when a cable presentation of a Broadway show might be financially viable was far in the future. It's closer now, but the time is still not yet right. In the next few years, however, I believe that there will be enough American homes wired for pay-per-view cable to make such shows possible.

Cable originated in the early 1950s, out of the need to bring TV signals to places broadcasts can't reach. Today about 80 percent of all American TV homes are accessible to cable. Most of the "unwired" areas in United States are heavily populated. Among them are three boroughs of New York—Brooklyn, the Bronx, and Queens—Washington, D.C., and Cleveland. Most communities without access to cable are those where average household income is in the lower third of the national average. In other areas, local politics have impeded installation of cable systems. That's especially true in New York City.

In the early days, I never thought the public would be willing to pay for what they were getting free on the commercial networks, such as football and baseball. By the late 1970s I came to understand that I was wrong about that. Eventually, many of the most desirable movies and sports events will be on cable. Since the programmers will have to pay as much or more than the commercial networks, the public will have to pay, whether by the event or by the month.

In 1979, at the urging of Herb Granath, who had succeeded Marty Pompadur as Elton's assistant, we started ABC Video Enterprises. This division is devoted to providing programming for new technologies such as video cassette and video disc, and to cable networks, including pay-per-view channels, "superstations," and other program originators who distribute product through cable and satellite broadcast systems. Herb became president of the video organization.

OTHER RECOLLECTIONS:
Herb Granath

We recognized that new distribution systems would, in time, erode network audiences. There was a clear and present danger from cable, video cassette, multiple-channel cable systems, low-power TV, direct broadcast satellites, and so forth.

By 1977, all of these things existed in some form, either completed or in development. From time to time, Leonard, Elton, Fred Pierce, and I would meet to discuss what this would mean to ABC.

This was just about the time ABC emerged as the leader in prime time, and was gaining in daytime and in other areas. There was quite a lot at stake. We thought it would be wise to look into how we might participate in the new arena.

Our thinking was very much like Procter & Gamble's approach to merchandising. If they have a brand of soap or something that is likely going to have a competitor, they always opt that the competitor be their own brand, instead of somebody else's—even if they have to create a new brand.

After many discussions, we decided against getting into the hardware side. That wasn't our area of expertise, while both RCA and CBS had experience as electronics manufacturers.

Since broadcast network ownership of cable systems was legally precluded by the FCC, that left only software—programming—an area where ABC has considerable experience, expertise, and clout.

Leonard was not merely receptive to the new technologies. He pushed for them. He was always asking, "What should we be doing?"

At the time, our affiliates were paranoid about the emergence of cable systems as competitors. All three networks and affiliates fought hard in Washington to keep the cable industry from getting what they thought were unfair advantages. So for us to get into a competitive business presented potential problems with affiliates.

When Leonard and Elton and Fred and I brainstormed, we asked ourselves, "As cable develops, what will it be? Several new networks to compete with the existing broadcast networks?"

We saw an opportunity to create cable networks that would be very specifically targeted to advertising groups. We called this "narrowcasting," and started looking for areas that could supplement programming to existing broadcast audiences. Specifically, we looked at audiences which were underserved by broadcasting.

❑ ❑ ❑

Through the early 1980s, cable developed several true narrowcasting services, such as CNN, Weather Channel, MTV, Nickelodeon, Arts & Entertainment, and ESPN. Each locked in a very specific target audience.

Simultaneously, there developed more broadly based entertainment networks such as USA. These were run somewhat like large independent stations, with children's programming at times when children watch, women's programming from midmorning through late afternoon, and, in prime time, general entertainment, off-network or self-produced programs, and a sprinkling of sports and other shows with broad appeal.

I knew our affiliates would object to ABC getting into cable. Fred Pierce brought this up several times in our planning sessions, and properly so. He was responsible for the network. But I said, "They may object, but if *we* don't go into cable, somebody else will. So, if it is going to happen, why shouldn't we do it?" I insisted we go into cable.

ABC entered narrowcasting with Alpha Repertory Television Service, or ARTS. It was aimed at the culturally deprived viewer. ARTS programming was, in a curious way, designed to satisfy the lofty vision once espoused by Newton Minow. Financially impractical for *broad*casting, we thought it might work in *narrow*casting.

In its first iteration, ARTS was a collection of cultural programs, including ballet, opera, and dance performances, as well as other programs appealing to the well-educated. That initial concept might be compared to the fare offered by PBS in the 1960s and 1970s. PBS, increasingly funded by grants from large corporations and by viewer subscription, has evolved to become more like the other broadcast networks. It offers less highbrow culture and more shows with popular appeal.

In 1981, ABC launched ARTS. It soon became an element in our partnership with the Hearst Corporation. It was advertiser-supported, and through affiliation with Warner Amex Satellite Entertainment Company, we immediately got satellite distribution to 700 cable systems reaching about 3.5 million people. Within one year that grew to 1,725 cable systems and an audience of 8 million.

Early in 1984, ARTS merged with the Entertainment Channel, an RCA project. RCA had a deal with the BBC for a cable network. It didn't do very well, and so they approached us about merging. Its one attractive asset was a ten-year contract to show BBC programs. We made a deal, and RCA wound up with one third of what we renamed the Arts & Entertainment Network.

A very important element in our cable ventures has been the ongoing involvement of the Hearst Corporation. When William Randolph Hearst died, his will named Dick Berlin as trustee of his estate. I was quite friendly with Dick, a client of my friend Ed Weisl.

Back in the 1960s, I was in Washington almost every week, trying to get drop-ins. One day, after leaving the FCC and getting on the shuttle to New York, I sat down next to Dick. I said, "Dick, you have a newspaper in Pittsburgh. I think you can buy into a television station there, WTAE. A lawyer I know owns a half-interest in it. It's losing money, and I think you can buy it for next to nothing. Interested?"

He said, "I sure am!"

I said, "Go after it; you'll get it."

He got it for about $1 million. Later they bought the other half for around $40 million.

At the time I told Dick about WTAE, I added one condition: that he affiliate with ABC and give us 100 percent clearances for our network programs. He agreed without hesitation.

After he got WTAE, Dick Berlin became very generous with contributing time and money to cerebral palsy. He realized I'd done him a real favor. And that support has continued to this day. Hearst established a chair at Harvard Medical School in the name of Isabelle, myself, and Jack and Ethel Hausman. They give at least $500,000 a year to cerebral palsy and often far more.

John Miller succeeded Dick Berlin; Frank Bennack succeeded Miller. I got to be very friendly with Frank.

OTHER RECOLLECTIONS:
Frank Bennack

Leonard has been a very good friend to me. I had come from restricted regional responsibilities in San Antonio as a newspaper publisher and editor. He was very helpful as I established myself in New York.

When I became CEO in 1979, the Hearst corporation had three stations, one affiliation with each of the networks. By 1986 we had six stations in all, of which five were affiliated with ABC, representing ABC's largest affiliate group. I believe no other network has a greater concentration of affiliation with a company than ABC has with us. Aside from their O&O's, we are its largest outlet.

Leonard's fine hand was involved almost from the beginning in Hearst broadcasting activities. He often spoke to me about ABC's publishing activities. We also talked a lot about cable, exploring areas where we could do something together.

In the early 1980s, we began to talk about prospects arising from our expertise in women's magazines. He envisioned that we could use our expertise and talent in women's programming to do something together in cable. I agreed almost immediately that we should consider launching a network.

We formed Hearst/ABC Video Services. We put money in to bring us to parity with ABC's investment in the ARTS part of it, and we launched a new network.

Originally our venture was called Daytime. It was largely targeted at the same subjects and type of material that appear in the leading women's magazines we own. *Good Housekeeping* had a show. Helen Gurley Brown had a show related to *Cosmo* matters. We explored a variety of other things.

As invariably happens, as we broadened both the broadcast day and the audience, the programming varied from the original, more literal attempt to re-create in a new medium (cable) something that was successful in another medium (magazines).

The cable ventures all lost money for their first few years. Leonard and I were individually getting advice that was in the nature of, "How long are you going to continue at this price?" But there was never a day that the life of those services was really at risk. We would occasionally examine the issue, I with my associates and he with his, but we had underlying faith in the concept.

Once we got the cable networks repackaged it was pretty clear that this was going to work. Among the three television networks and among all those who followed, Leonard was clearly the pioneer in seeing what cable networking was going to bring.

❑ ❑ ❑

As cable penetration grew, so did our investment. We bought satellite transponders, which were expensive and in short supply, to ensure room for future growth, and hired staff. The joint venture with Hearst was repackaged several times, even as our audiences continued to grow. We merged Daytime with a channel started by Viacom, the Cable Health Network, and called the new offering Lifetime. While our original concept was to create a women's network, by the mid-1980s we began to get substantial male viewership.

In the spring of 1982, ABC Video Enterprises launched another joint venture, this time with Group W Satellite Communications, a Westinghouse unit, as partner. Satellite News Channels (SNC) was designed as a pair of twenty-four-hour, all-news cable services. Only one of them even got off the ground.

In this area we went head-to-head with Ted Turner's Cable News Network, and with overnight news programming briefly established by CBS and NBC. Suddenly there was a news glut, especially late at night. Since CNN seemed so firmly established, it was soon apparent we would not be able to compete effectively for advertising revenue. In 1984 we sold SNC to Ted Turner for $25 million. He immediately shut it down.

Sometime after we sold the networks, Herb Granath ran into Turner at a party. While we competed against CNN, Turner, who had been getting 25 cents a month per subscriber from cable operators (while we asked nothing for SNC), had been forced to drop those fees to meet our competition. Turner told Herb that if he had had to compete with us for six months longer, "I would have been tapped out."

Turner was crowing about bluffing us out. Herb replied, "Okay, but we were going to fold SNC anyway, and then you came along and gave us $25 million so *you* could fold it."

Another flop was TeleFirst, a consumer-supported, entertainment recording service which we tried out in Chicago, in 1984. The idea was to use our Chicago station, WLS-TV, to broadcast first-run feature films in scrambled form to subscribers between 2 A.M. and 5:30 A.M., a time when the station was normally off the air. The movies were recorded by subscribers' VCRs; the scrambled cassette had to be played back through a TeleFirst decoder for viewing.

It was an unusual concept. It didn't work. Due to licensing restrictions on hit movies, the tapes automatically rescrambled a month later. If viewers hadn't watched them by then, it was too late. Even worse, very few subscribers knew how to set their own VCRs for delayed recording.

At about the same time, hundreds of video rental stores were opening, and rental prices for recent movies plunged. But we had to offset the cost of decoders and rights to hit movies. Our monthly fees were high. Subscribers shunned TeleFirst—it seemed too expensive for what they were getting.

TeleFirst was abandoned after a six-month test period. There was much clucking and finger pointing in the trade press, and for several years ABC was stuck with thousands of decoders. Ultimately we sold them to a hotel chain and recovered most of our hardware investment.

Unquestionably, ABC's greatest success in cable has been our involvement with ESPN. This round-the-clock sports cable network was started by Stu Evey, an executive of Getty Oil. His daughter, Susan, was the 1971 poster child for the Los Angeles UCP chapter, and so we got to know each other.

OTHER RECOLLECTIONS:
Stu Evey

I was the VP in charge of a unit within Getty called "diversified operations." One day in 1978 I got a call from an insurance executive I'd worked with on real estate investments. One of his neighbors, Bill Rasmussen, had a fascinating idea. We were introduced on the phone.

A satellite for cable distribution had been launched by RCA in 1976. Bill's thought was that one day there would be a lot of TV coming off satellites. So he got an option on one of that satellite's thirty-two channel transponders. These were not in demand. The only others that had them were HBO and a few emerging cable superstations.

Rasmussen had a certain period of time to exercise his option on a transponder. He had talked to the NCAA, and Walter Byers, the executive director, had expressed some interest in selling programming rights for a sports channel. But Rasmussen had no money. That is why he came to me.

I didn't know anything about cable. I got my staff together, and it was as foreign to us as anything could possibly be. However, I was a sports enthusiast. I had a business relationship with Art Keyler at Time-Life. And within the Time organization was HBO. I called Keyler and asked if he could introduce me by phone to the head of HBO. I wanted to find out what cable meant.

I had a long discussion with this fellow, Richard Munro, who went on to become head of Time, Inc. I said the concept would be similar to Time-Life's with movies, but we would offer sports. He said, "I can see all kinds of problems in that." He raised some very good issues. Finally he said, "I don't think I'd ever touch that."

So I did some more research. Getty was cash-rich then, and we were considering various alternative types of business which we could diversify into—e.g., insurance, financial, and communications. So this kind of fit the overall corporate criteria.

I made a presentation to the board of directors, a projection on the emerging cable business, and Getty funded the start-up of the Entertainment and Sports Programming Network, or ESPN.

We started ESPN in Bristol, Connecticut, in 1979. I was authorized to expend $10 million. It wasn't two months before we needed more money. I was asking Getty for more money all the time.

At that time only 20 percent of all TV households could even get cable, and of those, few were satellite-fed because cable operators hadn't set up the earth stations. We offered ESPN free to cable operators—but they had to have a satellite receiver to get it.

I wanted ESPN to become what the industry calls the "major lift" network. We became the vehicle that got the operator in the front door. They offered potential customers ESPN and CNN free so that they then had an opportunity to sell pay movie channels like HBO and Cinemax. That's where the profit is—pay channels.

Things started happening. Major companies came in and bought out the little guys. The majors saw the future and made capital expenditures. Cable became very volatile. It exploded. Our revenues increased, but expenditures increased faster than revenues.

Then personalities at Getty and economic conditions changed. Priorities changed. I was convinced by then that ESPN was potentially big. My only concern was how long Getty would keep giving me money.

I came up with a beautiful analogy that always worked. I would say, "Gentlemen, I would like to equate ESPN with an oil well. Seismic indicated there was a reservoir, and we determined that was true. Experience has shown that the reservoir is there and is a hell of a lot bigger than we originally thought. Unfortunately, it is also deeper than we thought. So I need more pipe."

The Getty board understood that, and so when I came in for a presentation, they always asked, "How much pipe?"

The most important rights were to the United States Football League. As bidding developed, we were at the limit of what we could spend. We knew that the USFL negotiators wanted us to get it. We had the facilities, the audience, and the staff, and Getty was behind us, so they knew we would last. It just came down to the deal. And I couldn't go any higher.

When our guys said we were going to need $2 million more or we would lose the USFL, I went out on a limb and committed for an extra million. Then I called a guy at Anheuser-Busch's ad agency, D'Arcy McManus. I got another million from Anheuser-Busch. They gave us the million, and Getty's board backed me. We got USFL for $11 million. It became a major drawing card for ESPN.

❑ ❑ ❑

ABC Sports also bought some of the USFL games. By demonstrating that ESPN could play in the same arena with ABC, ESPN acquired valuable prestige with cable operators as well as with audiences. It had come a long way from its opening show, a thirty-minute highlight tape of the slow-pitch softball World Series available to 1.4 million viewers.

By 1981, ESPN was costing Getty about $11 or $12 million a month in salaries, overhead, and capital expenditures. At the same time, the value of its equipment, especially the satellite transponders it had snapped up when they were going begging, had appreciated considerably. But the mood at Getty was changing, and Evey began to worry that at some point the oil company would decide ESPN was a dry hole.

OTHER RECOLLECTIONS:
Stu Evey

I had made the commitment to Getty that I wouldn't get them in so deep that they couldn't get out. And now I am not sure I can get them out.

I was getting to a credibility point within Getty. I decided it would be advantageous to us—and to me, internally—to affiliate with a major network. I wanted the prestige, and I wanted access to more programming.

I let it be known outside the company that we might be interested in affiliating with a major network. I waited to see who swam up. One was Gene Jankowski, then head of CBS. Ted Turner got the word. He wanted to get involved. I had them boiling out there.

Soon both CBS and ABC expressed an interest. There are tremendous egos involved. So I played them. I had ABC and CBS whipsawing one another. I had some negotiations with Herb Granath. Then Fred Pierce wanted to close the deal. Our negotiations with CBS were worrying ABC.

❑ ❑ ❑

I had been interested in getting a piece of ESPN for quite some time. And so, whenever I ran into Stu Evey at cerebral palsy meetings, I would always find a moment to take him aside and say, "Why don't you sell us a piece of it?"

At first he said they had no interest in selling. But after a time he said, "Well, maybe we might be interested." The next thing I knew, he had approached Herb Granath.

I told Fred Pierce, then ABC's executive VP, "You and Herb go out and work out a deal for as big a piece as you can get. One thing you must get is a commitment that, if they ever sell ESPN, we have either an option on the rest or at least the right of first refusal."

OTHER RECOLLECTIONS:
Fred Pierce

Herb, myself, and Mike Mallardi, our chief financial officer, started to negotiate a deal. Initially we bought 10 percent of the company at $20 million. We got an option for another 39 percent at a preset price, $2.2 million per point.

Stu Evey was a tough, unique individual, but the deal closed. And as we got going, we began to see the chemistry working between ABC Sports and ESPN. We had a lot of programming material that they could use. It was a perfect synergy.

❑ ❑ ❑

By taking 10 percent of ESPN for $20 million, Evey established a market value of $200 million for the whole network.

Among the details of our agreement was a system by which ABC Sports categorized its various rights and shared portions with ESPN for a very nominal price, and in some cases free. For example, "Wide World of Sports" often shot several times what it could use. The outtakes were made available to ESPN.

By early 1984 Stu Evey's internal situation at Getty forced him to consider selling the rest of ESPN.

OTHER RECOLLECTIONS:
Stu Evey

I heard something rumbling within Getty. I wasn't sure, but it looked like we were going to be bought out.

I was ABC's guest at the Winter Olympics in Sarajevo, and I spoke to Fred Pierce. I said, "Fred, do you have any interest in buying all of ESPN?"

He said, "What kind of deal do you think we could get?"

I said, "I am absolutely certain that I can get Getty to accept $175 million."

That was under the $200 million value that had been set earlier, and in the meantime we were in a lot more houses, which would increase the value. And I knew that had I sold it for $175 million at that time, I would have been a hero at Getty. But I also knew that it would take still more investment before this thing could become a real cash cow.

But there was no more pipe for ESPN at Getty. Our net losses up to then were $67 million.

Fred wanted to talk about it on a basis of projections of profitability. For example, if we hit this target, they'd pay so much, and if we did better they could go more. I said we didn't have time, and didn't want to get involved with that. So the bottom line was no.

❑ ❑ ❑

Stu, of course, was not at liberty to say that his company was on the block. Unfortunately, that didn't occur to Fred.

Before leaving Stu Evey, I should mention that beyond his contributions to ESPN, he earned another footnote in history. In the early 1980s, Stu played golf with Philippines dictator Ferdinand Marcos. Marcos had bodyguards all over the course, and Stu was astonished to see that on virtually every hole, one moved the dictator's ball to a more advantageous lie. After Marcos tried to steal the 1986 Philippines elections, Stu called columnist Joe Morgenstern at the Los Angeles *Herald* and told him about

Marcos's cheating. The story got extraordinary play on wire services and networks. For some reason, the revelation that Marcos was a golf cheat did almost as much to undermine his credibility in this country as the later discovery of his financial philandering.

In 1984, Texaco bought Getty. It borrowed a huge sum to make this purchase. As soon as the deal went through, it started looking for parts of Getty to sell off and help reduce its debt. Anything not closely connected to the oil business went to the top of the list.

I got a call from John McKinley, the head of Texaco, a fellow I knew quite well. He said, "Leonard, you have this option on ESPN, and I'd like to talk to you about it."

When I went to see McKinley, ESPN was losing millions each year. But it was clear to many in broadcasting that it would ultimately make money. And so, as I learned, there were several companies interested in buying it.

OTHER RECOLLECTIONS:
Fred Pierce

Leonard and I went up to see McKinley and one of his key lieutenants. It was tough because Turner was bidding against us, as was NBC and several other companies. We held an option to buy at least another 34 percent, which wouldn't have given us control. Had, say, NBC bought the other 51 percent, it might have led to a very weird situation.

The bottom line was we bought the rest of ESPN for $188 million and their distribution hardware for $14 million. ESPN was losing $25 million a year then, so it was all on the cuff.

It was the largest acquisition in ABC's history. And the timing was bad. Between 1980 and 1983, when ABC's profitability went up on a very high curve, most of our additional profit was plowed back in to establish daytime and our cable ventures. We lost $20–$25 million on Satellite News Channel. ARTS was still losing. TeleFirst cost us over $15 million. So for several years ABC's earnings were very flat.

So now here comes Fred and says, "Leonard, we are going to buy the rest of ESPN—and by the way, it's losing twenty-five million a year."

To cushion that a bit, I said, "There are two ex–ABC Sports guys, Don Ohlmeyer and John Martin, both very good, now working for Nabisco. And Ross Johnson, head of Nabisco, loves to merchandise sports.

"Nabisco wants to have some of their golfing events on ESPN. And they are very anxious to have a minority interest in ESPN."

My thinking was, here are Ohlmeyer and Martin, two *former* ABC Sports guys, who could serve on the ESPN Board with Bill Grimes, ESPN's CEO, and some other guys from ABC Sports.

And Nabisco would pay us $3 million a point for their 20 percent interest—$60 million.

With Herb Granath, I presented the proposal to Leonard and the board. When they heard the price, there were a few gulps. But most of the board thought it was the greatest thing since iced tea.

❑ ❑ ❑

After some discussion, the board approved the ESPN acquisition in June 1984. Owning ESPN enhanced ABC's capability to bid on major sports packages. We were able to maintain "Monday Night Football" at a profit only because we packaged those games with Thursday and Sunday night games on ESPN. Neither our network nor our affiliates cared to air them, since it conflicted with their local news programming.

Nevertheless, when the announcement of our acquisition was made, there was a flood of criticism, and not only from our broadcast affiliates. Many said they thought we'd been hornswoggled into buying a pink elephant. Others, echoing those who mocked my 1953 declaration that ABC would turn to Hollywood for programming, called me a traitor to broadcasting. And still others said I'd lost my mind to spend that much money on anything.

Howard Cosell, who knows more than a little about sports broadcasting, was not among these critics.

OTHER RECOLLECTIONS:
Howard Cosell

As I think of the people that Leonard's trained, the way he put this company together, I marvel all over again. I was a witness to what this man has created and developed. And yet over the years, they laughed at him.

When he bought ESPN, it was "Goldenson's Folly." Pouring all that money into an empty trap.

Leonard always was a great and understanding showman. He

knew what ESPN would become. ESPN would have been dropped by any other company in those years. It wasn't Goldenson's Folly. It was Goldenson's Vision. Look at them now. Leonard created one of the most profitable divisions of our company with ESPN.

❑ ❑ ❑

By the late 1980s, ESPN was the strongest service on cable, far more profitable than CNN, its closest competitor. It earned upward of $100 million a year. For a time ESPN was even more profitable than any of the three *broadcast* networks.

22

End Game

❑

In the decade of the 1970s, ABC had scrapped and clawed and worked overtime to bring itself first to parity and then to ratings and revenue leadership among the three broadcast television networks.

Fred Pierce, as head of television and then as executive VP of American Broadcasting Companies (and still running television), must get due credit. He had the benefit of a tremendously talented programming team, premier sports and news operations, top-rated O&O stations, and an expanding, high-quality affiliate lineup. But Fred was the man in the hot seat. He fit the pieces together. Under Fred Pierce, ABC's television operation became the world's finest and most successful.

As I predicted at the 1951 FCC hearings, competition from a viable third network spurred the entire industry to greater efforts. ABC achieved leadership by creating programming that appealed to America's young families. This lesson was not lost on the industry. When Grant Tinker replaced Fred Silverman at NBC in mid-1981, he adopted this programming philosophy and trumped our ace.

He had some help from ABC. Although I mentioned my concerns about complacency when we finally became number 1, parts of our organization nevertheless succumbed to some of the temptations of false pride. And so, for a time, we took our success for granted. We fell asleep. We became less willing to take chances with new ideas.

Some of our most creative programming executives, including Marcy Carsey, Tom Werner, and Brandon Tartikoff, became frustrated with the way management treated their ideas. First Carsey and then Werner left ABC. They formed their own production company. Tartikoff went to NBC, where his enormous talent quickly was recognized.

With nothing better to replace them, the sitcoms and other series that had helped to establish our dominance in prime time sometimes remained on our schedule beyond the time they should have been gracefully retired.

Thus ABC's network programming in the early 1980s was most notable for its presentation of long-form shows, including made-for-television movies and the miniseries we called Novels for Television. These were often compelling entertainment. Probably the most important was "The Winds of War," based on Herman Wouk's novel.

Disappointed with the film versions of his earlier works, notably *Marjorie Morningstar* and *Captain Newman, M.D.*, Wouk was extremely suspicious of Hollywood. So when Barry Diller approached him about "The Winds of War," he worried about the kind of commercials that would be used, he worried about the commercial interruptions themselves, and he worried about the presentation of his material. But Diller pursued the rights to his book for almost five years.

Before Diller went to Paramount, he got Fred Pierce excited about the project. Silverman, then head of ABC Entertainment, didn't want to do "Winds of War" at all. Pierce overruled him, and with Diller at Paramount finally made an extraordinary deal with Wouk. Besides a huge fee, there were specific limitations on the kinds of sponsors we could have, the number and length of commercials, how much network promotion the broadcast could include, the show's format, and guarantees that certain scenes from his book would be in the production.

This had never happened before, and I would bet everything I own that it will never happen again.

Fred Pierce's enthusiasm for the project remained undiminished during the nearly five years it took to bring it to network audiences in February 1983.

OTHER RECOLLECTIONS:
Fred Pierce

Herman Wouk was trying to protect the integrity of his material. Herman's vision was, "I want my novel on the air and there's no commercials except at the top and the bottom. Everything in the middle is just story." It was totally unrealistic with the world. But after some discussion, he agreed that commercials for automobiles or gasoline, or financial services, or computers would not detract from his work.

But interrupting a serious dramatic scene or a compelling love scene by going to a spot for a toilet-bowl cleaner, underarm deodorant, or for feminine hygiene products was unacceptable. After talking to our sales department, and getting a sense of the type of products we could sell spots for, I made an agreement with Wouk that prohibited certain kinds of commercials. We kept it a secret.

❑ ❑ ❑

Brandon Stoddard was intimately involved in "Winds of War" from the time we made the deal with Wouk.

OTHER RECOLLECTIONS:
Brandon Stoddard

We decided on Dan Curtis as producer, the luckiest decision we ever made. Everybody knew and trusted Dan. I had done many movies with him. Fred had known him for twenty years.

We had a dinner at Chasen's to celebrate the beginning of "Winds of War." Herman and Sarah Wouk, myself, Dan Curtis, and Gary Nardino, then head of television at Paramount. We talked about casting after dinner. We'd had a little wine, everybody was feeling good, and we were just throwing names out. I said, "Gee, wouldn't it be great if we could get Joanne Woodward for Rhoda and Paul Newman to play Pug."

Curtis says, "That's great," and Nardino says, "What a wonderful idea." Sarah looks up and says, "I don't think Paul Newman's right for Pug." I thought, This is going to be the longest five years anyone will ever have.

It took a couple of years to write the script. Herman had approval rights on casting and writers and so forth. We went through a couple of writers, and for one reason or another Herman didn't approve of them. So what you do in those kinds of situations is you say, "Well, there's only one man in the whole world who can write this, Herman, and that's you."

Herman is quick to remind people that he started as a writer on the "Fred Allen" radio show. And he'd written some screenplays. So he started writing the scripts for "Winds of War." Dan Curtis made what changes he thought necessary to make them more of a screenplay. He was very careful about how he did that, but Dan made a very strong contribution to the writing.

Casting was difficult. We wanted to give the show, through casting, the panache of a theatrical movie, not just another miniseries. So instead of using, say, Karen Valentine and Leslie Nielsen—television names—we went with Ali MacGraw, Robert Mitchum, and Jan-Michael Vincent.

We must have gone through 300 Natalies, the female lead. We tested actresses not just all over the country but all over the world, and chose Ali MacGraw. There was a lot of discussion about whether she should do this or not. Barry was not very much an Ali fan, and I was doubtful about her, but Dan liked Ali for the part.

Robert Mitchum was our first choice for Pug Henry, the male lead. No one's better than him in a uniform saying nothing. And Pug has nothing to say. He just walks around and is confident and makes you feel good.

Mitchum was sort of semiretired, living in Santa Barbara. I told Dan, "The only thing I'm worried about is his age."

Dan said, "He's willing to go to lunch."

"Great, we'll have lunch, take a look at the guy."

Mitchum comes down, and he's his imperious self, and we have lunch at Jimmy's in Beverly Hills. We sit outside so we can get the sun on him. But Mitchum's got these very dark glasses on, and he's not about to take them off.

So I can't see his eyes and I can't see how old this guy is. I'm trying to figure out how to get these damn glasses off. We came up with some trick, like, "Say, what kind of glasses are those, are those prescription?" to get them off, and so I finally got to look at his eyes and see how puffy they were. They seemed okay. The lidded look. So we cast him, and for the most part he really did a good job.

Making "Winds of War" almost killed Dan Curtis physically. It was a brutal show.

We started promoting the show almost three months before it went on the air. We ran seventeen different commercial strategies with about fifty commercials to promote it. It was the biggest promotion and marketing campaign of a television show—maybe of any entertainment show—ever, and since. It worked. We got our audience in.

There was a media frenzy. We owned radio, we were on the cover of every magazine, and everywhere you looked they were talking about "Winds of War." But there was a media backlash, which was painful for several people. I've never seen that before or since, but it definitely occurred.

With all the hype beforehand, it was impossible for anyone to measure up critically. Expectations were raised to such a fever pitch that critics were looking for anything to chomp on, anything to bring it to its knees a little. It destroyed Ali MacGraw. They buried her. She wasn't very good in the role, but there was a sort of "We're going to get you" attitude.

And that is why we haven't heard much from Ali MacGraw afterward. She did some weeks on "Dynasty," where everyone goes just before they become an interior decorator. Which is what Ali's doing now. She's a terrific lady, a marvelous person, really bright, very funny. I don't think acting was necessarily the best thing for her.

Dan Curtis also got whipped. He was very pained by the critical reaction to his work. It wasn't awful, but it was mixed. I think all of us expected better critical reactions. We did get a bunch of Emmy nominations, but few awards.

❑ ❑ ❑

"The Winds of War" got huge ratings and a 53 percent average share of all television viewers on the nights it ran, the third-highest-rated mini-series ever. A month later we aired "The Thorn Birds," produced by David Wolper and Stan Margulies. Stoddard again shepherded the production from concept to presentation.

OTHER RECOLLECTIONS:
Brandon Stoddard

I think most of the world, including ABC, had passed on *Thorn Birds*, the book by Colleen McCullough, at one point or another. Finally, Warners bought it as the basis for a theatrical feature. They wanted to do it for Robert Redford, but it didn't work, mainly because it's impossible to do a two-hour script from such a great big book.

Then Warners said, "We couldn't make it as a feature, are you interested in it as a novel for television?" And we said yes, because just then we needed some development. It wasn't that we were crazy in love with it. Or that I had searched this out and fallen to my knees and begged for it. That really wasn't the case. It just happened to hit at the right time.

David Wolper's production company is at Warner Bros., and they gave it to him. Casting was very difficult. Not Richard Chamberlain—that was easy. I think there's some kind of unwritten law that if a miniseries comes along, Chamberlain has to get right of first refusal. At least it sure seems that way.

The female lead got down to a choice between Jane Seymour and Rachel Ward. Jane did a test, but we finally decided to go with Rachel Ward. Jane would not talk to me for a year. I don't blame her. She wanted that part very badly.

It wasn't that Jane can't act. I'd already used her in "East of Eden" and in a lot of other things. But she is a little bit too uptown, too sophisticated and cool. The part was earthier, an off-the-land kind of girl, more innocent, less sophisticated. Rachel isn't the greatest actress in the world, but she was exactly what we wanted for this role.

We couldn't shoot in Australia, because we couldn't get the crews, and the weather was too hot. So we built a sheep station, Drogheda, in Simi Valley, about an hour north of Los Angeles.

I told David Wolper, "Right away we must establish that this thing is Australia. Audiences need that feeling of it."

I looked at the dailies of the first day's shooting. Richard Chamberlain drives up. He's hot and sweaty in his minister's getup. His old car goes putt-putt-putt and stops, and there's the Drogheda gate. He looks out and sees a kangaroo hopping across this huge field of stubbly grass. And it's the take on the kangaroo that says, "We're in Australia."

David, of course, ordered only one kangaroo. It was August, it must have been 110 out there, dryer than hell, and the kangaroo goes bounce-bounce-bounce, and falls over on its face, out cold with heat prostration or something. I thought kangaroos could take the heat a little better than that, but this one had been in captivity its whole life. And suddenly there are trainers running in, and everybody racing around, trying to revive the kangaroo. Needless to say, that did not show up in the final cut.

We opened on a Sunday night, and I came in on Monday morning and saw the overnight ratings. They were huge, 50 shares or something. I was really happy. The phone rang at a quarter of nine. It was Tony Thomopoulos, my boss at the time. He didn't say congratulations on the numbers, or it was great last night. He said, "Can we have a miniseries once a month next year?"

I said, "What?"

He said, "Well, these last two worked so well, it was really great, the numbers were so terrific, so we want to know if we can have one once a month?"

I said, "Tony, it took five years to make these shows. You want them once a month next year? It's April already."

This is what it means to be working at a network. If something works well, wham, "Let's have a dozen of them, and let's have them tomorrow."

❑ ❑ ❑

"The Thorn Birds" was the second-highest-rated miniseries of all time, giving ABC a sweep of the top three with "Roots" as number 1 and "Winds of War" number 3.

We aired another landmark program in November 1983, *The Day After*. This was a made-for-television movie depicting the effects of nuclear war on the residents of a small American city. Despite the controversial subject matter—or perhaps because of it—more than 100 million viewers tuned in. Afterward a special edition of our public affairs show, "Viewpoint," assembled leading statesmen and thinkers to discuss the issues raised by the film. *The Day After* was a very important program, but it would almost certainly not have made it to the network had not Brandon Stoddard several times put his job on the line to argue that we *must* broadcast it.

In general, our made-for-television movies and miniseries were fine television programs that touched the hearts and minds of huge audiences. But without the attraction of top weekly series, this kind of programming does not *keep* audiences tuning in to a network. In the early 1980s we slipped back into second place, and sometimes flirted with third. We needed strong weekly series, and they were not forthcoming.

Jackie Smith's daytime, however, was still going strong. By 1981 the rejuvenated "General Hospital" had become such a drawing card that some of the greatest names in show business were asking for guest appearances, a first for daytime dramas. Jackie will never forget the day one superstar asked to be on this show.

OTHER RECOLLECTIONS:
Jackie Smith

I was always doing promotional things. I had started something called Prime Time Stars for Daytime. We had an honorarium of

$1,000 a performance, so whether it was Sammy Davis or Milton Berle, whoever came on got $1,000 and that's it.

Elizabeth Taylor, a fan of "General Hospital," called up and wanted to play with Luke and Laura, then the stars of the show. We were all very excited about this and created a storyline for her. She was the villain whom Luke had destroyed and was coming back for revenge on Luke and Laura. I was so excited about this!

With the tightening of budgets, we were extremely cost-conscious. I thought, What a coup! Elizabeth Taylor for five performances, at $1,000 apiece! This was an executive's dream, we're really getting a bargain. We got thousands of dollars' worth of free publicity with the cover of *Newsweek*: "Liz and Luke and Laura."

Liz came in with an entourage of about twenty-five people. Her press agents, her footmen, her doormen, her hairdresser, and someone who sets up her fish tank. It was like a queen had arrived.

She insisted on fresh lavender roses every day in her dressing room, and the fish tank, and special foods—and all the bills came to ABC.

Plus, Taylor insisted that everyone in her entourage had to appear as an extra in each show. Of course they had to be paid for each performance. These people were constantly blowing their lines, which meant retakes. The studio was in chaos. Gloria Monty, the producer, handled her just magnificently. But with all these delays and all the little things to keep her happy, Elizabeth Taylor cost us a fortune.

Looking back, it was really very inefficient of me not to have imagined some of this. She cost us about $100,000 for her five days. Had I known about it beforehand, it would have been fine. "Elizabeth Taylor is coming, and it's going to cost us, but we'll gain in publicity."

Nevertheless it was a great tribute to daytime because Elizabeth Taylor is a star of such magnitude. An Academy Award winner. Her wanting to be on a soap opera gave us a great lift.

Luke and Laura's adventures culminated in their wedding. There was a whole audience that came in for the week and raised the ratings to about a 40 share. Then they disappeared and never came back to daytime, except maybe for one Oprah Winfrey show, when she talked about taking her weight off. It shows that you can excite an audience. You can captivate them.

❑ ❑ ❑

Our success in daytime was critical to ABC's bottom line; in 1983, 55 percent of network profits came from daytime, compared to only 20 percent from prime time.

Elton Rule had spent almost sixteen years in New York, far longer than he anticipated when I persuaded him to come back and run the network. In 1984, he retired as vice chairman of the board and returned to his beloved California. At the end of the same year, he started broadcasting investment and television production businesses. He died in March 1990 after a long struggle with cancer.

With Elton gone, I elevated Fred Pierce to president and chief operating officer. I retained the title and duties of chief executive. Fred had done a terrific job in the television area, and I hoped that he could stretch to accommodate the wider, longer playing field upon which he now found himself. He didn't know much about station operations, and even less about radio or publishing, but he's very bright and very industrious.

Fred's weakness, as Elton and I saw it, was his lack of communication with people both above and below. He was very loyal to his people, but discouraged them from offering views differing from his own. And he often acted without informing Elton or myself until long afterward, too late to benefit from any suggestions.

We felt that unless Fred learned to communicate more freely, to leaven his thinking with the counsel of his colleagues, he would have a tough time dealing with the very broad range of issues and problems confronting him.

Upon becoming president, Fred promoted Tony Thomopoulos, head of ABC Entertainment, to president of the ABC Broadcast Group, which included supervision of our Television, News & Sports, and Radio divisions. Elton and I opposed this promotion. While Tony is a fine fellow, and a most honorable gentleman, ABC's decline in network ratings had taken place under his stewardship of Entertainment. I could see no reason to reward this performance. I told Fred as much in very plain language.

Fred argued very strenuously for Tony. Ultimately, I decided that Fred was entitled to make this decision. It came with his new job. If he was to succeed, as I fervently hoped, then I had to support him or replace him. So, despite my misgivings, I backed him.

OTHER RECOLLECTIONS:
Tony Thomopoulos

Fred Pierce was my mentor. When I was the East Coast representative for programming, Fred was in charge of planning, so we had to build a professional relationship. It evolved. We became good friends. As Fred's power grew, mine grew along with it. We are of the same ilk, in the sense that we're both straightforward, direct, and basically honorable guys.

Fred's strong suit was in his concept of exploitation, of how to get something seen, how to get things moving, how to create excitement. While Fred sometimes shared his ideas with me, he usually kept his own counsel. I think he felt it would be a diminution of his power if he opened up more.

When I first went to work for Fred, and even when I became head of programming, I told him, "You have a responsibility to yourself as well as to this company. You're now a member of the board of directors. You've got to work with that board. You've got to know that board. You've got to go out with that board. You've got to socialize with that board. You have to get that board's confidence."

And he didn't do it. He never did. I pleaded and pleaded with him. But he didn't want to offend Leonard by intruding in his area.

I said, "Fred, don't you realize Leonard wants you to do that? Don't you realize Leonard wants you to come and take it from him? He's waiting for you to come and say, 'It's my turn, Leonard. I'm going to go for it.' "

Leonard might have been upset, but he would have respected him. But Fred never did it.

I said, "Fred, that's going to be your downfall. You've got to win them over. If someone comes to take this company over and the board doesn't support you, if they don't say, 'We want Fred too,' forget it. It's over."

And he said, "It's not in my nature. I can't do it. I'll just do a good job, and they'll have to recognize the fact I'm doing a good job."

I said, "Fred, that's not reality."

❑ ❑ ❑

Almost from the moment President Ronald Reagan took office in 1981, a great wind of change swept through the Federal government. While President Jimmy Carter had deregulated a few sectors of the economy, most notably the airline industry, Reagan's appointees to the regulatory agencies, and especially to the FCC, the Department of Justice, and the Securities and Exchange Commission (SEC), embraced deregulation almost as a religion.

Gene Cowen, ABC's in-house lobbyist, was closest to the changes taking place in Washington.

OTHER RECOLLECTIONS:
Gene Cowen

In 1981 Mark Fowler became chairman of the FCC. The FCC took a deregulatory posture which reflected Fowler's view in all matters: "Let the marketplace decide." Fowler began eliminating many restrictions on licensees. First, the FCC removed restrictions on combinations of broadcast property, thereby encouraging the purchase, takeover—hostile or friendly—of broadcast properties. As one of the FCC commissioners said at the time, "We find nothing in the law that says we must perpetuate existing management."

This came at a time when merger and takeover activities were occurring in all industries. Now, there's nothing wrong with mergers and takeovers. It is a basic fact of business life that some companies can be operated more efficiently through mergers or management changes.

But broadcasters had been protected, in a sense had a shield over them, for many years. For example, in the 1960s, they wouldn't permit someone like Howard Hughes to take over ABC.

There was—and is—general concern that broadcasters are too vulnerable to hostile takeovers and that financiers are trading broadcast licenses. Treating licenses like commodities. Like you trade pork bellies. Leonard spoke out against this trafficking in licenses.

❑ ❑ ❑

The FCC also changed the so-called 7-7-7 formula. This limited any entity, including networks, to ownership of not more than seven AM radio stations, seven FM radio stations, and seven television stations, only five of which could be VHF. Under the new rules, starting in January 1985, one could own up to twelve stations in each category, as long as the stations collectively reached no more than 25 percent of the total United States population.

At the same time, other Reagan appointees in the Department of Justice were signaling their intentions to allow virtually any merger or takeover. Many of the considerations that for decades had guided the Antitrust Division's scrutiny went out the window.

Before the Reagan era there was another constraint on mergers and acquisitions: money. For one company to take over another meant laying out the cash to buy enough stock to gain control. While many acquisitors borrowed a significant portion of these funds from investment banks, the banks almost always insisted buyers put up significant sums from their own resources. That guaranteed a certain degree of prudence, because buyers were risking their own assets.

But in the early 1980s, coincidental with the Reagan Era's deregulatory frenzy, takeover artists turned to a new device, the leveraged buyout, or LBO.

The money to finance LBOs often came from the sale of junk bonds. Promising to yield relatively high rates of interest, they also offered considerable risk to investors. They could lose their money if a company issuing such bonds went belly-up.

The brokerage houses that sold these bonds took in big sales commissions. In the Pittsburgh of my youth, there was no shortage of salesmen eager to peddle stocks of dubious quality. Likewise, in the America of my later years there was no shortage of junk-bond salesmen. In neither era did salesmen have difficulty finding investors in search of big yields.

Armed with the fearsome wealth of junk bonds, the corporate raiders of the 1980s were a threat to any cash- or asset-rich company.

By 1983, ABC was both attractive to takeover artists and vulnerable. ABC management owned less than 2 percent of the outstanding common stock. Most of it was held by large institutional investors, whose concerns are always centered on reaping the highest return on investments. So almost from the day Fred Pierce became president, ABC was in jeopardy of a hostile takeover.

Both CBS and NBC, each for different reasons, were also vulnerable. CBS was the first to come under attack. Bill Paley, who with the enormous contributions of Frank Stanton built the network that led the industry for decades, was eighty-two and ailing. In 1983 he stepped down from the chairmanship, although he maintained a seat on the board. The company was going through a slump, and its fabled news department was in chaos.

Ted Turner offered to buy CBS with a mountain of IOUs—100 percent of the sales price in junk bonds. CBS management turned him down, but Turner's audacity sent a ripple through the broadcasting industry. Everyone now realized how vulnerable the networks had become.

From the moment it became clear that Reagan's FCC was intent on deregulation, all three networks began to push for rescission of the Financial Interest and Syndication Rules, which since 1970 barred networks from syndicating network-developed programs, and from producing more than a small fraction of their own programs. These rules were the product of efforts by the Hollywood production community to curb what they insisted were the excessive power of the networks.

ABC took the lead in trying to change these rules. Ev Erlick, our general counsel, had a key role.

OTHER RECOLLECTIONS:
Ev Erlick

I spoke to Mark Fowler, the FCC chairman. Many others also talked to him. I said, "You are a free-market man, Mark. Here's what's happening in the broadcasting market." And I spoke of competition from cable and from independent stations, and all the things that were making it harder for networks to compete.

I said, "All those things are going to continue. In the meantime, with the world changing every time we blink, we're shackled with rules written for conditions, if they ever existed, that are twenty years old. The networks' hands are tied. We can't produce, we can't have a financial interest, we can't syndicate, we can't do this or that or the other. But all these other people can. That's wrong. And it's only going to get worse, not better.

"We're suggesting that this issue should be reopened. We can get to the merits later, but please take another look now. It's a new world."

Eventually they decided to reopen the proceedings. Every government agency that looked at this issue—the Department of Commerce, Justice Department, National Telecommunications Information Agency (NTIA)—came down on the side of throwing out the rules, either in whole or in part.

The FCC agreed. It came up for reconsideration, and they reached the same conclusion.

In the meantime the Hollywood boys got their act together. They collected a war chest and went to Capitol Hill. And they did a helluva job. They had a lot of credit slips from the past. They had had some big donors, people like Lew Wasserman and Steve Ross, a whole lot of heavy hitters.

And they had a lot of friends on the Hill. Jack Valenti had been very hospitable over the years. Largesse. Entertainment. Contributions. Gratuities, whatever you want to call them.

We'd won administratively, but we got rolled on the Hill. And ultimately got rolled by the President. Senator Goldwater chaired a hearing dealing with this question, at which the whole Hollywood celebrity crowd testified.

And in the course of the Goldwater hearings, the senator got a "Dear Barry" letter from President Reagan. "I know you're having hearings, and I have a certain interest in this issue," and so forth and so on, and, "We really ought to let everything stay put for two years. Let's not do anything now." That killed it.

❑ ❑ ❑

My old friend Lew Wasserman, chairman of MCA, which owns Universal, is a power behind the scenes in the movie industry. He was in the forefront of those who, in the late 1960s, pressured the FCC into barring networks from syndication and from more than token production of programming.

Lew is very active in Democratic politics, but, paradoxically and even more important, he was and is very close to Ronald Reagan. In the 1940s and 1950s MCA was a talent agency. Lew was Reagan's agent. He looked after Reagan very well in those years, and among other things, encouraged him to run for the head of the Screen Actors Guild. And he helped launch Reagan's political career.

I'm all but certain that Wasserman personally got Reagan to pressure Goldwater into derailing our efforts to rescind the Financial Interest and Syndication Rules.

So I was more than a little surprised and puzzled a few months later, early in 1983, when another old friend, Felix Rohatyn of Lazard Frères, took me to lunch and said that Wasserman wanted to merge MCA with ABC.

I said, "I've known Lew for more than fifty years. Why on earth would he ask somebody to speak to me on his behalf?" And I said, "A merger doesn't make any sense. Under the FCC rules, ABC cannot be in partnership with anyone to produce television shows. But Universal has partners on virtually everything they produce. So we would lose the benefit of that completely. And we cannot syndicate—but syndication is one of MCA's biggest businesses. Under those circumstances, I cannot see what advantage a merger would provide."

I thought that would be the end of the matter, but Lew came back to see me about a merger on several occasions. Each time I said the same thing: Under the FCC rules, a merger between MCA and ABC was a silly idea even to contemplate.

There is only one reason I can think of which might have prompted Lew to seek a merger with ABC. He must have thought that, since he got his pal Ronald Reagan to keep the Financial Interest and Syndication Rules in effect, then he could also get him to scrap the rules when it served Wasserman's interests.

Even before Lew Wasserman began pressing for a merger, I turned back what might have been a run at ABC by my old friend, Larry Tisch. Larry heads Loews, a company that had once been in the movie business—they owned MGM and, before 1950, hundreds of theaters. By 1981 it was a diversified conglomerate with hotels, financial services, and tobacco interests, among others.

Larry and I often discussed broadcasting. He was always full of questions about the business, which he found glamorous and exciting.

On January 7, 1981, Larry filed notice with the SEC that he held 6.5 percent of ABC's common stock, about 1.8 million shares. He continued buying stock through March. I began to worry about that, because with 6.5 percent he owned more shares than did ABC's management.

So, early in April, I met with Larry to discuss his holdings. Larry said he had no designs on ABC, that he had merely bought the stock as an investment. I said the size of his holdings made me nervous. With little prodding on my part, he agreed to get rid of most of his ABC stock. Fortunately, he came away with a nice profit.

I have no reason to impugn Larry's motives. He's a good friend, and he has a well-deserved reputation as one of the country's smartest investors. But a few years later, in 1985, he acquired control of CBS after accumulating more stock than Paley either owned or controlled.

As ABC moved into 1984, pressure on the company started to build. Mike Mallardi, our chief financial officer, began to hear rumors about various individuals who might be mounting takeover attempts.

OTHER RECOLLECTIONS:
Mike Mallardi

Nothing was clear-cut. There were rumors in newspapers, especially *The Wall Street Journal*, and the financial community picked them up. My contacts are at Morgan Stanley, First Boston, Goldman Sachs—people in the middle, partners. People we had relationships with, who were trying to cultivate ABC as a client.

So I'd hear things, but nothing really definitive. But of course that kind of talk tends to feed on itself, and ABC was such an attractive target. Management had very little equity. Leonard was getting close to eighty, so the era of the pioneer was coming to an end.

Then, the asset values of the company. As people became attracted to broadcast properties, started paying big prices, Wall Street analysts looked at ABC and said if we sold those properties they would be worth two, three, four times as much as our stock sold for on the exchanges.

We also owned a lot of New York real estate. I'm not sure anybody outside appreciated how much. We had been adding to it for a long time.

So just looking at that, people were saying, "Hey, all we have to do is buy ABC and break it up, and we'll have a fortune." And then junk bonds became a tool.

Now people buy stations and turn them over before the ink dries on the purchase agreements. And in an inflationary climate, at least attitudinally, prices go up by leaps and bounds.

And the industry itself was becoming more competitive. Cable was coming in. It wasn't just a question of competing with the other two networks down the block. It was a question of what HBO was going to do. And Viacom. And Hollywood. And independent stations.

We had a meeting in Jackson Hole, Wyoming, in June 1984. I made a presentation. I said, "All this stuff is going on with Wall Street. Realize what our stock is selling for, and if we broke this company up, it would be worth a helluva lot more, and if we don't start doing something, somebody else will."

❑ ❑ ❑

In 1981, anticipating that the company might soon come into play, we had retained attorney Joe Flom, one of the country's best takeover specialists. This was merely a precaution. There are only a handful of top people in this field, and we wanted at least one of them in our corner should something unexpected come up.

Early in 1984 two large uncertainties loomed across the company's future. One was the Summer Games, scheduled for Los Angeles in late July.

ABC's Olympics relationship had been very fruitful for us and for the international Olympic movement. But by 1984, rights fees were astronomical. We aired the Winter Games from Sarajevo, Yugoslavia, but snowstorms interrupted programming, and ratings weren't what we had hoped, although we certainly turned a profit.

The months before the Los Angeles Games were a period of increasing uncertainty. The United States had boycotted the 1980 Moscow Games, and it looked like the Russians would reciprocate by staying away from Los Angeles. No one knew if that meant that some or all the other Eastern European countries would also boycott.

An Olympics without the strong competition offered, for example, by East German swimmers and Romanian gymnasts, would lack drama and appeal. In addition, there were persistent worries about terrorists interrupting the Games, and about massive traffic tie-ups disrupting schedules. ABC had paid well over $300 million for broadcast rights, and many feared that if anything at all went wrong, it would cost us dearly.

The second uncertainty was connected to another huge investment. With the success of "The Winds of War," Pierce had committed $60 million to production of its twenty-hour sequel, "War and Remembrance." Producing on the epic scale required for this work meant shooting for years and all around the world. This multiplied the normal uncertainties of weather and cost inflation. To many people—me among them—the likelihood of recovering our investment appeared poor.

Moreover, as with "Winds of War," we were constrained from selling commercial time to broad categories of advertisers, and limited in the number and placement of spots. When word of our unusual arrangements with Wouk leaked out, rafts of second-guessers criticized Pierce.

Coupled with these two question marks were our declining ratings and the quarter-billion dollar investment we made in ESPN. Wall Street analysts began to raise questions about Fred Pierce's leadership ability.

Then, just days before the Los Angeles Games, in mid-August, an article appeared in *Forbes*. It ran under the byline of a staff writer, Subrata Chakravarty, but Fred Pierce believes it was spoon-fed to the writer.

OTHER RECOLLECTIONS:
Fred Pierce

It came from somebody who had designs on the company. Somebody trying to acquire us and who wanted to put the company in play. I was the "designated heir apparent," and if they took potshots at me, it would indicate that the company was in a vulnerable position.

So the story pointed out all the negatives without the positives.

It was a classic type of financial story. You see them all the time now when someone wants to see a certain company put into play or to raise question marks about the capability and qualifications of top management.

❑ ❑ ❑

The article said our reaction to the changing face of network broadcasting was "ill-considered and ineffective," and quoted unnamed outsiders as saying "management seems to have lost its bearings." This focused Wall Street's attention on ABC to an unprecedented degree. Moreover, judging from other information appearing with regularity in the press, there seemed to be a leak somewhere in the highest echelons of our company.

In mid-August Elissa von Tayn, an executive secretary, met secretly with Fred Pierce in our corporate suite at the Dorset. Her boss was Jim Abernathy, VP for Corporate Affairs. Abernathy's responsibilities included investor relations; he was ABC's chief spokesman to the financial community. At his request, Elissa routinely listened in on some of his telephone conversations as a way to keep herself informed about his hectic schedule.

Elissa had overheard Abernathy talking to a Boston-based portfolio manager who had bought up more than 5 percent of ABC's stock for his company. Their conversation dealt with details of what ABC's assets would be worth if the company were broken up. Abernathy seemed to be encouraging a group of investors to mount a leveraged buyout. If so, it was a treacherous act.

Shocked, Elissa reported the conversation to Pierce. After further investigation into his activities, Abernathy was summoned back from his vacation home in Nantucket to meet with Pierce and Ev Erlick. After a heated, two-hour meeting, Abernathy's relationship with ABC was terminated.

As it turned out, the Summer Games were the most successful in history. The Russians stayed home, but the Romanians came, and so did the Chinese—their first Olympics. American teams piled up dozens of medals. The weather was perfect. There were no traffic jams. Terrorists stayed away. Ronald Reagan, at the height of his popularity, officially opened the Games, and Dave Wolper's production of the opening and closing ceremonies provided the most spectacular Olympic television ever. More than 2 billion people around the world saw this production. We got tremendous ratings and, despite huge costs, turned a terrific profit.

By the end of the Games it was clear that all of our other problems notwithstanding, ABC was on its way to a year of record earnings. But that news did little to defuse criticism of our management.

By early August, we had very clear indications that people were accumulating our stock. The volume was unusually heavy, and the price was slowly rising. Once we began following and tracking the transactions, the rumors we'd heard became more than rumors.

I learned that Warren Buffett had bought a large chunk of our stock. That didn't bother me a bit. Warren is probably the most successful investor in the country, and he likes media companies. But Warren is no raider. He merely saw the value in ABC's stock and bought some for his portfolio.

Buffett was only one of several large buyers. I became somewhat alarmed when I learned Saul Steinberg was buying—a shrewd investor with a reputation for engineering takeovers. I wasn't so concerned that Steinberg would mount an attack, but I knew his activities would attract the attention of other raiders, more fearsome.

Saul and I are acquainted socially, and so I went to see him. I asked him to sell his ABC holdings and told him why. He sold.

While this was going on, Fred Pierce, Mike Mallardi, and Ev Erlick set about erecting takeover defenses. We retained First Boston Company, an investment banking house, against the possibility of suddenly finding ourselves at war with a raider.

We discussed our options. Among these was using an Employee Stock Option Plan (ESOP) to take the company private. An ESOP is a complex transaction whereby the company is sold to its own employees. The money to buy the stock on the open market is borrowed, and individual employees buy the stock from the company, usually in installments through payroll deductions.

It soon became obvious that wouldn't work for us. First, because it would take about a year to accumulate the stock at reasonable prices, and it was clear we couldn't wait that long. And second, going into the money markets to borrow the billions we would need would create a debt load that might have placed us in jeopardy. We could have sold assets to reduce the debt, but breaking up the company was precisely what I was trying to avoid.

In October, I had learned that Robert Bass had bought a large block of stock. With his brothers, Bass owned about 25 percent of Disney, one of our major suppliers. My friend Michael Eisner was just beginning to turn that troubled company around, and ABC was helping him.

As I described at the start of this book, I contacted Eisner, who determined that Robert was operating without the knowledge of his brothers. I was never sure what he had in mind, but as I mentioned earlier, after our meeting he agreed to get rid of our stock.

Along with Ev Erlick and Fred Pierce, Mike Mallardi attended the meeting with Robert Bass.

OTHER RECOLLECTIONS:
Mike Mallardi

Why should Robert Bass listen to Leonard? Because Leonard is unique as a pioneer, as Paley was unique. As Henry Ford was unique. So Leonard is accorded a lot of admiration, deference, and respect. Larry Tisch bought 6 percent and Leonard said, "I don't want you to do this," and Tisch says, "Okay."

Leonard lived his career. You hear stories about Donald Trump going to a black-tie event every night of the week. That's how he cultivates his relationships. I don't know if Leonard got to that point exactly, but he has always been very visible. Over the years, Leonard got to know an awful lot of important people. Really, the man knows everybody. The nature of our business is such that when advertisers place money in a TV network, they're spending millions. They're sensitive to the way things look. And all these people know and like Leonard.

In 1984, it began to dawn on us that at some point we must go through a changing of the guard. When, nobody knew. But with Leonard getting close to eighty, the idea that certain people were coming into our stock became a disturbing issue.

All these things began to converge on us at a time when Fred's leadership was being questioned. It wouldn't have mattered if Fred was the smartest guy in the world. The company probably would have been picked off. All the dynamics were there. Companies get picked off whether the guy running them is good or not. That's the way it is when there's so much money involved.

❑ ❑ ❑

Very soon after our conversation, Robert Bass severed the business relationship with his brothers and went out on his own.

But his withdrawal from ABC's stock was not the end of our woes.

Within the span of a few weeks, I heard from several other people. Martin Davis of Gulf + Western came up with an offer of a friendly merger. I was approached by the heads of Gannett, Coca-Cola, and Pepsico. Each wanted to buy or merge with ABC.

These were all very friendly offers, made by men I knew, liked, and respected. I said no to all of them, and in every case we parted friends.

Gradually I came to the view that these offers were not going to stop. And I also knew that, sooner or later, those making offers would not be gentlemen I could turn away with a smile and a handshake.

I have many friends on Wall Street, and as the autumn of 1984 faded into winter, I made it a point to see some of them. I picked their brains, as friends do, and by early December my fears were confirmed. The consensus was that the pressures on ABC would continue. The company was in play, and the stakes were very high.

Nearly everyone I spoke with, however, agreed that ABC was probably safe for the near term. As long as I remained in charge, they felt, it was unlikely that anyone would make a serious move on the company. But after my departure, in whatever fashion, the company would be quickly gobbled and very likely broken up for a quick and enormous profit.

On December 7, I celebrated my seventy-ninth birthday. It was a day spent largely in quiet contemplation. And as I started my eightieth year, I made a decision.

It is not given to many mortals to know in advance the time of their passing. But clearly I had reached the point when I had only a few years left. I could not allow the company I had watched over for more than thirty years to be dismembered by profit-hungry raiders.

Were I only seventy, I would have fought. And fought hard. But that time was long past for me. With the help of the men and women you have met on these pages, I had built ABC from near bankruptcy to one of the world's premier media companies. To keep faith with these people and the thousands of others that made ABC what it was, and most important of all, to keep faith with the American public whose interests we were licensed to serve, I would have to sell the company.

But sell it to *whom*?

It was plain I must sell to someone who would understand the very special responsibilities that go along with having a network license. Someone who would appreciate the care with which the disparate elements of the company had been assembled.

My first thought was IBM. This is a company that had always been run extremely well, moreover a company known for its high ethical standards. And as one of the biggest and strongest companies in the world, it was virtually invulnerable to a hostile takeover.

My friend Frank Cary, an ABC director, had recently been the chairman of IBM. I asked him to feel out IBM's board, see if they were interested.

And then I got lucky. Tom Murphy, chairman of Capital Cities, called to make an appointment. Capital Cities was a thirty-year-old company that owned and operated seven television and twelve radio stations. It also had a publishing division with daily and weekly newspapers and an assortment of trade and consumer magazines.

I've known Tom Murphy since 1954; several of Capital Cities' television stations were ABC affiliates.

OTHER RECOLLECTIONS:
Tom Murphy

My job had always been to grow Capital Cities. The secret was out that network-affiliated stations were highly profitable. So I figured the best opportunity for us was to see if I could make a deal on a wholesale basis. When the FCC dropped the limitation of only five VHF markets, it opened an opportunity for us to own up to twelve stations. The first person I went to see was Leonard.

I didn't think I could make a deal for the stations alone, because they were so entangled with the network. But the stations were what attracted me. That was the business I knew.

It looked to me that a combination of Capital Cities and ABC could own the network and stations covering 25 percent of the country. I went to Leonard and said, "Leonard, you can throw me out the window"—we were on the thirty-ninth floor—"but I have a suggestion to make. What about merging the two companies?"

He didn't throw me out the window. So I told him, "This is an idea that makes sense. I don't know quite how to put it together, but I want you to know that I'd like to try."

I frankly didn't think he was going to say yes. But I could see he was interested.

❑ ❑ ❑

I told Tom, "I can understand what you're talking about, but I'd like to think it over."

I was waiting to hear from IBM, but I couldn't tell that to Tom at the time. After the first of the year, he called again, and I said I wanted a little more time to consider his idea.

And then I heard from IBM. They had a new president, and he had a number of pressing matters needing his attention, and so they decided to pass. And in hindsight, I'm glad.

IBM's net annual profits were more than ABC's total revenues; we would have been a relatively small division of the company. And so we might well have had the same sort of problems that were anticipated when we talked about merging with ITT back in 1967. At the very least it presented a potential for IBM's customers, foreign and domestic, to react against their sales department because of something ABC News had done or might broadcast.

So when IBM turned me down, I decided that if I was going to save ABC, I had to make a deal with a broadcaster. And Capital Cities was a premier broadcaster. It was also an extremely well managed company that for many years had set industry standards on earnings. Tom Murphy, and his chief operating officer, Dan Burke, were very widely admired for their operating efficiency.

When Murphy called me in early February, I was ready to make a deal. Our discussions were held in the greatest secrecy. I told no one what was on my mind. I didn't want any third-party meddlers coming around to turn a friendly merger into a front-page dog fight.

OTHER RECOLLECTIONS:
Tom Murphy

At the time we were discussing it, our merger would become the biggest non-oil deal in history. Leonard would not have been interested in the deal unless we put into the equation someone who would be a substantial stockholder and who would protect the combined entity.

Fortunately, I've known Warren Buffett since the late 1960s. I called him.

❑ ❑ ❑

Warren Buffett, one of America's wealthiest men, owns 45 percent of Berkshire-Hathaway. Nominally a textile company, it serves as a vehicle for a very diverse stock portfolio. Warren is soft-spoken and genial, comfortable as an old shoe. He prefers to live and operate his business from Omaha, although he travels often.

OTHER RECOLLECTIONS:
Warren Buffett

I returned a phone call from Tom Murphy one day when I was down in Washington, seeing some people, and he said, "Pal, you're not going to believe this."

He'd just come back from ABC, and he'd had a meeting of the minds, essentially, with Leonard. He said, "I've just bought ABC. You've got to come and tell me how I'm going to pay for it."

So I went up to New York and saw Murph on Thursday morning. Dan Burke was there, too, and the first thing I told Murph was, "Are you sure you want to do this? Because your life is going to change." Meaning, he would be going from a very, very successful but quite obscure company to one that would be enormously in public view. His hours were not going to be spent the same way.

I said, "As a friend, I want you to be sure you know you're changing your life in a major way if you get into this. But if you want to do it, let's talk about how you do it."

One thing for sure, I said, is that, if Capital Cities owns ABC, there will be people with very big ambitions and relatively small pocketbooks lathering over the idea of owning a network. His company would be a potential takeover target, and the officers and directors of Capital Cities owned very little of its stock.

With Capital Cities, institutional ownership was even higher than ABC. You could put twenty money managers in one room and have half the stock of Capital Cities represented. Those people were totally happy with Capital Cities' management, but if somebody comes along and offers a big enough price, the company is gone.

You need a holder who will not sell, regardless of price. The Sulzberger family, for example, is totally insensitive to the price of *The New York Times*. No price would get them to sell. The same with the Graham family and *The Washington Post* and the Bancroft family at *The Wall Street Journal*. Otherwise those companies would have been gone long ago.

I said, "You better have a nine-hundred-pound gorilla. Somebody who owns a significant amount of shares who will not sell regardless of price. Or you can have two classes of stock, where only one votes. Or you can bring in a big life insurance company perhaps, a Prudential or an Equitable, something like that."

At that point I hadn't envisioned a role for myself. Murph brought it up. He said, "How about you being the gorilla?"

I said, "That would be fine with me." We made a deal in about thirty seconds. There's no one I'd rather be partners with than Tom Murphy.

There were a couple of problems. I was on the board of *The Washington Post*. I love the people there, and I've got strong feelings about that company. But under FCC rules I could not be a director of the *Post* and also a director of Capital Cities. I wanted to think it over for twenty-four hours, and I wanted to talk to the Grahams.

I had to resign from the board of the *Post*, but I kept our shares—we own 13 percent. It hasn't changed my relationship with them at all, except I'm not on the board anymore.

The second thing I said was, "I will not sell the Buffalo *News*." Capital Cities had a TV station in Buffalo, so there was a cross-ownership clash if we bought much stock in Capital Cities. I said, "I've got my life invested in that thing. I promised the people there that I would never sell it. I told them, when they wrote my obituary it would say, 'He owns the Buffalo *News*.' "

Murph said he would sell the station.

So I said, "Murph, how much would you like me to buy?"

He said, "What do you think?"

"How's three million shares?"

"That's fine."

"What should I pay?"

"What do you think?"

"$172.50."

"Fine."

And that was it. That was the deal. That gave us a percentage that Murph felt left us looking like King Kong to the rest of the world.

❑ ❑ ❑

Warren Buffett was the perfect man to play the role of Murphy's 900-pound gorilla. He wound up with 18 percent of the merged company's stock. This cost Warren a little over $517 million. And then he gave an irrevocable, eleven-year proxy on this stock to Murphy and Burke. Warren Buffett's involvement in this deal assured me of the continuing survival of ABC and that the company would be in excellent hands.

My negotiations with Murphy over the sales price were excruciating.

Eventually we settled on $3.5 billion, about seventeen times our record 1984 earnings. That amounted to $118 a share, plus $3 a share in warrants that could be used to buy a tenth of a share of Cap Cities/ABC stock within thirty months.

Maybe I could have got a dollar or so more per share. Maybe. But we both wanted to make the deal, and what we wound up with was very fair to both companies.

Just after we made that deal, Fred Pierce came back to me about "War and Remembrance." He wanted to increase the $60 million, twenty-hour project to thirty hours and $90 million. I said, "Fred, this will cost at least a hundred and five million and maybe as much as a hundred and ten before you're through."

And I told him the decision to commit these additional funds was properly Tom Murphy's—but if it were up to me, I would take a licking on the $14 million it would cost to scrap the project, and count myself lucky.

Fred wouldn't hear of it. He went to Murphy and pressed him to keep the project going despite the rising costs. Murphy went along—but I always felt he resented the way Fred had pushed him on it.

("War and Remembrance" aired in 1989, and won an Emmy as the best miniseries of the year. Despite respectable ratings, however, production expenses were such that the network lost about $70 million.)

The secrecy surrounding my talks with Murphy was virtually complete. Except for Pierce, Mallardi, and Erlick, no one at ABC knew.

When I took this deal to my board, Leon Hess, over the years one of my strongest outside directors, took me aside. He said, "Leonard, they're taking your baby away. Are you really sure you want to do this? What are you going to do with yourself after this deal is consummated? It's going to be a real letdown for you. You may find yourself depressed."

These were questions I had often asked myself. I had no answers, but I knew at my age I had to turn the company over to these younger and very credible people.

The board approved our deal with Capital Cities over the weekend of March 16, 1985. The announcement on March 18 stunned my friends and colleagues at ABC.

Dennis Swanson, who just days earlier been promoted to head our O&O television stations, was among those summoned to New York to hear the news.

OTHER RECOLLECTIONS:
Dennis Swanson

It was amazing. I'm sitting in this room with all the major executives from ABC. Fred Pierce is going to address the group. Leonard is there. And there are all these tremendously long faces. Everybody is sad. There were even some tears.

Looking around the room at all this remorse and sadness I thought, Holy smokes, our stock was somewhere in the 60's, and these people own way more of it than I do, and they are getting $121 a share. Leonard has done well by everybody in this room. They should be thanking him.

He did a tremendous thing. He sold his company at the most propitious time to an excellent broadcasting company. I don't know how he could have done better.

❑ ❑ ❑

I must confess to mixed feelings. Many of the people in that room had been with ABC through our darkest hours. They had met what once were thought to be insurmountable challenges. And in prevailing against all odds, ABC's thirty-two-year revolution had helped shape not only the broadcasting industry but our country and the whole world in ways I could not have imagined in 1953.

But every show must close, and mine had a long, long run. I'd had my time in the spotlight. The entertainment business is always a crapshoot, and at ABC we bet against long odds and fortunately succeeded in establishing a very competitive broadcast company. I worked through the years with many very interesting and exciting people.

One must come to the conclusion at my age that a younger and very able management must carry on. So although I felt regret at selling ABC, as broadcasting is a very exciting business with a fantastic future, I am pleased that I made the deal with Capital Cities. Its management is very effective in carrying out the ideals and standards we set at ABC.

Tom and Dan, I am passing the baton to you—good luck.

Afterword

❑

Throughout this book I've highlighted the people who helped build ABC. It just isn't possible to discuss them all, but I would be remiss if I didn't recognize the help I've had from the outside directors who have given their counsel and support—and an extraordinary degree of trust.

Over the years I've asked them to approve enormous budgets for programs. They rarely knew very much—if anything—about these programs. They went along because they believed in my judgment and in the competence of the people who picked and developed the shows. The same is true for some of the acquisitions we made. When it came to buying ESPN, for example, they bought Fred Pierce's enthusiasm and vision, perhaps because I backed him, and they believed in me.

So I'd like to single a few of these people out. I went to see John Coleman in 1950. He was chairman of the board of the New York Stock Exchange, and I needed help unraveling the Rube Goldberg arrangement the government had forced us to set up to complete the separation of Paramount Pictures and United Paramount Theatres. Our stock was put in a trust; stockholders could get their shares out of it either by signing an affidavit that they no longer held stock in Paramount Pictures, or by selling their stock to someone who didn't own any stock in Paramount Pictures.

John had never been on a board before. He agreed to join ours for five years, the period the government had given us to complete the severing of cross-connections between our stockholders and those of Paramount Pictures.

John became so enamored of our business that he remained on the board until the day he died, in 1976.

John Coleman was practically my godfather at ABC. Every day after morning Mass and before he went down to the floor of the Stock Exchange, he called to see how things were going. When I had a heart attack in 1971, he took it upon himself to calm the other board members and to give Si Siegel the operating room he needed to run the company until I returned. John Coleman was a dynamo, and his leadership and support were essential to the growth of ABC.

Leon Hess, chairman of Amerada Hess, had likewise never served on an outside board. In 1968, when I needed a strong outside director, I went to Harry Hagerty for a recommendation. Hagerty said that Leon, seeking $100 million to buy a position in Amerada, an oil company, had approached every bank and most of the insurance companies in New York. All turned him down. After looking at his balance sheet Harry said, "This doesn't warrant that large a loan. But I think you, as an individual, are entitled to it, so I'll lend you the $100 million."

I recall that Hagerty had also been instrumental in convincing my board, in 1951, that we ought to buy ABC. So when Hagerty recommended Hess, I had to accept his judgment. Likewise, when Hagerty suggested to Leon that he ought to join my board, Leon, though reluctant, felt obliged to honor Hagerty's request.

Leon was with ABC's board about twenty years, and he was always a tower of strength. He was very interested in sports—he owned the New York Jets—and so his advice on sports was always very cogent. He was also a dynamo when it came to getting anything important done. He was always the first to vote for it.

Frank Cary, who joined the board in 1978, was first president and then chairman of the board of IBM. He was a stabilizing influence on the board, and he always came up with very important questions on any issue that arose.

Tom Macioce, CEO of Allied Stores, and George Jenkins, who became chairman of Metropolitan Life, were both very strong and insightful financial analysts.

George Jenkins often kidded me. He'd say, "I see Howard Cosell's salary is a million and some odd dollars. Maybe I'm not worth a quarter of what he is, but why can't I go become a commentator or anchorman or a sports announcer?"

I'd say, "You've got to get a strong agent."

Ray Adam, CEO of NL Industries, was in charge of our compensation committee and spent a lot of time and effort ensuring that we were both prudent and fair to our management. He is an outstanding businessman who always raised excellent issues for board discussion.

Jack Hausman was chairman of Belding Heminway and a close and dear friend. With his wife, Ethel, he's a cofounder of United Cerebral Palsy. Jack should have been in show business, because he grew to love broadcasting.

Alan Greenspan, one of the world's leading economists, was at all times very pointed in his questions when it came to financial matters. His insights were very helpful to planning long-term strategies for a diverse media company.

I thank all these people, and all my other directors, for their support and encouragement.

Index

ABC (American Broadcasting Companies), 96; acquired by Ed Noble (as Blue Network), 96–97, 98; creation of (1927), 96; enters television, 98–115; rise to primetime dominance, 297, 318, 335, 337, 341–374. *See also specific divisions, networks, operations, personnel, programming, and stations*

"ABC Afterschool Specials," 350–351

ABC Broadcast Group, 449

ABC Communications, 391

ABC Entertainment. *See* Entertainment, ABC

ABC Entertainment Center, 424–426

ABC Films, 227–231

ABC International. *See* International Network, ABC

ABC Marine World, 424

ABC Radio Networks. *See* Radio Networks, ABC

"ABC Suspense Movie," 334

ABC Television Network. *See* Television Network, ABC

"ABC Theatre," 355, 366

ABC Video Enterprises. *See* Video Enterprises, ABC

Abernathy, Jim, 458

Academy Awards, 3, 55

Adam, Ray, 469

Adelaide TV Station (Australia), 214–215

Adelson, Merv, 398

"Adventures in Paradise," 146

Advertising: radio, 128, 139, 167, 170, 313; television, 105, 107, 115, 116, 128, 139, 148–149, 167–168, 251, 252, 329

Advertising, ABC-Radio, 139, 167, 307–313

Advertising, ABC-TV, 243, 315, 329, 377, 387, 457; ABC on-air promotion, 328; cable, 428–429, 432, 439; charge system, 116, 139; cigarette, FCC ban on, 335–337; daytime, 168–172, 354; early, 128, 129–131, 139–142, 148–149, 153, 154, 156–160, 167–172, 173, 179; fixed time slots, 167–168; international, 218, 219, 223–224, 227; and merger possibilities, 260, 262; mid-1970s, 366–367; networking charges, 172; news programming, 277, 278, 280, 285; 1962 rates, compared to other networks, 252; of 1980s, 442–443; Prime Time Access rule, 338–339; rotating spots, 169; scatter buys, 139; sports programming, 182, 185, 186, 187, 188, 192, 194, 195, 210, 213; and station compensation, 170–172; trend-setting in, 167–169, 328; Treyz strategies and problems, 139–142, 148–149, 156–160, 167–172, 175–176, 179. *See also specific sponsors*

Affiliates, ABC-Radio, 97, 140, 310–313

Affiliates, ABC-TV, 2, 3, 4, 104, 105, 161, 221, 273–274, 323, 338, 348, 374, 382–391, 392, 462; and cable, 428, 429, 436–439; and daytime programming, 170–172, 247–250, 352–353; drop-in issue, 165–166, 430; early lack of, 139, 149, 151, 165–166, 167, 194, 328, 382; Hearst, 430–431; increase in, during Rule era, 319, 386–391; international, 216–232; news programming, 273, 284, 287, 293, 376–378, 379, 409, 412; in North Carolina, 384, 391; promotion, 382; in Seattle, 382–383; sports programming, 190, 206; Taft stations, 384–386; UHF issue, 166. *See also specific cities and stations*

"Afternoon Film Festival," 134

Ain't Misbehavin', 426

Ali, Muhammad, 207

All About Eve, 138

Allied Group of Theatres, 70

"All in the Family," 321–322, 329

Index

"All My Children," 347, 369
All That Jazz, 153
Alsop, Joseph, 103
Alvarado, Ann, 60
Amadeus, 426
"AM America," 349, 353, 405
Ameche, Jim, 303
"American Bandstand," 161–165, 168; and payola scandal, 163–165
American Broadcasting–Paramount Theatres (AB-PT), 103, 200. *See also* ABC (American Broadcasting Companies)
American Cancer Society, 79
American Heart Association, 79
American Civil Liberties Union (ACLU), on UPT-ABC merger, 110
American Federation of Musicians, 40
American Graffiti, 348
American Information Network for Talk Radio, 310
American Type Founders, 97
Amos and Andy, 104
Amusement attractions, ABC, 423–424; Disneyland, 122–124, 423
Anderson, Loni, 385–386
Anderson, Marian, 286
Anderson, Richard Dean, 371
Andrews Sisters, 42
"Andy Griffith Show," 120
Animated programs, ABC, 347, 351–353
Annenberg, Evelyn, 80
Annenberg, Walter, 162
Ann-Margret, 355
Anti-Semitism, 9–10, 35, 66
Antismoking commercials, 336
Antitrust issues: in ABC-ITT merger attempt, 261–262; and cigarette advertising ban, 337; in FCC approval of UPT-ABC merger, 111–114; 1940s cases against movie-studio monopolies, 68–74, 95, 111, 114; 1980s deregulation of broadcasting industry, 3, 451–452; television coverage of national elections, 296. *See also* Federal Communications Commission (FCC)
Arafat, Yasir, 404
Arcade Theater (Scottdale, Pa.), 9, 10
Argentinian stations, ABC interests in, 218, 219–220
Arledge, Roone, 184, 320; as head of ABC News, 399–419; as head of ABC Sports, 184–213, 244, 335, 399–401
Army films, 55
Army-McCarthy hearings, 272–273
Arnold, Dr. Lee, 90, 91
Arnstein, Danny, 81, 85
"Arthur Godfrey Show," 139
ARTS (Alpha Repertory Television Service), 429, 438
Arts & Entertainment Network, 429–430
Asahi Shimbun, 221
Asian stations, ABC interests in, 221–223, 232
ASI testing, 246, 361
Associated Press, 294, 295–296
AT&T, 131, 168, 222, 287, 309
Atkinson, Brooks, 24
Aubrey, Jim, 126, 270, 375; as head of ABC-TV programming, 143–144, 182
Audiences, television, 104, 249–250, 329; and advertising strategies, 116, 141, 148–149; ASI testing of, 246, 361; cable, 428–429; demographic profile analysis of, 148–149; 1980s shrinking of, 326. *See also* Ratings, television
Austrialian television, 214; ABC interests in, 214–215, 229–230
"The Autobiography of Miss Jane Pittman," 318
Ayer, Marion, 315, 340, 343

Bader, Marvin, 198–201
Baker, George Pierce, 23
Baker, Seth, 422–423
Baker Dramatic Workshop (Harvard University), 23
Bakker, Jim, 422
Balaban, A. J., 27
Balaban, Barney, 26, 27, 28, 29, 40, 47, 52, 66, 67, 81, 85, 96; as Paramount president, 35, 36, 38, 39, 43, 52, 53, 55, 56–57, 60, 73, 105–106, 111–114; on UPT-ABC merger, 111–114
Balaban, Elmer, 27, 37
Balaban, Harry, 27, 37
Balaban, John, 85, 95, 112, 113
Balaban & Katz Theatres (Chicago), 26–30, 85, 112, 113, 121; early television broadcasting, 96
Ball, Jerry, 86–87
Ball, Lucille, 361
"The Barbara Walters Specials," 397, 398
Barbera, Joe, 352
Bare, Dick, 127
"Baretta," 361
Barnathan, Julius, 170, 179, 235, 240, 273, 359, 383–384; as head of ABC Broadcast Operations and Engineering, 197–198, 235, 241
"Barney Miller," 358–359, 361
Barris, Chuck, 247–248
Baruch, Bernard, 131–132

Index

Baseball, 194, 205
Bass, Robert, 1–2, 4, 459–460
Bass, Sidney, 1–2, 459–460
Bass brothers, 362–363; ABC takeover attempt by, 1–2, 4, 459–460
Bassett, John, 232
"Batman," 245–247
Bautzer, Gregson, 265, 267, 270
BBC, 345, 429; filming of Queen Elizabeth's coronation, 216; miniseries, 345; "Rainbow Sundae," 349; "Till Death Do Us Part," 321
BBD & O, 138–139, 247, 248, 328
Beard, Dita, 262
"Beat the Clock," 169
Beaudin, Ralph, 308–310
Beech-Nut Foods, 98, 100, 101
Beesemeyer, Dick, 387–388, 391
Begin, Menachem, 226–227, 394; meeting with Sadat, 406–408
Beirut, 404–405, 414; television stations, ABC interests in, 223–225
Belasco, David, 23
Bell, Steve, 411
"Ben Casey," 151–152, 153, 229, 230
Ben-Gurion, David, 225
Benjamin, Bob, 132–134
Bennack, Frank, 430–431
Bennett, Harv, 235
Bennington, Bill, 191
Benny, Jack, 30, 84, 104
Benson, Hugh, 147
Berenberg, Dr. Bill, 91
Bergen, Edgar, 104
Bergman, Ingmar, 340
Berle, Milton, 85, 448
Berlin, Dick, 430
Bernhard, Harvey, 228
Bernstein, Elmer, 279
Berry, Max, 198
"Beverly Hillbillies," 143, 149
"Bewitched," 243
"Big Joe's Happiness Exchange," 302
"Billy Rose's Playbill," 131
Bioff, Willie, 62
"Bionic Woman," 361, 366
Birney, Ben, 43
"Birth and Babies," 353
Blackmere, Sidney, 286
Blade Runner, 222
Blank, Abe, 30, 69, 73, 113
Black, Ben, 285
Blank, Myron, 69–70
Blinn, Bill, 364
Block booking, 70, 71
Blue Network, 96, 140, 170, 299, 308; acquired by Ed Noble, 96–97, 98, 140, 299; becomes American Broadcasting Company (1943), 97, 98
Bluhdorn, Charlie, 333, 355–356, 362
Blumberg, Nate, 64
Blumenstock, Mort, 125
Board of directors, ABC, 253; approval of UPT-ABC merger, 103–104, 109; and attempted merger with ITT, 260; and Capital Cities/ABC merger, 466; cumulative voting issue, 254–257; and Norton Simon's takeover bid, 253–257, 259, 260
Boland, Mike, 172, 261, 287
Bolger, Ray, 118, 119
Bombeck, Erma, 353
Bon Ami Corporation, 228–229
Bonsal, Judge Dudley, 267, 268, 269
Boston, Paramount theaters in, 30–34, 35
"Bourbon Street Beat," 146
Boxing, 185, 191, 206, 207
Brademas, John, 91
Brandeis, Louis, 24
Brandt, Otto, 382
"Breakfast Club," 307, 308
Brian's Song, 335
Brice, Fanny, 131
Bridging, 139, 160, 334, 345–346
Brinkley, David, 416; with ABC News, 416–418. *See also* "Huntley-Brinkley Report"
Briskin, Sam, 55, 58
Bristol Meyers, 243
British feature films, on ABC-TV, 134
British television, 233, 345; stations in Hong Kong, 223. *See also* BBC
Broadway Bill, 55
Broadway shows, ABC interests in, 424–427
Brokaw, Tom, 416
Brooklyn Paramount Theatre, 39, 40, 43, 67
Brooks, Jim, 368
Brown, Harold, 411
Brown, Helen Gurley, 431
Brown, Hilary, 392
Browning, Robert, 32
Buchwald, Art, 56–57
Buffalo *News*, 465
Buffett, Warren, 459, 463–465
"Bugs Bunny," 347, 351
Bundy, McGeorge, 288
Burke, Dan, 463, 464, 465, 467
"Burke's Law," 322–323
Burnett, Carol, 204
Burns, George, 104, 121, 237
Burns and Allen, 104, 121
Bush, George, 283
Bush, Jack, 284–285

Bushnell, Asa, 183
Business Week, 115
"Bus Stop," 177
Byrnes, Edd, 147, 148

Cabaret, 340
Cable broadcasting, 72, 272, 427, 456
Cable Health Network, 432
Cable Networks, ABC, 3, 427–440; advertising, 428–429, 432, 439; affiliates, 428, 429, 436–439; ARTS, 429, 438; Arts & Entertainment, 429–430; and ESPN, 433–440, 457; Hearst partnership, 429–432; narrowcasting, 428–429; profits, 431, 438, 440; programming development, 428–432; SNC, 432, 438; TeleFirst, 423–433, 438
Cabot, Sebastian, 332
Cadena Centroamericana, 217
Cahn, Sammy, 145
Caldwell, Erskine, 24
Calley, Lt. William L., 114
"Camel Newsreel," 139
Canada Dry, 256
Canadian broadcasting, 216, 290, 291, 292; ABC interests in, 232
Canadian theaters, 29, 214
"Caper" trend, 146
Capital Cities/ABC, 391; merger, 462–467
Capital Theatre (Hollywood), 236
Capitol Records, 35
Capone, Al, 29, 49, 62, 174
Capra, Frank, 55, 58
"The Captain and Tennille," 362
"Captain Kangaroo," 349, 353
"Captain Video," 105
Carsey, Marcey, 356, 441; as ABC program executive, 357–359, 367–369
Carson, Johnny, 208, 236, 237
Carter, Jimmy, 397, 408, 411–412, 450
Carter, Lynda, 362
Carter, Roslyn, 397
Cary, Frank, 462, 469
Casablanca (film), 125
"Casablanca" (TV show), 127
Castro, Fidel, 397
Cats, 426
"Cavalcade of Stars," 105
"CBS Evening News," 416
CBS Radio Network, 35
CBS Television Network, 43, 100, 101, 104, 106, 107, 108, 110, 111, 139, 142, 143–144, 151, 157, 176, 204, 232, 238, 318, 328, 330, 339, 347, 366, 372, 420, 428; ABC as trend-setter for, 129, 143, 345, 419; advertising rates, 168, 170, 252; affiliates, 100, 104, 115, 116, 167, 216–217, 349, 382, 384, 388, 391; "All in the Family" on, 322; attempts to acquire ABC, 100, 102; audiences, 104, 148, 149; cable interests, 436; children's programming, 349; color broadcasting, 251–252; daytime programming, 349, 369; and Disney Company, 122, 123, 235; early growth of, 116; foreign interests, 215–217; headquarters, 244–245; manufacturing interests, 251; merger possibilities, 258; movie schedules, 251–252; "My Three Sons" switched to, 153; news programming, 272, 273, 275, 277, 278, 280, 284, 286, 289, 291, 292, 293–297, 392, 395, 401, 402, 404, 407, 408, 409, 415–416, 419, 452; 1980s vulnerability to takeovers, 452, 455; -owned stations, 376–377, 382; profits, 252; ratings, 146, 149, 167, 243; Fred Silverman with, 359; sports programming, 182–184, 192, 194, 195, 197, 201, 206, 207, 244; WBKB-TV sold to, 102, 109. *See also specific programs*
"The CBS Thursday Night Movies," 252
Central Park Theatre (Chicago), 27, 28
Central States Theatres (Des Moines), 69
Cerebral palsy (CP), 75, 82; Goldensons' experience with, and charity work for, 75–94; misconceptions about, 76. *See also* United Cerebral Palsy (UCP)
"Challenge of the Yukon" (radio serial), 37
Chamberlain, Richard, 446
Chancellor, John, 404
Chandler, Raymond, 146
Chapman, Alger, 257
Charge system, in advertising, 116, 139
Charity work, entertainment industry involvement in, 79–94
Charles, Prince of Wales, 197
"Charlie's Angels," 348, 361–362
Chevrolet, 387
Cheyenne (film), 125
"Cheyenne" (TV show), 127–129, 139, 146, 155, 160, 238
Chicago, 99, 118, 175, 230, 275, 418; ABC News Bureau, 402, 414; ABC Northern Theatre Division, 230, 231; ABC-Radio stations in, 97, 298, 308, 420; ABC-TV O & O stations in, 85, 96, 100, 102, 109, 114, 293, 349, 375, 376–378, 380–381, 432; Paramount theaters in, 26–30, 85, 96, 112, 113, 121; World's Fair (1933), 30
Children of a Lesser God, 425–426
Children's programming, ABC-TV, 347; animated, 347, 351–353; early, 124, 132, 150, 161, 168; mid-1970s, 349–353. *See also specific programs*

Index

Child, Julia, 353
Chilton, 422
China, 283; television stations, ABC interests in, 222–223
"China Beach," 153
China Syndrome, The, 153
Chorus Line, A, 425
Christman, Paul, 191
Churchill, Winston, 134, 289
Cigarette advertising ban, 335–337
Cincinnati, 110; WKRC, 384–386
Cinderella, 122
Cineplex Odeon, 231
Cisneros, Diego, 218–219
CIT Financial Corporation, 267
Civil Aeronautics Authority, 98
Clark, Dick, 162–165, 170, 247; and payola scandal, 163–165, 301
Clark, Tom, 70, 72
Cleaver, Eldridge, 421
Cleveland, 110, 427
Clifford, Clark, 190, 274
Clipp, Roger, 161–162, 170–172
Clorox, 141–142
CNN (Cable News Network), 429, 432, 434, 440
Cobb, Lee J., 328
Coca-Cola, 4, 25, 461
Cochran, Ron, 284, 290
Cohen, Manny, 266
Cohn, Harry, 58–59
Cohn, Jack, 58
Cole, Nat King, 42
Coleman, John, 60, 104, 106, 215, 274, 341, 342, 468–469; and ABC takeover bids, 254–257, 265
Coleman, John (weatherman), 353, 377
Collier's, 171
Collingwood, Charlie, 284
Collins, Julius, 15
Color Purple, The, 381
Color television, 124, 251; ABC's slow conversion to, 251–252, 258, 263, 264; advertiser preference for, 251; CBS, 251–252; NBC, 142, 251–252
Columbia Pictures, 4, 55, 58, 142, 146, 153, 335, 363; 1940s antitrust suits against, 68, 70, 71
Columbia Presbyterian Hospital, 90, 341
Comaneci, Nadia, 203
"Combat," 229, 230, 376
Comedy programs, ABC-TV, 321–322, 348, 357–359, 367–369, 441. *See also specific programs*
Comic book series, ABC-TV, 245–247
Como, Perry, 42
Competitiveness in television industry, creation of, 110, 111
Concession sales, 32, 124
"Conflict," 146, 155
Congress, U.S., 177, 276, 338; involvement in medical research for human diseases, 78, 91; 1959 payola investigation of music industry, 163–165; on UHF issue, 166
"Congressional Investigators," 228, 229
Connery, Sean, 174
Contemporary Network for Top-40 Stations, 310, 311
Contracts, talent, 55–56, 71–72
Cooper, Gary, 26, 127
Co-Op Theatres (Detroit), 37
Cosby, Bill, 121
"The Cosby Show," 121, 153, 351
Cosell, Howard, 200, 400, 401, 439–440; with ABC Sports, 205–213
Cosmo, 431
Costa Rican television stations, ABC interests in, 217, 220
Costner, Kevin, 174
Court of Appeals, U. S., 269–270
"The Courtship of Eddie's Father," 328
Cousteau, Jacques, 279–280
Cox Broadcasting, 391
Cowen, Gene, 451
Coyle, Don, 215; as president of ABC International, 216–224
Cramer, Douglas, 235, 247, 249, 250, 326–327, 345
Crawford, Joan, 219
Crime programs, ABC-TV, 146, 172–174, 238–242, 323. *See also specific programs*
Cronkite, Walter, 184, 273, 284, 290, 402, 404, 407, 408, 415, 416
Crosby, Bing, 54, 55, 84, 104, 151, 202, 237, 303
Crosby, Dennis, 303
Crosby (Bing) Productions, 151
Crothers, Dr. Bronson, 82, 89–90
Crystal, Billy, 367, 368
Cuban missile crisis, ABC's role in, 280–282
Cumulative voting, 254–257
Curtis, Dan, 248; and "The Winds of War," 443–445
Curtis Publishing, 257

Daily Variety, 331
Dallas, 47, 118; ABC affiliate in (WFAA), 221, 287; Kennedy assassination in, 221–222, 285–288
"Dallas," 243
Dallas Cowboys, 208–209, 210
Daly, Joel, 377–378

Daly, John, 116, 205, 300; as head of ABC News, 273, 275, 277
Dann, Mike, 330
"Dark Shadows," 248–249
Dart, Justin, 98
"The Dating Game," 248
Davis, Martin, 4, 362
Davis, Marvin, 362
Davis, Ossie, 363
Davis, Sammy, Jr., 118, 119, 448
Day, Dennis, 308
Day, Doris, 204
The Day After, 447
"Day in Court," 169
Daytime, 431–432
Daytime programming, ABC-TV, 272, 326, 347, 391, 438; advertising, 168–172, 354; affiliates, 170–172, 247–250, 352–353; Army-McCarthy hearings, 272–273; early, 132–134, 161–165, 168–172; mid-1970s, 347–354, 369–371, 392; Moore era, 247–250; morning shows, 349, 353–354; of 1980s, 447–449; Operation Daybreak, 168–172; promotion of, 350–351, 371, 447–448; ratings, 349, 350, 353, 354; soap operas, 248, 347, 369–371, 447–448. *See also* Children's programming, ABC-TV; *specific programs*
DeBare, Chuck, 301–303
Dee, Ruby, 363
Deer Slayer, The, 349
De Laurentiis, Dino, 55
DeLorean, John, 387
DeMayo, Debby, 380, 381
De Mille, Cecil B., 54, 127, 421
Depinet, Ned, 65
Depression Era, 10, 20, 21, 22, 25, 30, 31, 39–40, 42, 97–98
Deregulation of broadcasting industry, 1980s, 3, 450–455
De Sylva, Buddy, 35
Detroit, 103, 118, 119; ABC-Radio stations in, 99, 119, 298–300, 308; ABC-TV O & O stations in, 100, 109, 375; Paramount theaters in, 36–39, 43, 105, 299
Devour the Snow, 425
"Dick Van Dyke Show," 120
Dietrich, Marlene, 26
Diller, Barry, 327, 328, 347; and ABC made-for-television movies, 330–335; and ABC miniseries, 345–346, 363, 442, 444; as chairman of Paramount, 356, 362, 442; at Fox, 362; leaves ABC, 355–356
Dillon, Read & Co., 97
Disney, Lilli, 318
Disney, Roy, 121, 124
Disney, Walt, 1, 2, 62, 121, 124, 184, 318, 352, 363; entertainment philosophy of, 62; and 1954 ABC/Disneyland deal, 122–124; relationship with ABC, 1–2, 121–124, 251
Disney (Walt) Company, 1, 62, 235, 350, 352, 363; amusement parks, 1, 2, 122–124, 235, 423; Michael Eisner as chairman and CEO of, 1–2, 347, 348, 363, 459–460; films, 121–122, 123; relationship with ABC, 1–2, 121–124, 142, 251, 423, 459; relationship with CBS, 122, 123, 235; relationship with NBC, 122, 123, 124, 251
Disneyland (amusement park), 2, 60, 122, 235, 352; ABC backing for, 122–124, 423
"Disneyland" (TV show), 124, 139, 146, 160, 175
"The Disney Sunday Movie," 1–2
"Disney's Wonderful World of Color." *See* "Walt Disney's Wonderful World of Color"
Distribution. *See* Affiliates, ABC-TV
"Divorce Wars," 355
Dixon, Pam, 359
"Dr. Kildare," 153
Dr. No (book), 223
Documentary films, ABC-TV, 278–280, 296
Dodge, 130
Donahue, Phil, 380–381
Donaldson, Sam, 404; with ABC News, 404, 408, 412, 417
"Donny and Marie," 361
"Doogie Howser, M. D.," 238
Dorsey, Tommy, 42
Downs, Hugh, 397, 403–404
"Do You Trust Your Wife," 168
Dozier, Bill, 245
Dreamgirls, 426
Drop-ins, ABC pursuit of, 165–166, 430
Drug, Inc., 97, 98
Duchin, Eddy, 42
Duffy, Jim, 320, 385; as president of ABC-TV Network, 343, 386, 387–391; as sales head of ABC-TV Network, 387
DuMont, Allen B., 105, 106
DuMont Labs, 137
DuMont TV Network, 81, 104–107, 110, 134, 184; decline of, 136–137; Paramount Pictures interest in, 105, 106, 110–111, 113, 114
"Dynasty," 243, 445
"Dynomutt," 352

Eckstine, Billy, 42
Ecuadorean television stations, 220–221
Eddy, Bill, 96
Edelman, Lou, 119

Index

Editing, film, 59
"Ed Sullivan Show," 43, 157–160, 236
Edwards, Douglas, 299
Edwards, Vince, 152
Egypt, 225; relations with Israel, 226–227, 406–408
"Eight Is Enough," 363
Eisenhower, Dwight D., 222, 276, 277
Eisner, Michael, 1, 321–322, 327, 333, 372, 424; as Disney chairman and CEO, 1–2, 347, 348, 363, 459–460; as head of ABC Entertainment program development, 346–353, 356–362; leaves ABC, 362; at Paramount, 362
Electrical Research Projects, Inc. (ERPI), 26
"The Elephant Man," 355
Elizabeth, Queen of England, 196–197; ABC broadcast of coronation of, 215–216
Ellsworth, Dick, 171
Emmy awards, ABC, 120, 279, 335, 369, 445, 466
Empire State Building (New York City), 99
Employee Stock Option Plan (ESOP), 459
Entertainment, ABC (after 1972), 345, 354; comedy programs, 348, 357–359, 367–369, 441; daytime programming, 347–354, 369–371, 392, 447–449; early 1980s complacency, 441–442, 447; Michael Eisner as head of program development, 346–353, 356–362; mid-1970s primetime hits, 358–369; miniseries, 345–346, 355, 363–366, 442–447, 457, 466; of 1980s, 441–450, 457, 466; Fred Silverman as president of, 359–373, 389, 442; Marty Starger as president of, 345–347, 356, 359, 363–364; Tony Thomopoulos as head of, 373, 446–447, 449. *See also* Programming, ABC-TV (1953–1972); *specific personnel and programs*; Television network, ABC
Entertainment Channel, 429
Entertainment Network, 310
Epstein, Arthur, 132–134
Erlick, Ev, 100, 164, 165, 240; as ABC attorney, 172, 179, 265–267, 269–270, 310, 335–339, 453–454, 458, 466; on Ed Noble, 100–101
Escape to Witch Mountain, 350
ESPN (Entertainment and Sports Programming Network), 429, 434; acquired by ABC, 438–440, 457; affiliated with ABC, 433–438
European television, American interests in, 233
European theaters, Paramount, 214
Evey, Stu, 433–438
"Expedition," 230
Exxon, 218, 225

Fabian, 177
Fahey, Flynn, 376–378, 380
Fairbanks, Douglas, Sr., 61
Fairness Doctrine, 336
Falkenberg, Jinx, 83
Fallen Idol, 134
Falstaff Beer, 182
"Family," 361
"Family Affair," 332
Famous Players, 33
Fantasia, 122
"Fantasy Island," 323
"Faraway Hill," 105
Farber, Dr. Sidney, 87–88, 90, 91
Farrow, Mia, 242
"Father Knows Best," 328
Fedder, Ted, 150
Federal Communications Commission (FCC), 3, 117, 232, 307, 441, 450, 462; on ABC's sequential networking, 310; "Bus Stop" hearings, 177; on cable industry, 428; chain broadcasting rules, 96–97, 100, 111, 115, 308–310; cigarette advertising ban, 335–337; drop-in issue, 165–166, 430; fifty-fifty rule, 338, 339; Financial Interest and Syndication Rules upheld by, 452–455; on ITT-ABC merger, 260–263; 1970 television broadcasting restrictions, 231, 452–453; 1980s deregulatory policies, 3, 450–455; Prime Time Access rule, 338–339; on radio network advertising fraud, 313; on transfer of station licenses, 257, 266, 268, 270; on TV channel allocations, 96, 98–99, 100, 165–166; UHF issue, 165–166; on UPT-ABC merger, 107, 110–115
Financial Interest and Syndication Rules, 231; upheld during Reagan era, 452–454
Firestone, Harvey, 129–130, 197
Firestone Rubber, 129–130
First Boston Company, 459
First National Pictures, 29
First-run theaters, 70, 71, 72
Fisher, O. D., 382–383
Flair Reports, 289
Fleming, Ian, 223
Fletcher, A. J., 383–384
"Flintstone Kids," 352
Flom, Joe, 456
Flynn, Jack, 96
FM Network, 310
Fomin, Alexandr, 282
Fonda, Jane, 398

Football, 185, 187, 197, 286, 337; ABC's televised NCAA games, 117–118, 137, 181–186, 189–191, 194, 195, 206; ABC's trendsetting technology in, 186, 191–192, 194, 196; on cable TV, 435, 439; importance of television to, 187–188; "Monday Night Football," 204–213. *See also* Sports, ABC-TV
Forbes magazine, 457–458
Ford, Henry II, 210
Ford, Jerry, 276
Ford Motors, 210, 387
"For Men Only," 184
Foss, Joe, 192
Foster, Jodie, 350
Fountain, Bob, 387–389, 391
Four Star Productions, 322, 323
Fowler, Mark, 451, 453
Fox. *See* Twentieth Century-Fox
Fox, William, 28
Fox Broadcasting, 233
Fox Movietone, 273
Francis, Arlene, 83
Frankle, Stanton, 183–184
Franklin, Charles, 23, 24
Fraser, Woody, 353
Freed, Alan, 302
Freeman, Frank, 33, 35–36, 40, 45, 421; as Paramount studio head, 53, 54
"Friday Night Fights," 182, 194
Friendly, Fred, 295, 296
Friendly, Henry, 24, 269–270
Friendly Persuasion, 55
From Here to Eternity, 144, 145
"The Fugitive," 151, 229, 230, 238–242

Gable, Clark, 67, 108
Gabor, Zsa Zsa, 308
Gallagher, Barbara, 360
Gallagher, Wes, 295, 296
Gallery, Tom, 182–184
Gambling, 20, 59, 64
Game shows, 338, 339; ABC-TV, 247–248
Gannett, 4, 461
Garbo, Greta, 108
Gardner, Ava, 58, 144
Garland, Judy, 58
Garner, James, 155, 156, 160, 161
Geneen, Harold, 258, 314; and attempted ITT-ABC merger, 258–264, 270–271
General Electric, 258
General Foods, 168, 169, 223–224
"General Hospital," 248, 347, 369, 370, 376, 447–448
General Mills, 140
General Motors, 30, 141, 153, 218
Gentry, Steve, 359
Gerber, David, 245
Geritol, 130–131
German television, 233
Gershwin, George, 16
Gersten, Chester, 104
Getty Oil, 433–438
Gifford, Frank, 207–213
Gillette, 182; ABC Sports sponsored by, 182, 185, 186, 188, 195
Ginsberg, Henry, 53–54
Glass, Charles, 404, 405
"The Glass Menagerie," 355
Gleason, Jackie, 105
Godfrey, Arthur, 104
Going My Way, 55
Goldberg, Leonard, 235, 347, 361; as head of ABC daytime programming, 247–250, 326; as head of ABC programming, 249, 250, 321, 326–335
Goldenson, Esther Broude, 6–10, 12, 13, 19, 21, 344
Goldenson, Genise (Cookie), 74; cerebral palsy of, and Goldensons' charity work due to, 75–94; death of, 94
Goldenson, Isabelle Weinstein, 44, 57, 59, 60, 61, 146, 153, 201, 215, 225, 226, 263, 340, 344, 351, 362, 383, 393, 430; on ABC takeover bids, 268; Goldenson's courtship of, 44–47; illness of daughter Cookie, and charity work due to, 75–94; marriage to Goldenson, 47
Goldenson, Lee, 6, 9, 10, 11, 12, 13, 17–18, 19, 20, 21
Goldenson, Leonard: birth of, 7; as chairman and CEO of ABC, 343–449; as CEO of ABC, 343–467; childhood of, 7–14; courtship of Isabelle Weinstein, 44–47; decision to sell ABC, 461; early interest in theater business, 10–11, 20, 23–24, 30; at Harvard, 14–20, 21; heart attack of, and lifestyle changes due to, 340–345; illness of daughter Cookie, and charity work due to, 75–94, 326; marriage to Isabelle Weinstein, 47; in post-reorganization Paramount, 35–44; in Paramount reorganization, 25–26, 30–35, 53; as Paramount theater division head, 52–74; as president of ABC, 116–344; religious background of, 8–10; as United Paramount Theatres head, 73, 95–115; views on television industry, 166–167
Goldenson, Levi, 6
Goldenson, Loreen, 46, 77, 163–164, 351
Goldenson, Maxine, 46, 77, 351
Goldenson, Dr. Samuel, 8

Goldman Sachs, 253
Goldwater, Barry, 295, 454
Goldwyn, Sam, 26, 28, 63–64
Gone With the Wind, 64
Good Housekeeping, 431
Goodman, Julian, 283, 285
"Good Morning America," 349, 353–354, 403, 411
"Good Times," 348
Gorshin, Frank, 246
Gothic serials, ABC-TV, 248–249
Gottlieb, Leo, 24
Gould, Jack, 278, 317
Gowdy, Curt, 191, 207
Graham, Billy, 136, 421–422
Graham, Virginia, 81
Graham family, 225, 464, 465
Granath, Herb, 426–428, 432, 436, 439
Grandinetti, Father, 219–220
Grant, Armand, 182
Grauman's Chinese Theatre, 27
Great Expectations, 134
"Great Grape Ape," 352
Green, George, 305
Green, Johnny, 16
"Green Acres," 143
"The Green Hornet" (radio serial), 37
Greenspan, Alan, 470
Grey, Joel, 118
Grey Advertising, 247
Griffith, Andy, 204
Gross, Walter, 72, 103
Group W Satellite Communications, 432
Guinness, Alec, 134
Gulf + Western, 4, 355, 362, 461
"Gunsmoke," 129
"The Guns of Will Sonnett," 324
Guntzelman, John, 385–386
Gymnastics, 203

Hagen, Jean, 120
Hagerty, Harry, 60, 106–107, 192, 469
Hagerty, Jim, 222, 276, 297; as head of ABC News, 276, 277, 281, 282, 283
Haley, Alex, 363; and "Roots," 363–365
Hamer, Rusty, 120
Hammerstein, Dorothy, 131
Hamerstein, Oscar, II, 131
Hand-held cameras, used in sports programming, 186, 198
"Hangman's Knot," 128, 330
Hanna/Barbera, 352
Hansen, Karen, 77, 87, 93–94
"Happy Days," 347, 348, 360, 366
Hargrove, Marion, 147
Harper, Pat, 392
Harris, Johnny, 49
"Harry O," 361
Hart, Phil, 337
Hartman, David, 353, 354, 393, 403
Harvard Medical School, 82, 87–90, 91, 92, 430
Harvard University, 23, 24, 222; Goldenson at, 14–20, 21
Harvey, Paul, 97, 307, 308
Hatfield, Mark, 421
Hausman, Jack and Ethel, 80–83, 146, 393, 430, 469–470
"Hawaiian Eye," 146
Hayden, Tom, 398
Hayworth, Rita, 58
HBO, 433, 434, 456
Headquarters, ABC (New York City): Avenue of the Americas, 244–245; 66th Street, 115, 137, 243–244
Hearst, William Randolph, 430
Hearst/ABC Video Services, 431–432
Hearst Corporation, ABC partnership with, 429–432
Hearst Telenews, 273, 284
Helms, Jesse, 384
Hennock, Frieda, 110, 115
Henry V, 134
Hepburn, Katharine, 355
Herman, Woody, 42
Hertz, John, 30, 35
Hertz Drive Yourself, 27, 30
Hess, Leon, 466, 469
Hesseman, Howard, 385
Heston, Charlton, 286
Hewitt, Don, 408
High Fidelity, 420
Hillbilly shows, 143, 149
Hilsman, Roger, 281, 282
Hilton, James, 138
Hiss, Alger, 277
Hitchcock Publishing, 422
Ho, George, 223
Hoberman, Ben, 303–305, 307, 311
Hoblitzelle, Karl, 30, 47, 70, 73; and Disneyland financing, 123–124
Hoffman, Dustin, 146, 340
Holbrook, Hal, 335
Hollywood, 104, 238, 242; as ABC-TV programming source, 104, 107, 108, 118, 143, 236–238, 242, 252, 325, 342; of 1940s, 53–71
"Hollywood Palace," 236–237
Homes magazine, 422
Homes Using Television (HUT), 170
Hon, Dr. Edward, 92
"The Honeymooners," 351

Hong Kong television stations, 222–223
"Hooperman," 238
Hoover, Herbert, 294
Hope, Bob, 30, 50–51, 54. 104, 121, 204; charity work of, 83–85
Hopkins, Anthony, 345
Horton, Robert, 332
"Hotel," 323
"Hour of Decision," 136
Howard, Ron, 348
Howard, Sandy, 228
Hubbard, Stanley E., 388–391
Huckster, The, 67
Hudson, Earl, 37; in charge of ABC West Coast operations, 103, 142–143
Huggins, Roy, 127–129, 361; and "The Fugitive," 238–242; and "Maverick," 155–156, 160, 161; and "Movie of the Week," 330–332; and "77 Sunset Strip," 146–148
Hughes, Bob, 403
Hughes, Howard, 1, 61, 98, 451; ABC takeover attempt by, 264–270
Hull, Henry, 24
Humphrey, Hubert, 288
Hunt Foods & Industries, 252, 253, 254
"Huntley-Brinkley Report," 273, 284, 290, 415
Hussein, King, 297
Hutchins and Wheeler, 31
Hutton, Betty, 42, 54
Hyde, Rosel, 261, 262, 266

Iacocca, Lee, 387
IBM, ABC offered for sale to, 461–463
I'll See You in My Dreams, 119, 120
"I Love Lucy," 361
Imitation of Life, 242
Independent television stations, 338, 339
Independent theaters, 70, 71
Ingram, Dan, 303
Insider trading, 112
Instant replays, 186, 191
"Interesting News for Kids," 349
International Federation of Stage Hands and Operators, 40
International Network, ABC, 214–234, 260; ABC Films (syndication), 227–231; advertising, 218, 219, 223–224, 227; Asian interests, 221–223, 232; Australian interests, 214–215, 229–230; broadcast of Queen Elizabeth's coronation, 215–216; Canadian interests, 232; Latin American interests, 216, 217–221, 232; Middle Eastern interests, 223–227; 1969 moon walk telecast, 231–232; programming, 227, 229, 230, 231–232; satellite communications, 221–222, 231–232
International television broadcast, first, 216
Interstate Theatres, 47, 70, 123
Iran, Shah of, 397, 413
"The Iran Crisis—America Held Hostage," 409–410
Iran hostage crisis, 409–410, 411–412
"I Spy," 121
Israel, 39, 224–227, 404, 405; relations with Egypt, 226–227, 406–408; television in, 224–225
Italian films, post-World War II, 55
Italian television, 233
It Happened One Night, 55
It's a Wonderful Life, 55
ITT, 258, 270–271; attempted merger with ABC, 258–264, 270–271, 296, 314

Jackson, Keith, 206, 208, 209
Jackson, Michael, 305
Jackson, Sherry, 120
"The Jackson Five," 347
Jacobs, Bernie, 424–426
Jaffe, Bill, 80
James, Dennis, 81
Jankowski, Gene, 436
Janssen, David, 242
Japan, 383; television stations, ABC interests in, 221–222, 232
Jazz Singer, The, 30, 109, 119
Jenkins, George, 253, 469
Jennings, Charles, 291
Jennings, Peter, 200, 289; with ABC News, 289–293, 404–408, 412–415, 418–419; as a foreign correspondent, 404–408, 412–414
Jerry Lewis Theatre (Hollywood), 236–237
Jessel, George, 118
John Paul II, Pope, 226
Johns Hopkins Medical School, 75, 82
Johnson, Lady Bird, 189
Johnson, Lyndon B., 72, 123, 131, 189, 262, 293; relationship with ABC, 189–190, 276–277; television station of, 189–190; and Vietnam War, 276
Jolson, Al, 35, 119
Jones, Quincy, 381
Joseloff, Stan, 23–24
Judaism, 8–10, 39, 227, 236, 254, 321; and anti-Semitism, 9–10, 35, 66
Junk bonds, 3, 452
Juntilla, James, 112–113
Justice Department, U.S., 450, 451, 453; on ITT-ABC merger attempt, 261–263; 1940s antitrust case against movie studio

monopolies, 68–74, 111, 114; on television coverage of national elections, 296

KABC (Los Angeles): Radio, 303–306; Television, 4, 130, 314–317, 375, 378–380
Kahn, Gus, 119
Kaiser, Henry, 141, 154; involvement with ABC, 156–161
Kalber, Floyd, 381
Kalmenson, Ben, 125, 137
Katz, Sam, 27, 29, 30, 35, 60
Kaufman, Irving, 39
Kaye, Danny, 42
KDKA (Pittsburgh), 8, 11
Kelly, Jack, 160, 161
Kennedy, John F., 190; assassination of, and television coverage, 189, 221–222, 285–289; and Cuban missile crisis, 280–282; disputed authorship of *Profiles in Courage*, 274–275; in 1960 Presidential televised debates, 275
Kennedy, Joseph P., 31, 274–275; as Paramount consultant, 35, 274
Kennedy, Robert, 190, 275, 282
"Kennedy and Co.," 349
Kenton, Stan, 42
KGO-Radio (San Francisco), 97, 302, 303, 311–312
KGTV (San Diego), 391
Khomeini, Ayatollah, 413
Khrushchev, Nikita, 282
Kilborn, William, 104
Killea, Marie, 82
Kincey, H. F., 73
Kinescope, 99, 184, 191, 216, 286, 421
King (né Kunsky), John, 36, 299
Kings Row (film), 125
"Kings Row" (TV show), 127, 160
KING-TV (Seattle), 382
Kinoy, Ernie, 364
Kintner, Bob, 103, 117–118, 137, 140, 150, 181, 285, 294, 382; decline at ABC, 137, 141, 142; as head of ABC, 103, 117–118, 134, 137, 139, 140–142, 149–150, 151, 167, 273; at NBC, 142, 150, 283, 285, 286, 294, 382
Kirkland, Jack, 23
Kissinger, Henry, 354
KFI (Los Angeles), 304
Klein, Terry, 173
Klutznick, Thomas, 231
Knotts, Don, 204
KNXT-TV (Los Angeles), 143
Kohn, Ralph, 35
Konysky, Hank, 306
Koppel, Ted, 289; with ABC News, 392, 404, 409, 410–412, 415
Korbut, Olga, 203
Kovac, Ed, 171–172
KQV (Pittsburgh), 308
Kramer vs. Kramer, 153
Kreisler, Fritz, 135, 136
Krim, Arthur, 333
KSTP-TV (Minneapolis), 388–391
KTLA-TV (Los Angeles), 96, 110–111, 114
Ku Klux Klan, 9
Kunsky-Trendle Radio Network, 36
Kuwait, Emir al Sabah of, 224

Laemmle, Carl, 28
Laine, Frankie, 42
"L.A. Law," 351
Lamour, Dorothy, 54
Lang, Jennings, 330
Langton, Baden, 290
Larman, Sig, 157, 158, 159, 169
Lasker, Albert and Mary, 78–80
Lasker Foundation, 79
Lasky, Sid, 28
Lastfogel, Abe, 118, 120, 143, 144, 145
Last Licks, 425
Latimer, George W., 113–114
Latin American stations, ABC interests in, 216, 217–221, 232
"Laugh In," 321
"Laverne & Shirley," 348, 360–361
Lavin, Leonard, 243
"Lawrence Welk's Dodge Dancing Party," 130
"The Lawrence Welk Show," 130–131
"Lawrence Welk's Top Tunes and New Talent," 130
Lazarsfeld, Dr. Paul, 148–149
League of Women Voters, 295
Lean, David, 134
Lear, Norman, 321–322
"Leave It to the Girls," 139
Lebanon, 404–405, 414; television, ABC interests in, 223–225
Lee, Peggy, 237
Lehman, Bobby, 243
Lehman Brothers, 243
Lenin, Vladimir Ilich, 44
Leonard, Sheldon, 120, 121, 323
LeShan, Eda, 350–351
Levathes, Pete, 63, 154, 159, 168–169, 239
Leveraged buyouts (LBOs), 452, 458
Levy, Gus, 253–255

Lewine, Bob, 126, 142, 150, 151, 155–156, 216
Lewis, Jerry, 42, 235–237
Lewis, Shari, 185
"Liberace," 169
Liberty Pictures, 55
Life magazine, 107, 117, 398
Life Savers, 97–98
Life Savers Corporation, 98
Lifetime, 432
Light, Judith, 371
Lights of New York, 30
Lincoln Mercury, 157, 158
Little, Dr. William, 82
Little League Baseball, 205, 350
"The Little Rascals" (animation), 351–352
Litton Industries, 260
Live programming, ABC-TV, 127, 128, 329
L & M Cigarettes, 195
Loan-outs, in movie industry, 65
Loeb, John, 265
Loew, Marcus, 28
Loews, 4, 28, 29, 30, 58, 108, 118, 258, 455; 1940s government antitrust suits against, 68, 70, 71
Logo, ABC, 244–245
London Bureau, ABC News, 402, 404, 414, 418
London *Sun*, 232–233
"The Lone Ranger" (radio serial), 37, 119, 299
Lord, Thomas, and Logan Advertising, 78
Loren, Sophia, 55
Lorillard Tobacco, 336, 337
Lorimar, 334
Los Angeles, 98, 301; ABC Entertainment based in, 345; ABC-Radio stations in, 298, 303–306, 308; ABC-TV O & O stations in, 4, 96, 109, 110–111, 114, 130, 314–317, 375, 378–380; 1940s Hollywood, 53–71; 1984 Olympics, 199, 279, 305–306, 456–459
Los Angeles Dodgers, 304
Los Angeles magazine, 422
Louisiana, Paramount theaters in, 43, 67
"Love, American Style," 348
"Love Boat," 323
"Love in the Afternoon," 371
Lower, Elmer, 283; as head of ABC News, 285–297, 392; with NBC, 283–285
Lubell, Jack, 186
Luce, Clare Boothe, 135
Lundy, Ron, 303
Lynch, Charles McKenna, 17–19, 20, 22
Lynch, Stephen A., 25–26, 31, 32, 33, 35, 57, 256
Ma and Pa Kettle at Home, 143
MacGraw, Ali, 444, 445
"MacGyver," 371
Macioce, Tom, 469
MacMurray, Fred, 153
Made-for-television movies, ABC-TV, 329–335, 447. *See also specific programs*
Madison Theatre (Detroit), 37, 38, 105
Maeda, Jiro, 221, 222
Mafia, 29, 274; and "The Untouchables," 172–174
Magazine programs, ABC-TV: cable, 431; news, 397–398, 403–404. *See also specific programs*
Mainichi Television, 221
"Make Room for Daddy," 119–121; broadcast in Lebanon, 223–224
"Making of the President, 1960" (TV documentary), 278–279
Making of the President, 1960, The (book), 278–279
Mallardi, Mike, 436, 455–456, 459, 460, 466
Management, ABC-TV, 109, 116, 342; of ABC Entertainment, 345–374; conflicts and changes, 117–118, 137–144, 176–179, 181, 235, 250, 275, 283, 297, 300–301, 314, 317–318, 342–345, 354, 359, 441, 449; "hands off" period (1953–1955), 103–104, 118–137; of International Network, 216–224, 227–231; and ITT merger attempt, 259, 260–261, 314; Moore era, 235–250, 280, 314; in news division, 276, 277, 281, 282, 283–285, 289, 297, 392–395, 399–419; 1972–1974 restructuring of, 342–345, 354; 1980s vulnerability of, 441–442, 449–450, 452, 455, 456, 457–461; of O & O stations, 378–381; Rule era, 314–340, 386; salaries, 229, 231; in sports division, 181–213; Treyz era and decline, 138–180, 300–301; working style of, 319–321, 347–348, 358. *See also specific divisions and personnel*
"The Man from 1999," 155
Manufacturer's Trust, 264
Man Who Came to Dinner, The, 138
March of Dimes, 62, 77, 85
Marcos, Ferdinand, 437–438
"Marcus Welby, M.D.," 328–329
Margulies, Stan, 364, 445
Markley, Sid, 123, 133–134
Marshall, Garry, 347, 348
Marshall, Walter, 104
Marshall Field, 97
Martin, Dean, 42
Martin, John, 438–439
Martin, Quinn, 172, 241–242
Martin, Tony, 42

Marvin, Lee, 127
Marx, Frank, 98, 190, 235; as head of ABC engineering, 98–99; on Ed Noble, 101–102
Marx, Groucho, 104
Marx Brothers, 30
Mary Poppins, 122
Masque Theatre (New York City), 24
Massachusetts Institute of Technology, 91
Mass appeal, importance in entertainment industry, 32–33, 55
Master agreements, 70
Masters Golf, 206, 208
"Maverick," 151, 155–161, 238
Maxwell, Robert, 232–233
"Mayberry, R.F.D.," 204
Mayer, Louis B., 57–58, 64
Mayes, Herbert, 254, 256, 257
MBS (Osaka station), 221, 222
MCA, 4, 333; merger with ABC sought by, 454–455
McAndrew, Bill, 283, 285
McCall Corporation, 252, 253, 254, 256–258
McCall's magazine, 252
McCann Erickson, 173
McCarey, Leo, 55
McCarthy, Senator Eugene, 292
McCarthy, Senator Joseph, 272; Army hearings televised by ABC, 272–273
McClintock, Earl, 96, 99
McCrary, Tex, 83
McCullough, Colleen, 445
McGranery, James, 114
McKay, Jim, 200, 201, 206
McKenna, Jim, 266, 339
McKinley, John, 438
McKinsey Company, 318
McLaughlin, Ed, 311–313
McNeill, Don, 307
McPhail, Bill, 244
Medical programs, ABC-TV, 151–152, 153, 328–329. *See also specific programs*
Medical research on human diseases, involvement of entertainment industry in, 79–94
"Meet the Press," 158
Meir, Golda, 225–226
Melbourne *Herald*, 214
Mellon family, 18, 97
Mellon Institute, 78
Melnick, Dan, 149, 235, 340; as ABC program development manager, 149–153, 172, 177–178, 240; on Ollie Treyz, 178–179
Meredith, Don, 206, 208–213
Mergers, ABC. *See* Capital Cities/ABC; Takeover and merger attempts, ABC; UPT-ABC merger
Merrill, Eugene, 115
Merritt, Dr. Houston, 90, 94
Mestre, Goar, 218–219
Metropolitan Life Insurance, 60, 106, 192, 253
Mexico City Olympics (1968), 198, 207
MGM (Metro-Goldwyn-Mayer), 20, 28, 58, 63–64, 69, 108, 110, 142, 455; in television, 108, 239
Michigan Theatre (Detroit), 37
"The Mickey Mouse Club," 124, 132, 150, 161, 168
Middle East: ABC News coverage in, 394, 405–410, 411–414; television stations, ABC interests in, 223–227
Midnight Express, 153
Midseason replacement shows, 247, 348, 359
Miller, Glenn, 42
Miller, Tom, 348
"Milton Berle," 139
Miniseries, ABC-TV, 345–346, 355, 363–366, 442–447, 457, 466. *See also specific programs*
Minneapolis, ABC affiliates in, 388–391
Minow, Newton, 166, 167, 429
Mississippi, Paramount theaters in, 43
Mitchum, Robert, 444
Modern Photography, 420
"Modern Romances," 140
"Mod Squad," 120, 323–324, 328
Mohrhardt, Fred, 33, 34, 81
Mondale, Walter, 397
"Monday Night Football," 187, 188, 204–213, 366, 439
Monogram Industries, 264
Monroe, Marilyn, 60, 62, 177
Monsanto Chemical, 128
Montgomery, Elizabeth, 243
Montgomery, George, 126, 127
Montreal Olympics (1976), 203, 306, 400
Monty, Gloria, 370, 448
Moon walk (1969), ABC's telecast of, 231–232
Moore, Leonard and Lynch (Pittsburgh), 17–19, 20
Moore, Tom, 143, 286, 387; as group vice president of ABC, 316–317, 318; as head of ABC-TV programming, 144, 145, 172, 174–176, 178, 179, 182, 183, 185, 186, 194, 235; leadership abilities of, questioned, 250, 314, 317, 318; leaves ABC, 318; as president of ABC-TV Network, 179, 194, 210, 235–250, 280, 314

Moore, Tom, Jr., 237–238
Morgan, Edward P., 288, 289
Morning shows, ABC-TV, 349, 353–354. *See also specific programs*
Morris (William) Agency, 118, 327, 363, 393
Morrow, Cousin Brucie, 303
Morse, Wayne, 262
Mosher, Jim, 151, 152
Motion picture industry, 2, 46; charity work of, 79–85; early growth of, 26–30, 60–61, 69–70, 112, 113; effects of television on, 67–68, 95, 104, 107–115, 118, 123, 124–129, 251–252, 298; feature films shown on television, 132–134, 137, 154, 251–252, 258, 264, 330, 334; mass appeal factor in, 32–33, 55; 1940s antitrust cases against, and subsequent theater divestment, 68–74, 95, 111, 114; 1940s Hollywood, 53–71; percentage deals in, 55–56; talkies introduced in, 27, 29–30, 32, 109, 298; theater chains controlled by, 26–30, 31, 53–55, 69–71, 112, 113. *See also* Theater industry
Motion Picture Pioneers of America, 51
"Movie of the Week," 204, 330–334
"Movie of the Weekend," 334
Movies, ABC-TV: cable, 432–433; feature films, 132–134, 137, 154, 252, 258, 264, 330, 334; made-for-television, 329–335, 447
Movie theme songs, 53
MTM, 368, 373
MTV, 429
Mudd, Roger, 416
Mullen, Martin, 31, 35
Munich Olympics (1972), 200–203, 206, 280, 399
"Murder, She Wrote," 323
Murdoch, Sir Keith, 214, 215
Murdoch, Rupert, 214–215; Fox Broadcasting started by, 233; on Leonard Goldenson, 233–234; involvement with ABC, 214–215, 229–230, 232–234
Murphy, Arthur, 257, 258
Murphy, Tom, 462; and Capital Cities/ABC merger, 462–467
Murrow, Edward R., 272, 284, 291
Musical variety programs, ABC-TV, 130–131, 144–145, 161–165, 347. *See also specific programs*
Music industry payola scandal (1959), 163–165, 301–302
Mutual Radio Network, 37
"My Body, My Child," 355
"My Mom Is Having a Baby," 350
"My Three Sons," 153
"My True Story," 140

Nabisco, 439
"Naked City," 146, 151
Namath, Joe, 193
Nardino, Gary, 443
Narrowcasting, 428–429
NASA-developed technology for the handicapped, 90–91
National Association of Broadcasters (NAB), 386, 389
National Conference of Christians and Jews, 421
National elections, television coverage of, 294–297
National Institutes of Health, 79, 91
Nazi Germany, 66
NBC Radio Network, 298; Blue, 96, 140, 299, 308; Red, 96, 140, 299, 308
NBC Television Network, 85, 101, 104, 107, 108, 110, 139, 151, 176, 204, 208, 232, 238, 328, 339, 357, 420; ABC as trendsetter for, 129, 153, 345, 419, 441; advertising rates, 168, 170, 171, 252; affiliates, 104, 115, 116, 382, 384, 388, 389, 391; Roone Arledge at, 184, 185; Army-McCarthy hearings covered by, 272–273; audiences, 104, 148, 149; cable interests, 438; color broadcasting, 142, 251–252; and Disney Company, 122, 123, 124, 251; early growth of, 116, 171–172; foreign interests, 215–217; headquarters, 244; Bob Kintner with, 142, 150, 283, 285, 286, 294, 382; morning shows, 349, 353, 354, 392, 393; movies, 251–252, 330, 332; news programming, 272, 273, 275, 279, 283–285, 286, 293–297, 392, 401, 404, 409, 415–417, 418, 419; 1980s success of, 441; 1980s vulnerability to takeovers, 452; -owned stations, 382; ratings, 146, 243, 349, 353, 354; Fred Silverman as president of, 372, 373; sports programming, 182–184, 192, 193, 194, 197, 201, 203, 204. *See also specific programs*
NCAA football games, 207, 208; on ABC-TV, 117–118, 137, 181–186, 189–191, 194, 195, 206; on Lyndon Johnson's television station, 189–190; on NBC-TV, 182, 183; network bidding for, 183–184
Neal, Hal, 299, 303, 304, 307
Neale, Jimmy, 182
"Ned Jordan, Federal Ace" (radio serial), 37
Nelson, Gaylord, 261
Nelson, Ozzie and Harriet, 104, 108, 118

Index

NET (Tokyo station), 221
"Never Too Young," 248
New England, Paramount theaters in, 25–26, 30–34, 35, 274
"The Newlywed Game," 248
Newman, Paul, 355, 443
"The New Original Wonder Woman," 362
New Orleans, 43, 44, 67
News, ABC-TV, 116, 117, 205, 272–297, 392–419, 449; advertising, 277, 278, 280, 285; affiliates, 273, 284, 287, 293, 376–378, 379, 409, 412; anchors, 277, 284, 288, 289–293, 392–418; Roone Arledge as head of, 399–419; John Daly as head of, 273, 275, 277; documentary films, 278–280, 296; early programming, 116, 132, 272–297; foreign affairs coverage, 280–282, 406–412; Jim Hagerty as head of, 276, 277, 281, 282, 283; and ITT merger attempt, 259, 261; on Lyndon Johnson, 276–277; Kennedy assassination coverage, 285–289; London Bureau, 402, 404, 414, 418; Elmer Lower as head of, 285–297, 392; magazine shows, 397–398, 403–404; mid-1970s to mid-1980s, 392–419; on Richard Nixon, 277–278; presidential election coverage, 275, 278–279, 294–297; *Profiles in Courage* authorship dispute coverage, 274–275; ratings, 293, 296, 297, 397, 412, 415, 416, 417; Reasoner/Walters team, 392–397, 399, 401–402; scheduling innovations, 293, 395, 409; Bill Sheehan as head of, 297, 392–395; three-desk format, 402–403, 405–408, 410, 412–416, 417; Barbara Walters with, 392–399, 401–402, 408, 415; Washington Bureau, 288, 293–294, 402, 409, 410, 412, 414. *See also specific anchors and programs*
News Election Service, 296
News Limited, 214; ABC interests in, 214–215, 232–233
Newsweek magazine, 448
New York Cerebral Palsy Telethons, 85
New York City, 118, 275, 427; ABC-Radio stations, 97, 298, 303, 308; ABC-TV O & O stations in, 375; early television industry in, 99, 105; Goldenson's early years in, 21–52; World's Fair (1939), 95
New York City Music Hall, 32
New York *Daily News*, 96
New Yorker, The, 138
New York Giants, 187, 286
New York Jets, 193, 210
New York *Mirror*, 131
New York Paramount Theatre, 39–43, 60, 67, 111
New York Post, 96
New York State Association for Cerebral Palsy, 82, 92–93
New York Times, The, 24, 57, 107, 115, 138, 178, 225, 243, 278, 295, 317, 464; *Magazine*, 371
New York Titans, 192–193
New York *World Telegram*, 295
Nickelodeon, 429
Nickelodeons, 32, 69
Nielsen rating system, 121, 181
"Nightline," 411–412
Night of the Stars for United Jewish Appeal, 81
Nighttime programming, ABC-TV, 211, 391; early, 116, 127–131, 132, 139, 142, 144, 146, 154–161; mid-1970s hits, 345–346, 348, 355, 358–369; Moore era, 236–237, 242–243, 247; news, 272–297, 392–419; of 1980s, 442–447, 449; Prime Time Access Rule, 338–339; Rule era, 329, 330–335, 337; sports, 204–213. *See also specific programs*
Nixon, Agnes, 369
Nixon, Richard M., 209–210; on foreign affairs, 277, 282–283; in 1960 Presidential televised debates, 275; relationship with ABC, 277–278
Nixon Administration, 262
Noble, Ed, 96, 97–98, 116, 118, 137, 382; ABC acquired by (as Blue Network), 96–97, 98, 140; ABC sold by, 99–103, 106, 107, 109–110; as major UPT-ABC stockholder, 109, 110, 115, 142
Nodella, Burt, 240
North Carolina, ABC-TV affiliate in, 384, 391
Northern Theatre Division (Chicago), 230, 231
Novels for television. *See* Miniseries, ABC-TV

O'Brien, Bob, 66, 72; as executive VP of ABC, 103, 116–118, 134, 137, 181; and UPT-ABC merger, 99, 100, 103
Odd Man Out, 134
O'Donnell, Bob, 47–51, 56, 123
O'Dwyer, Sloan Simpson, 83
Ohlmeyer, Don, 438–439
O'Leary, Dick, 320, 349; as head of ABC O & O's, 378, 381–382; at KABC-TV, 375; at WLS-TV, 376–378
Olivier, Laurence, 134
Olympics, ABC coverage of, 197, 198–204, 206, 279, 280, 456–459; *1960* Winter Games, 184, 197; *1964* Summer Games, 203; *1964* Winter Games, 197; *1968*

Olympics (*cont.*)
Summer Games, 198, 207; *1972* Summer Games, 200–203, 206, 280, 399; *1972* Winter Games, 203; *1976* Summer Games, 203, 306, 400; *1980* Summer Games, 203, 457; *1984* Summer Games, 199, 279, 305–306, 456–459; *1984* Winter Games, 456–457; *1988* Summer Games, 203; *1988* Winter Games, 203
O'Malley, Walter, 304
"Omnibus," 158
O'Neal, Ryan, 242
"One Life to Live," 347, 369, 370, 371
OPEC, 225
Operation Daybreak, 168–172
Orr, Bill, 125–128, 146, 147, 155
Orson Welles at Large, 143
Osgood, Charles, 289
"The Osmond Brothers," 347
Otterson, John, 26
Outlaw, The, 265
Owned and Operated (O & O) stations, ABC-TV, 216, 235, 244, 307, 308, 310, 316, 335, 349, 354, 374, 375–382; in Chicago, 85, 96, 100, 102, 109, 114, 198, 293, 349, 375, 376–378, 380–381, 432; in Detroit, 100, 109, 375; in Los Angeles, 96, 109, 110–111, 114, 130, 314–317, 375, 378–380; management of, 378–381, 466; in New York, 375; profits, 216, 375, 381–382; in San Francisco, 100, 109, 110. *See also specific cities and stations*; Television Network, ABC
"Ozzie and Harriet," 108, 118

Paley, William S., 35, 100, 102, 139, 245, 258, 452, 455; and Walt Disney, 122–123, 235
Palmer, Dr. Martin, 93
Paramount (Paramount Pictures; Paramount Theatres; up to 1948), 20, 24, 26–74, 118, 123, 127, 189, 214, 222, 238, 254, 256, 269, 389, 421; charity work by, 77; Chicago theaters, 26–30, 85, 95, 112, 113, 121; concession sales, 32; Detroit theaters, 36–39, 43, 105, 299; distribution division, 47; early growth of, 26–30, 33, 42, 60–61, 69–70, 112, 113; early television interests, 96; foreign interests of, 214; Goldenson as head of theater division, 52–74; Liberty Pictures acquired by, 55; Louisiana theaters, 43, 67; New England theaters, 25–26, 30–34, 35, 274; 1930s reorganization of, 25–26, 30–35, 53; 1940s operations, 53–68; in 1948 antitrust case, and subsequent theater divestment, 68, 70–74, 95, 111, 114; post-reorganization, 35–44; profitability, 36, 37–39, 40–41, 73; Rainbow Films acquired by, 55; Texas theaters, 47–50; theater chains controlled by, 26–30, 31, 53–55, 69–74, 112, 113. *See also* Paramount Pictures (after 1948); United Paramount Theatres
Paramount Building (New York City), 40, 132
Paramount Gulf Theatres, 67
Paramount Pictures (after 1948), 73, 97, 103, 254, 323, 333, 355, 362; Barry Diller as chairman of, 356, 362, 442; early television interests, 96; interest in Dumont TV Network, 105, 106, 110–111, 113, 114; relationship with UPT, 111–114, separation from UPT, 73, 95, 112, 114; stock, 111–112
Paramount Publix Corporation, 29
Pastore, John, 172–173, 177, 276
"Paul Harvey, News and Comment," 307, 308
Payola scandal in music industry (1959), 163–165, 301–302
Pay-per-view television, 213, 427
PBS, 167, 429
Pearl Harbor, attack on, 52, 66, 273
Pearson, Drew, 82, 274
Pepsico, 4, 218, 219, 461
Percentage deals, in entertainment industry, 55–56, 227–228, 229
Perry, Hart, 260
"Perry Como," 139
"Person to Person," 291
Peters, Jon, 397
Petrillo, James Caesar, 40
"Petticoat Junction," 143, 149
Peyton Place (film), 242
"Peyton Place" (TV show), 242–243
Phantom of the Opera, The, 109
Phelps, Dr. Winthrop, 82
Philadelphia, 161, 162
Picard, Paul, 235
Pickford, Mary, 61
Pierce, Fred, 318, 359, 426, 468; as executive VP of ABC, 441; leadership abilities, questioned, 449–450, 457; as president of ABC Television, 354–374, 392–393, 397, 399, 403, 410, 415, 416–417, 429, 436–439, 441, 442–443, 449; as president and COO of ABC, 449, 452, 457–458, 466–467
Pinanski, Sam, 31, 35
Pittsburgh, 6, 8, 105, 452; Goldenson's early years in, 17–19, 20–21; radio, 308; WTAE-TV, 430
Pleshette, Gene, 39
Pleshette, Suzanne, 39

Plitt, Henry, 66–68, 231; in charge of ABC films, 227–231
Plitt Theatres, 231
Plummer, Christopher, 286
Poland, 226, 227
Polio, 77, 82, 85
"The Political Obituary of Richard M. Nixon," 277
Pompadur, I. Martin, 318, 319, 320–321, 427
Ponti, Carlo, 55
Pooling agreements, 70
Posner, Vladimir, 411–412
Powell, Dick, 322, 323
Presidential elections, television coverage of, 277, 294–297; *1960*, 275, 278–279, 284; *1964*, 289, 294, 295; *1968*, 292, 296–297; pooling arrangement discussions, 294–295
Price Waterhouse, 85
Prime Time Access rule, 338–339
Primetime programming. *See* Nighttime programming, ABC-TV
Prime Time Stars for Daytime, 447–448
Procter & Gamble, 141–142, 168, 169, 428
Profiles in Courage (Kennedy), disputed authorship of, 274–275
Profits, ABC, 102, 258–259; cable, 431, 438, 440; early, 121, 144; international, 216, 231; loss of cigarette revenue, 337, 339; of 1960s, 252; of 1970s, 366–367, 391; of 1980s, 3, 4, 449, 457, 458–459; O & O, 216, 375, 381–382; publishing, 423; radio, 307, 310, 311, 313
Programming, ABC-TV (1953–1972), 104, 109, 238, 250, 264, 345, 359; accused of excessive sex and violence, 177; Jim Aubrey as head of, 143–144, 182; becomes ABC Entertainment (1972), 345; bridging, 139, 160, 334; color, slow conversion to, 251–252, 258, 263, 264; comedy, 321–322; comic book series, 245–247; crime shows, 146, 172–174, 238–242, 323; Disney involvement, 123, 124, 142, 251, 423; drop-in issue, 165–166; early, 116–136, 143–174; early budget difficulties, 109, 116, 117, 134, 170; early lack of, 116, 129, 132, 134, 136, 142, 143, 146, 161, 168, 181; ethnic groups offended by, 172–174, 321–322; feature films, 132–134, 137, 154, 252, 258, 264, 330, 334; game shows, 247–248; Leonard Goldberg as head of, 249, 250, 321, 326–335; Gothic serials, 248–249; Hollywood sources of talent, 104, 107, 108, 118, 143, 236–238, 242, 252, 325, 342; international, 227, 229, 230, 231–232; live, 127, 128, 329; made-for-television movies, 329–335; medical shows, 151–152, 153, 328–329; Dan Melnick as development manager, 149–153, 172, 177–178, 240; Tom Moore as head of, 144, 145, 172, 174–176, 178, 179, 182, 183, 185, 186, 194, 235; musical variety shows, 130–131, 144–145, 161–165; percentage of successful shows, 166–167; Prime Time Access rule, 338–339; religious, 134–136; scheduling innovations, 243, 246–247; Ed Scherick as head of, 194, 235, 236–237, 242–250, 261, 285–286, 326; series based on movies, 124–129; skeptical views on, 104, 106–108, 116, 118, 127, 141, 158, 168; soap operas, 242–243, 248; Aaron Spelling projects, 322–326, 328, 332–333; Marty Starger as head of, 335, 345; trendsetting in, 127–129, 143, 146, 151–153, 160, 167–168, 181, 186–192, 196, 211, 243–247, 293, 303–305, 323, 328, 345, 347, 367; variety shows, 235–237; Warner Bros. involvement, 124–129, 137, 142, 146, 155–161; Bob Weitman as head of, 116, 134–136, 142; Westerns, 127–129, 154–161, 238; youth, 148–149, 151, 273, 290, 291, 327, 350–351, 441. *See also* Advertising, ABC-TV; Daytime programming, ABC-TV; Entertainment, ABC (after 1972); News, ABC-TV; Nighttime programming, ABC-TV; *specific programs*; Sports, ABC-TV
Promotion, ABC-TV, 340, 371, 378; affiliate, 382; of "Batman," 246–247; of children's shows, 350–351; of daytime programs, 350–351, 371, 447–448; of movies, 123–129; on-air, 328; trendsetting in, 246–247, 328; of "The Winds of War," 444–445
Prowse, Juliet, 145
Publishing, ABC, 3, 420–324, 431
Publix Netoco Theatres, 31
Pyne, Joe, 304–305

QB VII, 345
Quinn, Anthony, 421

Rabb, Max, 265
Rabinovitz, Jay, 116–118
"The Race for Space," 278
Racism, in entertainment industry, 119, 365
Radio industry, 104, 128, 142, 298, 382; advertising, 128, 139, 167, 170, 313; Blue Network, 96, 140, 170, 299, 308; early, 8, 11, 27, 35, 36–37, 119, 139, 140, 251, 298–300, 388; FCC's chain broadcasting rules, 96–97, 100, 308–310; influence on

Radio industry (*cont.*)
television, 148, 170–171; 1980s deregulatory policies, 451; post-television identity crisis, 298, 307–308; Red Network, 96, 140, 299, 308. *See also specific networks and stations*
Radio Networks, ABC, 2, 3, 97, 139, 141, 164, 205, 288, 298–313, 335, 387, 420, 449; advertising, 139, 167, 307–313; affiliates, 97, 140, 310–313; Chicago stations, 97, 298, 308, 420; conflict-of-interest standards, 301–302; creation of, 97; Detroit stations, 99, 298–300, 308; as dominant force in radio industry, 313; Los Angeles stations, 298, 303–306, 308; multiple network concept, 309–312; New York stations, 97, 298, 303, 308; post-television identity crisis, 307–308; profits, 307, 310, 311, 313; program development and innovations, 303–313; ratings, 308, 309; religious programming, 302–303; San Francisco stations, 97, 298, 302, 303, 308, 311–312. *See also specific cities and stations*
Radio News Service, 388
Raibourn, Paul, 38, 105–106
Rainbow Films, 55
"Rainbow Sundae," 349
Rank, J. Arthur, 54, 132, 133
Rather, Dan, 384, 415–416
Ratings, ABC-TV, 121, 131, 252, 349, 385, 386; for daytime programming, 349, 350, 353, 354; early, 129, 142, 150, 158, 163; effect of "Roots" on, 366, 447; first time beating of CBS and NBC, 243; mid-1970s successes, 349, 350, 353, 361, 362, 366; Moore era, 236, 237, 242, 243, 252; for news programming, 293, 296, 297, 397, 412, 415, 416, 417; of 1980s, 445, 446, 447, 457, 458, 466; for sports programming, 204, 211
Ratings, television, 121, 146, 161, 171; Nielsen system, 121, 181
RCA, 96, 99, 106, 111, 217, 428; cable interests, 429–430, 433; color television, 124, 251–252; and Disney Company, 124; NBC as part of, 217
Reader's Digest, 258
Reagan, Nancy, 418
Reagan, Ronald, 98, 121, 450, 454, 455, 458
Reagan Administration, 405; deregulation of broadcasting industry, 3, 450–455
"Real McCoys," 120
Reasoner, Harry, 293; as ABC coanchor with Barbara Walters, 394–397, 399, 401–402; return to CBS, 402, 404
Rebel Without a Cause, 147
Redbook magazine, 252
Redford, Robert, 146, 445
Red Network, 96, 140, 299, 308
Red Shoes, The, 134
Reed, Carol, 134
Reger, Bob, 187
Religious programming, ABC: radio, 302–303; television, 134–136. *See also specific programs*
Remick, Lee, 355
Republic Bank (Dallas), 47, 123–124
Republic Pictures, 54, 55–56
Reruns, 339
Resnick, Leo, 110, 114
Reynolds, Frank, 293; with ABC News, 402, 408, 409, 410, 414–418; terminal illness of, 410, 411, 416, 417–418
Reynolds, John, 375
Reynolds, R. J., 195
Rich, Lee, 334
Rich, Raymond, 257–258
Richards, E. V., 30, 43–44, 67, 73
Richards, Reverend Bob, 182
"Richie Rich," 351
"Rich Man, Poor Man," 346, 360
Riddell, Jimmy, 232, 299–301, 303, 375
Ritz brothers, 30
Rivera, Geraldo, 274
Riviera Theatre (Chicago), 27
RKO (Radio Keith Orpheum), 51, 58, 61, 65, 123, 264; 1940s antitrust suits against, 68, 70, 71
Roberts, Oral, 422
Robinson, Max, 402; with ABC News, 402, 414–415, 418
Rockefeller, Nelson, 295
Rockefeller Foundation, 78
Rogers, Ginger, 51
Rohatyn, Felix, 454
Roman Holiday, 55
Romney, George, 141
"Rookie of the Year," 350
Rooney, Andy, 395, 396
Rooney, Mickey, 58
Rooney, Pat, 82
Roosevelt, Franklin D., 77, 85, 95, 278, 294
Root, Clark, Buckner, and Ballantine, 24
Roots (book), 363
"Roots" (TV show), 279, 363–366, 447
Rose, Billy, 131
Rose, Jack, 120
Rose, Pete, 354
"Roseanne," 351
Rosenberg, Meta, 151, 152
Rosenhaus, Matty, 130

Rosenwald, Julius, 27, 89
Rote, Kyle, Jr., 421
Roth, Gerard & Company, 258
Roxy Theater (New York City), 42
Rozelle, Pete, 204, 205, 208, 286, 337
Rubella, 75–76, 92
Rudner, Sam, 24
Rudolph, Lou, 364
Rukeyser, Bud, 185
Rule, Elton, 385, 420, 426; as manager of KABC-TV, 314–317, 375, 376, 386; as president of ABC-TV Network, 210, 314–340, 386; as president and CEO of ABC, 343–345, 354, 355, 364, 371, 401, 449; retirement of, 449; working style of, 319–321
Rushnell, Squire, 349, 359; as vice president of ABC's children's television, 349–354
Rusk, Dean, 281–282, 289
Russell, A. J., 370
Russell, Jane, 265
"Ryan's Hope," 369

Saatchi & Saatchi, 168
Sadat, Anwar, 226–227; ABC News coverage of, 394, 405–408; meeting with Begin, 406–408
"St. Elsewhere," 153
St. John, Jill, 332
St. Jude's Children's Research Hospital, 121
Salaries, ABC, 229, 231, 284, 292
"The Sammy Davis, Jr., Show," 119
Sampson, Harry LeBaron, 30–31
San Francisco, 301, 382; ABC-Radio stations in 97, 298, 302, 303, 308, 311–312; ABC-TV O & O stations in, 100, 109, 110
Sangster, Jimmy, 332
Saratoga Trunk, 127
Sarnoff, General David, 96–97, 100, 106, 108, 122, 131, 139, 140, 184, 251, 252, 285
Satellite communications, 196, 201, 214, 233, 309, 313, 402, 427, 428, 431, 433, 434; ABC's early use of, 201, 221–222, 231–232
Satellite News Channels (SNC), 432, 438
Saturday Evening Post, 107, 128, 171, 258
"Saturday Night at the Movies," 252
Saturday Review magazine, 252
Saudek, Robert, 286
Savalas, Telly, 205
Savitch, Jessica, 392
Sawyer, Diane, 393
Scali, John, 281–283, 289; role in Cuban missile crisis, 281–282
Scarface, 49
Scatter buys, 139
Schary, Dore, 58
Schenck, Joe, 62–63
Schenck, Nick, 58, 62, 108
Schenkel, Chris, 207
Scherick, Edgar, 181, 347; and ABC Sports, 181–184, 186, 194, 195; as head of ABC-TV programming, 194, 235, 236–237, 242–250, 261, 285–286, 326
Schiff, Dorothy, 96
Schoenfeld, Jerry, 424–426
Schuler, Robert, 421
Schwartz, Wally, 335
Science fiction serials, first television, 105
"Scooby Doo," 351, 352
"Scooby Doo and Scrappy," 352
Scottdale, Pa., Goldenson's early life in, 6–14, 20
Screen Gems, 146, 153, 224, 243, 332, 335
Scully, Vin, 207
Seamans, Bill, 406–407
Sears, 27
Seattle, ABC-TV affiliate in, 382–383
Second-run theaters, 70, 72
Securities and Exchange Commission (SEC), 264, 266, 450, 455
Seder, Madeline Goldenson, 7–8, 10, 12
Selassie, Haile, 289
Seligman, Selig, 376
Self, Bill, 245
Selznick, David O., 46, 58, 64
Selznick, Lewis J., 46, 64
Semple, Lorenzo, 245–246
Senate Communications Subcommittee, 276
Seoul Olympics (1988), 203
Sequential networking, 309–312
7-7-7 formula, 451
77 Sunset Strip (movie), 147, 148
77 Sunset Strip (novel), 127
"77 Sunset Strip" (TV show), 146–148, 151
Seymour, Dan, 179
Seymour, Jane, 446
"Shadow Box," 355
Shaker, Ted, 244, 284
Shanks, Bob, 353
Shavelson, Mel, 120
Shaw, Run Me, 222–223
Shaw, Sir Run Run, 222–223
Sheehan, Bill, 292, 293; as head of ABC News, 297, 392–395
Sheen, Bishop Fulton, 134–136
Sheen, Martin, 335
Sheinberg, Sid, 328, 330
Sherman Antitrust Act, 68, 70
Shock radio, 304–305
Shoda, Hidesaburo and Fumiko, 383
Shubert Organization, ABC involvement with, 424–427

Shubert Theatre (Los Angeles), 424, 425
Siegel, Bernie, 343
Siegel, Si, 33–34, 164, 170, 175, 179, 199, 205, 215, 286; as ABC executive vice president, 177, 216, 221, 229, 231, 244, 283, 284, 300, 317, 320, 341–343, 378; and ABC takeover bids, 255–256, 259–260, 263, 265; early recollections of Paramount, 33–34; retirement of, 342–343; on sequential radio networking, 309–310; on Ollie Treyz, 176–177
Siegel, Sol, 54
Silent motion pictures, 32, 109, 298
Silver, Arty, 127
Silverman, Fred, 320, 330, 441; leaves ABC, 372–373; as president of ABC Entertainment, 359–373, 389, 442; as president of NBC, 372, 373
Silver Springs park, 423–424
Simon, Burk, 23–24
Simon, Norton, 1, 252, 258, 314; ABC takeover bid by, 252–258, 259, 260, 270
Sinatra, Frank, 42, 56; relationship with ABC, 144–146
Sitcoms. *See* Comedy programs, ABC-TV
"The Six Million Dollar Man," 348
"60 Minutes," 395, 402, 408, 415
Skouras, Spyros, 81, 112, 242–243
Slow motion, 186, 191, 198
Small, Bill, 417
Smith, Howard K., 277, 286, 288, 293, 396
Smith, Jackie, 369; in ABC daytime programming, 369–371, 447–448
Smith, Kate, 84, 104
Smith, Red, 196
"The Smurfs," 351
Snow White, 62
Snyder, Tom, 365
"Soap," 367–368
Soap operas, 105; on ABC-TV, 242–243, 248, 347, 369–371, 447–448. *See also specific programs*
Sojo, Father, 219–220
Sorensen, Theodore, 274–275
Sound pictures, introduction of, 27, 29–30, 32, 109, 298
Soviet Union, 44, 282–283; ABC Sports in, 196; and Cuban missile crisis, 280–282; 1980 Olympics in, 203, 457; 1984 Olympics boycotted by, 457, 458; space program, 278
Special Interest Publishing Group, 423
Spelling, Aaron, 250, 322, 334; ABC projects of, 322–326, 328, 332–333, 361
Spelling, Torie, 325–326
Spielberg, Steven, 381
Spivak, Charlie, 42
Sponsors. *See* Advertising, ABC-TV
Sports, 105; importance of television to, 187–189; women's 203, 204. *See also specific sports*
Sports, ABC-TV, 2, 117, 181–213, 285, 337, 381, 449; advertising, 182, 185, 186, 187, 188, 192, 194, 195, 210, 213; AFL vs. NFL football rights, 192–194; announcers, 205–213; Roone Arledge as head of, 184–213, 244, 335, 399–401; competition from other networks, 182–184, 193–194, 195, 197, 201, 203; early deals reneged on, 184, 197; early programming, 117–118, 181–213; and ESPN, 435–440, 457; growth of, 184, 194; on Lyndon Johnson's television station, 189–190; "Monday Night Football," 204–213, 439; NCAA games, 117–118, 137, 181–186, 189–191, 194, 195, 206; 1972 Olympics crisis coverage, 200–203, 206, 280, 399; Olympics covered by, 197, 198–204, 206, 279, 280, 456–459; overseas, 196–197, 200–203; and Edgar Scherick, 181–184, 186, 194, 195; success of, 213; trend-setting technology and concepts, 186, 188, 190–192, 194, 196, 197, 198; USFL games, 435; "Wide World of Sports," 194–198, 201, 203, 204, 206. *See also specific programs*
Sports Illustrated magazine, 187, 319
Sports Programs, Inc., 182; acquired by ABC, 184, 194
Squaw Valley Winter Olympics (1960), 184, 197
Stanton, Frank, 102, 258, 286, 294–295, 452
Stapleton, Ruth Carter, 421
Starger, Marty, 320, 328, 332; as head of ABC programming, 335, 345; as president of ABC Entertainment, 345–347, 356, 359, 363–364
"Starsky and Hutch," 361
State Theatre (Detroit), 37
Stations. *See* Affiliates, ABC-Radio; Affiliates, ABC-TV; Owned and Operated (O & O) stations, ABC-TV
Staubach, Roger, 421
Steinberg, Saul, 4, 459
"Stella Dallas," 307
"Steve Allen," 160
Stevens, Gary, 125–126
Stevens, George, 55
Stewart, Jimmy, 55
Stock, ABC, 100, 101, 116, 179; Capital Cities/ABC, 465–467; cumulative voting issue, 254–257; and ITT merger attempt, 259, 260, 264; 1980s vulnerability of, 3, 4,

452, 455–461; and Norton Simon's takeover bid, 253–258; stockholder relations, 255; undervalued, 254; and UPT-ABC merger, 100, 101, 103, 107, 109–110
Stock market, 18–19; Goldenson's early experience with, 18–20; 1929 Crash, 20, 25, 30, 44, 97–98, 299; and 1980s deregulation of broadcasting industry, 3, 452
Stoddard, Brandon, 349; and ABC miniseries, 363, 364–365, 443–447; as head of ABC daytime television, 349, 350
Storz, Todd, 307
Strand Theater (New York City), 28, 42
Strand Theater (Scottdale, Pa.), 10, 11
Straw Dogs, 153, 340
"Streets of San Francisco," 361
Streicher, Julius, 66
Streisand, Barbra, 397
Sugar Bowl, 184, 197
Sullivan, Ed, 43, 81, 104, 193. *See also* "Ed Sullivan Show"
Sulzberger, Arthur Ochs, "Punch," 225, 295
Sulzberger family, 464
"The Sunday Night Movie," 132
"Super Friends," 347
Supreme Court, U.S.: 1948 case against movie studio monopolies, 71–74, 95, 111, 114
Susskind, David, 355
Swaggart, Jimmy, 422
Swanson, Dennis, 381; on Capital Cities/ABC merger, 466–467; as president of ABC Sports, 381; at WLS-TV, 378–381
Syndication, 227, 339; domestic, 231; international, 216–217; 1970 FCC restrictions, 231, 452–453; Reagan era policies, 452–455
Syndication, ABC, 214, 315, 381, 454–455; ABC Films (international), 227–231

Taft, Dudley, 384–386
Taft, Holbert, 384–385
Taft Broadcasting, 384–386
Takeover and merger activities, 1980s rise in, 3, 451
Takeover and merger attempts, ABC, 1–5, 258–264, 267, 270, 314, 341, 351–352; by Bass brothers, 1–2, 4, 459–460; by Howard Hughes, 264–270; by ITT, 258–264, 270–271, 296, 314; by MCA, 454–455; 1980s threat of, and ABC defenses against, 1–5, 452–461; by Norton Simon, 252–258, 259, 260, 270
Talk radio, 303–305, 308, 309, 310, 311
Talk programs, ABC-TV, 349, 380–381; morning, 349, 353–354. *See also specific programs*
Tartikoff, Brandon, 359, 441
"Taxi," 368–369
Taylor, Elizabeth, 397
Technology: ABC-Sports innovations, 186, 190–192, 194, 196, 197, 198; color, 251–252; early television, 99, 105, 166, 196, 214; microwave relay system, 379–380; of 1970s, 402; satellite, 196, 201, 221–222, 231–232, 233, 309, 313, 402, 427, 428, 431, 433, 434; slow motion, 186, 191, 198; video, 3, 196, 427–429, 432
TeleFirst, 432–433, 438
Telenews, 273, 284
Television Bureau of Advertising (TVB), 141
Television industry, 166–167; charity work of, 85–87; cigarette advertising ban effects on, 335–337; color, 124, 142, 251–252; considered an evil influence, 177; creation of competition in, 110, 111; development of, 67–68, 95–96, 98–99, 104–107, 141; early channel allocations, 96, 98–99, 100; early technology, 99, 105, 166, 196, 214; effects on movie industry, 67–68, 95, 104, 107–115, 118, 123, 124–129, 251–252, 298; effects of video technology on, 427–429; FCC freeze on network ownership, 96–97, 110, 111, 115; first international broadcast, 216; foreign interests, 214–234; 1980s deregulatory policies, 450–454; Prime Time Access rule, 338–339; radio's influence on, 148, 170–171. *See also specific networks*
Television Network, ABC, 2–5, 354, 449; attempted merger with ITT, 258–264, 270–271, 296, 314; beginnings of, 98–115; cable, 427–440; and cigarette advertising ban, 335–337; competitiveness in, 104–107, 110, 111, 116, 136, 146, 149, 151, 153, 155–160, 167, 182–184, 193–194, 204, 213, 215–216, 233, 238, 243, 258, 273, 293–297, 318, 329, 367, 409, 419, 420, 441; debt incurred during UPT merger period, 114–115, 116; drop-in issue, 165–166; Jim Duffy as head of, 343, 386, 387–391; early budget difficulties, 109, 116, 117, 134, 170, 296; early channel allocations, 98–99, 100; early growth of, 116–180; early 1980s complacency, 441–442, 447; financial maneuvers for color conversion, 264–271; "hands off" management period, 103–104, 118–137; headquarters in New York, 115, 137, 243–245; International, 214–234; Moore era, 235–250, 280, 314; 1961–1971

Television Network (*cont.*)
deficits, 375, 382; 1970s rise to prime-time dominance, 297, 318, 335, 337, 341–374; of 1980s, 441–450, 457, 466; payola scandal (1959), 163–165, 301–302; Fred Pierce as president of, 354–374, 392–393, 397, 399, 403, 410, 415, 416–417, 429, 436–439, 441, 442–443, 449; Prime Time Access rule, 338–339; reaches number one, 366–367; relationship with Disney Company, 1–2, 121–124, 142, 251, 423, 459; relationship with Warner Bros., 124–129, 137, 142, 146, 155–161; Rule era, 314–340, 386; Wally Schwartz as head of, 335; skeptical views on, 104, 106–108, 116, 141, 158, 168, 185; slow conversion to color programming, 251–252, 258, 263, 264; Ollie Treyz era, 138–180, 300–301; UPT merger, 99–115, 298, 376. *See also* Affiliates, ABC-TV; Cable Networks, ABC; Entertainment, ABC; International Network, ABC; News, ABC-TV; Owned and Operated (O & O) stations, ABC-TV; Programming, ABC-TV (1953–1972); Ratings, ABC-TV; Sports, ABC-TV
Temple, Shirley, 35
Terminal Cab Company, 81, 85
Texaco, 438
Texas, Paramount theaters in, 47–50
That Certain Summer, 335
"That Girl," 328
That's Entertainment, 153
Theater industry, 123; concession sales, 32; controlled by movie studios, 26–30, 31, 53–55, 69–71, 112, 113; divestment of, after 1948 antitrust case, 71–74, 95, 111, 114; early growth of, 26–30, 60–61, 69–70, 112, 113; effects of television on, 67–68, 95, 104, 107–115, 118, 123; 1970s decline, 231. *See also* Movie industry; *specific companies and theaters*
"This Week with David Brinkley," 417–418
Thomas, Danny, 119–121, 223–224, 323, 324, 327
Thomas, Marlo, 327, 328
Thomopoulos, Tony, 426; as head of ABC Entertainment, 373, 446–447, 449; as president of ABC Broadcast Group, 449–450
Thompson, Lord Roy, 224
Thompson (J. Walter) Agency, 179, 189, 193
Thorn Birds, The (book), 445
"The Thorn Birds" (miniseries), 279, 445–447
"Three's Company," 363, 368, 369
"Till Death Do Us Part," 321
Time, Inc., 4, 319, 433–434
Time-Life, 257, 433, 434
Time magazine, 75, 319, 403
Tinker, Grant, 185, 373, 441
Tisch, Larry, 4, 258, 263, 336–337; ABC stock owned by, 455, 460
Tivoli Theatre (Chicago), 28
Tobacco Road, 24
"Today Show," 349, 353, 354, 392, 393
Tokyo Olympics (1964), 203
Top-40 radio format, 307, 308, 309, 310
Touch, The, 340
Trachinger, Bob, 191
Trendle, George W., 36–37, 299
Treyz, Ollie, 137–180, 235, 314, 319; advertising strategies and problems, 139–142, 148–149, 156–160, 167–172, 175–176, 179; background of, 139–139; decline at ABC, 177–179; as president of ABC-TV Network, 142–180, 195, 223, 229, 275, 300, 301, 383
Trilling, Steve, 125–126
Trotsky, Leon, 44
Truman, Harry S., 62, 70
Trump, Donald, 460
Tsai, Gerry, 258, 263
Turner, Donald, 262
Turner, Lana, 242
Turner, Ted, 432, 436, 438, 452. *See also* CNN (Cable News Network)
"Turn On," 321
Twelve Angry Men, 328
Twentieth Century-Fox, 20, 29, 30, 42, 62–63, 110, 169, 180, 239, 242, 245, 246, 362, 424; 1940s antitrust suits against, 68, 70, 71
20th Century Limited (train), 61
"26 Men," 230
"20/20," 397, 398, 402, 403–404, 412

Ueberroth, Peter, 306
UHF stations, 190, 223, 273; controversy over, 165–166
United Artists, 28, 134, 333; 1940s antitrust suits against, 68, 70, 71
United Artists Theatre (Detroit), 37
United Cerebral Palsy (UCP), 82–93, 94, 326, 339, 393; research projects, 90–93; telethons, 85–87, 146
United Detroit Theatres, 36–39
United Nations, 283
United Paramount Theatres, 73, 85, 107, 116, 118, 123, 227; charity work of, 85; enters television industry, 95–96, 99–115; Goldenson as head of, 73, 95–115; merger with ABC, 99–115, 298, 376; relationship

with Paramount Pictures, 111–114; separation from Paramount Pictures, 73, 95, 112, 114; stock, 100, 102, 111–112. *See also* UPT-ABC merger
United Press, 294, 295, 296
U.S. Navy, 223
U.S. Steel, 167
"The U.S. Steel Hour," 167
Universal Pictures, 4, 20, 64, 69, 143, 328, 346, 454; and ABC's "Movie of the Week," 330–334; 1940s antitrust suits against, 68, 70, 71
Untouchables, The (film), 174
"The Untouchables" (TV show), 172–174, 241
UPT-ABC merger, 99–115, 298, 376; board approval, 103–104, 109; debt incurred during, 114–115, 116; FCC approval, 107, 110–115; "hands off" management period, 103–104, 118–137; negotiations, 99–107; stockholder approval, 109–110
Uris, Leon, 345
USA (cable network), 429
USFL games, on ABC Sports, 435

Variety, 126, 178, 330, 331
Variety Clubs, 49, 87, 88
Variety shows, ABC-TV, 235–237. *See also specific programs*
Vaudeville, 32, 50
VCRs, 3, 432–433. *See also* Video technology
Venezuelan stations, ABC interests in, 218–219
Veracker, Matt, 220
VHF stations, 165, 166
Video Enterprises, ABC, 231, 427–440. *See also* Cable Networks, ABC
Video technology, 3, 72, 196, 427, 428, 432
Vietnam war, 276, 398
"Viewpoint," 447
Vincent, Jan-Michael, 444
Vitagraph Studio, 109
Vogel, Joe, 118
"Voice of Firestone," 129
Voight, Jon, 146
Volpe, John, 91, 92
Von Tayn, Elissa, 458

WABC (New York), 303, 308
"Wagon Train," 332
Wald, Dick, 417
Walker, Norman, 127
Walker, Paul, 114
Wallace, George, 292
Wallace, Irving, 55
Wallace, Mike, 105, 299, 396; with ABC News, 274–275
Wallace-Homestead company, 420
Wallerstein, Dave, 26, 70, 121; and Disney Company, 122–124; on early movie industry, 27–30; on UPT-ABC merger, 113
Wall Street Journal, The, 1, 19, 115, 252, 455, 464
Walsh, Dick, 40
Walt Disney Company. *See* Disney (Walt) Company
"Walt Disney's Wonderful World of Color," 124, 251
Walters, Barbara, 392; ABC News shows of, 393–399, 401–402, 408, 415; as coanchor with Harry Reasoner, 394–397, 399, 401–402; leaves NBC, 393
"War and Remembrance," 457, 466
Ward, Rachel, 446
Waring, Fred, and the Pennsylvanians, 30
Warner, Jack, 59–60, 64, 95, 147; interests in television, 124–129, 159–160. *See also* Warner Bros.
Warner, John, 397
Warner Amex Satellite Entertainment Company, 429
Warner Bros. 28, 30, 42, 55–56, 59, 63, 65, 69, 95, 109, 119, 121, 148, 179, 238, 332, 445, 446; film library offered to ABC, 137; involvement with ABC-TV, 124–129, 137, 142, 146, 155–161
"Warner Bros. Presents," 126–129
Warren, Bill, 383
Washington, D.C., 105, 165, 275, 276, 291, 427; ABC News Bureau, 288, 293–294, 402, 409, 410, 412, 414
Washington Post, The, 225, 464, 465
Wasserman, Lew, 4, 330, 333, 334, 453; interest in ABC-MCA merger, 454–455
Watergate scandal, 278
Watson, George, 288–289
Wayne, John, 54, 55–56, 199, 421
WBBM (Chicago), 376–377
WBKB-TV (Chicago), 85, 96, 114, 198, 293; sold to CBS, 102, 109
Weather Channel, 429
Webb, Jim, 90, 91
Weeki Wachee Spring, 423
Weill, Sylvia Goldenson, 7, 9, 10, 12, 44
Weinstein, Isabelle. *See* Goldenson, Isabelle Weinstein
Weinstein, Max, 44, 45, 46, 89
Weisl, Ed, 81, 112, 123, 430
Weiss, Lou, 393

Weitman, Bob, 39, 66, 137; in charge of New York Paramount Theatre, 39–43; charity work of, 81, 83–85; as head of ABC-TV programming, 43, 103, 116, 134–136, 142, 144; leaves ABC for CBS, 142
Weitman, Sylvia, 134, 135
"Welcome Back, Kotter," 361, 366
Welk, Lawrence, 130–131. *See also* "The Lawrence Welk Show"
Welles, Orson, 143
WENR (Chicago): Radio, 97; Television, 102, 109
Werblin, Sonny, 193
Werner, Tom, 359, 441
Western Electric, 26
Western movies, 54, 55
Western series, ABC-TV, 127–129, 155–161, 238; as trendsetters, 129. *See also specific programs*
Westinghouse, 139, 172, 180, 307, 432
WFAA (Dallas), 221, 287
Wheeling Pittsburgh Steel Company, 253
"Wheel of Fortune," 381
"Where the Action Is," 247
Whitaker, Jack, 206
White, Theodore H., and *The Making of the President, 1960*, 278–279
White (R. L.) Co., 422
Whitney, Jock, 64
"Who Do You Trust?" 168
"Who's the Boss," 371
"Who Will Love My Children," 355
Why We Fight, 55
"Wide World of Sports," 187, 188, 194–198, 201, 203, 204, 206, 436–437. *See also* Sports, ABC-TV
Wilby, Bob, 73
Wilcox, John, 200
Wilder, Thornton, 138
Will, George, 417
Williams (J.B.) Company, 130
Willkie, Wendell, 98
Wilson, 63
Wilson, Tug, 117
Wilson, Woodrow, 63, 131
Winchell, Walter, 43, 82, 140
"The Winds of War," 442–445, 447, 457
Winfrey, Oprah, 380–381, 448
Winkler, Henry, 348
"Winnie the Pooh," 351
Wireless mikes, 196, 198
Wismer, Harry, 192
WJZ-Radio (New York), 97
WKRC (Cincinnati), 384–386
"WKRP in Cincinnati," 385–386
WLS (Chicago): Radio, 97, 298, 308, 420; Television, 293, 349, 376–378, 380–381, 432
WMAQ-TV (Chicago), 418
WMCA, 98
W9XBK-TV (WBKM, Chicago), 96
Wolper, David, 228, 458; and ABC miniseries, 363, 364, 365, 445–446; documentary films for ABC, 278–280
"Women's Room," 355
Wood, Bob, 149, 322, 375
Woodruff, Robert, 25
Woodward, Joanne, 443
Woollcott, Alexander, 138
Word, Inc., 420–422
"World News Tonight," 402–403, 405–408, 410, 412–418
"World News Tonight with Peter Jennings," 418–419
"World Premiere" movies, 330, 332
World's Fair: 1933 (Chicago), 30; 1939 (New York), 95
Worldvision, 217
World War I, 28, 97, 388
World War II, 51, 52, 54, 56, 57, 62, 66–67, 70, 78, 81, 96, 154, 258
Wouk, Herman, 442–443, 457
WPIX (New York), 369
Wright, Bob, 72, 73, 114
WSB-TV (Atlanta), 391
WTAE-TV (Pittsburgh), 430
WXYZ (Detroit): Radio, 36–37, 99, 119, 299–300; Television, 375
Wyler, William, 55

Xerox, 278

Yale School of Drama, 23
Young, Bob, 293
Young, Robert, 328–329
Young & Rubicam (Y & R), 100–101, 154, 172; involvement with ABC, 157–161, 168–169, 170, 227
Youth, ABC programming strategies for, 148–149, 151, 273, 290, 291, 327, 350–351, 441
Yudoss, Yale, 245

Zanuck, Darryl, 58, 62, 63, 64, 243
Zero-based budgeting, 422–423
Ziegfeld, Florenz, 131
Ziegfeld Theatre (New York City), 131

Zimbalist, Efrem, Jr., 146–147
Zionism, 39
Zoot Suit, 425
"Zorro," 124
Zousmer, Jesse, 291, 292
Zukor, Adolph, 26, 28, 60–61; and early growth of movie industry, 28, 29, 30, 60–61, 69; Paramount holdings lost by, 34–35, 60; on UPT-ABC merger, 108–109

Marvin J. Wolf, a Los Angeles-based writer, is past president of Independent Writers of Southern California, and a member of the American Society of Journalists and Authors. He is the author of four previous books.